Microprogrammed Systems

CHAPMAN & HALL COMPUTING SERIES

Computer Operating Series
For micros, minis and mainframes
2nd edition
David Barron

Microcomputer Graphics
Michael Batty

The Pick Operating System
Malcolm Bull

A Course of Programming in FORTRAN
3rd edition
V.J. Calderbank

Expert Systems
Principles and case studies
2nd edition
Edited by Richard Forsyth

Machine Learning
Principles and techniques
Edited by Richard Forsyth

Expert Systems
Knowledge, uncertainty and decision
Ian Graham and Peter Llewelyn Jones

Computer Graphics and Applications
Dennis Harris

Microprogrammed Systems
An introduction to firmware theory
Daniel Mange

Artificial Intelligence and Human Learning
Intelligent computer-aided instruction
Edited by John Self

Formal Concepts in Artificial Intelligence
Fundamentals
Rajjan Shinghal

Artificial Intelligence
Principles and applications
Edited by Masoud Yazdani

ACCESS
The Pick enquiry language
Malcolm Bull

Microprogrammed Systems

An introduction to firmware theory

Daniel Mange

Professor
Systems Laboratory
The Swiss Federal Institute of Technology, Lausanne
Switzerland

Translated by Jack Howlett CBE

CHAPMAN & HALL COMPUTING
London · Glasgow · New York · Tokyo · Melbourne · Madras

Published by Chapman & Hall, 2–6 Boundary Row, London SE1 8HN

Chapman & Hall, 2–6 Boundary Row, London SE1 8HN, UK

Blackie Academic and Professional, Wester Cleddens Road, Bishopbriggs, Glasgow G64 2NZ, UK

Van Nostrand Reinhold Inc., 115 5th Avenue, New York NY10003, USA

Chapman & Hall Japan, Thomson Publishing Japan, Hirakawacho Nemoto Building, 7F, 1-7-11 Hirakawa-cho, Chiyoda-ku, Tokyo 102, Japan

Chapman & Hall Australia, Thomas Nelson Australia, 102 Dodds Street, South Melbourne, Victoria 3205, Australia

Chapman & Hall India, R. Seshadri, 32 Second Main Road, CIT East, Madras 600 035, India

English language edition 1992

Original French language edition — *Systèmes microprogrammés: une introduction au magiciel* — © 1990, Presses polytechniques et universitaires romandes et CNET-ENST

Typeset in 10/12pt Palatino by Excel Typesetters Company, Hong Kong
Printed in Great Britain by T.J. Press, Padstow

ISBN 0 412 40800 7 0 442 31551 1 (USA)

A catalogue record for this book is available from the British Library

Library of Congress Cataloging-in-Publication data

Mange, Daniel, 1940–
[Systèmes microprogrammés. English]
Microprogrammed systems: an introduction to firmware theory / Daniel Mange; translated by Jack Howlett.
p. cm. — (Chapman & Hall computing series)
Translation of: Systèmes microprogrammés.
Includes bibliographical references and index.
ISBN 0–442–31551–1
1. Computer firmware. I. Title. II. Series: Chapman & Hall computing series.
QA76.765.M3613 1992
005.6 — dc20 91–41169
CIP

Contents

Introduction

OBJECTIVES

This book attempts to respond to three challenges:

- an educational challenge at the level of university teaching: to build a bridge between the standard theories of logic systems and of the microprogramming of processors;
- a scientific challenge: to achieve a synthesis of two theories that correspond to the two divisions of computer science, that of logic systems (the hardware division) and that of sequential programming (the software division);
- a technological challenge: to construct microprogrammed devices, implemented by means of bit-slice integrated circuits, to replace hard-wired logic systems or classical microprocessors.

To achieve this the book is based on the idea of equivalence between a hard-wired logic system (hardware) and a microprogram (software); and this equivalence, which at the mathematical level rests on the concept of the algorithm, is exhibited by means of one preferred representation, the binary decision tree. We shall see that any combinational algorithm can be represented by such a tree and that this tree can be implemented either in hardware (for example, as a network of demultiplexers and OR gates) or in equivalent software (as a set of **IF . . . THEN . . . ELSE . . .** and **DO . . .** instructions).

The book is addressed to those teaching or studying logic systems who would like to get a rigorously-based grasp of the theory and practice of processors, and offers in particular a methodology for the systematic design of microprograms. It will also interest electronic engineers who have the problem of designing real-time systems of medium complexity — of the order of 500 micro-instructions — to be implemented on bit-slice integrated circuits, and both simpler than hard-wired logic systems and faster than classical microprocessors.

All the necessary hardware concepts are explained in the first chapter; no further knowledge is needed for the understanding of the book.

METHOD ADOPTED

So as to give a consistent development of the material whilst avoiding the pitfall of too abstract a treatment, we start from the classical theory of logic systems and follow the usual sequence of combinational systems, counters and sequential systems. Simple examples, suitable to the medium level of the book, introduce the software concepts that form the chapter titles: binary decision trees and diagrams,

Le magiciel: l'art et la technique des transformations et équivalences entre matériel et logiciel. (Translator's note: Mange coined the word *magiciel* to convey the idea of the combination of hardware (*matériel*) and software (*logiciel*) which has almost magical powers, as indicated by the input to, and output from, the magician's hat. The English equivalent is **firmware** as used here. The pun, unfortunately, is essentially French and is untranslatable.)

sub-programs and procedures, incremental, structured and top-down programs, and the microprogramming of a universal processor.

The core of the book is the study of **firmware**, defined as **the art and technique of transformations and equivalences between hardware** (hard-wired logic systems) **and software** (microprograms). Classical microprogramming, which includes the art and technique of writing interpreters for assembly languages, is thus a particular case of firmware.

Chapter 1, devoted to hardware, describes the basic logic components: AND, OR and NOT gates, multiplexer, demultiplexer, D-latch, flip-flop and register. The idea of a high impedance (3-state) device is introduced here, as are the various elements needed for the construction of random access (RAM) and read only (ROM) memories.

Chapter 2 is devoted to binary decision trees and diagrams, which provide one form of representation of combinational systems. Such a tree can be constructed from a specification and then simplified to meet various cost criteria or broken down into a number of partial trees; this results in a binary decision diagram. A binary decision tree or diagram can be implemented either in hardware (as a network of demultiplexers or multiplexers) or in software; for the latter implementation we introduce a language **L1**, based on the two instructions of test and assignment. This language is interpreted by a special processor, a binary decision machine.

Counters and iterative combinational systems are characterized by the property of decomposability; these are studied in Chapter 3, and this study leads naturally to the idea of a sub-program or procedure, with or without parameter passing. The software implementation involves a language **L2**, formed from **L1** by adding the instructions *call* and *return* to and from a procedure; this language is interpreted by a binary decision machine provided with a stack.

Chapter 4 introduces incremental programs, in which each successive address is the preceding address incremented by one; this leads to a third language **L3**, an incremented version of **L2**, which is easily interpreted by a very popular form of stacked-based binary decision machine, the sequencer.

Chapter 5 first defines structured programming and then introduces two further languages, **L4**, a particular case of **L3**, and **L5** (MICROPASCAL), a high level language consisting of a minimal subset of PASCAL or MODULA instructions. The software implementation of sequential logic systems is considered, leading to the following fundamental result: any state table that has a minimum code leads to a structured program that can be expressed in **L4** or **L5**, whilst any state table with a 1-out-of-*m* code leads to a program that is generally unstructured and can be expressed in **L3**.

Chapter 6 introduces the idea of top-down programming, which enables a complex specification to be broken down in successive steps into a number of simpler problems that can be attacked by the methods of the preceding chapters. The example of a digital clock is treated in full detail, and shows how a number of compromises have to be made between hardware and software.

A larger-scale specification is considered in Chapter 7, a compiler for **L5** written in **L4** as object language. This provides an example for the writing of a complex micro-program and for considering the hardware of a processor that has two interpretation levels, a microprogrammed control unit and a general-purpose processing unit with arithmetical operations. Thus the interpretation of **L5** illustrates the scope of application of classical micro-programming.

Chapter 8 consists of a number of appendices; these give four methods for simplifying or combining binary decision trees and/or diagrams, two methods for structuring non-structured programs and a discussion of various number systems, including the representation of negative numbers.

Exercises for the reader are given in each chapter; 'projects' are also suggested, which will usually require more extended computations and in some cases experimental investigations. Bibliographical references are given in each chapter and these are collected together, in numerical order, at the end of the book.

STRUCTURE OF THE TEXT

The structure is chapter–section–paragraph; §4.5.6, for example, means Chapter 4, section 5, paragraph 6, and the numbering does not go into finer detail.

Figures and equations are numbered consecutively throughout each chapter, and equation numbers are given in parentheses; thus Figure 2.36 is in Chapter 2 and (5.37) is an equation in Chapter 5.

Technical terms are given in italics at their first appearance, when they are defined: for example, *multiplexer*. Bold is used to emphasize points of special importance.

1
Logic operators and memories

1.1 COMBINATIONAL LOGIC OPERATORS

1.1.1 Introduction

In this chapter we study the hardware of microprogrammed systems, confining ourselves to those devices that are essential to the realization of the binary decision machines and the processors that we shall describe in Chapters 2 to 7.

After a short résumé of the principal combinational logic operators (inverter, AND, OR and NAND gates, demultiplexer, multiplexer) and sequential operators (latch, flip-flop, register) we define various types of memory, emphasizing random access memory RAM, which can be constructed by linking a demultiplexer, several latches and a multiplexer. Introducing a state of high electrical impedance enables us to define a new logic device, the 3-state element; we show that an assembly consisting of 3-state elements and one demultiplexer can replace a number of multiplexers and can reduce the complexity of a memory. Furthermore, the 3-state element makes bi-directional transmission of logical information possible and thus the use of the same bus for both information input (writing) and output (reading) to or from memory; this latter suggests new structures for memories, with fewer connections to the outside world.

1.1.2 Definitions: asynchronous, combinational and synchronous systems

The theory of logic systems ([1], [59]) treats assemblages consisting of idealized elements of two types: combinational, for which the output state at any instant is determined completely by the input state at that instant, and delay, characterized by a delay Δt. The assemblage is governed by the rules:

- two output lines can never be tied together;
- in any feedback loop there is at least one delay element.

The most general assemblage of such elements provides an *asynchronous logic system,* in which time is a continuous variable. If there are no delay elements, and therefore no feedback loops, the assemblage is a *combinational logic system,* described later in this section.

In section 1.2 we describe two particular types of asynchronous system with feedback loops, the D-latch and the flip-flop. An assemblage of flip-flops and combinational elements gives what is called a *synchronous sequential system,* illustrated in section 1.2 by the shift register, a device in which time has become a discrete variable.

1.1.3 Definition: inverter

The symbol of Figure 1.1 represents a combinational logic system comprising one input a and one output a'. The truth table of Figure 1.2 defines the *logic function* a' as the *complement,* the *negation* or the *inverse* of a; it is also called the NOT *function.*

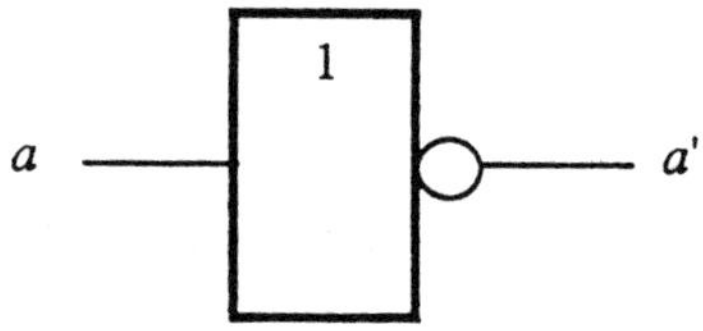

Figure 1.1

a	a'
0	1
1	0

Figure 1.2

Any system that realizes the NOT function is called an *inverter* or NOT-*operator;* thus the symbol is a graphical representation of the NOT-operator. If an inverter is associated with another operator this is usually represented by a small circle, as for example in Figure 1.5.

1.1.4 Definitions: AND, OR, NAND gates

The symbols of Figures 1.3–1.5 represent combinational systems having two inputs a, b and one output $X, Y,$ or Z. The truth table of Figure 1.6 defines the three functions as follows:

- $X = a \cdot b = ab$, logic function AND (*logic product* or *intersection* of a, b);
- $Y = a + b$ logic function OR (*logic sum* or *union*);
- $Z = (a \cdot b)' = a' + b' = a \uparrow b$ logic function NAND, i.e. NOT-AND.

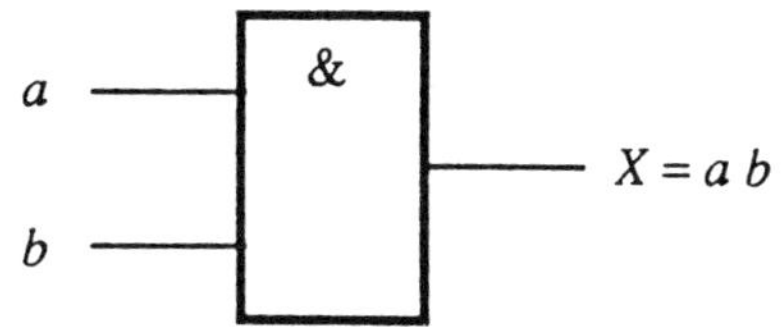

Figure 1.3

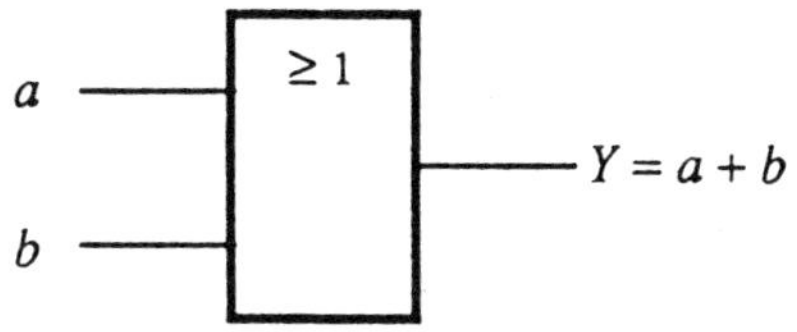

Figure 1.4

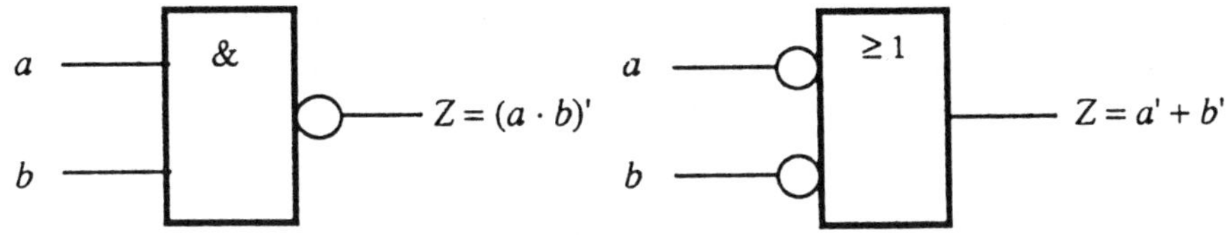

Figure 1.5

a	b	$X = ab$	$Y = a + b$	$Z = a \uparrow b$
0	0	0	0	1
0	1	0	1	1
1	0	0	1	1
1	1	1	1	0

Figure 1.6

The functions AND and OR extend immediately to three or more variables because they have the associativity property:

$$a(bc) = (ab)c = abc \tag{1.1}$$

$$a + (b + c) = (a + b) + c = a + b + c \tag{1.2}$$

NAND however does not have this property and therefore we must distinguish between three possible forms:

$$a \uparrow (b \uparrow c) = [a(bc)']' = a' + bc \tag{1.3}$$

$$(a \uparrow b) \uparrow c = [(ab)'c]' = ab + c' \tag{1.4}$$

$$a \uparrow b \uparrow c = (abc)' = a' + b' + c' \tag{1.5}$$

Hardware devices that perform these functions are called *operators* or, more usually, *gates;* thus Figures 1.3–1.5 represent the AND, OR, NAND gates respectively. Notice that there are two equivalent symbols for the NAND gate: their equivalence (having the same truth table) follows from de Morgan's theorem:

$$(a \cdot b)' = a' + b'; (a + b)' = a' \cdot b' \tag{1.6}$$

1.1.5 Definition: minterm

A *minterm* or *unit function* of n logic variables is any one of the 2^n products that can be formed by taking each variable either true of false; thus for $n = 2$ the four minterms are

$$Z8 = a'b'; Z4 = a'b; Z2 = ab'; Z1 = ab \tag{1.7}$$

The truth table of Figure 1.7 shows that each minterm has the value 1 for one and only one input state (a, b).

No	a	b	a'	b'	$Z8 = a'b'$	$Z4 = a'b$	$Z2 = ab'$	$Z1 = ab$	$Z9$
0	0	0	1	1	1	0	0	0	1
1	0	1	1	0	0	1	0	0	0
2	1	0	0	1	0	0	1	0	0
3	1	1	0	0	0	0	0	1	1

Figure 1.7

1.1.6 Comment

The algebraic expression for each minterm is a product of all the variables $(a, b$ here), each taken in its true or complementary form according as its logic value in the corresponding state is 1 or 0. Thus in Figure 1.7 $Z4 = 1$ for $a, b = 01$, from which we deduce $Z4 = a'b$.

1.1.7 Definition: canonical form

Any sum of minterms is called a *canonical algebraic form,* and for any given function this form is unique. Thus the function $Z9$ in Figure 1.7 can be written

$$Z9 = Z8 + Z1 = a'b' + ab$$

which is its canonical algebraic form.

With the variables taking the values 1 (true) and 0 (false), any input state can be assigned a binary number: e.g. for $a = 1$, $b = 0$ the binary number is 10, the decimal equivalent is 2. The *canonical decimal form* of a function is then the list of the decimal numbers of the input states for which the function has the value 1. Thus with an obvious notation

$$Z9(a, b) = \Sigma\ 0, 3$$

1.1.8 Definition: demultiplexer

The name *demultiplexer* (abbreviated to DMUX) is given to any combinational system that generates the 2^n minterms of n variables.

The logic diagram of Figure 1.8 is for one possible assemblage of NOT and AND gates that will generate all the four minterms of (1.7), provided that the auxiliary logic variable *IN* has the constant value 1.

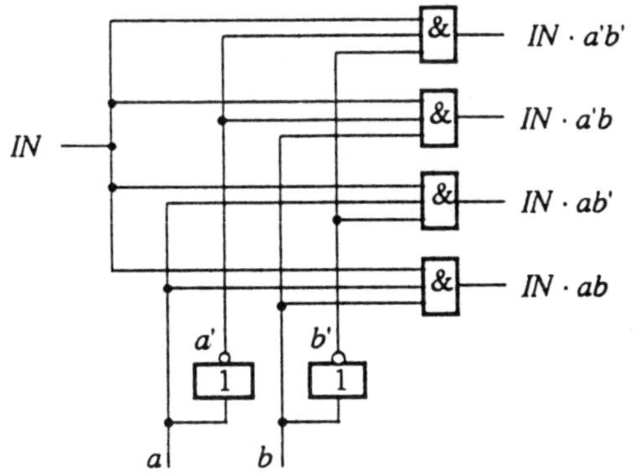

Figure 1.8

In what follows we shall say that this auxiliary variable *IN* is the *input* to the system, the products of the four minterms with *IN* are the *outputs OUT0 . . . OUT3* and the variables a, b are the *address* or *control variables* ADR_1, ADR_0 of the demultiplexer. Thus the system can be described by the following four relations:

$$OUT0 = IN \cdot ADR_1' \cdot ADR_0' \qquad (1.8)$$

$$OUT1 = IN \cdot ADR_1' \cdot ADR_0 \qquad (1.9)$$

$$OUT2 = IN \cdot ADR_1 \cdot ADR_0' \qquad (1.10)$$

$$OUT3 = IN \cdot ADR_1 \cdot ADR_0 \qquad (1.11)$$

Figure 1.9 is a simplified symbol for this 2-variable demultiplexer.

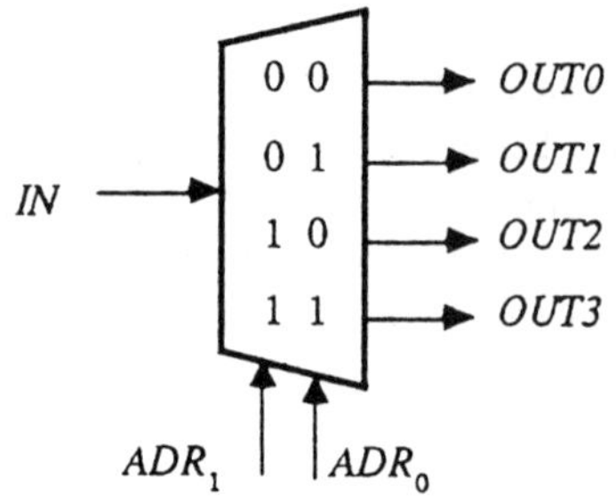

Figure 1.9

1.1.9 Conventions: state, word

Each of the 2^n possible combinations of the n logic variables $x1, \ldots xn$ is called a *state*; we shall denote it by the list $x1, \ldots xn$, or, if there is any doubt, by the same expression in parentheses: $(x1, \ldots xn)$.

In the definition of the demultiplexer in §1.1.8 we have two addressing variables ADR_1, ADR_0, both representing information of the same type, an address in this case. We shall adopt the following conventions:

- give the variables the same name (ADR) to indicate that they convey the same type of information, but distinguish them by suffixes (ADR_1, ADR_0);
- call each of the 2^2 combinations of the values of these two variables a *word* of two *bits;*
- represent such a word by any of the equivalent forms

  $$ADR = ADR_{1:0} = ADR_1, ADR_0 \qquad \text{(see Figures 1.9, 1.10)}$$

  or, in case of doubt, by these expressions in square brackets:

  $$[ADR] = [ADR_{1:0}] = [ADR_1, ADR_0]$$

We use letters without suffixes, e.g. $x1, \ldots xn$, to distinguish *free variables* from *bound variables*, e.g. ADR_1, ADR_0, with suffixes.

The value of a state is a combination of values of free variables; we shall generally denote this value by a binary number, e.g. $x1, x2, x3 = 101$. The value of a word is a combination of values of bound variables and we shall denote this by a binary, a decimal or a hexadecimal number, which can be distinguished by suffixes B, D, H respectively, e.g.

$$ADR = ADR_{3:0} = 1110_B = 14_D = E_H \qquad (1.12)$$

We shall use these suffixes only when doubt could arise.

Section 8.6 summarizes the features of these number systems and section 8.7 gives the conventions adopted in the book concerning operations on free variables and on words.

Finally, we use roman characters to denote the *name* of a system, e.g. MUX for a multiplexer, REG for a register; and italic for its *state* or for the *word* it gives rise to, e.g. $OUT = MUX$, $OUT = REG$. Thus the same string of letters can denote either a logic system (roman script) or its state (italic script).

1.1.10 Definition: bus

A *bus* is a group of n logic connections (n wires) that transmits a word of n bits; in logic diagrams it is represented by a doubled line with a label giving the number n of wires, e.g. $n = 2$ in Figure 1.10.

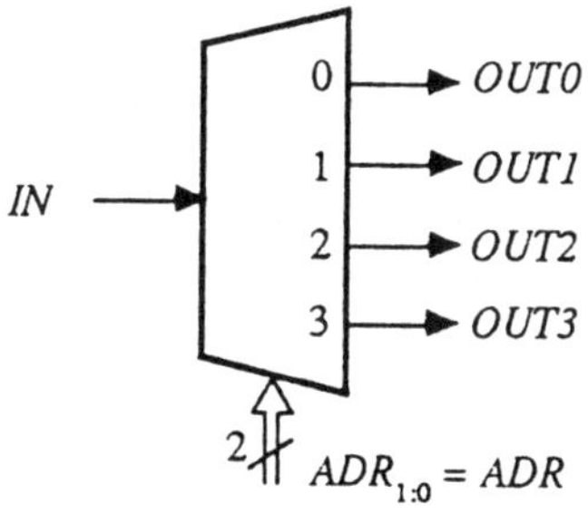

Figure 1.10

1.1.11 Representations: demultiplexer

The demultiplexer of Figure 1.9 with two address variables, can be represented as in Figure 1.10, using a single bus $ADR = ADR_{1:0}$ in place of the separate lines ADR_1 and ADR_0. The word $ADR = ADR_1, ADR_0$ is called the address word or simply the address of the demultiplexer.

The formal description of a demultiplexer with p address variables can thus be summarized as:

$$\begin{aligned} &OUTj = IN \quad \text{for } ADR = j \\ &OUTj = 0 \quad \text{for } ADR \neq j \\ &\text{with } 0 \leqslant ADR \leqslant 2^p - 1 \text{ and } 0 \leqslant j \leqslant 2^p - 1 \end{aligned} \tag{1.13}$$

Thus with this example, $p = 2$ and $0 \leqslant ADR \leqslant 3$, $0 \leqslant j \leqslant 3$.

Informally we may say that the demultiplexer uses a word of p bits to channel the input variable IN to one of the 2^p output lines OUT; the $2^p - 1$ lines that are not selected all output the logical value 0. If $IN = 1$

a single output is 1 and $2^p - 1$ are 0; we can express this by saying that the demultiplexer generates a *1-out-of-2^p code*.

1.1.12 Definition: universal logic function

The *universal logic function* of two variables a, b is defined as follows:

$$Z(a, b; K0, K1, K2, K3) = K0 \cdot a'b' + K1 \cdot a'b + K2 \cdot ab' + K3 \cdot ab \tag{1.14}$$

a, b are the principal variables of the function Z and the auxiliary variables $K0 \ldots K4$ are the *parameters*. The expression (1.14) is a polynomial, that is, a sum of monomials, each of which is the product of a parameter and a minterm.

The canonical form of any function of two variables can be obtained by giving each of the parameters the value 0 or 1; the 16 states $(K0, K1, K2, K3)$ define the 16 possible functions of two variables and each of these states is a *solution* for the universal function.

Generalizing, the universal function of n variables is expressed as a polynomial that is the sum of 2^n monomials, each of which is the product of a parameter and a minterm of n variables; it thus involves a total of $n + 2^n$ variables. The 2^{2^n} states of 2^n parameters define the 2^{2^n} functions of n variables which are the solutions for the universal function.

1.1.13 Definition: multiplexer

A *multiplexer* or *universal combinational system* of n variables, abbreviated to MUX, is any system that can generate the universal function of n variables. Figure 1.11 is an example of a multiplexer for the two variables a, b; it is an assemblage of AND, OR and NOT gates that can realize the relation (1.14).

We shall use the conventions that the universal function Z is the *output OUT*, the parameters $K0 \ldots K3$ are the inputs $IN0 \ldots IN3$ and the variables a, b are the address variables ADR_1, ADR_0 of the multiplexer. Thus this is defined by:

$$\begin{aligned} OUT = {} & IN0 \cdot ADR_1' \cdot ADR_0' + IN1 \cdot ADR_1' \cdot ADR_0 \\ & + IN2 \cdot ADR_1 \cdot ADR_0' + IN3 \cdot ADR_1 \cdot ADR_0 \end{aligned} \tag{1.15}$$

Figures 1.12 and 1.13 are simplified logic diagrams of this multiplexer. The formal description of a multiplexer with p address variables is:

$$OUT = INj \quad \text{with} \quad 0 \leqslant j = ADR \leqslant 2^p - 1 \tag{1.16}$$

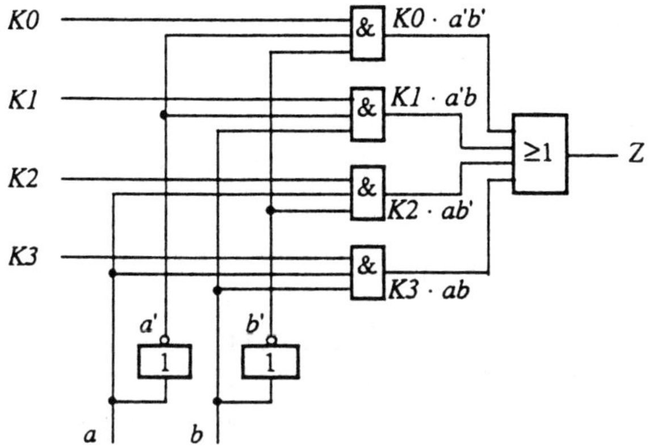

Figure 1.11

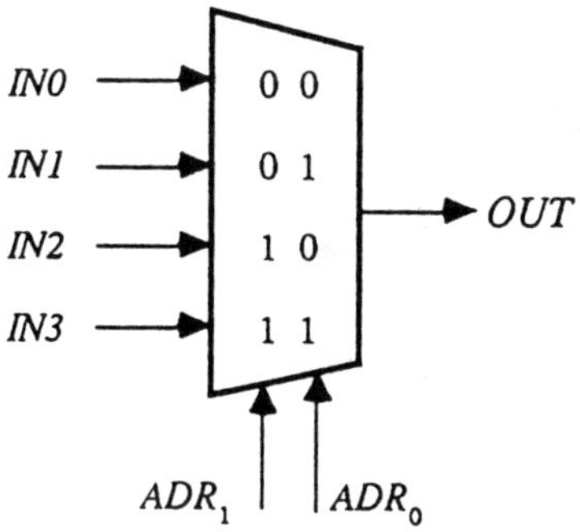

Figure 1.12

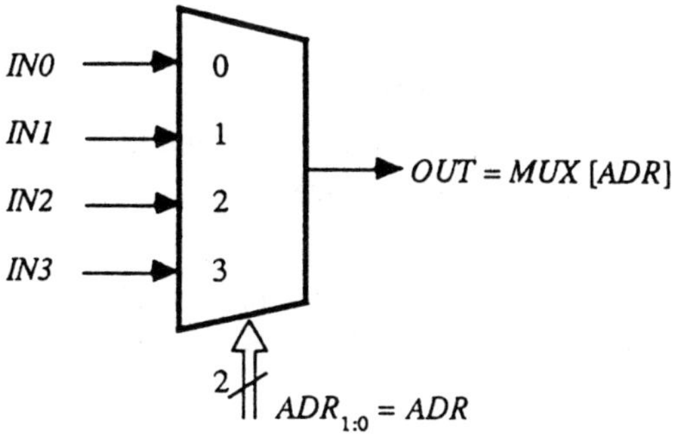

Figure 1.13

which is abbreviated to:

$$OUT = MUX\ [ADR] \tag{1.17}$$

Informally, the p-bit address ADR selects one of the 2^p inputs IN and channels it to the output OUT; the $2^p - 1$ inputs that are not selected have no effect.

1.1.14 Exercise: a comparator

The combinational system of Figure 1.14 consists of a demultiplexer and a multiplexer, each having four address variables. Analyse this system and show that the output OUT detects equality of the words $ADRA$, $ADRB$:

$$OUT = EG[ADRA, ADRB]$$

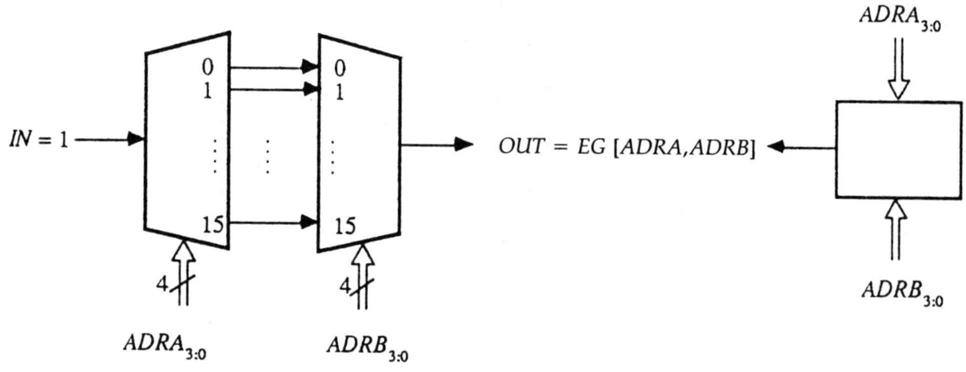

Figure 1.14

1.1.15 Definition: 3-state circuit

A *3-state circuit* (often abbreviated to *3-state*) is a device with three terminals, as in Figure 1.15. These are:

- an input terminal, defined by a variable IN;
- a control terminal, defined by a variable EN ($ENABLE$);
- an output terminal, defined by a variable OUT.

Given that IN and EN are logic variables, each able to take either of two states, the behaviour of the device is described by the operations table of Figure 1.16; here the symbol ∇ denotes a *high impedance* electrical state which does not have a definite logic value. Some writers denote this by Z, High-Z or HI-Z.

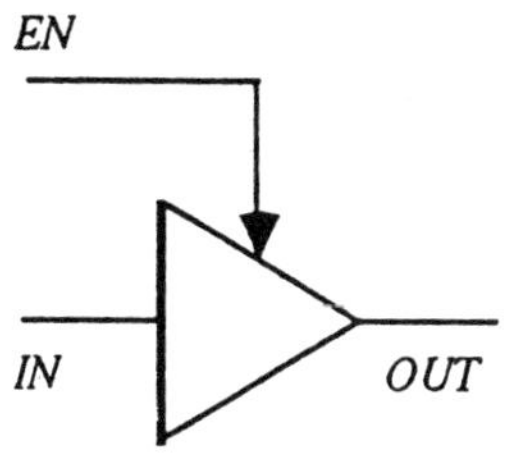

Figure 1.15

OPERATION	DESCRIPTION	*EN*
3-STATE	$OUT = \nabla$	0
TRUE	$OUT = IN$	1

Figure 1.16

1.1.16 Comment

Two consequences follow from the definition of ∇ and the operations table:

- the 3-state circuit is not a logic system in the strict sense of the term, that is, a device all of whose inputs and outputs are described by logic variables; rather, it is an electrical circuit that involves logic variables and one non-logic variable, the output *OUT* in the case of Figure 1.15;
- since the output *OUT* is determined at every instant by the states of the inputs *IN*, *EN*, the behaviour of the device is combinational; this is shown in the operations table by the equality sign '='.

A provisional mathematical formulation of the 3-state's behaviour is given in [19].

1.1.17 An application: construction of a multiplexer

The diagram of Figure 1.17 is for a system consisting of a demultiplexer with address word $B = B_1, B_0$ and four 3-states; its behaviour is described by the truth table of Figure 1.19 in which Φ denotes a *'don't care' condition*, meaning that the effect is the same whether this has the value 0 or 1; this is sometimes denoted by 'X'.

- For the state $ENABLE = 1$ the one of the four outputs $EN0 \ldots EN3$ that is selected by B has the value 1 and the others 0. Therefore one

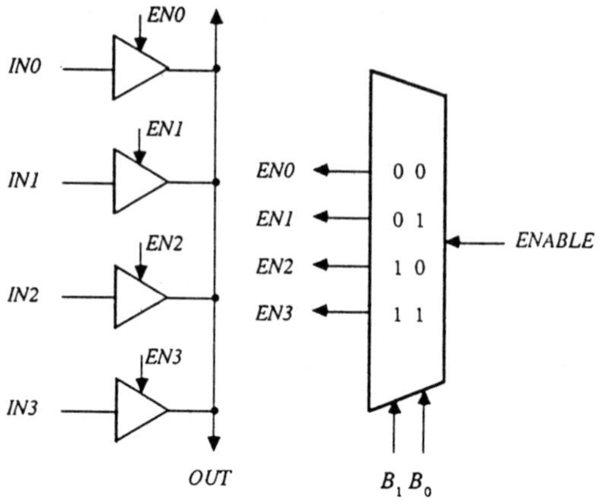

Figure 1.17

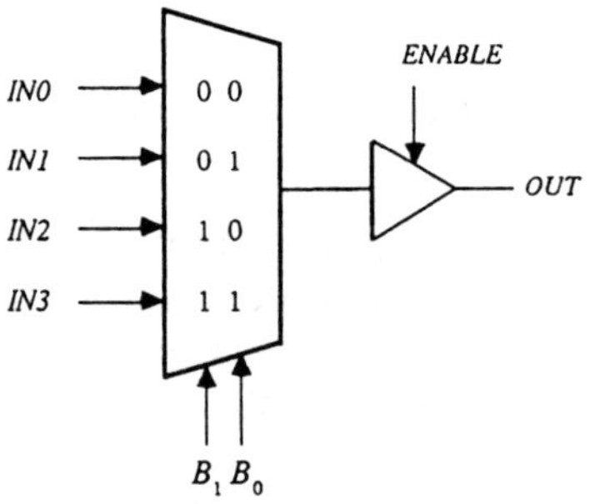

Figure 1.18

and only one of the 3-state circuits performs the operation TRUE, that is, $OUT = IN$, the others performing 3-STATE, that is, $OUT = \nabla$; the output *OUT* is thus the input to the 3-state that is addressed by *B*.

- For the state $ENABLE = 0$ all the outputs of the demultiplexer are 0 and therefore all the 3-state circuits perform 3-STATE and *OUT* takes the value ∇ of the high impedance state.

B_1	B_0	*ENABLE*	*EN3*	*EN2*	*EN1*	*EN0*	*OUT*
Φ	Φ	0	0	0	0	0	∇
0	0	1	0	0	0	1	*IN0*
0	1	1	0	0	1	0	*IN1*
1	0	1	0	1	0	0	*IN2*
1	1	1	1	0	0	0	*IN3*

Figure 1.19

OPERATION	DESCRIPTION	*ENABLE*
3-STATE	*OUT* = ∇	0
TRUE	*OUT* = *MUX* [*B*]	1

Figure 1.20

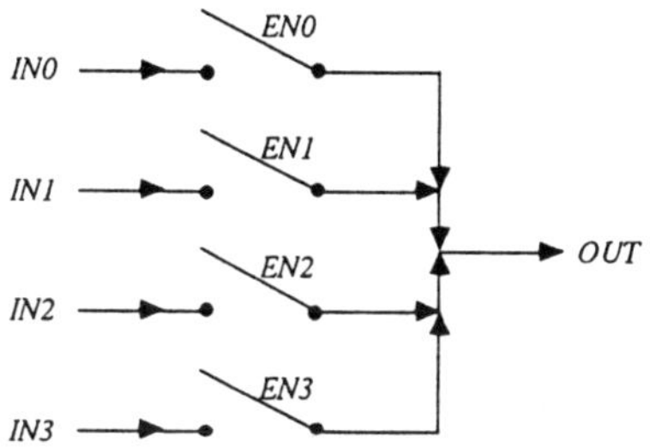

Figure 1.21

A logic connection in the high impedance state behaves like an open circuit, or a wire not connected to anything; this is a change from the usual rules that govern electrical wiring and has the following consequence, of fundamental importance:

- **the output lines of different 3-state circuits may be tied together.**

This completes the set of rules for connecting logic systems, the first two of which were given in §1.1.2; it requires that if the outputs of a number of 3-states are connected together then at most one device will be active at any one time.

1.2 SEQUENTIAL LOGIC OPERATORS

1.2.1 Definition: D-latch

Figures 1.22–1.24 are three diagrams for the logic system called a *D-latch* or *memory element*; 1.22 is the logic diagram in terms of NOT, AND and OR gates, 1.23 in terms of MUX and NOT, 1.24 the simplified symbol.

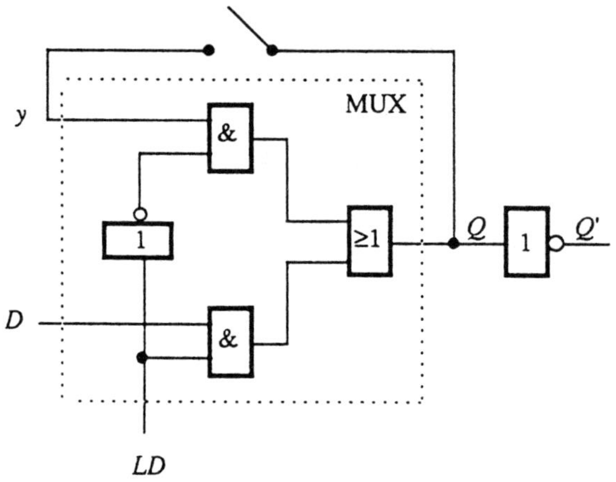

Figure 1.22

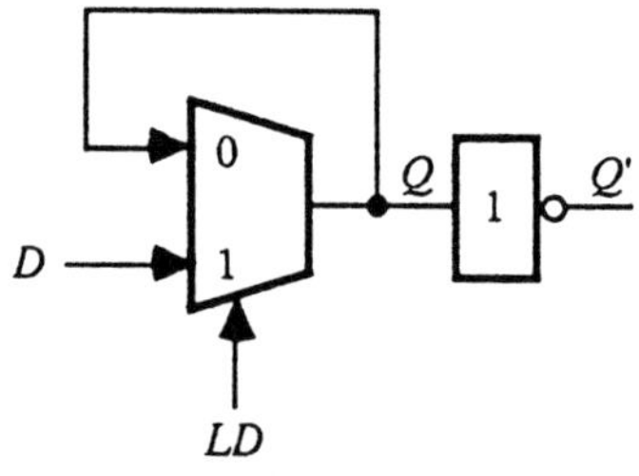

Figure 1.23

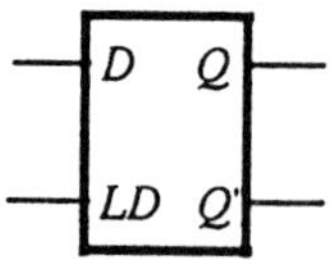

Figure 1.24

1.2.2 Representations

The feedback loop in Figures 1.22 and 1.23 makes the analysis awkward; if it is broken by opening the switch in Figure 1.22 the system becomes momentarily a combinational system for a function Q of three free variables, D, LD ($LOAD$), y:

$$Q = y \cdot LD' + D \cdot LD \tag{1.18}$$

The values of Q are given in the truth table of Figure 1.25; the output Q' is an auxiliary variable and can be neglected in what follows.

No	y	D	LD	$y \cdot LD'$	$D \cdot LD$	Q	
0	0	0	0			0	$y = Q$
1	0	0	1			0	$y = Q$
2	0	1	0			0	$y = Q$
3	0	1	1		1	1	$y \neq Q$
4	1	0	0	1		1	$y = Q$
5	1	0	1			0	$y \neq Q$
6	1	1	0	1		1	$y = Q$
7	1	1	1		1	1	$y = Q$

Figure 1.25

Closing the switch restores the original logic diagram and imposes the relation

$$y = Q \tag{1.19}$$

which must therefore hold in the truth table; a study of this shows:

- it does not hold for states 3 and 5 of (y, D, LD);
- the six remaining states 0, 1, 2, 4, 6, 7 for which it does hold, are therefore the only possible states for the system.

Taking this into account, the behaviour of the system is summarized in Figure 1.26.

No	D	LD	Q
0, 4	0	0	0, 1
1	0	1	0
2, 6	1	0	0, 1
7	1	1	1

Figure 1.26

1.2.3 Definition: sequential logic system

We have seen that for the input states $D, LD = 00$ and 10 of the D-latch there are two possible output states, $Q = 0$ or 1; this means that the output state at the instant t is not determined solely by the input state at that instant, but depends also on the input state at some preceding instant. Such behaviour is said to define a *sequential logic system.*

The behaviour of a sequential system separates into two regimes: a *permanent* or *stable* regime, described by the table in Figure 1.26, and a *transient* or *unstable* regime in which it passes from one stable regime to another.

1.2.4 Description: the transient regime

As an example, consider the following sequences of input states and corresponding output states (Figure 1.26):

- if the input state D, LD changes from 01 to 00, it is reasonable to expect that the output state $Q = 0$ will remain in that state (by 'inertia') since it is compatible with the new input state;
- if D, LD changes from 11 to 00 the initial output state $Q = 1$ will be conserved, for the same reason.

Experiments with the actual hardware show that this is the case.

1.2.5 Comment

This account of the transient regime calls upon an intuitive judgement; a rigorous treatment can be given, based on a more detailed model of the system, the *asynchronous model*. In this it is assumed that all the combinational elements in Figure 1.22 involve delays and that, to a first approximation, these can be assimilated into a single fixed delay Δt at the output of the OR gate; this gives a new assemblage, the asynchronous system. A detailed analysis of such systems is given in [1] and [59].

1.2.6 Representation: operations table

The truth table of Figure 1.26 makes clear that there are two types of behaviour: combinational, for input states $D, LD = 01$ and 11, and sequential, for $D, LD = 00$ and 10.

In the combinational state (for which $LD = 1$) the output Q at any instant is determined by the input at that instant, and from the truth table we see that in this case

$$Q = D \tag{1.20}$$

To express this cause–and–effect relation we write it

$$Q := D \tag{1.21}$$

the sign ':=' denoting *asynchronous assignment.*

In the sequential state (for which $LD = 0$) the value of Q remains unchanged, so we can say that the latch holds the memory of Q, and write simply

$$Q := Q \tag{1.22}$$

Such an asynchronous assignment is called a *neutral operation*, or NOP.

Figure 1.27 is the *operations table* for the latch; reading from left to right, the three columns give:

1. mnemonic names for the operations of the system: HOLD for the sequential state, LOAD for combinational;
2. the corresponding algebraic descriptions, relations (1.21) and (1.22);
3. the corresponding states of the logic variable LD.

OPERATION	DESCRIPTION	LD
HOLD	$Q := Q$	0
LOAD	$Q := D$	1

Figure 1.27

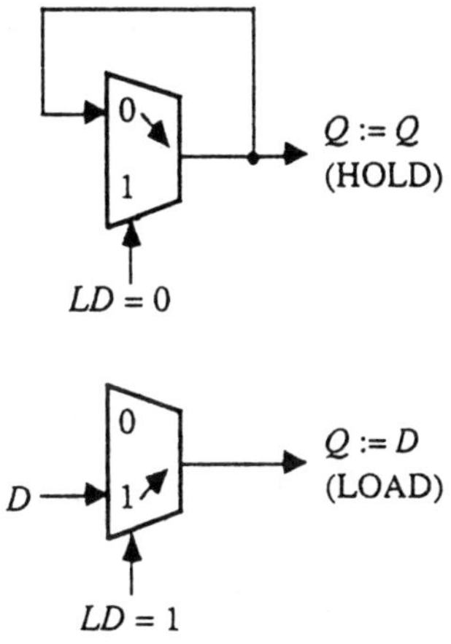

Figure 1.28

The diagrams of Figure 1.28 symbolize the two operations HOLD and LOAD.

The operations table can be reduced to the single algebraic expression

$$Q := (D)_{LD} \tag{1.23}$$

which states that the asynchronous assignment to Q is D when the control variable LD has the value 1; it is to be understood that when LD is 0 there is no operation and $Q := Q$. Thus (1.23) describes a *controlled asynchronous assignment*, the control being by the logic variable LD.

1.2.7 Definition: D flip-flop

Figures 1.29 and 1.30 each describe an assemblage consisting of two latches called a *D bistable circuit* or *D flip-flop*. The first latch (on the left) is usually called the *master* and the second (on the right) the *slave*.

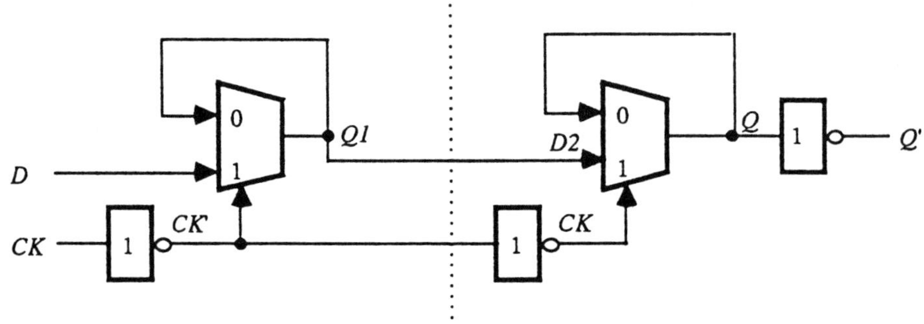

Figure 1.29

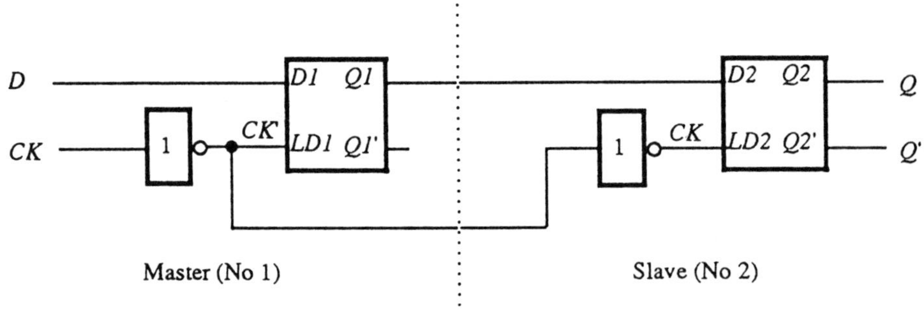

Figure 1.30

Figure 1.31 gives the inputs (D, CK) and the outputs (Q, Q'); we shall call D the *excitation input* and CK the *clock pulse*. The value of the output Q is the *state*, or *internal state*, of the flip-flop.

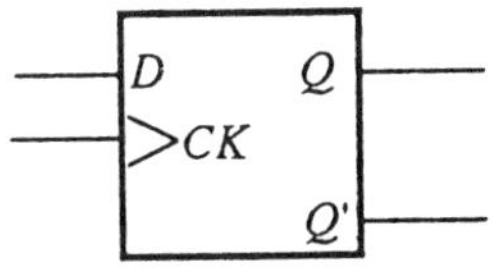

Figure 1.31

1.2.8 Definition: clock times

The clock pulse *CK* is a special logic variable that acts as a reference signal for the flip-flop; it may or may not be periodic. We give the name *clock periods* or, taking some freedom with the language, *clock times* to the time intervals during which $CK = 0$. If we take some arbitrary clock time as the *present clock time* t then the clock time immediately following is the *next clock time* t^+ (see Figure 1.32). The state Q of the flip-flop at time t is the *present state* and that at t^+ is the *next state* Q^+.

The change of *CK* from 0 to 1 is called its *rise*, from 1 to 0 its *fall*.

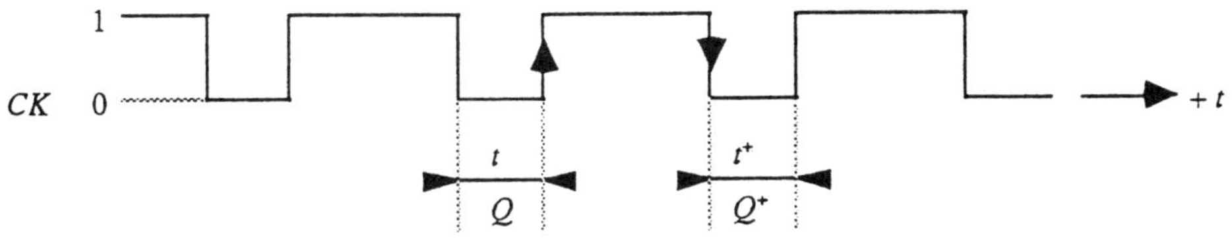

Figure 1.32

1.2.9 Timing diagram

The two regimes, permanent and transient, of the flip-flop can be represented by means of a *timing diagram*, as in Figure 1.33. This is constructed as follows.

1. Two sequences of square waves are drawn, representing respectively the clock pulse *CK* and its complement *CK'* at a number of consecutive clock times, *t1* to *t5* in the figure.
2. A third square wave is drawn, showing the time-variation of the excitation signal *D*, which in principle can be of any form: see §1.2.12 below.
3. From the logic diagram of Figure 1.30 it follows that for the first (master) latch

$$D1 = D, \quad LD1 = CK' \tag{1.24}$$

and therefore from (1.23)

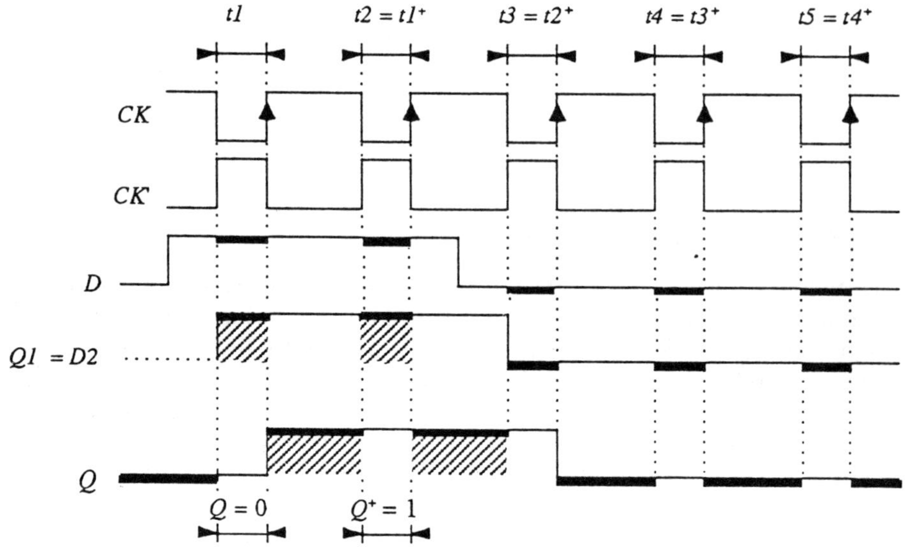

Figure 1.33

$$Q1 := (D1)_{LD1} \quad \text{or} \quad Q1 := (D)_{CK} \tag{1.25}$$

showing that $Q1$ takes the same value as D whenever the clock pulse is 0 (when $CK' = 1$): this is the LOAD operation for this latch.

4. Thus at each clock time ($CK = 0$) we can assign to $Q1$ a value equal to that of D at that instant (LOAD); whilst during the interval between two consecutive clock times ($CK = 1$) the value of $Q1$ remains what it was at the start of that interval (HOLD). Thus the diagram for $Q1$ is deduced directly from that of D, apart from the dashed line in Figure 1.33 which represents the (arbitrary) initial condition — here taken to be 0.
5. For the second (slave) latch

$$D2 = Q1, \quad LD2 = CK \tag{1.26}$$

whence from (1.23)

$$Q2 := (D2)_{LD2} \quad \text{or} \quad Q := (Q1)_{CK} \tag{1.27}$$

this last equation stating that Q takes the value of $Q1$ when the clock pulse CK has the value 1 (the LOAD operation).

6. In the interval between any two consecutive clock times ($CK = 1$) Q copies the value of $Q1$ (the LOAD operation); during each clock period ($CK = 0$) Q retains the value it had during the preceding interval (the HOLD operation). Thus the timing diagram for Q is determined completely by that of $Q1$.

1.2.10 Informal description

We see from Figure 1.33 that at the first clock time *t1*, which we are taking as the present clock time, the first latch loads the value of the input D ($Q1 = 1$) whilst the second retains the initial value ($Q = 0$): see Figure 1.34. At the rise of the clock pulse *CK*, that is, at the end of the present clock time, the roles of the two latches are interchanged: the first retains the value it has ($Q1 = 1$) whilst the second loads this value ($Q = 1$). Thus we may compare the flip-flop to a lock chamber, the top and bottom gates of which open and close alternately.

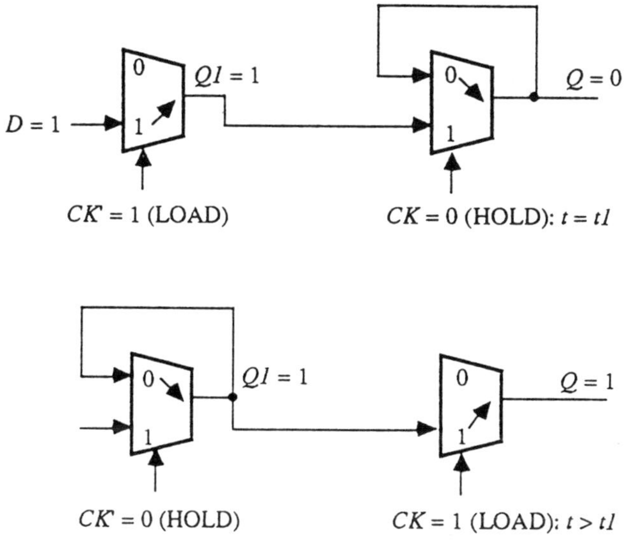

Figure 1.34

The flip-flop has three characteristics, that are of great importance.

- The state Q can change only at the clock pulse rise.
- The state Q does not change during any clock time ($CK = 0$).
- The values of the input D and the output Q at the present clock time t together determine the output Q^+ completely at the next clock pulse t^+.

1.2.11 Representation: operations table

Figure 1.35 is a *state table*, giving the next state Q^+ as a function of the present state Q and the input D; these three values can be read from the timing diagram of Figure 1.33. The table shows that

$$Q^+ = Q^+(D, Q) = D \tag{1.28}$$

which is the *characteristic equation* of the D flip-flop. So as to avoid using the superscript '+' we shall generally write this as

$$Q \leftarrow D \tag{1.29}$$

where the symbol '←' denotes *synchronous assignment*.

No	D	Q	Q^+
0	0	0	0
1	0	1	0
2	1	0	1
3	1	1	1

Figure 1.35

OPERATION	DESCRIPTION	D
CLEAR	$Q \leftarrow 0$	0
PRESET	$Q \leftarrow 1$	1

Figure 1.36

OPERATION	DESCRIPTION
LOAD	$Q \leftarrow D$

Figure 1.37

Figure 1.36 is the detailed operations table for the D flip-flop, giving the values of D explicitly; CLEAR and PRESET mean respectively 'reset to 0' and 'set to 1'. Figure 1.37 is the same table in abridged form, in which the values of D are implicit.

1.2.12 Comment

The state table and its consequences, the characteristic equation and the operations table, each provide an abridged representation of the behaviour of the flip-flop. This crude model is quite satisfactory in most applications, provided that the values of D, Q and Q^+ remain unchanged during any clock time, that is, while $CK = 0$; otherwise the table is invalid. Since the structure of the flip-flop is such that the values of Q and Q^+ cannot change while $CK = 0$ the only constraint is the following: **all variation of the excitation variable D is inhibited during any clock time** (that is, when $CK = 0$). This will be seen to hold in the timing diagram of Figure 1.33.

The majority of flip-flops on the market do not in fact insist on this constraint being satisfied; this is so in particular for those that are driven by the rising edge of the clock pulse, known as *edge-triggered flip-flops*. Flip-flop behaviour is studied in detail in [1] and [59].

1.2.13 Definitions: asynchronous, synchronous and quasi-synchronous behaviour

A sequential system that is described by one or more asynchronous assignments is said to exhibit *asynchronous behaviour* — for example, the latch of §1.2.6; and when described by one or more synchronous assignments, *synchronous behaviour*, controlled by a clock — for example, the flip-flop of §1.2.11.

We have said that the flip-flop is essentially an assemblage of two latches; it must therefore be possible to give a formal relation between the asynchronous assignments that describe the latches and the synchronous assignment that describes the flip-flop as an entity. To achieve this we start with the relations (1.25) and (1.27) for the master and slave latches respectively:

$$Q1 := (D)_{CK'}, \quad Q := (Q1)_{CK}$$

Substituting for $Q1$ from (1.25) into (1.27) gives

$$Q := ((D)_{CK'})_{CK} \tag{1.30}$$

We now define (1.30) to be equivalent to the synchronous assignment expressed by the characteristic equation (1.28) or (1.29); so we have three equivalent relations to describe the behaviour of the D flip-flop:

$$Q^{+} = D \tag{1.28}$$

$$Q \leftarrow D \tag{1.29}$$

$$Q := ((D)_{CK'})_{CK} \tag{1.30}$$

Finally, if the description of a sequential system involves both synchronous and asynchronous assignments we say that the behaviour is *quasi-synchronous*. An example is the Texas Instruments 7474 D flip-flop shown symbolically in Figure 1.38; this has two auxiliary logic

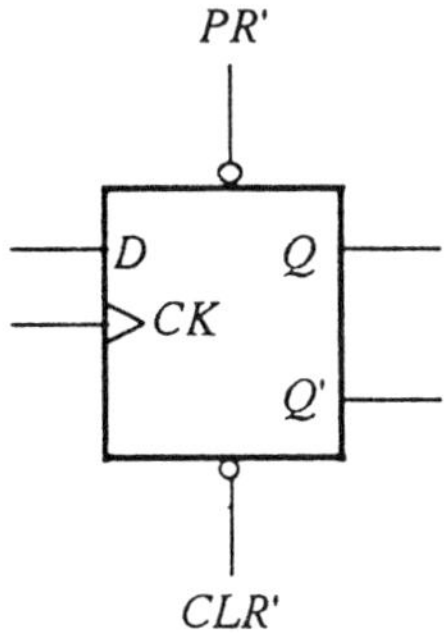

Figure 1.38

OPERATION	DESCRIPTION	PR'	CLR'
UNUSED	$Q := 1$ $(Q' := 1)$	0	0
PRESET	$Q := 1$	0	1
CLEAR	$Q := 0$	1	0
LOAD	$Q \leftarrow D$	1	1

Figure 1.39

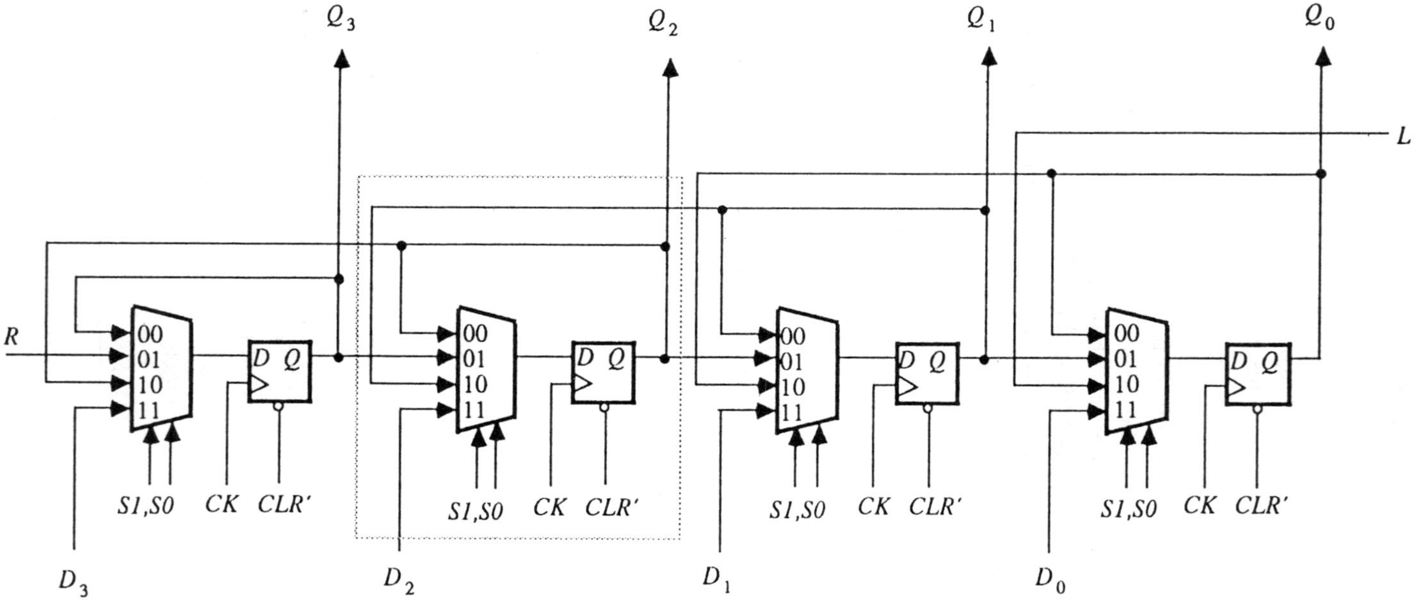

Figure 1.40

variables, the *asynchronous inputs PR* (*Preset*) and *CLR* (*Clear*). The operations table of Figure 1.39 shows both synchronous and asynchronous assignments, so the behaviour overall is quasi-synchronous. The operation UNUSED is forbidden: if it were allowed it would assign the value 1 to both Q and Q'. A detailed study of the asynchronous behaviour of *PR* and *CLR* is given in [1] and [59].

1.2.14 Definition: bi-directional shift register

The logic diagram of Figure 1.40 and the symbolic diagrams of Figure 1.41 are for a synchronous sequential system consisting of four D flip-flops and four multiplexers controlled by two variables *S1, S0*; this is a *4-bit bi-directional shift register*, abbreviated to REG.

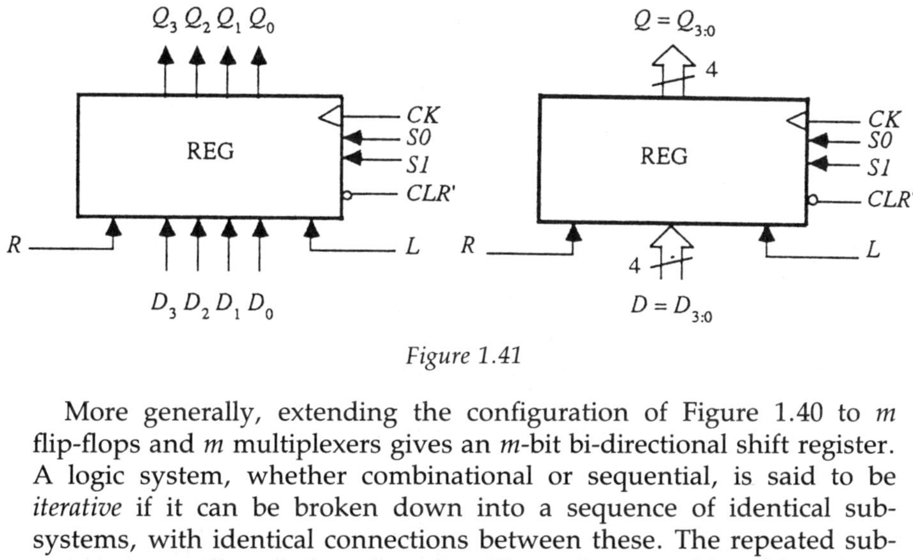

Figure 1.41

More generally, extending the configuration of Figure 1.40 to m flip-flops and m multiplexers gives an m-bit bi-directional shift register. A logic system, whether combinational or sequential, is said to be *iterative* if it can be broken down into a sequence of identical sub-systems, with identical connections between these. The repeated sub-system is usually called a *cell* or *slice*. The register considered here is an iterative system, one cell of which is shown in the box in Figure 1.40.

If the effect of asynchronous input *CLR'* is ignored the cell has a synchronous behaviour that can be described in terms of the variables *S1, S0* as follows:

for *S1, S0*	$= 00$	$Q_2 \leftarrow Q_2$	operation HOLD or NOP
	$= 01$	$Q_2 \leftarrow Q_3$	SHIFT RIGHT
	$= 10$	$Q_2 \leftarrow Q_1$	SHIFT LEFT
	$= 11$	$Q_2 \leftarrow D_2$	LOAD

The synchronous and the asynchronous behaviour of the complete device can be expressed in terms of words, as in the operations table of

Figure 1.42. Here the values of Q_3, Q_2, Q_1, Q_0 are regarded as the bits of a word Q and the operations SHIFT RIGHT, SHIFT LEFT as division and multiplication respectively of Q by 2:

$Q \leftarrow Q/2$ is equivalent to the shift $Q_3, Q_2, Q_1, Q_0 \leftarrow \Phi, Q_3, Q_2, Q_1$
$Q \leftarrow Q{*}2$ is equivalent to the shift $Q_3, Q_2, Q_1, Q_0 \leftarrow Q_2, Q_1, Q_0, \Phi$

where, as before, Φ denotes a 'don't care' condition.

OPERATION	DESCRIPTION	*CLR'*	*S1*	*S0*
CLEAR	$Q := 0$	0	Φ	Φ
HOLD	$Q \leftarrow Q$	1	0	0
SHIFT RIGHT	$Q \leftarrow Q/2,\ Q_3 \leftarrow R$	1	0	1
SHIFT LEFT	$Q \leftarrow Q{*}2,\ Q_0 \leftarrow L$	1	1	0
LOAD	$Q \leftarrow D$	1	1	1

Figure 1.42

The occurrence of Φ means that, as things stand, the most significant (leftmost) bit of $Q/2$ and the least significant (rightmost) bit of $Q * 2$ are undetermined. To remove this indefiniteness we add the synchronous assignments $Q_3 \leftarrow R$ (SHIFT RIGHT) and $Q_0 \leftarrow L$ (SHIFT LEFT), as shown in the table; the convention is that **synchronous assignments on the same line in an operations table and separated by a comma are performed simultaneously**.

A particular important case is that in which

$$S1 = S0 = LD \tag{1.31}$$

where the register performs only the HOLD and LOAD operations; the corresponding symbol has only a single input, labelled *LD,* instead of the pair *S1, S0* — as, for example, in Figure 2.60.

If LOAD is the only operation allowed the symbol is simplified still further and involves no control variable at all — again as Figure 2.60.

1.3 RANDOM ACCESS AND READ ONLY MEMORIES

1.3.1 Introduction

Memories are logic devices that are essential to the realization of microprogrammed systems in actual hardware. In this section we describe only their logical behaviour, that is, the relations between their inputs and outputs; these are summarized in the operations tables, in which the signs '=' and ':=' are used to denote equality and asynchronous assignment according as to whether the relevant behaviours are combinational or asynchronous respectively.

Nowhere in this book do we consider hardware technology or the methods by which integrated circuits (for memories, for example) can be designed; for this the reader should consult the references given in §1.3.12.

1.3.2 Definitions: random access and read only memory

A *memory* is a logic operator which makes possible the recording (writing), retaining and/or retrieving (reading) of binary information. It is usually represented by an array of 2^m *rows* (*words*), each of *n columns* (*bits*) (see Figure 1.43); the number of rows is the *depth* of the memory and the number of columns is the *width* or *breadth*. Each word is identified by a number *ADR*, its *address*, in the range $0 \leqslant ADR \leqslant 2^m - 1$.

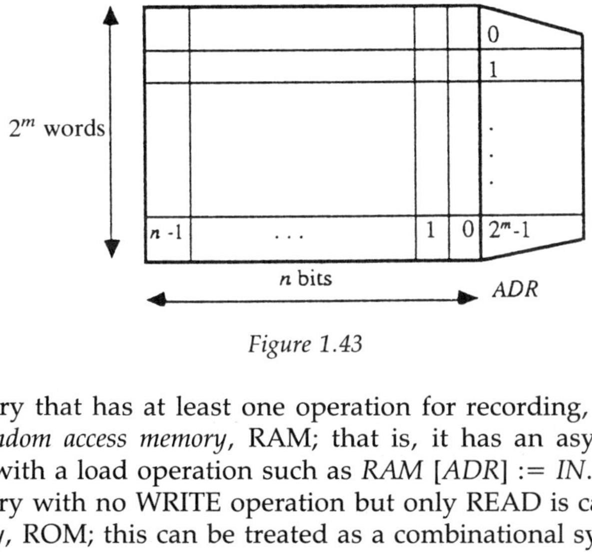

Figure 1.43

A memory that has at least one operation for recording, WRITE, is called a *random access memory*, RAM; that is, it has an asynchronous behaviour with a load operation such as *RAM* [*ADR*] := *IN*.

A memory with no WRITE operation but only READ is called a *read only memory*, ROM; this can be treated as a combinational system.

1.3.3 Description: RAM with four 1-bit words

Figure 1.44 shows an assemblage of a demultiplexer, four D-latches and a multiplexer that constitutes a random access memory for four words of one bit each.

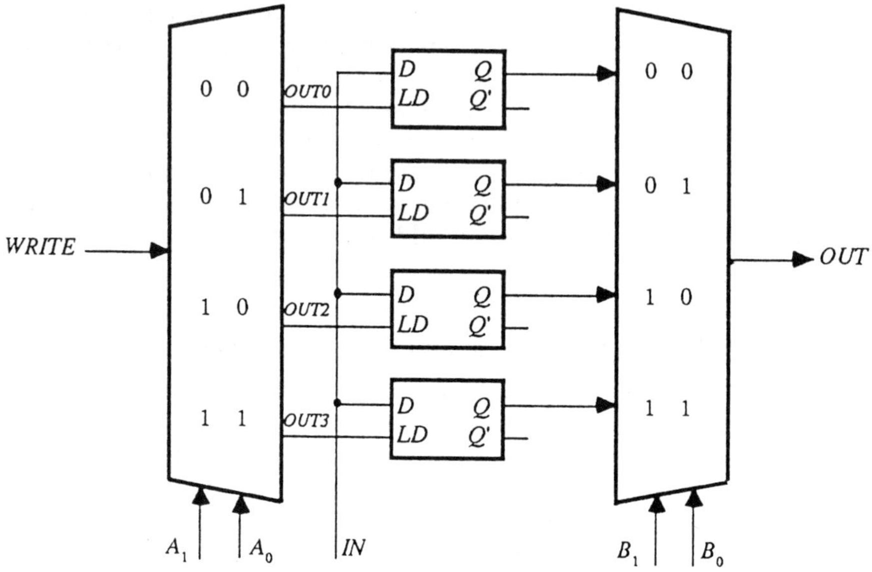

Figure 1.44

The output of the multiplexer is given by (1.17), which in this case becomes

$$OUT = MUX\ [ADR] = RAM\ [B] \tag{1.32}$$

showing that the output *OUT* of the RAM is always equal to the contents of the latch selected by the address $B = B_{1:0}$; the equality sign '=' is used here to indicate combinational behaviour. Since (1.32) does not involve the variable *WRITE* it appears in both lines of the operations table, Figure 1.46.

Each output *OUTj* ($0 \leqslant j \leqslant 3$) of the demultiplexer is the product of the input *WRITE* and one of the four minterms of A_1 and A_0, as in (1.8) . . . (1.11). Two cases arise:

- If *WRITE* = 0 all the outputs *OUT0* . . . *OUT3* are zero and therefore, since *OUTj* = *LDj* for $0 \leqslant j \leqslant 3$, all the latches perform the HOLD (neutral) operation (see Figure 1.27). We say that the memory performs the READ operation and retains the information that it contains; the asynchronous assignment *RAM* [*A*] := *RAM* [*A*] is a formal statement of the NOP by the latches.
- If *WRITE* = 1 one and only one of *OUTj* is 1, that for which $A = A_{1:0} = j$; then one and only one latch performs the LOAD operation

(Figure 1.27) and its output $Q = RAM\ [A]$ takes the value of the input *IN*:

$$RAM\ [A] := IN \tag{1.33}$$

which is an asynchronous assignment. We say that here the memory performs a READ AND WRITE operation.

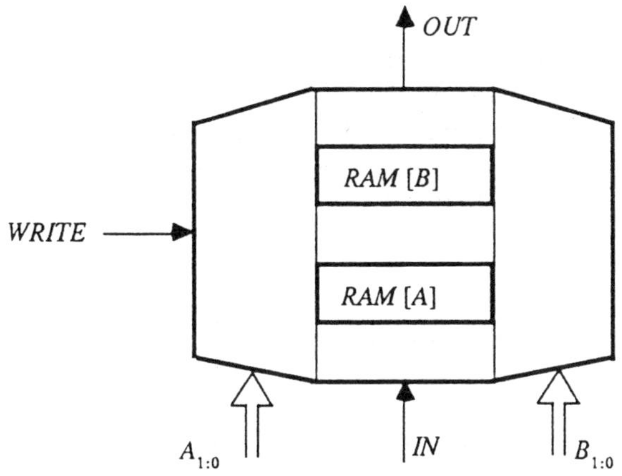

Figure 1.45

To summarize, the memory's operation is a superposition of an asynchronous behaviour $RAM\ [A] := IN$, performed only when $WRITE = 1$, (the WRITE operation) on a permanent combinational behaviour $OUT = RAM\ [B]$ (the READ operation); this is expressed by Figure 1.45. Note that the read address (*B*) is independent of the write address (*A*), so that at any instant a word can be read from an address *B* and, independently, another word written to an address *A*.

OPERATION	DESCRIPTION	*WRITE*
READ	$OUT = RAM\ [B]$, $(RAM\ [A] := RAM\ [A])$	0
READ AND WRITE	$OUT = RAM\ [B]$, $RAM\ [A] := IN$	1

Figure 1.46

1.3.4 Convention: the neutral operation

The asynchronous assignment *RAM* [*A*] := *RAM* [*A*] in Figure 1.46 is a formal description of a neutral operation. It is customary to ignore such an operation when it is accompanied by another operation, as it is in this table by *OUT* = *RAM* [*B*].

1.3.5 Description: random access memory of four 2-bit words

To hold in memory a word of two bits we need two latches connected as in Figure 1.47, simplified in Figure 1.48. A RAM for four 2-bit words can then be constructed by assembling four such latch pairs (one for each word), a demultiplexer and two multiplexers, as shown in Figure 1.49; each multiplexer outputs one of the two bits (OUT_1, OUT_0 in the diagram) of the word that is read.

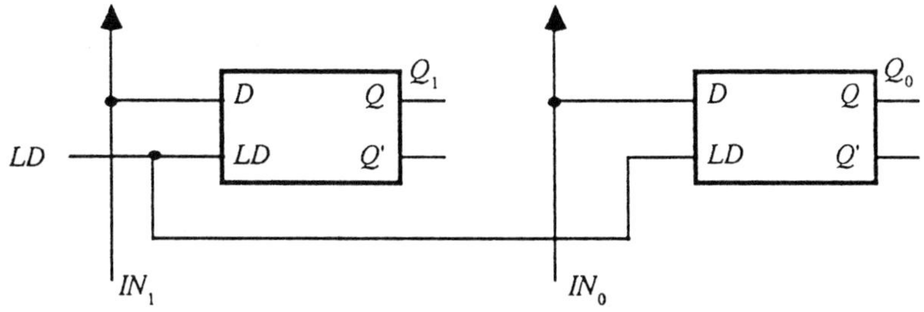

Figure 1.47

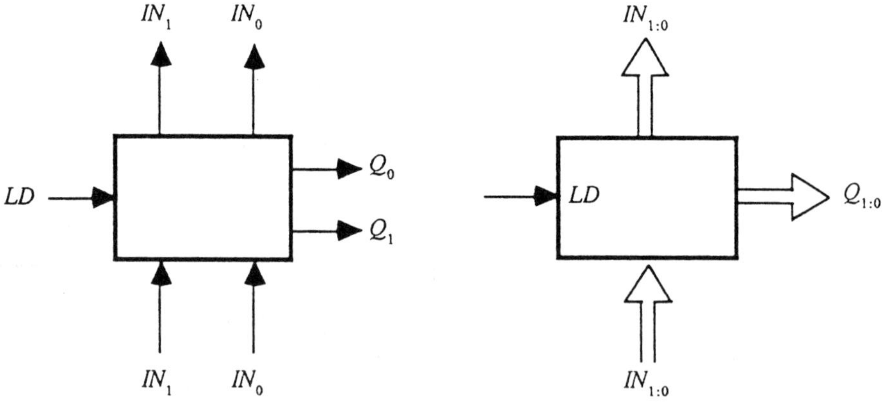

Figure 1.48

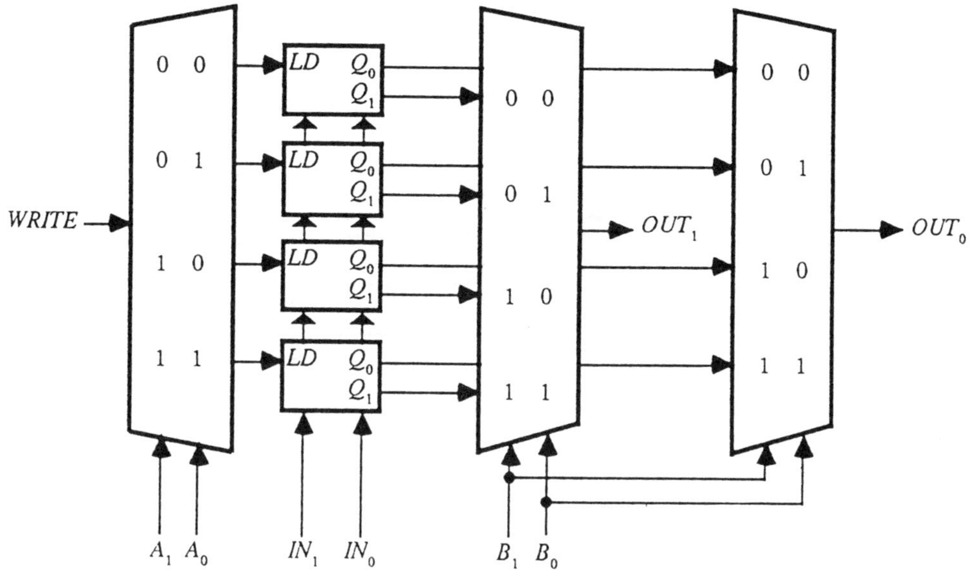

Figure 1.49

If we define the output word *OUT* by

$$OUT = OUT_1, OUT_0 = OUT_{1:0} \tag{1.34}$$

and the input word *IN* by

$$IN = IN_1, IN_0 = IN_{1:0} \tag{1.35}$$

then the operations table of Figure 1.46 remains valid: the final schema is shown in Figure 1.50.

1.3.6 Description: read only memory (ROM)

If we impose the constraint *WRITE* = 0 on the table of Figure 1.46 the resulting behaviour of the RAM is equivalent to a read only memory, ROM; it is described by the single relation

$$OUT = RAM\ [B] = ROM\ [B] \tag{1.36}$$

This behaviour is combinational; it is equivalent to that of the multiplexer of Figure 1.13, described by the relation

$$OUT = MUX\ [ADR] \tag{1.17}$$

One possible diagram is that of Figure 1.51, representing a ROM of 2^m

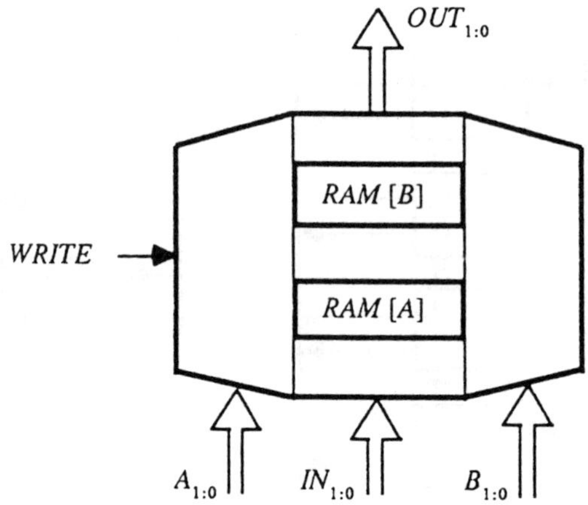

Figure 1.50

words of n bits each, with an address $ADR = B$ of m bits. Such a memory is functionally equivalent to n multiplexers with address $ADR = B$ for which each input INj is connected to the appropriate value of the logic constants (0 or 1).

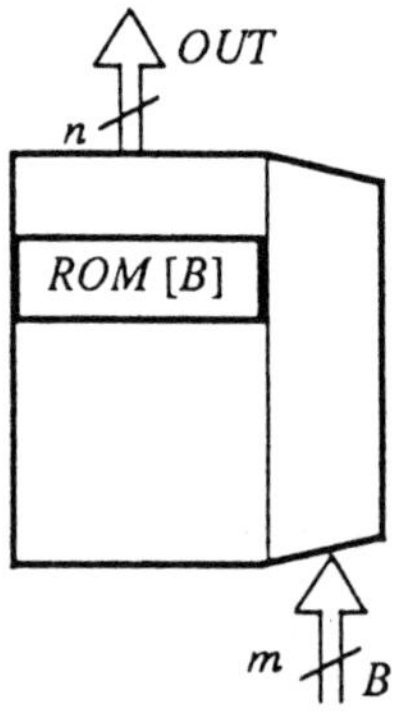

Figure 1.51

1.3.7 Description: RAM of four 2-bit words with 3-state circuits

We have shown that the multiplexer of Figure 1.18 is functionally equivalent to the assemblage of a demultiplexer and 3-state circuits of

Figure 1.17. In the RAM of Figure 1.49 it is usual, for both technological and economic reasons — reduction of the area of silicon needed for the integrated circuits and of the production costs, respectively — to replace the multiplexers by their equivalents of Figure 1.17. This leads to the new assemblage for a RAM of four 2-bit words, employing 3-state circuits, of Figure 1.53, in which we have used the schema of Figure 1.52 to represent a pair of 3-states on the end of the bus $Q_{1:0}$. Figure 1.54 is the corresponding simplified representation. As before, the symbol ∇ indicates that one or more output terminals can be in the high impedance state.

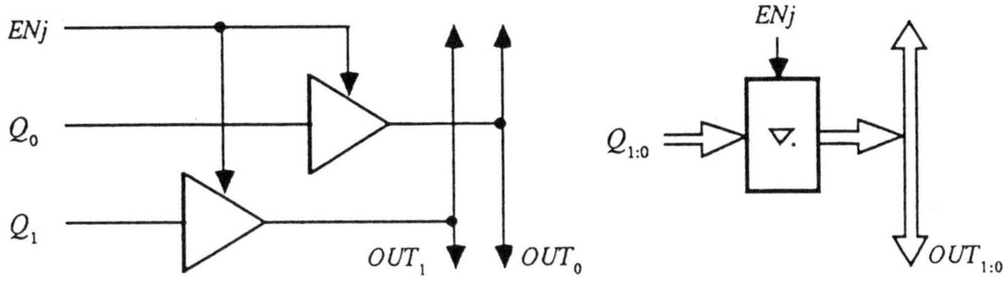

Figure 1.52

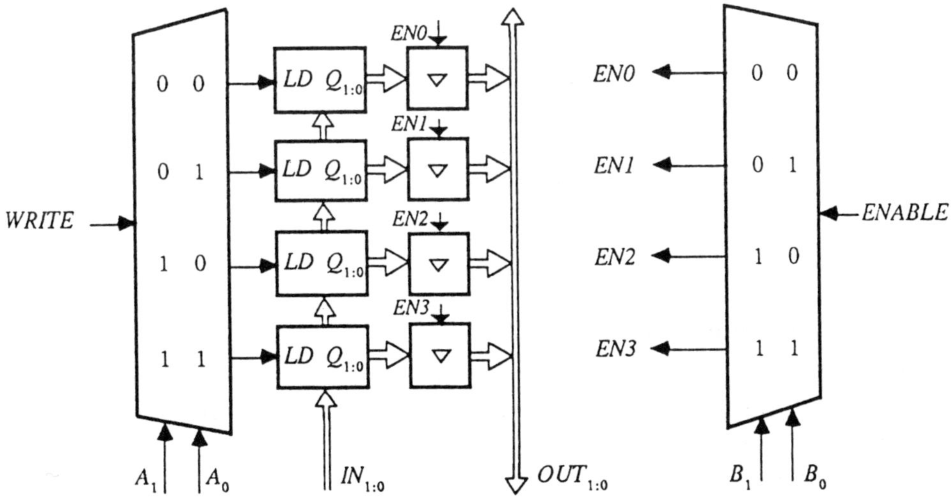

Figure 1.53

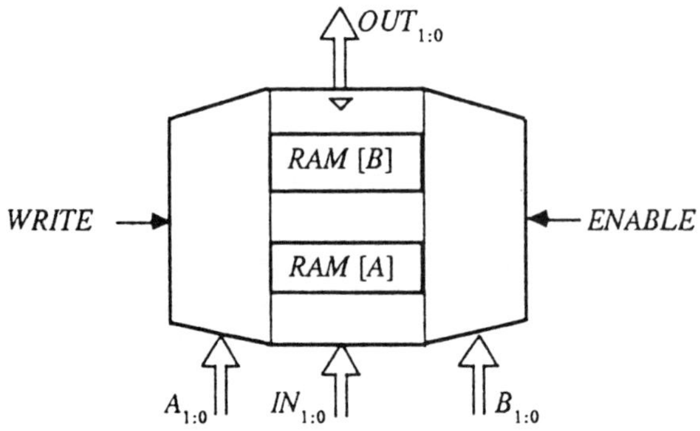

Figure 1.54

Introduction of a further control variable *ENABLE* extends the functionality of the memory; the original operations table (Figure 1.46) is now replaced by that of Figure 1.55 in which:

- for *ENABLE* = 1 the two lines of the original are reproduced exactly;
- for *ENABLE* = 0 the writing operation described by the asynchronous assignment *RAM* [*A*] := *IN* remains unchanged, whilst the reading operation described by the equality relation *OUT* = *RAM* [*B*] is replaced by the occurrence of a high impedance state *OUT* = ∇.

OPERATION	DESCRIPTION	*WRITE*	*ENABLE*
3-STATE	*OUT* = ∇	0	0
READ	*OUT* = *RAM* [*B*]	0	1
WRITE	*OUT* = ∇, *RAM* [*A*] := *IN*	1	0
READ AND WRITE	*OUT* = *RAM* [*B*], *RAM* [*A*] := *IN*	1	1

Figure 1.55

1.3.8 Definition: bi-directional bus

In the RAM of Figures 1.53 and 1.54, incorporating 3-state circuits, the rule established in §1.1.18 allows us to tie together the two *OUT* terminals so as to create a 2-bit output bus $OUT_{1:0}$.

The rules that apply to classical hardwired logic systems (§1.1.2) allow us to tie one of the output terminals (OUT_1, OUT_0 in this case) to one of the inputs (IN_1, IN_0), provided that we introduce at least one

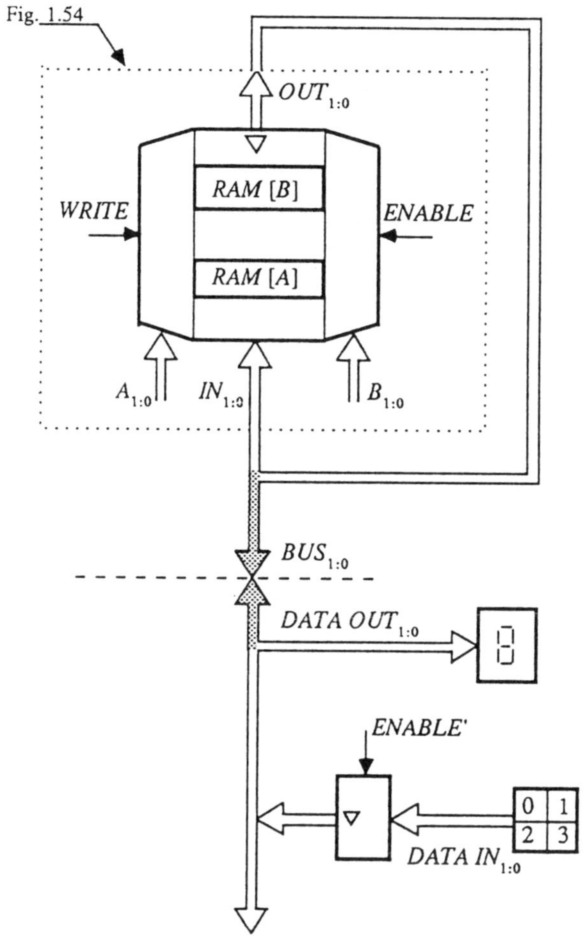

Figure 1.56

delay element into the feedback loop that this may create: the comment of §1.2.5 shows that this element will be an integral part of the latch. Making these linkages gives the systems of Figures 1.56 and 1.57, in which the memory has acquired a single bus, $BUS_{1:0}$, for both reading and writing.

A set of n logic connections (wires) along which n-bit words can be transmitted alternately in one direction and then the other is called a *bi-directional bus*; in Figures 1.56 and 1.57 the bus $B_{1:0}$ is bi-directional in the areas shaded.

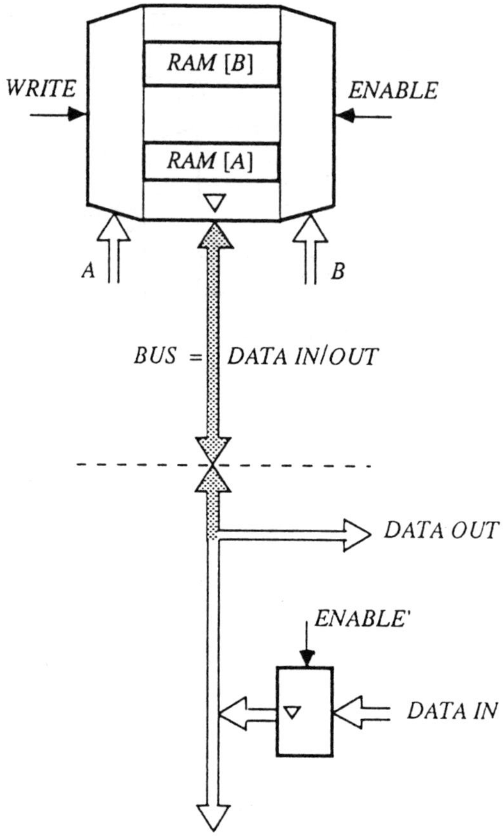

Figure 1.57

1.3.9 Description: 4 × 2-bit RAM with bi-directional bus

To show more clearly the behaviour of a random access memory with a bi-directional bus we consider this with the addition of:

- an input peripheral: a keyboard with four keys for entering any of the four binary numbers 00–11, connected to $BUS_{1:0}$ via a 3-state circuit which in turn is controlled by *ENABLE*. The information generated by this peripheral is called $DATA\ IN_{1:0}$;
- an output peripheral: a display consisting of seven line segments, connected directly to $BUS_{1:0}$. The information received by this peripheral is called $DATA\ OUT_{1:0}$.

Figure 1.58 is the operations table, derived from Figure 1.55 by taking into account the constraints concerning the bus (§1.3.8) and the

OPERATION	DESCRIPTION	*WRITE*	*ENABLE*
READ DATA	*DATA OUT* = *DATA IN*	0	0
READ RAM	*DATA OUT* = *RAM* [*B*]	0	1
WRITE DATA	*DATA OUT* = *DATA IN*, *RAM* [*A*] := *DATA IN*	1	0
WRITE RAM	*DATA OUT* = *RAM* [*B*], *RAM* [*A*] := *RAM* [*B*]	1	1

Figure 1.58

addition of the input/output peripherals. The variables *WRITE* and *ENABLE* define the following four operations, shown in Figure 1.59:

- for *WRITE, ENABLE* = 00 nothing is either written to or read from the memory; the information displayed is what is input via the keyboard:

  DATA OUT = *DATA IN* (operation READ DATA);

- for *WRITE, ENABLE* = 01 nothing is written to the memory; its contents, addressed by the word *B*, are displayed:

  DATA OUT = *RAM* [*B*]   (READ RAM);

- for *WRITE, ENABLE* = 10 the input information is written to the memory at address *A* and is displayed:

  DATA OUT = *DATA IN*,   *RAM* [*A*] := *DATA IN*   (WRITE DATA);

- for *WRITE, ENABLE* = 11 the information read from the memory at address *B* is displayed and simultaneously is written to the memory at address *A*:

  DATA OUT = *RAM* [*B*],   *RAM* [*A*] := *RAM* [*B*]   (WRITE RAM).

The last case, *WRITE, ENABLE* = 11, shows that a word in memory at one address *B* can be rewritten to another address *A*.

The system shown in Figures 1.56 and 1.57 is summarized, with less detail, in Figure 1.60; this gives a new arrangement with separate input and output terminals and two uni-directional buses *DATA IN*, *DATA OUT*. The operations table of Figure 1.58 still applies here.

1.3.10 Comment

The aim of using a single bus $BUS_{1:0}$ for both input and output is to minimize the number of connections to the outside world; but then it becomes impossible to read and write simultaneously, and the two

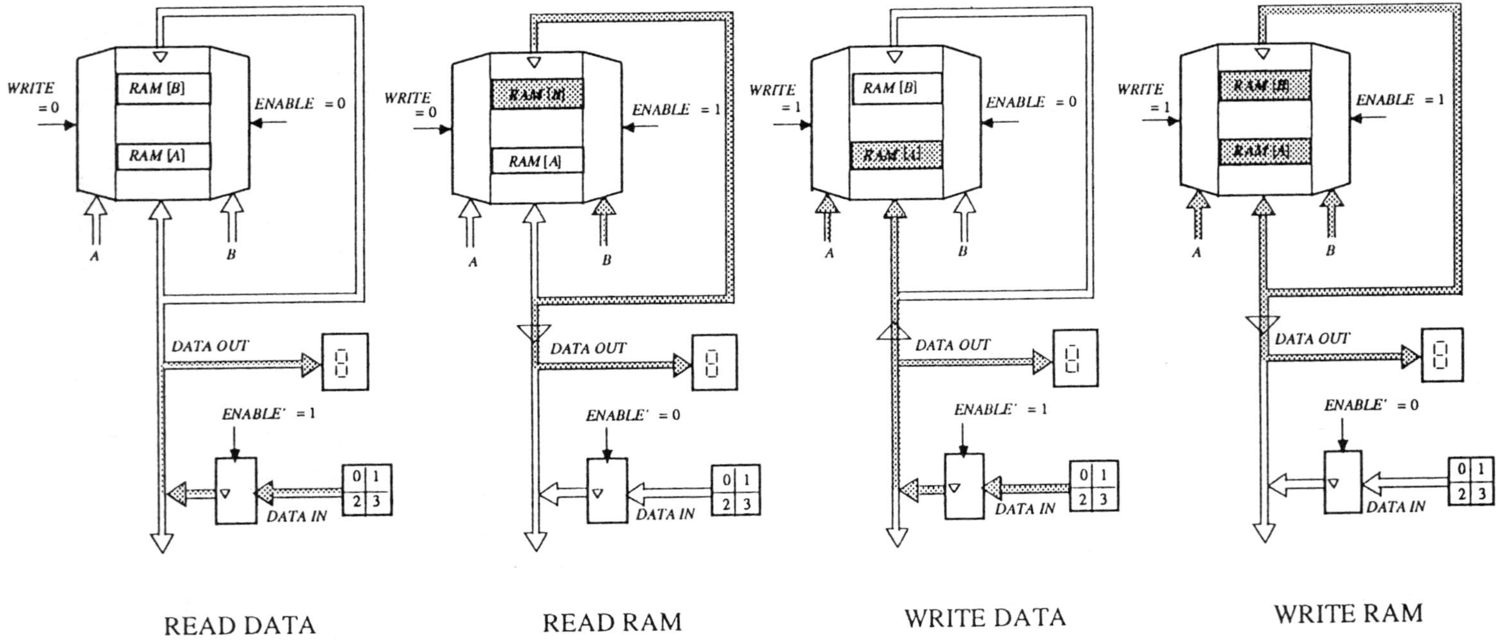
WRITE = 0
RAM [B]
RAM [A]
ENABLE = 0
A
B
DATA OUT
ENABLE' = 1
0 1 2 3
DATA IN
WRITE = 0
RAM [B]
RAM [A]
ENABLE = 1
A
B
DATA OUT
ENABLE' = 0
0 1 2 3
DATA IN
WRITE = 1
RAM [B]
RAM [A]
ENABLE = 0
A
B
DATA OUT
ENABLE' = 1
0 1 2 3
DATA IN
WRITE = 1
RAM [B]
RAM [A]
ENABLE = 1
A
B
DATA OUT
ENABLE' = 0
0 1 2 3
DATA IN
READ DATA
READ RAM
WRITE DATA
WRITE RAM

Figure 1.59

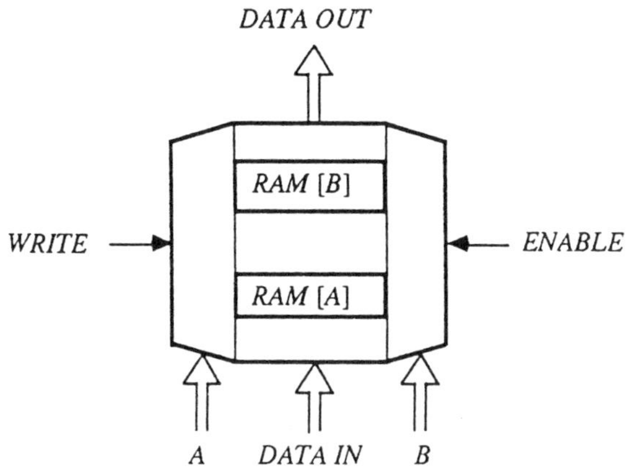

Figure 1.60

operations must be performed sequentially. Simultaneous reading and writing is possible only when the corresponding data are identical — the operation WRITE RAM of Figure 1.58.

The usual structure with separate input and output terminals and with uni-directional buses is achieved by simply adding a further 3-state circuit as in Figures 1.56, 1.57 and 1.60.

1.3.11 Application: 2048 × 8-bit RAM with bi-directional bus

Figures 1.61 and 1.62 represent the Texas Instruments TMS 4016 integrated circuit ([20], pp. 8.13–15), a 2048 × 8-bit word RAM. Figure 1.61 shows the basic differences between the organization of this device and that of Figures 1.56–1.57:

- there is only one address, *A*, for both reading and writing;
- the *WRITE* and *ENABLE* control variables depend on three new logic variables S' (chip select), W' (write enable) and G' (output enable), according to the relations

$$WRITE = S \cdot W, \quad ENABLE = S \cdot W' \cdot G \tag{1.37}$$

Figure 1.63 gives the operations table; this is derived from Figure 1.55 by tying the output terminal *OUT* of Figure 1.54 to the input terminal *IN* so as to form the bi-directional bus *DATA*, and introducing the new variables S', W', G'.

The two operations 3-STATE and DEVICE DISABLED have the same description and are functionally equivalent; the practical difference is that DEVICE DISABLED consumes less power. The same possi-

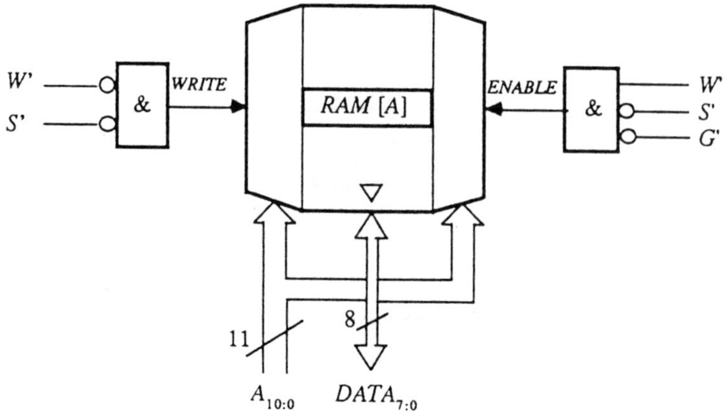

Figure 1.61

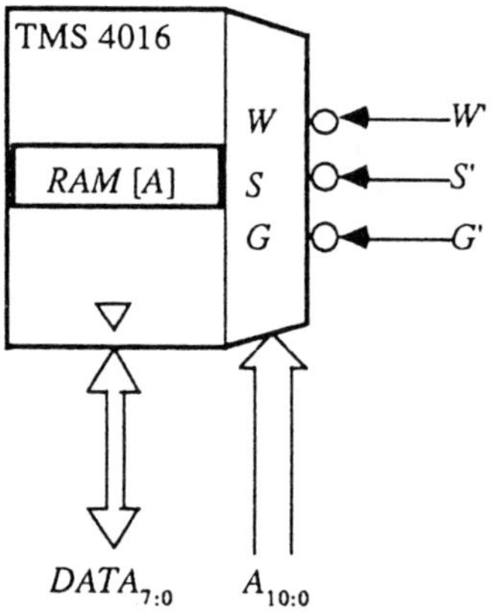

Figure 1.62

OPERATION	DESCRIPTION	*S'*	*W'*	*G'*	*WRITE*	*ENABLE*
WRITE	*RAM* [*A*] := *DATA*	0	0	Φ	1	0
READ	*DATA* = *RAM* [*A*]	0	1	0	0	1
3-STATE	*DATA* = ∇	0	1	1	0	0
DEVICE DISABLED	*DATA* = ∇	1	Φ	Φ	0	0

Figure 1.63

bility is offered in the equivalent Mitsubishi circuit M58725P ([21], pp. 2.3–8) by the operation POWER DOWN.

We can recover the convenience of independent input and output by putting on the *DATA* bus a 3-state circuit controlled by a variable x related to S', W', G'; one possible relation, shown in Figures 1.64 and 1.65, is

$$x = WRITE = S \cdot W \tag{1.38}$$

This leads to the table of Figure 1.66, which differs from Figure 1.63 only in that it is now possible to read ($OUT = IN$) at the same time as WRITE.

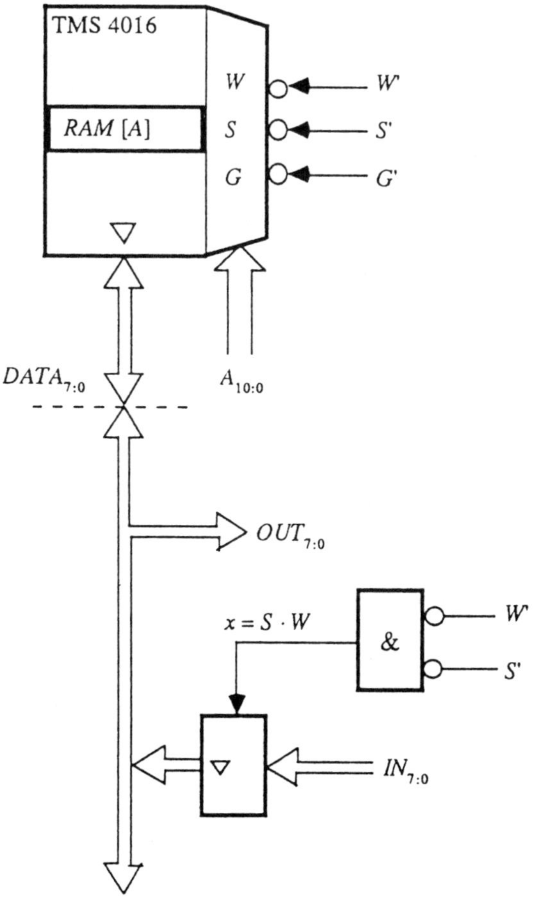

Figure 1.64

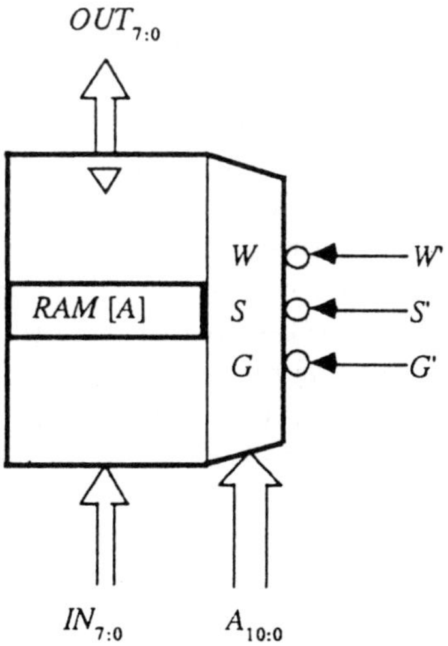

Figure 1.65

OPERATION	DESCRIPTION	S' W' G'	*WRITE*
WRITE	$OUT = IN, \quad RAM[A] := IN$	0 0 Φ	1
READ	$OUT = RAM[A]$	0 1 0	0
3-STATE	$OUT = \nabla$	0 1 1	0
DEVICE DISABLED	$OUT = \nabla$	1 Φ Φ	0

Figure 1.66

1.3.12 Bibliography

Reference [4], pp. 337–345 deals with the fabrication of magnetic core memories and the physico-chemical properties of their materials; bipolar and MOS (Metal Oxide Silicon) semiconductor memories are discussed in [4], [7] and [10].

The electrical and electronic properties of memories and their dynamic performance (e.g. cycle times) are studied in [9] pp. 195–228 (MOS transistors only) and [4], [5], [7] and [10] (bipolar and MOS transistors).

The logic analysis in which the memory is considered as an assemblage of combinational and sequential operators (gates, multiplexers, demultiplexers etc.) has been treated in section 1.3 of this chapter; there are similar treatments in [2] pp. 104–115, [3] pp. 18–20, [13] pp. 111–115, [16] pp. 75–76 and [33] pp. 173–176, 407–412.

For functional descriptions of memories summarizing the structures in simplified schemas which aim to show the basic architecture see [5] pp. 27–69, [7], [8] pp. 326–354 and [10]. This level of detail is usually sufficient for dealing with the problem of error correction [14], [15].

Finally, the use of read only (ROM) and random access (RAM) memories in the implementation of logic systems, whether combinational or sequential, is treated in [2], [4], [6] pp. 9–108, [8], [10], [11] pp. 381–413 and [12] pp. 246–316. Such systems can all be implemented by *programmable logic arrays* (PLA), or *programmable logic devices* (PLD), which, now form a fast developing field: see [2] pp. 115–128, [33] pp. 176–179, [140] and [141].

2

Binary decision trees and diagrams

2.1 ANALYSIS AND SYNTHESIS OF BINARY DECISION TREES

2.1.1 Introduction

This chapter is devoted to combinational systems. Using as a simple example a comparator for two numbers we show that any combinational system can be represented by a binary decision tree, that this can usually be simplified and in certain cases can be transformed into an equivalent but more compact representation, a binary decision diagram. After giving methods for synthesizing these trees and diagrams we show that both structures can be implemented in hardware by a network of demultiplexers or in software by a microprogram executed by a binary decision machine. The emphasis is on the software solution, for which we introduce a language which we call **L1**, consisting of instructions of two types: tests, **IF . . . THEN . . . ELSE . . .** , and assignments, **DO . . . GO TO . . .**

2.1.2 Example: a numerical comparator

Let A, B be decimal numbers each of which can be expressed by two binary digits, A_1, A_0 and B_1, B_0 respectively [33] pp. 57–59. The function of the logic system that we call a *comparator* (COMP) is to determine whether A is greater than, equal to or less than B (Figure 2.1). The truth table (Figure 2.2) is a representation of the behaviour of this system: the four variables A_1, B_1, A_0, B_0 determine $2^4 = 16$ input states, numbered 0 to 15, whilst the comparison leads to three distinct possible values for the output state Z, denoted by the symbols '>', '=' and '<'; these can be coded by the letters G, E, L respectively and we can say that Z is represented by a *1-out-of-3* code (cf. §1.1.11).

The algebraic forms of the logical functions G, E, L follow from the truth table, by summing the relevant minterms:

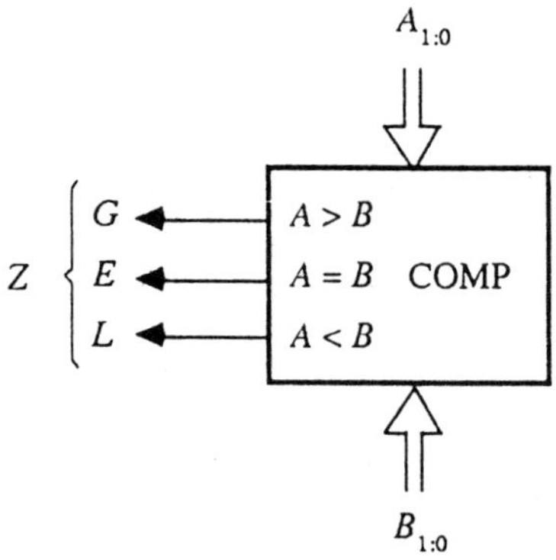

Figure 2.1

No	A_1	B_1	A_0	B_0	Z	G	E	L
0	0	0	0	0	=	0	1	0
1	0	0	0	1	<	0	0	1
2	0	0	1	0	>	1	0	0
3	0	0	1	1	=	0	1	0
4	0	1	0	0	<	0	0	1
5	0	1	0	1	<	0	0	1
6	0	1	1	0	<	0	0	1
7	0	1	1	1	<	0	0	1
8	1	0	0	0	>	1	0	0
9	1	0	0	1	>	1	0	0
10	1	0	1	0	>	1	0	0
11	1	0	1	1	>	1	0	0
12	1	1	0	0	=	0	1	0
13	1	1	0	1	<	0	0	1
14	1	1	1	0	>	1	0	0
15	1	1	1	1	=	0	1	0

Figure 2.2

$$G = A_1'B_1'A_0B_0' + A_1B_1'A_0'B_0' + A_1B_1'A_0'B_0 + A_1B_1'A_0B_0' + A_1B_1'A_0B_0 + A_1B_1A_0B_0' \qquad (2.1)$$

$$E = A_1'B_1'A_0'B_0' + A_1'B_1'A_0B_0 + A_1B_1A_0'B_0' + A_1B_1A_0B_0 \qquad (2.2)$$

$$L = A_1'B_1'A_0'B_0 + A_1'B_1A_0'B_0' + A_1'B_1A_0'B_0 + A_1'B_1A_0B_0' + A_1'B_1A_0B_0 + A_1B_1A_0'B_0 \qquad (2.3)$$

The traditional method for synthesizing combinational systems is that of implementing such expressions, possibly simplified, in terms of logical operators such as AND, OR, NOT, NAND [1], [59].

2.1.3 Representation: pseudo-boolean polynomial

The comparator of Figure 2.1 is a multiple-output logic system, and the code of Figure 2.2 expresses such a system in terms of the three logical functions G, E, L defined by (2.1)–(2.3). Generalizing, a combinational system having r outputs can always be described by r logical functions.

A function is said to be *pseudo-boolean* or *discrete* if it can take a finite number of distinct values; thus the function Z of Figure 2.2, which can take the three distinct values '>', '=', '<', is a discrete function that gives a complete description of the comparator. Further, Z can be expressed algebraically in the form

$$Z = G \cdot [>] + E \cdot [=] + L \cdot [<] \tag{2.4}$$

where the symbols $>$, $=$, $<$ are *non-logical* (or *discrete*) *constants*, which are always shown enclosed in square brackets. A polynomial such as (2.4), which expresses a discrete function, is called *pseudo-boolean*; its value can always be computed if the logical functions, here G, E, L, are disjoint, that is, if they are represented by a 1-out-of-3 code. Thus Z is discrete and can take as value $[>]$, $[=]$ or $[<]$. Generalizing, a combinational system with r output states can always be represented by a pseudo-boolean polynomial involving r non-logical constants.

If in (2.4) we replace G, E, L by their expression given by (2.1)–(2.3) we have the pseudo-boolean polynomial (2.5), defining in complete detail the comparator:

$$\begin{aligned} Z = {} & (A_1'B_1'A_0B_0' + A_1B_1'A_0'B_0' + A_1B_1'A_0'B_0 + \\ & A_1B_1'A_0B_0' + A_1B_1'A_0B_0 + A_1B_1A_0B_0') \cdot [>] + \\ & (A_1'B_1'A_0'B_0' + A_1'B_1'A_0B_0 + A_1B_1A_0'B_0' + A_1B_1A_0B_0) \cdot [=] + \\ & (A_1'B_1'A_0'B_0 + A_1'B_1A_0'B_0' + A_1'B_1A_0'B_0 + \\ & A_1'B_1A_0B_0' + A_1'B_1A_0B_0 + A_1B_1A_0'B_0) \cdot [<] \end{aligned} \tag{2.5}$$

Manipulation of pseudo-boolean polynomials, for example by factoring, may lead to expressions that are no longer simply sums of monomials; we shall call these *pseudo-boolean expressions*.

2.1.4 Representation: binary decision tree

In the truth table of Figure 2.2 the states A_1, B_1, A_0, B_0 are given in the natural order for the binary number system, from 0000 (decimal 0) to 1111 (decimal 15). An important property of this system is made clear in Figure 2.3: as the sequence is followed, the value of the least significant variable (B_0) changes at every step, that of the next-to-least significant (A_0) changes at every second step, of the next (B_1) at every four steps and of the most significant (A_1) at every eighth step. So turning Figure 2.3 through a right angle we have the equivalent new representation of Figure 2.4, the *binary decision tree*. Such a tree is constructed from two elements:

- a *test element*, represented by a diamond (see Figure 2.5) and defined by a logical *test variable* x or *predicate*; for each such variable there is an input terminal, an output terminal true for $x = 1$ and an output terminal false for $x = 0$. The false channel is indicated in the tree by a small circle, the conventional symbol for logical inversion;

- an *assignment element* (also called an *action element*, *output element* or *leaf*), represented by a rectangle (Figure 2.6) and defined by an assignment (or action or output) *s*; each such element has a single input terminal and no output terminals.

<table>
<tr><th>No</th><th>A_1</th><th>B_1</th><th>A_0</th><th>B_0</th><th>Z</th></tr>
<tr><td>0</td><td rowspan="8">0</td><td rowspan="4">0</td><td rowspan="2">0</td><td>0</td><td>=</td></tr>
<tr><td>1</td><td>1</td><td><</td></tr>
<tr><td>2</td><td rowspan="2">1</td><td>0</td><td>></td></tr>
<tr><td>3</td><td>1</td><td>=</td></tr>
<tr><td>4</td><td rowspan="4">1</td><td rowspan="2">0</td><td>0</td><td><</td></tr>
<tr><td>5</td><td>1</td><td><</td></tr>
<tr><td>6</td><td rowspan="2">1</td><td>0</td><td><</td></tr>
<tr><td>7</td><td>1</td><td><</td></tr>
<tr><td>8</td><td rowspan="8">1</td><td rowspan="4">0</td><td rowspan="2">0</td><td>0</td><td>></td></tr>
<tr><td>9</td><td>1</td><td>></td></tr>
<tr><td>10</td><td rowspan="2">1</td><td>0</td><td>></td></tr>
<tr><td>11</td><td>1</td><td>></td></tr>
<tr><td>12</td><td rowspan="4">1</td><td rowspan="2">0</td><td>0</td><td>=</td></tr>
<tr><td>13</td><td>1</td><td><</td></tr>
<tr><td>14</td><td rowspan="2">1</td><td>0</td><td>></td></tr>
<tr><td>15</td><td>1</td><td>=</td></tr>
</table>

Figure 2.3

2.1.5 Definition: binary decision tree

A binary decision tree can be defined rigorously as follows:

- every assignment element (as in Figure 2.6) is a tree;
- if *T1* and *T0* are trees then the assembly *T* of Figure 2.7 is a tree.

The tree *T* of Figure 2.7 can be defined by the pseudo-boolean polynomial

$$T = x' \cdot T0 + x \cdot T1 \tag{2.6}$$

where *T* is identified with the discrete function generated by the tree *T* and *T0, T1* are non-logical constants (assignments), or the discrete functions of the trees *T0, T1*.

It follows from the construction that there can be only one input terminal to the tree: this is called the *root*, and any path joining a leaf to the root is called a *branch*. Thus the tree of Figure 2.4 has 16 branches, each representing an input state A_1, B_1, A_0, B_0 of the combinational system of Figure 2.2 and also the associated output state *Z*.

It follows also from the construction that if *b* is the number of branches of the tree and *m* the number of test elements, then

$$b = m + 1 \tag{2.7}$$

or

$$m = b - 1 \tag{2.8}$$

Since the number of assignment elements is equal to the number of branches, the total number *t* of elements of both types is

$$t = m + b = 2b - 1 \tag{2.9}$$

2.1.6 Definitions: complete tree, partial tree

We see from the tree of Figure 2.4, and from the truth tables of Figures 2.2 and 2.3, that the input state $A_1, B_1 = 01$ leads to the output state $Z = [<]$ whatever the values of A_0 and B_0; and similarly 10 leads always to [>]. Figure 2.8 is a new binary decision tree, equivalent to Figure 2.4 but having fewer elements; and the associated truth table of Figure 2.9 is equivalent to Figure 2.2 but has fewer rows. In the table the symbols Φ indicate 'don't care' conditions (§1.1.17), expressing the fact that the values of A_0 and B_0 have no effect on the output state *Z*.

We now define a *complete* (or *canonical*) tree as a binary decision tree for *n* variables having 2^n branches corresponding to the 2^n possible input states: for the tree of Figure 2.4, $n = 4$ and $2^n = 16$. Thus any given variable can appear only once in the same branch, and each branch will consist of *n* test elements and 1 assignment element.

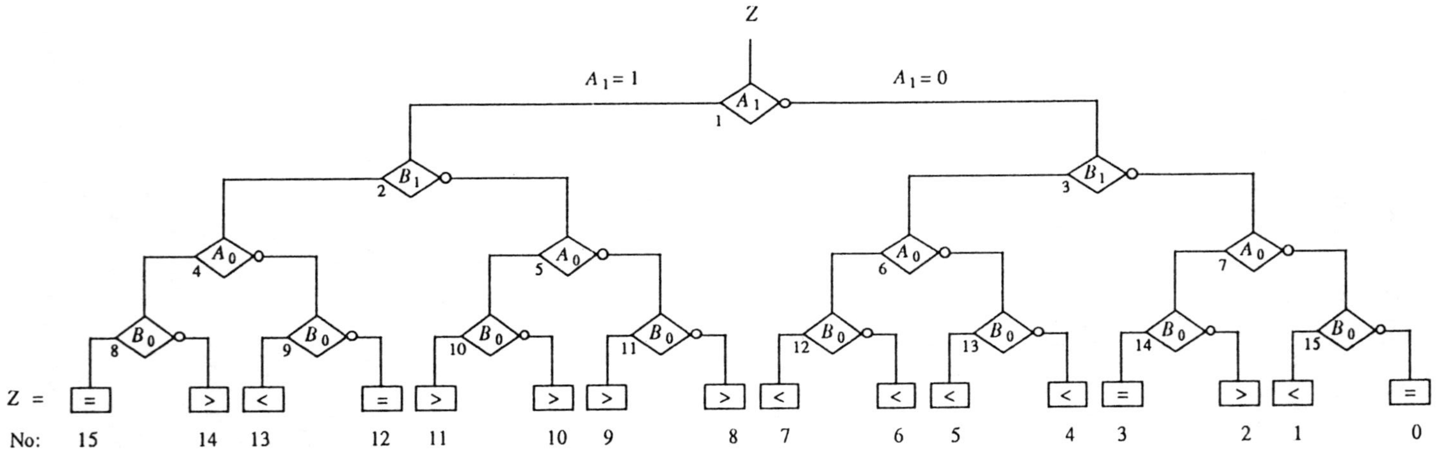
Z
$A_1 = 1$
$A_1 = 0$
A_1
1
B_1
2
B_1
3
A_0
4
A_0
5
A_0
6
A_0
7
B_0
8
B_0
9
B_0
10
B_0
11
B_0
12
B_0
13
B_0
14
B_0
15
Z = | = | > | < | = | > | > | > | > | < | < | < | < | = | > | < | =
No: 15 14 13 12 11 10 9 8 7 6 5 4 3 2 1 0

Figure 2.4

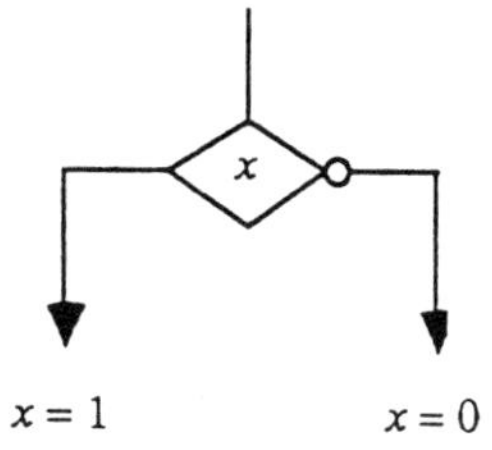

Figure 2.5

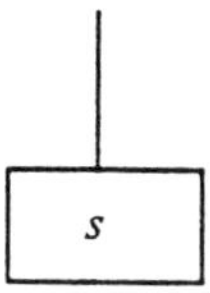

Figure 2.6

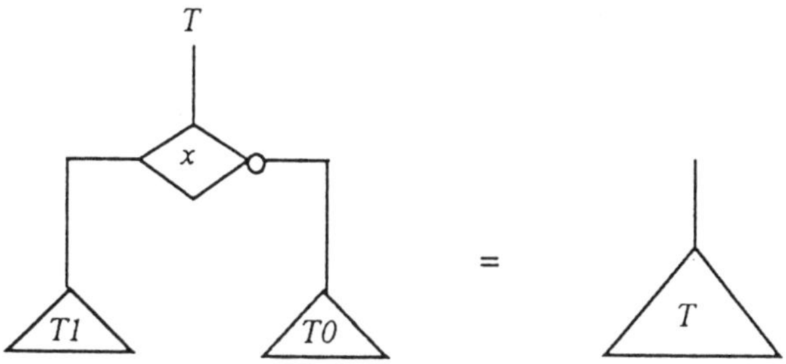

Figure 2.7

The *level of an element* is the number of elements between it and the root, plus 1; thus the first test element is at level 1 and in a canonical tree all the assignment elements (leaves) are at level $n + 1$. The *depth* of a tree is the number of elements in its longest branch; thus the depth of a canonical tree is $n + 1$.

If the number of branches b is less than 2^n the tree is *partial*: thus Figure 2.8, in which $b = 10 < 16$, is a partial tree. The corresponding truth table is also said to be partial, and has as many rows as there are branches in the tree: thus ten rows in Figure 2.9.

The complete tree of Figure 2.4 has 15 test elements and 31 elements (test + assignment) in total, agreeing with the formulae (2.8) and (2.9); the partial tree of Figure 2.9 has only nine test elements and 19 in total.

Each branch of a complete tree represents an input state of the complete set of variables (A_1, B_1, A_0, B_0 for Figure 2.4) and thus gives rise to one minterm in these variables. Each branch of a partial tree represents either a minterm or a partial product (monomial) of the input variables. From Figure 2.8 we see that the functions G, E, L can be expressed as follows:

$$G = A_1'B_1'A_0B_0' + A_1B_1' + A_1B_1A_0B_0' \qquad (2.10)$$

$$E = A_1'B_1'A_0'B_0' + A_1'B_1'A_0B_0 + A_1B_1A_0'B_0' + A_1B_1A_0B_0 \qquad (2.11)$$

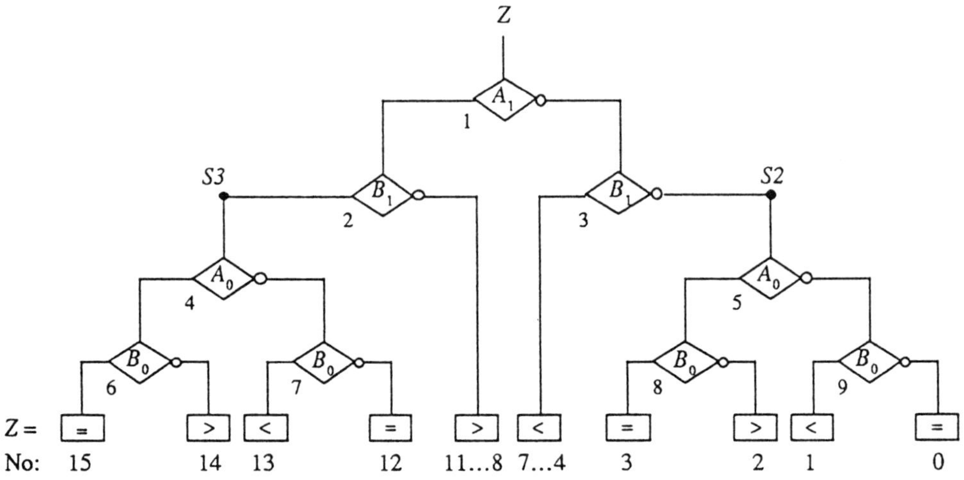

Figure 2.8

No	A_1	B_1	A_0	B_0	Z
0	0	0	0	0	=
1	0	0	0	1	<
2	0	0	1	0	>
3	0	0	1	1	=
4...7	0	1	Φ	Φ	<
8...11	1	0	Φ	Φ	>
12	1	1	0	0	=
13	1	1	0	1	<
14	1	1	1	0	>
15	1	1	1	1	=

Figure 2.9

$$L = A_1'B_1'A_0'B_0 + A_1'B_1 + A_1B_1A_0'B_0 \tag{2.12}$$

leading to what we call the *partial pseudo-boolean polynomial*, to distinguish the form from the *complete* or *canonical* form of (2.5):

$$\begin{aligned} Z = {} & (A_1'B_1'A_0B_0' + A_1B_1' + A_1B_1A_0B_0')\cdot[>] + \\ & (A_1'B_1'A_0'B_0' + A_1'B_1'A_0B_0 + \\ & A_1B_1A_0'B_0' + A_1B_1A_0B_0)\cdot[=] + \\ & (A_1'B_1'A_0'B_0 + A_1'B_1 + A_1B_1A_0'B_0)\cdot[<] \end{aligned} \tag{2.13}$$

Each minterm or monomial generated by a branch of a tree is called a *branch product*. For any given tree there are as many branch products as there are branches, that is, b.

2.1.7 Representation: Karnaugh map

The Karnaugh map [1], [59] shown in Figure 2.10 is a 2-dimensional representation of the truth table of Figure 2.2, in which the 16 cells of the former correspond to the 16 rows of the latter. Each cell defines a product of the four variables A_1, A_0, B_1, B_0, that is, a minterm, or branch product of the complete tree of Figure 2.4.

The Karnaugh map of Figure 2.10 represents the partial tree of Figure 2.8; here each of the ten branch products, given by the expression (2.13), is represented by a *block*, that is, either by a single cell (in the case of a minterm, e.g. $A_1'B_1'A_0'B_0'$) or by a group of four cells arranged in a square (in the case of a monomial, e.g. A_1B_1'). The general statement is that for any logical function each monomial is represented by a block in the Karnaugh map, where a block consists of $p = 2^n$ cells, $n = 0, 1, 2. \ldots,$ grouped in a square or rectangle [1], [59].

In Figure 2.11 the 4-cell blocks have been emphasized by the omission of the boundaries of the constituent cells; thus the number of subdivisions of the map is equal to the number of blocks, that is, ten; and this form is equivalent to the partial truth table of Figure 2.9, which has ten rows.

If Figure 2.11 is compared with the partial tree of Figure 2.8 it will be seen to illustrate three properties of binary decision trees: those of coverage, separation and compatibility.

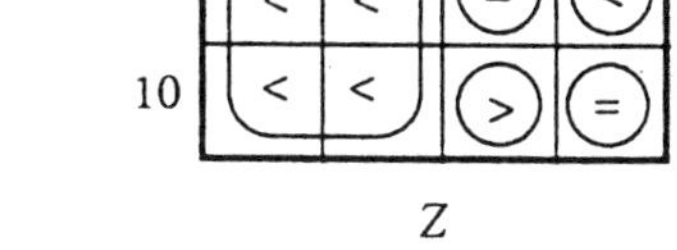

Figure 2.10

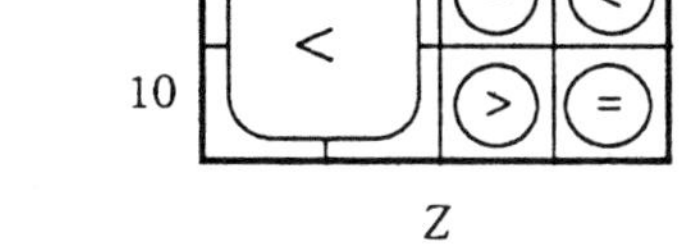

Figure 2.11

2.1.8 Definition: coverage

Taking Figures 2.10 and 2.11, we see that the ten branch products of the tree Z (i.e. the 10 blocks) cover the 16 minterms of the four variables. In general, the *coverage* property for a given tree states that the set of b branch products covers the set of 2^n cells of the corresponding Karnaugh map.

In graphical terms, this means that every cell of the table is included in a block.

2.1.9 Definition: separation

The set of branch products defines a partition of the set of minterms; each minterm is covered by one and only one branch product and each branch product contains one and only one output state — i.e. '>', '=' or '<' in the example of Figure 2.11. This is called the *separation* property.

Graphically, this means that each cell is included in one and only one block and that each block contains one and only one output state.

2.1.10 Definition: compatibility

Figure 2.12 gives the Karnaugh map representation of the partial tree Z of Figure 2.8; from a study of this we can say:

- the tree Z is represented by the Karnaugh map of Figure 2.11;
- in accordance with the definition of binary decision trees given in §2.1.5, Z can be broken into a test element and two new trees *S0*, *S1*, *sub-trees* of Z. The choice of A_1 as test variable gives a partition of the Karnaugh map into two *half-maps* representing *S0* and *S1*, and the value of Z can be expressed as a pseudo-boolean polynomial:

$$Z = A_1' \cdot S0 + A_1 \cdot S1 \tag{2.14}$$

- the sub-trees *S0*, *S1* can themselves be broken similarly; choosing B_1 as test variable for each, we get a further partitioning of the map into four *quarter-maps* representing two new sub-trees *S2*, *S3* and two assignment elements, [<] and [>]. Substituting the new values for *S0* and *S1* in (2.14) we get

$$Z = A_1' \cdot (B_1' \cdot S2 + B_1 \cdot [<]) + A_1 \cdot (B_1' \cdot [>] + B_1 \cdot S3) \tag{2.15}$$

- continuing, *S2* and *S3* can be decomposed; Figure 2.13 shows the partitions of *S2* by the use first of A_0 and then of B_0 as test variable; a similar operation on *S3* shows that the two trees are identical and can be described thus:

$$S2 = S3 = A_0'(B_0' \cdot [=] + B_0 \cdot [<]) + A_0(B_0' \cdot [>] + B_0 \cdot [=]) \tag{2.16}$$

- if finally we substitute for *S2, S3* in (2.15) the values given by (2.16) we get the following pseudo-boolean expression for *Z*:

$$Z = A_1'(B_1'(A_0'(B_0' \cdot [=] + B_0 \cdot [<]) + A_0(B_0' \cdot [>] + B_0 \cdot [=])) + B_1 \cdot [<]) + A_1(B_1' \cdot [>] + B_1(A_0'(B_0' \cdot [=] + B_0 \cdot [<]) + A_0(B_0' \cdot [>] + B_0 \cdot [=])) \tag{2.17}$$

which is equivalent to the partial pseudo-boolean polynomial (2.13), but of questionable readability.

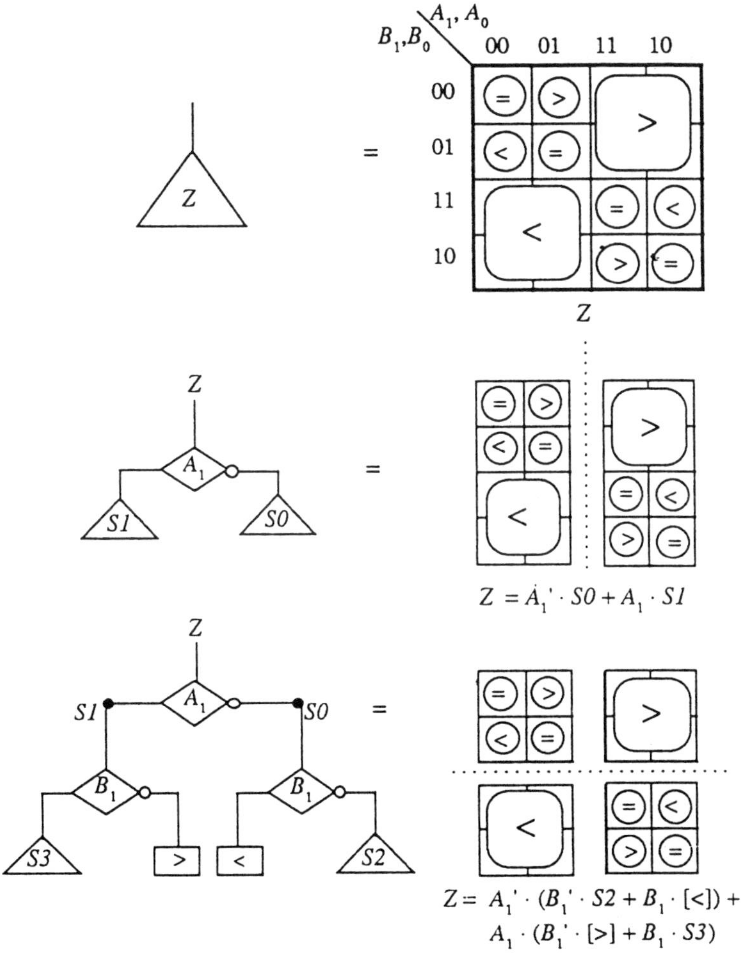

Figure 2.12

The *compatibility* property states that any binary decision tree T, and any of its sub-trees, can be expressed in the form

$$T = x' \cdot T0 + x \cdot T1 \tag{2.18}$$

where x is a test variable and $T0, T1$ are either sub-trees of T or assignment elements.

This property follows directly from the definition given in §2.1.5 and is verified formally, for the example of the comparator, by (2.17). Graphically, it means that no partitioning of the Karnaugh map by means of a test variable must separate an already-existing block: see for example Figures 2.12 and 2.13.

2.1.11 Comment

The result found in the example considered above, that the sub-trees $S2$, $S3$ are identical, is specific to this example and not one that holds generally. However, because of its importance the consequences of such an identity are studied in section 2.2 below.

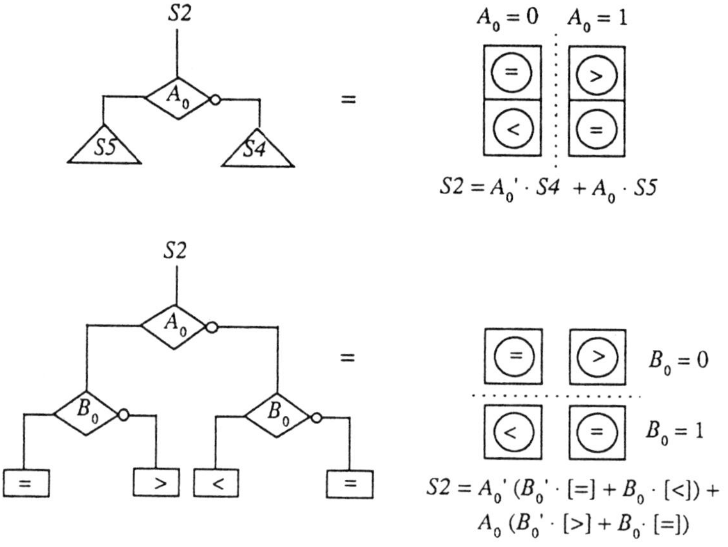

Figure 2.13

2.1.12 Definition: standard set

A set of branch products (represented by a set of blocks in the Karnaugh map) which has the three properties of coverage, separation and compatibility is called a *standard set*. Any such set can be represented by a binary decision tree, and conversely every binary tree leads to a standard set [27].

2.1.13 Definitions: minimal tree, simplification

In general, there will be several different but equivalent representations of a given discrete function by binary decision trees. Amongst these representations one or more will have fewer test elements than the others, and therefore, because of the relation (2.8), fewer branches: these are called the *minimal* or *simplified* trees for the function. The *simplification* of a discrete function is the determination, from the truth table or the Karnaugh map, of one or more minimal trees for the function.

2.1.14 Method: simplification of a discrete function

Simplication is essentially a search for a tree having the minimum number of branches, and therefore of branch products; it follows from the definition of §2.1.12 that this implies a search for a standard set having the minimum number of branch products. A systematic method, due to Cerny, Mange and Sanchez and designed for computer use, is given in section 8.1 [28], [29].

A fast graphical method for hand computation, using the Karnaugh map, is as follows.

1. Introduce the discrete function into the Karnaugh map.
2. Scan this visually to find a minimal set of blocks with the properties of coverage and separation.
3. Having found such a set, try to construct a tree by taking the test variables in turn and checking to see if the compatibility property is satisfied.
4. If this does not succeed, return to step 2 and repeat with another minimal set.

This is a subjective method and the quality of the result obtained depends greatly on the skill and experience of the user. For a rigorous treatment the algorithm of section 8.1 must be used.

2.1.15 Example 1: selection of an aircraft crew

Conscious of the risks of air travel, the Ruritanian National Airline will employ an individual as a member of a flight crew only if he or she satisfies at least one of the following criteria:

(a) male, unmarried, Ruritanian national;
(b) unmarried, Ruritanian national, age less than 25 years;
(c) female, unmarried, foreign national;
(d) male, age less than 25 years;
(e) unmarried, age at least 25 years.

They wish to construct a minimal binary decision tree to use in selecting candidates.

The problem reduces to the study of a function Z of four variables D, C, B, A, coded as follows:

D = nationality, 1 if Ruritanian, 0 if foreign;
C = civil state, 1 if unmarried, 0 if married;
B = sex, 1 if male, 0 if female;
A = age, 1 if <25, 0 if $\geqslant 25$;
Z = decision, 1 if accepted, 0 if rejected.

Acceptance ($Z = 1$) means that at least one of the five conditions (a) to (e) is satisfied; that is, with an obvious notation, at least one of the variables a to e has the value 1; so we can take

$$Z = a + b + c + d + e \tag{2.19}$$

Each condition can be expressed as a function of the variables A, B, C, D:

$$a = DCB, \quad b = DCA, \quad c = D'CB', \quad d = BA, \quad e = CA' \tag{2.20}$$

so $$Z = DCB + DCA + D'CB' + BA + CA' \tag{2.21}$$

for which the Karnaugh table is given in Figure 2.14. Z is a logical function, since it takes only the distinct values 0, 1; and it is *completely defined*, that is, there are no don't care conditions Φ as defined in §1.1.17.

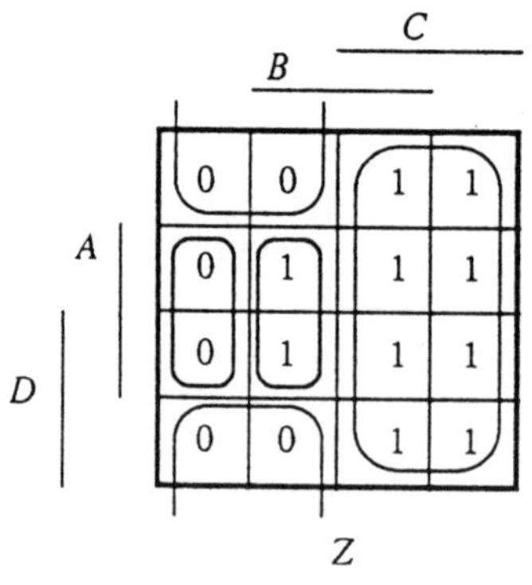

Figure 2.14

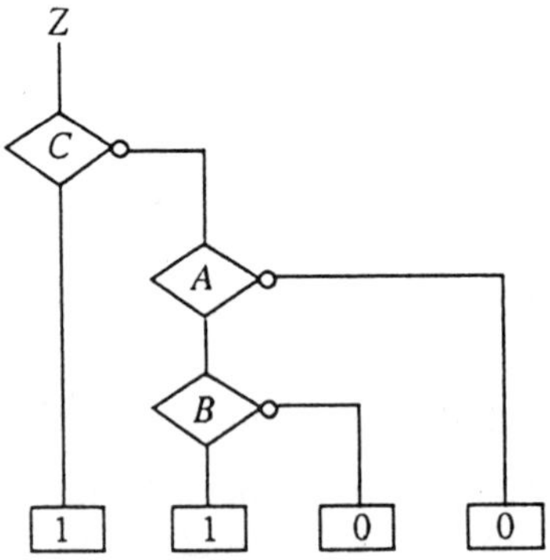

Figure 2.15

Figure 2.14 shows that ten input states give the output $Z = 1$ and that the corresponding cells are covered by a minimum of two blocks: one of eight cells (C) and one of two cells ($C'BA$); six input states give $Z = 0$ and the cells are in two blocks: one of four cells ($C'A'$) and one of two cells ($C'B'A$). The set of four blocks $\{C, C'BA, C'A', C'B'A\}$ has the properties of coverage and separation and in addition is minimal.

The first test variable is C: this is the only one that cuts the Karnaugh map into two half-maps without violating the compatibility condition. This gives the pseudo-boolean polynomial

$$Z = C \cdot [1] + C' \cdot S0 \tag{2.22}$$

where $S0$ is a sub-tree and [1] a non-logical constant indicating the assignment $Z = 1$. The only test variable compatible with $S0$ is A, so we next have

$$Z = C \cdot [1] + C'(A \cdot S1 + A' \cdot [0]) \tag{2.23}$$

where $S1$ is a new sub-tree and [0] indicates $Z = 0$. Finally, the only test variable compatible with $S1$ is B, giving

$$Z = C \cdot [1] + C'(A(B \cdot [1] + B' \cdot [0]) + A' \cdot [0]) \tag{2.24}$$

This pseudo-boolean polynomial gives the minimal tree of Figure 2.15; we see that Z does not depend on the variable D.

2.1.16 Comments

If Z is a completely defined logical function its expression as an algebraic polynomial such as (2.21) can be identified with the binary decision tree described by a pseudo-boolean polynomial such as (2.24). Thus in this particular case the equivalence of the two forms can be established by replacing the non-logical constants [0], [1] in the latter by the logical constants 0, 1 respectively.

For the example of §2.1.15 there is at least one minimal standard set, that is, a set of four branch products $\{C, C'BA, C'A', C'B'A\}$ which has the three properties of coverage, separation and compatibility. Starting from this set only one minimal tree can be constructed, that is, there is only one sequence of choices: first C, then A and finally B. In the general case several such sets can be found, and for each one there will be several possible choices for the sequence of test variables and hence several minimal trees.

Returning to the example, the number of branches is $b = 4$, so from (2.8) and (2.9) we have for the number of test elements in the minimal tree

$$m = b - 1 = 3 \tag{2.25}$$

and the total number t of elements, test + assignment,

$$t = 2b - 1 = 7 \tag{2.26}$$

It follows from the method of simplification that a discrete function having r distinct output states will have at least r blocks in its Karnaugh table and thus r branches, $r - 1$ test elements and $2r - 1$ elements in total.

2.1.17 Example 2: 7-bar numerical display

Figure 2.16 is a combinational system with four inputs D, C, B, A and seven outputs a–g; each output controls the lighting of a bar: 1 for illuminated, 0 for extinguished, and to each of the ten states D, C, B, A = 0000–1001 corresponds the display of one of the decimal digits 0–9 as shown in Figure 2.17. There are three possible forms for the digit 7, and nothing is specified for any of the six states 1010–1111: thus there are six don't care conditions (cf. §1.1.17). We require a minimal tree that generates the logical functions f, g, in other words the discrete function $Z = f, g$. We say that functions such as f, g and Z are *incompletely defined* since they have don't care (Φ) conditions.

We start by recording the binary values of f and g in the Karnaugh map (Figure 2.18), including the Φ conditions. We then translate each

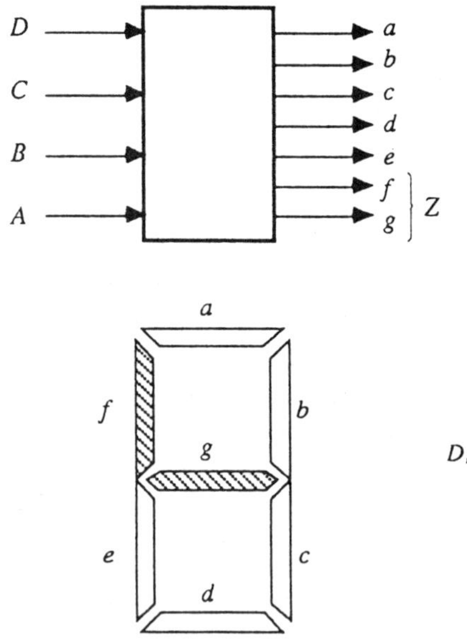

Figure 2.16

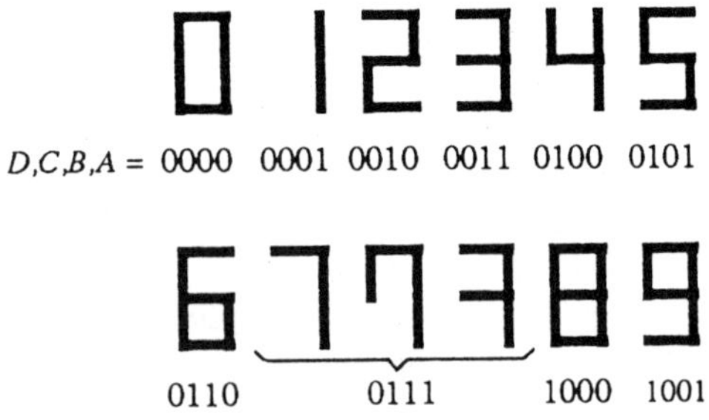

Figure 2.17

output state f, g into its decimal equivalent and record these in a Karnaugh map, as in Figure 2.19; this will make it easier to identify the blocks covering the same output state. The multiple choices resulting from the Φ conditions are shown explicitly, thus $f, g = \Phi\Phi$ describes the set of four states $00, 01, 10, 11$, and therefore the four decimal digits $0, 1, 2, 3$.

In this case the search for blocks in the map is complicated by the existence of the Φ conditions, since in seven cells these offer multiple choices for the output $Z = f, g$. Again, a rigorous treatment is given in section 8.1 and references [28], [29]; here we restrict the discussion to two minimal solutions found by the subjective process and checked subsequently.

B,A \ D,C	00	01	11	10
00	10	11	ΦΦ	11
01	00	11	ΦΦ	11
11	01	0Φ Φ0	ΦΦ	ΦΦ
10	01	11	ΦΦ	ΦΦ

$Z = f, g$

Figure 2.18

B,A \ D,C	00	01	11	10
00	2	3	0,1,2,3	3
01	0	3	0,1,2,3	3
11	1	0,1,2	0,1,2,3	0,1,2,3
10	1	3	0,1,2,3	0,1,2,3

Z

Figure 2.19

Figure 2.20 is the first of these solutions. The Karnaugh map shows a set of seven blocks, $S1 = \{D, D'CB', D'CBA, D'CBA', D'C'B'A', D'C'B'A, D'C'B\}$, with the coverage and separation properties; Figure 2.22 gives the tree $Z1$ corresponding to $S1$, which is a standard set. We

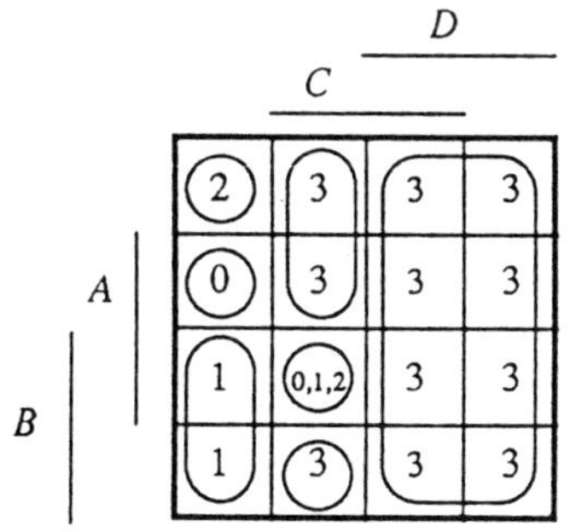

$Z1$

Figure 2.20

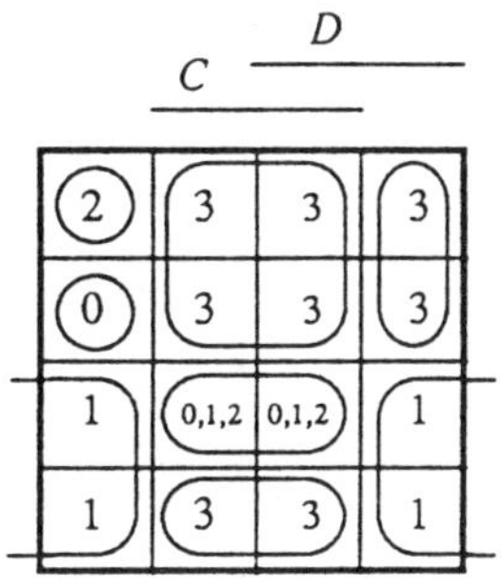

$Z2$

Figure 2.21

say that *Z1* is a particular solution for *Z*, since we have given the value 3 to the six Φ states (D, C, B, A = 1010–1111); *Z1* is an incompletely defined function, since the values $Z1 = 0, 1, 2$ are all given by the state $D, C, B, A = 0111$.

Figure 2.21 is the second solution, in which there is the standard set $S2 = \{D'C'B'A, D'B'C'A', C'B, CB', CBA', CBA, DC'B'\}$ and the corresponding tree *Z2* of Figure 2.23. The solution *Z2* is less obvious in the Karnaugh map than *Z1*; it is obtained by the systematic method of section 8.1, where it is shown that all minimal standard sets for this problem consist of seven branch products. *Z2* also is a particular solution for *Z*, and like *Z1* is incompletely defined since both input states 0111 and 1111 give the multiple outputs $Z2 = 0, 1, 2$.

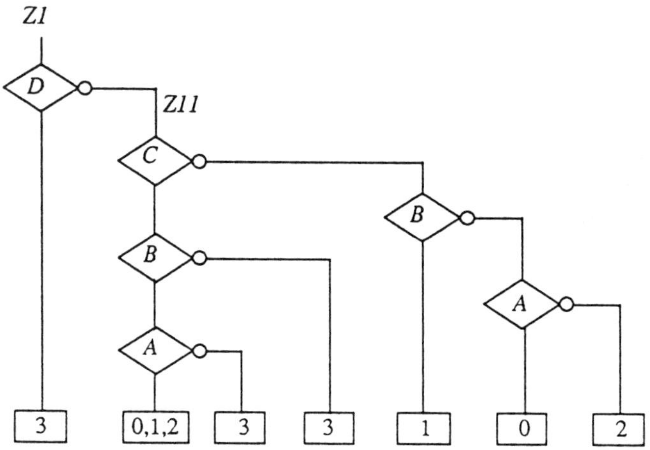

Figure 2.22

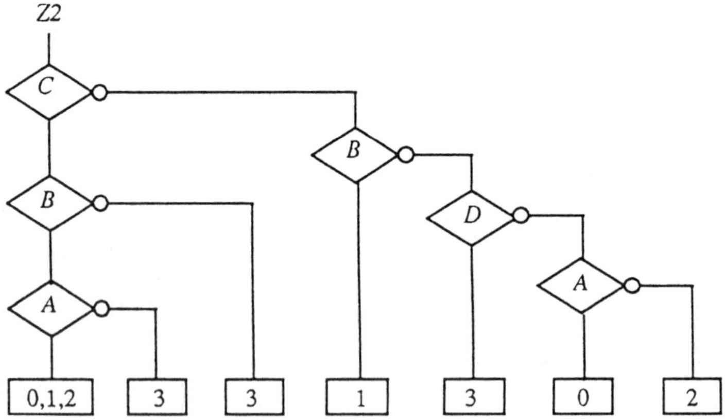

Figure 2.23

2.1.18 Comments

If a set of blocks has been found that has the coverage and separability properties it can be tested for compatibility and the sequence of test variables determined by a simple study of the branch products. Thus in the above example (§2.1.17) we have

$$S1 = \{D, D'CB', D'CBA, D'CBA', D'C'B'A', D'C'B'A, D'C'B\} \tag{2.27}$$

in which D is the only variable common to all seven branch products. It follows that D is the first test variable for $Z1$. The sub-tree $Z11$ of Figure 2.22 is then defined by

$$S11 = \{CB', CBA, CBA', C'B'A', C'B'A, C'B\} \tag{2.28}$$

in which C and B are seen to be candidates for the next test variable. In contrast, a set of branch products with no common variable (true of complemented) cannot give rise to a tree, since it does not satisfy the compatibility criterion.

The tree of Figure 2.23, in contrast to those of Figures 2.4, 2.8, 2.15 and 2.22, illustrates the more general case in which the test variables at any one level are all different. Here the test elements at level 3 are defined by A and D.

2.1.19 Example 3: months of the year

The months can be represented by BCD (*binary coded decimal*) numbers [1], [59] in the range 1–12 (decimal) with the aid of the following five logical variables:

- M_4 for the tens (0 or 1);
- M_3, M_2, M_1, M_0 for the units (0000–1001).

These are to be the inputs to a combinational system whose output Z is to be the number of days in that month: Z = 30, 31 or F for February. The problem is to construct a minimal binary decision tree for Z.

Of the 32 possible input states $M_4 \ldots M_0$, 12 are defined and 20 are Φ conditions for Z, which is thus an incompletely defined function. In the Karnaugh map of Figure 2.24 the set $S1$ of seven blocks

$$\{M_4M_0', M_4M_0, M_4'M_3M_0', M_4'M_3M_0, M_4'M_3'M_0, M_4'M_3'M_2M_0', M_4'M_3'M_2'M_0'\}$$

satisfies the coverage and separation criteria; thus a tree $Z1$, Figure 2.25, can be constructed from $S1$, which is thus a standard set.

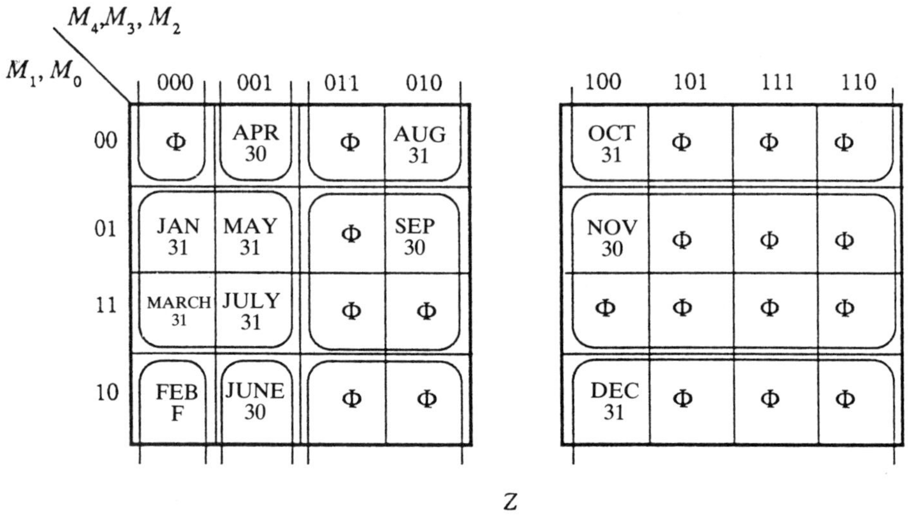

Figure 2.24

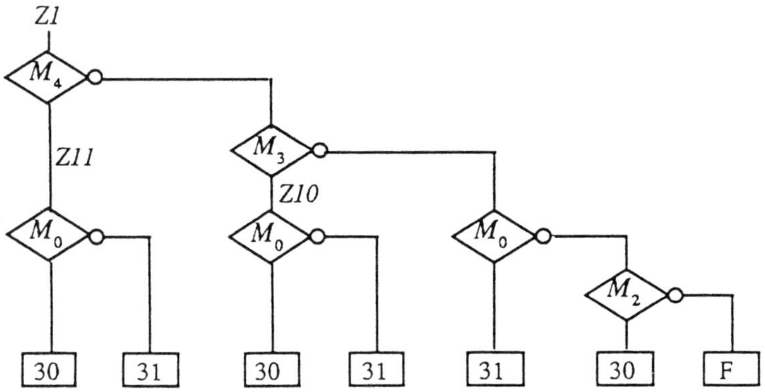

Figure 2.25

2.1.20 Comments

The method of section 8.1 must be used to show that the tree *Z1* is minimal. We see from the tree that the value of the discrete function *Z* depends only on the variables M_4, M_3, M_2, M_0, and not on M_1; this reduction in the number of variables reduces the volume of computation needed by that method.

We see also in Figure 2.25 that there are two identical sub-trees, *Z10* and *Z11*; this is an important property, which we return to in section 2.2.

The choice of the coding scheme for the 12 months has a strong influence on structure of the tree *Z*, a situation that is studied in more detail in [32].

2.1.21 Conclusion

The graphical method for simplifying a discrete function, using the Karnaugh map, is essentially visual and therefore subjective; further, it becomes very awkward, impractical even, if there are more than six variables. The systematic method of section 8.1 must be used whenever one needs to be certain of a minimal solution (or possibly several); but here the combinatorial explosion in the algorithm may again limit the application to problems with few variables.

When dealing with complex problems with many variables we may have to be satisfied with near-optimal solutions, or to break the original problem down into sub-problems of manageable size: see §2.2.14.

2.1.22 Exercise

For the completely defined logical function

$$F = W + X + Y + Z \qquad (2.29)$$

find all the minimal standard sets, and all the minimal trees for each set.

2.1.23 Exercise

Figure 2.26 is the state table for a sequential logic system. Find a minimal standard set and a minimal tree for the discrete function Y^+, Z.

x1 (columns 3–4), *x2* (columns 2–3); *y2* (rows 2–3), *y1* (rows 3–4)

1,0	0,0	0,0	0,0
1,0	2,0	0,0	0,0
1,0	0,0	0,0	0,1
Φ	Φ	Φ	Φ

Y^+,Z

Figure 2.26

2.1.24 Exercise

Figure 2.27 shows three incompletely defined logical functions R, S, T. Compare the numbers of test elements and of assignment elements in two distinct representations of these functions:

1. by three distinct minimal trees, one for each function;
2. by a single minimal tree for the global discrete function $Z = R, S, T$.

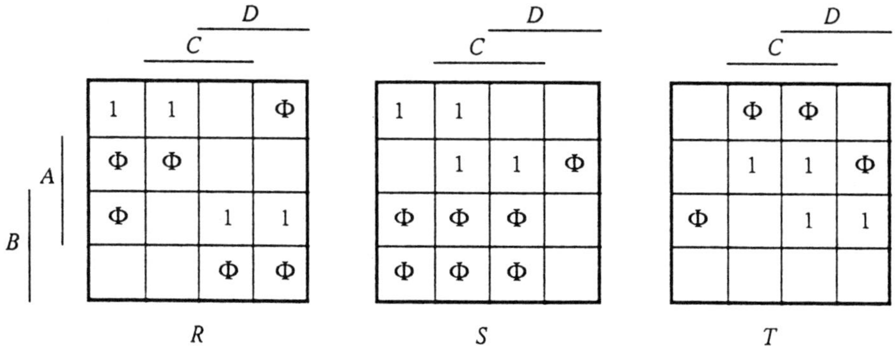

Figure 2.27

2.1.25 Exercise

For example §2.1.17, construct a minimal binary decision tree for the seven logical functions a to g (Figures 2.16, 2.17), that is, for the discrete function $Z = a, b, \ldots g$.

Can the minimum number of elements be determined directly from the specification given by Figure 2.17?

2.1.26 Exercise: minimal code, 1-out-of-M code

Figure 2.28 gives a discrete function F having the five distinct states $0, 1, 2, 3, 4$. Compare the minimal numbers of test and of assignment elements in two distinct trees for F:

1. using five variables $x0, x1, \ldots x4$ and a 1-out-of-5 code;
2. using only three variables $y0, y1, y2$ and a minimal code.

Show that both trees are minimal, each with five assignment elements, and that they differ mainly in their depths (see §2.1.6). Find the two depths for the general case of a discrete function with M distinct states.

$x4$	$x3$	$x2$	$x1$	$x0$	$y2$	$y1$	$y0$	F
0	0	0	0	1	0	0	0	0
0	0	0	1	0	0	0	1	1
0	0	1	0	0	0	1	0	2
0	1	0	0	0	0	1	1	3
1	0	0	0	0	1	0	0	4

Figure 2.28

2.1.27 Exercise: sorting numbers

Let $a1, a2, a3$ be three different integers, and with each pair ai, aj $(i \neq j)$ associate a logical variable Xij whose value is 1 if $ai > aj$ and 0 if $ai < aj$. Construct a minimal decision tree:

1. to sort the three numbers; that is, to generate assignments of the type $a1 > a3 > a2$;
2. to find the greatest of the three numbers, e.g. $a1$ [34].

Extend this to constructing a minimal tree to find the greatest of four numbers $a1, a2, a3, a4$.

2.2 ANALYSIS AND SYNTHESIS OF BINARY DECISION DIAGRAMS

2.2.1 Example: a comparator

Returning to Figure 2.8, we see that the partial tree Z for the comparator contains two identical sub-trees $S2, S3$; this is confirmed by the pseudo-boolean expressions of §2.1.10:

$$Z = A_1' \cdot (B_1' \cdot S2 + B_1 \cdot [<]) + A_1 \cdot (B_1' \cdot [>] + B_1 \cdot S3) \quad (2.15)$$

where

$$S2 = S3 = A_0'(B_0' \cdot [=] + B_0 \cdot [<]) + A_0(B_0' \cdot [>] + B_0 \cdot [=]) \quad (2.16)$$

2.2.2 Representation: decomposition of a tree

In Figure 2.29 the two trees $Z = pp$ and $S2 = S3 = sp$ together form a representation of Z that is equivalent to the single tree of Figure 2.8; we say that these trees, pp and sp, define a *decomposition* of the original tree.

In general, the decomposition of an arbitrary tree gives a *principal tree pp* and one or more *sub-trees sp*. To keep the notation meaningful we have to introduce a third type of element, to represent a *sub-tree call*: this is shown as a rectangle enclosing the name of the tree that is called, with four vertical bars to distinguish it from an assignment. This is illustrated in Figure 2.30. Any element of this type can have only one input terminal.

As we saw, the tree of Figure 2.8 has a total of 19 elements: nine tests and ten assignments; the decomposition shown in Figure 2.29 has a total of 14 elements: six tests, six assignments and two sub-tree calls. The two trees of this figure are described by the truth tables of Figure 2.32.

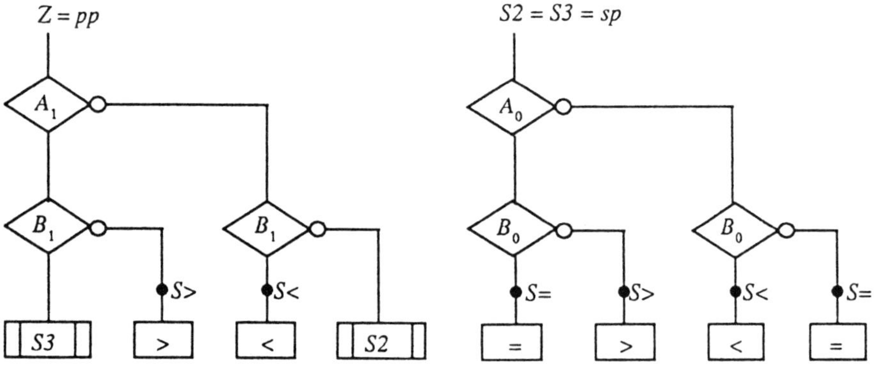

Figure 2.29

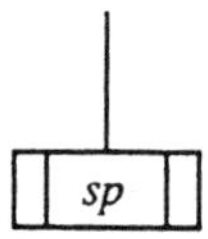

Figure 2.30

2.2.3 Comment

The decomposition of Figure 2.29 involves six assignment elements which are identical in pairs: two each of [>], [<] and [=]. This suggests a further decomposition as in Figure 2.31, in which these assignments are treated as further sub-trees *sp2, sp3, sp4* respectively, each consisting of a single element. But this increases the total number of elements to 17 without any compensating improvement in the representation of *Z*; from which we draw the lesson that de-

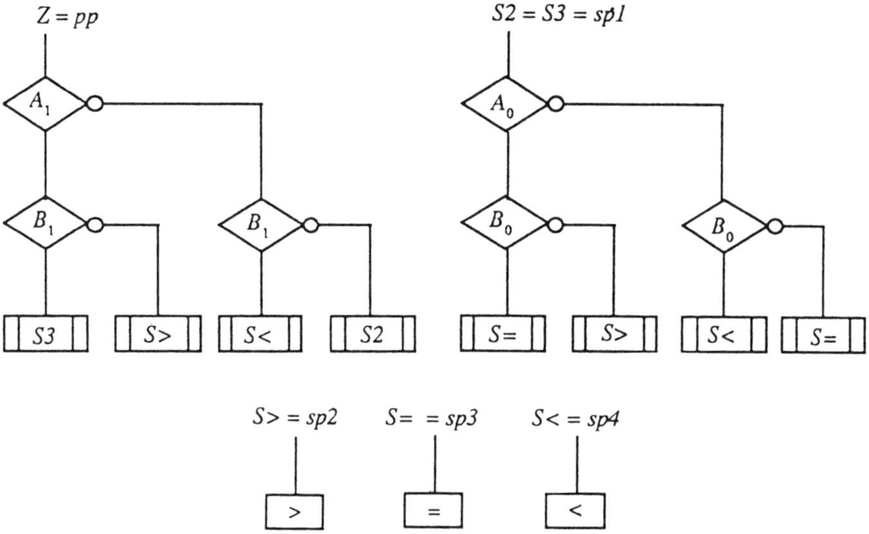

Figure 2.31

A_1	B_1	Z
0	0	*sp*
0	1	<
1	0	>
1	1	*sp*

pp

A_0	B_0	Z
0	0	=
0	1	<
1	0	>
1	1	=

sp

Figure 2.32

composition should not be taken down to the level of trivial sub-trees of a single element.

2.2.4 Representation: binary decision diagram

Figure 2.33 gives a different representation that is equivalent to both the single tree of Figure 2.8 and its decomposition of Figure 2.29; a new feature is a binary decision tree with two branches converging on the common sub-tree $S2 = S3$. Such a tree is called a *binary decision diagram* or *algorithm*.

This form differs from that of Figure 2.29 in that it uses only test and assignment elements, of which it has a total of 12, with no calls to

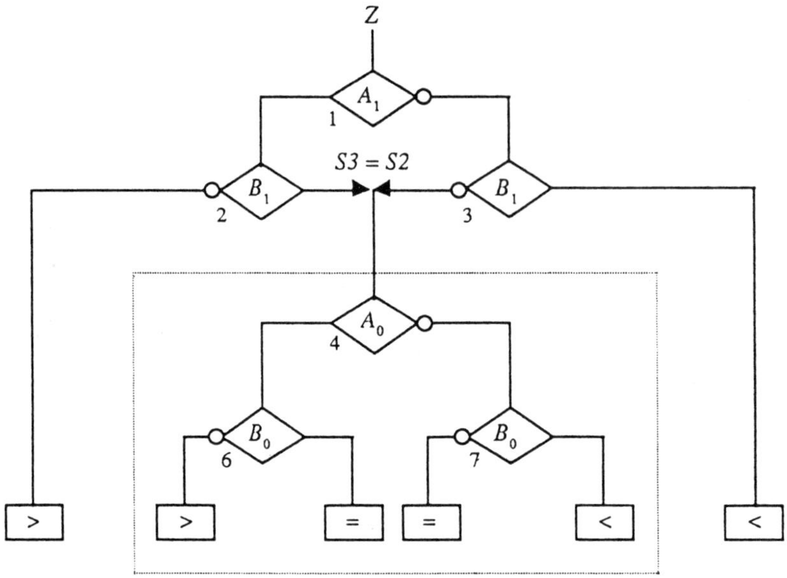

Figure 2.33

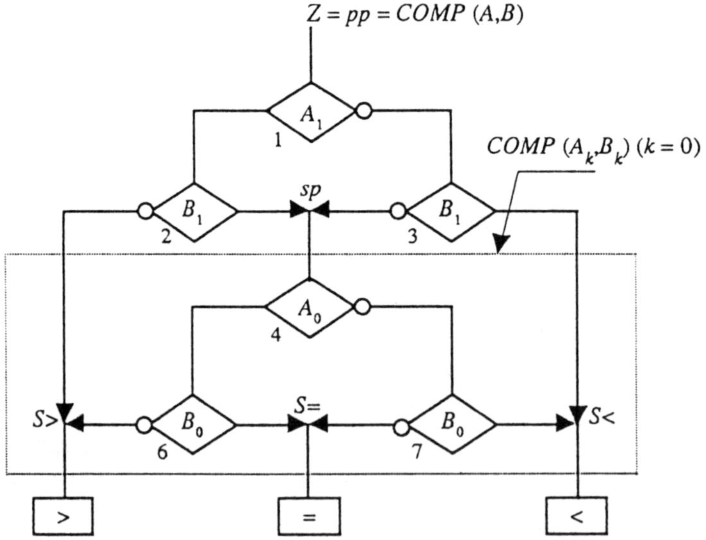

Figure 2.34

sub-trees. The convergence is highlighted in the diagram by arrows at the ends of the branches leading to the common sub-tree.

In §2.2.3 we commented that there was no advantage in continuing the decomposition of Figure 2.29 to the level of single-element trees as in Figure 2.31; but the corresponding conclusion does not follow for binary deçision diagrams, as is shown by Figure 2.34. This is equivalent to Figure 2.33, and has six branches converging in pairs on the three common sub-trees $S>$, $S=$, $S<$, reducing the total number of elements to nine.

2.2.5 Definitions: convergent and non-convergent diagrams

A binary decision diagram is thus an assembly of elements of two types, test and assignment; two possibilities arise:

1. There are no converging branches, the diagram is then said to be *non-convergent* and reduces to a binary decision tree;
2. There is at least one pair of converging branches, when the diagram is said to be *convergent*.

Throughout the rest of this book we shall generally take 'diagram' to imply 'convergent diagram'.

Any convergent diagram can be transformed into an equivalent non-convergent form, that is, a tree, by replicating common sub-trees. The converse is not true in general: non-convergent diagrams (trees) exist which cannot be decomposed, therefore have no pairs of identical sub-trees and consequently cannot be transformed into convergent diagrams.

2.2.6 Comment

If a decision tree can be shown to have at least one pair of identical sub-trees it can either be decomposed into two or more trees or transformed into a binary decision diagram. In either case the result is an equivalent representation that involves fewer elements and is therefore easier to implement.

The main advantage of decomposition is that this preserves the structure as trees, which, in contrast to decision diagrams, meet the requirements of structured programming (Chapter 5). However, a third type of element has to be introduced, the sub-tree call, the implementation of which is studied in Chapter 3. For these reasons the remainder of this chapter will deal mostly with binary decision diagrams only; but all the results obtained can be used for decomposition of decision trees.

2.2.7 Definitions: minimal diagram, reduction of a function

A discrete function Z can generally be represented by several distinct but equivalent binary decision diagrams. Among these will be one or more having the smallest number of test elements: these are called the *minimal* (or *reduced*) *diagrams for the function*. The *reduction of a discrete function* is the process of determining, from the truth table or other canonical form, the one or more minimal diagrams for the function.

A graphical method, based on the Karnaugh map, is described in §§2.2.9–2.2.13; this is derived from the corresponding method for simplifying a discrete function, given in §2.1.14. A computer algorithm due to Thayes, called the P-function algorithm, is given in section 8.2.

2.2.8 Definitions: minimal diagram and reduction of a tree

In general, any given tree T, whether complete or partial, has several equivalent but distinct representations as binary decision diagrams. Among these will be one or more having the smallest number of test elements: these are called the *minimal* (or *reduced*) *diagrams for the tree*. The *reduction of a tree* is the process of determining a minimal diagram for the tree.

Since a number of different trees can represent the same function Z, it is clear that a minimal diagram for a tree T is not necessarily minimal for the function Z that T represents.

A systematic method for reducing a tree is given in section 8.3; this has the virtues of:

- simplicity;
- applicability to a particular class of logical and discrete functions, the symmetric functions; the minimal diagram for any tree representing a function of this class coincides with that for the function itself.

2.2.9 Representation: Karnaugh map

The partial tree of Figure 2.8 for the comparator has two identical sub-trees $S2$, $S3$ and is described by these relations:

$$Z = A_1' \cdot (B_1' \cdot S2 + B_1 \cdot [<]) + A_1 \cdot (B_1' \cdot [>] + B_1 \cdot S3) \quad (2.15)$$

$$S2 = S3 = A_0'(B_0' \cdot [=] + B_0 \cdot [<]) + A_0(B_0' \cdot [>] + B_0 \cdot [=]) \quad (2.16)$$

We have already shown that $S2$ and $S3$ are represented in the Karnaugh map (Figures 2.12, 2.35) by two sub-maps (quarter maps), defined by $A_1, B_1 = 00$ and 11 respectively. Apart from a permutation these sub-tables are identical (Figure 2.37), so we can put the Karnaugh map in the more compact form of Figure 2.36. Note that the map $Z = pp$ of Figure 2.36 and the sub-maps $S2 = S3 = sp$ describe in detail the decomposition of the tree of Figure 2.29 — that is, the binary decision diagrams of Figures 2.33 and 2.34.

We conclude from this that any sub-tree of a given tree is represented in the Karnaugh map by a sub-map; this, according to the definition of §2.1.7, is a *block of blocks*, that is, a group of $p = 2^k$ cells arranged in a square or rectangle. It will contain at least two blocks that are distinct, that is, at least two distinct assignments, and thus at least two cells. Thus trivial sub-trees of a single assignment element are excluded. Figure 2.35 has two identical blocks each of four blocks that represent the sub-trees $S2$, $S3$. Every block of blocks represents some sub-tree and therefore has the coverage, separation and compatibility properties of §§2.1.8–10.

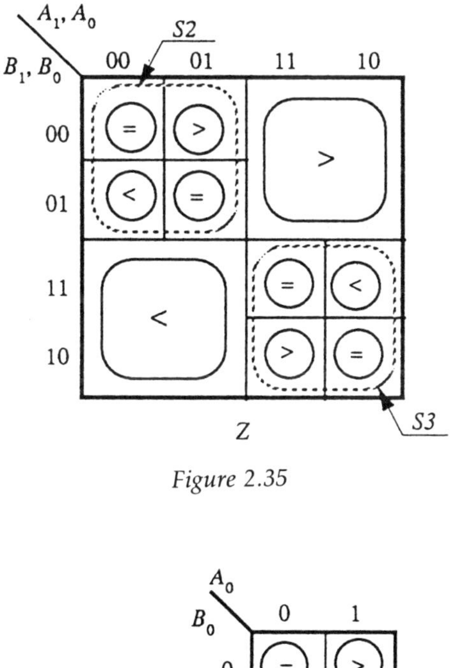

Figure 2.35

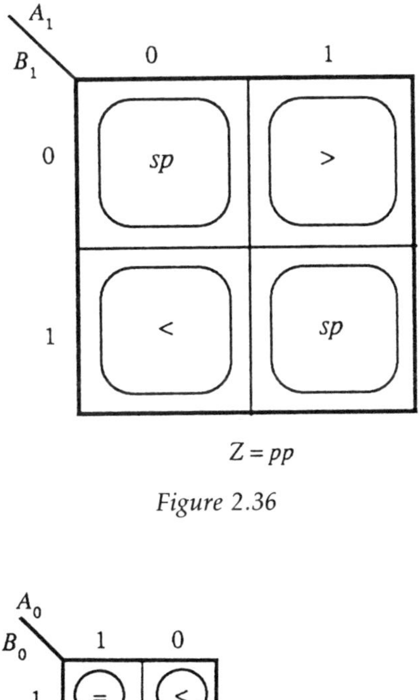

Figure 2.36

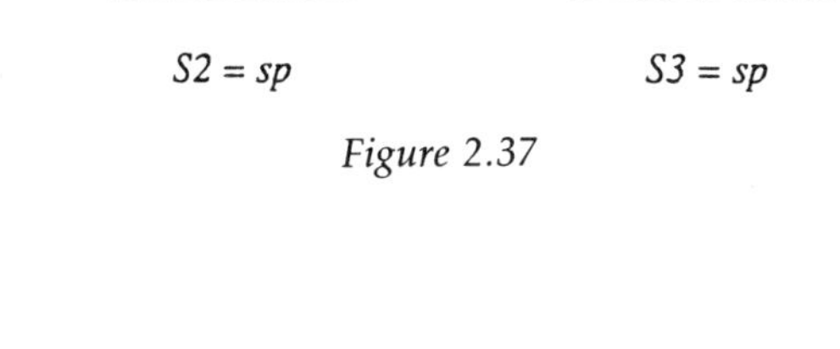

Figure 2.37

2.2.10 Example: months of the year

This is the example of §2.1.19. The original five-variable Karnaugh map of Figure 2.24 can be written more compactly as Figure 2.38 in which there are two identical blocks, each of two blocks, representing the common sub-tree *sp* (Figure 2.39). Figure 2.40 gives the decomposition of the function *Z* into a main tree *pp* and a sub-tree *sp*, equivalent to the decision diagram of Figure 2.41. The identical sub-trees of this example can be represented in the Karnaugh map by blocks each of the same

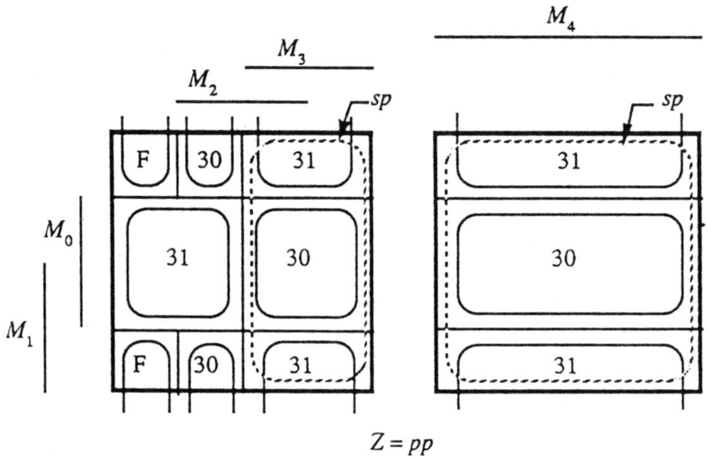

Figure 2.38

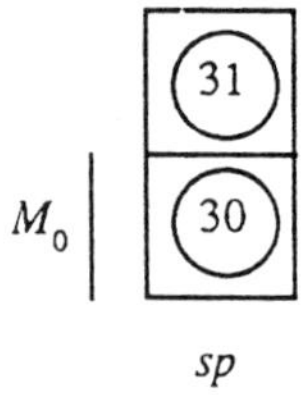

Figure 2.39

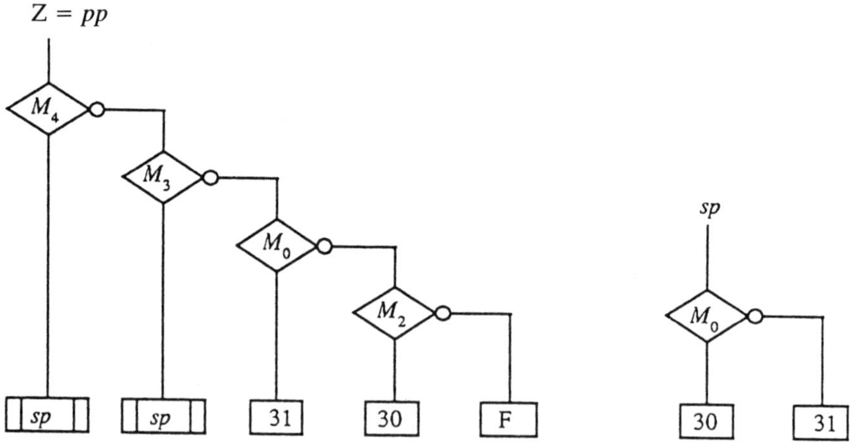

Figure 2.40

number of blocks but of different numbers of cells: $2^3 = 8$ for one and $2^4 = 16$ for the other.

Finding a minimal diagram requires the determination of a main tree and one or more sub-trees such that the combination has the least number of test elements and therefore, from (2.7), of branches, and so a minimum number of blocks in the corresponding Karnaugh map. The map *pp* of Figure 2.38 has five blocks, so the tree *pp* has five branches and four test elements; that for *sp* of Figure 2.39 has only two blocks, so the tree *sp* has two branches and one test element. Thus the final diagram has a total of five test elements.

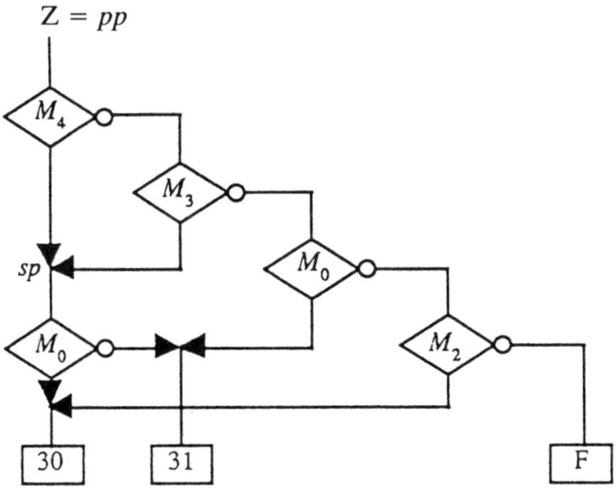

Figure 2.41

2.2.11 Example: the function *MAJORITY*

This is a logical function $MAJ(E, D, C, B, A)$ of five variables that has the value 1 if at least three of the variables have the value 1: the truth table is given in Figure 8.18 and a first form of the Karnaugh map in Figure 2.42.

We see in Figure 2.42, in succession:

1. six identical blocks each of two blocks, representing the sub-tree *sp4* which can be described by the pseudo-boolean polynomial

$$sp4 = A \cdot [1] + A' \cdot [0] \tag{2.30}$$

2. six blocks each of two blocks, representing the sub-trees *sp3* and *sp2* (Figure 2.43), written

$$sp3 = B \cdot sp4 + B' \cdot [0], \quad sp2 = B \cdot [1] + B' \cdot sp4 \tag{2.31}$$

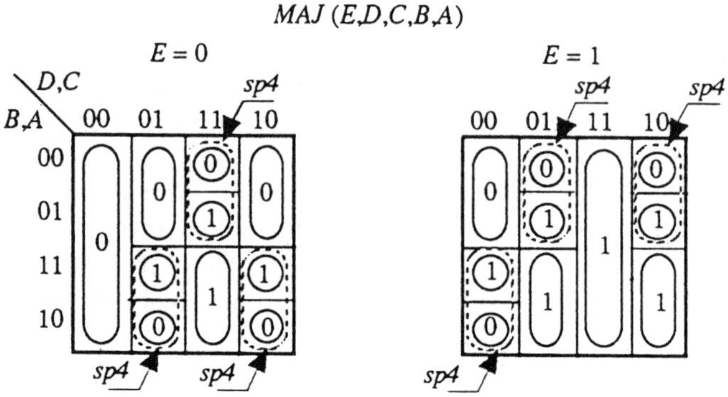

Figure 2.42

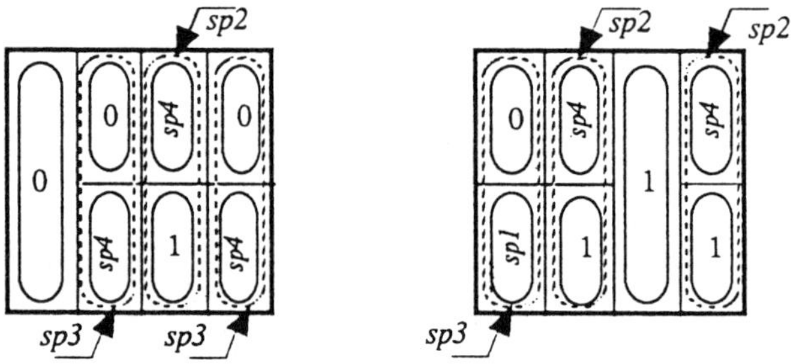

Figure 2.43

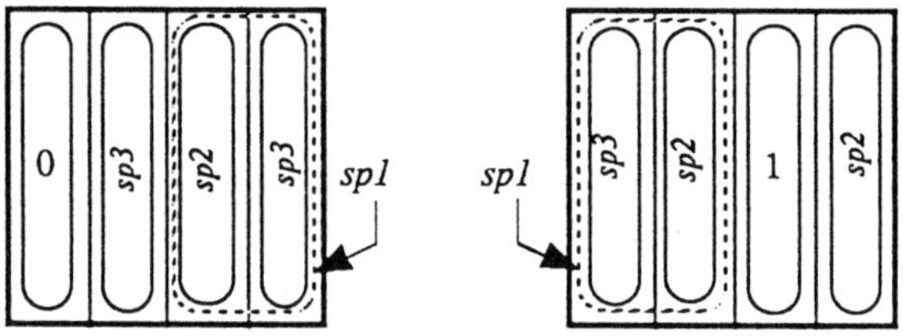

Figure 2.44

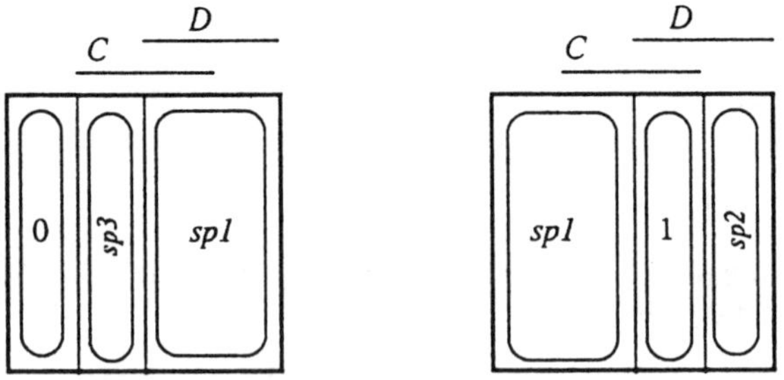

Figure 2.45

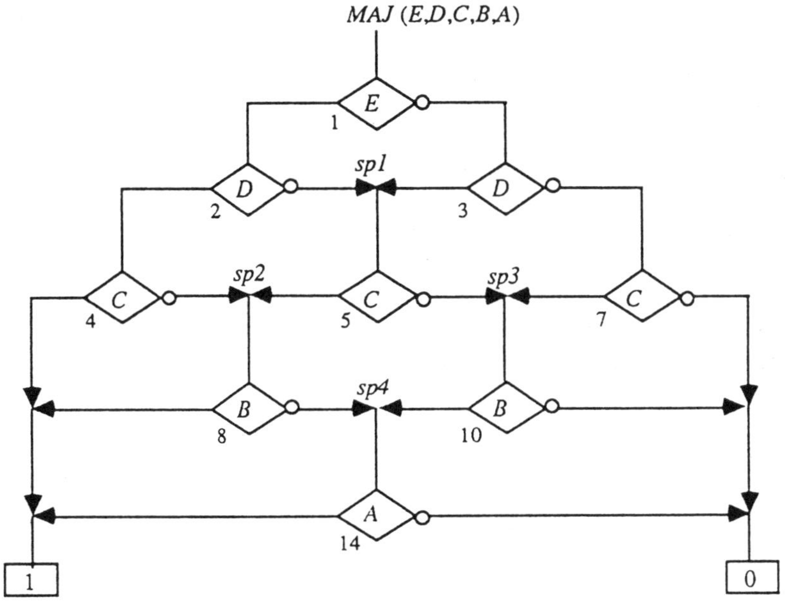

Figure 2.46

3. two blocks each of two blocks, each representing the sub-tree *sp1* (Figure 2.44), written

$$sp1 = C \cdot sp2 + C' \cdot sp3 \tag{2.32}$$

4. a main tree, consisting of six blocks (Figure 2.45):

$$MAJ(E, D, C, B, A) = E(D(C \cdot [1] + C' \cdot sp2) + D' \cdot sp1) + E'(D \cdot sp1 + D'(C \cdot sp3 + C' \cdot [0])) \tag{2.33}$$

Figure 2.46 gives the decision diagram for this set of four relations.

In this example there is considerable overlap among the sub-trees: *sp1* contains *sp2* which in turn contains *sp4;* this accounts for the progressive reduction brought about by the succession of Karnaugh maps, starting with blocks whose constituent blocks have the smallest number of cells (two for *sp4*) and ending with those with the largest number (eight for *sp1*). In a case of this kind the process of reducing a function in the Karnaugh map is very similar to that given in §8.3.6 for reducing a tree.

2.2.12 Example: an adder

Let A and B be two numbers each represented in binary by two bits, A_1, A_0 and B_1, B_0. The sum $S = A + B$ (the + sign here having its usual arithmetical meaning) is a discrete function, with the Karnaugh map of Figure 2.47. Here the minimal tree resulting from simplification is *complete*, having 16 blocks and therefore 16 branches and 15 test elements.

A first reduction (Figure 2.48) gives a single sub-tree *sp*. The ten blocks of the table *pp* and four of *sp* give nine and three test elements respectively, a total of 12.

A second reduction (Figure 2.49) gives two sub-trees *sp1* and *sp2*. The eight blocks *pp*, four blocks *sp1* and two blocks *sp2* give seven, three and one test elements respectively, a total of 11.

The difficulty in this example is to find any identical sub-trees, and hence a minimal or quasi-minimal solution.

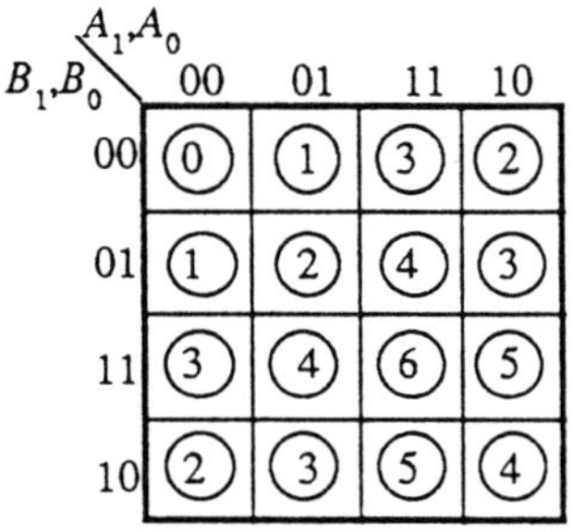

$S = A + B$

Figure 2.47

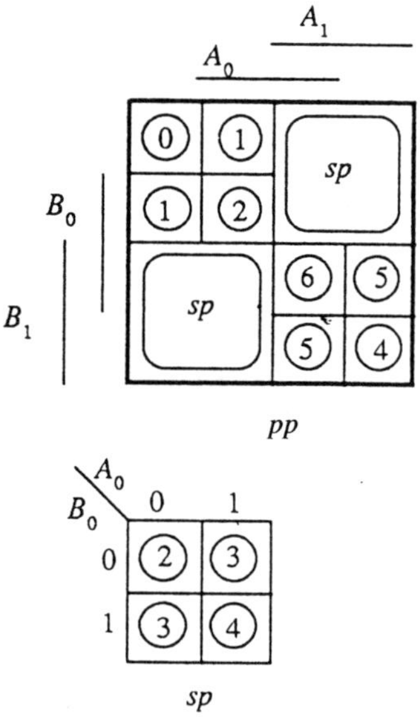

Figure 2.48

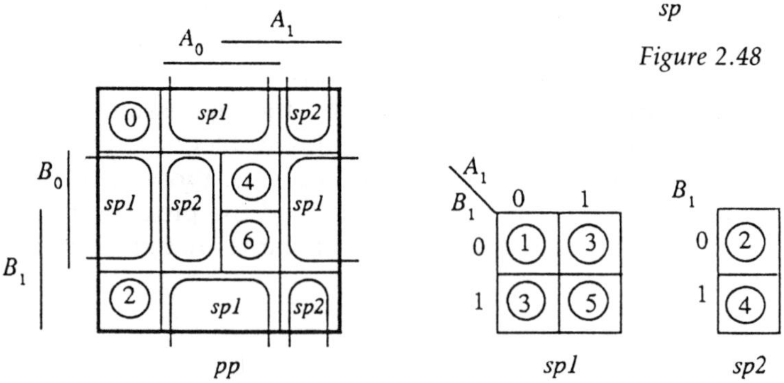

Figure 2.49

2.2.13 Method: reduction of a discrete function

The problem reduces to that of finding a decomposition (into a main tree and one or more sub-trees) that minimizes the total number of test elements; we know from (2.8) that in each Karnaugh map the number m of test elements is $(b - 1)$, where b is the number of branches and therefore of blocks. Thus we have to find a graphical representation of the discrete function with the aid of an initial Karnaugh map of b blocks and j sub-maps each of b_i blocks that minimizes the total number of test elements:

$$M = b - 1 + \sum_{i=1}^{j} (b_i - 1) \qquad (2.34)$$

Section 8.2 gives the P-function method of Thayse for performing this reduction [2] pp. 388–418, [3] pp. 115–142, [40], [41].

The Thayse method is intended primarily for computer use; a rapid graphical method for manual calculation is as follows.

1. A discrete function is introduced into the Karnaugh table.
2. As in the problem of simplifying a discrete function (§2.1.14), the table is scanned to find a minimal standard set, that is, a minimal group of blocks having the coverage, separation and compatibility properties.
3. Common sub-trees are looked for, that is, blocks of identical blocks; the latter must have at least two assignments and can be of different sizes (2^k and 2^{k+1} cells for example) and can have different forms resulting from permutations of the variables (cf. Figure 2.37). Any doubts can be resolved by applying the condition that for any pair of blocks to be identical they must have the same pseudo-boolean expression or the same Karnaugh sub-map representation.
4. Since the common sub-trees can overlap it is good practice to start with blocks of smallest size (two cells) and progress to larger.
5. Steps 2 to 4 will (probably) have to be repeated with different choices of minimal standard set, since it is unlikely that the first choice will suffice; it is even possible that a non-minimal set leads to a solution.
6. The minimal diagram follows from the Karnaugh maps finally arrived at by this process.

As in the case of §2.1.14, this method is very subjective and the comments made there apply here equally.

2.2.14 Conclusion

In this section we have studied the decomposition of a binary decision tree into a main tree and one or more sub-trees; this is equivalent to a transformation of the tree into a binary decision diagram.

When the tree is given the method of section 8.3 for reducing the number of tests is systematic and easily applied. In the more general case of starting from a discrete function, either the above subjective graphical method or the systematic P-function method of section 8.2 can be used; but both are limited by the combinatorial explosion to problems involving only a few variables. The following principles are likely to help in attacking a complex problem.

1. Make use of any properties that are inherent in the formulation of the problem. Thus in an arithmetical problem handle together all variables of the same weight: for the comparator of Figures 2.36 and 2.37 the most significant bits A_1, B_1 are tested first, followed by the least significant bits A_0, B_0. In the case of the adder (Figures 2.48 and 2.49) it is better to deal with the least significant bits first, and then the most significant [145].
2. Represent the given function by a number of partial diagrams of identical form. This applies particularly to the case of iterative diagrams, discussed in section 3.5.
3. Break the given problem down into sub-problems of manageable size, to be treated separately. This is 'top-down' programming, treated in section 6.1.
4. For a logical or discrete function of a large number of variables, construct the final diagram from the composition of a number of simple diagrams. This method, which can be very useful in practice, is described in section 8.4.

2.2.15 Bibliography

The representation of logical functions by binary decision diagrams, and the implementation of these by programs, was suggested by Lee in 1959 [25], whilst Akers [23] used the same diagrams for analysing and testing logic systems. Cerny, Mange and Sanchez [28], [29] developed a systematic method for simplifying discrete functions (finding minimal trees) and Thayse [2] pp. 388–418, [3] pp. 115–142, [40], [41], [43], [44] developed a general method for reducing such functions (finding minimal diagrams), based on the theory of P-functions; a more empirical treatment of the latter problem is given in [26]. The heuristic method for simplification and reduction using the Karnaugh map was developed independently by Warnier [46] pp. 91–221, [142] and Mange [45], [47], [48]. Finally, the theory of *decision tables* is treated in [50] pp. 249–252 and [72] pp. 100–111; these correspond closely to the partial and complete truth tables discussed in sections 2.1 and 2.2.

Moret [22] gives an exhaustive treatment of the definitions, properties and methods relevant to the optimization of binary decision trees and diagrams. Reference [51] gives a short summary of the history of the implementation of these structures in binary decision machines.

2.2.16 Exercise

A discrete function Z of 4 variables a, b, c, d can take 3 values:

Z = [>] if the number of 1s in the state (a, b, c, d) is greater than the number of 0s;
= [<] if the opposite is true;
= [=] if the numbers of 1s and 0s are equal.

Reduce Z by the Karnaugh map method and represent the solution thus found by means of a decomposition. Compare these results with those that follow from §8.3.9.

2.2.17 Exercise: the exclusive-OR function

This is a function of two variables a, b defined by

$$a \oplus b = a'b + ab' \tag{2.35}$$

Given that the operator $\oplus$ is associative, reduce the function $Z = a \oplus b \oplus c \oplus d$ by the Karnaugh map method; represent the solution by means of a decomposition and by a binary decision diagram.

2.2.18 Exercise

Figure 2.50 defines a discrete function Z. Using the Karnaugh map method, find two different binary diagram representations with eight and nine test elements respectively. For each of these represent Z by the equivalent decomposition.

C,R \ OR,E	00	01	11	10
00	b	a	c	d
01	b	a	a	b
11	c	d	d	c
10	c	d	b	a

Z

Figure 2.50

2.3 SOFTWARE REALIZATION OF TREES AND DIAGRAMS

2.3.1 Introduction

The binary decision trees and diagrams that we have been discussing are abstract representations of combinational systems. We now turn to the possibilities for concrete realization, using the logical operators of Chapter 1.

2.3.2 First hypothesis: sequential execution

In the example of the comparator, §2.1.2, the system itself is combinational but the diagram of Figure 2.34 suggests that this is traversed in time, that is, *sequentially*: we can imagine a synchronous sequential system which at each clock time reads an element of the diagram and executes the instruction, a test or an assignment, that it contains. Execution of a test instruction determines the next element to be read, according to the value of the logical variable, whilst execution of an assignment gives an output state. We say that the test and assignment elements constitute the two *primitives* of the specification.

A study of Figure 2.34 shows that if after the output state ([>], [<] or [=]) for the given input state A_1, B_1, A_0, B_0 has been determined, a different input state has to be considered, the calculation has to be restarted from the first test element: so in order to deal with a series of input states the diagram must loop back on itself, as shown in Figure 2.51. Execution of the complete diagram — that is, determining the value of Z for a given input state — requires at most five clock times (e.g. the branch product $A_1'B_1'A_0'B_0'$ and the output [=]) and at least three (e.g. A_1B_1' and output [>]).

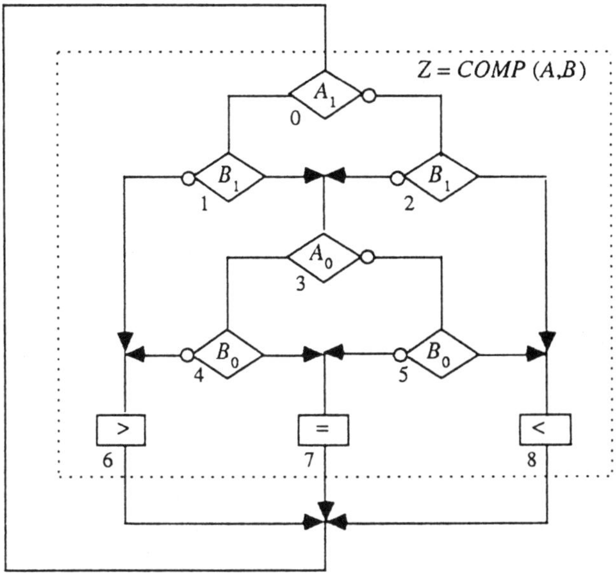

Figure 2.51

2.3.3 Second hypothesis: microprogrammed logic system

Excluding memories, any assemblage of logic elements, whether combinational (inverters, AND, OR, NAND gates, demultiplexers, multiplexers etc.) or sequential (latches, flip-flops, registers etc.) constitutes a *hardwired logic system*. If any memory is included it becomes a *logic system with memory*. If the content of the memory is that of the primitives of the specification (test or assignment elements) we say that we have a *microprogrammed logic system*, and this content is the *microprogram*.

For flexibility, we choose a microprogrammed system to realize the synchronous sequential system needed to execute the test and assignment primitives.

2.3.4 Definition: software realization

Given the concepts of sequential execution and a microprogrammed system we can now construct a realization of binary decision trees and diagrams: this is the *software realization*, the main concern of this book. The following stages are needed.

1. Detailed definition of the primitives and realization of these in memory as micro-instructions.

2. Representation of the tree or diagram by an assemblage of micro-instructions: the *flowchart*.
3. Translation of the flowchart into mnemonic microprogram, and then the conversion into the binary or hexadecimal equivalent.
4. Realization in hardware of the sequential system needed for execution of the microprogram.

2.3.5 Definitions: test and assignment micro-instructions

The content of each test or assignment element must be coded in binary, written into memory at a given address and finally executed by a sequential machine designed for the purpose. The realization in memory of an element produces a micro-instruction, for test or assignment as appropriate.

A *test micro-instruction* (Figure 2.52) is defined by an address *ADR* and a test variable *xi*; each such micro-instruction has one input and two output terminals leading to the next instruction to be executed, one to *ADR1* for the case $xi = 1$, the other to *ADR0* for $xi = 0$. This can be written symbolically (or *mnemonically*) as

IF *xi* **THEN** *ADR1* **ELSE** *ADR0* (2.36)

An *assignment micro-instruction* (Figure 2.53) is defined by an address *ADR* and a synchronous assignment $REG \leftarrow OUT$ (see §1.2.11) where *REG* designates a register and *OUT* an output state. Each such micro-instruction has one input terminal and one output terminal leading to the address *ADR+* of the next instruction. The mnemonic form is

DO $REG \leftarrow OUT$ **GO TO** *ADR+* (2.37)

This differs from the assignment element (§2.1.4) in having only one output terminal.

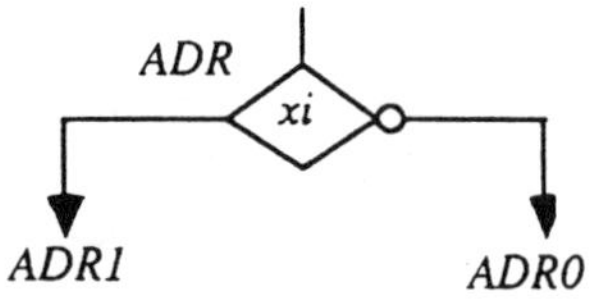

IF *xi* **THEN** *ADR1* **ELSE** *ADR0*

Figure 2.52

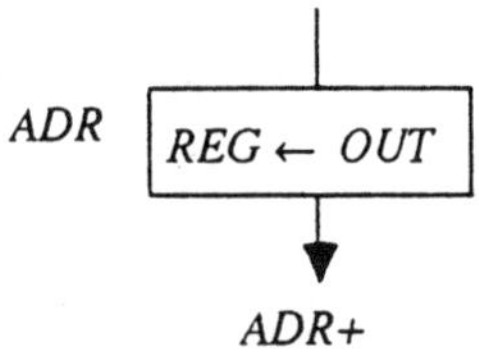

DO *REG* ← *OUT* **GO TO** *ADR+*

Figure 2.53

2.3.6 Representation: flowchart

An assemblage of test and assignment micro-instructions can be represented graphically in terms of the symbols of Figures 2.51 and 2.52, as for example in Figure 2.51; this representation is called a *flowchart* or *program schema*.

2.3.7 Definition: the language L1

The set of two micro-instructions, test and assignment respectively, constitutes what is called an *micro-instruction set*; usually, such a set is called a *language*. We shall call this set of two instructions the language **L1**:

$$\mathbf{L1} = \{\mathbf{IF\ldots THEN\ldots ELSE\ldots, DO\ldots GO\ TO\ldots}\} \quad (2.38)$$

2.3.8 Representation: mnemonic micro-program

If we give each micro-instruction in Figure 2.51 an address we can then list them, written in their mnemonic forms, to give the *mnemonic micro-program* for the comparator in the language **L1**, as in Figure 2.54.

ADR	L1
0	IF A_1 THEN 1 ELSE 2
1	IF B_1 THEN 3 ELSE 6
2	IF B_1 THEN 8 ELSE 3
3	IF A_0 THEN 4 ELSE 5
4	IF B_0 THEN 7 ELSE 6
5	IF B_0 THEN 8 ELSE 7
6	DO $REG \leftarrow [>]$ GO TO 0
7	DO $REG \leftarrow [=]$ GO TO 0
8	DO $REG \leftarrow [<]$ GO TO 0

Figure 2.54

2.3.9 Representation: binary and hexadecimal micro-programs

To write the micro-instructions in the memory we must have:

- a coding for the test variables *xi* and the assignments $REG \leftarrow OUT$;
- an organization of the constitutent elements in each micro-instruction, specified in every detail: this is the *format* of the instruction, and is made up of a number of *fields*.

A minimal binary coding of the 4 test variables $xi = A_1 \ldots B_0$ of our example requires 2 bits i_1, i_0 for the *index i* (Figure 2.55); a 1-out-of-3 coding of the output states Z requires 3 bits, $OUT_{2:0}$ (Figure 2.56); and the nine instructions of the mnemonic program require at least four bits, $ADR_{3:0}$, for the address.

xi	i	i_1	i_0
A_1	0	0	0
B_1	1	0	1
A_0	2	1	0
B_0	3	1	1

Figure 2.55

Z	$OUT_{2:0}$		
[>]	1	0	0
[=]	0	1	0
[<]	0	0	1

Figure 2.56

Lastly, we need to distinguish between the two types of micro-instruction in **L1**; this can be done by providing an *operating code OPC*, in the form of a single bit T: $T = 1$ identifies a test instruction, $T = 0$ an assignment.

We can now define a format for each micro-instruction, suitable layouts for which are given in Figure 2.57; and write the *binary micro-program*, as shown in Figure 2.58. The requirement that the micro-instructions are to be executed by a specially-designed machine imposes certain general restrictions on the formats; thus the two types must be of the same length (11 bits in this example) and there must be correspondences between the locations of the fields (*ADR1* and *ADR+* must be in the same memory position). It follows that some bits will not be defined and will correspond to Φ conditions: in Figure 2.57 these are marked '—'.

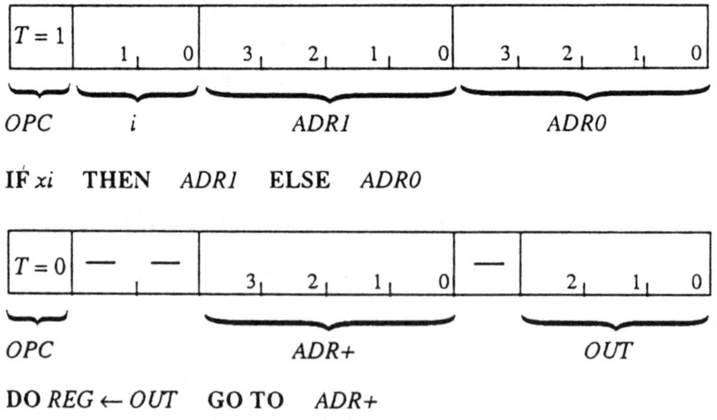

Figure 2.57

For convenience, a binary program is often converted into its *hexadecimal* equivalent, as in Figure 2.59; in this example the undetermined bits have been given the value 0.

ADR	*T*	$i_{1:0}$	*ADR1* *ADR+*	*ADR0* *OUT*
0000	1	0 0	0001	0010
0001	1	0 1	0011	0110
0010	1	0 1	1000	0011
0011	1	1 0	0100	0101
0100	1	1 1	0111	0110
0101	1	1 1	1000	0111
0110	0	- -	0000	-100
0111	0	- -	0000	-010
1000	0	- -	0000	-001

Figure 2.58

ADR	*T,i*	*ADR1* *ADR+*	*ADR0* *OUT*
0	4	1	2
1	5	3	6
2	5	8	3
3	6	4	5
4	7	7	6
5	7	8	7
6	0	0	4
7	0	0	2
8	0	0	1

Figure 2.59

2.3.10 A convention

In the rest of the treatment we shall, for the sake of simplicity, use *program, instruction* to mean *micro-program, micro-instruction*.

2.3.11 Hardware realization: interpreter for L1

As we have said, the synchronous sequential system that executes the two instructions of the language **L1** is called a *binary decision machine*; it can also be called an *interpreter* for **L1**, abbreviated to INT1. Since it includes a memory holding the primitives it is also, by §2.3.3, a micro-programmed system.

Figure 2.60 shows such a machine; it consists of:

- a *program memory* (here of 16 words of 11 bits each), compatible with the instruction formats of Figure 2.57. This can be RAM or ROM (cf. §1.3.2); if the latter, its behaviour is purely combinational (§1.3.6) and is described by the equation

$$OUT_{10:0} = ROM[ADR] \tag{2.39}$$

- an *address* or *instruction register* ADR, whose content *ADR* is the memory address. This is a particular case of the bi-directional register of §1.2.14, used in the operation LOAD($S1 = S0 = LD = 1$); it is defined by the equation

$$ADR \leftarrow ADR \tag{2.40}$$

- a multiplexer MUX1, controlled by the variable y; the purpose of this is to select the next address $ADR+$ in the various instruction fields ($ADR1 = ROM_{7:4}$, $ADR0 = ROM_{3:0}$, $ADR+ = ROM_{7:4}$)
- a second multiplexer MUX2, controlled by the variable T of the operating code and by the variables i_1, i_0 of the index; the purpose of this is to select the test variable xi ($xi = A_1, A_0, B_1$ or B_0)
- an *assignment* or *output register* REG, also a bi-directional register, used in the operations HOLD($S1 = S0 = LD = 0$) and LOAD($S1 = S0 = LD = 1$):

$$REG \leftarrow REG(S1 = S0 = LD = 0) \tag{2.41}$$

$$REG \leftarrow REG^{+}(S1 = S0 = LD = 1) \tag{2.42}$$

Figure 2.61 is the operations table for this machine, showing its general behaviour and in particular the transfers occurring in the registers ADR and REG for each test instruction (OP1, OP2) and each assignment (OP3).

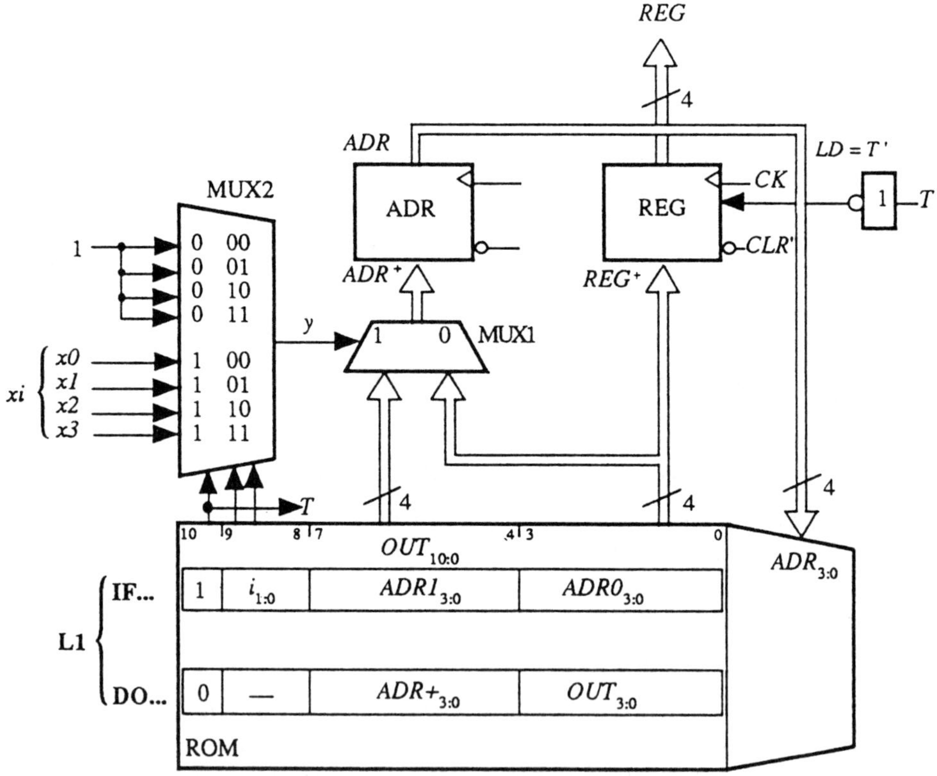

INT1

Figure 2.60

OPERATION	DESCRIPTION: ADR, REG	$T\ xi$
OP1 = **IF** 0 **ELSE** *ADR0*	$ADR \leftarrow ADR0$, $REG \leftarrow REG$	1 0
OP2 = **IF** 1 **THEN** *ADR1*	$ADR \leftarrow ADR1$, $REG \leftarrow REG$	1 1
OP3 = **DO** $REG \leftarrow OUT$ **GO TO** *ADR+*	$ADR \leftarrow ADR+$, $REG \leftarrow OUT$	0 Φ

Figure 2.61

The truth table (Figure 2.62) is deduced from the operations table; this gives the values of y (controlling MUX1) and LD (controlling REG) as functions of T (operating code) and xi (test variable). After simplification we find

$$y = T' + xi \tag{2.43}$$

$$LD = T' \tag{2.44}$$

The multiplexer MUX2 is a possible realization of (2.43): if $T = 1$ (indicating a test instruction) then $y = xi$, whilst if $T = 0$ (an assignment) then $y = 1$.

OPERATION	$T\ xi$	ADR^+	y	REG^+	LD
OP1	1 0	$ADR0 = ROM_{3:0}$	0	REG	0
OP2	1 1	$ADR1 = ROM_{7:4}$	1	REG	0
OP3	0 Φ	$ADR+ = ROM_{7:4}$	1	$OUT = ROM_{3:0}$	1

Figure 2.62

2.3.12 Comments

The binary decision machine of Figure 2.60 was tailored to the example of the comparator; it provides at most the following:

$2^4 = 16$ instructions $ROM_{10:0}$, with address $ADR_{3:0}$
$2^2 = 4$ input variables xi, with index $i_{1:0}$
$2^4 = 16$ different output states $OUT_{3:0}$

and a single assignment register REG.

These limitations are purely technological and can be lifted at will by the designer; in Chapter 4 (§4.2.2 and Figure 4.7) we give a different architecture providing greatly enhanced performance.

The clock signal CK in Figure 2.60 drives the two synchronous registers ADR and REG and thus sets the rate at which the program instructions are executed. We can assume that the clock interval is much shorter than that between any possible changes in the input state, so that even a transient in this, for example $A_1, B_1, A_0, B_0 = 0000 \rightarrow 0001 \rightarrow 0000$, will give the corresponding outputs, $[=] \rightarrow [<] \rightarrow [=]$.

The purpose of the variable CLR' is to enable the registers ADR, REG to be reset to zero asynchronously; this enables the first instruction of the program to be given the address $ADR_{3:0} = 0000$.

2.3.13 Bibliography

There are a great many architectures equivalent to that described in §2.3.11: we mention only those that execute **L1** or some very similar language, that is, one having a test and an assignment instruction. The forerunners are Clare [16] pp. 75–96 and Boute [24], whose work stimulated the joint researches of Davio, Deschamps, Thayse, Mange and Sanchez [2] pp. 353–387, [3] pp. 85–113, [45]; followed by Zsombor-Murray [52]. Other machines are described in [53] pp. 210–274, [54] pp. 600–612 and [55] pp. 44–64.

Reference [51] gives a brief historical review of the execution of trees and diagrams by binary decision machines.

2.3.14 Exercise: programming hazards

A study of Figure 2.51 shows that the state change

$$A_1, B_1, A_0, B_0 = 0000 \rightarrow 1001$$

occurring after the execution of instruction 0 and before that of instruction 2 will be interpreted by the machine as an input sequence

$$A_1, B_1, A_0, B_0 = 0000 \rightarrow 0001 \rightarrow 1001$$

thus producing the output sequence

$$Z = [=] \rightarrow [<] \rightarrow [>]$$

in which the transient state $[<]$ is incorrect. Such a state is called a *programming hazard*.

Find the hardware modifications needed to the machine of Figure 2.60 to eliminate all hazards of this kind.

2.3.15 Exercise

Write a mnemonic program in **L1** for the function $MAJ(E, D, C, B, A)$ of Figure 2.46. After having coded the test variables and the output states, design the formats for the instructions and then convert the program first to binary and second to hexadecimal. Can the machine of Figure 2.60 execute your program?

2.4 HARDWARE REALIZATION OF TREES AND DIAGRAMS

2.4.1 Introduction

The previous section has discussed the realization of trees and diagrams in software; and as we have said, this is the principal concern of the book and we shall take it up again in the following chapters. There is an equivalence between software and hardware, and as a first illustration of this it is helpful to consider some corresponding *hardware realizations*, in the form of assemblages of demultiplexers or multiplexers [2] pp. 414–417, [3] pp. 140–142, [28], [29], [45]. As defined in §2.3.3, such assemblages form *hardwired logic systems*.

2.4.2 Hardware realization: single-variable demultiplexers

The logic diagram {DMUX, OR} of Figure 2.63 is derived from the binary decision diagram Figure 2.34 as follows:

- each test element is implemented as a demultiplexer with a single address variable (§1.1.8);
- each information link between two elements is implemented as a physical connection (a wire);
- each convergence of k arrows (representing a common sub-tree) is implemented as an OR gate with k inputs;
- the input terminal in the logic diagram is given the value 1.

The outputs of the three OR gates in Figure 2.63 are the realizations of the three logical functions G, E, L of the comparator (Figure 2.2); an algebraic analysis of the logic diagram will lead to expressions equivalent to (2.10)–(2.12).

2.4.3 Hardware realization: demultiplexers with several variables

In the particular case where all the test elements act on the same variable at each level, a realization equivalent to Figure 2.63 can be constructed, in which a number of 1-variable demultiplexers are replaced by a single multi-variable demultiplexer. This is shown in Figure 2.64.

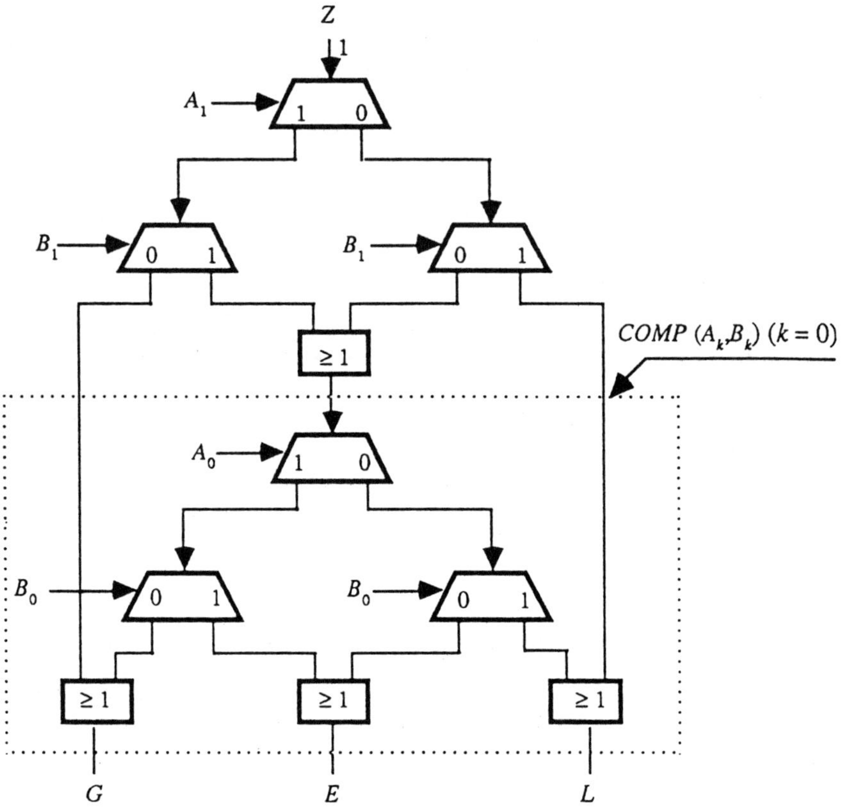

Figure 2.63

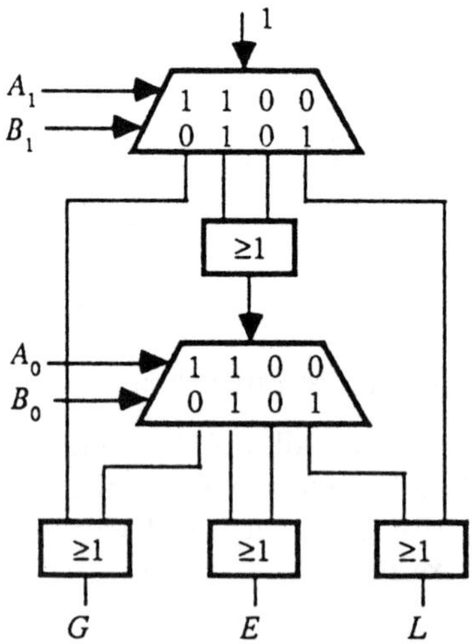

Figure 2.64

2.4.4 Hardware realization: multiplexers

The duality between demultiplexers and multiplexers suggests the possibility of a realization using the latter. This can be achieved as follows:

- each test element is implemented as a multiplexer with a single address variable (§1.1.13);
- each information link is implemented as a bus; for a minimal code 2 bits are needed, and for a 1-out-of-3 code 3 bits (see Figure 2.2), to represent the three values [>], [=], [<];
- the three input terminals in the logic diagram represent the constants [>], [=], [<] in the 1-out-of-3 code.

In Figure 2.65 the output is the realization of the discrete function Z = G, E, L in the 1-out-of-3 code.

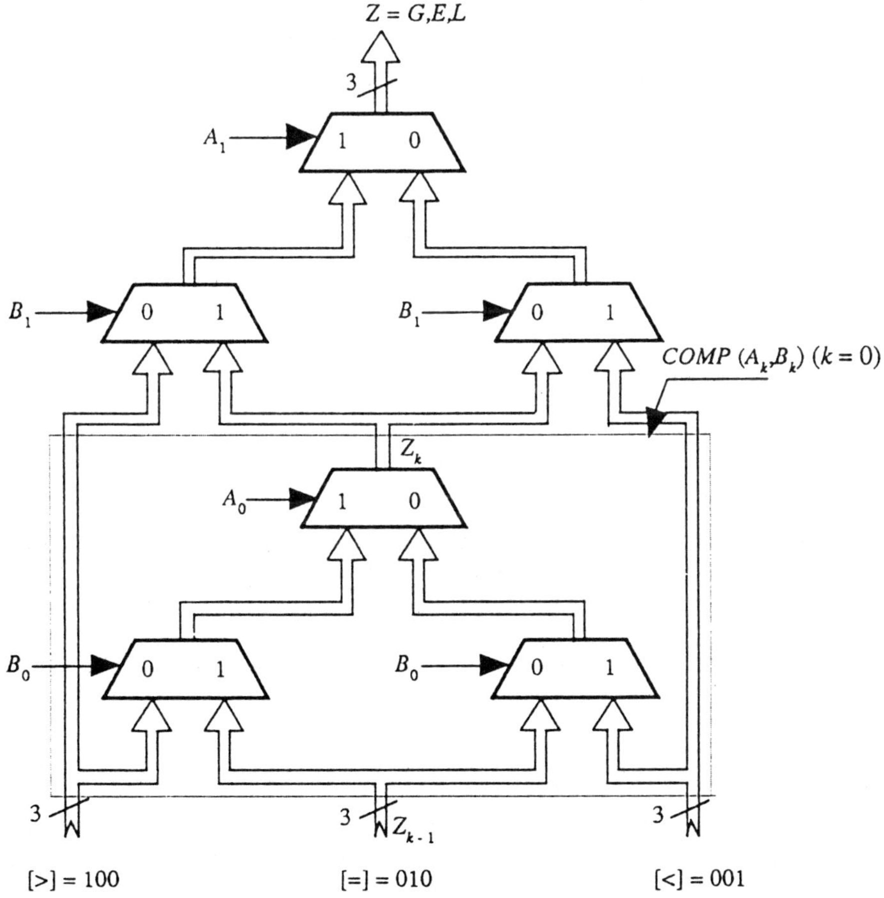

Figure 2.65

The need for multi-wire connections (buses) usually argues against a solution in terms of multiplexers, the simpler realization with demultiplexers being preferred. However, the two are equivalent if the function in question is logical and not discrete.

Corresponding to the possibility of §2.4.3 for demultiplexers, a number of 1-variable multiplexers can be replaced by a single multiple-variable multiplexer.

2.4.5 Exercise

Find a realization of the logical function

$$Z(D, C, B, A) = \Sigma\ 0, 3, 5, 6, 9, 10, 12, 15$$

1. as an assemblage {DMUX, OR} of 1-variable demultiplexers, minimizing the number of these;
2. as a minimal assemblage of 1-variable multiplexers.

Can such a function be realized by a network of a minimum number of switches, as Figure 2.66? (see [28]). Compare your results with those obtained as answers to the question of §2.2.17.

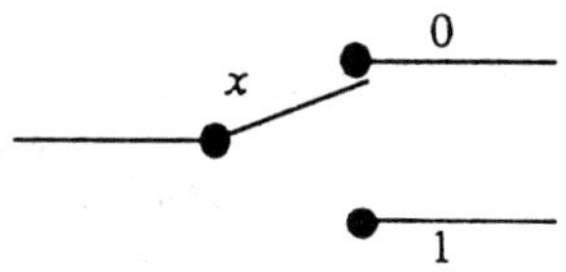

Figure 2.66

2.4.6 Exercise

1. Transform the logic diagram of Figure 2.65 (using a 3-wire bus) into three separate 1-wire diagrams, each realizing one of the logic functions G, E, L. Can this be done with a reduction in the amount of hardware?
2. Try to implement Figure 2.65 in terms of 3-state devices (§§1.1.15–1.1.18).

2.4.7 General conclusions

A logical or discrete function, whether or not completely defined, can always be represented by a binary decision tree or diagram; and this representation, possibly after simplification, can be realized either in software by a micro-programmed system or in hardware by a hard-wired system.

The microprogrammed system performs the evaluation sequentially, in time steps, and requires for this a certain number of clock times defined by a clock pulse. It requires also a hardware device (a binary decision machine, or interpreter for the language **L1**); the scale of this device does not increase to match the complexity of the function that it evaluates, but to a first approximation only the depth of memory, which is determined by the number of instructions, depends on the scale of the problem.

The hard-wired system constitutes a spatial (or combinational) realization of the decision tree or diagram. If we neglect the delays in the logic elements (multiplexers or demultiplexers) we can say that the evaluation is instantaneous. The scale of the hard-wired system increases with the complexity of the problem to be treated.

We can summarize this by saying that the software solution economizes space (or hardware) at the expense of the time required for the evaluation, whilst the hardware economizes time at the expense of space. The decision tree and diagram are modes of representation that are common to both software and hardware realizations; they make clear the hardware/software equivalences which are in fact a particular case of the trade-off between space and time.

Finally, we should recall that the aim of simplification and reduction of discrete functions is to reduce the number of test elements. This leads to shorter and therefore more efficient programs in the software realization and systems with fewer multiplexers or demultiplexers, and therefore less costly, in the hardware realization.

3

Sub-programs and procedures

3.1 LINEAR FLOWCHART

3.1.1 Introduction

Counters and iterative combinational systems, can be broken down into simpler systems; and the study of this process leads naturally to one of the fundamental concepts in software, that of the sub-program or procedure, with or without the passing of parameters.

We shall base our study on a 6-state counter and show first that the state diagram can be realized as a linear flowchart, itself consisting of an assemblage of the test (**IF. . . THEN. . . ELSE. . .**) and assignment (**DO. . . GO TO. . .**) instructions of the language **L1**. If this reveals a repetitive part of the program, that is, a sub-program, the linear flowchart can be transformed into a binary decision tree, which is itself programmed in **L1** and realizes the state table of the counter.

The execution of sub-programs can be made more direct if **L1** is enhanced by the addition of two new instructions, for calling a sub-program and returning to the main program respectively: **CALL. . . RET TO. . .** and **RET**; the sub-program thus becomes a procedure. We call the enhanced language **L2**, and this is to be interpreted by a binary decision machine provided with an auxiliary memory, a stack. This opens up new possibilities for treating decomposable systems, for example complex counters and digital clocks (serial decomposition), any combinational system that can be represented by a binary decision diagram (decomposition into a main tree and sub-trees) and iterative combinational systems (decomposition into sub-systems or slices). An example of the third type of decomposition is the comparator of two numbers studied in Chapter 2; procedures with parameters, and recursive procedures, can be used in this case.

3.1.2 Example: 6-state counter

A synchronous 6-state *counter* is a device driven by an external clock H (Figure 3.1) that outputs a cycle of states coded in binary as follows:

$$Q_2, Q_1, Q_0 = 000 \rightarrow 001 \rightarrow 010 \rightarrow 011 \rightarrow 100 \rightarrow 101 \rightarrow 000 \qquad (3.1)$$

This can be written with a synchronous assignment

$$Q \leftarrow Q + 1 \pmod 6 \qquad (3.2)$$

meaning that at each clock time the state of the counter is incremented by 1, from a lower limit $Q = 0$ to an upper limit $Q = 5 = p - 1$, where p (= 6) is the scale or *modulus* of the counter, abbreviated to *mod* in (3.2).

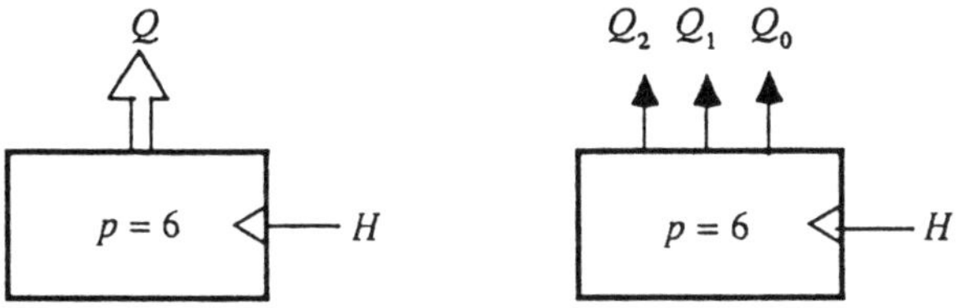

Figure 3.1

Figures 3.2, 3.3 are the state diagram and state table of the counter respectively; Figure 3.4 shows the synchronizing clock variable H, each rise of which ($H = 0 \rightarrow 1$) causes the change from the present state Q to the next state Q^+ (cf. [1] pp. 129–131, [59] pp. 163–164).

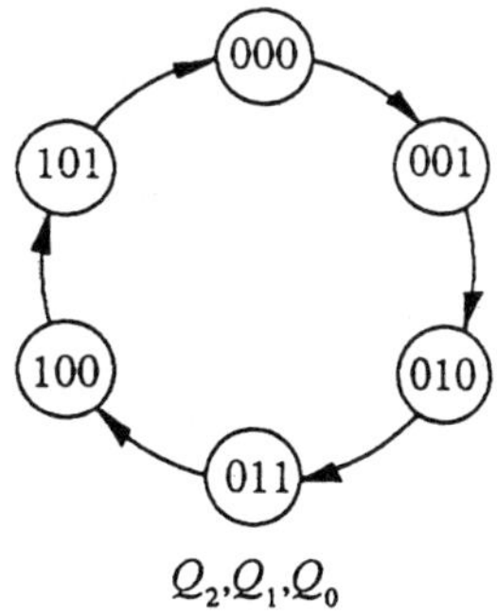

Figure 3.2

Q_2	Q_1	Q_0	Q_2^+	Q_1^+	Q_0^+
0	0	0	0	0	1
0	0	1	0	1	0
0	1	0	0	1	1
0	1	1	1	0	0
1	0	0	1	0	1
1	0	1	0	0	0

Figure 3.3

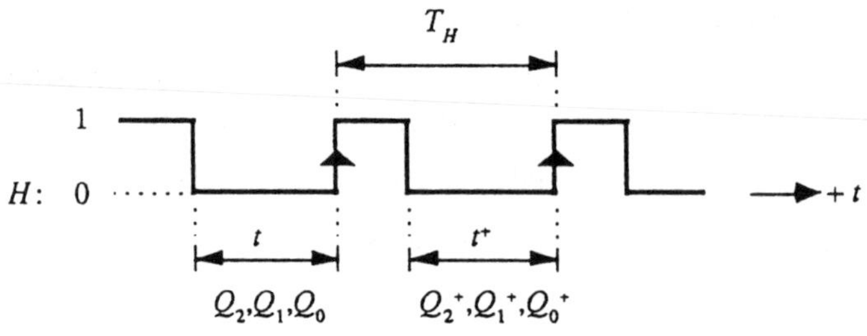

Figure 3.4

3.1.3 Software realization: linear flowchart

By a *linear flowchart* we mean a direct software realization of the state diagram, in terms of the test (Figure 2.52) and assignment (Figure 2.53) instructions of the language **L1**. Figure 3.5 gives this for the mod 6 counter; it can be checked that each state in the graph (that is, each vertex in Figure 3.2) generates an assignment instruction and each transition from a present state Q to the next Q^+ involves two successive tests of the clock variable H, in accordance with Figure 3.4.

3.1.4 Representation: mnemonic program

We give each of the 18 instructions in Figure 3.5 a hexadecimal address in the range $ADR = 00 - 11$, express them in the mnemonic code of (2.36–7) and list them as in Figure 3.7. This is the mnemonic program for the counter.

3.1.5 Definitions: cost, time

For each program in this chapter we shall calculate an evaluation represented by two parameters expressing spatial and temporal costs respectively: the first is the number c of instructions in the program, expressing the cost in memory required, the second is the number d of instructions that have to be executed between two successive rises of the clock variable H, that is, during one *clock cycle*. These two parameters depend on the number p of states of the counter, and from Figure 3.5 we find

$$c(p) = 3p \tag{3.3}$$

$$d(p) = \text{constant} = 3 \tag{3.4}$$

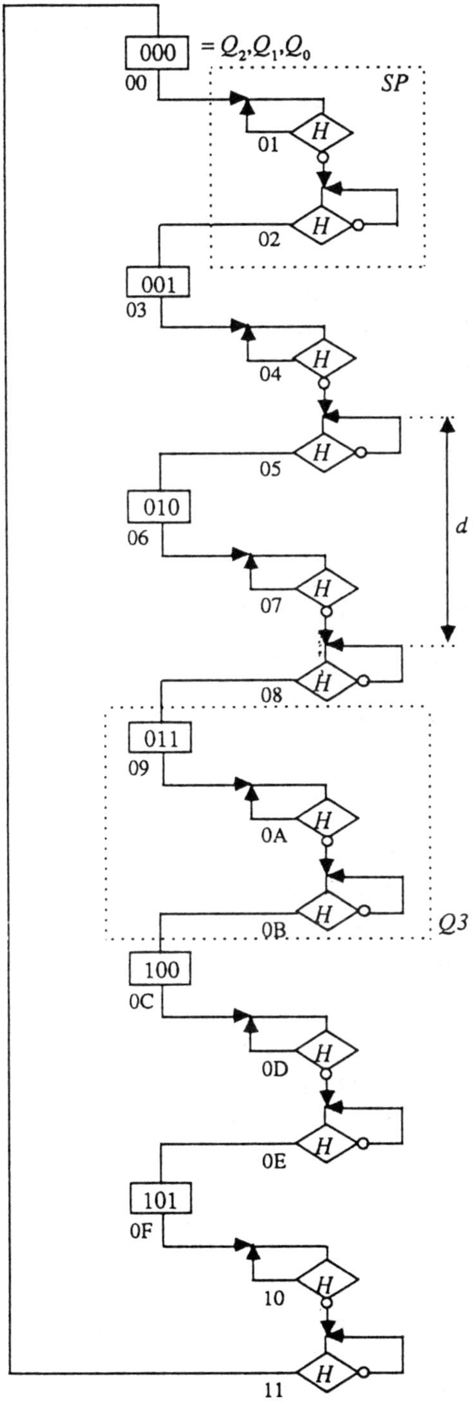

000
= Q_2,Q_1,Q_0
00
SP
H
01
02
001
03
04
05
010
06
d = 3
07
08
011
09
0A
0B
Q3
100
0C
0D
0E
101
0F
10
11

Figure 3.5

Finally, we define a *factor of merit* for the program as the product $c \cdot d$; for this example

$$c \cdot d = 9p \tag{3.5}$$

3.1.6 Assumption

In what follows we shall assume that the period T_{CK} of the internal clock *CK* of the binary decision machine (Figure 2.60) is always less than the period T_H of any external clock *H*; that is, that in all cases

$$d \cdot T_{CK} < T_H \tag{3.6}$$

Thus the cycle time d measures the speed of the microprogrammed system: the smaller d, the smaller must the minimum frequency of the internal clock *CK* be for a given frequency of the external clock *H*.

3.1.7 Hardware realization: interpreter for L1

A binary decision machine similar to that of Figure 2.60 (INT1) could execute the **L1** program of Figure 3.7; the only changes that might be needed would be to the formats of the test and assignment instructions (see the exercise of §3.1.9).

3.1.8 Hardware/software equivalence

The linear flowchart of Figure 3.5, coded and then executed by a binary decision machine such as the interpreter INT1, is equivalent to a hardwired logic system realizing a synchronous counter in a 1-out-of-6 code, that is, a *ring counter*: [1] pp. 142, 211; [59] pp. 179, 261. Each group of three successive instructions in Figure 3.5 is equivalent to one of the six D flip-flops, driven by the clock *H*, in the logic system of Figure 3.6: e.g. the group 09 (assignment) and 0A, 0B (tests) to *Q3*; and the double master/slave latch of the flip-flop (see Figure 1.29) is the hardware equivalent of the double software test of the clock signal *H* in Figure 3.5.

3.1.9 Exercise

For the mnemonic program of Figure 3.7, with the test variables and output states coded, find the format for the test and assignment instructions and then rewrite the program in binary and in hexadecimal.

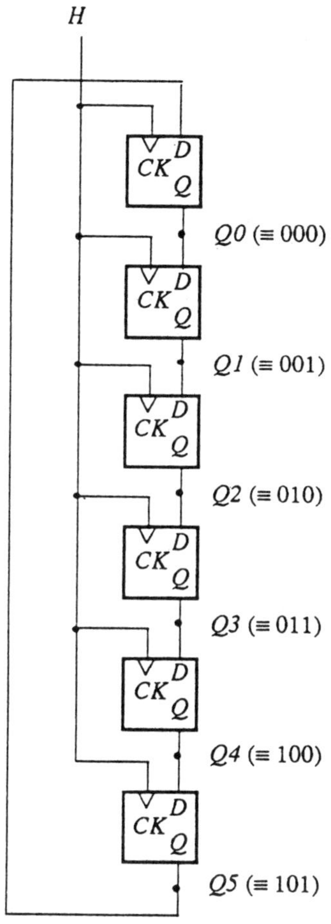

Figure 3.6

3.2 SUB-PROGRAMS AND DECISION TREES

3.2.1 Definition: sub-program

Any flowchart that has a single input and a single output terminal represents what we shall call a *sub-program*. Thus in Figure 3.5 the flowchart *SP* consisting of the two test instructions 01, 02 is a sub-program.

ADR	L1		
0 0	DO *REG* ← 000	GO TO 01	
0 1	IF *H*	THEN 01	ELSE 02
0 2	IF *H*	THEN 03	ELSE 02
0 3	DO *REG* ← 001	GO TO 04	
0 4	IF *H*	THEN 04	ELSE 05
0 5	IF *H*	THEN 06	ELSE 05
0 6	DO *REG* ← 010	GO TO 07	
0 7	IF *H*	THEN 07	ELSE 08
0 8	IF *H*	THEN 09	ELSE 08
0 9	DO *REG* ← 011	GO TO 0A	
0 A	IF *H*	THEN 0A	ELSE 0B
0 B	IF *H*	THEN 0C	ELSE 0B
0 C	DO *REG* ← 100	GO TO 0D	
0 D	IF *H*	THEN 0D	ELSE 0E
0 E	IF *H*	THEN 0F	ELSE 0E
0 F	DO *REG* ← 101	GO TO 10	
1 0	IF *H*	THEN 10	ELSE 11
1 1	IF *H*	THEN 00	ELSE 11

Figure 3.7

3.2.2 Software realization: decision tree

The sub-program *SP* is repeated six times in Figure 3.5; this suggests that the original flowchart could be simplified by transforming it so that *SP* appeared only once, as in Figure 3.8. However, the resulting assemblage of instructions no longer defines a flowchart completely, because it does not specify how the output from *SP* is to be input to the six assignment instructions. There are two ways of solving this problem: by software, using a binary decision tree, which we consider next, or by hardware, using a stack, which we consider in section 3.3.

The present state of the counter determines unambiguously the next state, for example $Q_2, Q_1, Q_0 = 000$ is always followed by $Q_2^+, Q_1^+, Q_0^+ = 001$; this information is contained in the state diagram and in the state table, Figures 3.2, 3.3. Thus a binary decision tree with test variables Q_2, Q_1, Q_0 can be constructed with which we can determine, at the output from *SP*, the next state Q_2^+, Q_1^+, Q_0^+.

The original state table (Figure 3.3) can be put into the form of a Karnaugh map, as Figure 3.9. The presence of the Φ conditions

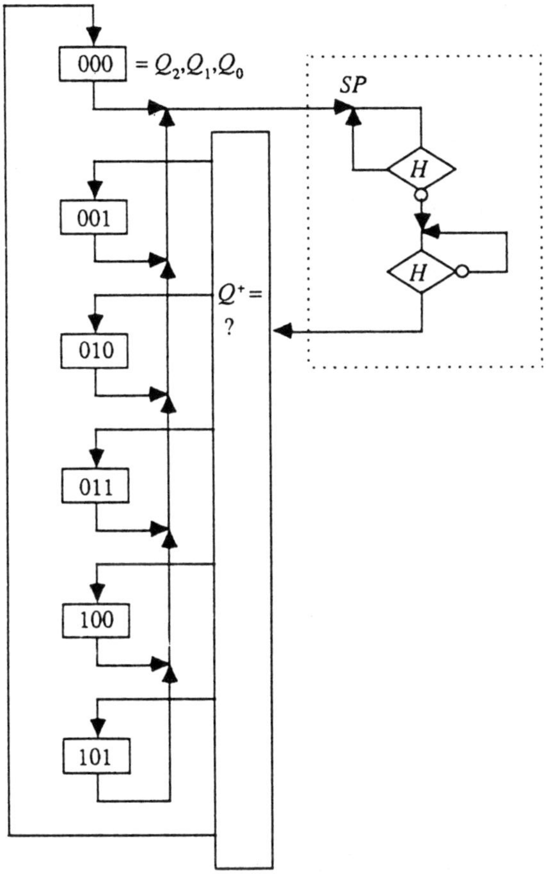

Figure 3.8

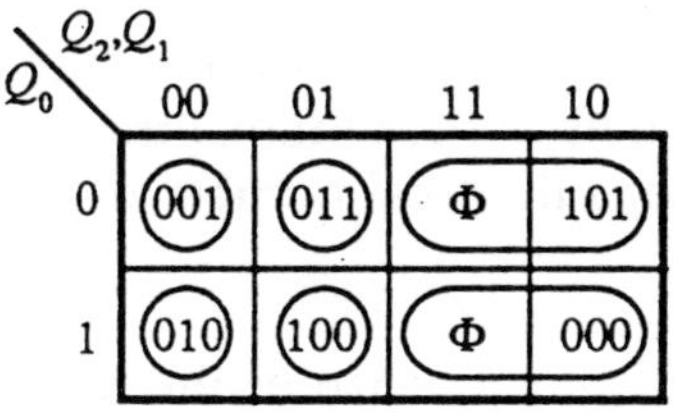

$Q^+ = Q_2^+, Q_1^+, Q_0^+$

Figure 3.9

$Q_2, Q_1, Q_0 = 110, 111$ makes simplification of this possible, and this can be done by the graphical method of §2.1.14; the resulting tree for Q^+ in Figure 3.10 is minimal. The combination of this tree with the sub-program *SP* gives the flowchart of Figure 3.10, which is thus a possible software realization of Figure 3.8; this has achieved the aim of requiring only one copy of *SP*, at the cost of a certain amount of software, the five test instructions in the tree.

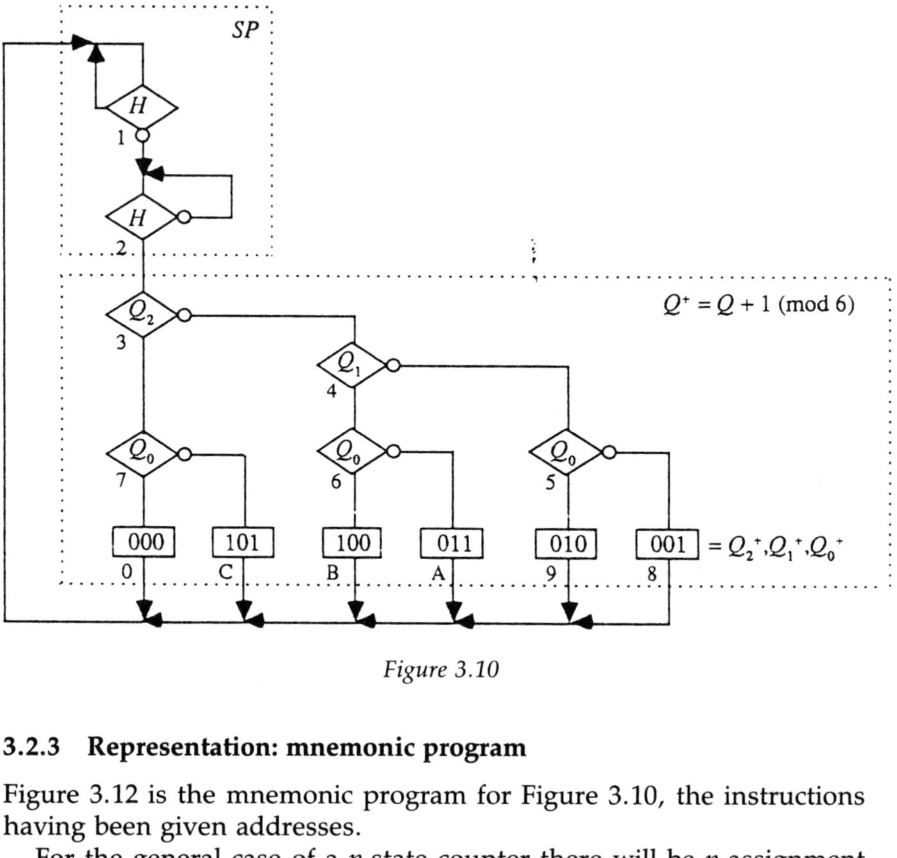

Figure 3.10

3.2.3 Representation: mnemonic program

Figure 3.12 is the mnemonic program for Figure 3.10, the instructions having been given addresses.

For the general case of a p-state counter there will be p assignment and $p - 1$ test instructions in the minimal tree and two test instructions in the sub-program; thus the total number of instructions is

$$c(p) = 2p + 1 \tag{3.7}$$

The cycle time depends on the size of the tree; in the worst case (the canonical tree)

$$d(p) = 3 + \lceil \log_2 p \rceil \tag{3.8}$$

where $\lceil x \rceil$ means the smallest integer greater than or equal to x. Thus the factor of merit is

$$c \cdot d = (2p + 1)(3 + \lceil \log_2 p \rceil) \cong p(6 + 2\lceil \log_2 p \rceil) \qquad (3.9)$$

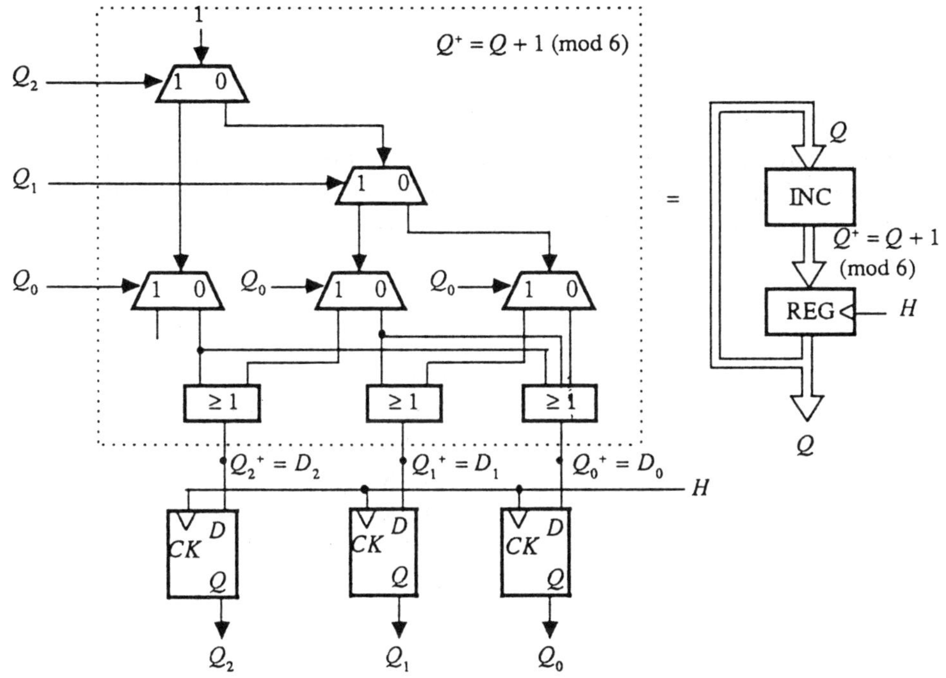

Figure 3.11

3.2.4 Hardware realization: L1 interpreter

The **L1** program of Figure 3.12 could be executed by the binary decision machine INT1 of Figure 2.60; the reader can check that no change would be needed to the formats of Figure 2.57 for the test and assignment instructions.

Notice that the machine must test the values Q_2, Q_1, Q_0; in this case, in contrast to that of the linear flowchart of 3.1.7, there is a hardware feedback between the outputs $REG_{2:0} = Q_2, Q_1, Q_0$ and the inputs of the test variables xi of the multiplexer MUX2 (Figure 2.60).

3.2.5 Hardware/software equivalence

The flowchart of Figure 3.10, coded and then executed by a binary decision machine such as INT1, is equivalent to the hardwired logic system of Figure 3.11 which realizes the synchronous counter in a *minimal code*: [1] p. 205, [59] p. 254. Using the rules of §2.4.2 to construct the {DMUX, OR} assemblage for Figure 3.10, we get the following relations

$$Q_0^+ = D_0 = Q_2'Q_1'Q_0' + Q_2'Q_1\,Q_0' + Q_2\,Q_0' \tag{3.10}$$

$$Q_1^+ = D_1 = Q_2'Q_1'Q_0 + Q_2'\,Q_1\,Q_0' \tag{3.11}$$

$$Q_2^+ = D_2 = Q_2'Q_1\,Q_0 + Q_2\,Q_0' \tag{3.12}$$

which provide a possible hardware realization of the state table of Figure 3.9: [1] pp. 135–137, [59] pp. 169–172. In Figure 3.11 the sub-program *SP* is realized by the master/slave flip-flops, switched by the clock signal *H*.

ADR	L1				
0	DO	*REG* ← 000	GO TO	1	
1	IF	*H*	THEN	1	ELSE 2
2	IF	*H*	THEN	3	ELSE 2
3	IF	Q_2	THEN	7	ELSE 4
4	IF	Q_1	THEN	6	ELSE 5
5	IF	Q_0	THEN	9	ELSE 8
6	IF	Q_0	THEN	B	ELSE A
7	IF	Q_0	THEN	0	ELSE C
8	DO	*REG* ← 001	GO TO	1	
9	DO	*REG* ← 010	GO TO	1	
A	DO	*REG* ← 011	GO TO	1	
B	DO	*REG* ← 100	GO TO	1	
C	DO	*REG* ← 101	GO TO	1	

Figure 3.12

3.2.6 Exercise

A scale-of-7 counter has to produce the cycle

$$\begin{aligned} Q_{3:0} = {} & 0001 \rightarrow 0010 \rightarrow 0011 \rightarrow 0101 \rightarrow 0111 \rightarrow \\ & 1011 \rightarrow 1101 \rightarrow 0001 \end{aligned} \tag{3.13}$$

Find two software realizations, one as a linear flowchart, the other as a minimal decision tree. Give the mnemonic program for each, determine the format for the **L1** instructions and rewrite the programs in binary and in hexadecimal.

3.3 PROCEDURES AND STACKS

3.3.1 Hardware realization: the stack

As we have seen, the present state Q of the counter determines the next state Q^+ completely and unambiguously; and in §3.2.2 this determination is brought about by a software structure, the decision tree of Figure 3.10.

If we introduce into the interpreter a special register, a *stack* (also called a *push-down stack*, or *last-in-first-out*, *LIFO*, *register*) we can record in this, at the instant of leaving the present state Q (= 000, say) the address of the next state Q^+ (= 001 after Q = 000), to be set up after the sub-program has been executed. The presence of this hardware operator has consequences for the software, in particular requiring two new instructions. In the example of the counter (Figure 3.13) there is the following sequence of events:

1. at the initial address 0, the assignment $Q \leftarrow 000$;
2. at address *ADR* = 1, the new instruction **CALL** to enter the sub-program *SP*, beginning at address *ADSP* = C, and record in the stack the return address *ADRT* = 2;
3. execution of the sub-program instructions at addresses C, D in that order;
4. at address E, the new instruction **RET** to take the address *ADRT* = 2 from the stack and return from the sub-program to re-enter the main program at this address;
5. at address *ADRT* = 2, execution of the assignment Q ← 001.

3.3.2 Definitions: call and return instructions

A *call instruction* (Figure 3.14) is defined by an address *ADR* and the address *ADSP* of first instruction of the sub-program *SP* that is to be entered. Graphically, every such instruction has a single input and a single output terminal, the latter leading to the return address *ADRT*. The mnemonic form is

CALL *ADSP* **RET TO** *ADRT* (3.14)

A *return instruction* (Figure 3.15) is defined by its address *ADR* and the simple mnemonic expression

RET (3.15)

Each such instruction has a single input terminal.

By using the graphical symbols of Figures 3.14 and 3.15, the flowchart of Figure 3.13 can be transformed into that of Figure 3.16.

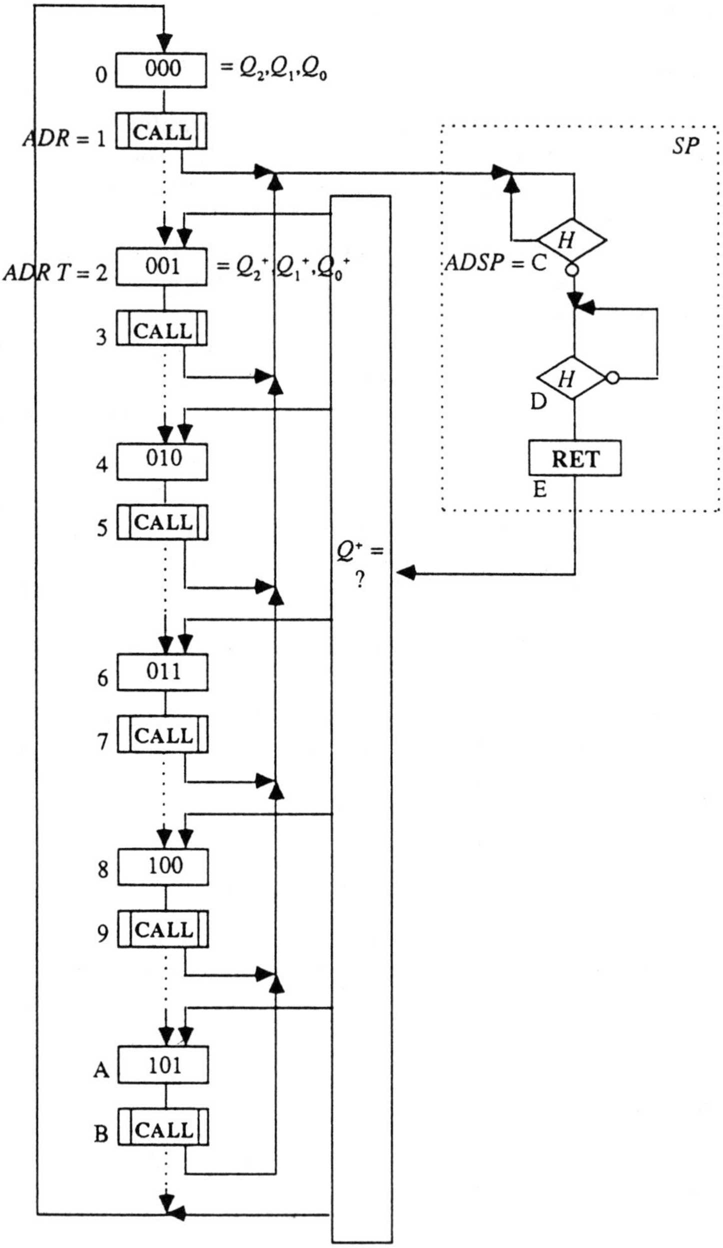

0
000
$= Q_2, Q_1, Q_0$
ADR = 1
CALL
SP
H
ADSP = C
ADR T = 2
001
$= Q_2^+, Q_1^+, Q_0^+$
3
CALL
H
D
4
010
RET
E
5
CALL
$Q^+ =$
?
6
011
7
CALL
8
100
9
CALL
A
101
B
CALL

Figure 3.13

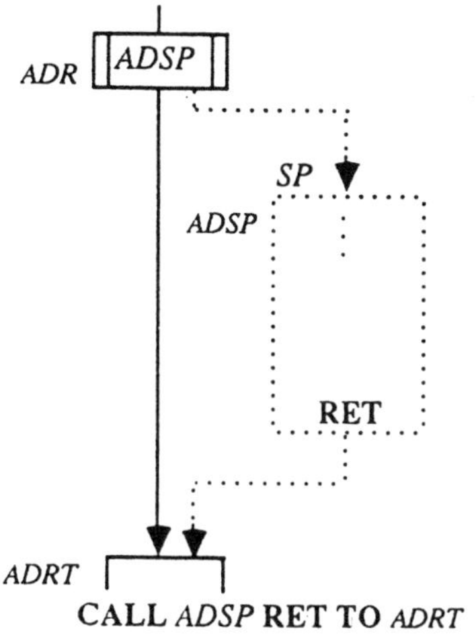

Figure 3.14

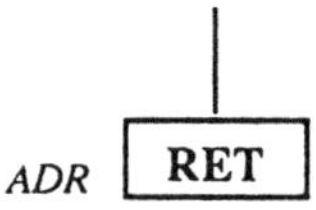

Figure 3.15

This breaks down into a *main (principal) program PP* and a sub-program *SP* and provides a possible realization of Figure 3.8. Thus we have again achieved the aim of requiring only a single copy of the sub-program *SP*, this time at cost of some hardware (the stack) and some software (the new **CALL** and **RET** instructions).

3.3.3 Definition: procedure

We define a *procedure* as any sub-program entered from a *calling program* or *calling procedure* by a **CALL** instruction belonging to the calling program or calling procedure. A procedure is always represented by a flowchart that has a single input terminal and no output terminal, and terminates with a return instruction (Figure 3.16).

If the call instruction belongs to the procedure itself then the procedure is said to be *recursive*.

3.3.4 Definition: indexed assignment instruction

In applications we often want to use several distinct assignment registers; for this we generalize the assignment instruction of §2.3.5 and Figure 2.53 to the form

DO *REG*[*j*] ← *OUT* **GO TO** *ADR*+ (3.16)

Here *j* is an *index*, distinguishing a particular register.

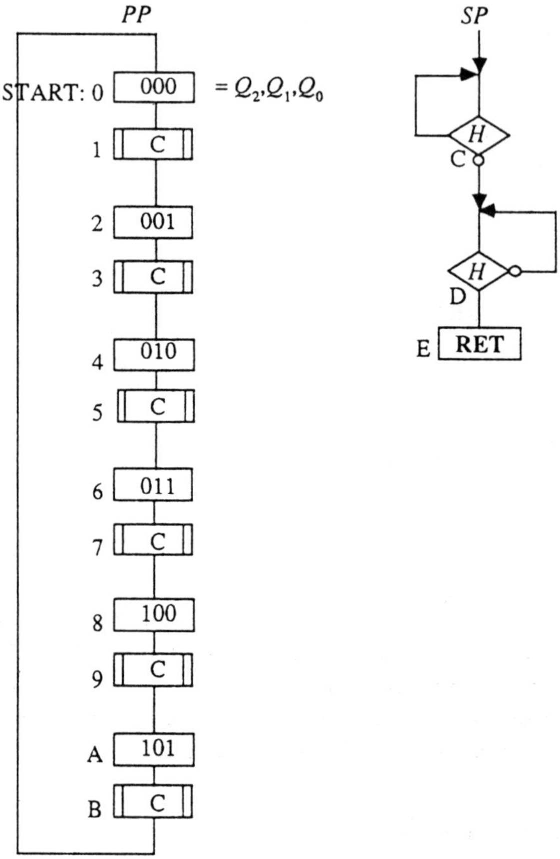

Figure 3.16

3.3.5 Definition: the language L2

The set of four instructions: test (2.36), indexed assignment (3.16), call (3.14) and return (3.15) form the language **L2**; this is defined symbolically as

$$\mathbf{L2} = \{\mathbf{IF...THEN...ELSE...,\ DO...GO\ TO...,\ CALL...RET\ TO...,\ RET}\} \tag{3.17}$$

3.3.6 Representation: mnemonic program

If the instructions in Figure 3.16 are given addresses the mnemonic expressions can be listed as in Figure 3.17, where we have assumed that there is only a single assignment register, with index $j = 0$.

ADR	L2		
0	DO *REG* [0] ← 000	GO TO 1	
1	CALL C	RET TO 2	
2	DO *REG* [0] ← 001	GO TO 3	
3	CALL C	RET TO 4	
4	DO *REG* [0] ← 010	GO TO 5	
5	CALL C	RET TO 6	
6	DO *REG* [0] ← 011	GO TO 7	
7	CALL C	RET TO 8	
8	DO *REG* [0] ← 100	GO TO 9	
9	CALL C	RET TO A	
A	DO *REG* [0] ← 101	GO TO B	
B	CALL C	RET TO 0	
C	IF *H*	THEN C	ELSE D
D	IF *H*	THEN E	ELSE D
E	RET		

Figure 3.17

For the p-state counter there are p call and p assignment instructions in the main program and two test and one return instructions in the sub-program; the total number is thus

$$c(p) = 2p + 3 \tag{3.18}$$

The cycle d time is constant:

$$d = 5 \tag{3.19}$$

and therefore the figure of merit is

$$c \cdot d = 10p + 15 \tag{3.20}$$

3.3.7 Representation: binary and hexadecimal programs

Figure 3.23 gives a possible format for the instructions of **L2**; we note:

- the operating code must have at least two bits, to distinguish between the four instructions; hence $OPC_{1:0}$;
- the index $i_{1:0}$ enables four different variables xi to be tested; for the present example we choose

$$H = x0, \quad i_{1:0} = 00 \tag{3.21}$$

- the index j enables four different output registers REG[j] to be addressed; in the present example

$$j = 0, \quad j_{1:0} = 00 \tag{3.22}$$

- the index $k_{1:0}$ is defined in §3.5.9 below; for the present we can say simply that it provides two undefined bits, Φ conditions;
- four address bits are needed for the 15 instructions, hence $ADR_{3:0}$; the output state Q_2, Q_1, Q_0 needs three bits, $OUT_{2:0}$

The binary and hexadecimal forms are given in Figures 3.18, 3.19 respectively, in which it is assumed that all the undefined bits are set to 0.

Notice that if the various fields of the four instructions coincide with groups of four bits, as is the case for all the addresses in Figure 3.23, for example, the hexadecimal program of Figure 3.19 can be derived directly from the mnemonic program of Figure 3.17 without the need to go through the tedious process of first transforming the latter to binary.

ADR	*OPC*	*i* *j*	*ADR1* *ADR+* *ADSP*	*ADR0* *OUT* *ADRT*
0000	10	00	0001	-000
0001	00	- -	1100	0010
0010	10	00	0011	-001
0011	00	- -	1100	0100
0100	10	00	0101	-010
0101	00	- -	1100	0110
0110	10	00	0111	-011
0111	00	- -	1100	1000
1000	10	00	1001	-100
1001	00	- -	1100	1010
1010	10	00	1011	-101
1011	00	- -	1100	0000
1100	01	00	1100	1101
1101	01	00	1110	1101
1110	11	- -	- - - -	- - - -

Figure 3.18

ADR	*OUT* = *ROM* [*ADR*]		
0	8	1	0
1	0	C	2
2	8	3	1
3	0	C	4
4	8	5	2
5	0	C	6
6	8	7	3
7	0	C	8
8	8	9	4
9	0	C	A
A	8	B	5
B	0	C	0
C	4	C	D
D	4	E	D
E	C	0	0

Figure 3.19

3.3.8 Description: stack

An *m-level stack*, for words of one bit, is a bi-directional register of m bits, consisting of m D flip-flops (cf. §1.2.14).

The logic diagram of Figure 3.20, and the schema of Figure 3.21, represent a four-level stack ($Q_0 \,..\, Q_3$) for 1-bit words, based on the register of Figure 1.40; *IN* is the input and $OUT = Q_0$ the output. The uppermost word Q_0 (= *OUT*) is the *head*, *top* or *front* of the stack, the lowermost Q_3 is the stack *base* or *bottom*.

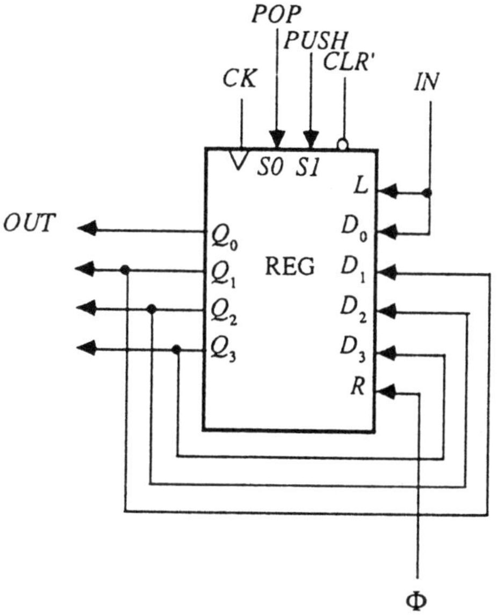

Figure 3.20

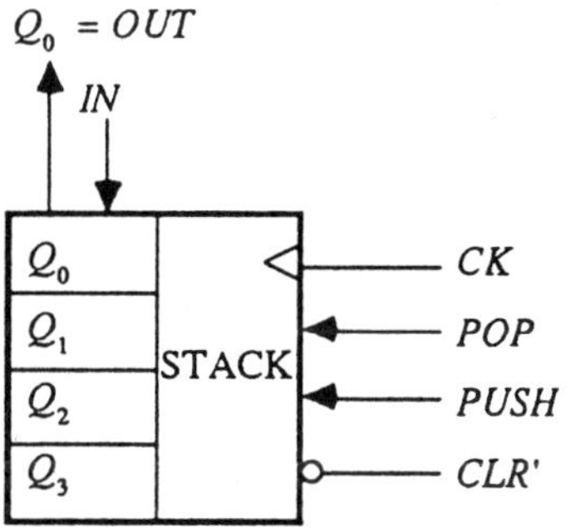

Figure 3.21

Ignoring the effect of the asynchronous input *CLR'*, the operations table is as in Figure 3.22. The four operations are:

- the neutral operation HOLD, for *PUSH, POP* = 00;
- *'unstack'*, POP, for *PUSH, POP* = 01; this results in a 1-bit shift from the base towards the head;
- *'stack'*, PUSH, for *PUSH, POP* = 10; this results in a 1-bit shift from the head towards the base;
- the loading operation, LOAD, for *PUSH, POP* = 11.

The bi-directional shift register becomes a stack if the following relations hold; they are taken from the corresponding tables of Figures 1.42 and 3.22:

OPERATION	DESCRIPTION	$PUSH = S1$	$POP = S0$
HOLD	$Q_3 \leftarrow Q_3,\ Q_2 \leftarrow Q_2,\ Q_1 \leftarrow Q_1,\ Q_0 \leftarrow Q_0$	0	0
POP	$Q_3 \leftarrow \Phi,\ Q_2 \leftarrow Q_3,\ Q_1 \leftarrow Q_2,\ Q_0 \leftarrow Q_1$	0	1
PUSH	$Q_3 \leftarrow Q_2,\ Q_2 \leftarrow Q_1,\ Q_1 \leftarrow Q_0,\ Q_0 \leftarrow IN$	1	0
LOAD	$Q_3 \leftarrow Q_3,\ Q_2 \leftarrow Q_2,\ Q_1 \leftarrow Q_1,\ Q_0 \leftarrow IN$	1	1

Figure 3.22

$$S1 = PUSH, \quad S0 = POP \tag{3.23}$$

$$R = \Phi \text{ (SHIFT RIGHT = POP)} \tag{3.24}$$

$$L = IN \text{ (SHIFT LEFT = PUSH)} \tag{3.25}$$

$$D_3 = Q_3, \quad D_2 = Q_2, \quad D_1 = Q_1, \quad D_0 = IN\text{(LOAD)} \tag{3.26}$$

An m-level stack for n-bit words is an iterative assemblage of n bi-directional shift registers, each of m flip-flops. Figure 3.23 shows a 4-level stack for 4-bit words.

3.3.9 Comments

The number m of levels is the *depth* of the stack and the word length n is the *width* or *breadth*. With m levels m successive calls can be made to nested procedures (see §3.4.5).

Stacks of large depth and width are usually implemented as a combination of a random access memory and a counter called a *stack pointer*: this is described in §§7.4.6–7, and in [84].

3.3.10 Hardware realization: interpreter for L2

The microprogrammed system for executing **L2** is a *stack-based binary decision machine*, or *interpreter* for **L2**, INT2. This is shown in Figure 3.23; it consists of:

- a program memory ROM for 16 words of 12 bits, defined by $OUT_{11:0} = ROM_{11:0}[ADR]$;
- an address register ADR, defined by

$$ADR \leftarrow ADR^{+} \tag{3.27}$$

- a 4-level stack STACK for 4-bit words, whose input IN and output OUT are

$$IN_{3:0} = ADRT_{3:0}, \quad OUT_{3:0} = STACK_{3:0} \tag{3.28}$$

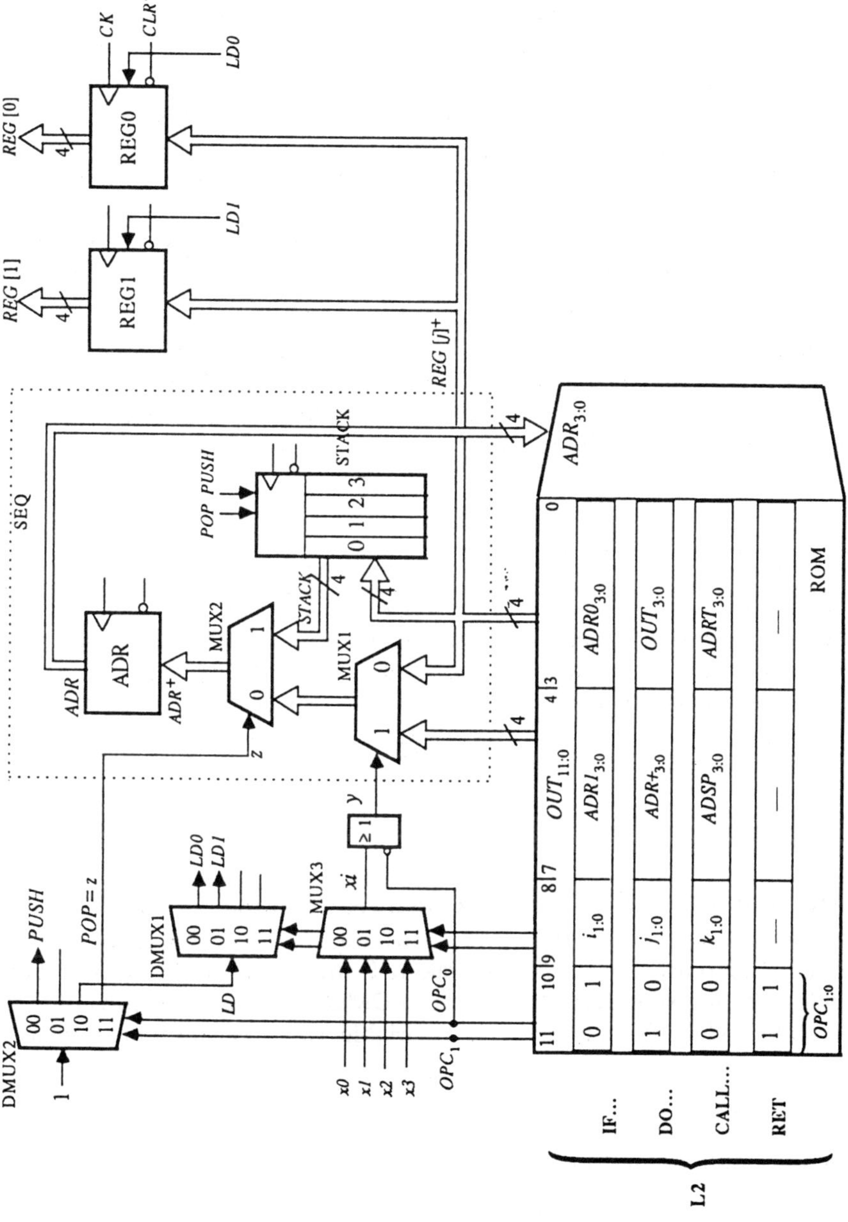

REG [0]
REG [1]
REG0
REG1
CK
CLR'
LD0
LD1
REG [j]+
SEQ
STACK
POP PUSH
ADR
ADR+
MUX1
MUX2
MUX3
DMUX1
DMUX2
PUSH
POP = z
LD
xi
y
≥ 1
OPC0
OPC1
x0
x1
x2
x3
ADR3:0
OUT11:0
i1:0
j1:0
k1:0
ADR03:0
ADR13:0
OUT3:0
ADR+3:0
ADRT3:0
ADSP3:0
OPC1:0
ROM
INT2
IF...
DO...
CALL...
RET
L2

Figure 3.23

- two multiplexers MUX1, MUX2 driven by the variables y, z, for selecting the next address ADR^+ ($ADR1 = ROM_{7:4}$, $ADR0 = ROM_{3:0}$, $ADR+ = ROM_{7:4}$, $ADSP = ROM_{7:4}$, $STACK$);
- a multiplexer MUX3 driven by the variables i_1, i_0 of the index i, for selecting the test variable xi;
- two assignment registers REG0, REG1, driven by the variables $S1 = S0 = LD0$ and $S1 = S0 = LD1$ (cf. §1.2.14);
- a demultiplexer DMUX1, driven by the variables j_1, j_0 of the index j, to select one or other of the assignments $REG[j] \leftarrow OUT$, $j = 0$ or 1;
- a demultiplexer DMUX2 to decode the operating code $OPC_{1:0}$.

The operations table of Figure 3.24 describes the global behaviour of the stack machine, in particular of the transfers between the registers ADR, STACK and REG for each of the instructions: the tests OP1, OP2, the assignment OP3, the call OP4 and the return OP5.

OPERATION	DESCRIPTION: ADR, STACK, REG	$OPC_{1:0}$	xi
OP1 = IF 0 ELSE *ADR0*	$ADR \leftarrow ADR0$, HOLD, HOLD	01	0
OP2 = IF 1 THEN *ADR1*	$ADR \leftarrow ADR1$, HOLD, HOLD	01	1
OP3 = DO $REG[j] \leftarrow OUT$ GO TO *ADR+*	$ADR \leftarrow ADR+$, HOLD, $REG[j] \leftarrow OUT$	10	Φ
OP4 = CALL *ADSP* RET TO *ADRT*	$ADR \leftarrow ADSP$, PUSH, HOLD	00	Φ
OP5 = RET	$ADR \leftarrow STACK$, POP, HOLD	11	Φ

Figure 3.24

The truth table of Figure 3.25 is deduced from the operations table. We calculate the values of y and z (driving MUX1, MUX2), of *PUSH* and *POP* (driving the stack and taken from Figure 3.22), and of *LD* (driving the registers REG and input to DMUX1), all as functions of the operating code $OPC_{1:0}$ and the test variable xi. After simplification we find

$$y = OPC_0' + xi \tag{3.29}$$

which is implemented by an OR operator; and

$$z = POP = OPC_1 \cdot OPC_0 \tag{3.30}$$

$$PUSH = OPC_1' \cdot OPC_0' \tag{3.31}$$

$$LD = OPC_1 \cdot OPC_0' \tag{3.32}$$

which are implemented by the demultiplexer DMUX2.

OPERATION	$OPC_{1:0}$	*xi*	ADR^+	*y*	*z*	*PUSH*	*POP*	$REG[j]^+$	*LD*
OP1	01	0	$ADR0 = ROM_{3:0}$	0	0	0	0	$REG[j]$	0
OP2	01	1	$ADR1 = ROM_{7:4}$	1	0	0	0	$REG[j]$	0
OP3	10	Φ	$ADR+ = ROM_{7:4}$	1	0	0	0	$OUT = ROM_{3:0}$	1
OP4	00	Φ	$ADSP = ROM_{7:4}$	1	0	1	0	$REG[j]$	0
OP5	11	Φ	*STACK*	Φ	1	0	1	$REG[j]$	0

Figure 3.25

3.3.11 Comments

A program that consists of a main program *PP* and *m* procedures *P1 . . . Pm* can be represented by $m + 1$ distinct flowcharts, as for example in Figures 3.16 ($m = 1$) and 3.30 ($m = 2$). In the worst case, that is when the instruction to be executed is in the procedure *Pm* ($ADR = C$ in Figure 3.16, $= B$ in Figure 3.30) the machine has to store $m + 1$ addresses:

- the present address *ADR*, held in the address register;
- *m* return addresses, held in the *m* levels of the stack.

The initial instruction ($ADR = 0$: START) must be in the main program (as in Figures 3.16 and 3.30), not in a procedure. If it were in a procedure a general resetting to zero would destroy the contents of the stack registers and prevent a correct return from the procedure to the main program or to the calling procedure.

3.3.12 Hardware/software equivalence

The two flowcharts of Figure 3.16 constitute a decomposition in time of the linear chart of Figure 3.5; thus 3.16 is formally equivalent to the hardwired system of Figure 3.5 for the realization of the counter in a 1-out-of-6 code (Figure 3.6).

3.3.13 Conclusion

From the above results we can say that, at least so far as the implementation of a counter is concerned, the hardware realization with a stack, together with the new call and return instructions of the language **L2**, is equivalent to the software realization as a binary decision tree (Figure 3.10). The stack-based solution has the advantages of clarity of the **L2** program (Figures 3.16–7), constant cycle time *d*, no hardware feedback (from the assignment register to the inputs to the test variables) and above all the possibility of partitioning complex problems by the use of successive calls to nested procedures: this last feature is discussed in the next section.

3.3.14 Bibliography

Procedures and their execution by a stack-based machine, using either bi-directional shift registers or random access memories with pointers, are discussed in the following references: [2] pp. 443–448, [3] pp. 166–171, [54] pp. 613–618, [56] pp. 47–50, [57] pp. 67–83, [67] pp. 245–249.

3.3.15 Exercise

Draw the flowcharts for main and sub-programs that constitute the **L2** program for the 7-state counter of §3.2.6. Determine the instruction formats and write out the mnemonic, binary and hexadecimal programs. Construct the detailed logic diagram for a 1-level stack that is adapted to these formats, minimizing the number of components of the type described in Chapter 1.

3.4 DECOMPOSITION OF COUNTERS

3.4.1 Introduction

We know from the theory of hardwired logic systems that provided the decomposition is in fact possible, the problem of designing a p-state counter can be reduced to that of designing a number of counters of scales less than p; the decomposition will then simplify the calculation by reducing the number of variables involved.

We shall show in this section that serial decomposition of the counter problem lends itself particularly well to solution in terms of procedures (as described in section 3.3), and to a lesser extent to the use of sub-programs and decision trees (as in section 3.2). Consequently serial decomposition is a favoured method of attack on complex counter problems; later we shall illustrate this with the example of a digital clock.

3.4.2 Definition: serial decomposition

Figure 3.26 shows a p-state counter constructed as an assemblage of counters of smaller scales $p1, p2, \ldots pq$; clearly for this to be possible we must have

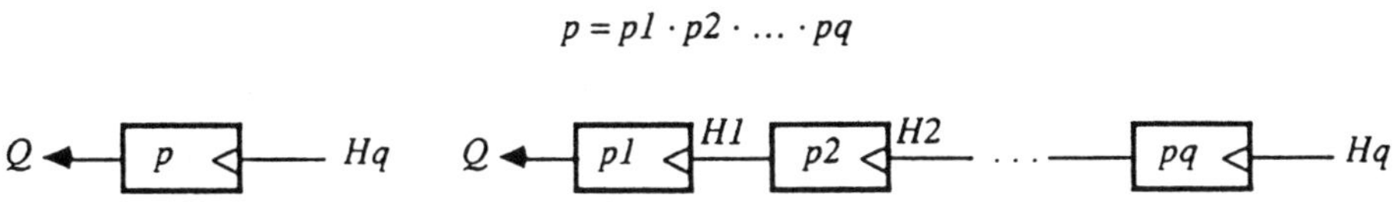

Figure 3.26

$$p1 \cdot p2 \cdot \ldots \cdot pq = p \tag{3.33}$$

If this holds we say that the p-counter admits of a *serial decomposition* (cf. [1] pp. 148–157, [59] pp. 186–197); and that the q counters $p1, p2 \cdot \ldots \cdot pq$ are *partial counters* for the *full p-counter.*

Since all the numbers here must be integers, it is clear that such a decomposition is possible only if p is composite, that is, is not a prime number. Further, for any given decomposition $p1, p2 \cdot \ldots \cdot pq$ there will in general be several distinct permutations of the factors, e.g. $6 = 2 \cdot 3 = 3 \cdot 2$, and each will be represented by a different schema and will have a different coding. Thus serial decomposition is not a commutative operation, and the different permutations of the factors are distinct entities.

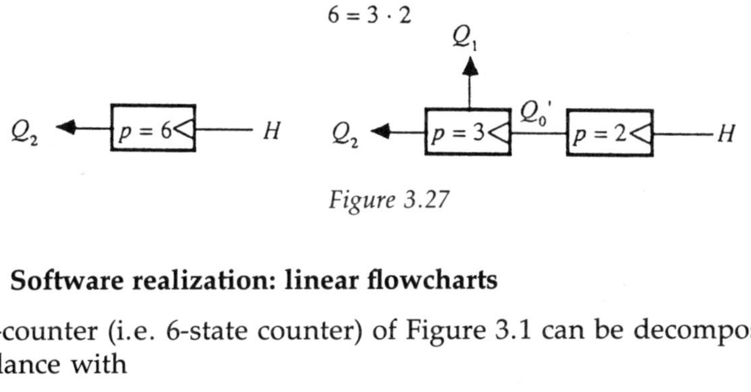

Figure 3.27

3.4.3 Software realization: linear flowcharts

The 6-counter (i.e. 6-state counter) of Figure 3.1 can be decomposed in accordance with

$$6 = 3 \cdot 2 \tag{3.34}$$

giving the schema of Figure 3.27 and the decomposition of the original state graph of Figure 3.2 into the two partial graphs of Figure 3.28:

- one of two vertices, describing the 2-counter whose state Q_0 changes at each rise of the clock signal H ($H \leftarrow 1$);
- one of three vertices, describing the 3-counter whose state Q_2, Q_1 changes at each fall of Q_0 ($Q_0 \leftarrow 0$).

Using §3.1.3, the two flowcharts of Figure 3.29 can be deduced directly from these graphs.

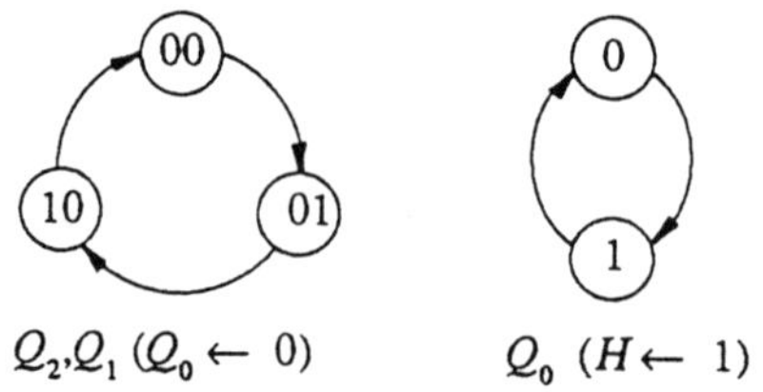

Figure 3.28

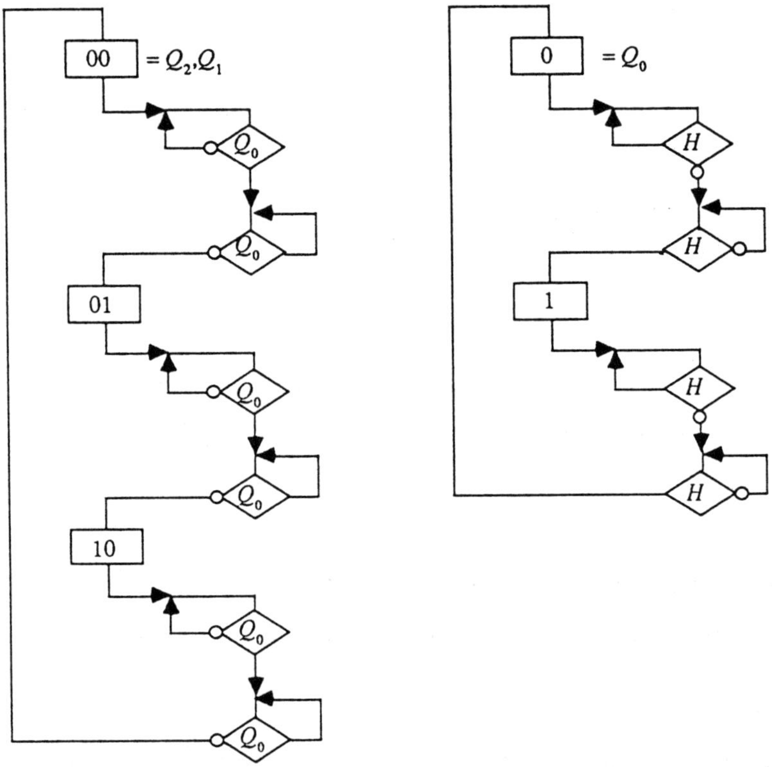

Figure 3.29

Unfortunately, implementation of the two charts requires two different programs that have to be executed on two different machines: we say that they represent *parallel processes*. In the interests of simplicity we shall not, in the present book, consider any system of parallel processes that requires several processors.

3.4.4 Software realization: procedures

We have already demonstrated the value of the procedure call and return instructions for reducing a complex problem to a set of simpler sub-problems. Consideration of the serial decomposition (3.34), described by the pair of graphs of Figure 3.28 and by the pair of flowcharts of Figure 3.29, leads to the solution of Figure 3.30 comprising:

- the main program *PP*, for the counting by 3 (states Q_2, Q_1);
- a procedure *P1*, for the counting by 2 (state Q_0);
- a procedure *P2*, for the double test of *H*.

The program for this can be written in **L2** and executed by the machine of Figure 3.23; two separate registers are needed for the assignments $REG[1] \leftarrow Q_2, Q_1$, $REG[0] \leftarrow Q_0$.

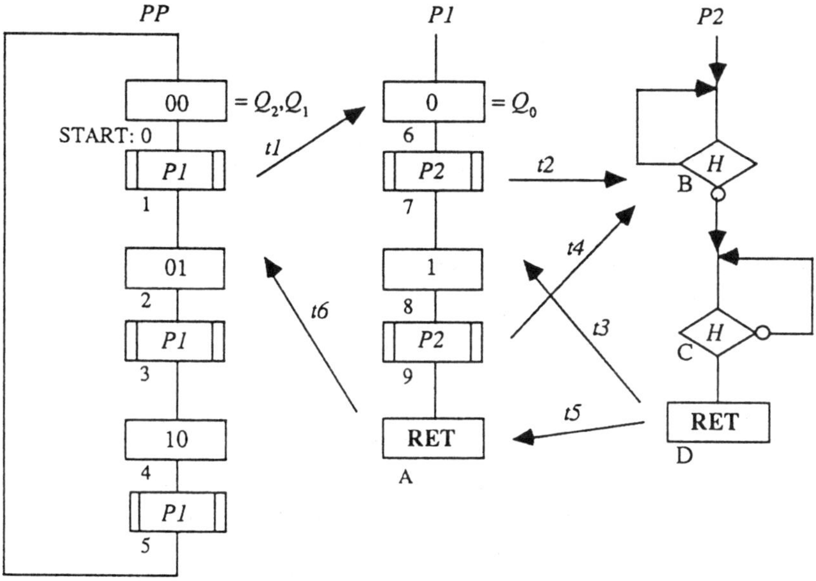

Figure 3.30

3.4.5 Definition: nested procedures

If a procedure *P2* is called, not by the main program, but by another procedure *P1* (as in Figure 3.30, for example) then *P2* is said to be *nested* in *P1* and *P1* is said to be the *calling procedure* for *P2*. Figure 3.31 shows the contents of the stack of Figure 3.30 at the six clock times *t1, t2, . . . t6* that correspond to three procedure calls (*t1, t2, t4*: operation PUSH) and three returns (*t3, t5, t6*: operation POP).

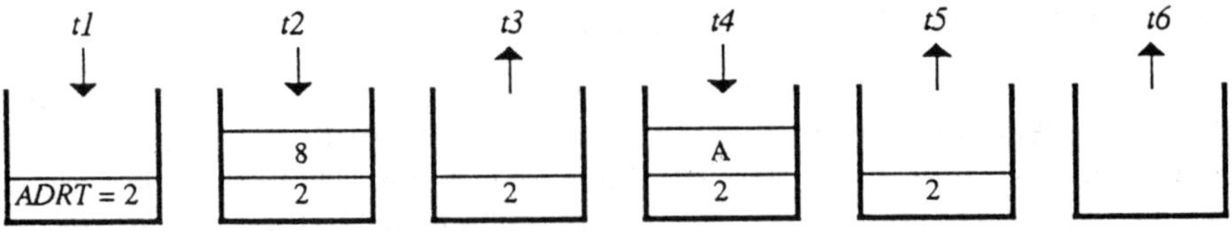

Figure 3.31

3.4.6 Software realization: decision trees

The decomposition of (3.34) can equally be realized by the flowchart of Figure 3.32, in which neither the call nor the return instruction is used. We have here:

- the sub-program *SP*, performing the double test of the clock signal *H*;
- a tree described by the relation

$$Q^+ = Q + 1 \pmod 2 \tag{3.35}$$

  realizing the 2-counter (state Q_0), as §3.2.2
- a second tree described by the relation

$$Q^+ = Q + 1 \pmod 3 \tag{3.36}$$

realizing the 3-counter (states Q_2, Q_1) as in §3.2.2; from Figure 3.28, the state changes of this counter are driven by the fall of Q_0 ($Q_0 \leftarrow 0$).

The program for Figure 3.32 can be written in **L2**, provided that two indexed assignments are available, $REG[1] \leftarrow Q_2, Q_1$ and $REG[0] \leftarrow Q_0$.

3.4.7 Method: synthesizing a counter

A counter is usually specified by its scale *p*, with possibly a code in addition, such as binary, BCD (Binary Coded Decimal) etc. The general method for synthesis is as follows.

1. One or more serial decompositions are found, compatible with any code that may have been specified; each must of course satisfy the condition

$$p1 \cdot p2 \cdot \ldots \cdot pq = p \tag{3.37}$$

2. One of the three main software realizations is constructed for each decomposition: linear flowchart, procedure or decision tree.
3. (a) *Linear flowchart*. This requires *q* separate linear flowcharts for the *q* parallel processes, and *q* separate binary decision machines, interpreting **L1**, to execute them. Each flowchart can be derived

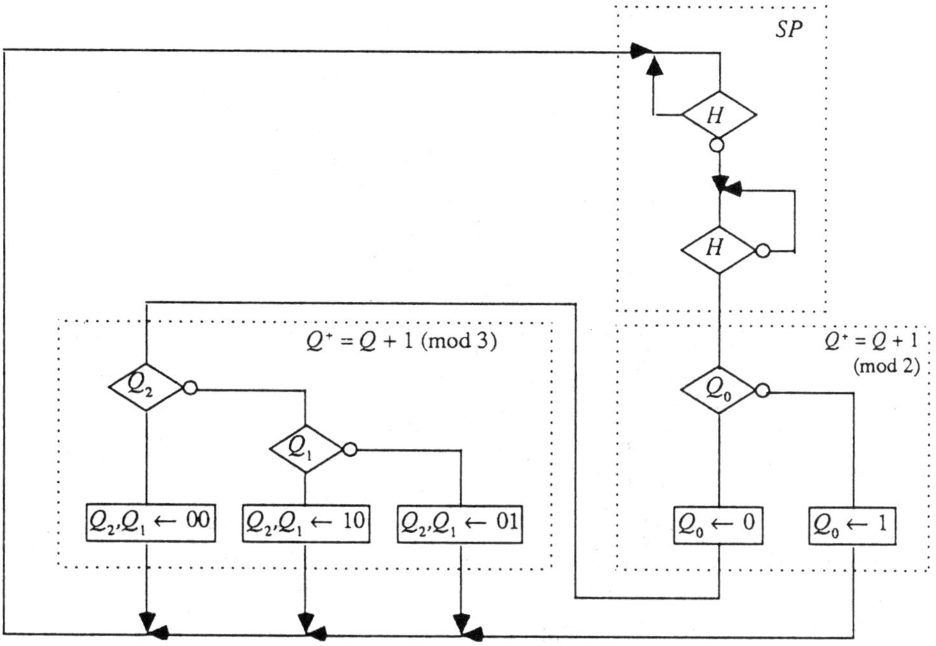

Figure 3.32

directly from the state graph for each partial counter, as described in §3.1.3.

(b) *Procedures*. This requires a main program and q procedures, to be executed by a machine with a stack of depth q, interpreting **L2**. The main program and $q - 1$ procedures follow directly from the state graphs for the q partial counters (§3.3.1); the remaining procedure is for the double test of the clock signal H.

(c) *Decision tree*. This requires a sub-program (for the double clock test) and q trees, executed by a machine that interprets **L1**. Each tree realizes one partial counter and can be derived from the state table for that counter, in which the next state Q^+ is given as a function of the present state according to §3.2.2.

3.4.8 Application: a digital clock

The problem is to design a 60-state counter for displaying the seconds or minutes of a digital clock. The specification is as follows:

- the scale $p = 60$;
- the sequence of states is, in decimal: $00 \rightarrow 01 \rightarrow 02 \rightarrow \ldots \rightarrow 59 \rightarrow 00$.

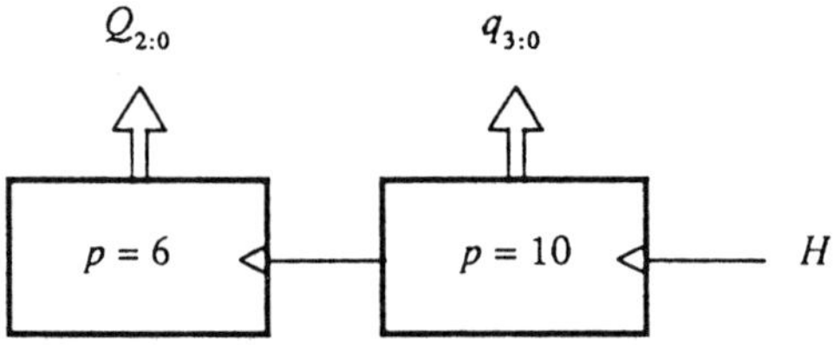

Figure 3.33

It is usual to have separate displays for the tens and units; thus we use BCD, needing four bits $q_{3:0}$ for the units (0000 to 1001) and three bits $Q_{2:0}$ for the tens (from 000 to 101): see Figure 3.33.

Even if we restrict ourselves to a single machine and a single program, and therefore exclude the use of parallel processes, we find that many equivalent flowcharts can be constructed to meet this specification, representing combinations of one or other of the basic methods (linear flowchart, procedures, tree) and of the possible decompositions of the counter. Figure 3.34 summarizes the main variants, giving in each case the cost c, the cycle time d (always calculated for the worst case) and the figure of merit $c \cdot d$. The table gives also the number of stack levels, which is the number of successive calls to nested procedures.

Variants 3 and 7 have the best factor of merit. Variant 3 is given in Figure 3.35, showing the main program *PP* and the procedures *P1*, *P2*; these latter make clear the simplicity of the realization, which is particularly well adapted to structured programming (Chapter 5).

3.4.9 Conclusion

A p-state counter with $p = p1 \cdot p2 \cdot \ldots \cdot pq$ can be realized:

1. by a linear flowchart; no decomposition is possible if parallel processing is excluded but the cycle time is minimized;
2. by a main program and q procedures; the cost is, to a first approximation, proportional to the sum of the partial scales, $p1 + p2 + \ldots + pq$;
3. by a sub-program and q decision trees, when again the cost is approximately proportional to the sum of the partial scales.

For Cases 2 and 3 it follows that the lowest cost will correspond to decomposition into the smallest possible partial scales.

Thus decomposition reduces the cost, but it increases the cycle time, the occurrence of transient output states, and, possibly, the size of the

No	Realization	Cost c	Cycle time d	Figure of merit $c \cdot d$	Stack level
	Linear flowchart				
1	$p = 60$	180	3	540	–
	Procedure(s)				
2	$p = 60$	123	5	615	1
3	$p = 6 \cdot 10$	36	8	288	2
4	$p = (3 \cdot 2) \cdot (5 \cdot 2)$	30	14	420	4
	Tree(s)				
5	$p = 60$	121	10	1210	–
6	$p = 6 \cdot 10$	32	11	352	–
7	$p = (3 \cdot 2) \cdot (5 \cdot 2)$	22	13	286	–

Figure 3.34

stack. It is nevertheless the preferred basis for the design of complex counters.

3.4.10 Bibliography

Reference [60] gives a general treatment of the software realization of counters by the methods discussed above, and applications to micro-programmed clocks are treated in [42], [51], [61] and [62]. In the case of the sub-program plus tree solution (method 3 of §3.4.9) a very fine-grain decomposition can be achieved by the use of 2-state counters, together with some possible feedback; this method, which is equivalent to the hardware realization of *frequency dividers*, is discussed in [60].

3.4.11 Exercise

What modifications must be made to the stack machine of Figure 3.23 if it is to interpret the flowcharts of Figure 3.35 for the 60-state counter? Determine the formats for the **L2** instructions and write the mnemonic, binary and hexadecimal programs.

3.4.12 Exercise

In Figure 3.34, solution 7 uses a sub-program and several binary decision trees; simplify each of these trees and construct the complete flowchart for the counter.

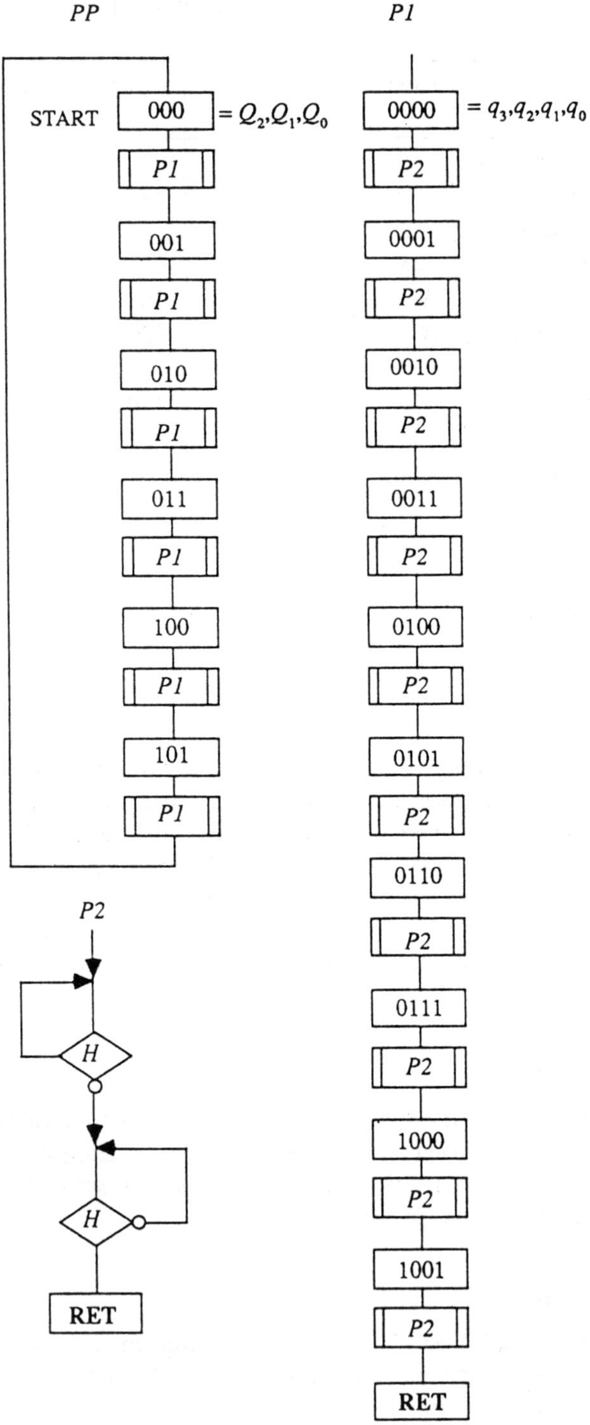

PP
P1
START
000
$= Q_2, Q_1, Q_0$
P1
001
010
011
100
101
0000
$= q_3, q_2, q_1, q_0$
P2
0001
0010
0011
0100
0101
0110
0111
1000
1001
RET
P2
H
H
RET

Figure 3.35

3.4.13 Exercise

Draw the flowchart for each solution of the 60-state counter listed in Figure 3.34 and check the values given for cost and cycle time (and hence for the factor of merit).

3.4.14 Exercise

A 12-state counter is to be realized in BCD, counting from 00 to 11 (decimal). Develop three programs for this, using the methods of linear flowcharts, procedures and decision trees respectively, without any decomposition; calculate for each the cost, the cycle time and the figure of merit. Determine the instruction formats and write the programs in mnemonic code, binary and hexadecimal.

What modifications would be needed if the counting were in binary, from 0000 to 1011?

3.4.15 Exercise

A 12-state counter operates in pure binary, from 0000 to 1011. Find all the possible serial decompositions (cf. [1] pp. 148–157, [59] pp. 186–197); select the one with minimum cost and realization by

(a) procedures and a stack;
(b) a sub-program and trees.

Compare the cycle times and figures of merit for these solutions.

3.5 DECOMPOSITION OF TREES

3.5.1 Definition: iterative binary decision diagram

A binary decision diagram that can be decomposed into a number of identical partial diagrams, linked by identical connections, is said to be *iterative*. An example is Figure 2.34, for the 2-bit comparator; this consists of copies of the partial diagram $COMP(A_k, B_k)$, each a *slice* of the complete diagram, enclosed in the dotted lines in the figure.

To be more precise, we say that two slices of a diagram are identical if they are represented by the same assemblage of test and/or assignment elements; the indices i of the test variables xi, and j of the assignment registers $REG[j]$ are usually different for the different slices.

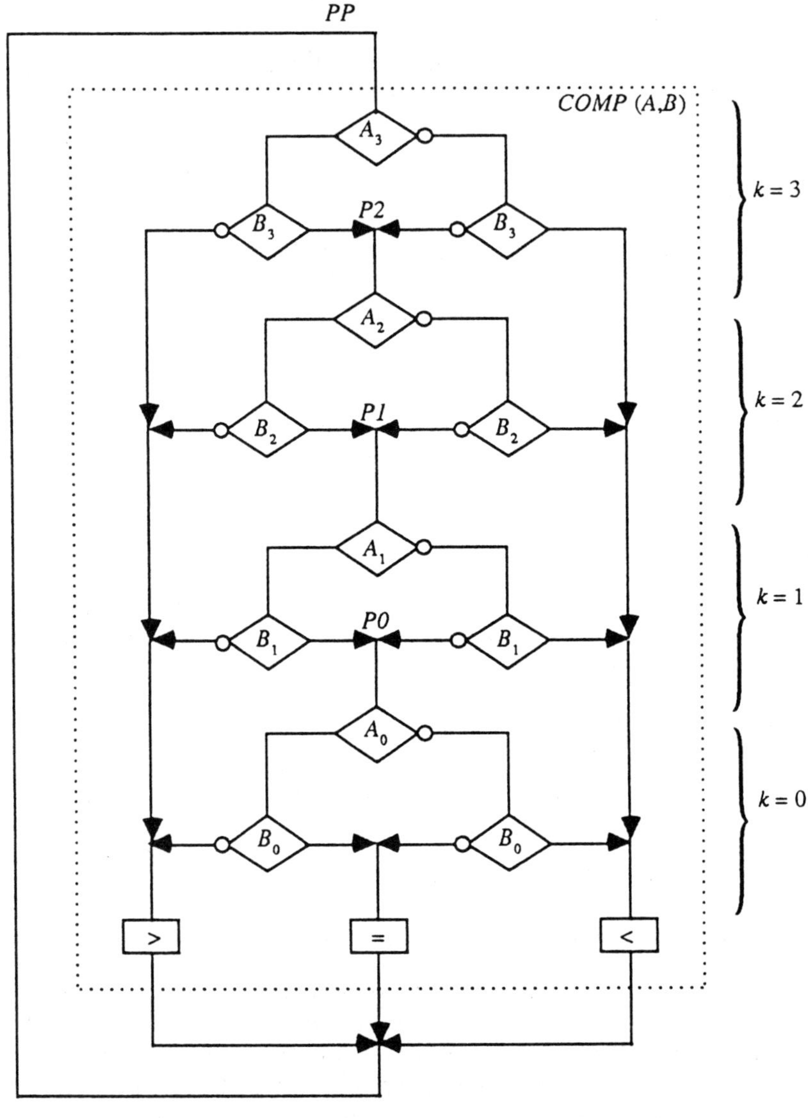

Figure 3.36

3.5.2 Application: 4-bit comparator

Figure 3.36 (enclosed in the dotted lines) is the iterative diagram for a comparator *COMP*(A, B) for two numbers $A = A_{3:0}, B = B_{3:0}$, each of four bits; this is constructed by simple juxtaposition of four slices similar to Figure 2.34. The looping back of the diagram on to itself

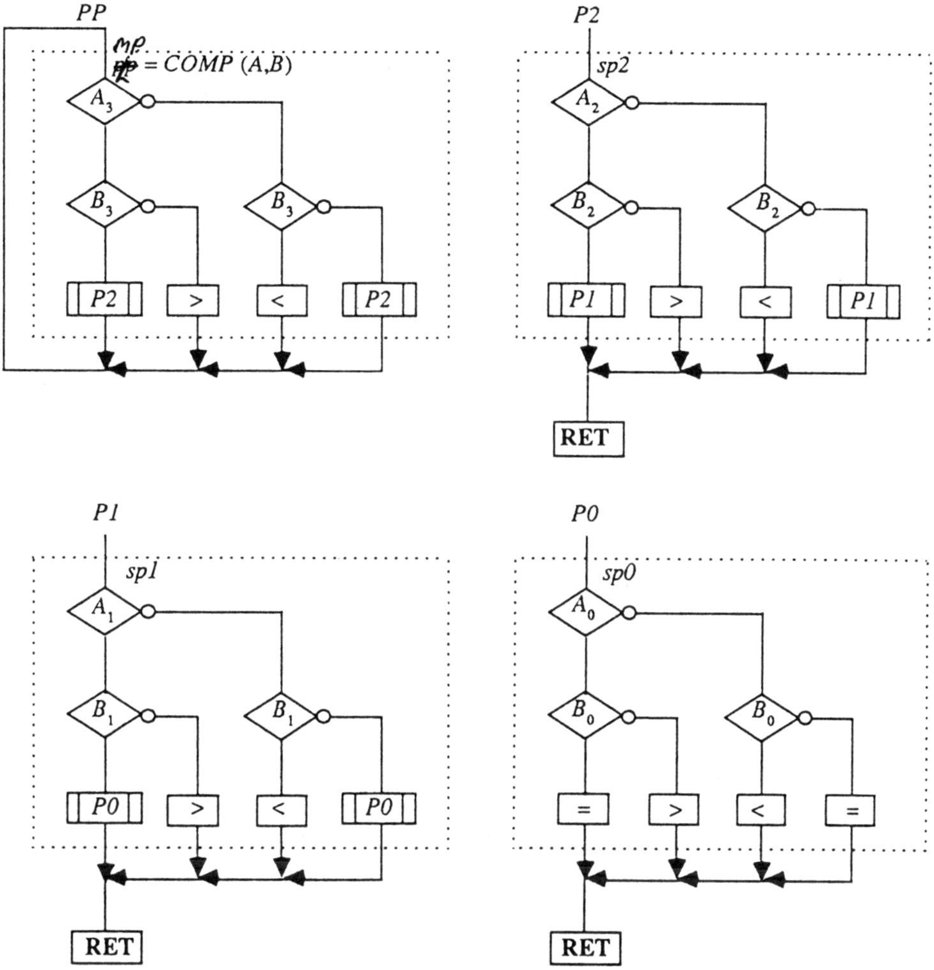

Figure 3.37

gives the *iterative flowchart* of Figure 3.36, consisting solely of test and assignment instructions, which can be written in **L1** and executed by a machine such as Figure 2.60.

3.5.3 Résumé: decomposition of a tree

We have already seen (§2.2.2) that any binary decision diagram is equivalent to a combination of a main tree with one or more sub-trees; thus Figure 2.34 is equivalent to combination of the main tree *pp* and sub-tree *sp* of Figure 2.29.

3.5.4 Application: 4-bit comparator

Figure 3.36 is equivalent to the combination of the main tree *pp* and the three sub-trees *sp2, sp1, sp0* of Figure 3.37, all shown enclosed in dotted lines.

3.5.5 Software realization: procedures

This representation (§3.5.4) of the 4-bit comparator leads at once to the software realization of Figure 3.37, consisting of:

- a main program *PP*, obtained simply by looping the main tree *pp*;
- three procedures *P2, P1, P0* obtained by converging each of the sub-trees *sp2, sp1, sp0* on to a single terminal instruction **RET**, as defined in §3.3.3.

The four flowcharts of Figure 3.37 consist of test, assignment, call and return instructions; thus they can be expressed in **L2** and executed on a stack machine such as Figure 3.23.

3.5.6 Hardware/software equivalence

The 4-bit comparator can be realized by the iterative combinational system of Figure 3.38. This consists of four functionally equivalent sub-systems ([1] pp. 82–86, [59] pp. 104–109), each of the form of COMP(A_k, B_k) of Figure 3.39. The *k*th sub-system compares the bits of order *k* in the two numbers and outputs an intermediate result Z_k([>], [=] or [<]) which depends on the variables A_k, B_k and the output Z_{k+1}

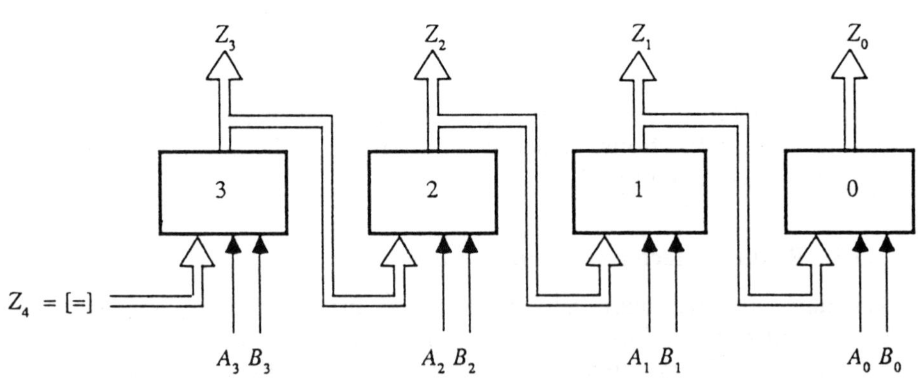

Figure 3.38

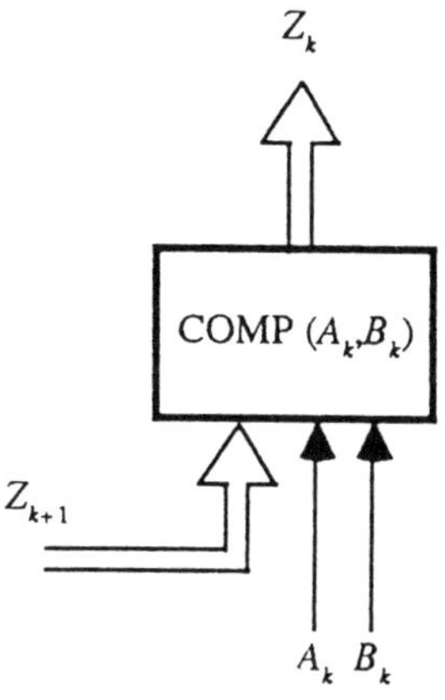

Figure 3.39

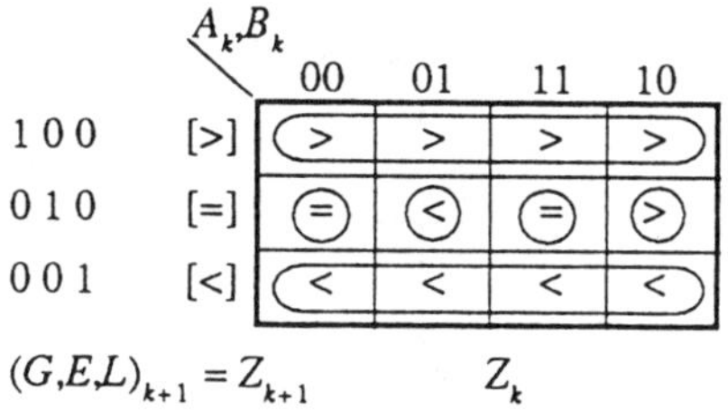

Figure 3.40

of the preceding stage. Thus the comparison is made in the order of most significant bits first.

The discrete variable Z_k is represented as a function of the logic variables A_k, B_k and the discrete variable Z_{k+1} by a special form of truth table, the *state table* of the iterative system, Figure 3.40. If we use a 1-out-of-3 code (Figure 2.2) and if we represent each row of Figure 3.40 by a binary decision diagram we get the three diagrams $G_{k+1}, E_{k+1}, L_{k+1}$ of Figure 3.41, the union of which gives a possible representation of the sub-system COMP(A_k, B_k). Using the method of §2.4.2 this can by realized in hardware by an assemblage of {DMUX, OR} operators identical to Figure 2.63, or, using the method of section 2.3, in software by an assemblage of test and assignment instructions. For the software solution we get the flowchart of Figure 3.36 with:

- four repetitions of the partial flowchart of Figure 3.41, for $k = 3 \ldots 0$; $3 \ldots 0$;
- suppression of the *intermediate states* Z_3, Z_2, Z_1 and therefore of the assignment instructions in the slices $k = 3, 2, 1$; here the output is the single state Z_0, from the final slice $k = 0$;
- inclusion of an *initial condition* expressed as $Z_4 = [=]$; this reduces the slice $k = 3$ to the single diagram $E_{k+1} = E_4$.

Finally, we say that the flowchart of Figure 3.41, or the slice of Figure 3.36 (and equally the logic diagram Figure 2.63) is a *1-out-of-3 code realization*, or a *3-channel flowchart*, that is, having three inputs and three outputs; such realizations are not structured in the sense defined in Chapter 5 (§5.5.9).

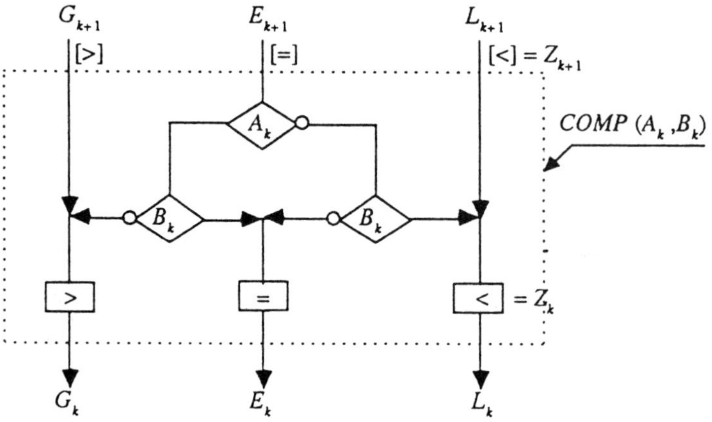

Figure 3.41

3.5.7 Software realization: parametrized procedure

The iterative diagram Figure 3.36 for the 4-bit comparator breaks down into four identical slices, each consisting of three test elements for the bits $A_k, B_k, k = 3, \ldots 0$; and in the solution of Figure 3.37 each slice is realized either by the main program or by one of the three procedures. This can be simplified by writing the program with a single procedure $P(k)$ whose execution varies with the value of the parameter k, here $3, 2, 1$ or 0. This is shown in Figure 3.42, where we have a main program *PP* and *parametrized procedure* $P(k)$, the former consisting of four successive calls to $P(k)$, with the appropriate value of k passed with each call; $P(k)$ consists of the following:

- a 3-channel flowchart $COMP(A_k, B_k)$ identical to that of Figure 3.41; the test variables A_k, B_k and the register (Z_k) depend on the parameter k;
- two test instructions for G_{k+1}, E_{k+1} ($ADR = 4, 5$) to determine the output of slice $k + 1$ (Z_{k+1} = [>], [=] or [<]) and therefore the corresponding input in $COMP(A_k, B_k)$: this decision tree is necessary because, by the definition of §3.3.3, a procedure can have only a single input;
- a terminal instruction **RET**.

In contrast to Figures 3.36 and 3.37, the intermediate states Z_k for $k = 3, 2, 1$ are preserved, since they are needed in the tests of G_{k+1}, E_{k+1}; the single output Z_0 is produced by $P(0)$. Finally, the initial condition Z_4 = [=] is expressed as

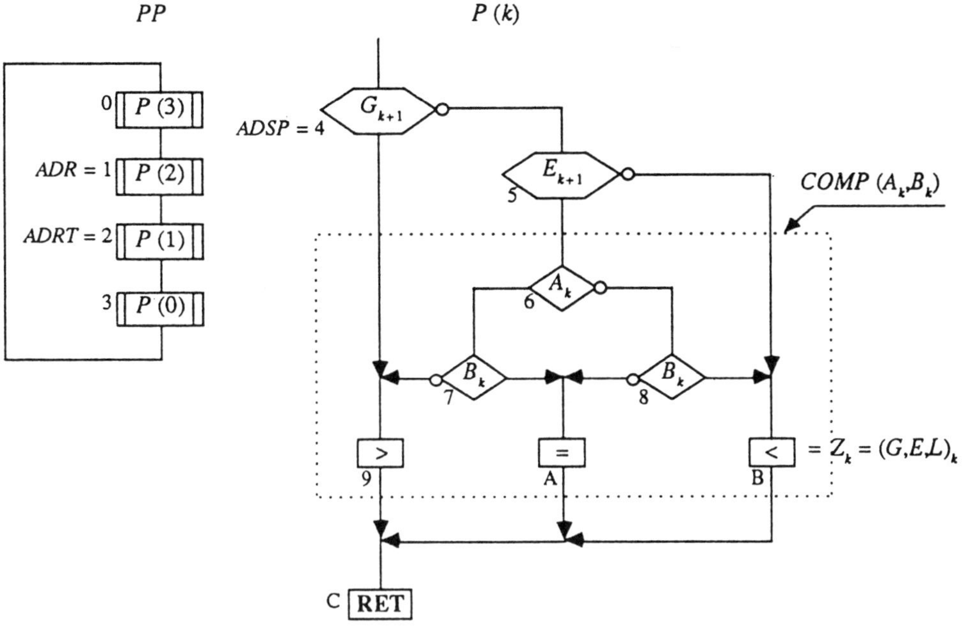

Figure 3.42

$$G_4 = 0, \quad E_4 = 1 \tag{3.38}$$

which is hardwired into the machine (cf. §3.5.9).

3.5.8 Definitions: parametrized procedure call instruction, language L2.1

A *parametrized call instruction* (Figure 3.42) consists of an address *ADR*, the address *ADSP* of the first instruction of the parametrized procedure *P*(*k*) and the value of the parameter *k*. It has one input and one output terminal, the latter leading to the return address *ADRT*. The mnemonic form is

CALL *ADSP*(*k*) **RET TO** *ADRT* (3.39)

The four instructions — test (2.36), indexed assignment (3.16), parametrized call (3.39) and return (3.15) — constitute an extension of **L2**, which we call **L2.1**.

Having given addresses to the instructions of Figure 3.42 we can write the mnemonic program as in Figure 3.43; we have assumed the availability of four registers $REG[j,k] = REG[0,k]$, $k = 3\ldots0$ for storing in succession the successive states $Z_k = (G,E,L)_k$.

ADR	L2.1		
0	CALL 4 (3)	RET TO 1	
1	CALL 4 (2)	RET TO 2	
2	CALL 4 (1)	RET TO 3	
3	CALL 4 (0)	RET TO 0	
4	IF G_{k+1}	THEN 9	ELSE 5
5	IF E_{k+1}	THEN 6	ELSE B
6	IF A_k	THEN 7	ELSE 8
7	IF B_k	THEN A	ELSE 9
8	IF B_k	THEN B	ELSE A
9	DO *REG* [0,*k*] ← [>] GO TO C		
A	DO *REG* [0,*k*] ← [=] GO TO C		
B	DO *REG* [0,*k*] ← [<] GO TO C		
C	RET		

Figure 3.43

3.5.9 Hardware realization of the interpreter for L2.1

This requires a stack machine, such as Figure 3.23; the addition of the new instruction (3.39) necessitates the following modifications:

- an *auxiliary stack*, similar to the main stack (§3.3.8) and having the same number of levels; this is to stack and unstack the successive values of the parameter *k*;
- auxiliary multiplexers, driven by the value of *k* at the head of its stack, to select the test variable xi_k: thus in Figure 3.42, $x0_k = G_{k+1}$, $x1_k = E_{k+1}$, $x2_k = A_k$, $x3_k = B_k$;
- $k \cdot j$ output registers $REG[j, k]$ controlled, through auxiliary demultiplexers, by the value of *k* at the head of its stack: thus in Figure 3.42 there are 4 registers $REG[0, k] = Z_k = (G, E, L)_k$.

The detailed design of the system is given as an exercise, §3.5.15.

Notice that in the example of Figure 3.42 the call of the procedure *P*(*k*) by the main program *PP* requires a main stack and an auxiliary stack with only one level.

3.5.10 Hardware/software equivalence

The realization of *COMP*(*A*, *B*) by the main program *PP* and a single parametrized procedure *P*(*k*) of Figure 3.42 is equivalent to the hardware realization ([1] pp. 185–188, [59] pp. 228–233) consisting of:

- two auxiliary shift registers REGA, REGB for storing the numbers $A_{3:0}$, $B_{3:0}$ (Figure 3.44);
- a synchronous sequential system consisting of a combinational system (C) and a parallel register (REG), giving the next state Z_k as a function of the present state Z_{k+1} and the input variables A_k, B_k.

Figure 3.40 is the state table for the sequential system. If instead of the 1-out-of-3 code of the figure we choose a minimal code, based for example on the logical variables G_{k+1}, E_{k+1}, we can partition the table into six blocks (Figure 3.45) and so represent it by the single minimal diagram $P(k)$ of Figure 3.42, the minimal code realization. This can easily be structured in the sense of Chapter 5 (§5.5.7).

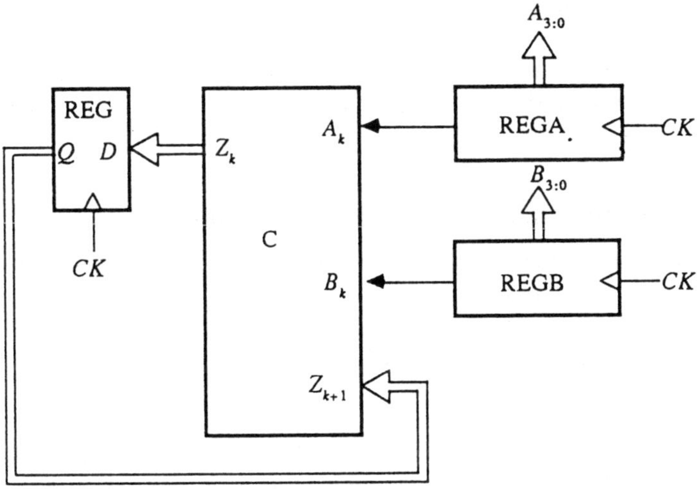

Figure 3.44

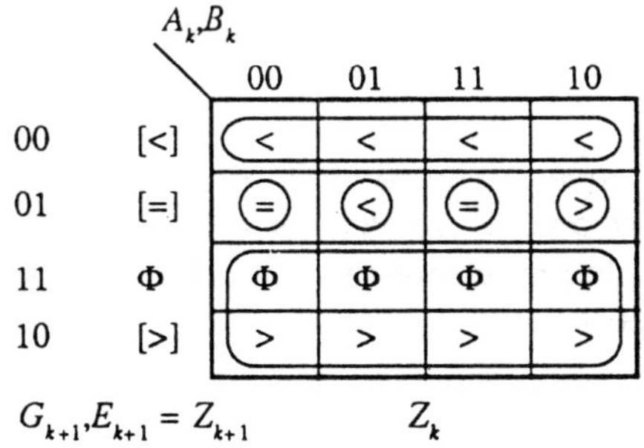

Figure 3.45

3.5.11 Method: parametrized procedure

The outcome of §3.5.10 leads to the following method for software realization of an iterative combinational system, using a parametrized procedure.

- The state table for the sequential system is set up, giving the next state Z_k as a function of the present state Z_{k+1} and the input variables A_k, B_k.
- The present state Z_{k+1} is coded by a minimum number of binary internal variables (G_{k+1}, E_{k+1}).
- Determine the minimal tree or diagram for the next state as a function of the input and internal variables.
- The tree or diagram thus obtained is made to converge on a single terminal **RET** instruction: this forms the parametrized procedure *P*(*k*).
- The main program *PP* is made to call this procedure as many times as is required by the problem before closing the loop on itself.

3.5.12 Software realization: recursive procedure

The hardware realization with multiplexers of Figure 2.65 suggests a new solution, similar to that of Figure 3.38 but with least significant bits first.

The discrete function Z_k for the slice *k* can be written

$$Z_k = A_k'(B_k' \cdot Z_{k-1} + B_k \cdot [<]) + A_k(B_k' \cdot [>] + B_k \cdot Z_{k-1}) \tag{3.40}$$

The same variable *Z* appears in both sides of this equation: we therefore say that it is a *recursive* relation ([2] pp. 155–158). Combined with (3.41) and (3.42) below, which give respectively the range of values for *k* and the end condition, it forms a complete description of the 4-bit comparator:

$$3 \geqslant k \geqslant 0 \ (k \leftarrow k-1;\ k_{max} = 3, k_{min} = 0) \tag{3.41}$$

$$Z_{-1} = [=] \tag{3.42}$$

A software equivalence to Figure 3.42, consisting of a main program *PP* and a parametrized procedure *P*(*k*), is given in Figure 3.47. The main program is the single procedure call with the value $k = k_{max} = 3$, whilst the procedure consists of:

- a diagram Z_k producing the discrete function of (3.40), represented by the Karnaugh map of Figure 3.46;
- a tree Z_{k-1} for the *recursive call* of the parametrized procedure; this

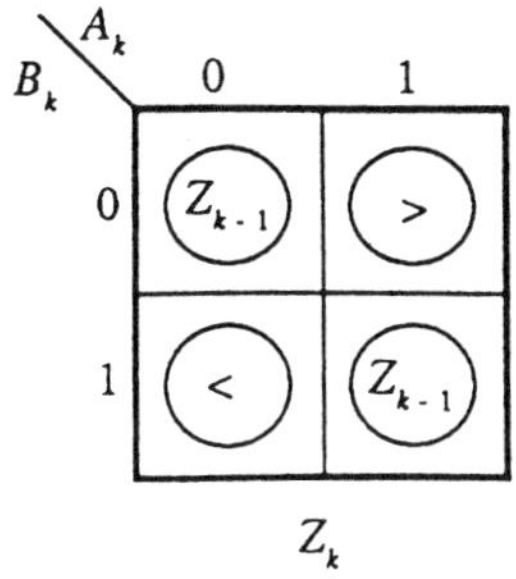

Figure 3.46

computes the value of $k-1$, given k, with $k = k_{1:0}$; it terminates at $k = k_{min} = 0$, giving $Z_{-1} = [=]$ in agreement with (3.42);
- a terminal instruction **RET**.

Thus $P(k)$ calls itself, so in conformity with the definition of §3.3.3 we say it is a *recursive procedure* (in this case, parametrized). The program for Figure 3.47 can be written in **L2.1** and executed by a machine such as that of §3.5.9, provided that the test variables k_0, k_1 are accessible at the head of the auxiliary stack.

Successive recursive calls can need a greater number of stack levels than the calls of parametrized procedures discussed in §3.5.7: four levels in Figure 3.47, for example; notice however that in this example the intermediate states Z_k are never calculated, and the final state Z_0 is given directly.

3.5.13 Conclusion

In the first part of this section we explained the special importance of iterative combinational systems. The diagrams for these are themselves iterative and consequently are easy to determine for complex problems involving many variables.

We next showed that any combinational system, whether iterative or not, that can be represented by a binary decision diagram can be realized by a combination of a main program and one or more procedures. This may seem complex, since it requires an extended language **L2** and a special interpreter provided with a stack, but it has the fundamental advantage that the main program and the procedures are structured in the sense of Chapter 5, in contrast to the original diagram.

For iterative diagrams this realization gives, with the main program, procedures all of the same form and differing only in the indices of the

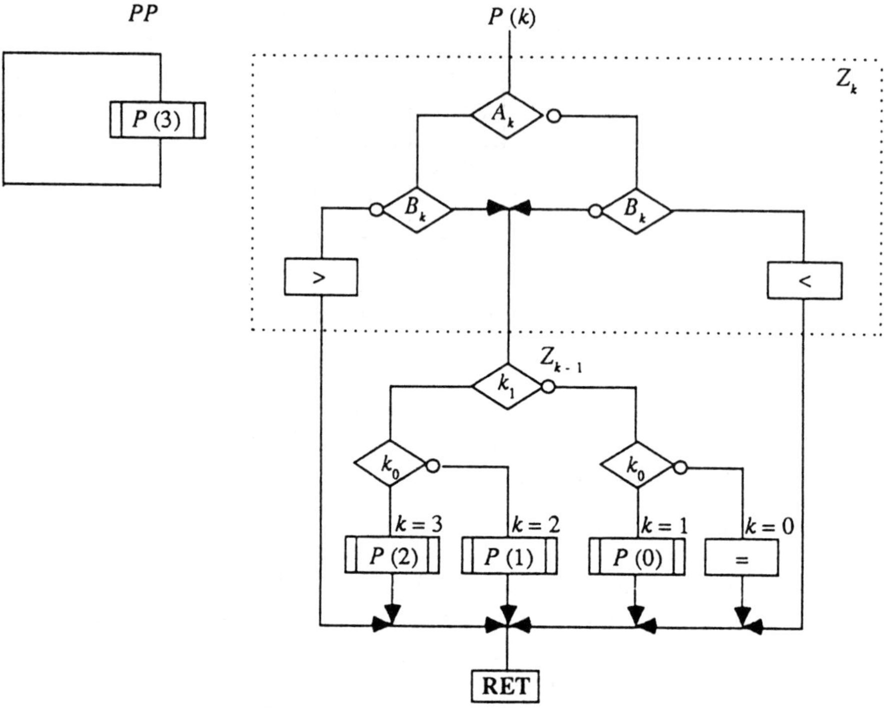

Figure 3.47

test variables and/or assignment registers. Thus the set of procedures can be replaced by a single parametrized procedure, which can be called by the main program; this reduces the number of instructions in the complete program, at the cost of some extensions to **L2** to give a new language **L2.1**, and a new, more complex interpreter.

Finally, given this new language and interpreter, the main program can be simplified drastically by the use of recursive calls.

Lastly we have shown that there is a close correspondence between software realizations of counters and of iterative combinational systems:

- the linear flowchart (§3.1.3) has a repetitive structure analogous to that of the iterative flowchart (§3.5.2);
- the combination of a main program calling a single procedure (§3.3.2) results from the discovery of a sub-program *SP* that forms a repeated feature in the linear flowchart; the discovery of a slice of the iterative flowchart leads to the calling of a parametrized procedure (§3.5.7);

- the same sub-program *SP* can be associated with a binary decision tree (§3.3.2) that performs the counting function $Q \leftarrow Q + 1$, and correspondingly the slice of the iterative flowchart can be associated with the decision tree that counts down through the parameter values, $k \leftarrow k - 1$: this is the recursive procedure of §3.5.12.

3.5.14 Exercise

1. Give the decision diagrams, using a main tree and sub-trees, for:
   - the MAJORITY function for 5 variables, $MAJ(E, D, C, B, A)$, as defined in Figure 2.46;
   - the function $Z(a, b, c, d, e, f, g, h, i)$ of Figure 8.27.
2. Give a realization of each of these functions as a main program and sub-programs, and the flowcharts and the **L2** mnemonic programs. What depth of stack is needed in each case?

3.5.15 Exercise

Taking account of §3.5.9, design an interpreter for **L2.1** that can execute the programs of Figures 3.43 (parametrized procedure) and 3.47 (recursive procedure). In each case give the programs in mnemonic, binary and hexadecimal.

3.5.16 Exercise

The *exclusive–OR* function of two variables is defined by equation (2.35), §2.2.17. Construct an iterative combinational system for realizing the function $Z = A_0 \oplus A_1 \oplus A_2 \oplus A_3$ and determine the state table for a sub-system, the iterative decision diagram for the complete system and a realization using a main program and a single parametrized procedure: give the flowchart and the mnemonic program. Is it possible to express Z as a recursive expression and to realize it by a recursive procedure? If your answer is yes, give the flowchart and the mnemonic program and determine the depth of the stack.

3.5.17 Exercise

It is required to produce an iterative combinational system $ADD(A, B)$ to add, arithmetically, two 4-bit binary numbers (cf. §8.2.4); the result is to be 5 bits, a 1-bit carry R_3 and a 4-bit sum $S_{3:0}$. Construct the state table for a sub-system and then give the mnemonic program for the complete system based on (1) an iterative flowchart; (2) a main program and a parametrized procedure. Can this flowchart be deduced from that of the realizations of §2.2.12? Can the parametrized procedure be deduced from the calculations of §§8.2.4–9? Try to construct a program with a recursive procedure, and determine the number of levels in the stack; if you do not succeed, repeat the attempt for the carry alone.

If one of the numbers A, B is 1 the adder becomes an *incrementer*, $INC = ADD(A, 1)$. Change the programs obtained above so that they are oriented to this particular case.

4
Incremental programs

4.1 INCREMENTATION

4.1.1 Introduction

So far we have assumed that addressing — assigning addresses to instructions — was free of all constraints; in this chapter we introduce a number of restrictions by requiring that in certain paths in the flowchart addresses must be given incrementally: that is, that the address of each instruction is obtained by adding 1 to that of its predecessor. This leads to a new language, **L3**, and a number of rules for writing the programs.

The constraints imposed on the software by **L3** are compensated for by considerable savings in hardware; the width of the **L2** instructions — the number of bits in a word in memory — is almost halved, with the result that problems much larger than those discussed in the previous chapters can be handled by interpreters of reasonable size.

We end the chapter with the hardware design of an interpreter for **L3**, which can be realized by an assemblage of a memory, several logic operators (multiplexer, demultiplexer, register) and a complex subsystem called a *sequencer*. With this language and the interpreter — a binary decision machine equipped with a sequencer — we can meet realistic specifications, such as that for a digital alarm clock.

4.1.2 Definition: incrementation path

A *path* in a flowchart is a sequence of consecutive instructions, the input to each being linked to the output from its predecessor. An *incrementation path* is a path in which the addresses *ADR*, *ADR+* of each pair of consecutive instructions are related by

$$ADR+ = ADR + 1 \qquad (4.1)$$

Figures 3.10 ($ADR = 0 \ldots 5$) and 3.16 ($ADR = 0 \ldots \mathrm{B}$) show two incrementation paths.

4.1.3 Definition: the language L3

When the flowchart contains incrementation paths the language **L2** can be simplified, as follows:

- for $xi = 1$ the test instruction leads to the next address, $ADR1 = ADR + 1$, and has the simplified mnemonic form

  IF *xi* **ELSE** *ADR0* (4.2)

- the address *ADR+* following that of the assignment instruction satisfies (4.1), so the corresponding mnemonic form is

  DO $REG[j] \leftarrow OUT$ (4.3)

- the return address in a call instruction is $ADRT = ADR + 1$, so the mnemonic form is

  CALL *ADSP* (4.4)

- the return instruction is unchanged:

  RET (4.5)

This set of four instructions constitutes the language **L3**:

L3 = {**IF...ELSE...,DO...,CALL...,RET**} (4.6)

Any program written in **L3** is an *incremental program*.

In Figure 4.1 the incrementation paths are shown by heavy lines.

4.1.4 Comments

Figure 4.7 gives a possible format for each of the instructions of **L3**; comparing this with the **L2** interpreter of Figure 3.23 we see that we have gained one field in each of test, assign and call: *ADR1*, *ADR+*, *ADRT* respectively. If we ignore the fields for the operating code *OPC* and the indices i, j, k we can say that for an n-bit address the width of a word in memory is n for **L3**, against $2n$ for **L2**.

In the test instruction we can replace the relation $ADR1 = ADR + 1$ for $xi = 1$ by $ADR0 = ADR + 1$ for $xi = 0$. The former is necessary in the context of structured programming, as will be shown in section 5.2.

4.1.5 Description: flowcharts in L3

Whilst the **L3** representation of a linear sequence of instructions (e.g. $ADR = 0 \ldots B$ in Figure 3.16) or of a binary decision tree (e.g. $Q^+ = Q + 1$ of Figure 4.4) can be derived directly from that in **L2** (cf. Figure 3.10), this is not the case for the following configurations:

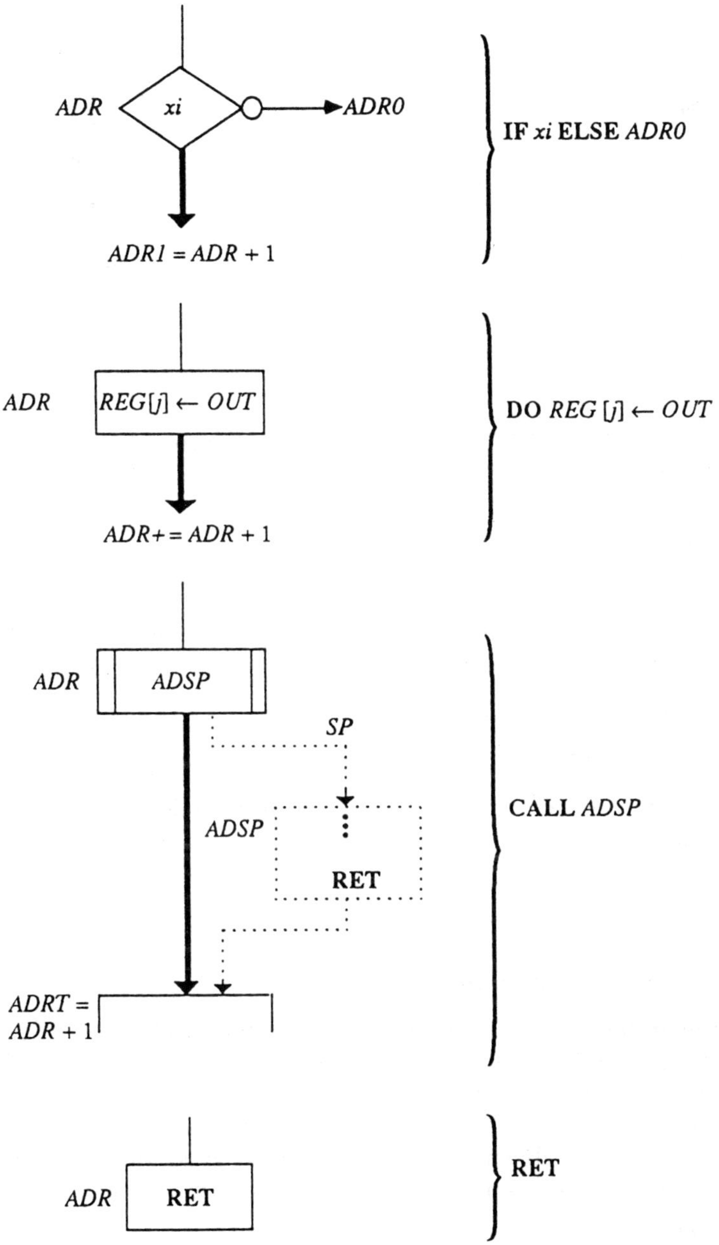
ADR
xi
ADR0
IF xi ELSE ADR0
ADR1 = ADR + 1
ADR
REG[j] ← OUT
DO REG [j] ← OUT
ADR+ = ADR + 1
ADR
ADSP
SP
ADSP
RET
CALL ADSP
ADRT =
ADR + 1
ADR
RET
RET

Figure 4.1

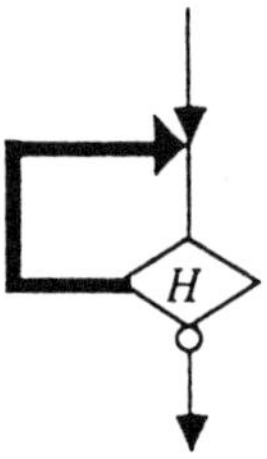

Figure 4.2

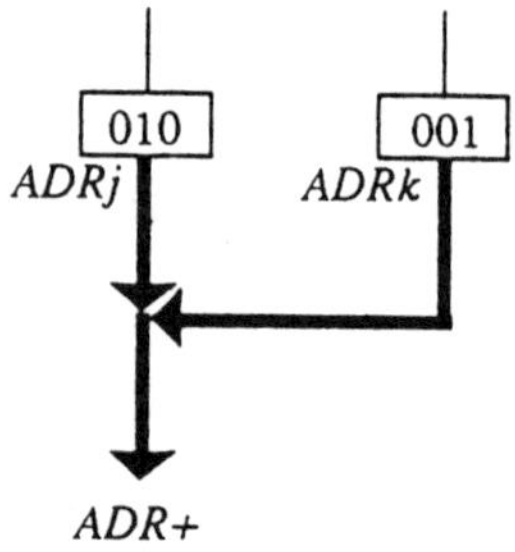

Figure 4.3

- a *loop* in an incrementation path, as in Figures 3.10, 4.2; here the addresses of a pair of consecutive instructions do not satisfy the relation (4.1): thus in Figure 4.2

  $$ADR+ \neq ADR + 1 \neq ADR;$$

- the *convergence* of a number of incrementation paths at the end of a tree or in a decision diagram, as in Figures 3.10 and 4.3; here the condition (4.1) would require

  $$ADRj = ADRk = ADR+ - 1 \tag{4.7}$$

  i.e. the identity of what should be distinct addresses.

Software transformations are needed in order to derive the **L3** program from the **L2** in these cases; these involve a new instruction, the *unconditional jump*.

4.1.6 Definition: jump instruction

The (unconditional) jump instruction is shown in Figure 4.5. It consists of an address *ADR*, an input and an output terminal, the last leading to the next instruction, with address *ADR+*.

Figure 4.5 suggests a realization by means of a test instruction in which the test variable *xi* is set to the logical constant 0. This gives the jump instruction as a special case of the test, which we can express as

$$\textbf{GO TO } ADR+ = \textbf{IF } 0 \textbf{ ELSE } ADR0 \tag{4.8}$$

and can use either form indifferently.

This has no effect on **L3**: all that is required is that the interpreter has available the special test variable $xi = 0$.

4.1.7 Software realization: flowchart in L3

Consider the **L2** flowchart of Figure 3.10 for the 6-state counter and its **L3** equivalent of Figure 4.4. The transformation requires these additions:

- a jump instruction (*ADR* = 01), to deal with the loop in the incrementation path testing *H* (*ADR* = 00);
- six jump instructions (*ADR* = 06, 08, 0C, 0E, 11, 13) to deal with the convergence of six incrementation paths (branches of the tree) and their looping on the initial instruction (*ADR* = 00).

Taking note of the incrementation paths, shown by heavy lines in Figure 4.4, we can set up an addressing scheme that is compatible with **L3** and so obtain the mnemonic program, as in Figure 4.6. With the instruction formats and operating code of Figure 4.7 we then get the hexadecimal form, also shown in Figure 4.6, in which the test variables have been coded as follows: $x0 = H$, $x1 = Q_2$, $x2 = Q_1$, $x3 = Q_0$, $x4 = 0$ (the last as required by the **GO TO** instruction).

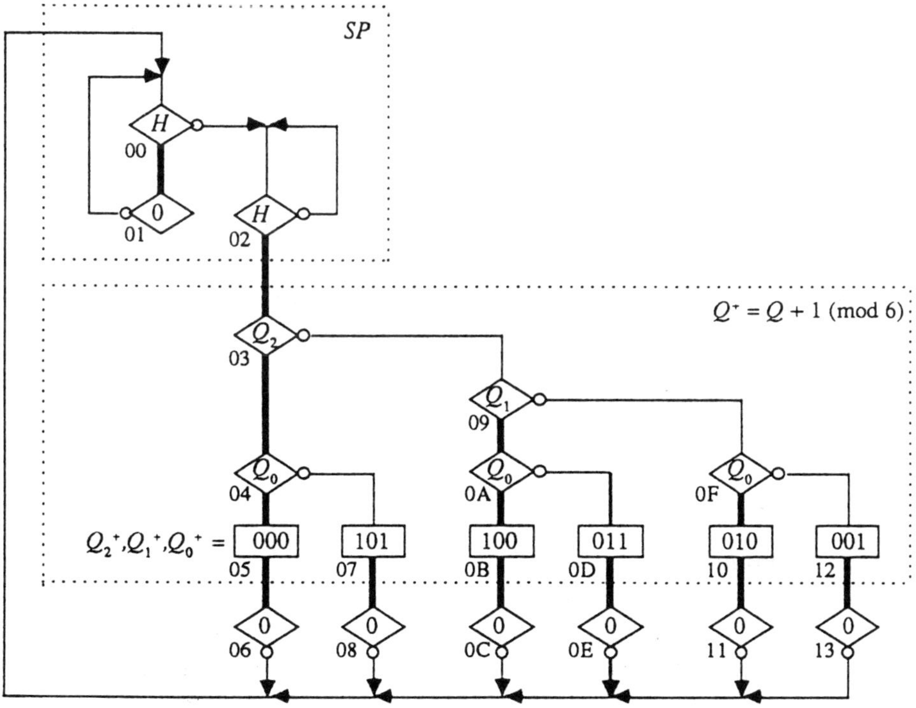

Figure 4.4

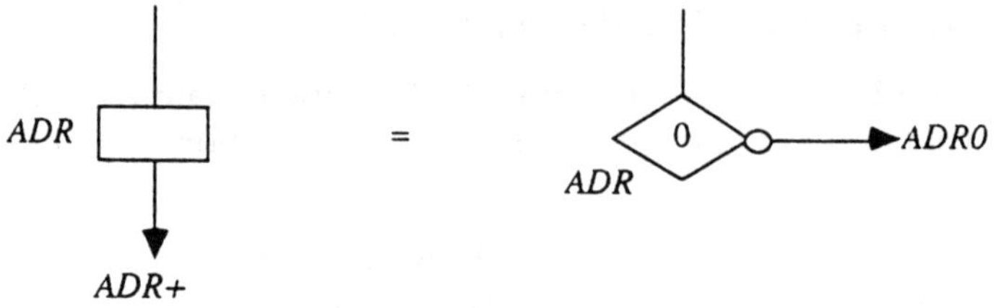

GO TO *ADR+* = IF 0 ELSE *ADR0*

Figure 4.5

ROM [*ADR*]	*ADR*	L3	
0002	00	IF *H*	ELSE 02
0400	01	GO TO 00	
0002	02	IF *H*	ELSE 02
0109	03	IF Q_2	ELSE 09
0307	04	IF Q_0	ELSE 07
1000	05	DO *REG* [0] ← 00	
0400	06	GO TO 00	
1005	07	DO *REG* [0] ← 05	
0400	08	GO TO 00	
020F	09	IF Q_1	ELSE 0F
030D	0A	IF Q_0	ELSE 0D
1004	0B	DO *REG* [0] ← 04	
0400	0C	GO TO 00	
1003	0D	DO *REG* [0] ← 03	
0400	0E	GO TO 00	
0312	0F	IF Q_0	ELSE 12
1002	10	DO *REG* [0] ← 02	
0400	11	GO TO 00	
1001	12	DO *REG* [0] ← 01	
0400	13	GO TO 00	

Figure 4.6

4.1.8 Comment

As with its predecessors **L1** and **L2**, **L3** is defined by an instruction set — that given in §4.1.3. No rule has been laid down concerning the assembling of these instructions into a program apart from what commonsense would require: for example, that the initial instruction, defined by $ADR = 00$, must be in the main program, or are imposed by the definitions, for example, that a procedure must have only a single input terminal and must terminate with a **RET** instruction. It follows that there cannot be a rigidly systematic method for addressing the instructions of an **L3** program, or for transforming an **L2** program into **L3** [105]. However, displaying the incrementation paths (as by heavy lines in the flowchart) will aid the insertion of jump instructions in configurations such as loops or branch convergences in which the address relation of (4.1) is violated.

A further new language, **L4**, that does have assembly rules is introduced in Chapter 5; with this a systematic method for writing incremental programs can be developed.

4.1.9 Conclusion

By introducing the software constraint of incremental addressing, giving the language **L3**, we have reduced the width of the instructions considerably. This gives a saving in hardware, at the cost of changes to programs in **L2** — insertion of jump instructions where there are loops or branch convergences — which may increase the depth of memory required. There is also the need for an interpreter for **L3**: this is taken up in section 4.2.

4.1.10 Exercise

Transform the **L2** flowchart of Figure 3.35, for a 60-state counter, to **L3**. Address the new flowchart and construct the corresponding mnemonic program.

4.1.11 Exercise

Transform to **L3** the **L2** flowchart of Figure 3.36, for a comparator for two 4-bit numbers. Address the new flowchart and construct the mnemonic program; then choose an operating code and instruction formats for **L3** and rewrite the program in binary and in hexadecimal.

4.1.12 Exercise

An *atomic binary decision diagram* (§8.4.5) is defined as one in which all the test elements are in one branch. For Figure 8.26, taking this branch as the incrementation path, construct the flowchart and the mnemonic program in these realizations:

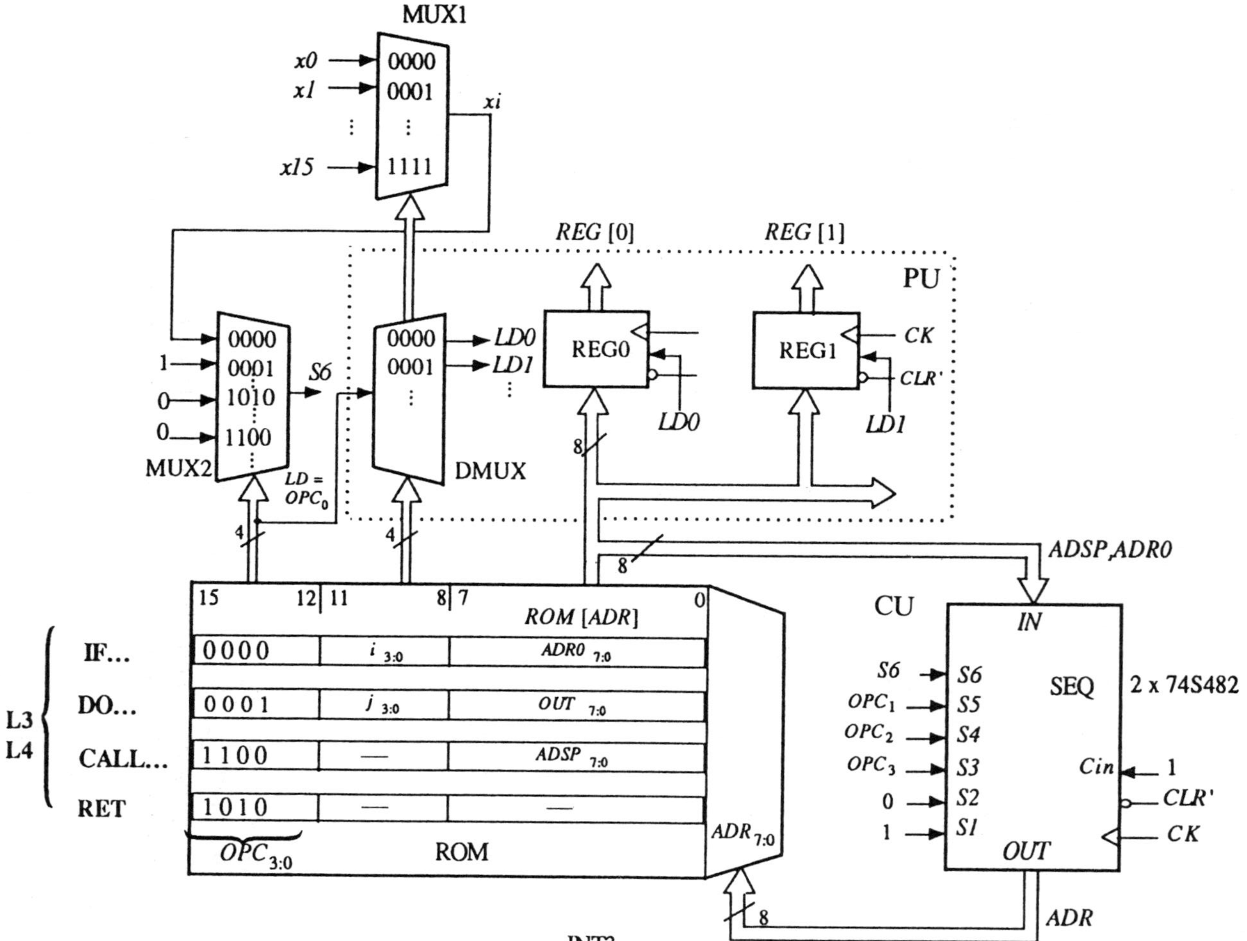

INT3

Figure 4.7

- in **L3**, using tests of variables xi and of their complements xi';
- in the extended language **L3.2**, obtained from **L3** by adding to the definition (4.6) the complementary test instruction

  IF *xi* **THEN** *ADR1* **ELSE** (*ADR* + 1)

4.2 SEQUENCER AND INTERPRETER FOR L3

4.2.1 Description: L3 instruction format

In Figure 4.7 the read only memory ROM contains a possible format for the four **L3** instructions. The 8-bit addresses *ADR*, *ADSP*, *ADR0* each allow $2^8 = 256$ memory words to be addressed and the 4-bit indices i, j allow any of 16 test variables xi and of 16 assignment registers $REG[j]$ to be selected.

The operating code $OPC_{3:0}$ suggested here is not optimal, since it is of four bits although two would suffice; we shall see the reason for this in §4.2.5 below.

4.2.2 Description: interpreter for L3

The microprogrammed system designed to execute the four **L3** instructions, the *interpreter* (INT3), is a *stack-based binary decision machine*. Figure 4.7 gives a possible design, consisting of:

- a program memory ROM of 256 words of 16 bits;
- a *sequencer* SEQ or *controller*, type Texas Instruments 74S482, whose output state *OUT* is the memory address *ADR*; this component is a complex synchronous sequential system;
- up to 16 assignment registers, REG0 . . . REG15, controlled by the 16 variables *LD0* . . . *LD15* (cf. §1.2.14);
- a demultiplexer DMUX, controlled by the indexing variables $j_3 \ldots j_0$, for selecting one of the 16 assignments $REG[j] \leftarrow OUT$ ($j = 0 \ldots 15$);
- a multiplexer MUX1, controlled by the indexing variables $i_3 \ldots i_0$, for selecting the test variable xi;
- a second multiplexer MUX2, to generate the input *S6* to the sequencer SEQ as a function of five variables, the test variable xi and the four bits $OPC_3 \ldots OPC_0$ of the operating code.

The instruction and operating code formats, discussed in §4.2.1, are given in Figure 4.7. We shall analyse the sequencer in §4.2.3, enabling us in §4.2.5 to determine the quantities that at this stage are unknown: the variables controlling the assignment registers *LD* and the control variables *S6* . . . *S1*, *Cin* for the sequencer.

4.2.3 Description: the sequencer

An *n-bit sequencer* or *controller* is a synchronous sequential system whose purpose is to calculate the next address ADR^+, of n bits, in a microprogrammed memory from the present address *ADR*, further addresses *ADR0*, *ADSP* or *STACK*, and supplementary information provided by the operating code *OPC* and the test variable *xi*.

A large variety of such devices are available on the market, the most popular of which are listed in §4.2.8; here we analyse an 8-bit sequencer (Figure 4.8) constructed from two Texas Instruments 74S482 circuits. This circuit was chosen for two reasons: it is particularly well adapted to the present requirements, and it has an iterative structure (a

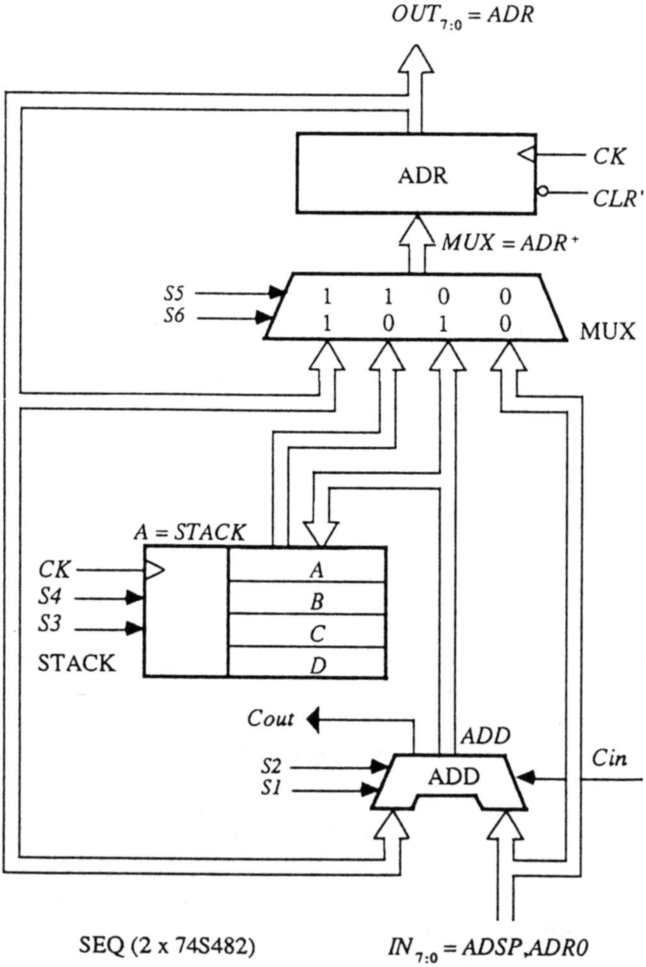

Figure 4.8

bit-sliced circuit) that enables it to compute any address that is a multiple of 4 bits: such a circuit is *cascadable*.

The sequencer of Figure 4.8 breaks down into two parts: a sequential part consisting of an address register ADR and a stack STACK, and a combinational part consisting of a multiplexer MUX aand an adder ADD. All the buses are 8 bits wide and:

- the address register ADR is defined by

$$OUT = ADR \leftarrow ADR^{+} = MUX \tag{4.9}$$

- the stack STACK has 4 levels and 4 operations, HOLD, LOAD, POP, PUSH, controlled by the variables $S3, S4$ in accordance with the operations table of Figure 4.10;
- the multiplexer MUX is controlled by the variables $S5, S6$ (Figure 4.11) and selects the next address $ADR^{+} = MUX$ from amongst four possible words: the input IN to the sequencer, the output ADD from the adder, the head of the stack, $STACK$, and the present address ADR;
- the adder ADD forms the arithmetical sum of one (in which case there is no addition) or more of the values ADR, IN, Cin — respectively the present address, sequencer input and, if there is one, the carry from the preceding stage in the sequencer; there are four modes for this addition, given in Figure 4.9 and selected by the variables $S1, S2$: the symbol '+' means ordinary arithmetical addition. The final result $Cout, ADD$ is given as the computed sum ADD together with any carry $Cout$ that may arise.

OPERATION	DESCRIPTION: ADD	$S1$	$S2$
ADD	$Cout,ADD = ADR + IN + Cin$	0	0
INCREMENT IN	$Cout,ADD = IN + Cin$	0	1
INCREMENT ADR	$Cout,ADD = ADR + Cin$	1	0
CARRY	$Cout,ADD = Cin$	1	1

Figure 4.9

OPERATION	DESCRIPTION: STACK	$S3$	$S4$
HOLD	NOP	0	0
LOAD	$A \leftarrow ADD$	0	1
POP	$A \leftarrow B, B \leftarrow C, C \leftarrow D, D \leftarrow \Phi$	1	0
PUSH	$A \leftarrow ADD, B \leftarrow A, C \leftarrow B, D \leftarrow C$	1	1

Figure 4.10

OPERATION	DESCRIPTION: MUX	*S5*	*S6*
SELECT IN	*MUX* = *IN*	0	0
SELECT ADD	*MUX* = *ADD*	0	1
SELECT STACK	*MUX* = *STACK*	1	0
SELECT ADR	*MUX* = *ADR*	1	1

Figure 4.11

4.2.4 Comment

The sequencer of Figure 4.8 is equivalent to the assemblage labelled SEQ in stack machine of Figure 3.23: the address register and the stack are identical, whilst the single multiplexer MUX of Figure 4.8 replaces the pair, MUX1, MUX2 of Figure 3.23 and so offers a further choice of the future address, here $ADR^+ = ADR$.

The essential difference between the two lies in the inclusion of the adder ADD in the sequencer; it is this that enables incremental programs to be executed, by performing the incrementation $ADR + 1$ of the present address *ADR*.

4.2.5 Hardware realization: L3 interpreter

The realization of the interpreter INT3 requires, finally, a combinational logic system C (Figure 4.14) that will generate the control signals to drive SEQ (the variables *S1* . . . *S6*) and DMUX (the variable *LD* of Figure 4.7); the demultiplexer DMUX selects the assignment registers. These control signals are functions of the test variable *xi* and of the four bits of the operating code *OPC* . . . OPC_3.

For this purpose we set up the operations table of Figure 4.12, which describes the global behaviour of the interpreter; in particular, it gives the transfers in the registers ADR, STACK and REG for each instruction: tests (OP1, OP2), assignments (OP3), calls (OP4) and returns

OPERATION	DESCRIPTION: ADR, STACK, REG	$OPC_{3:0}$	*xi*
OP1 = **IF** 0 **ELSE** *ADR0*	*ADR* ← *ADR0*, HOLD, HOLD	0000	0
OP2 = **IF** 1 **THEN** *ADR* + 1	*ADR* ← *ADR* + 1, HOLD, HOLD	0000	1
OP3 = **DO** *REG* [*j*] ← *OUT* **GO TO** *ADR* + 1	*ADR* ← *ADR* + 1, HOLD, *REG* [*j*] ← *OUT*	0001	Φ
OP4 = **CALL** *ADSP* **RET TO** *ADR* + 1	*ADR* ← *ADSP*, PUSH, HOLD	1100	Φ
OP5 = **RET**	*ADR* ← *STACK*, POP, HOLD	1010	Φ

Figure 4.12

OPERATION	$OPC_{3:0}$	xi	ADR^+	$S1$	$S2$	$S5$	$S6$	Cin	$S3$	$S4$	$REG[j]^+$	LD
OP1	0000	0	$ADR0 = IN = ROM_{7:0}$	Φ	Φ	0	0	Φ	0	0	$REG[j]$	0
OP2	0000	1	$ADR + 1 = ADD$	1	0	0	1	1	0	0	$REG[j]$	0
OP3	0001	Φ	$ADR + 1 = ADD$	1	0	0	1	1	0	0	$OUT = ROM_{7:0}$	1
OP4	1100	Φ	$ADSP = IN = ROM_{7:0}$	1	0	0	0	1	1	1	$REG[j]$	0
OP5	1010	Φ	$STACK$	Φ	Φ	1	0	Φ	1	0	$REG[j]$	0

Figure 4.13

(OP5). From this we can deduce the partial truth table of Figure 4.13 and the operations tables for the sequencer; these latter describe the adder (the variables *S1, S2, Cin* in Figure 4.9), the multiplexer (*S5, S6* of Figure 4.11) and the stack (*S3, S4* of Figure 4.10). We easily derive the following relations from the truth table:

$$S1 = 1 \quad S2 = 0 \quad S3 = OPC_3 \quad S4 = OPC_2 \quad S5 = OPC_1$$
$$Cin = 1 \quad LD = OPC_0$$

Only the variable *S6* cannot be identified with either a constant or a logical variable. The Karnaugh map of Figure 4.15 gives a possible representation, from which we can derive a realization of *S6* by the multiplexer MUX2 of Figure 4.7: this is driven by four address variables, with four of its inputs linked to the constants 0, 1 or the test variable *xi* and the remaining 12 left undefined (Φ).

This choice of operating code leads to the minimal hardware realization of the combinational system C of Figure 4.14. A minimal code, of two bits in this example, could be obtained at the cost of a more complex decoder which would generally be realized as a ROM or a programmable logic array.

4.2.6 Comments

The main limitations of the interpreter INT3 of Figure 4.7 are:

- the maximum number of instructions is $2^8 = 256$;
- the maximum number of test variables, and of assignment registers, is $2^4 = 16$;
- the maximum number of nested procedures is four (the number of levels in the stack).

These are purely technological limitations. The first two could be relaxed by choosing a longer word, and providing a wider memory: bit-sliced circuits make this a simple matter. Those due to insufficient depth of the stack are more serious, since this is an integral part of the

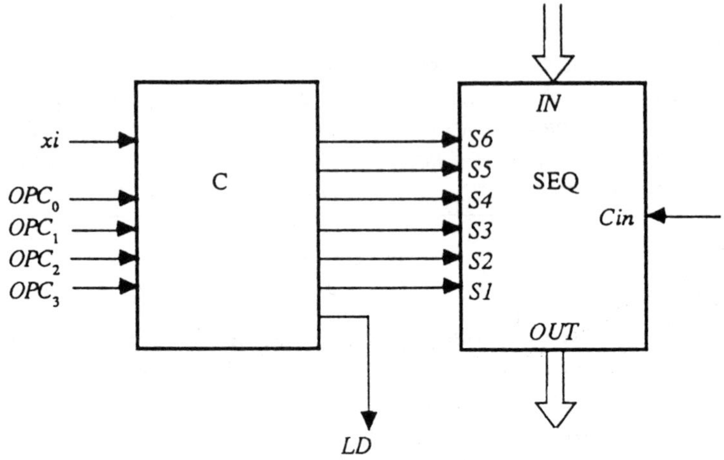

Figure 4.14

$OPC_{1:0}$ \ $OPC_{3:2}$	00	01	11	10
00	xi	Φ	0	Φ
01	1	Φ	Φ	Φ
11	Φ	Φ	Φ	Φ
10	Φ	Φ	Φ	0

S6

Figure 4.15

sequencer and cannot be changed; thus stack depth is a crucial parameter in the design of an interpreter and the corresponding choice of sequencer — see the bibliography in §4.2.8.

The address register ADR of Figure 4.8 has an asynchronous reset (*ADR* := 0), executed when *CLR* = 1 (or *CLR'* = 0). Therefore the first instruction of the program is always *ADR* = 0, and this must be in the main program and not in a procedure (cf. §3.3.11).

Finally, since implementation of the jump instruction (§4.1.6) requires a test of the logical constant 0, this is one of the test variables at the input to the multiplexer MUX1 of Figure 4.7.

4.2.7 Conclusion

The combination of a new software concept, the incremental program, and a new hardware operator, the sequencer, has enabled us to develop an interpreter with a very simple architecture — an assemblage of a memory, a sequencer and a few elementary logic operators — that can execute relatively complex programs: in the example we have used, up to 256 instructions and four levels of procedure. Thus the language **L3** and its interpreter INT3 provide a very significant alternative to traditional hardwired logic systems.

4.2.8 Bibliography

A rigorous proof of the equivalence of **L2** and **L3**, together with an evaluation of the cost (number of instructions) of an **L3** program, can be found in [2] pp. 419–430 and [3] pp. 143–154.

Many sequencers that can interpret a language identical with or very similar to **L3** are available on the market; the most popular are the following.

- Advanced Micro Devices Am2909, 2911: 4-bit bit-sliced circuits, 4-level stack; see [53] pp. 275–321, [54] pp. 613–648, [63] pp. 140–210, [64] pp. 125–141, [65] pp. 11–89.
- Advanced Micro Devices Am2910: 12-bit circuit, 5-level stack; see [63], [64], [65] *loc. cit.*, [143] pp. 139–159.
- Fairchild 9408: 10-bit circuit, 4-level stack; see [53], [63] *loc. cit.* Monolithic Memories 67110: 9-bit circuit, 1-level stack; see [63] *loc. cit.*
- Motorola MC10801: 4-bit bit-sliced circuit, 4-level (extendable) stack; see [53], [63] *loc. cit.*
- Signetics 8X02: 10-bit circuit, 4-level stack; see [2] pp. 448–453, [3] pp. 171–176, [53], [63], [54] *loc. cit.*
- Texas Instruments 74S482 (cf. §4.2.3): 4-bit bit-sliced circuit, 4-level stack; see [48], [54], [63] *loc. cit.*, [114].

For a comparative study of the performance of sequencers of all types see [63], [64] *loc. cit.*, [66].

What are called *pipeline* architectures, component assemblages designed specifically to speed up the interpretation of instructions, are described in [2] pp. 453–456, [3] pp. 176–178, [63] pp. 212–230.

4.2.9 Exercise

Given a minimal (2-bit) operating code, construct a new decoder for the **L3** interpreter (Figure 4.7) in which the number of combinational components is minimized. Give two variants, one using only NAND gates, the other a {DMUX, NAND} assemblage.

Do the same for an interpreter also based on Figure 4.7 but for **L3.2**, defined in §4.1.12.

4.2.10 Exercise

L3.1 is the language derived from **L3** by replacing the **CALL** *ADSP* instruction by the parametrized instruction **CALL** *ADSP(k)* (see §3.5.8). Show that the 74S482 sequencer (§4.2.3) can be transformed into a 5-level stack, in accordance with the definitions of §3.3.8. Use this to construct an interpreter for **L3.1**, adapting the formats and general layout of Figure 4.7 (with $ROM_{11:8} = k_{3:0}$ for the new **CALL** instruction).

4.2.11 Project: digital clock

The following is the specification for a digital alarm clock.

- The counting of the minutes, from 00 to 59, is to be done according to the results of §4.1.10, which themselves are derived from the flowchart of Figure 3.35.
- The hours are to be counted from 00 to 23 by a combination of a main program for the tens and a procedure for the units.
- A comparator, based on the results of §4.1.11, compares the time currently displayed with a pre-set time (both in hours and minutes) and causes the alarm to be sounded if the two agree.

Given the availability of a signal *H* of period one minute, construct the flowchart and the memonic **L3** program; adapt the **L3** interpreter, the operating code and the instruction format of Figure 4.7 to the execution of this program. Finally, give the hexadecimal version.

4.2.12 Exercise: relative addressing

Changing the **L3** instructions, **IF** *xi* **ELSE** *ADR0* and **CALL** *ADSP* to

$$\textbf{IF } xi \textbf{ ELSE } ADR + \Delta ADR0 \tag{4.10}$$

$$\textbf{CALL } ADR + \Delta ADSP \tag{4.11}$$

and give a *relative* or *indexed addressing* scheme, in which the *absolute addresses ADR0, ADSP* stored in memory are replaced by the *increments* $\Delta ADR0$, $\Delta ADSP$, to be added to the current address *ADR*. This enables the instruction length to be reduced in some cases, since the increments are generally smaller numbers than the actual addresses; further, a part of the program can then be moved without changing the contents of the instructions — the code is said to be *relocatable*: see [63] pp. 190–194.

Call the new language thus obtained **L3.3**. Retaining the operating code and instruction formats of Figure 4.7, give the hardware changes that must be made to the original interpreter INT3. Finally, give the mnemonic and hexadecimal programs for the digital clock of §4.2.11 in **L3.3**, paying particular attention to the case of negative increments (see section 8.6).

4.2.13 Project: an iteration loop

We wish to execute a certain sub-program n times, which we can do by putting it in a *loop* and then traversing the loop n times — in Pascal: **for** $k := n$ **downto** 1 **do**. . . .

As a first step, add to **L3** such instructions as you consider needed to enable the interpreter of Figure 4.7 to deal with a single loop. Then consider the more complex situation of *nested loops*, attempting two solutions:

1. using a number of distinct reversible counters, one for each nested loop;
2. using a single reversible counter together with a stack to hold intermediate results, one level for each nested loop; for this case base the solution on the Texas Instruments 74S482 sequencer.

For each solution give the instruction set for the extended language **L3**.

5

Structured programming

5.1 STRUCTURING PROGRAMS

5.1.1 Introduction

We begin by defining structured programming and continue with a study of the process of structuring a program, that is, given an arbitrary program, of transforming it to an equivalent structured program (section 5.1). We give several methods for structuring, both global and local, with two aims in mind:

1. theoretical: to prove that the functions of any program can be performed by a structured program, and thus to establish the universality of the structuring concept;
2. practical: to show how to write a structured program that meets a given unstructured specification — for example, a flowchart.

Writing structured programs requires new languages; two, which we call **L4** and **L5**, are given in section 5.2. These are derived immediately from the four instructions of **L3** by imposing certain formal rules governing how they may be used, that is, a syntax.

Software realization of sequential systems forms the heart of the chapter; the behaviour of these can be either synchronous (section 5.4) or asynchronous (section 5.3), according as the output state does or does not depend on a synchronizing signal. We give three methods in each case: one based on a global state table, assigned with internal variables (the table tree method); one in which each state is implemented directly, without any use of internal variables (the state tree method); and thirdly, an interesting compromise between the first two — the method of separation of the variables. It will appear that methods that use internal variables (of the first and third types) always give structured programs whilst those that do not use such variables (the second type) usually give instructured programs.

A method for writing structured programs for combinational systems is given in section 5.5. If the system is iterative, each slice can be defined by a state table and implemented by one of the methods for sequential systems. The final flowchart will or will not be structured according as internal variables are or are not used.

5.1.2 Description: structured programming

Structured programming means program writing using only a limited number of structures, that is, assemblages of instructions, which can be hierarchically organized and nested. The structures allowed are described in §5.1.5; they are

sequencing: **do** . . .
conditional iteration: **while** . . . **do** . . .
choice: **if** . . . **then** . . . **else** . . .

The aim of structured programming is to increase the likelihood that a program is correct, efficient and adaptable:

- *correct* because error-free; checking is made easier;
- *efficient* because optimal; optimization of certain factors is made easier, including cycle time (time parameter) and memory requirement (space parameter);
- *adaptable* because easily modifiable: a part of the program can be changed without affecting the rest — structured programming is *modular*. The modularity makes the program easier to read, and also helps in the writing of a program by several programmers in collaboration.

These aims are achieved at the cost of some redundancy in the software. More instructions are required, and they are more complex; this increases the demands on memory and the time needed to perform a given action. This redundancy can to some extent reduce the efficiency of the structured program and thus act against the declared aims.

5.1.3 Definitions: control and action instructions

A *control instruction*, written with the diamond symbol of Figure 5.1, has the mnemonic form

$$\textbf{IF}\ a\ \textbf{THEN}\ ADR1\ \textbf{ELSE}\ ADR0 \qquad (5.1)$$

This generalizes the test instruction of §2.3.5; here a can be either a test variable xi or the logical result of a more complex test, for example the comparison of two binary numbers, the test $A_{3:0} = B_{3:0}$, say.

An *action instruction*, written with the rectangle symbol of Figure 5.2, has the mnemonic form

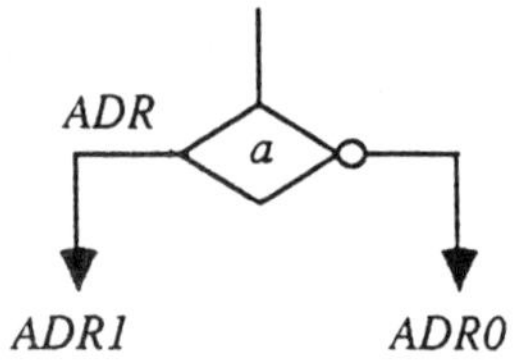

Figure 5.1

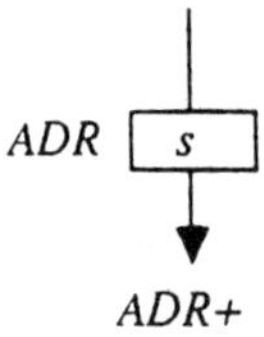

Figure 5.2

DO *s* **GO TO** *ADR+* (5.2)

This generalizes the assignment instruction of §2.3.5; here the *action*, *s*, can be the assignment to a register of a value, e.g. $REG[j] \leftarrow OUT$, a function, e.g. $REG[j] \leftarrow REG[j] + 1$, a sub-program (cf. §3.2.1) or a procedure call (cf. §3.3.2).

(5.1) and (5.2) form in effect a generalization of the language **L1**; their functions are clearly complementary: decision or sequencing for the first, action for the second.

5.1.4 Definition: proper program

A *program* — Figure 5.13, for example — is an arbitrary assemblage of instructions of the two types defined above.

A *flowchart* or *program schema* — Figure 5.13 for example — is a graphical representation of a program, in terms of the symbols of Figures 5.1 and 5.2.

A *proper program*, represented graphically by a *proper flowchart* (Figure 5.14) has these features:

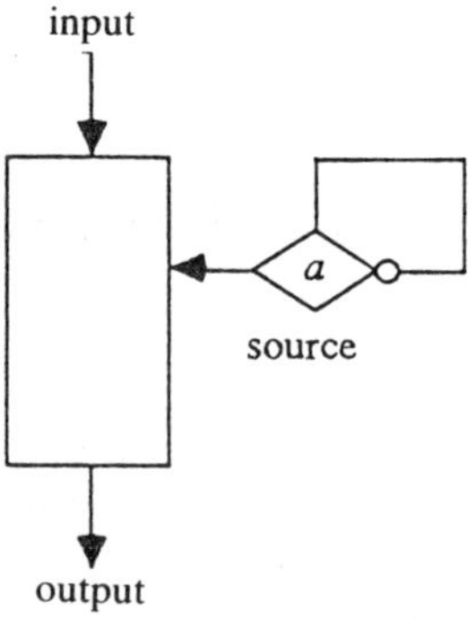

Figure 5.3

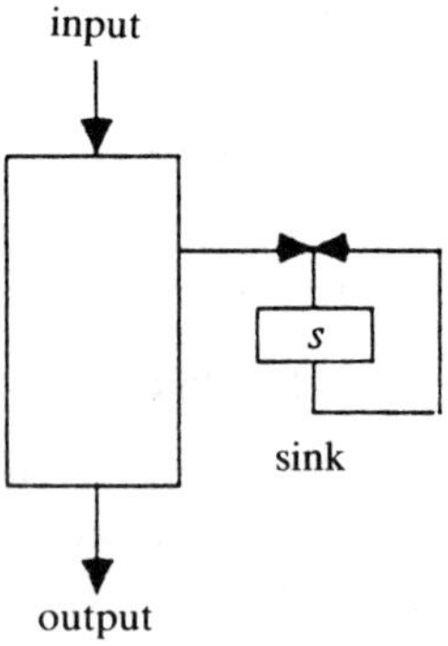

Figure 5.4

- one and only one input terminal, one and only one output terminal;
- all instructions accessible from the input: that is, no *source*, as there is in Figure 5.3;
- all instructions lead to the single output: that is, no *sink*, as there is in Figure 5.4.

A proper program is thus a sub-program (cf. §3.2.1) with neither source nor sink.

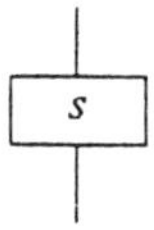

do *s*

Figure 5.5

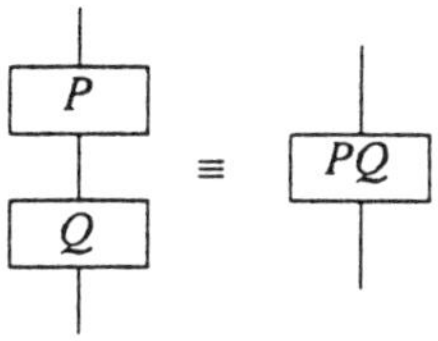

do *PQ*

Figure 5.6

5.1.5 Definition: structured program

1. The action instruction **do** s represented by the rectangle of Figure 5.5 is a *structured program*; it is defined by the action s and has a single input terminal, connected to a single preceding instruction, and a single output terminal, connected to a single following instruction. Then:
2. The *sequence* or *composition* of two successive action instructions P, Q — **do** PQ, written PQ and meaning **do** (P then Q), Figure 5.6 — is a structured program, of which the structured programs P, Q are the *elements*.
3. The choice of either P or Q — **if** a **then** P **else** Q, written $<_a P | Q>$, Figure 5.7 — is a structured program; P, Q are the *terms* or *alternatives* of the choice.
4. The *iteration* or *conditional repetition* of P — **while** a **do** P, written $\{_a P\}$, Figure 5.8 — is a structured program; such a program has a *feedback loop*.
5. Any combination of finite numbers of these four forms, and only such a combination, is a structured program.

Thus any structured program has a single input and a single output terminal; and any combination of structured programs is a structured program.

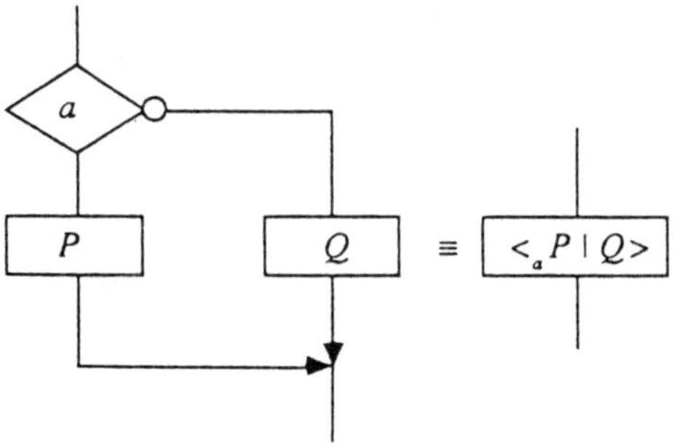

if a **then** P **else** Q

Figure 5.7

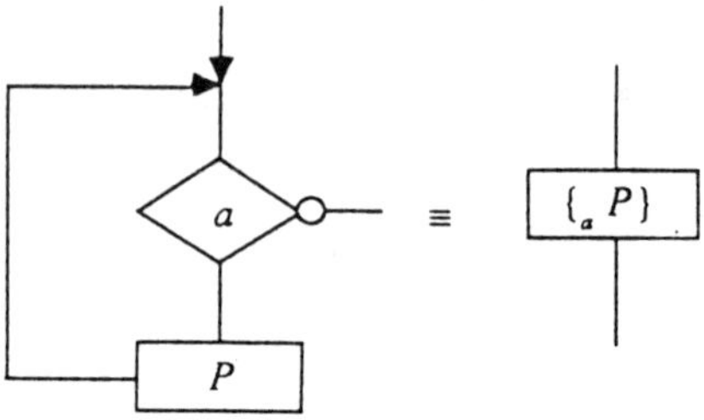

while a **do** P

Figure 5.8

5.1.6 Representation: characteristic equation

It follows from the above that a structured program can be represented by the concatenation of the algebraic expressions P, Q, PQ, $<_aP|Q>$, $\{_aP\}$ that represent its elements; this concatenation is the *characteristic equation* for the program.

For example, the equation for the program x of Figure 5.21 is

$$x = s1\ \{_s <_T T0 <_i s0\,|\,Ti\ s1>|\,s0>\}.$$

where the final point '.' indicates the end.

5.1.7 Definition: structuring

Structuring is the process of transforming a proper program into an equivalent program that is structured according to the definition of §5.1.5. The structuring is *local* if the change affects only a part of the original, unstructured program, *global* otherwise.

To complete this definition we need to define equivalence: two proper programs having the same input and the same output variables are said to be *equivalent* if, from the same initial state and for the same sequence of input states, either they both do not halt or both halt with the same sequence of output states [100].

5.1.8 Method: local structuring

This consists of successive applications, possibly with repetitions, of the following three rules, which follow from the definitions of §5.1.5.

5.1.9 Rule 1: composition

By definition, any structured program has a single input and a single output and can be represented by a single action instruction (Figure 5.2). The composition of two or more structured programs, as $p = \{_aP\}$ and $q = <_bQ|R>$ in Figure 5.9, is a structured program; for Figure 5.9 this can be written $r = pq$.

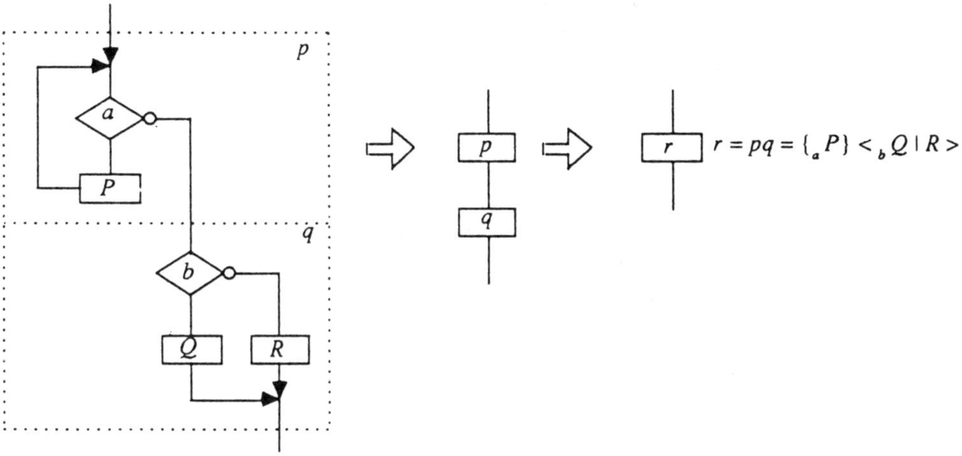

Figure 5.9

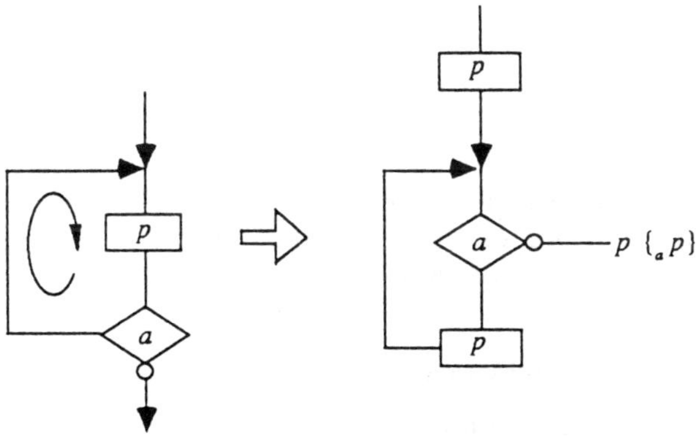

Figure 5.10

5.1.10 Rule 2: breaking loops

Suppose that an unstructured flowchart contains a loop having a single input terminal, as in Figures 5.10 and 5.11; the number of output terminals is called the *fan-out*. Any loop with a fan-out of one (i.e. a single output terminal) can be replaced by a structured program containing an element **while** . . . **do** . . . : thus in Figure 5.10 by $p\{_a p\}$.

5.1.11 Rule 3: reducing loops

If the fan-out is greater than one, as in Figure 5.11, then in general the global method given in §5.1.18 has to be used to find the equivalent structured program. However, if its first element is a proper program p the loop can be *reduced*: this is illustrated by Figure 5.11, where p has been duplicated.

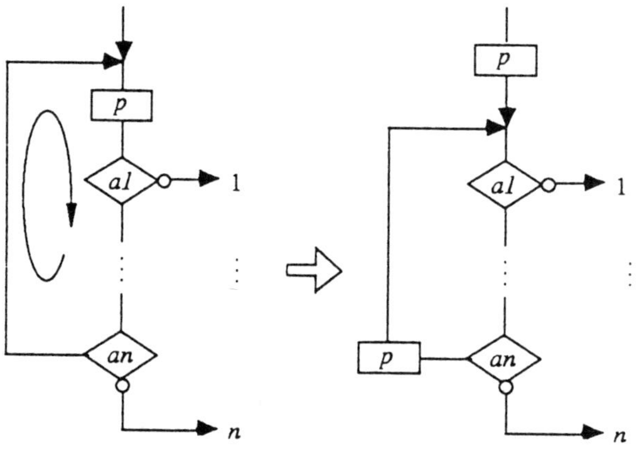

Figure 5.11

5.1.12 Comment

The transformations suggested by Rules 2 and 3 are elementary and we shall not give a proof of their validity here; a formal proof can be derived from the results of §8.5.14.

5.1.13 Example: digital clock

A digital clock, driven by a clock pulse H, is to count and display the time as follows:

- seconds from 00 to 59;
- minutes from 00 to 59;
- hours from 00 to 23.

H is a logical variable with period 1 second; the seconds count is incremented at each rise of H, $H = 0 \rightarrow 1$.

Index i	i_2 i_1 i_0	Time variable $T[i]$	Constant $G[i]$
0	0 0 0	$T[0]$ = seconds units	$G[0] = 10$
1	0 0 1	$T[1]$ = seconds tens	$G[1] = 6$
2	0 1 0	$T[2]$ = minutes units	$G[2] = 10$
3	0 1 1	$T[3]$ = minutes tens	$G[3] = 6$
4	1 0 0	$T[4]$ = hours units	$G[4] = \begin{cases} 10 \text{ for 00–19 hrs, } T_1[5] = 0 \\ 4 \text{ for 20–23 hrs, } T_1[5] = 1 \end{cases}$
5	1 0 1	$T_{3:0}[5]$ = hours tens	$G[5] = 3$
6 (max)	1 1 0	—	—
7	1 1 1	—	—

Figure 5.12

5.1.14 Description: clock algorithm

There is a universally-applicable algorithm for reckoning time, generally called the *clock algorithm* [93]; Figure 5.13 gives the flowchart, with the notation of Figure 5.12. This implements the above specification as follows:

- the index i, range 0–5, specifices the variable to be calculated: in turn, seconds, minutes, hours; in each case first units, then tens;
- the *time variable* $T[i]$ is the quantity calculated; its decimal value is in the range 0–9;
- the constant $G[i]$ is the upper limit for $T[i]$.

Starting with the first test of H (START in Figure 5.13), the program detects the rise of the clock signal (second test of H) and sets i to 0 ($i \leftarrow 0$, counting the seconds units) and increments $T[0]$, $T[0] \leftarrow T[0] + 1$. If the new value is not equal to the upper limit $G[0] = 10$ the incrementation is repeated at each rise of H; when $T[0] = 10$ the seconds units digit is reset to 0, $T[0] \leftarrow 0$, and i is incremented, $i \leftarrow i + 1$ giving $i = 1$. The program then starts to count the tens of seconds, incrementing $T[1] \leftarrow T[1] + 1$, and so on until the limit $i = imax = 6$ is reached, when the whole system is reset to zero.

5.1.15 Software realization: proper flowchart

The program of Figure 5.13 is not proper in the sense defined in §5.1.4, because it has neither an input nor an output terminal. However, it is easily transformed into a proper program by introducing the auxiliary variable $EN = ENABLE$ as in Figure 5.14: here it is labelled as the main program PP, and some of the complex instructions are abbreviated to simple names.

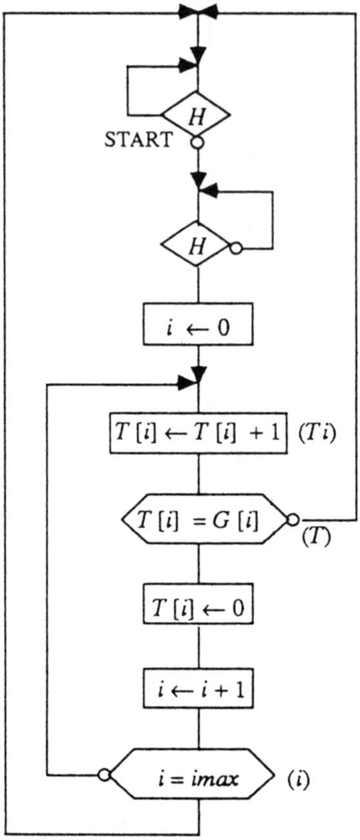

Figure 5.13

Notice that the proper flowchart has been obtained from the original form by breaking a loop and inserting a test of the *EN* variable, to be applied each second. A further cut could be made, so that the test was applied each time *i* reached its maximum value *imax*, that is, each day.

In the new chart the original second test of *H* has been replaced by a test of its complement *H'*; this is to ensure compatibility with the **while** . . . **do** . . . construction of structured programming (Figure 5.8).

5.1.16 Application: local structuring

The structuring rules are applied to this problem as follows.

- Rule 1 (§5.1.9) transforms the flowchart of Figure 5.14 into the pair of charts of Figure 5.15, in which the new proper programs are

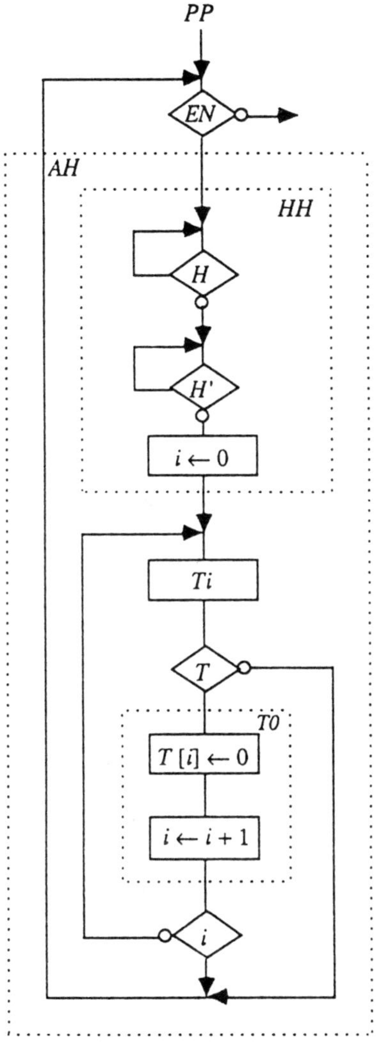

Figure 5.14

derived from the originals by composition. The new labels *PP*(∗), *HH*(∗), *T0*(∗) show that these proper programs are structured.

- Rule 3 (§5.1.11) transforms the flowchart for *AH* of Figure 5.15 into that of Figure 5.16, by reduction of a loop.
- Rule 1 transforms the flowchart for *AH* of Figure 5.16 into that for *AH*(∗) of Figure 5.17, by composition; *h* and *x* are proper programs and both *h* and *AH* are structured.

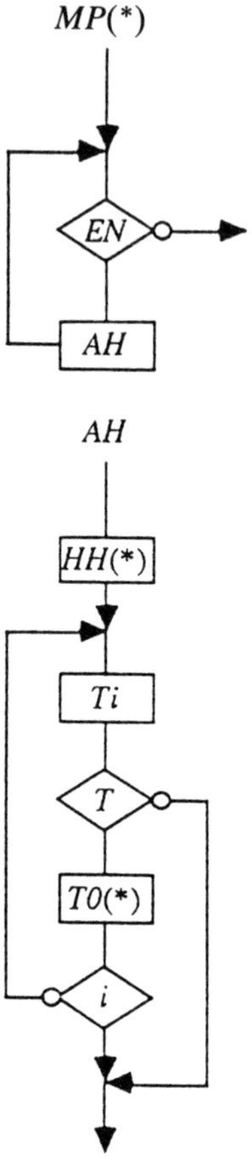

Figure 5.15

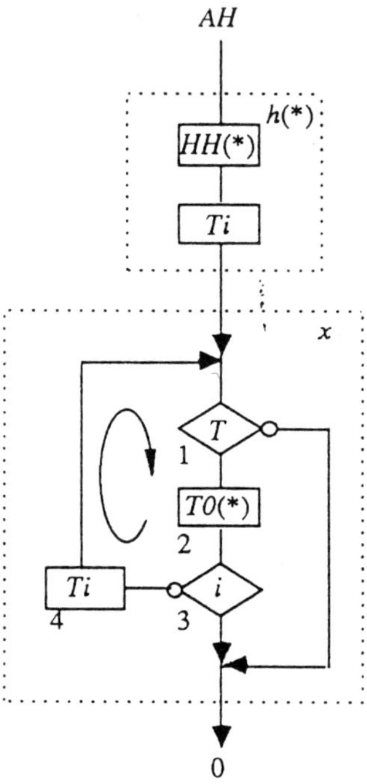

Figure 5.16

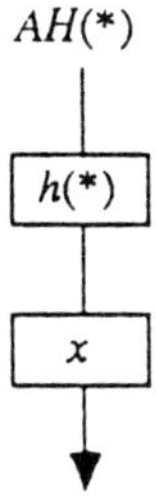

Figure 5.17

At this stage, all the programs except x (Figure 5.16) are structured; we cannot apply the rules for local structuring to this program, so we have to use the global rules to be given in §5.1.18.

5.1.17 Conclusion

Whilst the method of local structuring is easy to use, it is not systematic and the result can depend on the order in which the rules are applied. Further, if there are loops with fan-out greater than one only a partial structuring can be achieved, and for full structuring the global method has to be used.

5.1.18 Method: global structuring

We illustrate this by structuring the program x of Figure 5.16, the last stage in transforming the non-structured clock algorithm.

1. The instructions of the program are given addresses, which can be arbitrary; here we take $ADR = 1, 2, 3, 4$. $ADR = 1$ is always reserved for the first instruction encountered at the input terminal, and $ADR = 0$ for the output terminal.
2. Each control and each action instruction is replaced by a structured program as in Figure 5.18 (control) and 5.19 (action); with this a discrete auxiliary variable s is introduced, $0 \leqslant s \leqslant 4$.
3. The required structured flowchart (Figure 5.20) will consist of a standard part, common to all structuring problems, a decision tree T and a part R that is tailored to the particular problem:
   - the standard part consists of an initial condition, the assignment $s \leftarrow 1$ and a conditional iteration **while** $s > 0$ **do . . .**

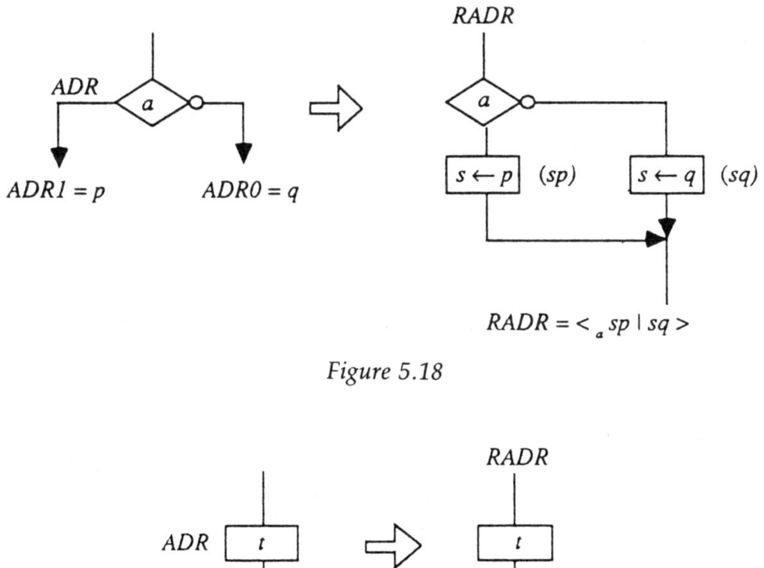

Figure 5.18

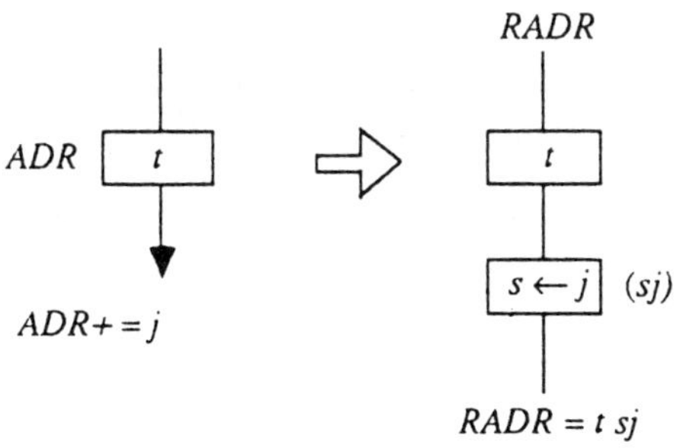

Figure 5.19

- the tree T has n branches and $n-1$ test elements, where n is the number of instructions in the original program (four in this case);
- the specialized part R is a grouping of the n structured programs ($R1$ to $R4$ here) resulting from step 2.

5.1.19 Definition: canonical structured flowchart

The structured flowchart given by the global method is called *canonical;* for a given unstructured original proper program, with given addressing, it is unique. The following statements are easily verified:

- it is equivalent to the original unstructured chart, in the sense of §5.1.7;
- it has only a single **while . . . do . . .** element, and therefore only a single loop;
- the decision tree T has n branches and $n-1$ test elements, where n is the number of instructions in the original program;
- the auxiliary discrete variable s takes the $n+1$ values $0 \ldots n$.

5.1.20 Comment

If a proper but unstructured program has N instructions, then in the worst case, which arises when every instruction is a control, the canonical structured flowchart will have $N+1$ instructions in the standard part and the tree T, and $3N$ in the specialized part R, giving a total of $4N+1$. Thus in the worst case the structured form has four times as many instructions as the unstructured equivalent.

5.1.21 Software realization: simplified structured flowchart

We now attempt to simplify the canonical structured flowchart, by reducing the number of instructions. The general method is to replace each action instruction **do** $s \leftarrow j$ (abbreviated to **do** sj) by the corresponding structured program Rj, except for **do** $s0$ which remains unchanged, as it leads to the exit from the program. In the case of the present example (Figure 5.20) this goes as follows.

- in $R1$ the assignment $s2$ is replaced by $R2$; from the characteristic equations for $R1$, $R2$

$$R1 = <_T s2 \,|\, s0> \tag{5.3}$$

$$R2 = T0\ s3 \tag{5.4}$$

this gives

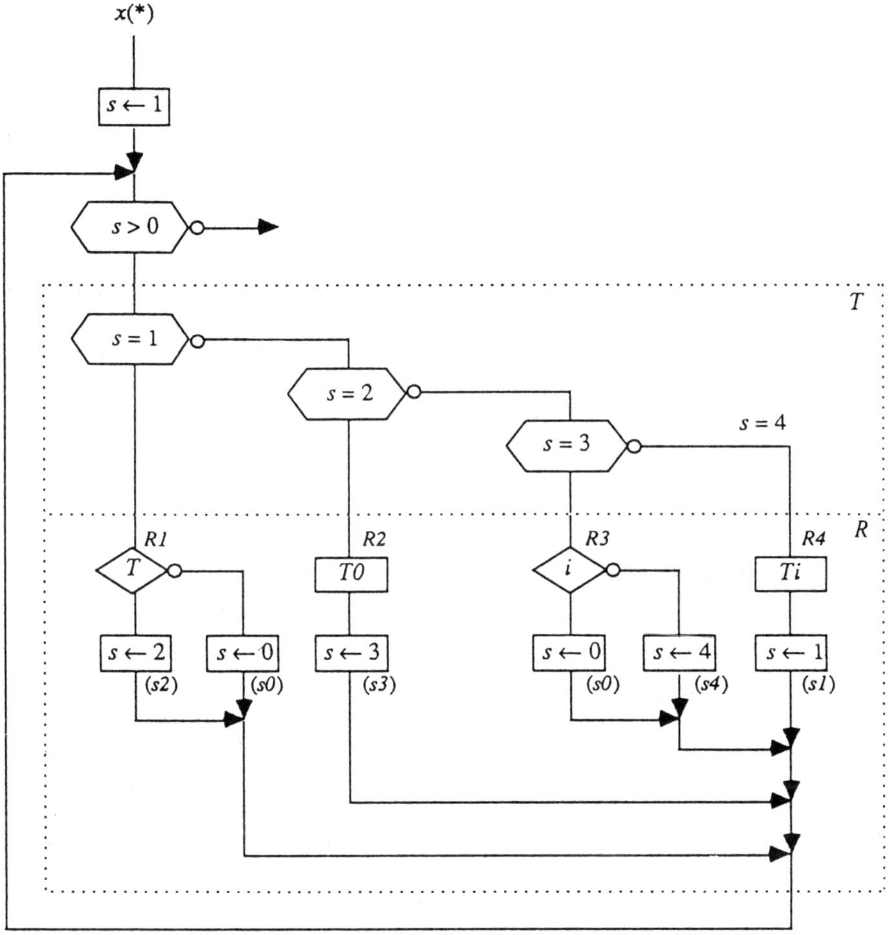

Figure 5.20

$$R1 = <_T T0\ s3 \mid s0> \tag{5.5}$$

- replacing *s3* by *R3* in (5.5):

$$R1 = <_T T0 <_i s0 \mid s4> \mid s0> \tag{5.6}$$

- replacing *s4* by *R4* in (5.6):

$$R1 = <_T T0 <_i s0 \mid Ti\ s1> \mid s0> \tag{5.7}$$

The right side of (5.7) contains an assignment *s1*, which should be replaced by *R1*; but then *R1* would occur on both left and right sides and we should have a recursive expression. This replacement is thus not possible, and the characteristic equation for the final structured program is

$$x = s1 \; \{_s \; R1\}$$
$$= s1 \; \{_s <_T T0 <_i s0 \,|\, Ti \; s1> \,|\, s0>\} \qquad (5.8)$$

for which the *simplified structured flowchart* is Figure 5.21. In this:

- the number of instructions is less than in the canonical chart: nine, instead of 15;
- there is only a single **while . . . do . . .** element, and therefore only a single loop;
- the decision tree T has k branches and $k - 1$ test elements, where k is the number of *essential loops*, that is, loops in the original unstructured flowchart that cannot be broken. In the general case, $k \leq n$ where n is the number of instructions in the original flowchart; in our example the flowchart of Figure 5.16 has only one essential loop, so in Figure 5.21 the tree T reduces to a single branch with no test elements — in effect, there is no tree;
- the auxiliary variable s takes the $k + 1$ values $0 \ldots k$, which in this case means the values 0, 1: thus s is a logical variable.

5.1.22 Comment

For any given canonical flowchart there are many equivalent simplified structured charts, whose form and number of instructions depend on the order in which the successive replacements of §5.1.21 are made; it is possible, in particular, to derive a tree with more than k branches. The method described in §§8.5.1–9, using the graph of equations, is systematic and gives a tree with k branches, which is therefore minimal.

An unstructured program can be represented by a state table and the latter realized by one of the methods developed for sequential systems, as described later in §5.3.15; this approach leads to a second systematic method for structuring, the state table method, which is described in §§8.5.10–15.

5.1.23 Software realization: final structured program

The assemblage of Figure 5.22 is the final fully-structured program *PP*; it is the result of combining the structured programs x (Figure 5.21), *T0* (Figure 5.14), h (Figure 5.16), *HH* (Figure 5.14) and *PP* (Figure 5.15). The original full forms are given instead of the abbreviations *Ti*, *T*, *i* and in the interests of clarity the flowchart is shown as a main program

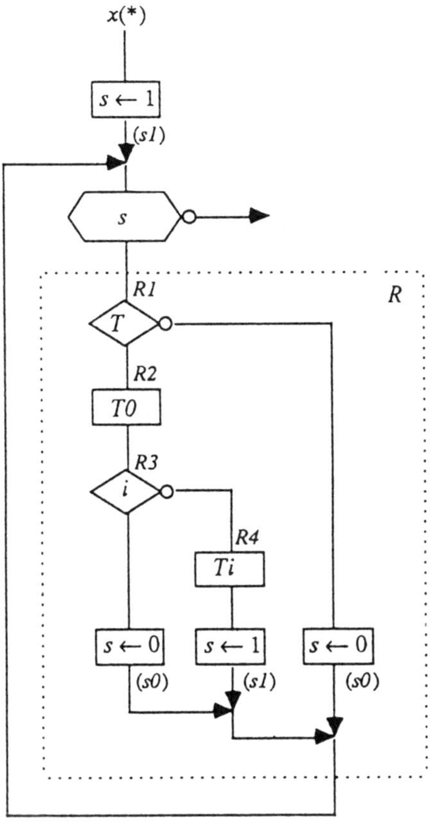

Figure 5.21

PP and a sub-program *SP1*. Also in Figure 5.22 the incrementation paths are the vertical lines marked with a downwards-pointing arrow and all the other lines are jumps paths (§5.2.6); this helps in implementing the program in the languages **L4**, **L5**, to be described in section 5.2.

5.1.24 General conclusion

In the example treated the global structuring of a proper program of nine instructions (Figure 5.14) resulted in canonical structured flowchart with a single **while** . . . **do** . . . element (and therefore a single loop) and a tree *T* with nine branches and eight test elements. Local structuring has reduced the complexity of global structuring, which has been applied only to the part *x* of the original program. In the final

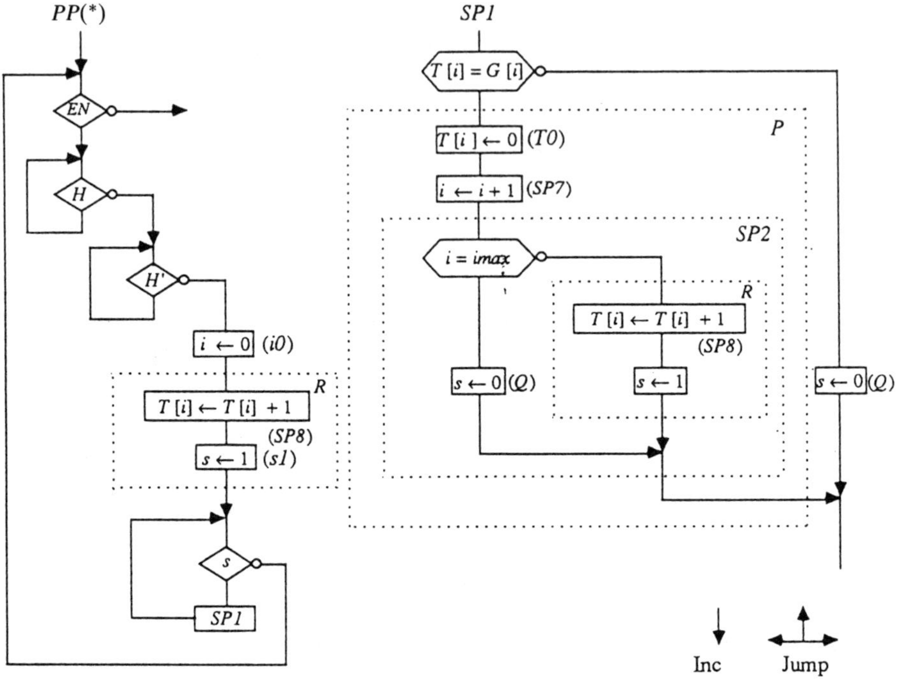

Figure 5.22

structured program (Figure 5.22) the tree *T* has disappeared, but there are four **while** . . . **do** . . . elements and therefore four loops; thus the process has preserved certain topological features of the original program, in particular the double test of the clock signal *H*.

The main interest of local structuring, apart from its simplicity, is the reduction in complexity it can achieve when used in conjunction with global structuring; and also the preservation of topological features. Thus the two methods are complementary.

5.1.25 Bibliography

The history and definition of structured programming, and the underlying motivation, are treated in [72], pp. 136–153 and [69], [76], [77], [78] and [88] are devoted entirely to its implementation. Bohm & Jacopini's classical paper [74], proving that any program can be expressed in terms of three constructions only: sequence (composition), choice and iteration, is reproduced in [71] (pp. 13–25).

The various representations of structured programs, including structured flowcharts and *Nassi-Shneiderman Tables*, or *structograms (N-S charts)* are discussed in [50] pp. 244–265.

The general global method is well known, cf. [69] pp. 91–146, [72] pp. 153–168, [83]; it is based on the theorem that to any proper program there is an equivalent structured program containing a single **while . . . do . . .** element and a tree of n branches testing an $(n + 1)$-valued auxiliary variable. Harel [89] gives the detailed history and a formal proof of this theorem and attributes it to Jacopini [74], von Neumann [90] and Kleene [91].

The local method derives from [92] and [99], and the equivalence of programs is treated in depth in [100].

5.1.26 Exercise

Give a formal proof of the validity of Rule 2, §5.1.10 (breaking loops). Try to use the state table method of §8.5.14.

5.1.27 Exercise

Figure 5.46 is the unstructured **L3** flowchart for an automobile starter. Transform this into a proper flowchart in **L1** (introducing the auxiliary variable *EN*) and apply the local structuring process. Can a structured program be obtained directly, without introducing further auxiliary variables? — if so, draw the flowchart for this and give the number of loops (**while . . . do . . .** elements).

5.1.28 Exercise

Apply local structuring to the proper flowchart of Figure 5.23 (taken from [100]); give the sequence in which the various rules are applied and draw the final chart, which may or may not be structured. How many loops does it contain?

5.1.29 Exercise

First apply local structuring to the proper flowchart of Figure 8.30 and then global structuring to the parts that remain unstructured. Draw the chart finally obtained, give the number of loops (**while . . . do . . .** elements) and compare the complexity (number of instructions) and readability with Figure 8.32.

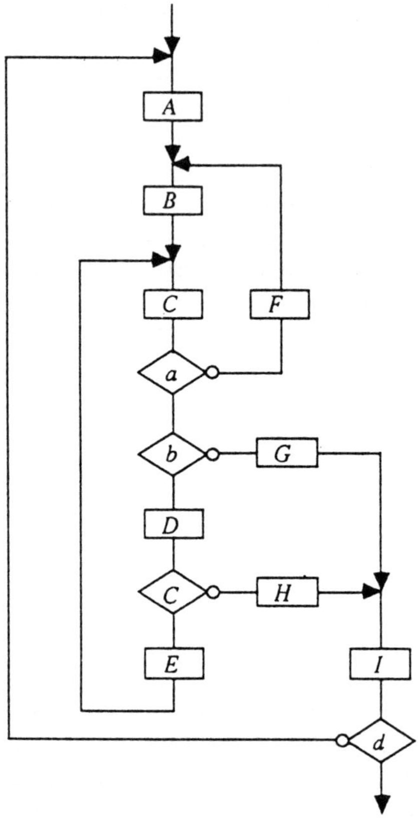

Figure 5.23

5.1.30 Exercise

The tree T in Figure 5.20 has four branches and three test elements on the 5-valued discrete variable s (or on three logical variables $s1$, $s2$, $s3$ in a 1-out-of-4 code). Give an equivalent tree using two new logical variables $S1$, $S2$ and a minimal code and change the original flowchart appropriately. What are the respective merits of the two types of tree? — see also the exercise of §2.1.26.

5.1.31 Exercise

Apply global structuring (§5.1.18, possibly with the variant of §8.5.8) to the proper flowchart of Figure 5.14, without any preliminary local structuring. Find the minimum number k of loops and compare the simplified structured chart finally obtained with Figure 5.22, from the points of view of complexity (number of instructions) and readability (conservation of topological elements of the original flowchart, in particular of the original loops).

Apply the graphical method of §8.5.14 to Figure 5.14, without preliminary local structuring; pay particular attention to the determination of the internal states, as defined in §8.5.10. Find the minimal number *Ns* of rows in the state table and compare the simplified structured chart with that found in the first part of this exercise.

5.1.32 Exercise

Solve the equations (8.61) to (8.70) for the variables *t5*, *t7*, using the results of §8.5.6, and construct the corresponding simplified structured flowchart, showing any sub–programs that you use. Compare the complexity (number of instructions) of your result with Figure 8.32.

5.2 STRUCTURED LANGUAGES

5.2.1 Introduction

In Chapter 4 we introduced the language **L3**, with the instruction set **IF . . . ELSE . . . , DO . . . , CALL . . . , RET**; the motivation for this was the efficiency of the new language, in particular its significantly smaller demands on memory than **L2**, and its simplicity of execution, thanks to the commercial availability of hardware sequencers, essential to the interpreter. Then in section 5.1 we defined structured programming, basing our definition on two instructions only, control and action (§5.1.3), which can be regarded as an extension of the language **L1**.

In this section we bring the two concepts together in structured programs written in **L3**; this leads to the language **L4**, a particular case of **L3**, having the same instruction set but with formal rules governing their use that ensure compatibility with the definitions of structured programming. For convenience we shall associate with **L4** a new high-level language which we call **L5**, or MICROPASCAL, which can be regarded simply as another representation of **L4** structured programs.

5.2.2 Assumptions

From here on in this chapter, for simplicity, we shall take the control instruction defined in §5.1.3 as being identical with the test instruction, and the variable *a* in (5.1) as a test variable *xi*; and correspondingly the action instruction as identical with the assignment, with the *s* of (5.2) as the assignment of a constant to a register, $REG[j] \leftarrow OUT$.

In Chapter 6 we shall study the hardware and software realization of the control and action instructions, treated more generally as defined in §5.1.3; there, the variable *a* may be the result of a complex logical test and *s* the assignment of a function to a register.

5.2.3 Software realization: sequence 'do *PQ*'

If we set out to realize the sequence of Figure 5.6 in **L3**, noting the assumption of §5.2.2, we get at once the solution of Figure 5.24 in which *P*, *Q* are synchronous assignments of the form $REG[j] \leftarrow OUT$. The characteristic equation for this structured program is thus simply

$$P1 = PQ. \tag{5.9}$$

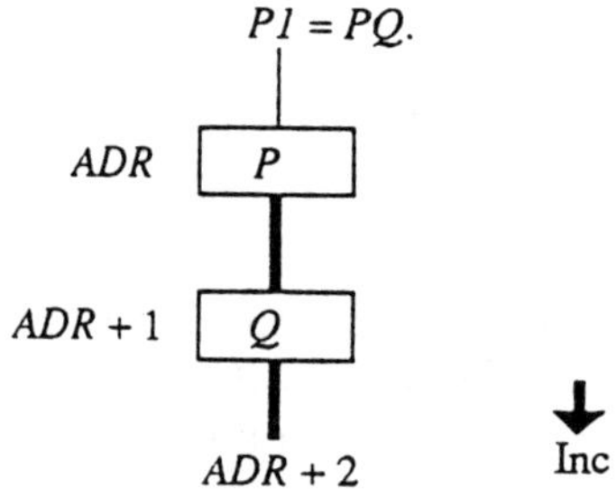

Figure 5.24

5.2.4 Software realization: choice 'if *a* then *P* else *Q*'

Similarly for the realization of Figure 5.7 we get the solution of Figure 5.25, in which the convergence of the two branches requires an unconditional jump instruction (§4.1.6), with address $ADR + 2$. Since *P*, *Q* are synchronous assignments, we have the characteristic equation

$$P2 = <_a P \mid Q>. \tag{5.10}$$

5.2.5 Software realization: iteration 'while *a* do *P*'

Continuing, for the realization of Figure 5.8 we have Figure 5.26, in which the loop requires an unconditional jump instruction with address $ADR + 2$. The characteristic equation is

$$P3 = \{_a P\}. \tag{5.11}$$

$P2 = \langle_a P \mid Q \rangle.$

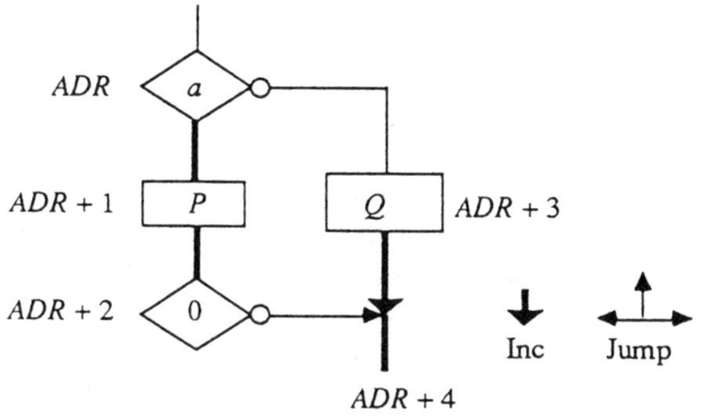

Figure 5.25

$P3 = \{_a P\}.$

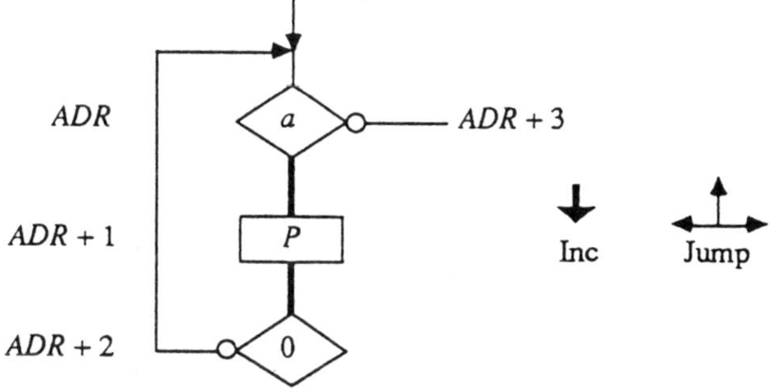

Figure 5.26

5.2.6 Representation: structured L3 flowchart

A *structured flowchart* or *structured programming schema* is a two-dimensional graphical representation of a structured program (as defined in §5.1.5). Figure 5.24–6 are examples for **L3**, with these features:

- the vertical paths marked with heavy lines and downward-pointing arrows are incrementation paths (Inc), characterized by $ADR+ = ADR + 1$;
- all other paths are jump paths (Jump), characterized by an unconditional jump to the address $ADR+ = ADR0$.

5.2.7 Representation: indented mnemonic programs, symbolic programs

Figures 5.27–9 give the programs *P1* (Figure 5.24), *P2* (Figure 5.25), *P3* (Figure 5.26) written in three different forms; each form can be said to be *literal* or *textual*, since each is a linear sequence of instructions or symbols, given in the order of increasing address.

- The list of **L3** instructions, together with the *keywords* **PROGRAM . . . , END PROGRAM, ENDIF, PROCEDURE** (instructions without addresses), constituting the **L4** mnemonic program. **L4** is a new language, to be defined in §5.2.8.
- The list of instructions or **L5** mnemonic program; **L5** is a new high-level language, to be defined in §5.2.9; in this the assignments *P, Q* of the choice (Figure 5.28) and the assignment *P* of the iteration (Figure 5.29) are displaced to the right. We say that mnemonic **L4** and **L5** programs are *indented*.
- The list of *symbols* belonging to the set **S**, where

  $$\mathbf{S} = \{Pj = P,\ Q,\ <_a, \mid, >,\ \{_a\ \},\ \cdot\}$$

  which constitutes the *symbolic program* for *P1, P2, P3*; when read from top to bottom the sequence in each case is identical with the corresponding characteristic equation, read from left to right.

ADR	L4	S	L5
—	PROGRAM *P1*	*P1*=	**program** *P1*
ADR	DO *P*	*P*	**do** *P*
ADR + 1	DO *Q*	*Q*	**do** *Q*
—	END PROGRAM	•	**end program**

Figure 5.27

ADR	L4	S	L5
—	PROGRAM *P2*	*P2*=	**program** *P2*
ADR	IF *a* ELSE *ADR* + 3	$<_a$	**if** *a*
ADR + 1	DO *P*	*P*	**do** *P*
ADR + 2	GO TO *ADR* + 4	|	**else**
ADR + 3	DO *Q*	*Q*	**do** *Q*
—	ENDIF	$>$	**endif**
—	END PROGRAM	•	**end program**

Figure 5.28

ADR	L4	S	L5
—	PROGRAM *P3*	*P3*=	**program** *P3*
ADR	IF *a* ELSE *ADR* + 3	$\{_a$	**while** *a*
ADR + 1	DO *P*	*P*	**do** *P*
ADR + 2	GO TO *ADR*	}	**end while**
—	END PROGRAM	•	**end program**

Figure 5.29

Generally, the first instruction of each of the programs *P1, P2, P3* is the initial instruction, with address *ADR* = 0.

5.2.8 Definition: language L4

This is defined by:

- the **L3** instruction set (4.6) with the addition of the jump instruction (4.8);
- a set of keywords, which are not executed by the interpreter;
- a set of *assembly rules*, defining the *syntax* of the language.

The instructions and keywords are:

L4 = {**IF. . .ELSE. . ., GO TO. . ., DO. . .,**
CALL. . ., RET, PROGRAM. . ., ENDIF,
PROCEDURE. . ., END PROGRAM} (5.12)

The syntax is given in the *syntactic diagram* of Figure 5.30, in which each path describes a syntactically correct program or part of a program. The rectangles, for example 'statement', are *non-terminal symbols*, the details of which will be given elsewhere in the diagram; whilst the ovals, for example **END PROGRAM**, are *terminal symbols*, that is, either instructions or keywords of (5.12).

The syntactic diagram is equivalent to the *Backus-Naur notation* (or *Backus-Naur Form, BNF*) ([124] pp. 25–82), given in Figure 5.31 in which we have used the following conventions:

- word in light type (e.g. statement) = non-terminal symbol;
- word in bold type (e.g. **PROGRAM**) = terminal symbol;
- word in braces (e.g. {statement}) = repetition: any number of times, including zero;
- words separated by a vertical bar (e.g. **DO | CALL**) = alternative: execution of one but not the other.

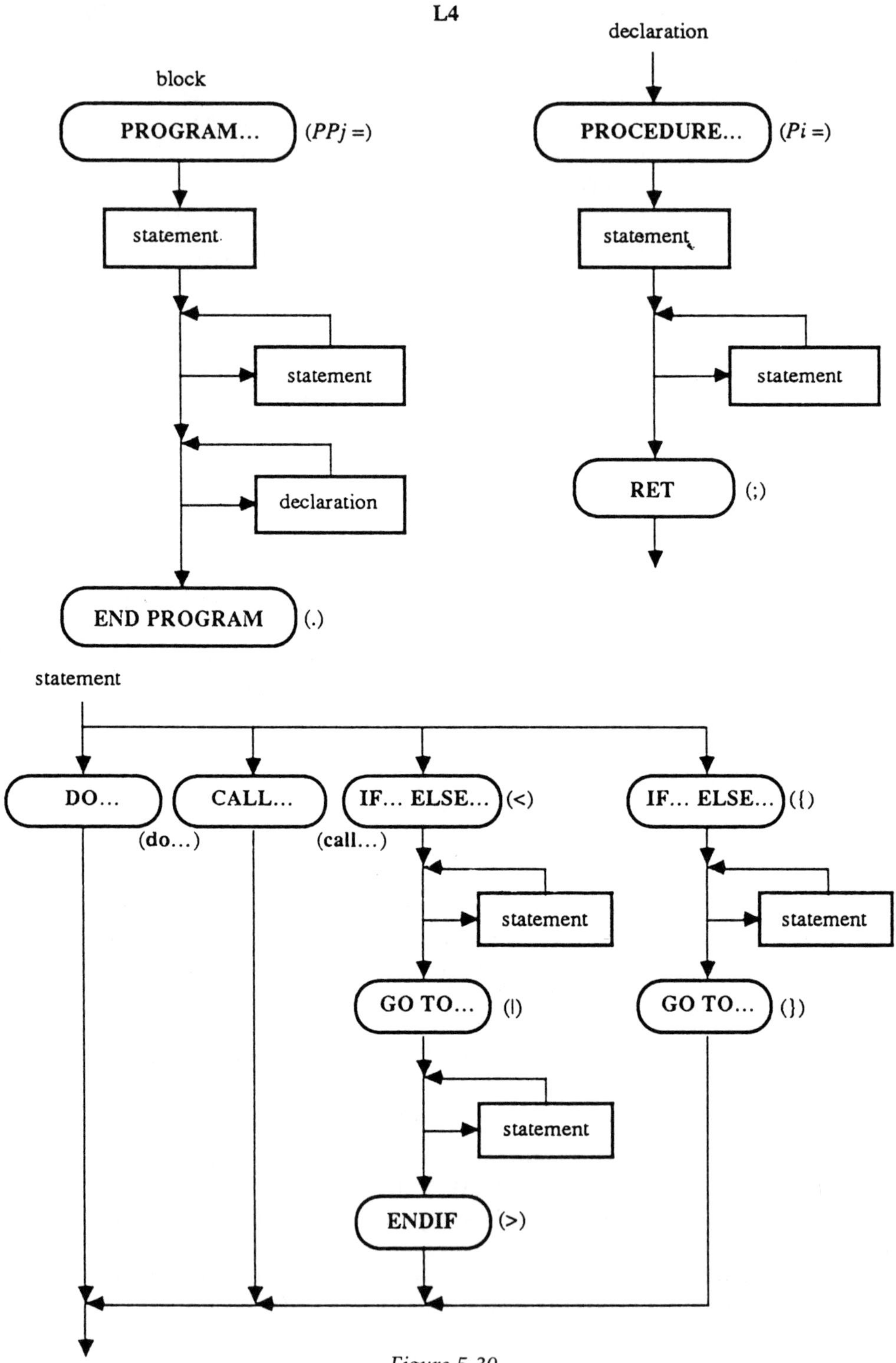
L4
block
PROGRAM...
(PPj =)
statement
statement
declaration
END PROGRAM
(.)
declaration
PROCEDURE...
(Pi =)
statement
statement
RET
(;)
statement
DO...
CALL...
IF... ELSE...
(<)
IF... ELSE...
({)
(do...)
(call...)
statement
statement
GO TO...
(|)
GO TO...
(})
statement
ENDIF
(>)

Figure 5.30

block	:	**PROGRAM** statement {statement} {declaration} **END PROGRAM**;
statement	:	**DO** ǀ **CALL** ǀ **IF** {statement} **GO TO** {statement} **ENDIF** ǀ **IF** {statement} **GO TO**;
declaration.	:	**PROCEDURE** statement {statement} **RET**.
		L4

Figure 5.31

Thus **L4** programs are written with the same primitives (the same instructions) as **L3** but must conform to the formal assembly rules, that is, to the syntax. **L4 programs are therefore a subset** of **L3 programs, from which it follows that any L3 interpreter, in particular the binary decision machine with a sequencer of Figure 4.7** (INT3) **can execute L4 programs without change**.

5.2.9 Definition: language L5

This high-level language, also called MICROPASCAL [49] for historical reasons, is actually a minimal subset of the MODULA-2 language [73]. It is defined by the syntactic diagram of Figure 5.32; the 11 terminal symbols form the instruction set, and there are no keywords. The equivalent Backus-Naur notation is given in Figure 5.33.

L5, in contrast to **L4**, cannot be executed directly by an **L3** interpreter; we discuss the interpretation and compilation of **L5** in Chapter 7.

5.2.10 Comments

A general distinction to be made between **L4** and **L5** is that the first is a *low-level language* and the second a *high-level language*. In **L4** future addresses have to be given explicitly, e.g. **IF** *a* **ELSE** *ADR0*, **GO TO** *ADR+*, **CALL** *ADSP*, whilst in **L5** these are determined by the interpreter or compiler and not by the programmer. Thus the latter is relieved of the need to concern himself with such fine detail and can give all his attention to the design of the program.

Comparison of the syntactic diagrams or the BNF notations for **L4** and **L5** shows the following:

- both conform to the rules of structured programming (§5.1.5);
- each part labelled 'statement' calls itself (instructions **if . . . else . . . endif** and **while . . . end while** in Figure 5.32); we therefore say that the diagram includes recursive calls;
- given any sequence of terminal symbols, that is, a list of instructions

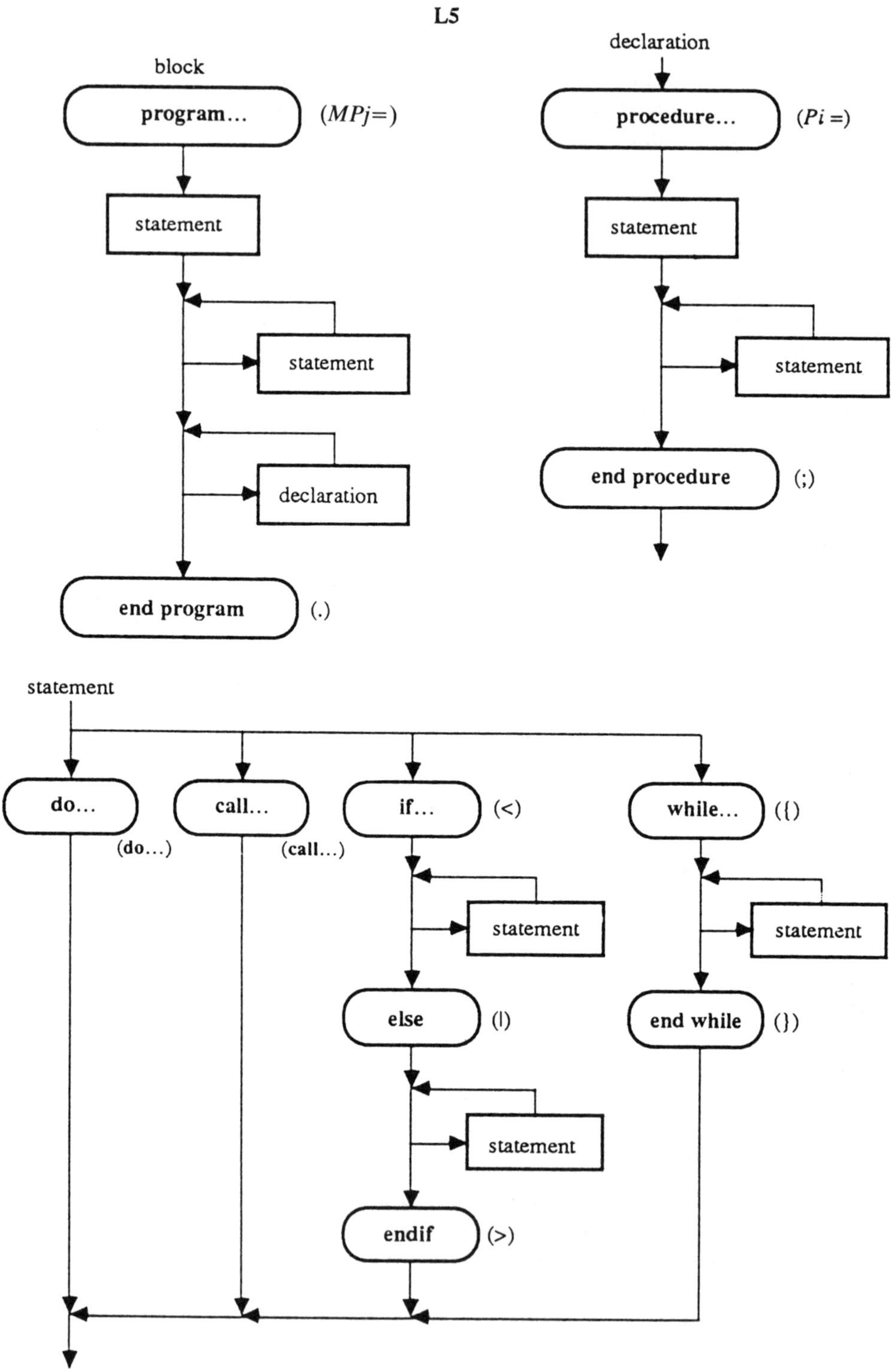

L5
block
program...
(MPj=)
statement
statement
declaration
end program
(.)
declaration
procedure...
(Pi =)
statement
statement
end procedure
(;)
statement
do...
(do...)
call...
(call...)
if...
(<)
statement
else
(|)
statement
endif
(>)
while...
({)
statement
end while
(})

Figure 5.32

block	:	**program** statement {statement} {declaration} **end program;**
statement	:	**do** | **call** | **if** {statement} **else** {statement} **endif** | **while** {statement} **end while;**
declaration	:	**procedure** statement {statement} **end procedure.**
		L5

Figure 5.33

and/or keywords, one and only one path can always be found in the **L5** diagram (Figure 5.32), which is therefore said to be *deterministic;* this is not the case for **L4** (Figure 5.30), where the instruction **IF . . . ELSE . . .** leads to two distinct paths.

5.2.11 Definition: the symbolic language S

Any program in the high-level language **L5** can be written more compactly as an algebraic expression, called in §5.2.7 a symbolic program and equivalent to the characteristic equation of §5.1.6. The *symbolic language* **S** is a convenient abbreviation of **L5**. It is defined by the syntactic diagram of Figure 5.32 and consists of the 11 symbols of (5.13), where the commas separate the different symbols; these represent the terminal symbols (ovals) of **L5** (Figure 5.32) or **L4** (Figure 5.30):

$$\mathbf{S} = \{PPj=,\ \mathbf{do}\ldots,\ \mathbf{call}\ldots,\ <, |, >,\ \{,\ \},\ Pi=,\ ;,\ .\} \tag{5.13}$$

Points to note here are:

- specific symbols are given for main programs ($PPj=$) and procedures ($Pi=$);
- for the sake of clarity, the mnemonic expressions **do . . .**, **call . . .** are generally used to specify assignment and call instructions respectively;
- the symbols '.' (point) and ';' (semi-colon) indicate the end of a program (**end program**) and of a procedure (**end procedure**) respectively.

5.2.12 Definition: structured languages

Any main program and any procedure written in **L4** or **L5** is a structured program in the sense of §5.1.5; we say therefore that these are *structured languages.*

L1, **L2**, and **L3**, defined only by their instruction sets, are not structured; as was done with **L3**, assembly rules can be devised for **L1** and **L2**, so giving other new structured languages.

5.2.13 Conclusion

By imposing a syntax, that is, a set of formal assembly rules, on **L3** we have derived our first language, **L4**, that conforms to the rules of structured programming; and this, being a subset of **L3**, can be executed directly by the **L3** interpreter described in Chapter 4.

The immediate argument for structuring a low-level language such as **L4** is that this helps to produce programs that are correct, efficient and adaptable. But further, a close relationship can be established between the structured low-level language and a new high-level, also structured, language, such as **L5**; the consequence is that a program written in the high-level language (the source program) is easily transformed to the low level (the object program) which can then be executed directly by an interpreter.

The execution or compilation of **L5** programs through the medium of an interpreter or a compiler requires hardware and software resources that are discussed later, in Chapter 7.

5.2.14 Bibliography

Reference [85] deals with the application of the concepts of structured programming to microprograms and their implementation in commercially available computers, and [84] describes an interpreter specially designed for the execution of structured microprograms.

Patterson [121] is one of the earliest publications on high-level microprogramming languages. The motivation for developing such languages, a survey of their advantages and disadvantages, and descriptions of the most important among them are given in [115], [119], [134] (pp. 125–135) and [148] (pp. 145–190).

5.3 SEQUENTIAL SYSTEMS WITH ASYNCHRONOUS BEHAVIOUR

5.3.1 Definition: synchronous sequential system

Using the notation of [1] (p. 159) and [59] (p. 199), we say that a *synchronous sequential system* or *Mealy machine* is any assemblage of flip-flops and a combinational system of the form of Figure 5.34, having:

- n independent variables $x1, x2, \ldots xn$, the *input variables;* any combination of values of these constitutes an *input state* x;
- r dependent variables $Z1, Z2, \ldots Zr$, the *output variables;* any combination of values of these constitutes an *output state* Z;
- m type D flip-flops, used in synchronous mode ($PR' = CLR' = 1$) and all driven by the same clock signal ($H = CK1 = CK2 = \ldots =$

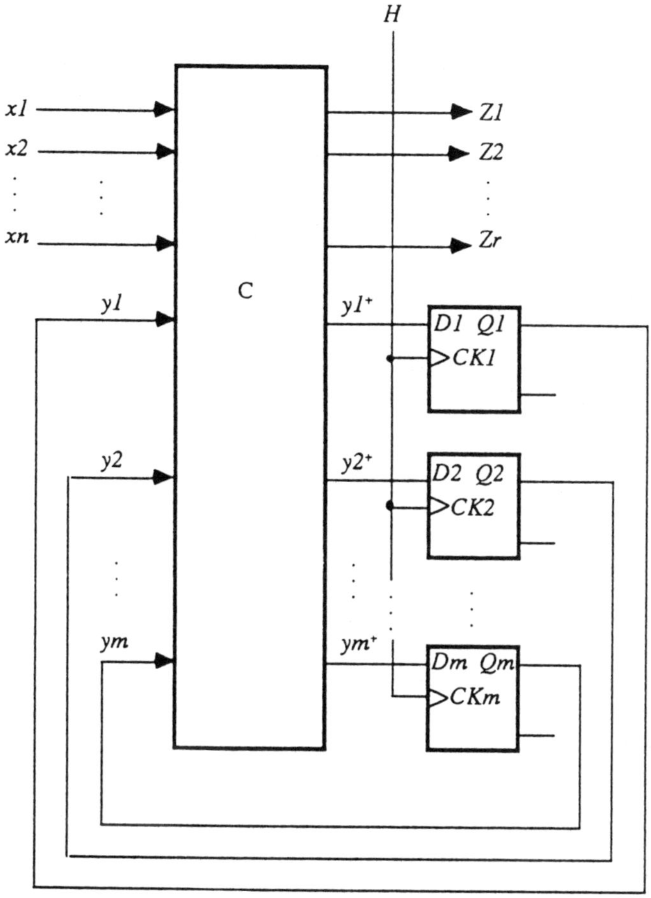

Figure 5.34

CKm); the outputs $Q1, Q2, \ldots Qm$ are the *internal variables* $y1, y2, \ldots ym$, and the inputs $D1, D2, \ldots Dm$ which trigger the flip-flops are the *future internal variables* $y1^+, y2^+, \ldots ym^+$; any combination of values of the internal variables constitutes an *internal state* y.

Any combination of values of the n variables x and the m variables y is a *total state* of the system, written x, y; and of the y^+ and Z is a *resultant state*, written y^+, Z. A total state is *stable* if

$$x, y = x, y^+ \tag{5.14}$$

and *unstable* if this does not hold, that is if, for the same input state, $y \neq y^+$.

5.3.2 Example: car starter motor

A sequential system for controlling the starting of a car consists of two input variables, the ignition key *x1* and the seat belt switch *x2*, and three outputs, the ignition switch *Z1*, the warning light *Z2* and the buzzer *Z3*. The specification for the system lays down four main sequences [79]:

1. If the seat belt is fastened, inserting and then turning the key starts the engine.
2. If the belt is not fastened, turning the key puts on the warning light and sounds the buzzer but does not start the engine.
3. If after (2) the belt is fastened, the buzzer is turned off but the light is left on and the engine does not start; it can be started only by returning to (1), when the light is turned off.
4. If the belt is unfastened while the car is in motion with the engine running, the light is turned on.

5.3.3 Definition: asynchronous behaviour

If in the case of the self-starter the frequency of the clock pulse *H* is much higher than that of either of the inputs *x1*, *x2* an important feature follows: the **output state** $Z = Z1, Z2, Z3$ **is independent of the duration of the input states** $x = x1, x2$ (measured in clock periods) but **depends only on the order in which they occur**. We describe this by saying that the behaviour is *asynchronous*.

In this example we can assume also that the values of the input variables can never change simultaneously, that is, within the same clock period.

5.3.4 Representation: state table

Figure 5.35 is the *primitive state table* for the example, constructed in accordance with the treatment of logic systems given in [1] (pp. 195–231) and [59] (pp. 241–285). The columns correspond to the four possible input states *x* and the rows to the six possible internal states $y \in \{a, b, \ldots f\}$, as required by the specification.

Each cell in the table, the intersection of a row and a column, defines a total state x, y and gives the resultant state y^+, Z, again as required by the specification and taking for granted the assumptions of §5.3.3. Undefined values of the next states y^+ and output states *Z* are shown by a dash (—), defined output states are shown by the decimal equivalent of the binary word $Z = Z1, Z2, Z3$.

The table can be reduced by using methods developed in the theory

y^+,Z	$x1,x2$ 00	01	11	10
a	a,0	b,0	–	e,–
b	a,0	b,0	c,–	–
c	–	b,–	c,4	d,–
d	a,–	–	c,–	d,6
e	a,–	–	f,–	e,3
f	–	b,–	f,2	e,–
y				

Figure 5.35

of logic systems [35], [37]. The first step is to construct the graph of *compatible states,* as Figure 5.36, from which a unique *minimal reduced table T1,* Figure 5.37, of two states, can be deduced.

Other reduced tables that are not minimal can be derived from Figure 5.36; an example is *T2* of Figure 5.38, with three states: this is a *non-mininal reduced table.*

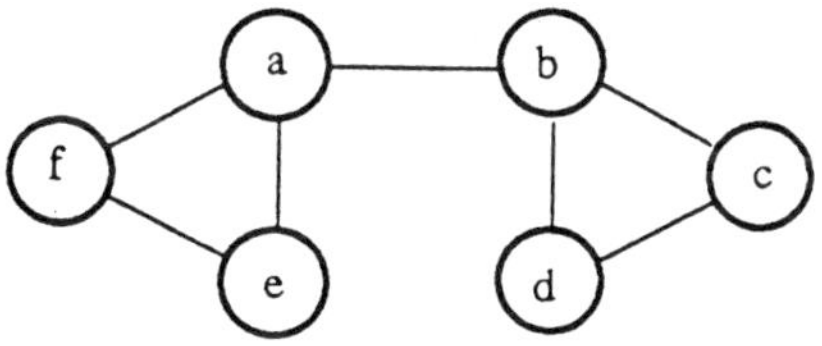

Figure 5.36

y^+,Z	$x1,x2$ 00	01	11	10
0 = A = {a,f,e}	A,0	B,0	A,2	A,3
1 = B = {b,c,d}	A,0	B,0	B,4	B,6
y				
	T1			

Figure 5.37

y^+,Z	$x1,x2$ 00	01	11	10
F = {a,b}	F,0	F,0	E,–	D,–
E = {c,d}	F,–	F,–	E,4	E,6
D = {e,f}	F,–	F,–	D,2	D,3
y				
	T2			

Figure 5.38

5.3.5 Representation: tree, for minimal table

The minimal table *T1* of Figure 5.37 can be represented by a binary decision tree by associating with each row a state of the m internal variables *y1, y2, . . . ym*: this is called *coding* the table, and the code is *minimal* if the number Ny of rows, and therefore of states, satisfies

$$2^{m-1} < Ny \leqslant 2^m \tag{5.15}$$

If $Ny = 2$, $m = 1$ and the minimal code of Figure 5.37 involves only a single internal variable y; and we are brought back to the classical problem of determining the minimal tree for a combinational system, in this case where each resultant state y^+, Z depends on a total state x, y. The Karnaugh map method of §2.1.14 can be applied to *T1*; the six resultant states form six blocks, giving the 6-branch tree of Figure 5.39 with a total of 11 elements, made up of six assignment and five test elements.

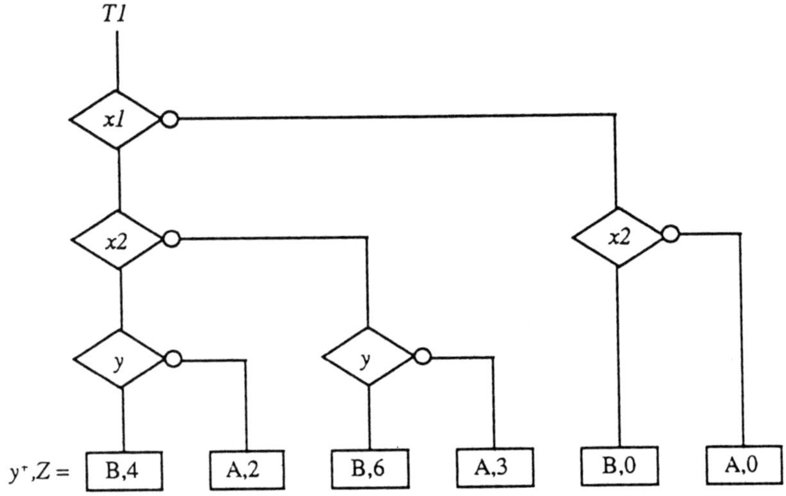

Figure 5.39

5.3.6 Coding

Once the number m of internal variables has been determined there is complete freedom to code the Ny states with any of the 2^m combinations of values. This can be done in K ways where [1] (pp. 205–206), [59] (pp. 253–255)

$$K(Ny, m) = (2^m)!/(2^m - Ny)! \tag{5.16}$$

5.3.7 Representation: tree for non-minimal table

The minimal code for the non-minimal table *T2* of Figure 5.38 requires two variables, $y1, y2$. One possible coding is given in Figure 5.40; we can see here that the state $y1, y2 = 11$ is unnecessary: it implies the undefined resultant states shown by dashes. We call *T3* the coded state table.

There are five different resultant states here, enabling the table to be partitioned into five blocks and so giving a tree of only five branches (Figure 5.41); this has nine elements: five assignments and four tests.

y^+,Z \ *x1,x2*	00	01	11	10
00 = F	F,0	F,0	E,-	D,-
01 = E	F,-	F,-	E,4	E,6
11 = C	–	–	–	–
10 = D	F,-	F,-	D,2	D,3

y1,y2 = y

T3

Figure 5.40

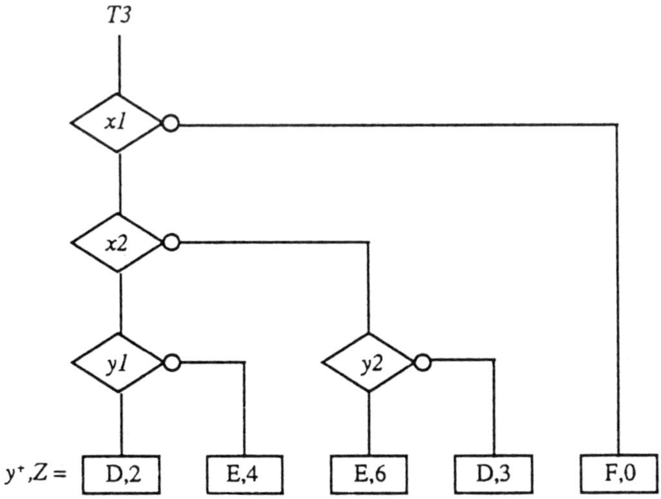

Figure 5.41

5.3.8 Definition: minimal tree for a sequential system

In general, the same sequential system can be represented by a number of different, but equivalent, trees; among these, those with the smallest number of test elements are the *minimal trees* for the system.

It follows from §2.1.16 that the minimal number of different blocks in the Karnaugh map is equal to the number Nr of different output states. For a sequential system this last is equal to or greater than the greatest of Ny, the number of internal states (= 2 in the example studied) and NZ, the number of different output states determined by the specification (= 5 in the example); that is,

$$Nr \geqslant \text{Max}\,(Ny, NZ) \tag{5.17}$$

Thus from (2.9) the theoretical minimum number of elements in the tree for a sequential system (the *lower bound*) is

$$t_{\min} = 2 \cdot Nr_{\min} - 1 = 2 \cdot \text{Max}\,(Ny, NZ) - 1 \tag{5.18}$$

In our example, the tree *T3* of Figure 5.41 has exactly $t_{\min} = 2 \cdot \text{Max}(2, 5) - 1 = 9$ elements; so this is a minimal tree for the starter-motor system.

5.3.9 Conclusion

The above results show that the minimal reduced state table for a sequential system does not necessarily lead to a minimal tree; in fact, the problem of reducing a primitive state table to a number Ny of rows, and determining the number m of internal variables with which to code these rows in one of the K ways given by (5.16), so as to give a minimal tree, or even a minimal decomposition, is formidable, and is still unsolved.

In practice, the complexity of the necessary calculations has to be limited by working with strongly reduced, even minimal, tables, making use of the result (5.18) which sets the lower bound $t_{\min}$ to the number of elements in the minimal tree.

5.3.10 Software realization: structured L4 flowchart

A structured **L4** flowchart *PP3* for the minimal tree *T3* of Figure 5.41, using the structures of Figures 5.24–6, can be constructed as follows:

- by definition, each choice structure **if . . . then . . . else . . .** has a single output; therefore to each test element in the tree there corresponds a test instruction in the flowchart (Fig. 5.42) and a path closure after the test, the latter consisting of the convergence of the two branches of the choice together with a jump instruction, as in §5.2.4 and Figure 5.25. The tests nearest to the leaves (*y1*, *y2* in Figure 5.42) are made first, and each convergence is labelled with the corresponding test variable, e.g. '*y1>*', '*y2>*', then *x2* and finally *x1*;

- the real-time nature of the problem implies that the calculation of the resultant states y^+, Z has to be repeated indefinitely, and this requires that the tree *T3* is looped back on itself. This in turn requires the introduction of a **while** . . . **do** . . . structure (§5.2.5 and Figure 5.26), an auxiliary test variable *EN* (*ENABLE*) and a jump: in Figure 5.42 this last is labelled '*EN*}', meaning that if *EN* = 1 the tree *T3* is executed by the interpreter, otherwise it is abandoned and some another part of the program, indicated by '?' in the figure, is taken up.

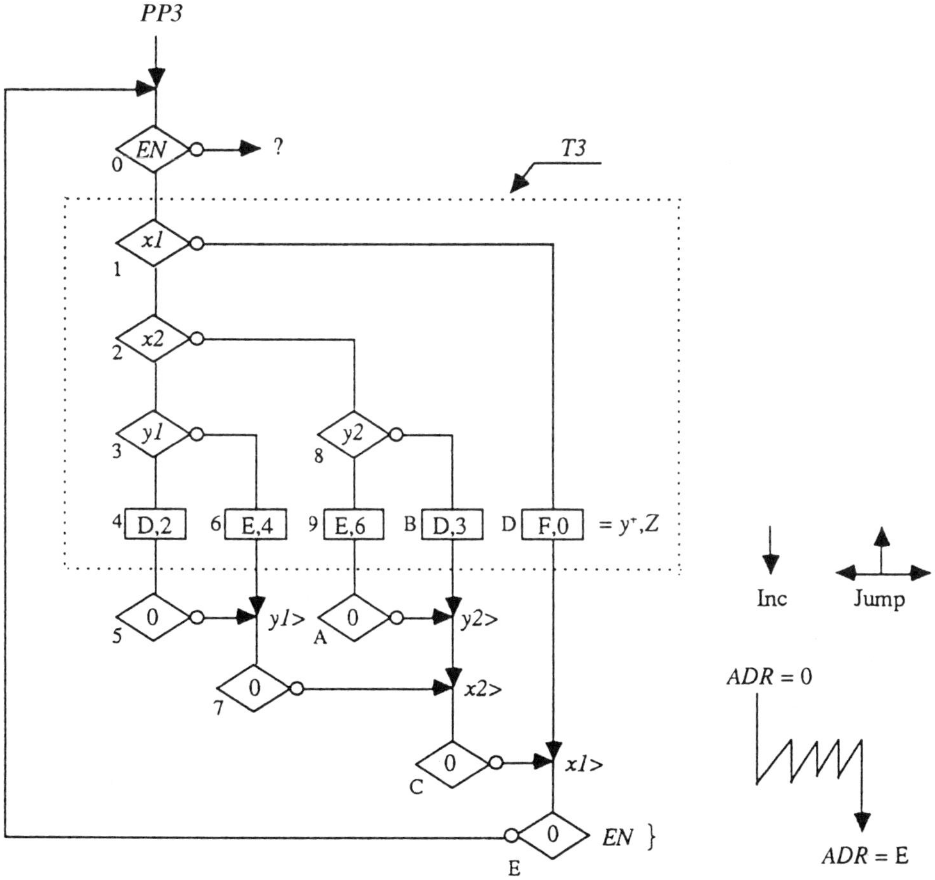

Figure 5.42

To sum up, the original representation of *T3*, enclosed in dotted lines in Figure 5.42, remains unchanged; the only changes made necessary by the language **L4** are the successive closings of the choices originally left open after the test instructions and the introduction of the auxiliary variable *EN* to enable the final loop to be closed.

5.3.11 'Zig-zag' addressing

With the three basic constructions of structured programming (sequence, choice, iteration) represented as in Figures 5.24–6, the following applies to any **L4** structured flowchart, following from the graphical representation of incrementation paths and jumps (cf. §5.2.6):

- the list of addresses *ADR* is read from top to bottom (following the incrementation paths), starting at the extreme left and completing the columns in order from left to right: thus in Figure 5.42 the sequence is *ADR* = 0 . . . 5, then 6, 7 and so on, ending with D,E on the extreme right.

This is called *zig-zag* addressing; it is related directly to the graphical representation of the structured language **L4**.

5.3.12 Representation: indented mnemonic programs, symbolic programs

In the structured flowchart of Figure 5.42, with its zig-zag addressing, we have given the first test instruction, $xi = EN$, the first address, $ADR = 0$. We can construct the characteristic equation for the program by scanning the list of instructions from there to the last (ADR = E), and this is equivalent to the symbolic program given in the column **S** in Figure 5.43, read from top to bottom:

$$PP3 = \{_{EN}{<}_{x1}{<}_{x2}{<}_{y1}\ \mathbf{do}\ \mathrm{D},2\,|\,\mathbf{do}\ \mathrm{E},4{>}\,|\,{<}_{y2}\ \mathbf{do}\ \mathrm{E},6\,|\,\mathbf{do}\ \mathrm{D},3{>}{>}\,|\,\mathbf{do}\ \mathrm{F},0{>}\}. \qquad (5.19)$$

Each symbol of **S** translates into **L4** either by an addressed instruction or by an unaddressed keyword, or into an **L5** instruction, in either case conforming to the syntactic diagram for the language (Figures 5.30, 5.32). This gives the indented mnemonic programs in **L4** and **L5** for the starter motor, shown in Figure 5.43.

ADR	L4	S	L5
	PROGRAM *PP3*	*PP3=*	**program** *PP3*
0	IF *EN* ELSE ?	$\{_{EN}$	while *EN*
1	IF *x1* ELSE D	$<_{x1}$	if *x1*
2	IF *x2* ELSE 8	$<_{x2}$	if *x2*
3	IF *y1* ELSE 6	$<_{y1}$	if *y1*
4	DO D,2	do D,2	do D,2
5	GO TO 7	$\vert$	else
6	DO E,4	do E,4	do E,4
	ENDIF	>	endif
7	GO TO C	$\vert$	else
8	IF *y2* ELSE B	$<_{y2}$	if *y2*
9	DO E,6	do E,6	do E,6
A	GO TO C	$\vert$	else
B	DO D,3	do D,3	do D,3
	ENDIF	>	endif
	ENDIF	>	endif
C	GO TO E	$\vert$	else
D	DO F,0	do F,0	do F,0
	ENDIF	>	endif
E	GO TO 0	$\}$	end while
	END PROGRAM	.	end program

Figure 5.43

5.3.13 Hardware realization

The **L3** interpreter INT3 of Figure 4.7 can execute the **L4** program of Figure 5.43 immediately; the internal variables $y1, y2$ are supplied as the output of the single assignment register, $REG = y^+, Z$, with the conventions of Figure 5.40 ($y1, y2$ = 00 = F, 01 = E, 10 = D) and form the hardware feedback for the sequential system.

In Figure 5.42, in contrast to the hardwired system of Figure 5.34 which provides a future state y^+ at every clock beat, a loop in the flowchart has to be traversed for every evaluation of a resultant state y^+, Z, the time for which, measured by the number of instructions, varies from a minimum of 4 for F,0 to a maximum of 9 for D,2. The assumptions made in §5.3.3 must therefore be modified to read as follows: (1) the frequency of the interpreter clock pulse *CK* is much higher than that of the input signals $x1, x2$; (2) the two input variables cannot change simultaneously, that is, in the course of an evaluation and therefore within the same loop of the flowchart.

5.3.14 Hardware/software equivalence

As for the 6-state counter of §3.2.5, each of the trees *T1* (Figure 5.39), *T3* (Figure 5.41) is equivalent to the combinational system C of the hardwired sequential system of Figure 5.34. Such a tree can be realized by an assemblage {DMUX, OR}, as in §2.4.2, and gives both the output variables Z and the triggers $y^+ = D$ for the flip-flops.

T1 represents the minimal state table and implies the existence of a single internal variable y and therefore of a single flip-flop; *T3* represents a non-minimal table and requires two internal variables $(y1, y2)$ and therefore two flip-flops.

5.3.15 Method 1: state table tree

The following is a possible method for performing the calculation for the starter-motor example.

1. From the specification, the primitive state table is constructed, and possibly the state diagram also.
2. The graph of compatible states is deduced.
3. A reduction of the primitive table is sought, and a coding that minimizes the number of different resultant states y^+, Z — that is, the number of blocks in the Karnaugh map and therefore the number of branches in the tree.
4. The minimal or quasi-minimal tree, possibly decomposed, is constructed as a structured flowchart after the various choices and loop have been closed; a zig-zag addressing is applied.
5. The characteristic equation is derived by scanning this flowchart, and hence the symbolic program **S** and the indented mnemonic **L4**, **L5** programs. The **L4** program can be coded in hexadecimal and executed by the **L3** interpreter; the **L5** program requires the methods to be described in Chapter 7 for interpretation or compilation.

Steps 1 and 2 are those of the general method for synthesis of sequential systems given in [1] (pp. 195–201) and [59] (pp. 241–249), based on the classic work of Huffman [75], [80]. Step 3 follows Huffman's general procedure but has different objectives: here we are looking for a minimal tree rather than an optimal combinational system with a minimal number of internal variables. Steps 4 and 5, which are new, are specific to the software realization of sequential systems.

Finally, we can say that the global representation of a state table, with the *Ny* rows coded by *m* internal variables, gives a unique binary decision tree or decomposition of a tree, having a single loop as in Figure 5.42 and always realizable by a structured flowchart and a structured language.

5.3.16 Representation: state tree

The minimal table *T1* of Figure 5.37 has two internal states $y \in \{A, B\}$, each of which (each row in the table) can be represented by a *partial state table* (Figure 5.44) giving the resultant state y^+, Z for each input state $x1, x2$. The graphical method of §2.1.14, based on the Karnaugh map, can be applied to each of the tables A, B separately, leading in each case to the minimum number of blocks and hence to the minimal tree: in the case we are considering these trees are canonical. The union of the two minimal trees gives a new representation of the minimal table, in terms of *state trees* or *partial trees* for *T1* (Figure 5.45).

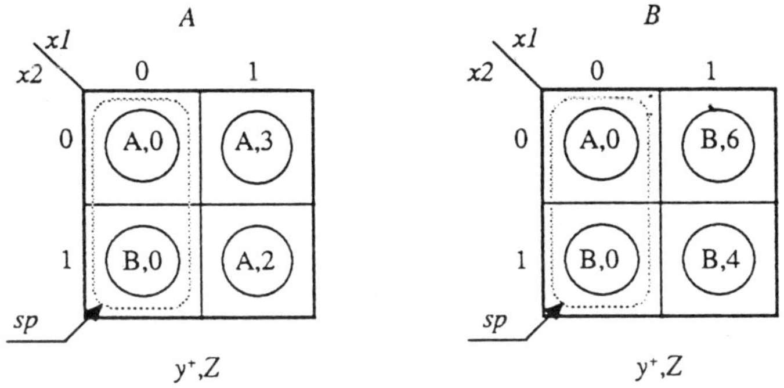

Figure 5.44

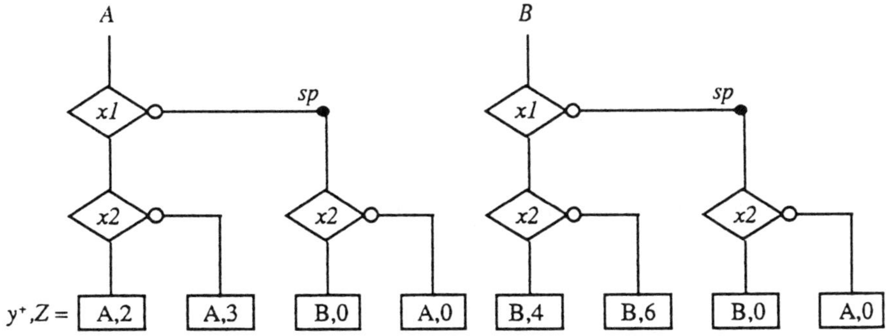

Figure 5.45

5.3.17 Comment

The method of state trees poses the problem of the simultaneous simplification of a number of decision trees. In the most general case the solution requires the trees for all the states in the primitive table, or in any one of its reductions, to be simplified simultaneously, in order to find sub-trees that may be common to several trees. The general calculation is complex, and we simplify as follows. Starting from the minimal table with *Ny* rows we simplify simultaneously the *Ny* trees for the corresponding states:

- either by the P-function method given in §8.2.11, obtaining two decision diagrams *ZA*, *ZB* with a common sub-tree *sp*;
- or by applying the Karnaugh map graphical method of §2.2.13 to the tables *A*, *B* simultaneously; this reveals any block of blocks that is common to the two tables (*sp* in Figure 5.44), and hence any common sub-tree (Figures 5.45, 8.14).

5.3.18 Conclusion

Representing a table as *Ny* decision trees or diagrams has the following consequences:

- the internal variables $y1, y2, \ldots ym$ have gone, the internal state being given by the corresponding tree; thus the trees are simpler, since they now depend only on the input variables $x1, x2, \ldots xm$, but there are *Ny* of them instead of the previous single tree;
- whilst the output state *Z* is produced as before, by synchronous assignment to a register, production of the future state y^+ requires an unconditional jump to the root of the corresponding tree; this has a profound effect on the structure of the flowchart for the *Ny* state trees, and in general will prevent the design of a structured program.

In the treatment that follows we reduce the amount of calculation needed by simplifying the *Ny* state trees separately and ignoring the possibility of common sub-trees.

5.3.19 Software realization: L3 flowchart

An unstructured **L3** flowchart (*PP4*, Figure 5.46) is constructed as follows:

- the trees *A*, *B* of Figure 5.45 are copied, omitting the assignment y^+ that gives the next state; this is shown inside the dotted lines in Figure 5.46;

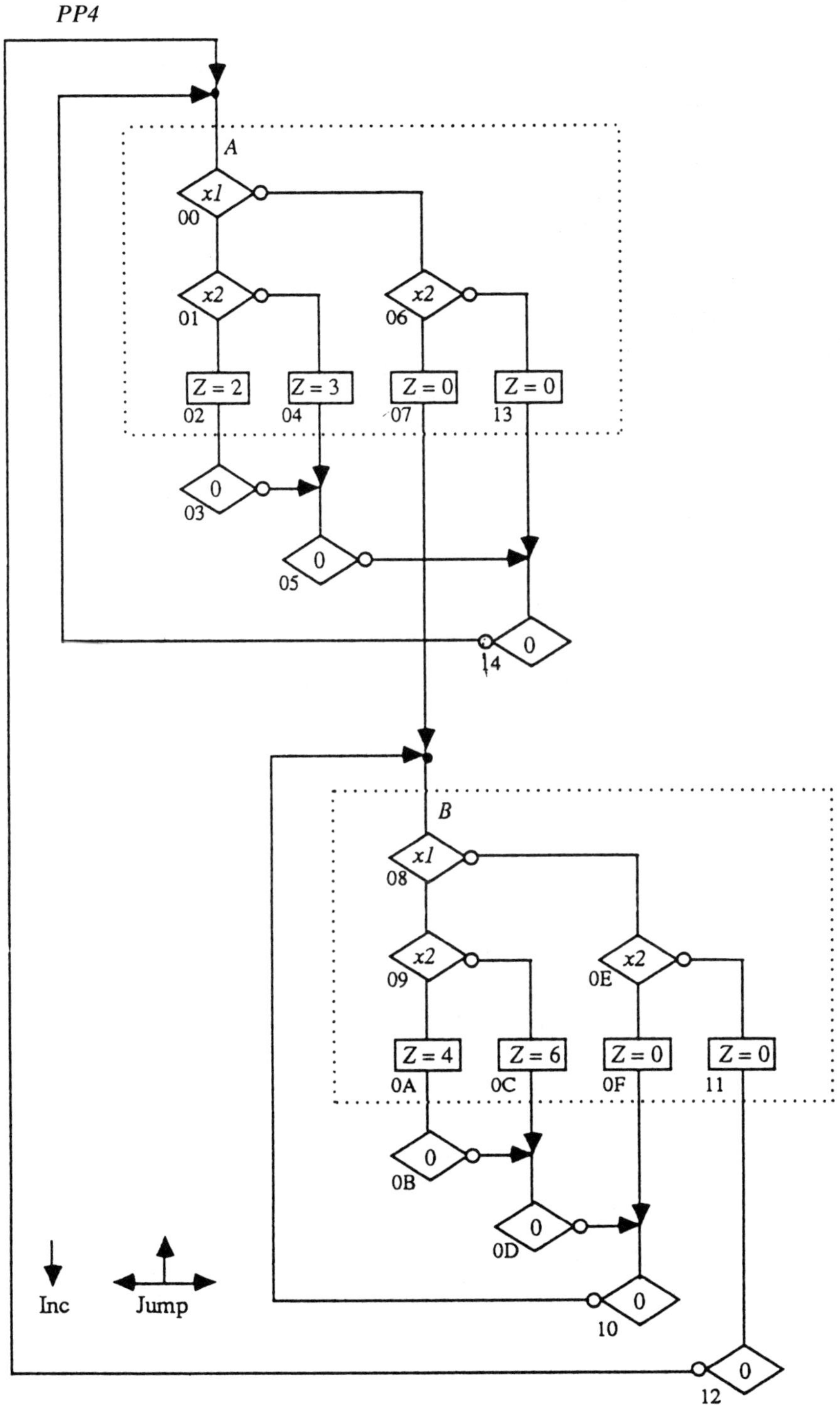

PP4
A
x1
00
x2
01
x2
06
Z = 2
02
Z = 3
04
Z = 0
07
Z = 0
13
0
03
0
05
0
14
B
x1
08
x2
09
x2
0E
Z = 4
0A
Z = 6
0C
Z = 0
0F
Z = 0
11
0
0B
0
0D
0
10
0
12
Inc
Jump

Figure 5.46

- the assignments $y^+ = A$, $y^+ = B$ are implemented by means of unconditional jumps linking the assignment instructions to the roots of the relevant trees;
- in accordance with the rules for **L3**, a jump instruction **GO TO . . .** is introduced at each convergence of two or more incrementation paths and into each loop;
- a possible addressing scheme is set up as in Figure 5.46, in which we have left the conventional representation of incrementation paths (Inc) and jump paths (Jump) unchanged.

The instruction list for the mnemonic **L3** program of Figure 5.47 follows from the flowchart; unlike the latter, the program is not structured and it cannot be expressed as a characteristic equation or in any of the languages **S**, **L4** or **L5**. It can however be executed by the **L3** interpreter of Figure 4.7: since there are no internal variables, there is no hardware feedback from the assignment register to the test variables.

ADR	**L3** (*PP4*)	
00	**IF** *x1*	**ELSE** 06
01	**IF** *x2*	**ELSE** 04
02	DO Z = 2	
03	GO TO 05	
04	DO Z = 3	
05	GO TO 14	
06	**IF** *x2*	**ELSE** 13
07	DO Z = 0	
08	**IF** *x1*	**ELSE** 0E
09	**IF** *x2*	**ELSE** 0C
0A	DO Z = 4	
0B	GO TO 0D	
0C	DO Z = 6	
0D	GO TO 10	
0E	**IF** *x2*	**ELSE** 11
0F	DO Z = 0	
10	GO TO 08	
11	DO Z = 0	
12	GO TO 00	
13	DO Z = 0	
14	GO TO 00	

Figure 5.47

5.3.20 Hardware/software equivalence

The realization in software of the *Ny* trees for a table of *Ny* states is equivalent to the realization in hardware of a sequential system in a 1-out-of-*Ny* code [1] (pp. 211–218), [59] (pp. 261–268): each node of the tree is implemented by a flip-flop provided with an OR gate at the excitation input D, each test element by a demultiplexer having a single control variable, and the set of assignment elements y^+, Z by the combination of one set of OR gates for the output states Z and a second set of OR gates (the flip-flops) for the next states y^+.

5.3.21 Method 2: state trees

This new software method follows from the previous work.

1. The primitive state table or diagram is constructed as before (§5.3.15).
2. The graph of compatible states is deduced, giving a minimal table with *Ny* states; these are represented by *Ny* partial tables.
3. The *Ny* trees for these partial tables are either simplified, to give minimal trees, or reduced, to give minimal diagrams; they can be treated either simultaneously or separately.
4. The assemblage of simplified trees or diagrams is implemented in **L3** by an unstructured flowchart, and addressed.
5. A mnemonic **L3** program is derived from the list of instructions; this can be coded in hexadecimal and executed by the **L3** interpreter.

As for Method 1 of §5.3.15, steps 1 and 2 are those of the general method for synthesis of sequential systems, whilst steps 3 to 5 are particular to the realization of such systems in software.

5.3.22 Method 3: separation of variables

This, which forms a bridge between Methods 1 and 2, keeps the second method's advantage of separate simplification of each state in the table while preserving the properties of structured programming.

1. The primitive state table or diagram is constructed.
2. The graph of compatible states is deduced, leading to a minimal table of *Ny* states which are given a minimal coding; in the example of the starter motor the table *T1* (Figure 5.37) has two states and a single internal variable y, and these states are represented in the partial tables of Figure 5.44.
3. The *Ny* partial trees (diagrams) are simplified (reduced), either

simultaneously or separately: cf. in Figure 5.45, trees *A*, *B* with common sub-tree *sp*.

4. A new main tree is constructed, with *Ny* branches and *Ny* − 1 test elements, providing the choice of any of the *Ny* partial trees through the medium of the *m* internal variables *y1*, *y2*, . . . *ym*; in Figure 5.48, *Ny* = 2, *m* = 1 and only a single internal variable *y* is needed to mediate the choice of one or other of the partial trees *A*, *B*.
5. The assemblage of this main tree and the *Ny* partial trees (possibly decomposed) forms the single tree sought, which also may be decomposed, as in Figure 5.48; this is then realized as a structured flowchart (*PP5*) and given a zig-zag addressing.
6. The characteristic equation is derived from the flowchart, and from

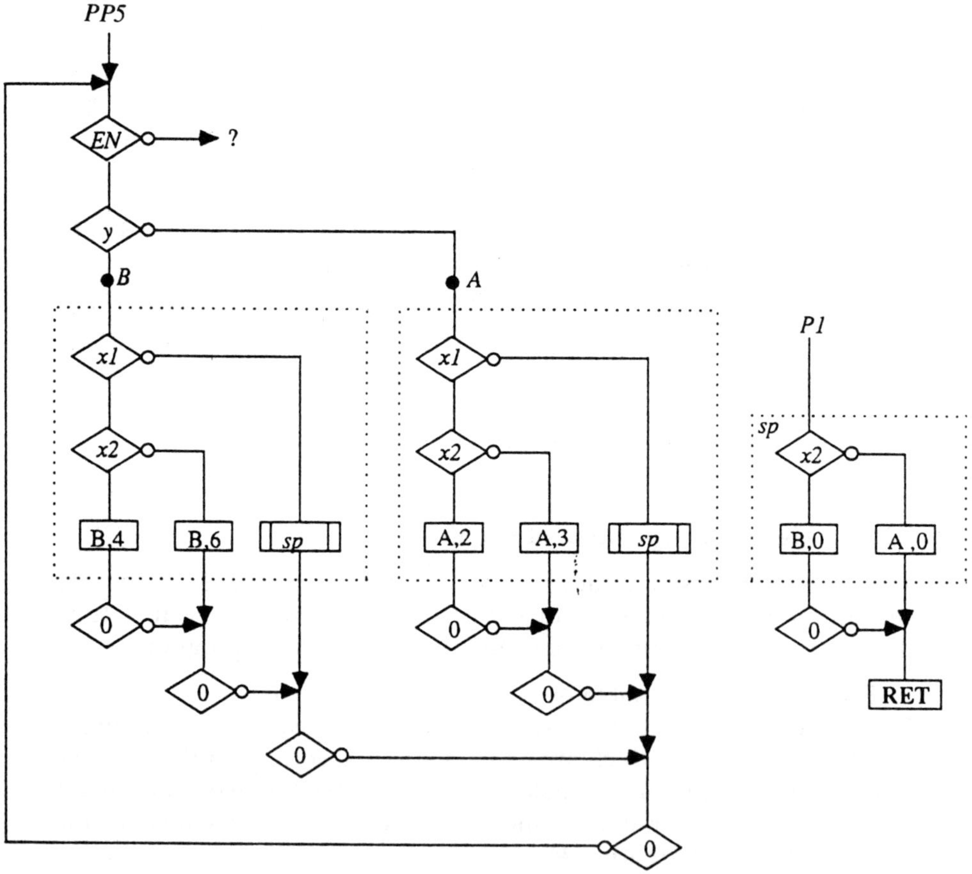

Figure 5.48

this the symbolic program **S** and the mnemonic programs in **L4** and **L5**.

This method is in fact a particular case of the first (§5.3.15), obtained by imposing a minimal coding and a separate realization of each internal state. This leads to a single tree, and thus a structured program, with a strict separation of the *m* internal variables (placed at the root, for selection among the *Ny* partial trees) from the input variables to these partial trees. The result is not, in general, minimal, as can be seen in the present example by comparing Figure 5.48 with Figure 5.42.

5.3.23 General conclusion

For the Method 2 we can say that the representation of the *Ny* rows of the state table by means of *Ny* partial tables, without any coding and therefore without internal variables, results in *Ny* distinct binary decision trees, possibly reduced as diagrams, which can be realized as an unstructured flowchart with *Ny* loops. Breaking down the overall specification (the state table) into *Ny* partial specifications (the internal states) reduces the complexity of the calculation, because of the removal of the internal variables, but precludes structured programming.

Thus **coding of the internal states is the price that has to be paid for structuring an unstructured program**. A new algorithm for systematic structuring can be derived by representing the unstructured program by a state table, coding this by means of the internal variables and applying the first (§5.3.15) or the third (§5.3.22) method; this is described in §§8.5.10–15.

5.3.24 Exercise

Taking note of §5.3.14, construct logic diagrams for the sequential systems defined by the trees *T1* (Figures 5.37, 5.39) and *T3* (Figures 5.40, 5.41), using D flip-flops, OR gates and a demultiplexers with a single control variable.

Repeat the exercise for the trees *A, B* of Figure 5.45, taking account of §5.3.20: does the existence of the common sub-tree *sp* lead to further simplifications? Compare the amounts of hardware required by the different logic diagrams.

5.3.25 Exercise

In the second (state trees) method the realization of the output state *Z*, by a synchronous assignment to a register, is distinct from that of the future state y^+, by an unconditional jump to the root of the tree; and this offers a possibility of further reductions in the number of assignment instructions in the final flowchart. Figure 5.49 is a detail from Figure 5.46, with a simplified but equivalent realization involving a *migration* of the assignment instruction $Z = 0$ to a higher point in the flowchart.

1. Show this change in the partial tables of Figure 5.44.
2. Modify accordingly the flowchart *PP4* of Figure 5.46.
3. Simplify further the flowchart *PP4*, by realizing a single copy of the sub-tree *sp* shown in Figure 5.45 (see also the equivalent Figure 8.14).
4. Address the modified *PP4* and derive the mnemonic **L3** program.

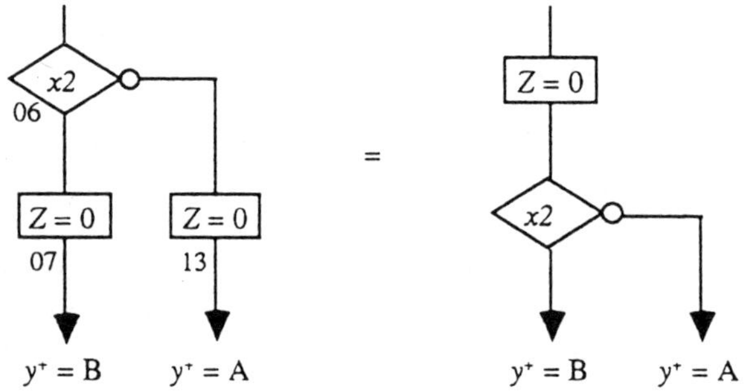

Figure 5.49

5.3.26 Exercise

Application of Method 3 to the starter-motor problem gives the structured flowchart of Figure 5.48; construct the zig-zag addressing schema, the characteristic equation and the symbolic (**S**) and mnemonic (**L4, L5**) programs.

Using the same method try to find two forms of structured flowchart for the non-minimal table *T*2 for the starter (Figure 5.38): one with decompositions (common sub-trees), the other without. Compare the total number of instructions in each solution with that in Figure 5.48.

5.3.27 Exercise

Figure 5.50 is the primitive state table for the rotational direction *discriminator* described in [1] (pp. 196–201) and [59] (pp. 242–249). Find the following realizations.

y^+,Z	$x1,x2$ 00	01	11	10
1	1,0	2,0	–	5,1
2	8,1	2,0	3,0	–
3	–	7,1	3,0	4,0
4	1,0	–	6,1	4,0
5	1,0	–	6,1	5,1
6	–	7,1	6,1	4,0
7	8,1	7,1	3,0	–
8	8,1	2,0	–	5,1
y				

Figure 5.50

1. The tree, decomposed or not, for the primitive table, by Method 1.
2. The tree, decomposed or not, for the minimal reduced table, by Method 1. Can it be shown that this is a minimal tree for the sequential system?
3. The state trees, reduced or not, by Method 2; show any possible migrations of assignment instructions (cf. §5.3.25).
4. The tree, decomposed or not, for the minimal reduced table, with a minimal code, by Method 3.

In each case give either a structured flowchart with zig-zag addressing, the characteristic equation and the **S**, **L4** and **L5** programs, or an unstructured, addressed flowchart and the **L3** program. Compare the total number of instructions in the four solutions.

5.3.28 Exercise

An electronic lock can be opened ($Z1 = 1$) only by means of a particular sequence of input states $x1, x2$; any other sequence will set off an alarm ($Z2 = 1$). Two further input sequences will turn off the alarm and close the lock respectively, returning the system to its initial state. On the assumption that $x1, x2$ cannot change simultaneously the primitive states table is as in Figure 5.51: find and compare four different realizations of this, as defined in §5.3.27.

The table of Figure 5.51 shows that this sequential system has an important special feature: the output states $Z = Z1, Z2$ depend only on the internal states y and not on the input states $x1, x2$. Such a system is

y^+,Z1,Z2	x1,x2 00	01	11	10
1	1,00	2,00	–	5,0Φ
2	5,0Φ	2,00	3,00	–
3	–	4,Φ0	3,00	5,0Φ
4	7,10	4,10	5,ΦΦ	–
5	5,01	6,01	5,01	5,01
6	1,0Φ	6,01	5,01	–
7	7,10	8,10	–	5,ΦΦ
8	1,Φ0	8,10	5,ΦΦ	–
y				

Figure 5.51

called a *Moore machine*. Show that for any such system Method 2 leads to *Ny* trees, each containing a single output state *Z* which is determined by the migrations (§5.3.25) in the partial tables.

5.4 SEQUENTIAL SYSTEMS WITH SYNCHRONOUS BEHAVIOUR

5.4.1 Example: a reversible counter

A synchronous system, driven by an external clock signal *H*, is to generate:

for $x = 0$ the sequence $Q_1, Q_0 = 00 \rightarrow 01 \rightarrow 10 \rightarrow 11 \rightarrow 00$

for $x = 1$ the inverse $Q_1, Q_0 = 00 \rightarrow 11 \rightarrow 10 \rightarrow 01 \rightarrow 00$

Figures 5.52, 5.53 give the state diagram and table respectively, in which the role of the clock signal *H* (Figure 5.54) is understood: at each rise $H = 0 \rightarrow 1$ the present state Q changes to a next state Q^+, the next in the sequence. Such a device is called a *4-state reversible counter*.

5.4.2 Definition: synchronous behaviour

A synchronous sequential system, with a logic diagram such as Figure 5.34, is said to have a *synchronous behaviour if* **the output state** $Z = Z1, Z2, \ldots Zr$ **depends on both the durations of the input states** $x1, x2, \ldots xn$ **and the order in which they occur,** where the duration is measured in periods of the clock pulse *H*.

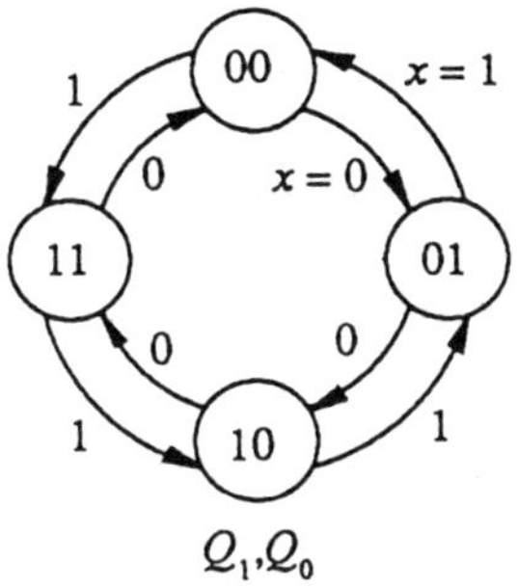

Figure 5.52

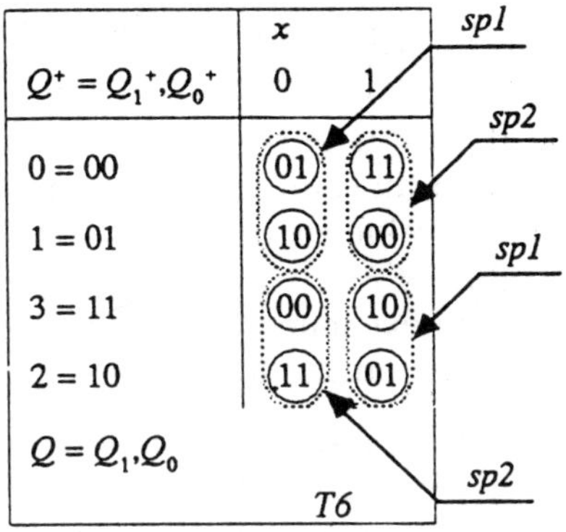

Figure 5.53

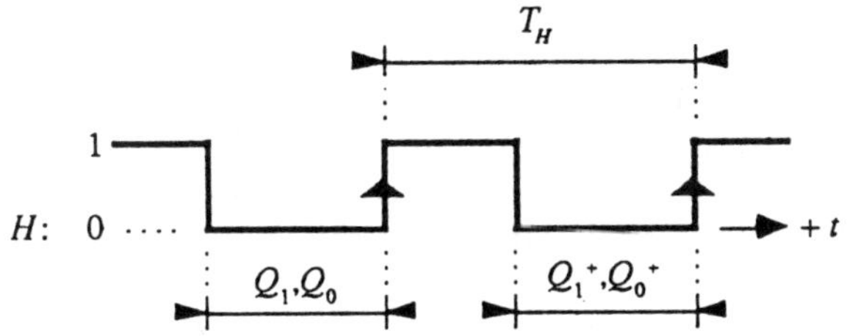

Figure 5.54

Thus for the table of Figure 5.53 the same input state, $x = 0$ for example, will give a new output state Q_1, Q_0, different from the preceding one, at each clock pulse; and we say that the behaviour of the counter is *synchronous*, as distinct from the asynchronous behaviour of §5.3.3 in which successive input states are not distinguished if they are identical. Synchronous behaviour can be expressed also as the absence of stable total states (§5.3.1) from one or more rows in the state table.

5.4.3 Assumptions

Thus a system with synchronous behaviour distinguishes between identical successive input states, that is, identical input states separated by a single period T_H of the clock signal H. This signal is therefore a new explicit variable for which a test must be provided in any software realization, so that the necessary distinction can be made; and from now on we shall distinguish between *CK*, the clock signal which drives all the flip-flops and registers of the interpreter (the hardware level) and H, which we call the *synchronizing signal* (the software level). We now assume that:

1. the value of the synchronizing signal H changes much more rapidly than those of the input variables $x1, x2, \ldots xn$;
2. the value of the clock signal CK changes much more rapidly than that of H;
3. the next state y^+ is determined immediately after the rise $H = 0 \rightarrow 1$, based on the total state x, y at that instant.

The third assumption is in accordance with the use, in the hardware, of *edge-triggered* D *flip-flops* [1] (pp. 270–271), [59] (pp. 333–334), for which the next state Q^+ depends on both the present state Q and the state of excitation of D measured at the instant of the clock pulse rise.

5.4.4 Representation: state table tree

The state table for the reversible counter, *T6* in Figure 5.53, is a reduced table and already has a minimal coding since Q_1, Q_0 are the two internal variables for the device. Further, the output state Z coincides with the internal state Q, so the system is a Moore machine as defined in §5.3.28.

Application of the Karnaugh map method of §2.2.13 to *T6* gives a decomposition into a main tree *pp* and two sub-trees *sp1*, *sp2*, as in Figure 5.55.

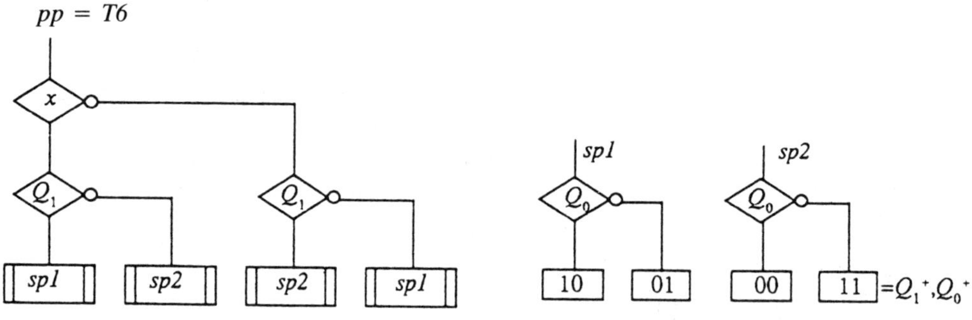

Figure 5.55

5.4.5 Software realization: L4 structured flowchart

The construction of a structured flowchart *PP6* in **L4** (Figure 5.56) for the trees of Figure 5.55 proceeds as in §5.3.10:

- the tests in *pp*, *sp1*, *sp2* are closed;

- the main tree *pp* is turned into a closed loop by introducing a test for the auxiliary variable *EN*;
- each procedure (*P1* for *sp1*, *P2* for *sp2*) is terminated with a **RET** instruction;
- a double test of the synchronizing signal *H* is introduced, to meet the needs of synchronous behaviour (cf. §5.4.3); this, in **L4**, is performed by the sub-program *SP* and is equivalent to that of Figure 3.10 (in **L1**) and to that of Figure 4.4 (in **L3**).

After the zig-zag address scheme has been set up the characteristic equations are determined:

$$PP6 = \{_{EN}\ \{_{H}\ \}\ \{_{H'}\ \} <_x <_{Q_1} \textbf{call } P1 \,|\, \textbf{call } P2 > | <_{Q_1} \textbf{call } P2 \,|\, \textbf{call } P1 >>\}$$

$$P1 = <_{Q_0} \textbf{do } 10 \,|\, \textbf{do } 01>;$$

$$P2 = <_{Q_0} \textbf{do } 00 \,|\, \textbf{do } 11>;. \qquad (5.20)$$

This is equivalent to the symbolic program **S** of Figure 5.57, from which the mnemonic programs in **L4** and **L5** can be derived. Provided that the assumption (2) of §5.4.3 holds, the **L4** program, after coding in hexadecimal, can be executed by the **L3** interpreter INT3 of Figure 4.7.

5.4.6 Comments

The sub-program *SP* is located in the flowchart of Figure 5.56 so that assumption (3) of §5.4.3 is valid; this has these consequences:

- at the rise $H = 0 \rightarrow 1$ the counter goes from address 03 to 05;
- the main tree *pp* and one or other of the sub-trees *sp1*, *sp2* perform the evaluation of the total state $x, y = x, Q_1, Q_0$ and then generate the new internal state $y^+ = Q_1{}^+, Q_0{}^+$;
- the counter then returns to the sub-program *SP* and waits there until the next rise of *H*.

In contrast to the **L3** realization given in Figure 4.4, both the synchronizing signal *H* and its complement *H'* are needed here: this is to satisfy the requirements of the **while . . . do . . .** construction used in the **L4** language (Figure 5.26).

5.4.7 Hardware/software equivalence

The main tree *pp* and the sub-trees *sp1*, *sp2* are together equivalent to the combinational system (C) of the hardwired sequential system of Figure 5.34; they can be realized as an assemblage {DEMUX, OR}, as in §2.4.2, and generate the excitation variables $Q_1{}^+ = D_1$, $Q_0{}^+ = D_0$ for

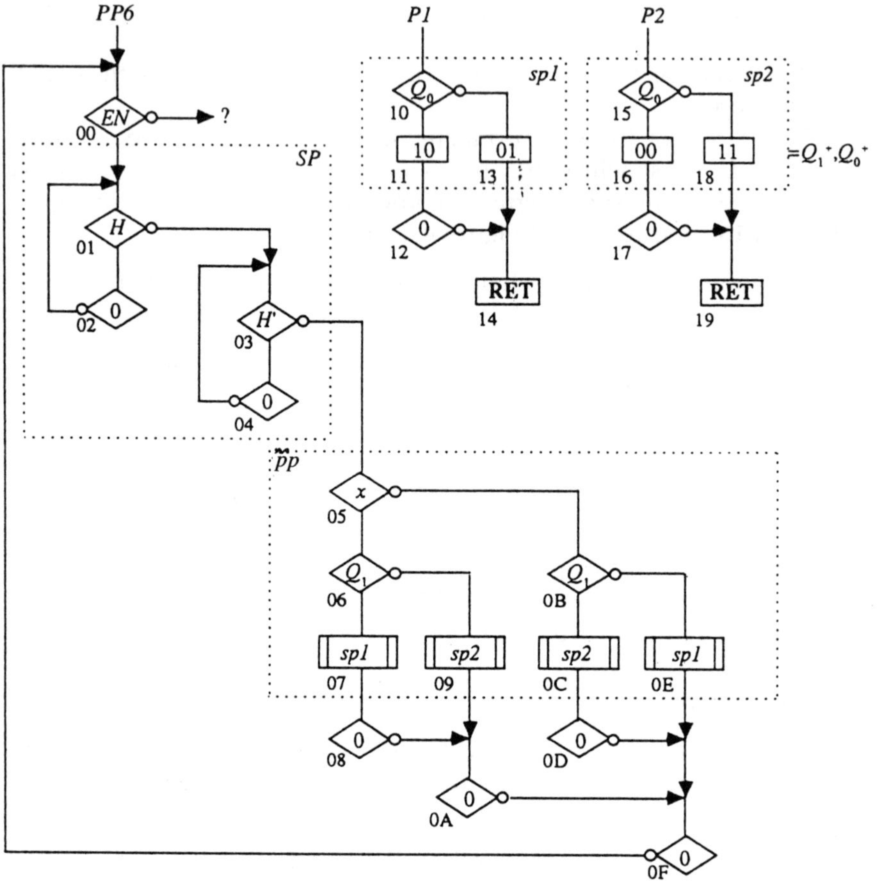

Figure 5.56

the flip-flops. The provision of two edge-triggered D flip-flops, clocked by the signal *H*, fulfills the requirements of assumption (3) of §5.4.3 and in effect implements the sub-program *SP* of Figure 5.56; this sub-program is equivalent to the double master/slave latch which is the essence of each flip-flop (cf. Figure 1.29).

5.4.8 Method 1: state table tree

Whilst the synchronizing signal *H* can be ignored in considering asychronous behaviour, it must be used explicitly when synchronous behaviour is concerned; the method of §5.3.15 has therefore to be modified, and in fact only a single modification is needed, to step (4), which becomes:

Code	*ADR*	L4	S	Code	*ADR*	L5
		PROGRAM *PP6*	*PP6=*	F-02	00	**program** *PP6*
0110	00	**IF** *EN* **ELSE** ?	$\{_{EN}$	7--1	01	**while** *EN*
0203	01	**IF** *H* **ELSE** 03	$\{_{H}$	7--2	02	**while** *H*
0801	02	**GO TO** 01	}	6---	03	**end while**
0305	03	**IF** *H'* **ELSE** 05	$\{_{H'}$	7--3	04	**while** *H'*
0803	04	**GO TO** 03	}	6---	05	**end while**
040B	05	**IF** *x* **ELSE** 0B	$<_x$	B--4	06	**if** *x*
0609	06	**IF** Q_1 **ELSE** 09	$<_{Q1}$	B--6	07	**if** Q_1
C-10	07	**CALL** *P1* = 10	**call** *P1*	3-FF	08	**call** *P1*
080A	08	**GO TO** 0A	$\vert$	A---	09	**else**
C-15	09	**CALL** *P2* = 15	**call** *P2*	3-FE	0A	**call** *P2*
		ENDIF	>	9---	0B	**endif**
080F	0A	**GO TO** 0F	$\vert$	A---	0C	**else**
060E	0B	**IF** Q_1 **ELSE** 0E	$<_{Q1}$	B--6	0D	**if** Q_1
C-15	0C	**CALL** *P2* = 15	**call** *P2*	3-FE	0E	**call** *P2*
080F	0D	**GO TO** 0F	$\vert$	A---	0F	**else**
C-10	0E	**CALL** *P1* = 10	**call** *P1*	3-FF	10	**call** *P1*
		ENDIF	>	9---	11	**endif**
		ENDIF	>	9---	12	**endif**
0800	0F	**GO TO** 00	}	6---	13	**end while**
		PROCEDURE *P1*	*P1=*	D-FF	14	**procedure** *P1*
0513	10	**IF** Q_0 **ELSE** 13	$<_{Q0}$	B--5	15	**if** Q_0
1102	11	**DO** 10	**do** 10	2102	16	**do** 10
0814	12	**GO TO** 14	$\vert$	A---	17	**else**
1101	13	**DO** 01	**do** 01	2101	18	**do** 01
		ENDIF	>	9---	19	**endif**
A---	14	**RET**	;	C---	1A	**end procedure**
		PROCEDURE *P2*	*P2=*	D-FE	1B	**procedure** *P2*
0518	15	**IF** Q_0 **ELSE** 18	$<_{Q0}$	B--5	1C	**if** Q_0
1100	16	**DO** 00	**do** 00	2100	1D	**do** 00
0819	17	**GO TO** 19	$\vert$	A---	1E	**else**
1103	18	**DO** 11	**do** 11	2103	1F	**do** 11
		ENDIF	>	9---	20	**endif**
A---	19	**RET**	;	C---	21	**end procedure**
		END PROGRAM	.	E---	22	**end program**

Figure 5.57

4a. The minimal or quasi-minimal tree, possibly decomposed, is realized as a structured flowchart, after the various choices and the loop have been closed; **the sub-program** *SP* **is inserted, to provide the double test of the synchronizing signal** *H*; a zig-zag addressing is applied.

In practice *SP* would be placed immediately before the tree (possibly decomposed) of the state table (Figure 5.56), thus satisfying assumption (3) of §5.4.3 which implies the use of edge-triggered D flip-flops. The use of special types of flip-flop (for example *data lock-out flip-flops*) could cause the position of this sub-program, or a part of it, to shift: this is the subject of the exercise of §5.4.19.

5.4.9 Representation: state trees

There are four internal states in the table of Figure 5.53, each of which can be represented by a partial table giving, for each input state x, the resultant state $y^+, Z = Q_1{}^+, Q_0{}^+; Q_1, Q_0$ (cf. Moore machine, §5.4.4).

As an example, Figure 5.58 is the partial table for the state $Q_1, Q_0 = 00$, for which the output state Z is identical to the internal state Q_1, Q_0. Application of the Karnaugh map method (§2.1.14) gives a partitioning into two blocks, that is, a tree with two branches, as in Figure 5.59.

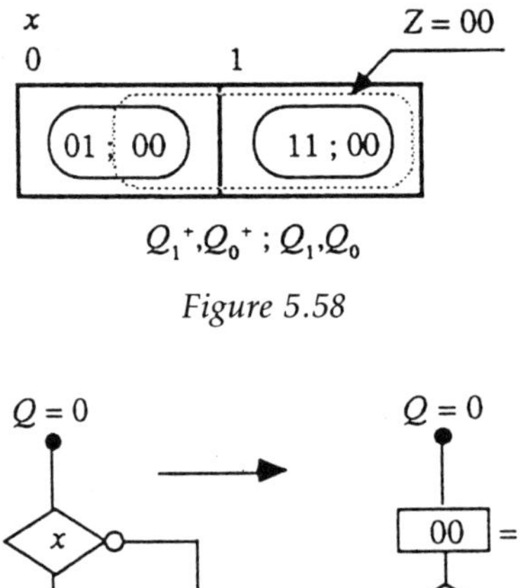

Figure 5.58

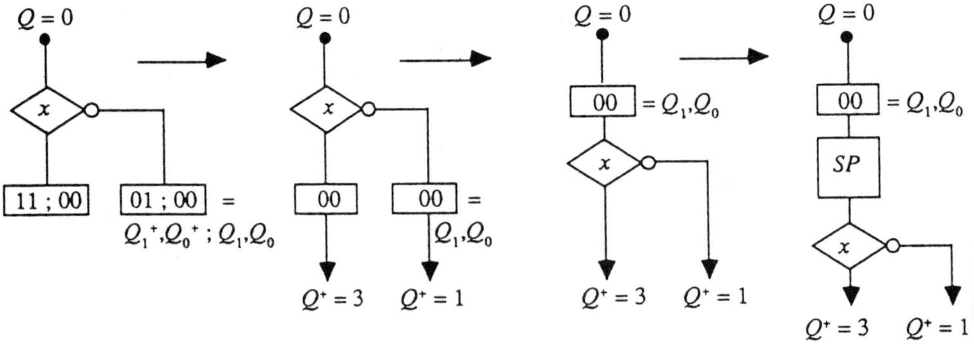

Figure 5.59

5.4.10 Software realization: L3 flowchart

Using the representations of Figures 5.59, 5.61 we can construct an unstructured **L3** flowchart *PP7* for the counter as follows.

1. The four partial trees, similar to Figure 5.59, are copied, omitting the assignment $Q_1{}^+, Q_0{}^+$ of the next state.
2. Since in a Moore machine the output state Z is the same for all input states x, the two assignment elements $Z = Q_1, Q_0$ in each partial tree can be replaced by a single resultant element: this is the migration shown in Figure 5.49 and discussed in §5.3.25.
3. To meet the essential needs of synchronous behaviour and assumption (3) of §5.4.3, a sub-program *SP* that performs the double test of the synchronizing signal H is inserted in each partial tree between the assignment and test elements.
4. The assignments $Q^+ = 3$, $Q^+ = 1$ etc. are realized by means of unconditional jumps linking the output of each partial tree to the root of the corresponding tree.
5. A jump instruction **GO TO . . .** is inserted at each convergence of incrementation paths and in each loop in such a path, as is required by **L3**.

Figure 5.61 is the flowchart obtained, in which the sub-program *SP*, identical with that of Figure 4.4, is labelled; the drawing also makes clear the 4-slice iterative structure.

Provided that assumption (2) of §5.4.3 holds, the **L3** interpreter INT3 of Figure 4.7 can execute *PP7*.

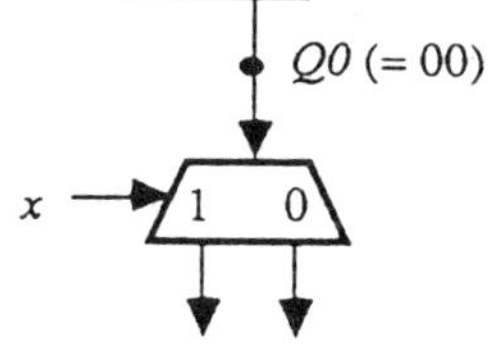

Figure 5.60

5.4.11 Hardware/software equivalence

The software realization of the four partial trees of table *T6* is equivalent to the hardware realization of a synchronous sequential system in a 1-out-of-4 code. Each slice in the flowchart Figure 5.61 is equivalent to an assemblage such as Figure 5.60, of a D flip-flop for the assignment instruction and the double test of the synchronizing signal *H*, an OR gate for the convergences of unconditional jumps, and a demultiplexer driven by the variable *x*, for testing this variable. Assumption (3) of §5.4.3 requires the flip-flop to be edge-triggered.

5.4.12 Method 2: state trees

Again only a single step in the corresponding method for systems with asynchronous behaviour, §5.3.21, has to be changed; we now have:

4a. **a sub-program** *SP* **that performs the double test of the synchronizing signal** *H* **is incorporated into each partial tree or diagram**; the collection of *Ny* simplified partial trees (diagrams) is realized by an unstructured flowchart in **L3** and addressed.

If a behaviour similar to that of edge-triggered flip-flops is required, then in response to any migration of the output state *Z*, *SP* must be located in the partial trees so that assumption (3) of §5.4.3 continues to hold.

5.4.13 Method 3: separation of variables

Only step 5 of the corresponding method for asynchronous behaviour, §5.3.22, has to be changed; we now have, according to the modifications of §5.4.8:

5a. the assemblage of this main tree and the *Ny* partial trees, possibly decomposed, forms the single tree sought, which also may be decomposed; **after incorporating the sub-program** *SP* **for the double test of the synchronizing signal** *H* this is realized as a structured flowchart and given a zig-zag addressing.

5.4.14 Application: counters

p-state counters (§3.1.2) are a particular case of sequential systems with synchronous behaviour, one for which there are no input variables; thus they can be treated by any of the methods developed for the general case.

Method 1, §5.4.8, always gives a structured program, consisting of a main tree, possibly with sub-trees, and a sub-program *SP* that tests the

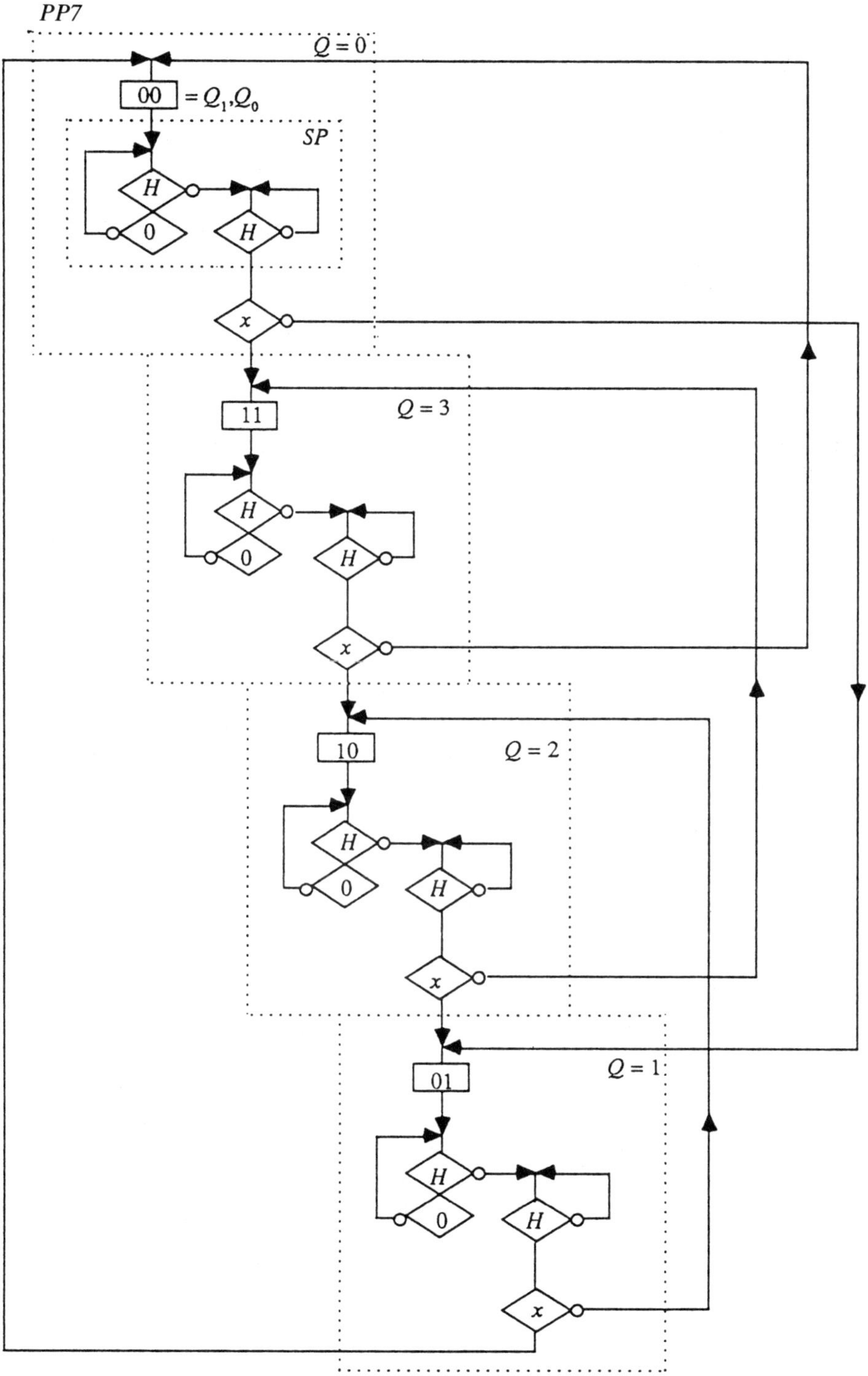

Figure 5.61

synchronizing signal H (Figure 5.56). This way of proceeding is equivalent to software implementation with a decision tree (section 3.2, Figure 3.10).

Method 2, §5.4.12, gives an unstructured program consisting of Ny partial trees or diagrams, each with a sub-program SP as before (Figure 5.61); this is equivalent to software implementation with a linear flowchart (section 3.1, Figure 3.5). A variant derived by implementing SP as a procedure (see Exercise §5.4.18) is equivalent to implementing the counter as a procedure (see section 3.3, Figure 3.16).

5.4.15 Conclusion

In contrast to the construction of hardwired logic systems, where the same methods can be used for both asynchronous and synchronous behaviour, in the software realization of synchronous systems the synchronizing signal H plays an explicit role which is implemented in the form of a double test; the location of this test in the program depends on the assumptions made concerning the timing of the signals, and possibly also on the type of flip-flop used. If there are any doubts concerning the role of H and the location of the double test an equivalent sequential system with asynchronous behaviour can always be constructed, by drawing up a new state table in which H is an explicit input variable; the required result is then obtained by the methods developed for systems with asynchronous behaviour, given in section 5.3: see Exercise §5.4.20.

Whether the behaviour is synchronous or asynchronous, the general type of result produced by each method will always be the same: minimal structured program (Method 1), separate calculation of each state by an unstructured program (Method 2) or by a structured program (Method 3).

The need to set up one or more state tables limits these methods to problems with only a small number of input and/or internal variables. An important point is that each resultant state can be realized either as a simple assignment instruction, as in the examples of the starter motor and the reversible counter, or as a procedure or a sub-program, each in turn decomposable. Thus a complex but hierarchically-structured program can be expressed as a succession of state tables, or truth tables, of moderate size: this approach is the subject of Chapter 6.

5.4.16 Bibliography

Methods 1 (state table) and 2 (state trees) are due to Mange and Sanchez [82]; they are based on the equivalence between a sequential system, described by a state table or diagram, and a program, described by a flowchart: [70] (pp. 285–296), [95] (pp. 51–52, 118–125), [96] (pp. 11–64), [132] (pp. 111–119), [133] (pp. 131–139). Method 3 (separation of variables), due to Sanchez is illustrated by the design of a microprogrammed watch [61]. Other examples of the application of Method 1 are given in [47], [48] and [49], in which the structured languages **L4**, **L5** (MICROPASCAL) are used and an interpreter for **L4** and a compiler for **L5** are described.

Method 2 is discussed also in [86] and [144], where the use of trees, diagrams and binary decision machines is extended to cases in which K (>1) variables have to be tested simultaneously. Grass [107] also treats the software realization of sequential systems and the equivalences between Mealy and Moore machines (§§5.3.1, 5.3.28 respectively), and pays special attention to the algorithms associated with Method 2.

The classic work of Clare [16] and the use of *Algorithms State Machine (ASM)* charts to describe sequential systems are particular cases of Method 2 in which each internal state is realized separately and the only test variables are the inputs. An industrial application, the design of a signature analyser, is described in [87] (pp. 221–245), and [54] (pp. 457–465) introduces a variant of ASM diagrams, *MDS — Mnemonic Documented State* diagrams.

5.4.17 Exercise

Construct a logic diagram for the trees *pp*, *sp1*, *sp2* for the reversible counter of Figure 5.55, using D flip-flops, 1-variable demultiplexers and OR gates (§5.4.7).

Each slice of a hardware realization equivalent to that of §5.4.11 consists of a flip-flop and a multiplexer driven by the variable x; construct a logic diagram of this type that implements the iterative flowchart of Figure 5.61 and show how this can be realized by the bi-directional shift register of §1.2.14 (Figure 1.40).

5.4.18 Exercise

1. Give a suitable addressing scheme for the flowchart Figure 5.61 and write the mnemonic **L3** program.
2. Give a variant of this flowchart in which the double test of H in *SP* is performed by a procedure. Draw the unstructured flowchart, address it and write the **L3** program.
3. Find a further variant by using Method 3 (§5.4.13) to produce a structured flowchart; compare the number of instructions with those for the solution given by Methods 1 and 2, Figures 5.56, 5.61

respectively and by (2) above. Give a zig-zag addressing and write the symbolic program **S** and the mnemonic **L4**, **L5** programs.

5.4.19 Exercise

A *data lock-out flip-flop* [1] (p. 275), [59] (p. 338) has these characteristics: the values of the excitation variables (D for example) are stored at the rise of the clock signal CK, and the next state Q^+ is not issued until the next fall of this signal.

Revise the software realizations of the 4-state reversible counter to allow for the use of such flip-flops and give the flowcharts corresponding to the use of the three methods described (Figures 5.56 and 5.61, Exercise §5.4.18).

5.4.20 Exercise

A 3-state counter, driven by an external clock signal H, is to generate the following binary sequence:

$$Q_1, Q_0 = 00 \to 01 \to 10 \to 00$$

with each rise $H = 0 \to 1$ changing the present state to the next in the sequence.

Construct the state table, involving H explicitly as an input variable, and realize this table:

1. as a structured **L4** flowchart, by Method 1, §5.3.15;
2. as an unstructured **L3** flowchart, by Method 2, §5.3.21.

Show that the second method gives a linear flowchart similar to Figure 3.5, and therefore justifies the introduction of the double test of H required by sequential systems with synchronous behaviour (§§5.4.5, 4.5.10).

5.4.21 Exercise

The following ([81]) is an account of a haunted house.

Dear Charles

I bought this old house some time ago, and it has turned out to be haunted by two voices from beyond the grave — a ribald song and a sardonic laugh: it's practically uninhabitable. But I'm not entirely without hope, because I've found that they obey certain rules which, though complicated, are infallible, and I can affect what they do by playing the organ or burning incense. This is what I've found.

In any one minute each voice either sounds or does not, and what each does in the next minute depends on what has happened during the present minute:

- *each does the same — sounds or keeps quiet — as it did before, unless during that previous minute I played the organ so loudly as to drown the laugh, in which case the song does the opposite;*
- *if I'm burning incense the laugh sounds or doesn't according as the laugh sounded or didn't in the previous minute — that is, it imitates the laugh after a minute's delay; if I'm not burning incense the laugh always does the opposite to what the song did.*

I've been hearing both the song and the laugh, together, for some minutes. I'd be very grateful if you could tell me how I should go about things with the organ and the incense so that I get some peace and quiet in the shortest delays.

Represent this haunted house as a sequential system, with two input variables O, I (Organ, Incense) and two internal variables $y1 = S$, $y2 = L$ (Song, Laugh) which are also the output variables — a Moore machine. Find four different realizations of this:

1. The tree, decomposed or not, of the reduced minimal state table, using Method 1.
2. The state trees, reduced or not, using Method 2. Use the special properties of a Moore machine (§5.3.28) to show the migrations of the output states.
3. As (2), but using a procedure call for the double test of the synchronizing signal.
4. As (1), but using Method 3.

For each solution give either a structured flowchart, with zig-zag addressing, characteristic equation and the **S**, **L4** and **L5** programs, or an unstructured flowchart, with addressing and **L3** program. Compare the total numbers of instructions in the different solutions.

5.4.22 Exercise

A *sequence detector* [1] (pp. 218–222), [59] (pp. 270–274) is a sequential system with a reading head for two variables, which at every clock time reads a new input state $x = x1, x2$; the output state Z takes the value 1 at each clock time that terminates any sequence $x = 00 \rightarrow 01 \rightarrow 10$. Given the state table of Figure 5.62, find and compare four different realizations as in §5.4.21.

y^+,Z	x1,x2 00	01	11	10
0	1,0	0,0	0,0	0,0
1	1,0	2,0	0,0	0,0
2	1,0	0,0	0,0	0,1
y				

Figure 5.62

5.4.23 Exercise

A sequential system providing a *programmable delay* has two inputs *x1*, *x2* and an output Z such that:

- if *x2* = 0 the value of Z at the present clock time is that of *x1* the previous clock time;
- if *x2* = 1, the value of Z at the present clock time is that of *x1* two clock times earlier.

Set up the state table, possibly reduced, and give and compare four solutions as in §5.4.21.

5.4.24 Exercise

A *programmable synchronous counter* provides four functions: no action (quiescent state), counting by 2, by 3 or by 4. Set up the state table and give and compare four solutions as in §5.4.21.

5.5 AN APPLICATION: COMBINATIONAL SYSTEMS

5.5.1 Introduction

Method 1, §§5.3.10–12, for constructing the structured flowchart and **L4**, **L5** programs for a sequential system with asynchronous behaviour, can be applied without restriction to combinational systems. We shall now consider two cases, iterative (§5.5.6–7) and non-iterative (§5.5.2) respectively.

5.5.2 Method: general combinational system

The Karnaugh map method gives either a simplified tree (§2.1.14) or a reduced diagram (§2.2.13), and the latter is always equivalent to a decomposition into a main tree and a number of sub-trees — excluding the trivial case of trees with only a single element (§2.2.3). The structured program for an arbitrary combinatorial system is found as follows.

1. The system is represented by a main tree and, if necessary, one or more sub-trees.
2. The tests in these trees are closed in the opposite order to that in which they were opened.
3. The main tree is made into a closed loop by introducing the auxiliary variable EN.
4. Each procedure, realizing a sub-tree, is terminated by a **RET** instruction.
5. The structured flowchart is given a zig-zag addressing, usually with the test of $xi = EN$ at $ADR = 0$, and the characteristic equation is determined for the main program and the procedures.
6. The symbolic program **S** and the mnemonic programs in **L4**, **L5** are deduced.

The resulting **L4** program can be executed by the **L3** interpreter of Figure 4.7.

5.5.3 Exercise

Apply the above method to these cases:

(a) The discriminator for the calendar months given either by the diagram of Figure 2.41 or by the equivalent decomposition of Figure 2.40.
(b) The function MAJORITY given by the diagram of Figure 2.46.

For each give the structured flowchart, the characteristic equation, the symbolic program and the mnemonic **L4**, **L5** programs. Give also the depth of stack required, that is, the maximum number of nested procedures.

5.5.4 Comment

The maximum number of nested procedures can be greater than the depth m of the stack in the interpreter used ($m = 4$ for the **L3** interpreter of Figure 4.7), and in such a case some procedures will have to be deleted. If a procedure is called by p different call instructions it can always be implemented as p copies of itself, replacing the separate calls.

5.5.5 A project

The method of composition of diagrams described in section 8.4 is perticulary well suited to programming logical expressions involving a large number of different variables but a small number of letters (i.e. a small number of occurrences of these variables). The project is the study of the application of structured programming to this method, with the following suggested procedure.

1. Construct the set of diagrams of Figure 8.27, using the method of §5.5.2. Reduce the number of procedures by deleting those that are called only once, so as to reduce the depth of the stack and also the total number of instructions.
2. For the example of Figure 8.27 express each elementary composition (product or sum) as a system of characteristic equations. For example, the logical expression

   $$Z6 = Z3 + Z4 = g' + hi \tag{5.21}$$

   is equivalent to the characteristic equations, and therefore structured programs

   $$sp3 = <_g \mathbf{do}\ 0 \mid \mathbf{do}\ 1>; \tag{5.22}$$

   $$sp4 = <_h <_i \mathbf{do}\ 1 \mid \mathrm{do}\ 0> \mid \mathbf{do}\ 0>; \tag{5.23}$$

   the sum composition *sp6* of which is obtained by replacing all the assignments [0] of *Z3* by the diagram *Z4*, that is, by replacing every **do** 0 in *sp3* by **call** *sp4* (cf. §8.4.3):

   $$sp6 = <_g \mathbf{call}\ sp4 \mid \mathbf{do}\ 1>; \tag{5.24}$$

   The pair of characteristic equations (5.23), (5.24) thus represents the composition of diagrams that realizes the logical equation (5.21).
3. Investigate the possibility of generalizing these results to derive a method for obtaining for an arbitrary logical expression, involving only the operators AND, OR, NOT, the characteristic equations for a composition of diagrams and from this a structured flowchart.

5.5.6 Reminder: iterative combinational system

Suppose an iterative combinational system has n slices; we have already shown (§3.5.6) that each slice, of rank k, can be described by a state table with Ny rows. For example, the comparator for two numbers studied in section 3.5 has $n = 4$ slices (Figure 3.38) and each slice can be described by a state table with $Ny = 3$ rows (Figure 3.40).

Since any iterative combinational system can be represented by a state table, it is clearly possible to find a realization of such a system by the methods already given for sequential systems. Only a few minor modifications need to be made, to allow for purely combinational behaviour of the new systems.

5.5.7 Method 1: state table tree

For the example of the comparator (section 3.5), Method 1 of §5.3.15 suggests the following approach.

1. Set up the state table for a slice of index k, based on the specification given (Figure 3.40 in this example).
2. After possible reduction of this table, find a coding that minimizes the number of distinct resultant states y^+, Z: that is, the number of branches in the tree. Thus Figure 3.45 represents a minimal code, obtained by using two internal variables G_{k+1}, E_{k+1}; and since this is a Moore machine the resultant and next states coincide, $y^+, Z = y^+ = Z_k$.
3. Realize the minimal tree, possibly decomposed, by a structured flowchart, after closing the choices in succession (Figure 5.63). This gives what is called a *single-track flowchart*, because it has only one input one output terminal.
4. Replicate this flowchart n times (for n slices) with suitable values for the test variables xi_k and the assignment registers $REG[j, k]$. Loop this set of n flowcharts on to the test of the auxiliary variable EN.
5. Give a zig-zag addressing to this structured global flowchart and construct the characteristic equation.
6. Derive the symbolic program **S** and hence the mnemonic **L4**, **L5** programs.

As before, the **L4** program can be executed by the **L3** interpreter of Figure 4.7.

5.5.8 Comment

The structured flowchart thus obtained has n slices. A program of this type can be simplified drastically by realizing a single slice — e.g. $COMP(A_k, B_k)$ in Figure 5.63 — as a procedure with a parameter $P(k)$ and calling this n times by the main program (§3.5.7). This requires an extension to the **L4**, **L5** languages, which is the subject of the exercise of §5.5.11.

5.5.9 Method 2: state trees

With the same example, Method 2 of §5.3.21 suggests the following approach.

1. Set up the state table for a slice of index k, based on the specification given (Figure 3.40).

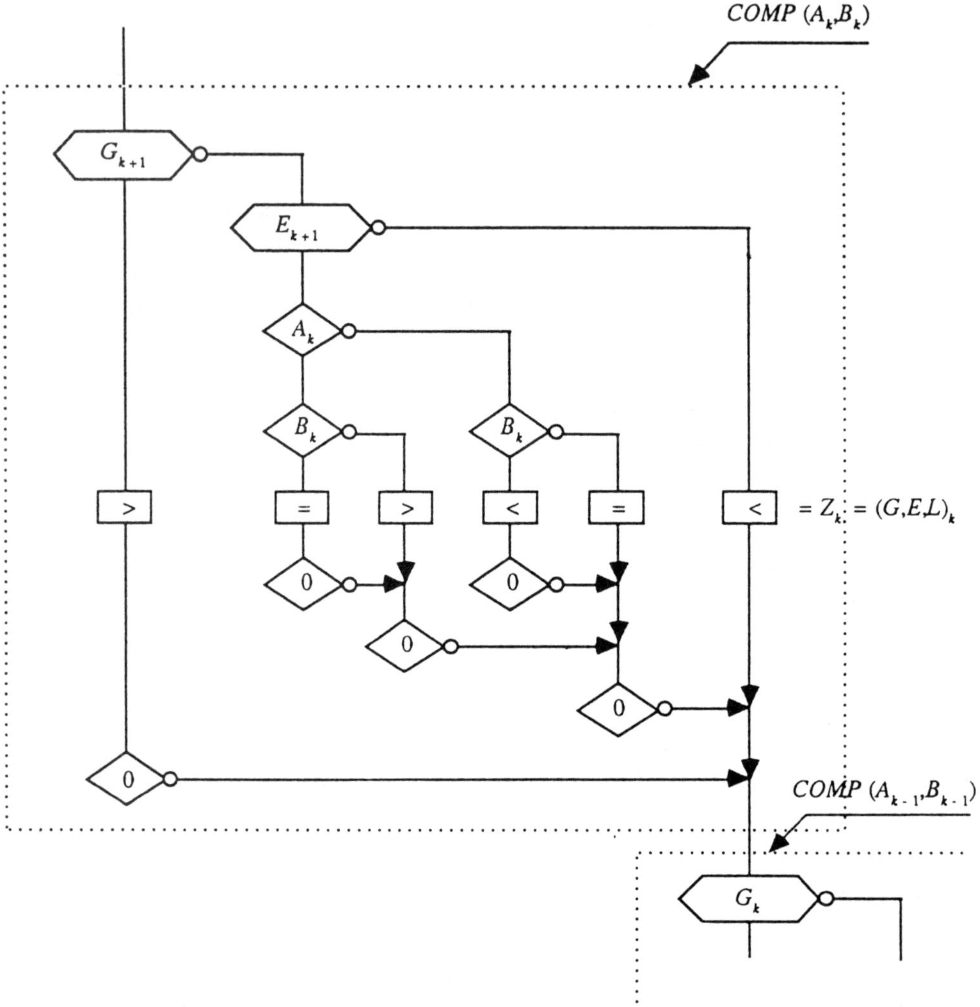

Figure 5.63

2. After possible reduction find the minimal table, with *Ny* states, and represent this by *Ny* partial tables.
3. Simplify/reduce the trees/diagrams for these *Ny* partial tables, simultaneously or separately: this is done in Figure 3.40.
4. Realize the assemblage of *Ny* trees or diagrams by an unstructured flowchart with *Ny* tracks, that is, with *Ny* inputs and *Ny* outputs: cf. Figure 3.41, language **L2**.
5. Replicate this unstructured flowchart *n* times (for *n* slices), with

suitable values for the test variables xi, and the assignment registers $REG[j,k]$; put these n flowcharts in a loop, as in Figure 3.36 (language **L2**) and give an addressing.

6. The list of instructions so formed constitutes the **L3** program for the system, which can be executed by the **L3** interpreter of Figure 4.7.

Note that the table of Figure 3.40 does not define the output states, but gives the next states $y^+ = Z_k$ uniquely. It follows that the assignment instructions of Figure 3.41 are unnecessary and need only be given in the last slice of the final flowchart, Figure 3.36.

5.5.10 Comment

Naturally, Method 2 gives a flowchart with n slices, which is unstructured (Figure 3.36). This in turn can be realized by a structured flowchart consisting of a main program and $n - 1$ procedures by using the method of §5.5.2 (applicable to any combinational system) and in particular the decomposition of Figure 3.37 into a main tree PP and three sub-trees $sp2, sp1, sp0$. This decomposition is in fact equivalent to the diagram $COMP(A,B)$ of Figure 3.36.

5.5.11 Exercise

First, complete the construction of the structured flowchart for the comparator for two 4-bit numbers of §3.5.2, sketched in Figure 5.63: follow the method of §5.5.7 for this and determine the flowchart with its zig-zag addressing, the characteristic equation, the symbolic program **S** and the mnemonic **L4** and **L5** programs.

Then, taking note of §§3.5.7 and 5.5.8, obtain a structured solution, using a procedure for $P(k) = COMP(A_k, B_k)$ with parameter k. Give the necessary extensions to the **L4**, **L5** languages and the modifications to the interpreter, as discussed in §4.2.10.

5.5.12 Exercise

Realize the main tree and the three sub-trees of Figure 3.37 by a structured **L4** flowchart; give this a zig-zag addressing and construct the characteristic equation, the symbolic (**S**) progam and the mnemonic **L4**, **L5** programs. How must this flowchart be modified if the depth of the stack is 2?

6

Top–down programming

6.1 SOFTWARE REALIZATION: SUCCESSIVE REFINEMENTS

6.1.1 Introduction

Good programming style is conducive to the design of structured flowcharts, which in effect means programming in a language such as **L4**. A study of that language shows that, apart from calls to and returns from procedures, each instruction performs either a test of an input variable *xi* (4.2) or an assignment of a constant *OUT* (a binary word) to an output register *REG*[*j*] (4.3): these are the *primitive instructions* of the language.

Specifications often require the comparison of two words, each of several bits — e.g. test of $A_{3:0} = B_{3:0}$ — or the assignment of a function to a register — e.g. $REG[j] \leftarrow REG[j] + 1$: these are *complex instructions*, the *control* (5.1) and *action* (5.2) instructions of §5.1.3. Software realization of such instructions in terms of primitive instructions is the process of successive refinements, which forms the basis of *top-down programming*; this is the subject of section 6.1. Refinement is the main tool for attacking complex problems; we shall illustrate its use by applying it to the problem of the digital clock, as described by the algorithm of Figure 5.22. As we have seen, the primitive instructions of **L4** can be executed directly by the interpreter INT3 of Figure 4.7; this is a binary decision machine with two essential units: a processing unit (PU in the figure), consisting of a set of registers and a demultiplexer to select the appropriate one, and a control unit (CU), consisting of the sequencer, the memory and a number of logic operators.

This interpreter can be made to execute complex instructions directly, without the need for any decomposition of the software, by adding to it certain hardware operators, of both combinational and sequential types. The resulting system is a specialized processor, consisting of the original control unit and a new processing unit tailored to the specification. The construction of such a processor, illustrated by the example of the digital clock, is the subject of section 6.2.

If the processing unit contains universal hardware operators, in particular an arithmetic and logic unit, it is said to be a universal processor. The analysis and programming of such a processor is the subject of Chapter 7.

6.1.2 Description: primitive instructions

A study of the flowchart of Figure 5.22 shows that it contains a number of primitive test and assignment instructions which can be realized directly by languages such as **L1**—**L5**. These test an input variable *xi* or assign a constant *OUT* (a binary word) to a register *REG*[*j*]:

- tests: *EN*, *s* (auxiliary variables); *H*, *H'* (clock variables);
- assignments: $T[i] \leftarrow 0$ (time variable), $i \leftarrow 0$ (index), $s \leftarrow 1$, $s \leftarrow 0$ (auxiliary variable).

These instructions can be executed directly by the INT3 interpreter, and therefore no refinement is necessary.

6.1.3 Description: complex instructions

Further study of Figure 5.22 reveals the complex instructions:

- control: $T[i] = G[i]$, $i = imax$;
- action: $T[i] \leftarrow T[i] + 1$, $i \leftarrow i + 1$.

Realization of these in terms of primitives involves breaking them down into simpler elements that are equivalent to the primitives, a process that may have to be done in a series of stages. This is the method of *successive refinements*.

6.1.4 Declarations

In order to make the design of the final program and the relevant interpreter as clear as possible it is advisable, at each stage in the refinement process, to *declare* the test variables *xi* and the assignment registers *REG*[*j*]; and to state the width of the register explicitly, for example $REG_{3:0}$ [*j*] for a 4-bit register. Thus for §6.1.2 we have the *declarations*:

- ***test variables*** *xi*: *EN*, *s*, *H*, *H'*;
- ***assignment registers*** *REG*[*j*]: $i_{2:0}$, $T_{3:0}[i_{2:0}]$, *s*.

The width of the register $i_{2:0}$ follows from Figure 5.12; that of $T_{3:0}$ is found from the specification of §5.1.14, where it is stated that *T*[*i*] can vary from 0 to 9 (decimal), which is from 0000 to 1001 in binary. Since s takes only the values 0 and 1 its register needs only one bit.

Before embarking on the refinement process we must explain how a new operator, the addressable register $T_{3:0}[i_{2:0}]$, is realized in hardware.

6.1.5 Hardware realization: addressable register $T[i]$

The time variable $T[i]$ represents any of the measures units of seconds, tens of seconds, etc., up to tens of hours — six in all — according to the value of the index i in the range 0–5 (Figure 5.12). Therefore six independent registers $T[0]$—$T[5]$ are needed, of which any one can be selected by the index i. We call such a set of registers an *addressable register*; it can be implemented as an assemblage of a demultiplexer, multiplexers and registers, each of the last being a particular version of the bi-directional register of Figure 1.41 with $S1 = S0 = LD$. Figure 6.1 gives the logic diagram, Figure 6.2 the block diagram and Figure 6.3 the operations table.

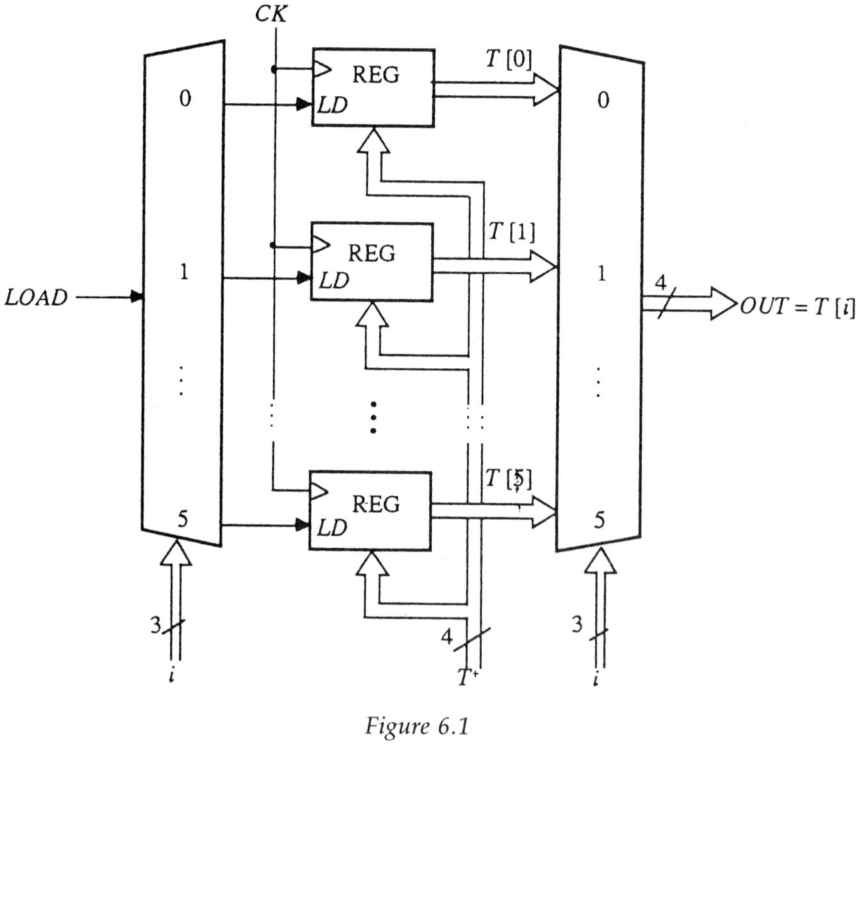

Figure 6.1

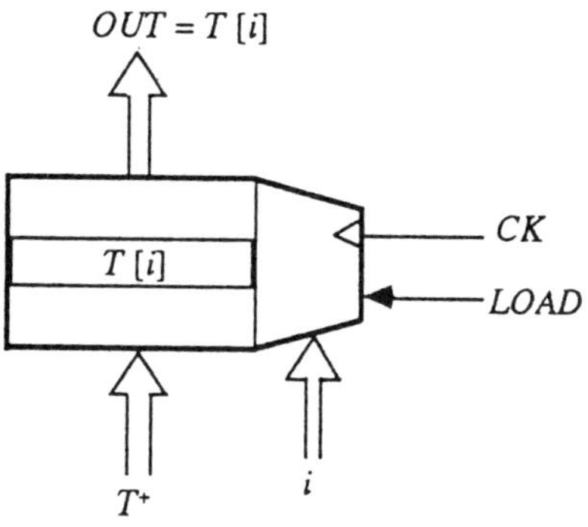

Figure 6.2

OPERATION	DESCRIPTION	*LOAD*
HOLD	$OUT = T[i]$	0
LOAD	$OUT = T[i], T[i] \leftarrow T^+$	1

Figure 6.3

6.1.6 Hardware realization: synchronized RAM $T[i]$

The solution of Figure 6.1 requires six 4-bit registers, an input demultiplexer and four output multiplexers (or the equivalent in a system using 3-state devices). A more compact system can be constructed by using *synchronized random access memory* ([87], pp. 295–301), as shown in Figure 6.4; it consists of the following.

- A random access memory $RAM[A]$, as shown in Figures 1.65 and 1.66, used here only in the state $S', G' = 00$ since WRITE and READ are the only operations allowed. It is described by the asynchronous assignment

$$OUTRAM = RAM[A] := (IN)_W \qquad (6.1)$$

which states that the content of address A of RAM is the value of the input IN when $W = 1$ (§1.2.6).

- A 4-bit latch, described by the asynchronous assignment (1.23)

$$Q := (D)_{LD} \qquad (6.2)$$

- An input multiplexer, driven by the variable *LOAD*.

The connections in Figure 6.4 ensure the following relations:

$$W = LD = CK, D = OUTRAM, Q = OUT = T[i] \qquad (6.3)$$

which through the asynchronous assignments (6.1), (6.2) lead to

$$OUT = T[i] := ((IN)_{CK})_{CK} \qquad (6.4)$$

This is equivalent to the synchronous assignment (§1.2.13)

$$T[i] \leftarrow IN \qquad (6.5)$$

which when $LOAD = 1$, i.e. when $IN = T^+$, becomes

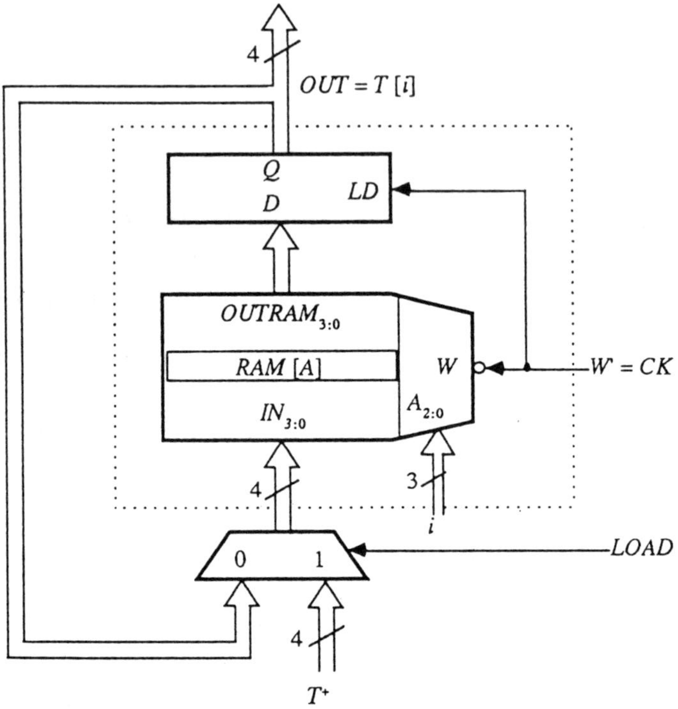

Figure 6.4

$$T[i] \leftarrow T^{+} \tag{6.6}$$

The operations table for this memory is the same as that for the addressable register of Figure 6.3, so the logic diagrams of Figures 6.1 and 6.4 are equivalent.

It follows that the part of Figure 6.4 within the dotted line frame is similar in structure to a flip-flop (Figure 1.30): the memory *RAM*[*A*] is the master unit and the latch is the slave.

6.1.7 Assumption

To avoid possible ambiguity in the interpretation of a synchronous assignment such as (6.6) we postulate that any variations in the word *i* are synchronized to the assignment itself, that is, are made immediately after the rise of the clock signal *CK*. In other words, we ensure that both the register *i* and the addressable register (or the synchronized memory) are driven by the same clock signal.

6.1.8 Refinement: the control instruction $i = imax$

The complex control instruction $i = imax$ occurs in the structured sub-program *SP2* of Figure 5.22. If we call Q, R the sub-programs that are alternative outcomes then *SP2* has the characteristic equation

$$SP2 = <_{i=imax} Q\,|\,R> \tag{6.7}$$

and the flowchart of Figure 6.5.

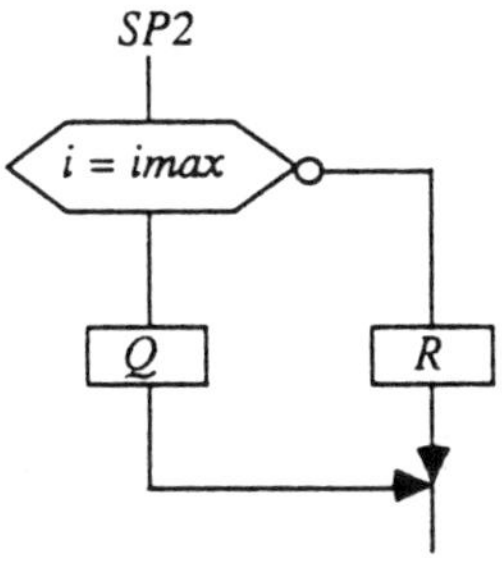

Figure 6.5

The specification (Figure 5.12) requires $imax = 6$, that is, $imax_{2:0} = 110$. The combinational behaviour is therefore as follows, where $f(SP2)$ is a discrete function of the variables i_2, i_1, i_0:

- for $i = 0$ ($i_{2:0} = 000$), $f(SP2) = \Phi$, i.e. is a don't care condition; in effect, the test $i = imax$ follows the assignment $i \leftarrow i + 1$ (Figure 5.22);
- for $1 \leqslant i < imax$, ($001 \leqslant i_{2:0} < 110$), $f(SP2) = R$;
- for $i = imax$, ($i_{2:0} = 110$), $f(SP2) = Q$;
- for $i > imax$ ($i_{2:0} = 111$), $f(SP2) = \Phi$.

Figure 6.7 is the Karnaugh map for $f(SP2)$. The graphical method of §2.1.14 gives a partitioning into three blocks, and hence a tree with three branches (Figure 6.6). The new sub-program *SP2.1*, equivalent to *SP2*, has the characteristic equation

$$SP2.1 = <_{i2}<_{i1} Q\,|\,R>\,|\,R> \tag{6.8}$$

SP2.1 involves only tests of the logical variables i_2, i_1 and therefore can be written in terms of the primitive test instructions; the declarations can be summarized as

- ***test variables*** *xi*: i_2, i_1.

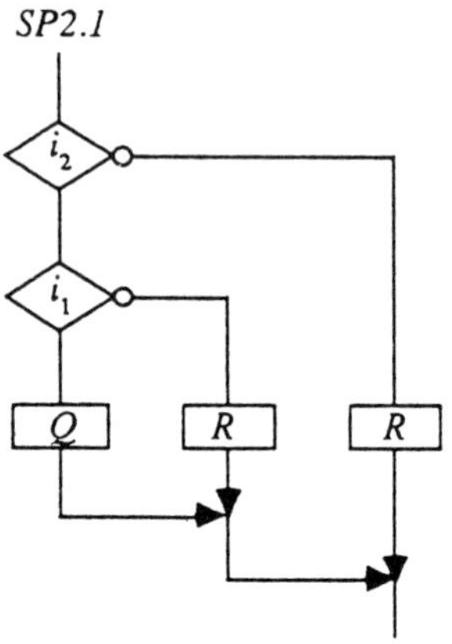

Figure 6.6

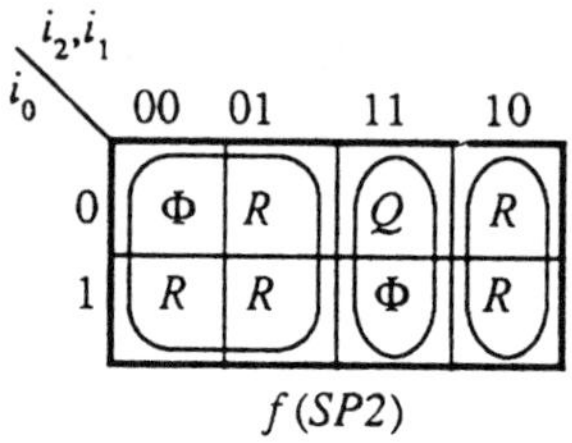

Figure 6.7

6.1.9 First refinement: control instruction $T[i] = G[i]$

This occurs in the structured sub-program *SP1* of Figure 5.22; it has the flowchart of Figure 6.10 and the characteristic equation

$$SP1 = <_{T[i]=G[i]} P \mid Q> \qquad (6.9)$$

The specification gives the value of $G[i]$ for each value of i; when $i = 4$, $G[i]$ (for units of hours) depends on $T[i]$ as well as on i.

Recalling that the suffixes B, D distinguish between binary and decimal numbers (§1.1.9), we can express $G[4]$ as a function of the time in hours as follows:

$$\begin{aligned} G[4] &= 10_D = 1010_B \quad \text{for} \quad 00 \leqslant t \leqslant 19 \\ &= \ \ 4_D = 0100_B \quad \text{for} \quad 20 \leqslant t \leqslant 23 \end{aligned}$$

This states that the upper limit to the units of hours is 10_D for times between 0 and 19 hours, and 4 for times between 20 and 23. A test of the 1-bit variable $T[5]$, representing the tens of hours, suffices to detect the value of $G[4]$:

$$\begin{aligned} G[4] &= 10_D = 1010_B \quad \text{if} \quad T_1[5] = 0 \\ &= \ \ 4_D = 0100_B \quad \text{if} \quad T_1[5] = 1 \end{aligned}$$

The reduced truth table for the discrete function $G[i]$ follows; this is shown in Figure 6.8. Figure 6.9 is the Karnaugh map; application of the graphical method of §2.1.14 gives a partitioning into five blocks, and hence a tree with five branches, as Figure 6.11.

A system based on either an addressable register (Figure 6.1) or a synchronized memory (Figure 6.4) will produce at each clock time a

i	$i_{2:0}$	$T_1[5]$	$G[i]$
0	0 0 0	Φ	10
1	0 0 1	Φ	6
2	0 1 0	Φ	10
3	0 1 1	Φ	6
4	1 0 0	0	10
4	1 0 0	1	4
5	1 0 1	Φ	3

Figure 6.8

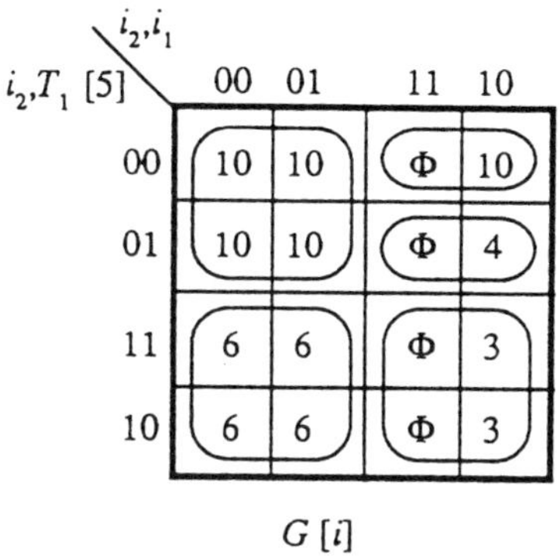

Figure 6.9

4-bit word $T_{3:0}[i]$ which in general is determined by the value of i at that instant; but when $i = 4$ the value of this index must be changed to enable the test of the 1-bit variable $T_1[5]$ to be performed. This is done as follows:

1. i is given, temporarily, the value 5 ($i \leftarrow 5$);
2. $T_1[i] = T_1[5]$ is tested;
3. the value 4 is restored ($i \leftarrow 4$).

The part of the flowchart which does this is enclosed in the dotted line frame in Figure 6.11.

Finally, the comparison $T[i] = G[i]$ (= a constant, 3, 4, 6 or 10) has to be implemented for each of the five branches of the tree; this is done by the sub-programs *SP3—SP6*, the design of which constitutes the second refinement, the subject of §6.1.11.

The characteristic equation for the new sub-program *SP1.1*, equivalent to *SP1*, is as follows, in which, for example, the assignments $i \leftarrow 5$, $i \leftarrow 4$ are abbreviated to *i5*, *i4* respectively,

$$SP1.1 = <_{i2}<_{i0}\ SP3 \mid i5 <_{T1[5]} i4\ SP4 \mid i4\ SP6>> \mid <_{i0}\ SP5 \mid SP6>> \tag{6.10}$$

The declarations are

test variables *xi*: i_2, i_0, $T_1[i] = T_1[5]$;
assignment registers *REG*[*j*]: $i_{2:0}$

6.1.10 A convention

To simplify the writing we shall represent the individual bits of the 4-bit time variable $T[i]$ as follows:

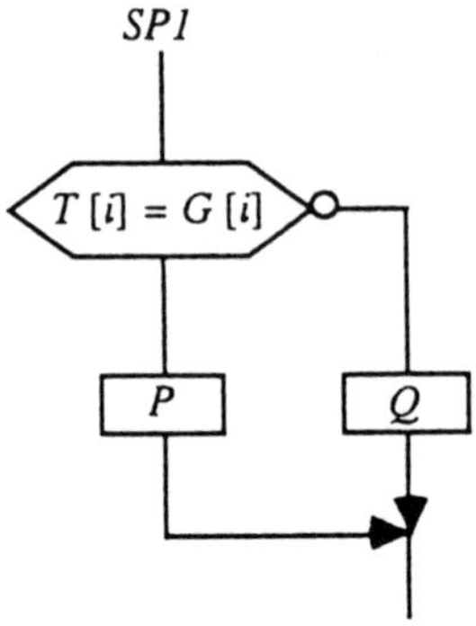

Figure 6.10

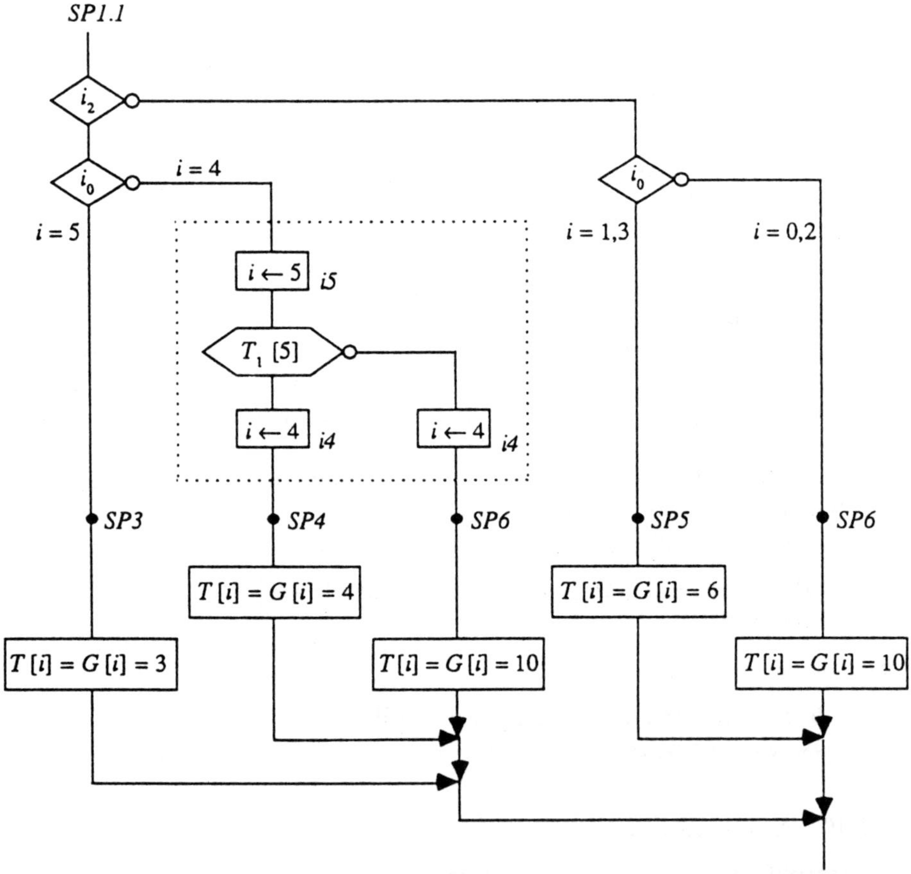

Figure 6.11

$$T_j = T_j[i], \quad j = 3, 2, 1, 0 \tag{6.11}$$

We shall however use this convention only when there is no risk of confusion, that is, only when the value of i is clearly defined.

6.1.11 Second refinement: the control instruction $T[i] = G[i]$

Consider as an example the instruction $T[i] = G[i] = 3$ (Figure 6.11), which occurs in the structured sub-program *SP3* of Figure 6.13; the details of the sub-programs *P*, *Q* are given in Figure 5.22. The test $T[i] = 3$ is a combinational system which can be described by a discrete function $f(SP3)$ of the four variables T_3—T_0:

- for $0 \leq T < 3$ ($0000 \leq T_{3:0} < 0011$) then $f(SP3) = Q$;
- for $T = 3$ ($T_{3:0} = 0011$) $f(SP3) = P$;
- for $T > 3$ ($0011 < T_{3:0} \leq 1111$) $f(SP3) = \Phi$.

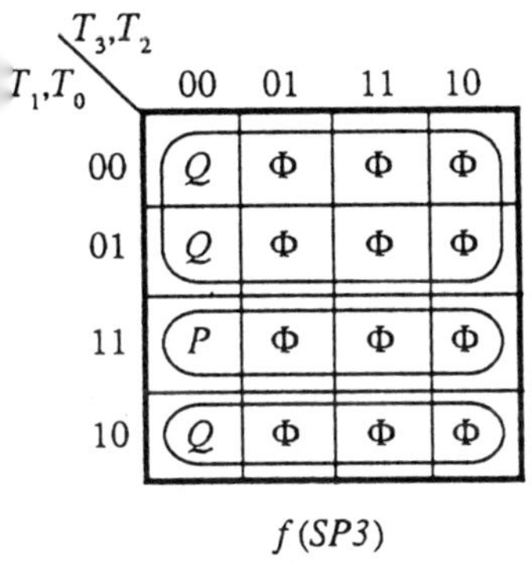

Figure 6.12

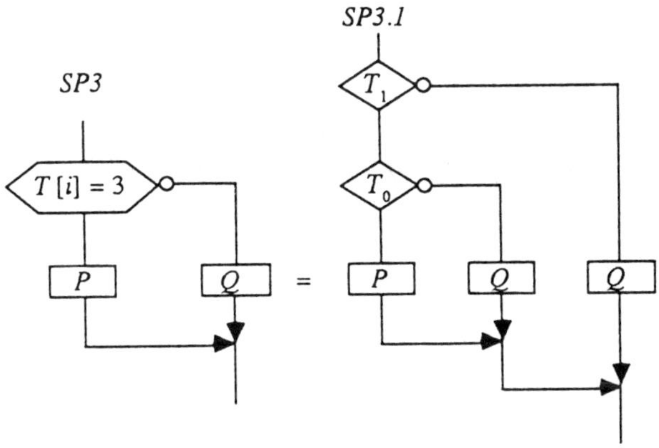

Figure 6.13

Figure 6.12 is the Karnaugh map for $f(SP3)$, for which the graphical method of §2.1.14 gives a partitioning into three blocks and hence the tree Figure 6.13 with three branches. The characteristic equation for the new sub-program *SP3.1*, equivalent to *SP3*, is

$$SP3.1 = <_{T1}<_{T0} P \,|\, Q> \,|\, Q> \tag{6.12}$$

Application of the same method to the cases $T[i] = 4, 6, 10$ (Figure 6.11) gives the Karnaugh maps of Figures 6.14, 6.16, and 6.18 respectively and the corresponding simplified trees; and finally the three structured subprograms of Figures 6.15, 6.17, and 6.19 with characteristic equations

$$SP4.1 = <_{T2} P \,|\, Q> \tag{6.13}$$

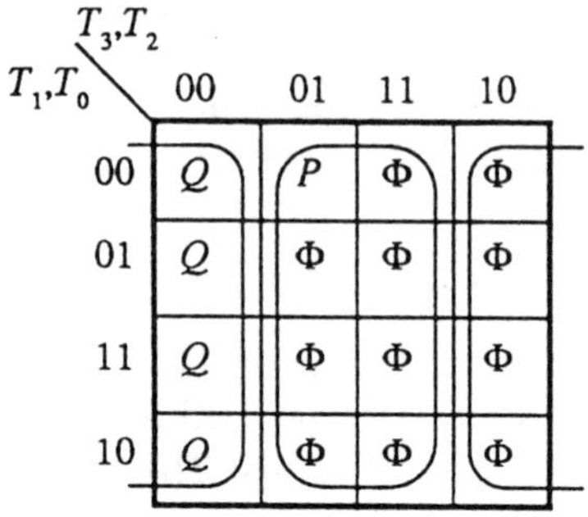

$f(SP4)$

Figure 6.14

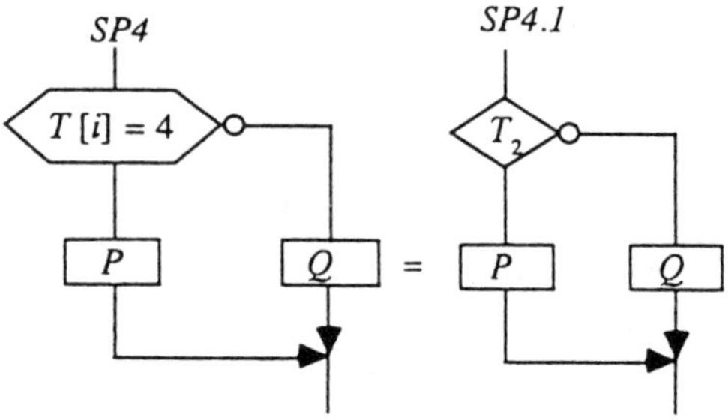

Figure 6.15

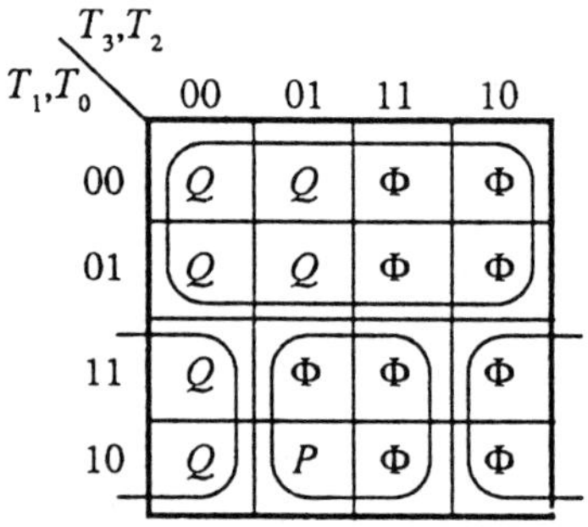

$f(SP5)$

Figure 6.16

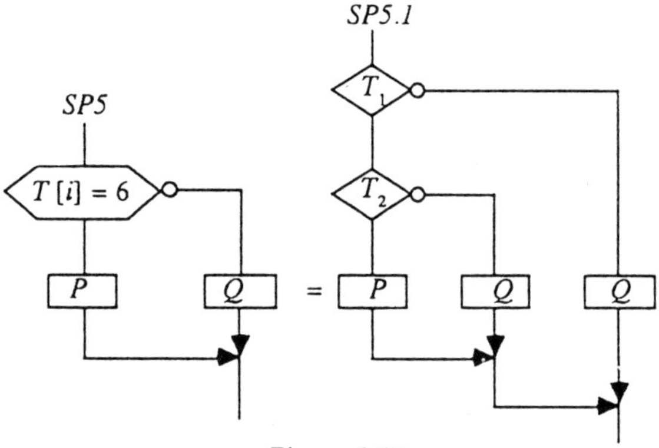

Figure 6.17

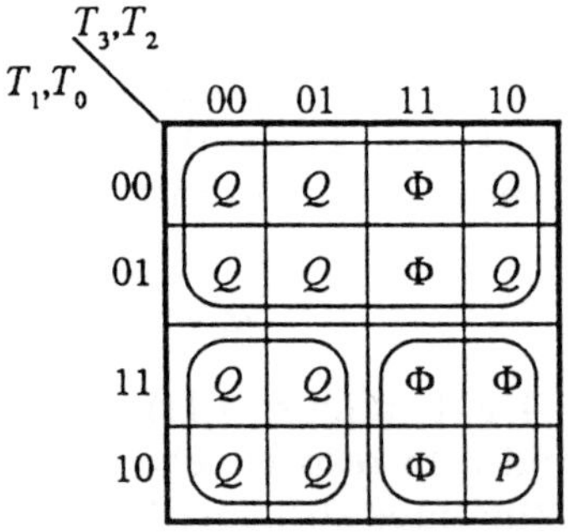

$f(SP6)$

Figure 6.18

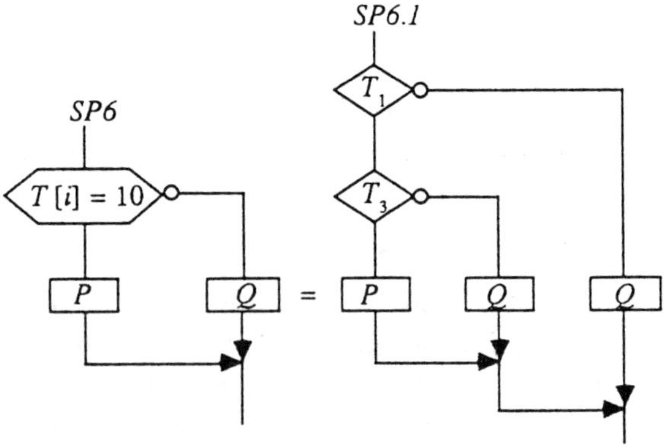

Figure 6.19

$$SP5.1 = <_{T1} <_{T2} P \mid Q> \mid Q> \tag{6.14}$$

$$SP6.1 = <_{T1} <_{T3} P \mid Q> \mid Q> \tag{6.15}$$

The declarations are

- ***test variables*** *xi*: $T_3[i]$, $T_2[i]$, $T_1[i]$, $T_0[i]$

6.1.12 Refinement: the action instruction $i \leftarrow i + 1$

This complex instruction (sub-program *SP7*) increments the index *i*; recalling that the value of this must not exceed *imax* = 6 (see Figure 5.12) we can construct the Karnaugh map or truth table as follows:

- for $0 \leqslant i < imax$ ($000 \leqslant i_{2:0} < 110$), $i^+ = i + 1$;
- for $i \geqslant imax$ ($110 \leqslant i_{2:0} \leqslant 111$), $i^+ = \Phi$.

This is shown in Figure 6.20. Proceeding as before we get a partitioning into six blocks and a tree (Figure 6.21) with six branches. The new sub-program *SP7.1*, equivalent to *SP7*, has the following characteristic equation, where the assignments $i \leftarrow 6 \ldots i \leftarrow 1$ are abbreviated to $i6 \ldots i1$.

$$SP7.1 = <_{i2} <_{i0} i6 \mid i5> \mid <_{i1} <_{i0} i4 \mid i3> \mid <_{i0} i2 \mid i1>>> \tag{6.16}$$

The declarations are

- ***test variables*** *xi*: i_2, i_1, i_0;
- ***assignment registers*** *REG*[*j*]: $i_{2:0}$

The sub-program *SP7.1* is very similar to that of the 6-state counter of Figure 3.10, the two differing only in the next state following the present state 101. This is 110 for the incrementer of Figure 6.20 and 000 for the counter of Figure 3.9.

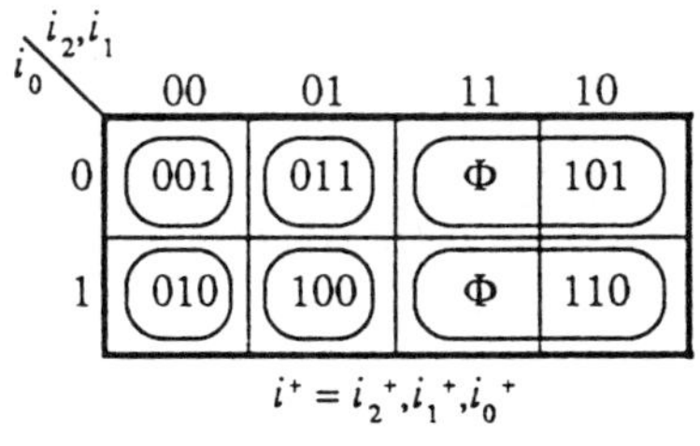

Figure 6.20

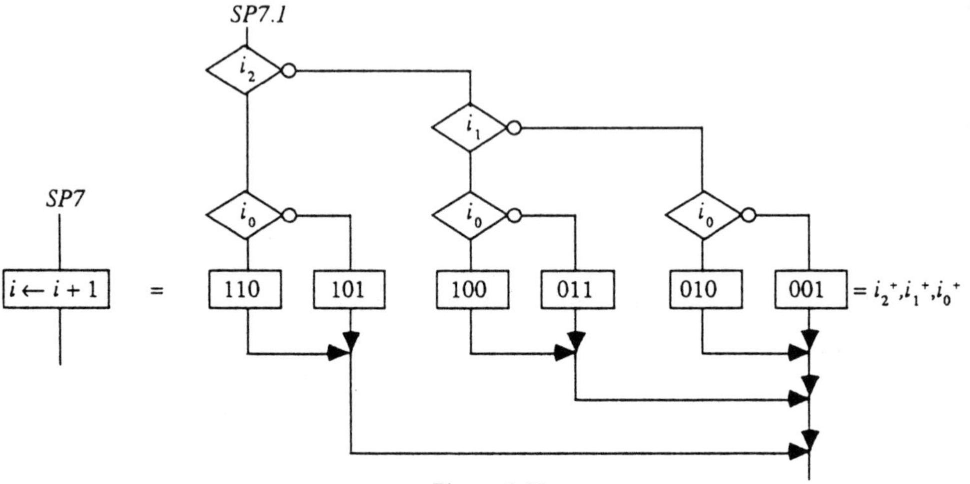

Figure 6.21

6.1.13 Refinement: the action instruction $T[i] \leftarrow T[i] + 1$

Recalling that the value of the time variable $T[i]$ must not exceed the upper limit $G[i] = 10$ (decimal), we can construct the Karnaugh map as follows.

- for $0 \leqslant T[i] < 10$ $(0000 \leqslant T_{3:0}[i] < 1010)$, $T^{+}[i] = T[i] + 1$;
- for $T[i] \geqslant 10$ $(1010 \leqslant T_{3:0}[i] \leqslant 11)$, $T^{+}[i] = \Phi$.

This is shown in Figure 6.22. Proceeding as before we get a partitioning into ten blocks and hence a tree (Figure 6.23) with ten branches. The

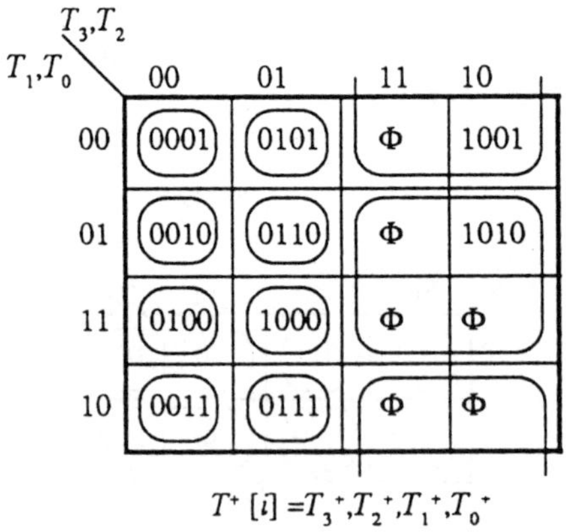

Figure 6.22

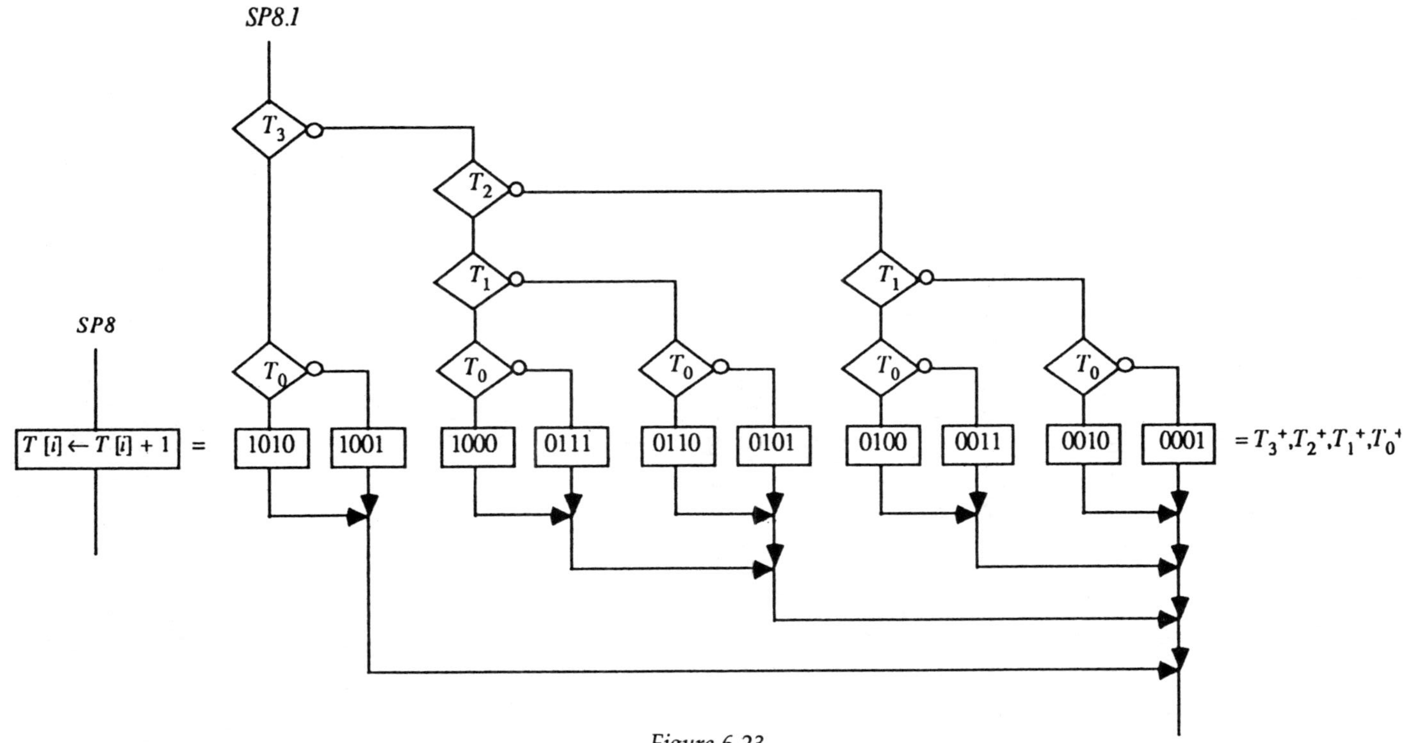

SP8
T [i] ← T [i] + 1
=
SP8.1
T3
T2
T1
T1
T0
T0
T0
T0
T0
1010
1001
1000
0111
0110
0101
0100
0011
0010
0001
= T3+,T2+,T1+,T0+

Figure 6.23

new program *SP8.1*, equivalent to *SP8*, has the following characteristic equation, in which the assignments $T[i] \leftarrow 10$ etc. are abbreviated to *T*10 etc.

$$SP8.1 = <_{T3} <_{T0} T10 \mid T9> \mid <_{T2} <_{T1} <_{T0} T8 \mid T7> \mid <_{T0} T6 \mid T5>> \mid <_{T1} <_{T0} T4 \mid T3> \mid <_{T0} T2 \mid T1>>>> \qquad (6.17)$$

The declarations are

- ***test variables*** *xi*: $T_3[i]$, $T_2[i]$, $T_1[i]$, $T_0[i]$;
- ***assignment registers*** $REG[j]$: $T_{3:0}[i_{2:0}]$

6.1.14 Software realization: mnemonic L5 program

We are now in a position to write the program for the clock algorithm in the structured language **L5**. Starting from Figure 5.22, consisting of the main program *PP* and the sub-program *SP1*, we deal systematically with all the constituent sub-programs, together with their successive refinements, and from their characteristic equations we form the list of **L5** instructions.

The following list summarizes the set of characteristic equations that describes the main and sub-programs of Figure 5.22, using only the primitive instructions of test and assignment.

	$PP = \{_{EN} \{_{H}\} \{_{H'}\} i0\ R\ \{_{s}\ SP1\}\}$	(6.18)
where	$R = SP8\ s1$	(6.19)
where	$SP8 = SP8.1$	(6.17)
and where	$SP1 = SP1.1$	(6.10)
where	$SP3 = SP3.1$	(6.12)
where	$SP4 = SP4.1$	(6.13)
where	$SP5 = SP5.1$	(6.14)
where	$SP6 = SP6.1$	(6.15)
where	$Q = s \leftarrow 0$	(6.20)
where	$P = T0\ SP7\ SP2$	(6.21)
where	$SP7 = SP7.1$	(6.16)
where	$SP2 = SP2.1$	(6.8)
where	R	(6.19)
where	Q	(6.20)

If *PP* (6.18) is the main program and if all the sub-programs except for the trivial *SP8.1* and *Q* are implemented by procedures, then the mnemonic **L5** program can be derived directly from the equations listed above; it is given in Figure 6.24.

As an exercise, the reader should construct the mnemonic **L4** program, with a zig-zag addressing.

```
program PP
while EN
        while H
        end while
        while H'
        end while
        do i←0
        call R
        while s
                call SP1.1
        end while
end while

procedure R
if T3
        if T0
                do T←10
        else
                do T←9
        endif
else
        if T2
                if T1
                        if T0
                                do T←8
                        else
                                do T←7
                        endif
                else
                        if T0
                                do T←6
                        else
                                do T←5
                        endif
                endif
        else
                if T1
                        if T0
                                do T←4
                        else
                                dc T←3
                        endif
                else
                        if T0
                                do T←2
                        else
                        do T←1
                        endif
                endif
        endif
endif
do s←1
end procedure
```

```
procedure SP1.1
if i2
        if i0
                call SP3.1
        else
                do i←5
                if T1 [5]
                        do i←4
                        call SP4.1
                else
                        do i←4
                        call SP6.1
                endif
        endif
else
        if i0
                call SP5.1
        else
                call SP6.1
        endif
endif
end procedure

procedure SP3.1
if T1
        if T0
                call P
        else
                do s←0
        endif
else
        do s←0
endif
end procedure

procedure SP4.1
if T2
        call P
else
        do s←0
endif
end procedure

procedure SP5.1
if T1
        if T2
                call P
        else
                do s←0
        endif
else
        do s←0
endif
end procedure
```

```
procedure SP6.1
if T1
        if T3
                call P
        else
                do s←0
        endif
else
        do s←0
endif
end procedure

procedure P
do T←0
call SP7.1
call SP2.1
end procedure

procedure SP7.1
if i2
        if i0
                do i←6
        else
                do i←5
        endif
else
        if i1
                if i0
                        do i←4
                else
                        do i←3
                endif
        else
                if i0
                        do i←2
                else
                        do i←1
                endif
        endif
endif
end procedure

procedure SP2.1
if i2
        if i1
                do s←0
        else
                call R
        endif
else
        call R
endif
end procedure


end program
```

Figure 6.24

6.1.15 Definition: calls graph

Figure 6.25 is the *calls graph* for the clock algorithm; it is constructed as follows:

- the main program *PP* and each procedure (cf. Figure 6.24) are represented by vertices;
- each procedure call is represented by an arrow, directed from the calling vertex (*PP* or a procedure) to the called (a procedure).

The longest path, starting from *MP* and following the arrows, gives the maximum number of nested procedures, that is, the depth of the stack needed by an interpreter for **L4**; in this example the number is five. It is good practice to use procedures freely, because this generally gives programs that are clear and easy to read; departure from this practice is shown only by the limited depth of the stack in certain interpreters.

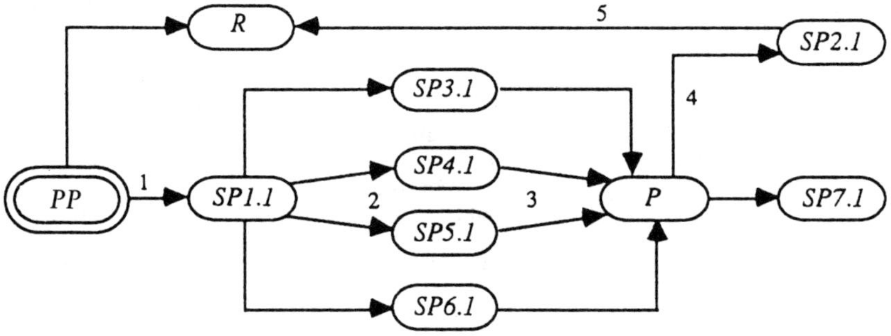

Figure 6.25

6.1.16 Hardware realization: interpreter INT3.1

The declarations for the clock algorithm are given in §§6.1.4–13; the complete set is as follows:

- ***test variables*** *xi*: $T_3[i]$, $T_2[i]$, $T_1[i]$, $T_0[i]$, i_2, i_1, i_0, s, EN, H, H', 0
- ***assignment registers*** $REG[j]$: $T_{3:0}[i_{2:0}]$, $i_{2:0}$, s

The test variable $xi = 0$ is needed by the **L4** instruction

GO TO *ADR+* = **IF** 0 **ELSE** *ADR0*

The interpreter INT3 of Figure 4.7 will be able to execute the **L4** program if it is provided with:

- the twelve test variables (*x0, . . . x11*) listed above;
- the three assignment registers listed above ($j = 3, 2, 1$); $REG[1] = T_{3:0}$ must be an addressable register, implemented by synchronized RAM (§§6.1.5–6).

We call the new interpreter, with these provisions, INT3.1; it is shown in Figure 6.26.

6.1.17 Definitions: control and processing units

In any interpreter, for example Figure 4.7, we can distinguish between the set of output registers *REG*[*j*], associated with a demultiplexer DMUX, and the rest of the machine; we call the former the *processing unit*, PU, and the latter the *control unit*, CU. In Figure 4.7, for INT3, the PU is shown by the dotted line frame. For INT3.1 (Figure 6.26) the units are as follows:

- a control unit CU identical with that of Figure 4.7;
- a processing unit PU specially adapted to the clock algorithm, with three registers, one of which is addressable.

As can be seen in Figures 4.7 and 6.26, each register has inputs of two quite distinct types:

- a *data input* $OUT_{3:0} = ROM_{3:0}[ADR]$, directly from the interpreter memory and common to all three — a *bus;*
- a *control input LD1 . . . LD3*, from the demultiplexer DMUX, which itself is controlled by the fields $j_{3:0} = ROM_{11:8}$ and $LD = ROM_{12}$ of the memory.

In contrast to other hardware realizations, in particular that of section 6.2, we say that Figure 6.26 is a *software-dominated architecture*, because it consists of:

- a minimal processing unit, consisting solely of registers;
- a control unit characterized by a relatively large program, Figure 6.24; a measure of the complexity of this is given by the number *Ni* of **L5** instructions, which will be found to be 154.

6.1.18 Method: programming by successive refinements

The special case of the clock algorithm suggests a general method for constructing the software implementation of programs of significant complexity.

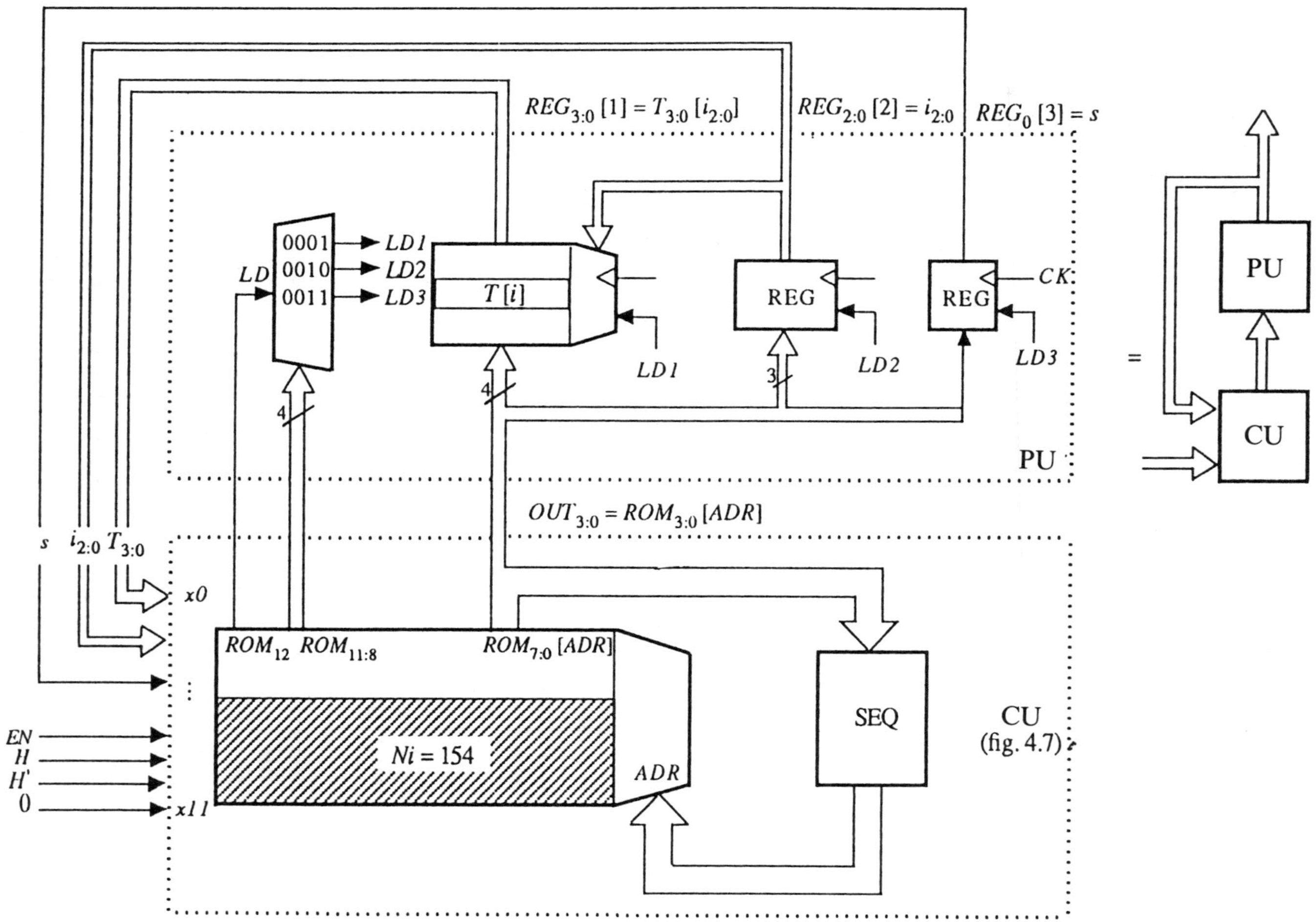

INT3.1

Figure 6.26

1. The original specification is represented by a flowchart; in the general case this will be an arbitrary — that is, unstructured — assemblage of complex control and action instructions.
2. If necessary, this is modified so as to be a proper flowchart, and structured. Local structuring, according to the rules of §§5.1.9–11, is attempted first, followed by the application of the global methods of §5.1.18 or section 8.5 for those parts of the program that remain unstructured.
3. The resulting structured flowchart will contain both primitive instructions, which can be executed directly, and complex instructions, each of which must be broken down by successive refinements and implemented by a sub-program which is a structured assemblage of primitive instructions. The methods for simplification and reduction given in Chapter 2 can be used in the refinement process.
4. Each sub-program is described by its characteristic equation and each, with the exception of certain trivial sub-programs (and the main program itself) is implemented by a procedure. The set of equations is equivalent to the symbolic program **S**, from which the mnemonic program in **L4** or **L5** can be derived. The calls graph can be constructed if there is a need to check the number of nested procedures.
5. The set of declarations gives the number of test variables *xi* and the number and widths of assignment registers *REG*[*j*]. The set of registers forms the processing unit of the interpreter and the zig-zag addressing and hexadecimal coding of the **L4** program enable the control unit to be designed.

6.1.19 Conclusion

The programming method of §6.1.18 is based on the policy decision that the processing unit shall consist solely of registers, any or all of which may be addressable, and the control unit shall execute only primitive instructions (tests or assignments); this requires that complex instructions are broken down into sequences of primitive instructions by the process of successive refinements. The final outcome is a software-dominated architecture.

We shall give a complementary method in section 6.2, in which hardware dominates and complex instructions are implemented without software breakdown. This illustrates once again the duality and equivalence between software and hardware realizations: in the former by a program of significant size resident in the control unit, in the latter by a processing unit specially adapted to the particular problem.

6.1.20 Bibliography

Many methods have been developed for the design and realization of programs, summaries of which are given in [50] (pp. 230–241) and [102]. The top-down method by successive refinements described in this section has certain similarities to the method of Jackson [50] (pp. 208–215), [68], [103], but is closer to the formal method LCP (*Logical Construction of Programs*) due to Warnier [46], [50] (pp. 215–228).

6.1.21 Exercise

Extend the clock algorithm by adding a general *reset to zero*, of the hours, minutes and seconds. This is to be done automatically each time the clock is started and must be available at any time when it is running. Modify the **L5** program (Figure 6.24) to incorporate this, limiting the maximum number of nested procedures, and therefore the depth of the stack, to four. Derive the symbolic program **S**, the **L4** program and the hexadecimal coding of the latter, assuming the use of the interpreter INT3.1 of Figure 6.26, supplemented by a logic system that gives a permanent display of the time in hours, minutes and seconds.

6.1.22 Project: extensions to the clock algorithm

Add one or more of the following determinations to the original specification.

(a) Day of the week, Monday to Sunday.
(b) Day of the month, 1 to 28, 29, 30 or 31, according to the calendar month and the year. See §§2.1.19 and 2.2.10.
(c) Month, January to December.
(d) Year.
(e) Leap years: all years whose serial number (AD) is divisible by four, except for century years that are not divisible by 400.

Use the method of §6.1.18, with successive refinements, to construct a program for your specification, first in **L5** and then in **L4**; the **L4** program is to be executed by an interpreter similar in principle to Figure 6.26.

6.1.23 Project: determination of the interval between two given dates

The problem is to compute the number of days between two arbitrary dates in the same year. The data are two couples (Month 1, Day 1 and

Month, 2, Day 2) and the year: it can be assumed that the first is the earlier and that both are correct in the sense that each is a possible date (thus excluding, for example, 31 February); also that an interpreter similar to INT3.1 (Figure 6.26) is available. Apply the method of successive refinements to construct a program first in **L5** and then in **L4**.

6.2 HARDWARE REALIZATION: SPECIALIZED PROCESSOR

6.2.1 Introduction

We now show how the complex instructions defined in §6.1.1 can be realized without breaking them down into sequences of primitive instructions; the effect is that the clock algorithm instructions (Figure 5.22):

- control: $T[i] = G[i], \quad i = imax$
- action: $T[i] \leftarrow T[i] + 1, \quad i \leftarrow i + 1$

become primitive instructions of languages such as **L1...L5**. This is achieved at the cost of providing hardware in the processing unit for the realization of certain operations, both combinational (the comparisons $T[i] = G[i]$, $i = imax$) and sequential (the incrementations $T[i] \leftarrow T[i] + 1$, $i \leftarrow i + 1$), which was previously performed by software, that is, by the sub-programs of Figures 6.5–6.23. The method thus represents a shift from software to hardware.

If we add the primitive assignments of §6.1.2 — $T[i] \leftarrow 0$, $i \leftarrow 0$, $s \leftarrow 1$, $s \leftarrow 0$ — and the neutral operations on the three registers, $T[i] \leftarrow T[i]$, $i \leftarrow$ i and $s \leftarrow$ s, we obtain the final specification of the processing unit of Figure 6.27.

6.2.2 Definitions: computing resources and transfer registers

By *computing resources* we mean the combinational systems in the processing unit that realize the control instructions; these, labelled C in Figure 6.27, are usually comparators. The *transfer registers*, labelled S, form the sequential part of the processing unit and realize the action instructions, for example the incrementation of a variable.

It is convenient to declare the test variables *xi*, the results of comparisons made by the computing resources, and the *control variables* Z_j that are needed for the various operations of the transfer registers.

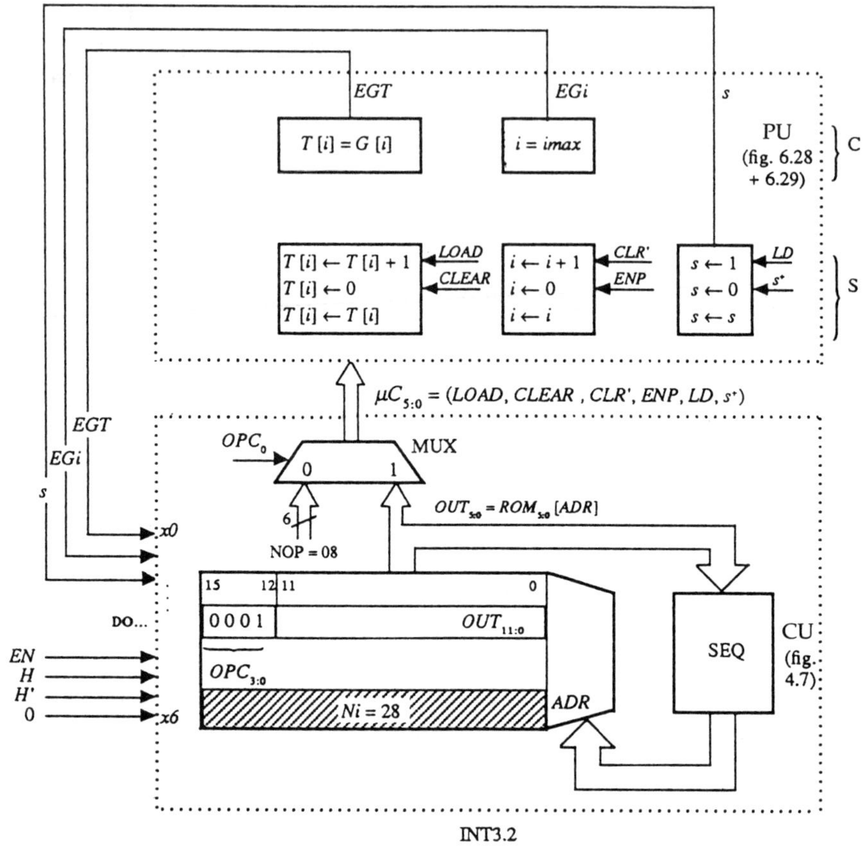

Figure 6.27

6.2.3 Computing resource: control instruction i = *imax*

If in the comparator of Figure 1.14, §1.1.14, we set $ADRA_{3:0} = imax_{3:0} = 0110$ and $ADRB_{3:0} = i_{3:0}$, this device will realize the comparison $i = imax$, and its output

$$EG[ADRA, ADRB] = EG(0110, i_{3:0}) = EGi$$

has the value 1 if $i = imax$ (see Figure 6.28). The declarations are:

- ***test variable*** *xi*: *EGi*

6.2.4 Computing resource: control instruction $T[i] = G[i]$

This test requires a knowledge of the value of $G[i]$, which is the discrete function of the state $i_{2:0}$ and the 1-bit $T_1[5]$ given in the truth

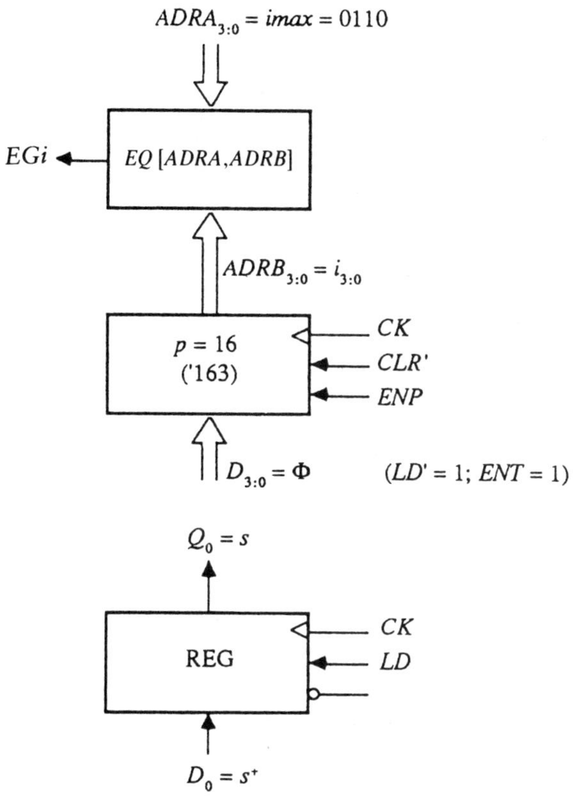

Figure 6.28

table of Figure 6.8. A possible realization of $G[i]$ uses the read only memory ROM[B] of Figure 1.51, consisting of the words $ROM_{3:0} = G_{3:0}$ of $n = 4$ bits and the addresses $B_{3:0} = i_{2:0}$, $T_1[5]$ of $m = 4$ bits. If now we set $ADRA_{3:0} = G_{3:0}[i]$ and $ADRB_{3:0} = T_{3:0}[i]$, the comparator of Figure 1.14 will realize the test and its output

$$EG[ADRA, ADRB] = EG[G_{3:0}[i], T_{3:0}[i]] = EGT$$

has the value 1 if $T[i] = G[i]$ (see Figure 6.29). The declarations are:

- ***test variable*** *xi*: *EGT*

6.2.5 Transfer register *i*

The requirements of this are summarized in Figure 6.27; if the following conditions are imposed:

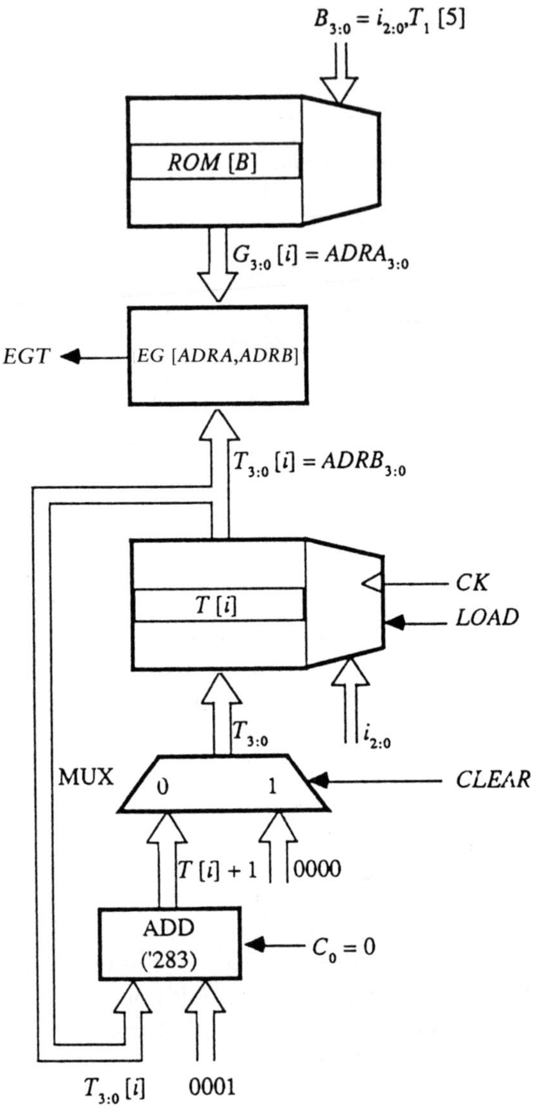

Figure 6.29

$$LD' = 1; \quad ENT = 1; \quad Q = i \tag{6.22}$$

they can be met by the Texas Instruments '163 *programmable counter* [17] (pp. 7.190–205).

With these conditions the original operations table Figure 6.30, in which the symbol '+' has its normal arithmetical meaning, becomes

OPERATION	DESCRIPTION: '163	*CLR'*	*LD'*	*ENP*
CLEAR	$Q \leftarrow 0$	0	Φ	Φ
LOAD	$Q \leftarrow D$	1	0	Φ
HOLD	$Q \leftarrow Q$	1	1	0
COUNT	$Q \leftarrow Q + ENT$	1	1	1

Figure 6.30

OPERATION	DESCRIPTION: '163	*CLR'*	*ENP*
CLEAR	$i \leftarrow 0$	0	Φ
HOLD	$i \leftarrow i$	1	0
INC	$i \leftarrow i + 1$	1	1

Figure 6.31

that of Figure 6.31, which satisfies the requirements of the problem as shown in Figure 6.28. The declarations are

- ***control variables*** Z_j: *CLR', ENP*

6.2.6 Transfer register *T*[*i*]

This is defined by the operations table of Figure 6.3 (§6.1.5) and can be realized by either a battery of registers or a synchronized RAM. The table must be transformed into that of Figure 6.32 (where again '+' is the arithmetical operator) so as to meet the specification as summarized in Figure 6.27. The assemblage of a multiplexer MUX and an adder ADD (for example, a Texas Instruments '283, [17] pp. 7.415–419), shown in Figure 6.29, is a possible solution, for which the declarations are

- ***control variables*** Z_j: *LOAD, CLEAR*

OPERATION	DESCRIPTION	*LOAD*	*CLEAR*
HOLD	$T[i] \leftarrow T[i]$	0	Φ
INC	$T[i] \leftarrow T[i] + 1$	1	0
CLEAR	$T[i] \leftarrow 0$	1	1

Figure 6.32

6.2.7 Transfer register *s*

The specification for this, derived from Figure 6.27, is given by the operations table of Figure 6.33; it can be realized by a bi-directional shift register with $S1 = S0 = LD$ (Figure 6.28 and §1.2.14). The declarations are

control variables Z_j: LD, s^+

OPERATION	DESCRIPTION: REG	LD	s^+
HOLD	$s \leftarrow s$	0	Φ
CLEAR	$s \leftarrow 0$	1	0
PRESET	$s \leftarrow 1$	1	1

Figure 6.33

6.2.8 Hardware realization: processing unit

The processing unit finally arrived at is the assemblage of two computing resources — comparators $i = imax$, $T[i] = G[i]$ — and the three transfer registers — addressable incrementer $T[i]$, incrementer i, register s; this is shown in the logic diagrams of Figures 6.28–29 and the block diagram of Figure 6.27.

6.2.9 Definition: micro-commands

The declarations of §§6.2.5–7 total to

- ***control variables*** Z_j: $LOAD$, $CLEAR$, CLR', ENP, LD, s^+

In the software-dominated realization of Figure 6.26 each register in the processing unit has one input for common data, $OUT_{3:0}$, and one for data special to that register, LD_j (§6.1.17); but the control unit of Figure 6.27 has tu establish a particular state of the control variables for the execution of each instruction of the program. Such a state is called a *micro-command*, μC; here it is a word of six bits, defined by the above declaration:

$$\mu C_{5:0} = (LOAD, CLEAR, CLR', ENP, LD, s^+) \qquad (6.23)$$

Finally, the complete operation of the control unit is summarized in the operations table of Figure 6.34:

- When a test, procedure call or return instruction is being executed, these being characterized by the operating code $OPC_0 = 0$ of Figure

OPERATION	DESCRIPTION	OPC_0
NOP	μC = NOP = 08	0
DO *OUT*	$\mu C = OUT$	1

Figure 6.34

4.7, all the transfer registers in the processing unit are inhibited, that is, they perform the neutral operation. The corresponding *neutral micro-command* NOP is given in §6.2.11.

- When an assignment instruction ($OPC_0 = 1$) is being executed, the appropriate transfer register performs the relevant operation, the micro-command for which is in the field *OUT* of the **DO...** instruction:

$$\mu C_{5:0} = OUT_{5:0} = ROM_{5:0}[ADR] \tag{6.24}$$

6.2.10 Comment

In the hardware-dominated realization the assignment instruction in **L4** **DO** $REG[j] \leftarrow OUT$ does not need to have the register stated explicitly and can therefore be abbreviated to

$$\textbf{DO } OUT \tag{6.25}$$

The micro-command μC can occupy the memory fields $j_{3:0}$ and $OUT_{7:0}$ (Figure 4.7), a total of 12 bits: $\mu C_{11:0} = OUT_{11:0} = ROM_{11:0}[ADR]$.

6.2.11 Description: table of micro-commands

This is given in Figure 6.35. It is constructed by taking each of the assignments of Figure 6.27 in turn, excluding the neutral operations, and proceeding as follows.

- The values of the control variables for the specified assignment are noted; these are found from the corresponding operations tables and are shown in bold type in Figure 6.35: thus for $T[i] \leftarrow T[i] + 1$, $LOAD, CLEAR = 10$ is found in Figure 6.32.
- When a particular assignment is being considered it can be assumed that all other transfer registers are performing only the neutral operation; the values of the control variables for these registers, found from the corresponding operations tables, are shown in normal type; thus for $i \leftarrow i$, Figure 6.31 gives $CLR', ENP = 10$ and for $s \leftarrow s$ Figure 6.33 gives $LD, s^+ = 0\Phi$.

DESCRIPTION	*LOAD*	*CLEAR*	*CLR'*	*ENP*	*LD*	s^+	$\mu C_{5:0}$
$T[i] \leftarrow T[i]+1$	**1**	**0**	1	0	0	Φ	28
$T[i] \leftarrow 0$	**1**	**1**	1	0	0	Φ	38
$i \leftarrow i+1$	0	Φ	**1**	**1**	0	Φ	0C
$i \leftarrow 0$	0	Φ	**0**	Φ	0	Φ	00
$s \leftarrow 1$	0	Φ	1	0	**1**	**1**	0B
$s \leftarrow 0$	0	Φ	1	0	**1**	**0**	0A
NOP	0	Φ	1	0	0	Φ	08

Figure 6.35

- The neutral micro-command NOP is obtained by juxtaposing the neutral operations of the several registers involved.
- Each micro-command μ*C* corresponds to a state of the set of control variables; the column $\mu C_{5:0}$ gives the hexadecimal representations of these states.

6.2.12 Comment

A study of Figure 6.35 shows that a suitable choice of the Φ conditions would enable the relation $CLEAR = s^+$ to be checked, thus reducing the number of micro-command variables. A systematic method of reduction, based on the use of a *compatibility graph* in which each vertex is a micro-command variable, is given in [105] and [107] (pp. 96–117).

6.2.13 Software realization: mnemonic L5 program

This program, which can be derived directly from Figure 5.22, is given in Figure 6.36; no refinement is necessary, since each complex instruction can be realized by a single primitive test or assignment instruction.

The **L4** program is shown for comparison. This is given a zig-zag addressing and the assignments replaced by the corresponding micro-commands from Figure 6.35, represented here by their hexadecimal codes. As an exercise the reader should construct the hexadecimal coding for the complete **L4** program.

6.2.14 Hardware realization: the interpreter INT3.2

If we add to the test variables declared in §§6.2.3–4 those of the primitive test instructions of Figure 5.22 we get the following list:

- ***test variables*** *xi*: *EGT, EGi, EN, H, H', 0*

where $xi = 0$ is needed by the **L4** instruction

GO TO *ADR+* = **IF** 0 **ELSE** *ADR0*

The declaration of the control variables Z_j (§6.2.9) is:

- ***control variables*** Z_j: *LOAD, CLEAR, CLR', ENP, LP,* s^+

These determine the micro-command $\mu C_{5:0}$ of (6.23).

The interpreter INT3.2 of Figure 6.27 will be able to execute the **L4** program of Figure 6.36 if it has:

ADR	L4	L5
	PROGRAM *PP*	**program** *PP*
00	**IF** *EN* **ELSE** 0C	**while** *EN*
01	**IF** *H* **ELSE** 03	**while** *H*
02	**GO TO** 01	**end while**
03	**IF** *H'* **ELSE** 05	**while** *H'*
04	**GO TO** 03	**end while**
05	**DO** 00	**do** $i \leftarrow 0$
06	**DO** 28	**do** $T[i] \leftarrow T[i] + 1$
07	**DO** 0B	**do** $s \leftarrow 1$
08	**IF** *s* **ELSE** 0B	**while** *s*
09	**CALL** 0C	**call** *SP1*
0A	**GO TO** 08	**end while**
0B	**GO TO** 00	**end while**
	PROCEDURE *SP1*	**procedure** *SP1*
0C	**IF** *EQT* **ELSE** 15	**if** $T[i] = G[i]$
0D	**DO** 38	**do** $T[i] \leftarrow 0$
0E	**DO** 0C	**do** $i \leftarrow i + 1$
0F	**IF** *EQi* **ELSE** 12	**if** $i = imax$
10	**DO** 0A	**do** $s \leftarrow 0$
11	**GO TO** 14	**else**
12	**DO** 28	**do** $T[i] \leftarrow T[i] + 1$
13	**DO** 0B	**do** $s \leftarrow 1$
	ENDIF	**endif**
14	**GO TO** 16	**else**
15	**DO** 0A	**do** $s \leftarrow 0$
	ENDIF	**endif**
16	**RET**	**end procedure**
	END PROGRAM	**end program**

Figure 6.36

- a control unit CU similar to that of Figure 4.7, with seven test variables $x0 \ldots x6 = EGT \ldots 0$ and a multiplexer MUX, this last driven by the variable OPC_0 of the operating code and implementing the table of Figure 6.34;
- a specialized processing unit PU driven by the micro-command $\mu C_{5:0}$; this is described in §6.2.8 and shown in Figures 6.28–9.

To distinguish it from the software-dominated realization of section 6.1 we say that Figure 6.27 is a *hardware-dominated architecture*, since it consists of:

- a control unit characterized by a minimal program: the number *Ni* of instructions in the **L5** program of Figure 6.36 is only 28, against 154 for the previous solution;
- a processing unit that is relatively complex, since for the example of the clock algorithm it has two comparators, a ROM to hold the values of *G*[*i*], an addressable register *T*[*i*] with a multiplexer and an adder, a programmable counter *i* and a register *s*.

6.2.15 Definition: specialized processor

The combination of a control unit and a specialized processing unit constitutes a *specialized processor*: Figure 6.27 is an example, a *clock processor*. We have not attempted any exhaustive treatment of the hardware construction of such processors, since the orientation of the book is primarily towards software realization; §6.2.18 gives a number of references the reader may care to consult, and in Chapter 7 we take up the subject of more general systems with universal processing units.

6.2.16 Method: synthesis of a specialized processor

The analysis of the problem of the digital clock suggests the following general method for the design of interpreters for the **L4** language that (a) are able to execute complex instructions, in the sense of §6.1.3, and (b) consist of a standard control unit such as Figure 4.7 linked to a specialized processing unit.

1. The specification is represented by a flowchart.
2. If necessary this is structured, using either the local methods of §§5.1.9–11 or the global methods of §5.1.18 or section 8.5.
3. The complex instructions are examined individually and the hardware components of the processing unit deduced: the control instructions determine the computing resources (the combinational

components), and the action instructions the transfer registers (the sequential components).

4. The structured flowchart can then be implemented in primitive instructions and programmed in **L4** or **L5**.
5. The table of micro-commands is derived from the declarations of the control variables Z_j of the processing unit and the operations tables for the transfer registers: it may prove possible to reduce the table of micro-commands by studying the graph of compatibilities between variables, cf. §6.2.12. Zig-zag addressing and hexadecimal coding lead to the **L4** program.
6. The declarations in the processing unit and the structured flowchart fix the number of test variables *xi*. The required processor then follows as the combination of a control unit similar to Figure 4.7, a multiplexer to generate the micro-command μC, and the computing resources and transfer registers needed for the processing unit.

6.2.17 Conclusion

The method of §6.2.16 is based on the following policy decisions:

(a) the processing unit is to consist of a variety of hardware components, both combinational and sequential, able to execute any complex instruction directly, that is, during one clock time;
(b) software decomposition, with programming by successive refinements, is to be replaced by a specialized processing unit in which hardware operators perform the functions of the sub-programs of Figures 6.5–23: thus the combinational logic system *EG*[*ADRA*, *ADRB*] of Figure 6.28 is equivalent to the sub-program *SP2.1* of Figure 6.6, realizing the test $i = imax$.

This can be expressed as the replacement of the sequential (temporal) realization of a sequence of primitive instructions by a standard processing unit, by the combinational (spatial) realization of a single complex instruction by a specialized processing unit designed for that purpose. We can say that this represents a shift from software to hardware, which in turn is a particular case of the trade-off between time and space.

6.2.18 Bibliography

The operators, whether combinational (the computing resources such as comparators, adders etc.) or sequential (transfer registers such as programmable counters, addressable registers etc.) that constitute the processing unit can be described by operations tables or by *transfer register languages*: see [18] (pp. 305–344), [33] (pp. 522–540), [67] (pp. 83–112), [104]. Some novel attempts have been made to give formal descriptions of complex logic operators: thus Lee [109] (pp. 48–72) has suggested a vectorized logical algebra for handling words rather than bits, whilst Hayes [111] has introduced the idea of *expansibility*, meaning the property of components such as multiplexers by virtue of which numbers of them can be interconnected in a systematic manner to provide more powerful components — that is, to perform the same operation on more operands and/or operands of greater size, that is, consisting of more bits.

The formal description of processors consisting of a control unit combined with a processing unit is based on the *Glushkov model*; an exhaustive study of this model, the interface between the two units and the migrations across this interface that bring about the shifts between hardware and software dominance is given by Davio, Deschamps and Thayse in [2] (pp. 251–336) and [3] (pp. 49–67).

Methods for synthesizing specialized processors are given by many authors; applications to the addition, subtraction and multiplication of two binary numbers are given in [18] (pp. 407–458) and [67] (pp. 83–112, 244–267, 288–295); to division in [104], [105] and to the clock algorithm in [138]. Several authors emphasize top-down design for the processing unit, in which the successive refinements lead to novel specification for the final logic diagram: [106] (pp. 136–165, 241–265, 333–367), [110]; the relation of this method to that of top-down programming described in section 6.1 is clear.

Finally, [108] and [139] give very full treatments of the basic arithmetical operations (addition, subtraction, multiplication, division), of certain special (trigonometric) operations and of their realization in hardware and software; and [112] treats in detail so-called *pipeline* architectures, in which a basic operator such as a multiplier is broken down into a sequence of partial operators separated by memory elements (latches), so as to increase the rate at which such operations can flow through the system.

6.2.19 Exercise

If the addressable register $T[i]$ in the digital clock is implemented in synchronized RAM the variable $T_1[5]$, required for the determination of $G[i]$ (cf. Figure 6.29) is not immediately available, nor can a permanent display of the time (hours, minutes, seconds) be provided. Extend the logic diagram of Figure 6.29 by adding a means for producing $T_1[5]$ and making possible the permanent display.

To support the hardware design of the processing unit of Figure 6.27 construct the truth table for $G_{3:0}[i]$ as a function of $i_{2:0}$ and $T_1[5]$: that is, program the read only memory *ROM*[*B*] of Figure 6.29.

6.2.20 Exercise

In Figure 6.28 the hardware equivalent of the sub-program *SP2.1* of Figure 6.6 (the test $i = imax$) is the comparator *EG*[*ADRA*, *ADRB*], taken from Figure 1.14; this produces a logical variable *EGi*. Use the method of §2.4.2 to obtain an alternative hardware equivalent, derived directly by implementing the tree *SP2.1* by means of demultiplexers controlled by a single variable. A procedure such as this demonstrates the complete equivalence between the software-dominated architecture of section 6.1 and the hardware-dominated architecture of section 6.2.

Repeat this for the test $T[i] = G[i]$ (the sub-program *SP1* of Figure 6.10).

7

Microprogramming a universal processor

7.1 UNIVERSAL PROCESSING UNIT

7.1.1 Introduction

The subject of this chapter is the realization of a universal processor and the design of the micro-program for this in the **L4** language. Section 7.1 gives a classification of the various architectures discussed in the book, based on a functional parameter, the set of *primitive specifications* (defined in §7.1.2); this distinguishes between sequential systems, binary decision machines, specialized processors and universal processors. The last, the universal processor, consists of a processing unit, built around an arithmetic and logic unit (described in section 7.1) and itself universal, and a control unit of standard design that interprets a particular 32-bit format of **L4** (described in section 7.2).

The application of the universal processor is illustrated by a fairly complex case study, the micro-program for a small compiler for the **L5** language, *PASCALINE*. Section 7.3 studies the proposed specification and section 7.4 the design of the micro-program, and also a variant of the control unit characterized by containing a 'nano-program'.

Section 7.5 gives some applications and a general conclusion. Here we compare the results obtained in the present book with what has been obtained with 'classical' micro-programming, the usual aim of which is the interpretation of an assembly language. Finally, we explain the two levels of interpretation — program and micro-program — of a micro-programmable universal processor.

7.1.2 Description: architectures

In our progress from the binary decision machine of Figure 2.60, the interpreter INT1, to the specialized processor of Figure 6.27, the interpreter INT3.2 for the clock algorithm, we have met a variety of hardware logic systems, with and without memory. Each of these constitutes an *architecture* and each architecture defines an interface between the hardware realization — the logic system — and the software realization — the program residing in the memory — of the specification. These architectures can be classified in various ways, one of the most popular being according to the technology used — small, medium or large scale integrated circuits, bit-sliced circuits, programmable logic arrays, custom chips, 32-bit micro-processors etc.

In view of the speed of technological development we have chosen a basis that avoids the need for frequent revisions, the *functional parameter*. We define this as the set of *primitive specifications*, each of which — an internal state or an instruction — describes the set of items of information processed by the hardware during a single clock time. This gives four principal architectures, described briefly in the following paragraphs: sequential system (§7.1.3), binary decision machine (§7.1.4), specialized processor (§7.1.5), universal processor (§7.1.6).

7.1.3 Type 1 architecture: sequential system

The *synchronous sequential system* or *finite state machine*, defined in §5.3.1, is represented by Figure 5.34. The set of primitive specifications reduces to a single element, the internal state or *general instruction* represented either by a row in the state table of Figure 5.35 or by a vertex in the state diagram, Figure 5.52. Such an instruction can be written, in a language such as Pascal, as a mnemonic expression:

case $(x1, x2, \ldots xn)$ **of**
$00\ldots0$: $y^+ = \ldots;\ Z = \ldots;$
$00\ldots1$: $y^+ = \ldots;\ Z = \ldots;$
.
.
$11\ldots1$: $y^+ = \ldots;\ Z = \ldots$
end (7.1)

The test of the n input variables $x1, x2, \ldots xn$ and the generation of a future state y^+ and an output state Z are all performed during the same clock period, so the speed of the system is very high. Against this, the need to represent the 2^n states of the n input variables severely limits the size of problem that can be handled.

7.1.4 Type 2 architecture: binary decision machine

This is defined in §2.3.11 and several variants have been discussed: INT1 (Figure 2.60), INT2 (Figure 3.23), INT3 (Figure 4.7), INT3.1 (Figure

6.26), the purpose of all of which is to interpret a set of instructions, that is, a language. Neglecting the call and return instructions, the set of primitive specifications reduces to a single test instruction:

$$\textbf{IF } xi \text{ (}\textbf{THEN } ADR1\text{) } \textbf{ELSE } ADR0 \tag{7.2}$$

and a single assignment instruction:

$$\textbf{DO } REG[j] \leftarrow OUT \text{ (}\textbf{GO TO } ADR+\text{)} \tag{7.3}$$

The fundamental difference from the sequential system is that here either a single input variable is tested or a single output state is generated during one clock time; thus the general instruction (7.1) has been broken down in time and made sequential. This has three consequences: it reduces the speed of the system, it makes handling of complex problems more feasible and it leads naturally to the partitioning of the machine into two systems, a control unit that computes the next addresses and a processing unit consisting of the assignment registers (discussed in section 7.3).

There are in fact architectures that are intermediate between these two types; the corresponding machines test K input variables during a single clock time, where K lies between 1 (the value for the binary decision machine) and n (the value for the sequential system): cf. [86], [144].

7.1.5 Type 3 architecture: specialized processor

This is defined in §6.2.15, with the processor INT3.2 for the clock algorithm (Figure 6.27) as an example. Neglecting again the call and return instructions, the set of primitive specifications reduces to a single control instruction:

$$\textbf{IF } xi \text{ (}\textbf{THEN } ADR1\text{) } \textbf{ELSE } ADR0 \tag{7.4}$$

where xi is either a test variable or the result of a comparison of a given pair of words and a single action instruction:

$$\textbf{DO } s \text{ (}\textbf{GO TO } ADR+\text{)} \tag{7.5}$$

where s is a micro-command that assigns a constant or a function to a register.

The clock algorithm contains both comparisons of words:

$$T[i] = G[i], \quad i = imax \tag{7.6}$$

and assignments of functions to registers:

$$T[i] \leftarrow T[i] + 1, \quad i \leftarrow i + 1 \tag{7.7}$$

Whilst the control unit of such a processor is essentially the same as that of a binary decision machine, the processing unit is specially designed to implement comparisons and assignments such as (7.6) and (7.7). Thus an entire sub-program that would need several clock times for execution by a binary decision machine can be expressed here by a single instruction and executed in a single clock time: thus we have a shift from software to hardware, the extra speed provided by the specialized processor being paid for in extra hardware.

7.1.6 Type 4 architecture: universal processor

Preservation of the speed of the specialized processor whilst avoiding the need to design a special processing unit for each problem specification is the motivation for the design of a general purpose, or universal, processing unit. The main features of such a unit are suggested by the example of the clock algorithm and are described in detail in §§7.1.8–15, together with their implementation in bit-slice integrated circuits. The exploitation in a fairly complex application, the micro-program for an **L5** compiler, is given in section 7.4.

The word comparisons in the clock algorithm recalled in (7.6) are equivalent to:

$$T[i] - G[i] = 0, \quad i - imax = 0 \tag{7.8}$$

which can be implemented as the arithmetical subtraction of the two terms or operands on the left, followed by a test of the result for zero. The assignments (7.7) can be implemented by the arithmetical addition of the operands on the right, followed by assignment of the result to a register designed for the purpose. Thus the universal processing unit must have at least the following components:

- an arithmetic unit, RALU in Figure 7.1, able to add and subtract two binary numbers and test the result for zero;
- an addressable register, or synchronized RAM, able to store and return functions such as $T[i]$ and $G[i]$; such a memory, labelled RAM in Figure 7.1, is addressed by a specific register MAR;
- one or more assignment registers, either under the direct control of the control unit (REG, DMUX in Figure 7.1) or included in the arithmetic unit; for example, to hold the variable i;
- an input unit (IN in Figure 7.1) to read the data into the memory RAM, for example the values of $G[i]$ in Figure 6.8;
- a single bi-directional bus BUS, to provide all the necessary information transfers between the components.

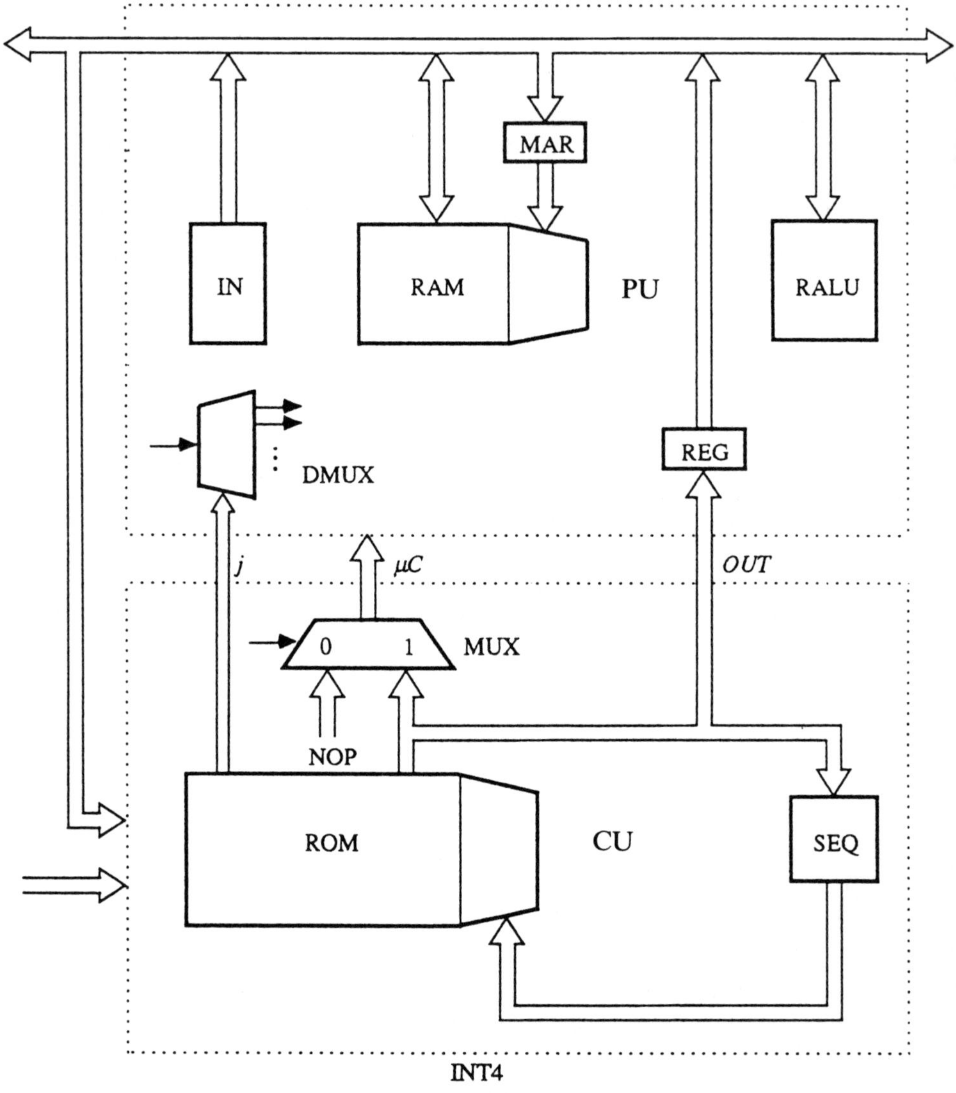

Figure 7.1

Neglecting the call and return instructions, the set of primitive specifications consists of (a) a control instruction:

IF *xi* (**THEN** *ADR1*) **ELSE** *ADR0* (7.9)

where *xi* is either a test variable or the result of a word comparison; (b) an assignment instruction, typical of the binary decision machine:

$$\textbf{DO } REG[j] \leftarrow OUT \ (\textbf{GO TO } ADR+) \tag{7.10}$$

and (c) an action instruction, typical of the specialized processor:

$$\textbf{DO } s \ (\textbf{GO TO } ADR+) \tag{7.11}$$

where s is a universal micro-command, in this case

$$s \equiv BUS = BUS[\mu C_{23:20}], \quad RAM[B] \leftarrow F1, \quad Q \leftarrow F2 \tag{7.12}$$

We shall study this micro-command later, in §7.2.8, where we show that in each clock time it performs two assignments simultaneously, from the arbitrary origins $F1$, $F2$ to the internal registers $RAM[B]$ and Q of RALU.

The processing unit shown as PU in Figure 7.1, and described by a micro-command s such as (7.12), forms a *universal processing unit*; the combination of this with a control unit (CU) similar to that of the specialized processor of Figure 6.27, forms a *universal processor* (or *micro-processor*), the interpreter INT4 to Figure 7.1.

The remainder of this section gives a detailed analysis of this processing unit; the next section, 7.2, deals with the control unit.

7.1.7 Principles adopted

Many variants of the architecture are possible within the general framework of Type 4, the universal processor, differing mainly in the characteristics of the arithmetic and logic unit, the number of buses, the functions performed by the universal micro-command, etc; references are given in the bibliography, §7.1.17. The position we have adopted, with the aim of simplifying the hardware realization, is that a complex operation that would require several transfer registers and/or several computing resources operating in parallel — that is, during the same clock time — shall be broken down into a sequence of elementary operations, each using a single register and/or resource and the sequence taking several clock times to complete. In other words, we sacrifice speed, which requires parallel computations, to simplicity, which implies sequential operation.

This approach explains the choice of a single bi-directional bus rather than a number of separate buses, and of a 1-out-of-n coding of the variables that control the registers, which excludes the possibility of simultaneous transfers (§7.1.14).

7.1.8 Description: random access memory RAM

This has to fulfil two essential general conditions:

- it must be *synchronized*, to ensure that it keeps in step with the clock

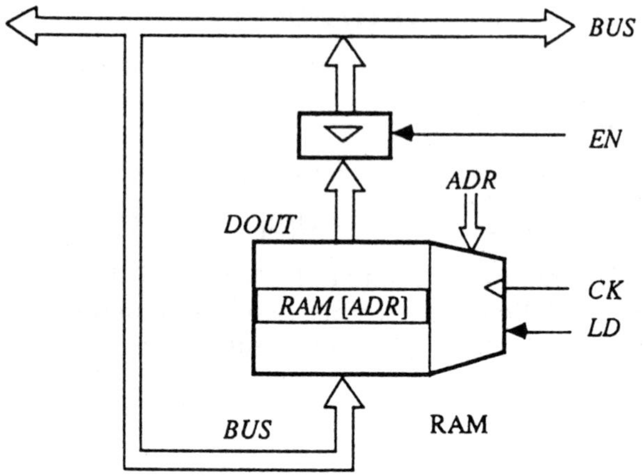

Figure 7.2

signal *CK* and is equivalent to an addressable register (§6.1.5);

- it must include a *bi-directional bus*, to limit the number of connections and so simplify the hardware — the principle stated in §7.1.7.

This is easily achieved by combining a synchronized random access memory (§6.1.6, Figures 6.2 and 6.3) with a 3-state device (§1.1.15, Figures 1.15 and 1.16), as shown in Figure 7.2. Putting

$$T^+ = BUS,\ OUT = DOUT,\quad T[i] = RAM[ADR],\quad LOAD = LD \tag{7.13}$$

we get the schema of Figure 7.3 and the operations table of Figure 7.4.

The size and the organization of the memory may depend on the particular application. In the case of the clock algorithm, $RAM[ADR]$ has to hold the functions $T[i]$ and $G[i]$, for which a 4-bit address, for $i_{2:0}$ and $T_1[5]$, and two independent 4-bit words, for $T_{3:0}$ and $G_{3:0}$, will suffice. For more complex problems, such as the compiler we shall discuss in section 7.4, we can need over a hundred addresses; so we choose an 8-bit address, $ADR_{7:0}$, giving a memory size of 256 words, and for the sake of simplicity in the addressing an 8-bit bus, $BUS_{7:0}$, also. Only the width of the memory now remains to be settled, and for this we take 16 bits, divided into three independent words, two of four bits and one of eight bits: $RAM_{15:12}$, $RAM_{11:8}$, $RAM_{7:0}$; this gives a very flexible organization, particularly well adapted to the problem of section 7.4. Thus the memory finally arrived at is in three parts RAM1, RAM2, RAM3 as shown in Figure 7.5, defined by the words $RAM_{15:12}[ADR]$, $RAM_{11:8}[ADR]$, $RAM_{7:0}[ADR]$ respectively. Each of

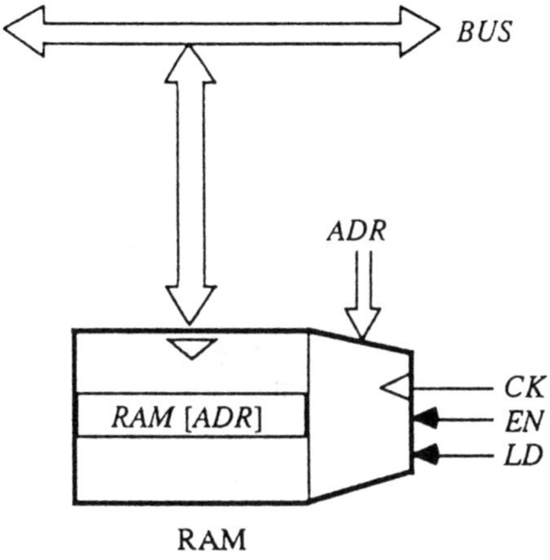

Figure 7.3

OPERATION	DESCRIPTION: RAM	*EN*	*LD*
HOLD	$BUS = BUS, \quad DOUT = RAM\ [ADR]$	0	0
WRITE	$BUS = BUS, \quad DOUT = RAM\ [ADR], RAM\ [ADR] \leftarrow BUS$	0	1
READ	$BUS = DOUT, DOUT = RAM\ [ADR]$	1	Φ

Figure 7.4

these partial memories has its own read (*EN*) and write (*LD*) control variable, but all share the same address $ADR_{7:0}$, generated by the *memory address register* MAR.

7.1.9 Description: input unit IN

The design of the *input unit* IN will be influenced by the intended applications. For the example of section 7.4, a compiler, we must be able to write 4- or 8-bit words into the memory RAM through the medium of the single bus BUS of Figure 7.5 and in conformity with the organization shown. A 4-bit word is equivalent to a hexadecimal character, which can be produced by a keyboard K with 16 keys labelled 0–9, A–F as in Figure 7.6. Four hexadecimal characters form a full 16-bit memory word; they are distributed over three registers REG1 ($INL_{15:12}$), REG2 ($INL_{11:8}$), REG3 ($INL_{7:0}$), a partitioning compatible with that of the memory.

The specification of §7.4.2 gives up to 16 types of operation such as compilation, writing of data, etc; the selection of a particular one is

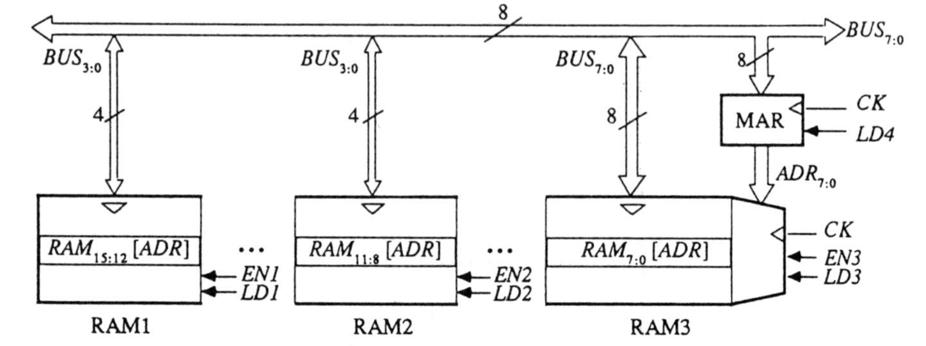

Figure 7.5

made by means of a single hexadecimal character $FLAG_{3:0}$, generated by the keyboard and stored in the register REG4. Some further logic systems, not shown in Figure 7.6, are needed to load the characters generated by the keyboard into the registers REG1–4; the outputs of these registers are connected to the bus via 3-state circuits whose control variables *EN*6–9 will be discussed later in §7.1.13.

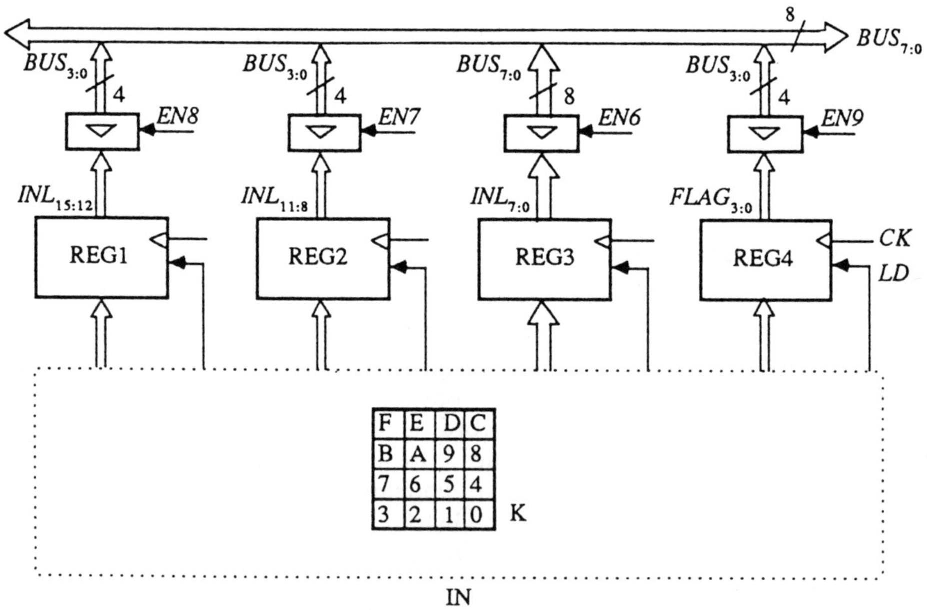

Figure 7.6

7.1.10 Description: arithmetic and logic register RALU

Many RALUs are available on the market, of which the most popular are given in §7.1.17. We shall describe an 8-bit unit, shown diagrammatically in Figure 7.7, constructed by combining two Am2901 integrated circuits from Advanced Micro Devices [125]. We have chosen this type of circuit for the same reasons as for the sequencer of §4.2.3: it is particularly well adapted to the specification we have to meet (section 7.4) and its iterative (bit-slice) structure enables it to operate on binary words of any multiple of four bits.

The RALU of Figure 7.7 falls into two parts: a sequential part S (transfer registers), consisting of a synchronized memory RAM and a register QREG, and a combinational part (computing resource) consisting of an 8-function ALU, two *shifting registers* RAMSHIFTER, QSHIFTER, an input multiplexer ALUMUX, an output multiplexer OUTMUX and a 3-state circuit. Apart from the two for the addresses $A_{3:0}$, $B_{3:0}$ all the buses are eight bits wide.

7.1.11 Description: RALU transfer registers

The key element in the sequential part of the RALU (S in Figure 7.7) is a synchronized memory of sixteen 8-bit words (§6.1.6), constituting a bank of 16 registers. The addresses $A_{3:0}$, $B_{3:0}$, taken as a pair, enable the words $RAM[A]$, $RAM[B]$, held in the memory, to be read to the outputs $A = AOUT$, $B = BOUT$; whilst the address $B_{3:0}$ alone enables the writing of a new word $RAM[B]$ coming from RAMSHIFTER. The memory RAM is described formally by the relations

$$AOUT = RAM[A], \quad BOUT = RAM[B], \quad RAM[B] \leftarrow BIN \tag{7.14}$$

The second element in this sequential part is the register QREG described by the transfer

$$Q \leftarrow D \tag{7.15}$$

7.1.12 Description: computing resources of the RALU

Figure 7.8 is the operations table for the multiplexer ALUMUX. Each of the eight states I_2, I_1, I_0 selects, for each of the two outputs (destinations) R, S one of the five inputs (sources): $D = BUS$, $A = AOUT$, $B = BOUT$, Q and the constant 0; here D means 'direct', A, B are the two outputs from RAM, Q is the output from QREG and 0 (zero) is $0_D = 00_H = 0000\ 0000_B$.

The key element in the combinational part is the arithmetic and logic

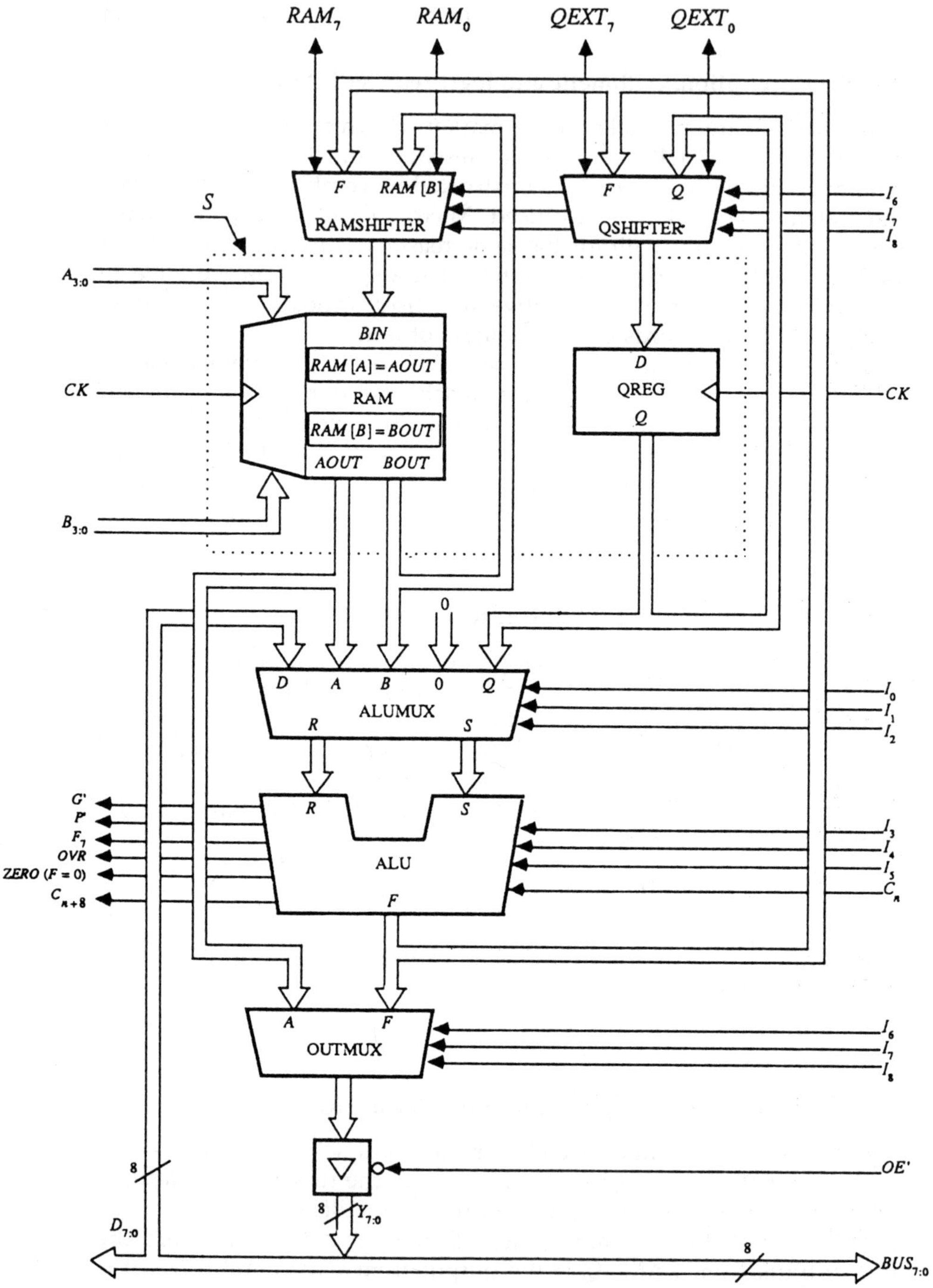

RALU (2 x Am2901)

Figure 7.7

OPERATION	DESCRIPTION: ALUMUX		I_2	I_1	I_0
OP0	$R = A,$	$S = Q$	0	0	0
OP1	A	B	0	0	1
OP2	0	Q	0	1	0
OP3	0	B	0	1	1
OP4	0	A	1	0	0
OP5	D	A	1	0	1
OP6	D	Q	1	1	0
OP7	D	0	1	1	1

Figure 7.8

OPERATION	DESCRIPTION: ALU	I_5	I_4	I_3
OP0 = ADD	$C_{n+8}, F = R + S + C_n$	0	0	0
OP1 = SUB R	$= S - R = R' + S + C_n$	0	0	1
OP2 = SUB S	$= R - S = R + S' + C_n$	0	1	0
OP3 = OR	$F = R \vee S$	0	1	1
OP4 = AND	$= R \wedge S$	1	0	0
OP5 = R' AND S	$= R' \wedge S$	1	0	1
OP6 = EXOR	$= R \oplus S$	1	1	0
OP7 = EXNOR	$= (R \oplus S)'$	1	1	1

Figure 7.9

unit itself, ALU, described by the operation table of Figure 7.9. The eight states I_5, I_4, I_3 determine the following eight operations.

- Three arithmetical operations, OP0–2, for addition or subtraction of two words R, S (denoted by '+', '−' respectively), taking into account a possible carry C_n from a previous slice; in the final result C_{n+8}, F, C_{n+8} is the possible carry and $F_{7:0}$ is the output from ALU. The details of binary subtraction are given in section 8.6.
- Five logical operations OP3–7, each acting on each pair of bits R_j, S_j of the words R, S and holding to the conventions given in section 8.7. The operations are as follows:

  OP3: logical OR, denoted by $\vee$
  OP4, 5: logical AND, denoted by $\wedge$
  OP6, 7: exclusive–OR, denoted by $\oplus$

  The result is given as an 8-bit word $F_{7:0}$.

The ALU produces the following set of signals, the details of which are given in [125], [63] (pp. 48–65) and [65] (pp. 91–127):

- the variables P' (*propagation*) and G' (*generation*), which are needed by the *look-ahead carry* system;
- the variable *OVR*, which indicates *overflow;*
- the flag F; if $F = 0$ then the monomial

$$ZERO = F_7' \cdot F_6' \cdot F_5' \cdot F_4' \cdot F_3' \cdot F_2' \cdot F_1' \cdot F_0' = 1$$

Figure 7.10 is the operations table for the output multiplexer OUTMUX and the shift registers RAMSHIFTER, QSHIFTER. Each state I_8, I_7, I_6 determines the functioning of the sequential part, that is, of the memory RAM, described by the state $RAM[B]$, and of the register QREG, described by the state Q.

In conformity with the conventions of §1.2.14, $F/2$, $Q/2$ and $F*2$, $Q*2$ mean shifts to the right and to the left respectively (see also section 8.7). Here RAM_7, RAM_0, $QEXT_7$ and $QEXT_0$, which represent bi-directional terminals, are the input variables to the two shift registers.

Each state I_8, I_7, I_6 also describes the behaviour of the combinational part of RALU, that is, of the output Y and the bi-directional terminals RAM_7, RAM_0, $QEXT_7$, $QEXT_0$; for this:

- the output state Y corresponds to $OE' = 0$, that is, that the 3-state circuit is in the state TRUE; if $OE' = 1$ then $Y = \nabla$ whatever the values of I_8, I_7, I_6;
- according to the type of operation, the terminals RAM_7, RAM_0, $QEXT_7$, $QEXT_0$ are either output variables designated by F_7, F_0, Q_7, or Q_0, or input variables designated by IN_7 or IN_0;
- the values of some bits are undefined, corresponding to Φ conditions; these bits are marked '—' in the table.

OPERATION	DESCRIPTION: RAM, QREG		DESCRIPTION: Y	RAM_7	RAM_0	$QEXT_7$	$QEXT_0$	I_8	I_7	I_6
OP0	$RAM[B] \leftarrow RAM[B]$,	$Q \leftarrow F$	F	–	–	–	–	0	0	0
OP1	$RAM[B]$,	Q	F	–	–	–	–	0	0	1
OP2	F ,	Q	A	–	–	–	–	0	1	0
OP3	F ,	Q	F	–	–	–	–	0	1	1
OP4	$RAM_7.F/2$,	$QEXT_7.Q/2$	F	IN_7	F_0	IN_7	Q_0	1	0	0
OP5	$RAM_7.F/2$,	Q	F	IN_7	F_0	–	Q_0	1	0	1
OP6	$F*2.RAM_0$,	$Q*2.QEXT_0$	F	F_7	IN_0	Q_7	IN_0	1	1	0
OP7	$F*2.RAM_0$,	Q	F	F_7	IN_0	Q_7	–	1	1	1

Figure 7.10

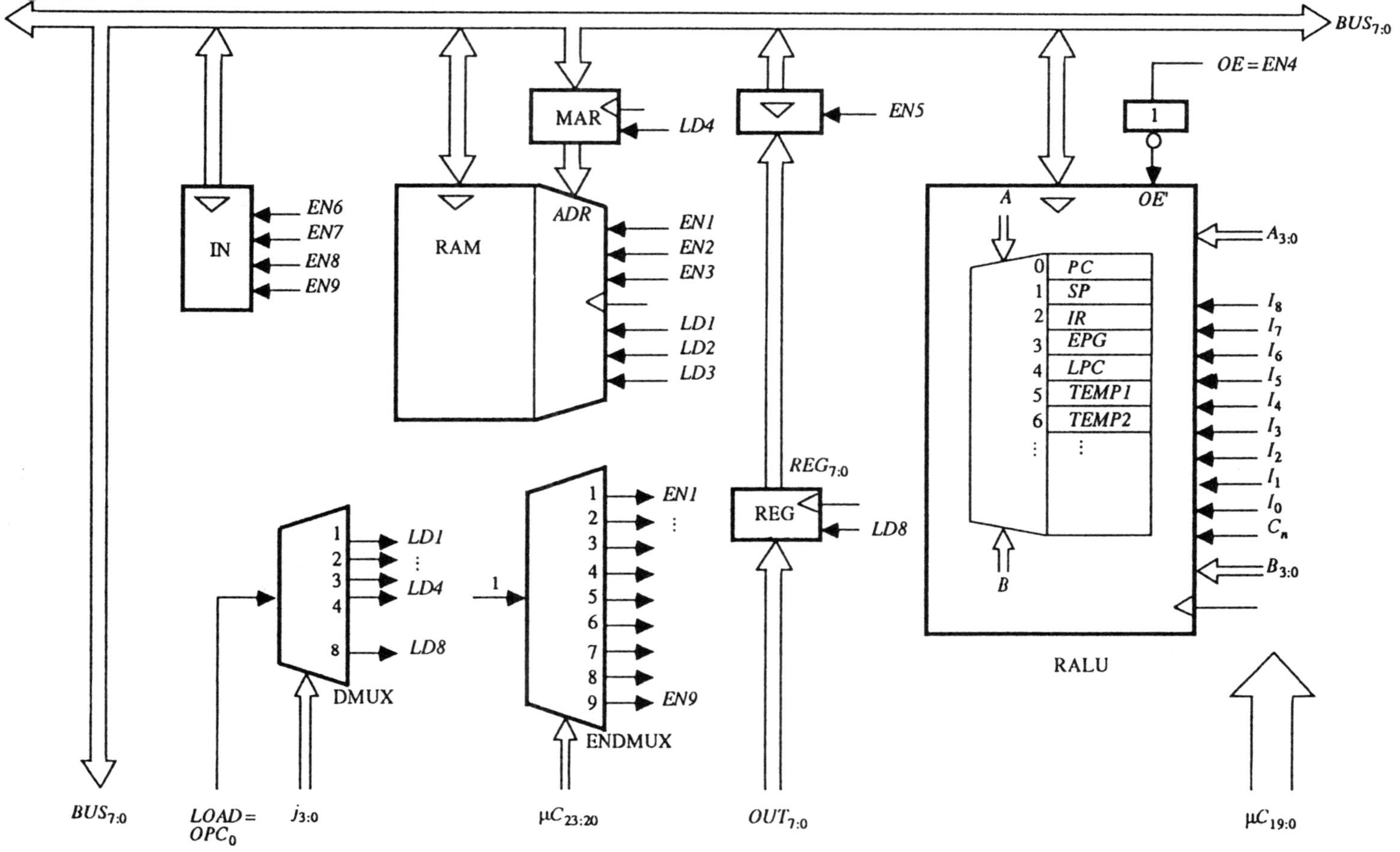

INT4: PU

Figure 7.11

7.1.13 Description: bi-directional bus BUS

As was explained in §7.1.7, we have opted for a single bus, an 8-bit bi-directional bus $BUS_{7:0}$, to carry all the information transfers between the input unit IN, the memory RAM and its address register MAR, the arithmetic and logic unit RALU and a further register REG. This last, as shown in Figure 7.1, transfers a state *OUT*, produced by the control unit, directly to the bus via a 3-state circuit.

We saw in §1.1.18 that we can connect the outputs of any number n of 3-state circuits together provided that we can guarantee that only one is active at any one time, and that this implies a 1-out-of-n coding of the control variables of a group of n circuits. Such a coding is easily achieved by means of a demultiplexer.

In Figure 7.11 nine circuits are connected to the one bus BUS; their control variables *EN1–9* are generated by the demultiplexer ENDMUX, itself controlled by four new variables $\mu C_{23:20}$. From §1.1.17 we see that this combination is equivalent to a multiplexer with nine inputs; the output state of the assemblage is the state of the bus, $BUS_{7:0}$, described by the operations table of Figure 7.12. We can show this state as a function of the four control variables $\mu C_{23:20}$:

$$BUS = BUS[\mu C_{23:20}] \tag{7.16}$$

Finally, Figure 7.12 shows that in the case of OP1, OP2 and OP7–9 only half of the bus ($BUS_{3:0}$) is defined and the remaining half $BUS_{7:4}$ is in the high impedance state ∇.

OPERATION	DESCRIPTION: BUS	$\mu C_{23:20}$
OP0	$BUS_{7:0} = \nabla$	0000
OP1	$BUS_{7:4} = \nabla, BUS_{3:0} = RAM_{15:12}$	0001
OP2	$BUS_{7:4} = \nabla, BUS_{3:0} = RAM_{11:8}$	0010
OP3	$BUS_{7:0} = RAM_{7:0}$	0011
OP4	$BUS_{7:0} = Y_{7:0}$	0100
OP5	$BUS_{7:0} = REG_{7:0}$	0101
OP6	$BUS_{7:0} = INL_{7:0}$	0110
OP7	$BUS_{7:4} = \nabla, BUS_{3:0} = INL_{11:8}$	0111
OP8	$BUS_{7:4} = \nabla, BUS_{3:0} = INL_{15:12}$	1000
OP9	$BUS_{7:4} = \nabla, BUS_{3:0} = FLAG_{3:0}$	1001
OP10...15	$BUS_{7:0} = \nabla$	1010...1111

Figure 7.12

7.1.14 Description: demultiplexer DMUX

In Figures 7.5 and 7.11 there are five registers RAM1–3, MAR, REG that are controlled by the five independent control variables *LD1–4*, *LD8*. It is of course quite possible to load a number of registers simultaneously, but in the interests of simplicity we restrict the loading to one register at a time, that is, at most one loading in any one clock time: this is consistent with implementation of the interpreter INT3 (Figure 4.7), whose demultiplexer DMUX, controlled by the word $j_{3:0}$ and the variable $LOAD = LD = OPC_0$, can load one out of the 16 registers. Figure 7.13 describes the control of the five registers of Figure 7.11, as provided by DMUX.

OPERATION	DESCRIPTION: RAM, MAR, REG	$j_{3:0}$
OP0	NOP	0000
OP1	$RAM_{15:12} \leftarrow BUS_{3:0}$	0001
OP2	$RAM_{11:8} \leftarrow BUS_{3:0}$	0010
OP3	$RAM_{7:0} \leftarrow BUS_{7:0}$	0011
OP4	$ADR_{7:0} \leftarrow BUS_{7:0}$	0100
OP5...7	NOP	0101...0111
OP8	$REG_{7:0} \leftarrow OUT_{7:0}$	1000
OP9...15	NOP	1001...1111

Figure 7.13

7.1.15 Hardware realization: universal processing unit

The assemblage of the memory RAM together with its register MAR (Figure 7.5), the input unit IN (Figure 7.6), the arithmetic and logic unit RALU (Figure 7.7), the bi-directional bus BUS, the register REG with its 3-state circuit, and the demultiplexers ENDMUX, DMUX constitutes the universal processing unit PU shown in Figure 7.11.

7.1.16 Conclusion

Within the restricted framework of a single-bus Type 4 architecture the schema of Figure 7.11 is an entirely representative example of the universal processing unit. The essential components are the arithmetic and logic unit RALU (Figure 7.7) and the synchronized memory RAM (Figure 7.3) with its register MAR; their characteristics provide the scope for truly universal application. The remaining components, the input unit IN, the register REG and the demultiplexers ENDMUX, DMUX (Figure 7.11) play a secondary role and can be tailored to particular applications: in our case, to the compiler to be discussed in section 7.4.

Figure 7.11 does not give anything explicit concerning the output unit, whose purpose is to display the results; this can be achieved by direct reading of the bus or by transfer of the bus state $BUS_{7:0}$ or that of the control unit $OUT_{7:0}$ to one or more registers provided for the purpose and controlled by DMUX.

7.1.17 Bibliography

Universal processing units, involving arithmetic and logic units, can be realized in very different ways. Various architectures, using one bus or several, and the associated timings, are described in [2] (pp. 336–341) and [3] (pp. 69–73). The Am2901 RALU is described in detail in [2] (pp. 341–346), [3] (pp. 73–77), [63] (pp. 48–65), [64] (pp. 147–152), [114] and [129] (pp. 155–165). Tables of comparisons and detailed analyses of the most popular circuits such as Intel 3002, Motorola MC10800, Texas Instruments SBP0401A and 74S481, Advanced Micro Devices Am2901 and 2903, Monolithic Memories 6701 and Fairchild 9405 are given in [63] (pp. 48–139) and [64] (pp. 143–160). Uses of Am2901 and 2903 are given in [65] (pp. 91–127). The design of an ALU and the analysis of shifters are treated in [18] (pp. 358–406) in particular.

7.2 THE CONTROL UNIT

7.2.1 Specification

With the definition of Type 4 architecture of §7.1.6, the universal processor will combine the characteristics of the interpreter INT3 or 3.1, which make possible the assignment $REG[j] \leftarrow OUT$, with those of INT3.2, which lead to the micro-command μC of §6.2.9.

The control unit we are thus led to is shown in Figure 7.14. Whilst the formats of the instructions **IF. . .**, **CALL. . .** and **RET** remain as in Figure 4.7, that of **DO. . .** has been modified as follows:

- for a value of j between 0 and 7 ($j_{3:0} = 0000\ldots0111$ or $j_3 = 0$) **DO. . .** simultaneously loads the register $REG[j]$ and executes a micro-command $\mu C_{23:0} = ROM_{23:0}$:

$$\textbf{DO}\ REG[j], \mu C_{23:0} = \textbf{DO}\ ROM_{27:0} \tag{7.17}$$

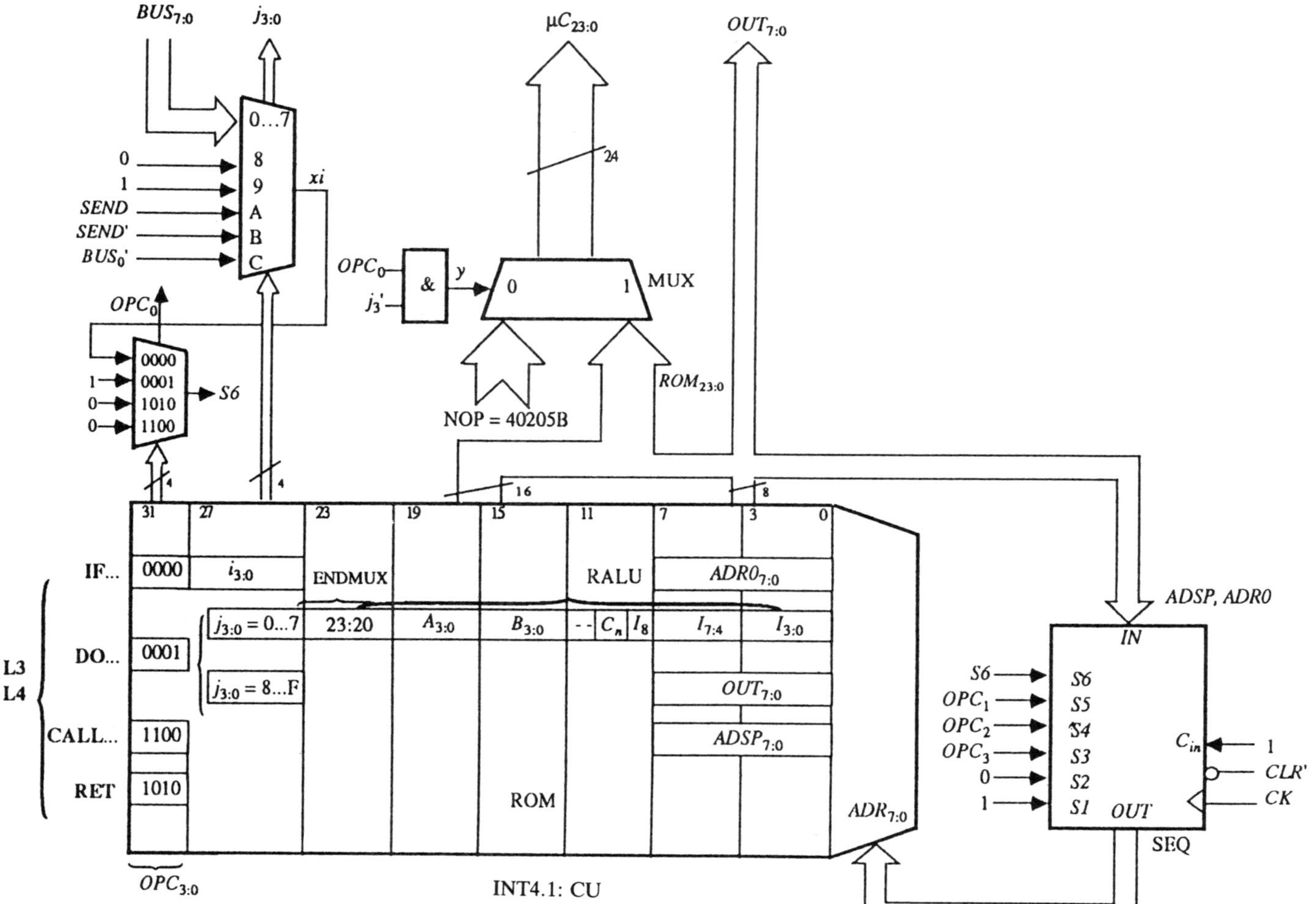

INT4.1: CU

Figure 7.14

where $REG[j]$, defined by Figure 7.13 (RAM or MAR), is loaded with the state of the bus; so this is in effect a transfer $REG[j] \leftarrow BUS$;

- for j between 8 and F_H ($j_{3:0} = 1000\ldots1111$ or $j_3 = 1$) **DO...** loads the register $REG[j]$ with the state $OUT_{7:0}$, which is a constant, held in the memory ROM

$$\textbf{DO}\ REG[j] \leftarrow OUT \tag{7.18}$$

In what follows we shall distinguish between *micro-command instructions*, described by (7.17), and assignment instructions, described by (7.18).

7.2.2 Hardware realization: control unit

The functioning of the control unit of Figure 7.14 is summarized in the operations table of Figure 7.15.

OPERATION	DESCRIPTION: μC, $REG[j]$	OPC_0	j_3	$LOAD$	y
IF..., CALL..., RET	$\mu C_{23:0}$ = NOP , HOLD	0	Φ	0	0
DO $ROM_{27:0}$	$\mu C_{23:0} = ROM_{23:0}$, $REG[j] \leftarrow BUS$	1	0	1	1
DO $REG[j] \leftarrow OUT$	$\mu C_{23:0}$ = NOP , $REG[j] \leftarrow OUT$	1	1	1	0

Figure 7.15

- During the execution of a test, call or return instruction, characterized by $OPC_0 = 0$ ($j_3 = \Phi$), all the control variables of the processing unit are inactive (neutral micro-command NOP) and also all the registers $REG[j]$ (operation HOLD).
- During that of a micro-command instruction, with $0 \leqslant j \leqslant 7$ ($OPC_0 = 1$, $j_3 = 0$) the control variables of the processing unit are active ($\mu C_{23:0} = ROM_{23:0}$), also those of the registers $REG[j]$ ($REG[j] \leftarrow BUS$).
- During that of an assignment instruction, with $8 \leqslant j \leqslant F_H$ ($OPC_0 = 1$, $j_3 = 1$) the control variables of the processing unit are inactive (NOP) but those of the registers are active, $REG[j] \leftarrow OUT$.

Thus the equations for the variables $LOAD$ (demultiplexer DMUX, Figure 7.11) and y (multiplexer MUX, Figure 7.14) are

$$LOAD = OPC_0; \qquad y = OPC_0 \cdot j_3' \tag{7.19}$$

7.2.3 Description: universal micro-command

Having dealt with the variables $LOAD = OPC_0$, $j_{3:0}$ and $OUT_{7:0}$, we can see from Figure 7.11 that there remain those required for control of the processing unit:

- the control variables of the demultiplexer ENDMUX (Figure 7.12):

  $\mu C_{23:20}$

- the control variables of the arithmetic and logic unit RALU (Figures 7.7–10):

  $$\mu C_{19:0} = A_{3:0}, B_{3:0}, (\Phi, \Phi, C_n, I_8), I_{7:4}, I_{3:0} \qquad (7.20)$$

  where the two bits $\mu C_{11:10}$ are not used in the application discussed in section 7.4 and are therefore shown as Φ; they can be held in reserved for other applications.

The state $\mu C_{23:0} = \mu C_{23:20}, \mu C_{19:0}$ is the final, or *universal micro-command*, represented by a 24-bit word, for which a possible format is shown in Figure 7.14. We have sought to make this easier to read by partitioning it into 4-bit words, each word assigned to one type of function.

We say, as a definition, that each part of the micro-command, for example the word $\mu C_{19:0}$, forms a *command state* or *micro-order*.

7.2.4 Determination of the command state of the RALU

In order to perform an arithmetical (addition, subtraction etc.) or a logical (AND, OR, exclusive-OR) operation by means of an RALU we have to determine one or more command states $\mu C_{19:0}$ that can produce, at each clock time, the required values of $A_{3:0}$, $B_{3:0}$, C_n (the carry bit) and $I_8, \ldots I_0$. As an example, consider the determination of a state that will, in the same clock time, write the input state D (see Figure 7.7) to the register $RAM[B]$ at address $B = 5$ and read the register $RAM[A]$ at address $A = 0$ to the output Y:

$$RAM[B{=}5] \leftarrow D, \quad Y = RAM[A{=}0] \qquad (7.21)$$

We see from Figure 7.10 that the only operation that can generate $Y = RAM[A]$ directly is OP2:

$$RAM[B] \leftarrow F, \quad Y = A = RAM[A] \text{ for } I_8, I_7, I_6 = 010 \qquad (7.22)$$

To obtain $F = D$ was choose first, from Figure 7.9, the logical operation OP3 (OR):

$$F = R \vee S \quad \text{for} \quad I_5, I_4, I_3 = 011 \qquad (7.23)$$

and then, from Figure 7.8, the operation OP7:

$$R = D,\ S = 0 \quad \text{for} \quad I_2, I_1, I_0 = 111 \tag{7.24}$$

Substitution from (7.24) into (7.23) gives the command state (7.21) required; and substituting into (7.20), noting that $C_n = \Phi$, we have the binary form

$$\mu C_{19:0} = 0000,\ 0101,\ (\Phi, \Phi, \Phi, 0),\ 1001,\ 1111 \tag{7.25}$$

which in hexadecimal is

$$\mu C_{19:0} = 0509\text{F} \tag{7.26}$$

where all the Φ conditions have been replaced by 0.

7.2.5 Command state table for the RALU

We see from (7.20) that in the state $\mu C_{19:0}$, $A_{3:0}$ and $B_{3:0}$ represent addresses of RALU registers and act as numbers or operands rather than as control variables. It follows that the operation performed by the RALU is determined by the command state $\mu C_{11:0}$:

$$\mu C_{11:0} = (\Phi, \Phi, C_n, I_8),\ I_{7:4},\ I_{3:0} \tag{7.27}$$

We shall see in section 7.4 that the example of the compiler requires only eight distinct command states $\mu C_{11:0}$, given in the operations table, or *command state table*, of Figure 7.16. Here we have adopted the conventions that: (1) in deriving the hexadecimal values all the Φ conditions have been given the value 0; (2) '+', '−' are the normal arithmetical operators; and (3) FF_H is 1111 1111 in binary.

OPERATION	DESCRIPTION: RALU		C_n	$I_8 \ldots I_6$	$I_5 \ldots I_3$	$I_2 \ldots I_0$	$\mu C_{11:0}$
OP1 = WRITE	$RAM[B] \leftarrow D$	$, Y = RAM[A]$	Φ	010	011	111	09F
OP2 = READ		$Y = RAM[B]$	Φ	001	011	011	05B
OP3 = INC	$RAM[B] \leftarrow RAM[B] + 1$	$, Y = RAM[B] + 1$	1	011	000	011	2C3
OP4 = CLEAR	$RAM[B] \leftarrow 0$	$, Y = 0$	Φ	011	100	010	0E2
OP5 = READ INC		$Y = RAM[B] + 1$	1	001	000	011	243
OP6 = DEC	$RAM[B] \leftarrow RAM[B] - 1$	$, Y = RAM[B] - 1$	0	011	001	011	0CB
OP7 = STACK	$RAM[B] \leftarrow FF_H - RAM[A]$	$, Y = FF_H - RAM[A]$	0	011	010	100	0D4
OP8 = CLEAR OUT		$Y = 0$	Φ	001	100	010	062

Figure 7.16

7.2.6 Comments

The complexity of the Am2901 RALU is such that the command state $\mu C_{11:0}$ can be implemented in several different ways; thus Figure 7.16 is only one possible realization of the states OP1–8.

The reader will find it of advantage to study the manufacturer's documentation [125]; this gives tables for more complex operations, involving the six variables $I_5 \ldots I_0$ and thus combining the tables of Figures 7.8 and 7.9.

7.2.7 Analysis of the neutral micro-command

Here we are interested in the details of the neutral micro-command NOP, which in Figure 7.14 is given the value 40205B:

$$\mu C_{23:0} = \mu C_{23:20}, A_{3:0}, B_{3:0}, \mu C_{11:0} = 40205\text{B} \qquad (7.28)$$

It follows from Figure 7.16 that the operation of the RALU, which is determined completely by the relation $\mu C_{11:0} = 05\text{B}$, is

$$Y = RAM[B] \quad (\text{OP2} = \text{READ})$$

whilst from (7.28) $B_{3:0} = 2$, and so

$$Y = RAM[2] = IR$$

where IR is the state of the register $RAM[2]$ of the RALU, as in the mnemonic expression in Figure 7.11. Then Figure 7.12 shows that $BUS = Y$ for $\mu C_{23:20} = 4$, and consequently NOP is

$$BUS = Y = IR \qquad (7.29)$$

which means that the RALU sends the state of the register IR directly to the bus BUS.

The justification for this choice for NOP, and the precise role of the register IR, is given in §7.4.2.

7.2.8 Micro-command instructions

The output state F of the ALU (Figure 7.7) is a function Fj depending on $\mu C_{19:0}$ and the operands $RAM[A]$, $RAM[B]$, Q, $D{=}BUS$; so we can write

$$Fj = Fj(RAM[A], RAM[B], Q, BUS, \mu C_{19:0}) \qquad (7.30)$$

If we ignore the operations that concern shifts, OP4–7 of Figure 7.10, we can determine from $\mu C_{19:0}$ the following three RALU functions that appear in Figures 7.8–11:

$$\mu C_{19:0} = RAM[B] \leftarrow F1, \quad Q \leftarrow F2, \quad Y = F3 \tag{7.31}$$

The state $\mu C_{23:20}$ defines the bus state $BUS[\mu C_{23:20}]$ as in Figure 7.12 and the index $j_{3:0}$ specifies the register $REG[j]$ that is to be loaded, as in Figure 7.13.

Thus the detailed form of the micro-command instruction (7.17) is:

$$\textbf{DO } ROM_{27:0} = \textbf{DO } REG[j] \leftarrow BUS, \quad BUS = BUS[\mu C_{23:20}], \\ RAM[B] \leftarrow F1, \quad Q \leftarrow F2 \tag{7.32}$$

which shows that in any one clock time the processing unit performs at most three transfers, one to a register $REG[j]$ and two to RALU registers, $RAM[B]$ and Q.

With the action of NOP as obtained in §7.2.7, the assignment instruction (7.18) becomes simply

$$\textbf{DO } REG[j] \leftarrow OUT, \quad BUS = IR \tag{7.33}$$

7.2.9 Hardware realization: interpreter INT4.1

The assemblage of the universal processing unit of Figure 7.11 and the control unit of Figure 7.14 constitutes our first universal processor, the interpreter INT4.1. This can execute the languages **L3** and **L4**, provided that the instruction format is compatible with the memory ROM, which uses 32-bit words. It must be emphasized that it cannot execute these languages if the instructions have the normal 16-bit format, as in Figure 4.7.

7.2.10 Conclusion

The control unit of Figure 7.14 combines the characteristics of the interpreter INT3 (Figure 4.7), which executes the assignment instruction **DO** $REG[j] \leftarrow OUT$, with those of INT3.2 (Figure 6.27), which executes the micro-command instruction **DO** *ROM*. The large number of control variables of the universal processing unit, and in particular of the RALU, requires a 24-bit micro-command $\mu C_{23:0}$ in place of the eight bits needed for the state $OUT_{7:0}$ of the traditional assignment instruction. The consequences of this are:

- poor use of the read only memory ROM, whose width of 32 bits is determined by the needs of the single micro-command instruction;
- considerable redundancy of information in the micro-command. In the example of section 7.4 the 12 bits $ROM_{11:0} = \mu C_{11:0}$ control only eight distinct operations (OP1–8 in Figure 7.16), for which minimal code would need only three.

In section 7.4 we shall make a detailed study of the program in the memory, leading in §7.4.13 to a new realization INT4.2 (Figure 7.40) in which these disadvantages are reduced. The universal nature of INT4.1, the programming of which enables 2^{24} different states of the 24 variables of $\mu C_{23:0}$ to be generated, requires a ROM of large width, 32 bits, and therefore high cost; specializing in INT4.2 to a particular application reduces the width to 16 bits and so reduces the cost. A more detailed comparison of the two solutions is made in §7.4.15.

7.2.11 Bibliography

The design of simple micro-programs is illustrated in [18] (pp. 424–429) by the algorithms for addition and subtraction and in [67] (pp. 288–295) for multiplication. The complete development of a micro-program for multiplying two binary numbers, using the Am2901 RALU, is given in [3] (pp. 77–82).

One approach to the optimization of micro-programs, meaning the reduction of the number of micro-command instructions needed for a given task, is to look for the greatest possible amount of parallelism, which can be done systematically with the help of a graph of functional dependences; this is discussed in [110].

7.2.12 Exercise

Using §7.2.4 as an example, verify the command state $\mu C_{11:0}$ for each operation of Figure 7.16. Investigate the possibility of there being more than one solution for the same operation, in particular for OP6 and OP7 which involve arithmetical subtractions (see section 8.6).

7.2.13 Exercise

To simplify the architecture of the processing unit, Figure 7.11, we could consider omitting the register REG and recording the state $OUT_{7:0}$, generated by the control unit, in one of the other registers (RAM, MAR, RALU), via the bus. If the instruction formats of Figure 7.14 were not to be changed, what hardware and/or software changes would have to be made to INT4.1?

7.3 CASE STUDY: SPECIFICATION FOR A COMPILER FOR L5

7.3.1 Introduction

With the two-fold aim of designing a complex micro-program and illustrating the use of a universal processor, we study in this and the next sections a fairly substantial problem, the production of a small compiler for the **L5** language. Section 7.3 is devoted to the analysis of the specification proposed and section 7.4 to the design of the microprogram and the interpretation of this by two variants of a universal processor.

The high-level language **L5** (MICROPASCAL), defined in §5.2.9, cannot be executed directly by the interpreters described in this book; we therefore study the *compilation* of the language, that is, the design of a new program, the *compiler*, that will transform a program written in **L5** into the low-level **L4** and so be executable by one of the interpreters already described. In principle, any compiler is a program written in any language, for example PASCAL, and executed by any computer, for example a VAX. To show the possibilities offered by microprogrammed systems we consider a very special compiler:

- written in **L4**, defined in §5.2.8;
- executed by a universal processor, the interpreter INT4.1 defined in §7.2.9.

7.3.2 Definition: compiler

A *compiler* is a translation program; its function is to transform algorithms expressed in one language, the *source language*, into equivalent algorithms expressed in another, the *object* or *target language*. In general, the source language is a high-level language, for example **L5**, and the object language is low-level, for example **L4**. Thus the role of the compiler is to transform a high-level language program into a form that can be executed. We say that the algorithms in the source language, which form the input data for the compiler, are the *source programs* and their equivalents, the results produced by the compiler, are the *object programs*.

7.3.3 Representation: T-diagram

Figure 7.17 is a symbolic representation of a compiler. *N* (central) is its name, **Ls** (on the left) is the source language, **Lo** (on the right) is the object language and **Lc** (at the base) is the language in which the compiler is written. This is called a *T-diagram* [123] (pp. 1–9), [124] (pp. 725–729).

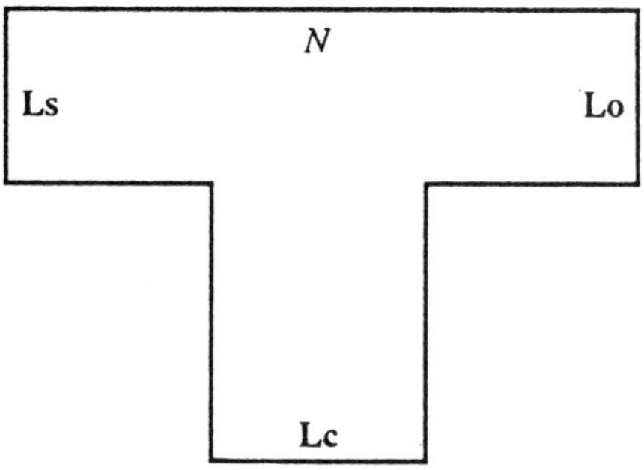

Figure 7.17

7.3.4 Example: the compiler *PASCALINE*

Figure 7.18 is the T-diagram for the compiler we study here. Its name is *PASCALINE*; the source language **Ls** is **L5** (MICROPASCAL); the object language **Lo** into which it is to be translated is **L4**; and it is to be written in **L4**.

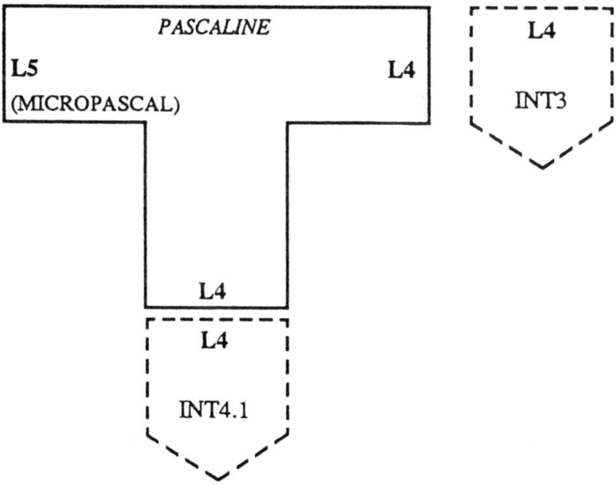

Figure 7.18

7.3.5 Definition: interpreter

An *interpreter* is an execution program; its function is to execute algorithms expressed in a given language, the source language for the interpreter: this means the application of the algorithms to given data and production of the corresponding results.

7.3.6 Representation: I and V-diagrams

Figure 7.19 is a symbolic representation of an interpreter. N (central) is the name, **Ls** (at the top) is the source language, **Li** (bottom) is the language in which it is written. This is called an *I-diagram* [123] (pp. 4–9).

If the interpreter is itself a hardware system, as for example is the case of INT3 for **L3** and **L4**, Figure 4.7, the diagram takes the form of Figure 7.20, the *V-diagram*.

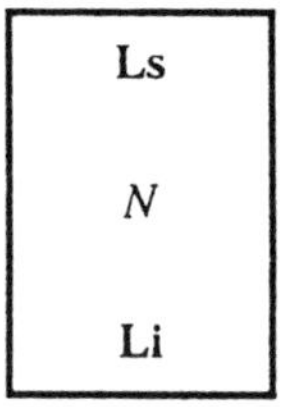

Figure 7.19

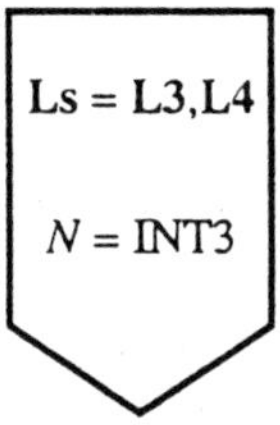

Figure 7.20

7.3.7 Example: *PASCALINE*

This compiler, written in **L4**, is to be executed by a universal processor, the interpreter INT4.1 of §7.2.9 (Figures 7.11, 7.14); the object language **L4** which it produces can be executed by a simpler interpreter, for example the INT3 of Figure 4.7. Thus we can add to Figure 7.18 two V-diagrams, as shown in the dotted lines, and the figure thus completed summarizes the broad specification for the compiler.

7.3.8 The source language L5

This has been described already, in §5.2.9. It is defined by the syntactic diagram of Figure 5.32 and in Backus-Naur notation by Figure 5.33; in the latter there are 11 terminal symbols, shown in the ovals in Figure 5.32, each of which constitutes an instruction or *line* of **L5**.

Each line is a 16-bit word and is coded in a standard form of four hexadecimal characters, with the conventions of Figure 7.21:

- each line is described by a mnemonic **L5** expression, a symbol from the set **S** of (5.13) and a *format* giving the 16-bit function $L_{15:0}$ and/or the four hexadecimal characters $L_{15:12}$, $L_{11:8}$, $L_{7:4}$, $L_{3:0}$;
- each line is identified by its first hexadecimal character, which has been chosen arbitrarily; it is called the *line code*, $LC_{3:0} = L_{15:12}$;

L5	S	Format $L_{15:0}$ bits 15–12	11–8	7–4	3–0
program *np*	$PPj =$	F	–	$np_{7:0}$	
do *REG* [*j*] ← *OUT*	**do...**	2	$j_{3:0}$	$OUT_{7:0}$	
call *p*	**call...**	3	–	$p_{7:0}$	
if *xi*	$<_{xi}$	B	–	–	$i_{3:0}$
else	|	A	–	–	–
endif	>	9	–	–	–
while *xi*	$\{_{xi}$	7	–	–	$i_{3:0}$
end while	}	6	–	–	–
procedure *p*	$Pi =$	D	–	$p_{7:0}$	
end procedure	;	C	–	–	–
end program	.	E	–	–	–
		$LC_{3:0}$			

Figure 7.21

- in the line **program** *np* the variable $np_{7:0}$ gives the maximum number of procedures in the program, from 00 to FF_H;
- in the line **do** $REG[j] \leftarrow OUT$ the address $j_{3:0}$ and the output state $OUT_{7:0}$ are identical to those of the instruction **DO** $REG[j] \leftarrow OUT$ of the object language **L4** (Figure 7.22);
- in the lines **call** *p* and **procedure** *p* the variable $p_{7:0}$ gives the name of the procedure called, from 00 to FF_H;
- in the lines **if** *xi* and **while** *xi* the index $i_{3:0}$ is that of the **L4** instruction **IF** *xi* **ELSE** *ADR0* (Figure 7.22).

Since the indices $i_{3:0}$, the register addresses $j_{3:0}$ and the output states $OUT_{7:0}$ are identical with those of the object language **L4**, which corresponds directly with the interpreter INT3 of Figure 4.7, we can say that the high-level language **L5** is *dependent on the machine that executes it*, that is, on the interpreter INT3. This has the advantage of greatly simplifying the compiler, which however can then be used only by this specialized machine.

L3, L4	Format $ROM_{15:0}$			
	15 12	11 8	7 4	3 0
IF *xi* ELSE *ADR0*	0	$i_{3:0}$	$ADR0_{7:0}$	
(GO TO *ADR+* = IF 0 ELSE *ADR0* : *xi* = 0)				
DO *REG* [*j*] ← *OUT*	1	$j_{3:0}$	$OUT_{7:0}$	
CALL *ADSP*	C	–	$ADSP_{7:0}$	
RET	A	–	–	–
	$OPC_{3:0}$			

Figure 7.22

7.3.9 Example: reversible counter

Figure 5.57 gives the **L4** and **L5** programs for the reversible counter described in §5.4.1. The hexadecimal code for the object language **L4** is derived from the mnemonic expressions, taking the following into account:

- the formats of the four INT3 instructions, repeated in Figure 7.22;
- the hexadecimal coding of the index i, given in Figure 7.23, with $i = 8$ reserved for the logical constant 0;
- the single assignment register $REG[j] = REG[1]$;
- the use of key words **PROGRAM...**, **ENDIF**, **PROCEDURE...**, **END PROGRAM**; in accordance with the definition of **L4** (§5.2.8); these do not generate any instruction.

xi	*i*
EN	1
H	2
H'	3
x	4
Q_0	5
Q_1	6
0	8

Figure 7.23

The hexadecimal code for the source language **L5** is derived from the mnemonic **L5** expressions, taking into account the following:

- the format of Figure 7.21;
- the hexadecimal coding for *i*, of Figure 7.23;
- the single assignment register *REG*[1];
- the number of procedures in the program: $np = 02$;
- the choice, essentially arbitrary, of the procedure names: $P1 = \text{FF}$, $P2 = \text{FE}$ (see also §7.4.11).

This example, although very simple, illustrates the use of each of the eleven lines of **L5**.

7.3.10 Specification for the compiler *PASCALINE*

PASCALINE has to translate **L5** source programs into **L4** object programs; the hexadecimal code of the source program forms the *data* whilst that of the object program is the *result* of the computation performed by the compiler. The rules governing the translation form the *compilation algorithm* and must specify how each of the eleven lines of Figure 7.21 is to be translated by one or other of the four instructions of Figure 7.22.

A comparison of the source and object programs of Figure 5.57 shows that the eleven **L5** lines can be grouped into the four classes of Figure 7.24, as follows.

- Class 1: the **L5** instructions with $LC_{3:0} = 2$, C are translated directly without the need for any further information, becoming the **L4** instructions with $OPC_{3:0} = 1$, A.
- Class 2: these four **L5** instructions produce on **L4** instructions; they are however essential to the correct functioning of the compiler.
- Class 3: each of these four **L5** instructions is replaced by either a test, **IF . . . ELSE . . .**, or a jump, **GO TO . .** ; the compiler's task here is to compute the address *ADR0* or *ADR+*.
- Class 4: the line **call** *p* produces the **L4** instruction **CALL** *ADSP*; the compiler has to replace the name of the procedure *p* (where $0 \leqslant p \leqslant \text{FF}$) by the address *ADSP* in the object program.

7.3.11 Comment

From Figure 7.24 we see that to each **L5** instruction of the source program there corresponds to at most one **L4** instruction in the object program; thus the object program will have fewer instructions than the source. This result, which simplifies the final realization of the

No	$LC_{3:0}$	L5	$OPC_{3:0}$	L4
1	2 C	**do** $REG\,[j] \leftarrow OUT$ **end procedure**	1 A	**DO** $REG\,[j] \leftarrow OUT$ **RET**
2	F 9 D E	**program** *np* **endif** **procedure** *p* **end program**	– – – –	– – – –

3	B
	A
	7
	6
		if *xi*
		else
		while *xi*
		end while
			0
			0
			0
			0
				IF *xi* **ELSE** *ADR0*
				GO TO *ADR+*
				IF *xi* **ELSE** *ADR0*
				GO TO *ADR+*

4	3	**call** *p*	C	**CALL** *ADSP*

Figure 7.24

PASCALINE compiler, is quite specific to the pair of languages **L4, L5,** for in general a source program will compile into an object program with many more instructions.

7.3.12 Compilation of the construction if . . . else . . . endif

There are several occurrences of this construction in the program of Figure 5.57. The algorithm for its compilation can be divided into three stages:

(a) the line **if** *x* (*ADR* = 06) produces **IF** *x* **ELSE** *ADR0*, where *ADR0* is not yet known and has to be computed later;
(b) the line **else** (*ADR* = 0C) produces **GO TO** *ADR+* (*ADR*= *ADRELSE* = 0A), where *ADR+* has to be determined later; but the knowledge of the address *ADRELSE* = 0A enables the missing address in (a) to be filled in:

$$\textbf{IF}\ x\ \textbf{ELSE}\ ADR0 = \textbf{IF}\ x\ \textbf{ELSE}\ ADRELSE + 1 = \textbf{IF}\ x\ \textbf{ELSE}\ \mathrm{0B} \tag{7.34}$$

(c) the line **endif** (*ADR* = 12) produces no new instruction but enables the address of the last instruction of the object program to be determined: *ADREND* = 0E. The instuction of stage (b) can then be completed:

$$\begin{aligned}\textbf{GO TO}\ ADR+ &= \textbf{GO TO}\ ADREND{+}1\\ &= \textbf{GO TO}\ \mathrm{0F}\end{aligned} \tag{7.35}$$

S	*ADR*	Code	L5	*ADR*	Code	L4
$<_x$	06	B--4	**if** *x*	05	04??	**IF** *x* **ELSE** ? = **IF** *x* **ELSE** *ADR0*

(a)

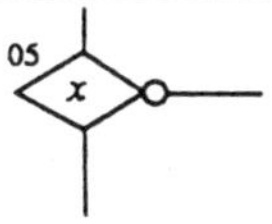

S	*ADR*	Code	L5	*ADR*	Code	L4
$<_x$	06	B--4	**if** *x*	05	040B	**IF** *x* **ELSE** 0B = **IF** *x* **ELSE** *ADRELSE* + 1
⋮	⋮	⋮	⋮	⋮	⋮	
|	0C	A---	**else** →	0A	08??	**GO TO** ? = **GO TO** *ADR+*

(b)

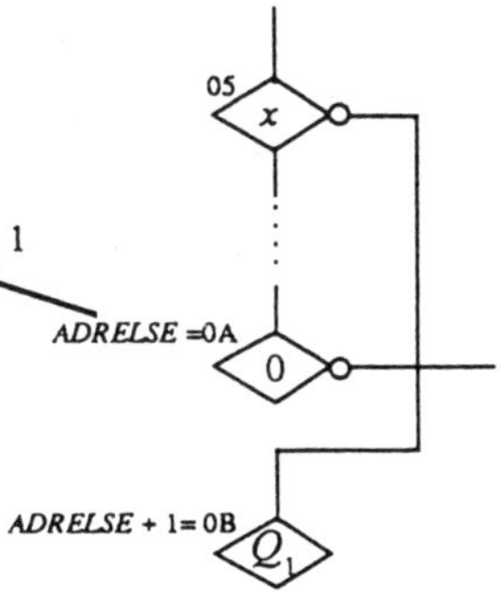

S	*ADR*	Code	L5	*ADR*	Code	L4
$<_x$	06	B--4	**if** *x*	05	040B	**IF** *x* **ELSE** 0B
⋮	⋮	⋮	⋮	⋮	⋮	
|	0C	A---	**else**	0A	080F	**GO TO** 0F = **GO TO** *ADREND* + 1
⋮	⋮	⋮	⋮	⋮	⋮	
				0E	C-10	**CALL** *P1*
>	12	9---	**endif** →	–	–	**ENDIF**

(c)

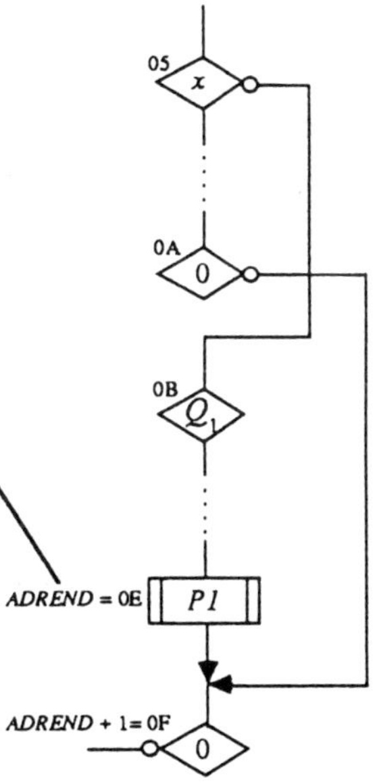

Figure 7.25

7.3.13 Compilation of the construction while . . . end while

This construction also occurs in Figure 5.57, and again the compilation can be divided into three stages (Figure 7.26):

(a) the line **while** *H* (*ADR* = 02) produces **IF** *H* **ELSE** *ADR0*, where *ADR0* is to be computed later; the address of the current instruction (*ADRWHILE* = 01) is held in memory for subsequent processing;

(b) the line **end while** (*ADR* = 03) produces **GO TO** *ADR+*, where *ADR+* is known since it follows from the previous stage:

$$\textbf{GO TO } ADR+ = \textbf{GO TO } ADRWHILE = \textbf{GO TO } 01 \tag{7.36}$$

S	*ADR*	Code	L5	*ADR*	Code	L4
{$_H$	02	7--2	**while** *H*	01	02??	IF *H* ELSE ? = IF *H* ELSE *ADR0*
			(a)			
{$_H$	02	7--2	**while** *H*	01	02??	IF *H* ELSE ? = IF *H* ELSE *ADR0*
}	03	6---	**end while** →	02	0801	GO TO 01 = GO TO *ADRWHILE*
			(b)			
{$_H$	02	7--2	**while** *H*	01	0203	IF *H* ELSE 03 = IF *H* ELSE *ADRENDWHILE* + 1
}	03	6---	**end while**	02	0801	GO TO 01
			(c)			

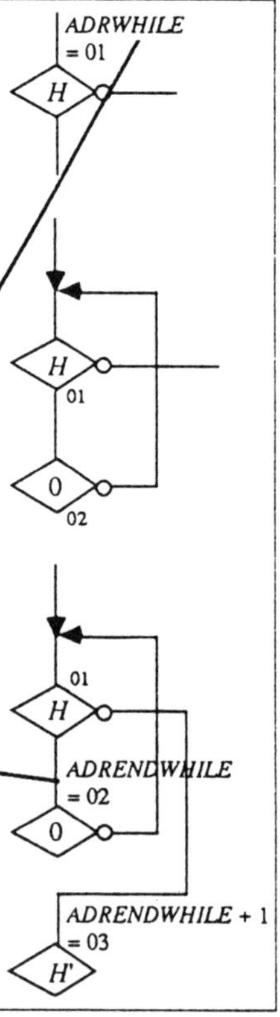

Figure 7.26

(c) this line also enables the missing address *ADR0* of stage (a) to be determined:

$$\begin{aligned}\textbf{IF } H \textbf{ ELSE } ADR0 &= \textbf{IF } H \textbf{ ELSE } ADRENDWHILE{+}1\\ &= \textbf{IF } H \textbf{ ELSE } 03\end{aligned} \qquad (7.37)$$

7.3.14 Compilation of call . . . , procedure . . . , end procedure

The term *pass* is used to denote the process of reading through a program from the first instruction to the last, in ascending order of addresses. In a first pass through the source (**L5**) program, with *ADR* = 00. . .22 (Figure 5.57), the compilation algorithm produces the full set of instructions in the object language **L4** (cf. Figure 7.22) but lacking the address *ADSP* in each instruction **CALL** *ADSP*. For each procedure the compiler preserves the names that have been chosen (in the example of Figure 5.57 *P1* = FF, *P2* = FE) and determines the address *ADSP* of the first instruction of each:

$$\begin{aligned}ADSP &= 10 \quad \text{for} \quad P1 = \text{FF}\\ &= 15 \quad \text{for} \quad P2 = \text{FE}\end{aligned}$$

In a second pass all the **CALL** . . . instructions in the program resulting from the first pass (**CALL** FF, **CALL** FE in Figure 5.57) are transformed by replacing each procedure name (e.g. FF, FE) by the corresponding address *ADSP* (here, 10 and 15 respectively). The compilation is then complete.

7.3.15 Compilers generally

The classical compilers, whose function is the translation of high-level languages such as, for example, PASCAL, operate in two phases: analysis, or checking, followed by synthesis, or production. The analysis phase generally falls into three stages:

- *lexical analysis*, in which the source program is scanned character by character (hexadecimal in our example), to check that the symbols used are only those allowed by the language (here, the 11 lines of **L5**);
- *syntax analysis*, which checks that the order in which the symbols are used is correct according to the syntactic diagram for the language (for **L5**, Figure 5.32);
- *semantic analysis*, which checks that each phrase (succession of symbols) is meaningful, in particular that the various types of data used are compatible with one another.

The sole purpose of this phase is to detect any errors that may have been made in writing the program, and to issue messages describing any errors found.

The synthesis phase is in two stages:

- *code generation*, which produces the object program;
- *code optimization*, which derives an improved version of this object program.

It will be seen that our specification for *PASCALINE* (§7.3.10) bears only on the code generation stage, and thus concerns only a small part of the complete compilation process.

7.3.16 Conclusion

The value of a compiler is that by allowing programs to be written in high-level languages it eases the programmer's task. For the use of the particular language **L5**, a compiler such as *PASCALINE* allows the methods for realizing a variety of systems, described in previous chapters, to be simplified; in particular:

- the state table tree (§§5.3.15, 5.4.8);
- the separation of the variables (§§5.3.22, 5.4.13);
- the design of combinational systems generally (§5.5.2);
- the design of iterative combinational systems (§5.5.7);
- programming by successive refinements (§6.1.18);
- the synthesis of a specialized processor (§6.2.16).

In each of these methods the **L5** program can be derived directly from the tree or the standard flowchart, using the characteristic equations if necessary. There is no need to give a zig-zag addressing, as the compiler itself generates all the addresses in the object program.

7.3.17 Bibliography

As an introduction to compilers it is helpful to study the compilation of some simplified high-level languages, for example SampleC, a sub-set of C [116] and PASCAL Minus, a sub-set of PASCAL [122]. An exhaustive treatment is given in [124].

7.3.18 Exercise

The format $L_{15:0}$ chosen here for the eleven **L5** lines is quite arbitrary (Figure 7.21). By comparing these lines with the four **L4** instructions of

Figure 7.22 investigate the possibility of modifying this so as to simplify the compilation.

7.3.19 Exercise

A comparator for two numbers $A(A_{1:0})$, $B(B_{1:0})$ can be realized by a combination of a main tree (*sp1*) and a sub-tree (*sp0*) as in Figure 3.37, using the method of §5.5.2 (see also the exercise of §5.5.12). Starting from the characteristic equations, write the **L5** program for this, give the addressing and the hexadecimal code with the conventions of Figure 7.21, and carry out a manual compilation to derive the **L4** object program, giving the mnemonic expressions, the addresses and the hexadecimal code.

7.4 MICROPROGRAM FOR THE *PASCALINE* COMPILER

7.4.1 Introduction

The specification for this compiler was given in §7.3.10 and some details concerning the compilation algorithm in §§7.3.12–14. The **L5** source program is the data required by the compiler program, and to ensure that this can be loaded into the processor, that is, the INT4.1 interpreter of §7.2.9, this specification must be completed by the addition of certain elementary operations for writing, reading and editing words in the memory RAM of Figure 7.11.

PASCALINE is to be written in **L4**. The INT4.1 interpreter (Figures 7.11, 7.14) provides, in addition to the standard assignment instruction **DO** $REG[j] \leftarrow OUT$, a micro-command instruction **DO** $REG[j]$, $\mu C_{23:0}$ of which the states j, $\mu C_{23:20}$, $\mu C_{11:0}$ are described in Figures 7.13, 7.12 and 7.16. The micro-command instructions are the new primitive instructions of **L4**; they will be used to steer the process of breaking down the original specification by the top-down programming process of successive refinements (§6.1.3).

7.4.2 Main program *PASCALINE*

Figure 7.27 is the flowchart for this. There are four modes of operation, controlled by the variable *FLAG*, as follows:

- *address mode*, $FLAG_{3:0} = 0000$; procedure *ADDRESS*;
- *write mode*, $FLAG_{3:0} = 0001$; procedure *WRITE*;
- *incrementation mode*, $FLAG_{3:0} = 0010$; procedure *INCREMENT*;
- *compilation mode*, $FLAG_{3:0} = 0011$; procedure *COMPILATION*.

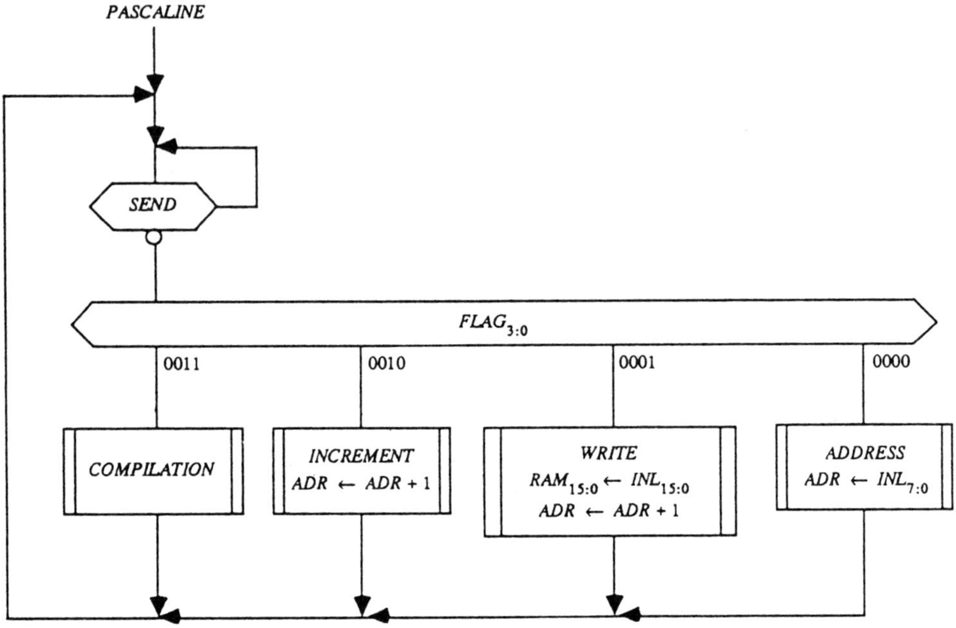

Figure 7.27

The program is started by a pulse that sets $SEND = 0$; the state $FLAG_{3:0}$, generated by the register REG4 of the input unit Figure 7.6, is sent over the bus and stored in the *instruction register* IR of the RALU, using the micro-command instruction

$$\textbf{DO } BUS_{3:0} = FLAG_{3:0}, \quad IR \leftarrow BUS \tag{7.38}$$

The neutral micro-command NOP, defined by (7.29) as $BUS = IR$, ensures that the content of IR is on the bus whenever any test instruction **IF** . . . is executed (Figure 7.15); thus the value of $FLAG_{3:0}$ can be tested directly on the bus $BUS_{3:0}$ after an execution of (7.38) and used to call one of the above four modal procedures.

Figure 7.28 gives the *PASCALINE* main program finally arrived at, in both **L4** and **L5**; the declarations are

- ***test variables*** *xi*: 1, $SEND$, BUS_1, BUS_0;
- **RALU** ***register*** $RAM[B]$: $RAM[2] = IR$.

7.4.3 Procedure *ADDRESS*

In *address* mode we wish to load the MAR register, which addresses the memory RAM, with some address *ADR* in the range 00 to FF_H which

$ROMA_{15:0}$	$ROM_{31:0}$	ADR	L4	L5: *PASCALINE*
			PROGRAM	program 11
090F	09....0F	00	IF 1 ELSE 0F	while 1
0A03	0A....03	01	IF *SEND* ELSE 03	while *SEND*
0801	08....01	02	GO TO 01	end while
1000	1090209F	03	DO 000	do *BUS*3:0 = *FLAG*3:0, *IR* ← *BUS*
010A	01....0A	04	IF *BUS*1 ELSE 0A	if *BUS*1
0008	00....08	05	IF *BUS*0 ELSE 08	if *BUS*0
C.22	C.....22	06	CALL 22	call FF {*COMPILATION*}
0809	08....09	07	GO TO 09	else
C.1D	C.....1D	08	CALL 1D	call FE {*INCREMENT*}
			ENDIF	endif
080E	08....0E	09	GO TO 0E	else
000D	00....0D	0A	IF *BUS*0 ELSE 0D	if *BUS*0
C.14	C.....14	0B	CALL 14	call FD {*WRITE*}
080E	08....0E	0C	GO TO 0E	else
C.0F	C.....0F	0D	CALL 0F	call FC {*ADDRESS*}
			ENDIF	endif
			ENDIF	endif
0800	08....00	0E	GO TO 00	end while
			END PROGRAM	end program

Figure 7.28

$ROMA_{15:0}$	$ROM_{31:0}$	ADR	L4	L5: *ADDRESS*
			PROCEDURE FC	procedure FC {*ADDRESS*}
0B11	0B....11	0F	IF *SENDBAR* ELSE 11	while *SENDBAR*
080F	08....0F	10	GO TO 0F	end while
1001	1060009F	11	DO 001	do *BUS*7:0 = *INL*7:0, *PC* ← *BUS*
1402	1440005B	12	DO 402	do *ADR* ← *BUS*, *BUS* = *Y*, *Y* = *PC*
A...	A.......	13	RET	end procedure

Figure 7.29

has been set up on the register REG3 of the keyboard K of Figures 7.5 and 7.6:

$$ADR_{7:0} \leftarrow INL_{7:0} \qquad (7.39)$$

The transfer (7.39) is executed when $SENDBAR = SEND' = 0$, that is, when the starting signal has its initial value $SEND = 1$; the address

ADR is always copied into the *source program counter* PC of the RALU before being loaded into MAR. The declarations are (Figure 7.29):

- ***test variable*** *xi*: *SENDBAR* = *SEND'*;
- ***assignment register*** *REG* [*j*]: *REG*[4] = $ADR_{7:0}$;
- **RALU** ***register*** *RAM*[*B*]: *RAM*[0] = PC.

7.4.4 Procedures *WRITE, INCREMENT*: Figure 7.30

In *write* mode (procedure *WRITE*) the data $INL_{15:0}$ in the registers REG1-3 have to be written to the memory RAM at the current address *ADR;* this is always the content of PC at that instant, and has to be incremented after the transfer in preparation for the next write operation:

$$RAM_{15:0}[ADR] \leftarrow INL_{15:0} \tag{7.40}$$

$$ADR \leftarrow ADR + 1 \tag{7.41}$$

This sequence of transfers enables the complete source program to be transfered, line by line, into the memory RAM.

It will be seen in the final procedure, Figure 7.30, that a simple transfer such as that described by (7.40) has to be broken down into the

$ROMA_{15:0}$	$ROM_{31:0}$	*ADR*	L4	L5: *WRITE, INCREMENT*
			PROCEDURE FD	procedure FD {*WRITE*}
1402	1440005B	14	DO 402	do *ADR* ← *BUS*, *BUS* = *Y*, *Y* = *PC*
1103	1180005B	15	DO 103	do *RAM*15:12 ← *BUS*3:0, *BUS*3:0 = *INL*15:12
1204	1270005B	16	DO 204	do *RAM*11:8 ← *BUS*3:0, *BUS*3:0 = *INL*11:8
1305	1360005B	17	DO 305	do *RAM*7:0 ← *BUS*7:0, *BUS*7:0 = *INL*7:0
0B1A	0B....1A	18	IF *SENDBAR* ELSE 1A	while *SENDBAR*
0818	08....18	19	GO TO 18	end while
1006	104002C3	1A	DO 006	do *BUS* = *Y*, *Y* = *PC* + 1, *PC* ← *PC* + 1
1402	1440005B	1B	DO 402	do *ADR* ← *BUS*, *BUS* = *Y*, *Y* = *PC*
A...	A.......	1C	RET	end procedure
			PROCEDURE FE	procedure FE {*INCREMENT*}
0B1F	0B....1F	1D	IF *SENDBAR* ELSE 1F	while *SENDBAR*
081D	08....1D	1E	GO TO 1D	end while
1006	104002C3	1F	DO 006	do *BUS* = *Y*, *Y* = *PC* + 1, *PC* ← *PC* + 1
1402	1440005B	20	DO 402	do *ADR* ← *BUS*, *BUS* = *Y*, *Y* = *PC*
A...	A.......	21	RET	end procedure

Figure 7.30

three elementary transfers *ADR* = 15, 16, 17; this is made necessary by the architecture of the processing unit, in particular by the width of the bus and the partitioning of the memory RAM into three fields (Figure 7.5). This shows that consequences for the software — here, sequential decomposition of a simple operation — follow from the choice of hardware architecture — here, adoption of the principles of §7.1.7, leading to a simple architecture with little parallelism.

In *incrementation* mode (procedure *INCREMENT*) the current address *ADR*, held in PC, has to be incremented, as (7.41); this enables the program to be read from RAM, line by line, for checking before compilation. The mode is realized by a sub-set of the instructions of the *WRITE* procedure, as shown in Figure 7.30; the declarations are:

- ***assignment registers*** *REG*[*j*]:
  $REG[1] = RAM_{15:12}$; $REG[2] = RAM_{11:8}$; $REG[3] = RAM_{7:0}$

7.4.5 Procedure *COMPILATION*

In *compilation* mode, as was explained in §7.3.14, two passes have to be distinguished (Figure 7.31). In the first, the procedure *COMPILATION*, all the instructions of the **L4** object code are determined but not the addresses *ADSP* needed in the **CALL...** instructions; these are determined in the second pass, the procedure labelled *2ND PASS* in Figure 7.31, described in §7.4.9.

The first pass (Figure 7.32) begins by resetting to zero the two registers PC, EPG (*end program register*) of the RALU; PC then sets the memory address register MAR to zero: RAM($ADR_{7:0} \leftarrow 00$). The procedure *COMPILATION* reads each line of the source program in succession into RAM so long as $EPG_0 = 0$, beginning with the first line at the address $ADR_{7:0} = 0$ and then decoding the line code $LC_{3:0}$ after executing the transfer

$$IR \leftarrow RAM_{15:12} = LC_{3:0} \tag{7.42}$$

The state $EPG_0 = 1$ indicates that the last line of the source program (**end program**, Figure 5.32) has been compiled.

The test of the line code $LC_{3:0}$ is performed in accordance with the definitions of Figure 7.21 and for each of the 11 lines of that figure calls the corresponding procedure. After this procedure has been executed the address *ADR* is incremented, enabling the next source line to be dealt with. The delarations are:

- ***test variables*** *xi*: $BUS0BAR = BUS_0'$, BUS_2, BUS_3;
- **RALU** ***register*** *RAM*[*B*]: *RAM*[3] = *EPG*

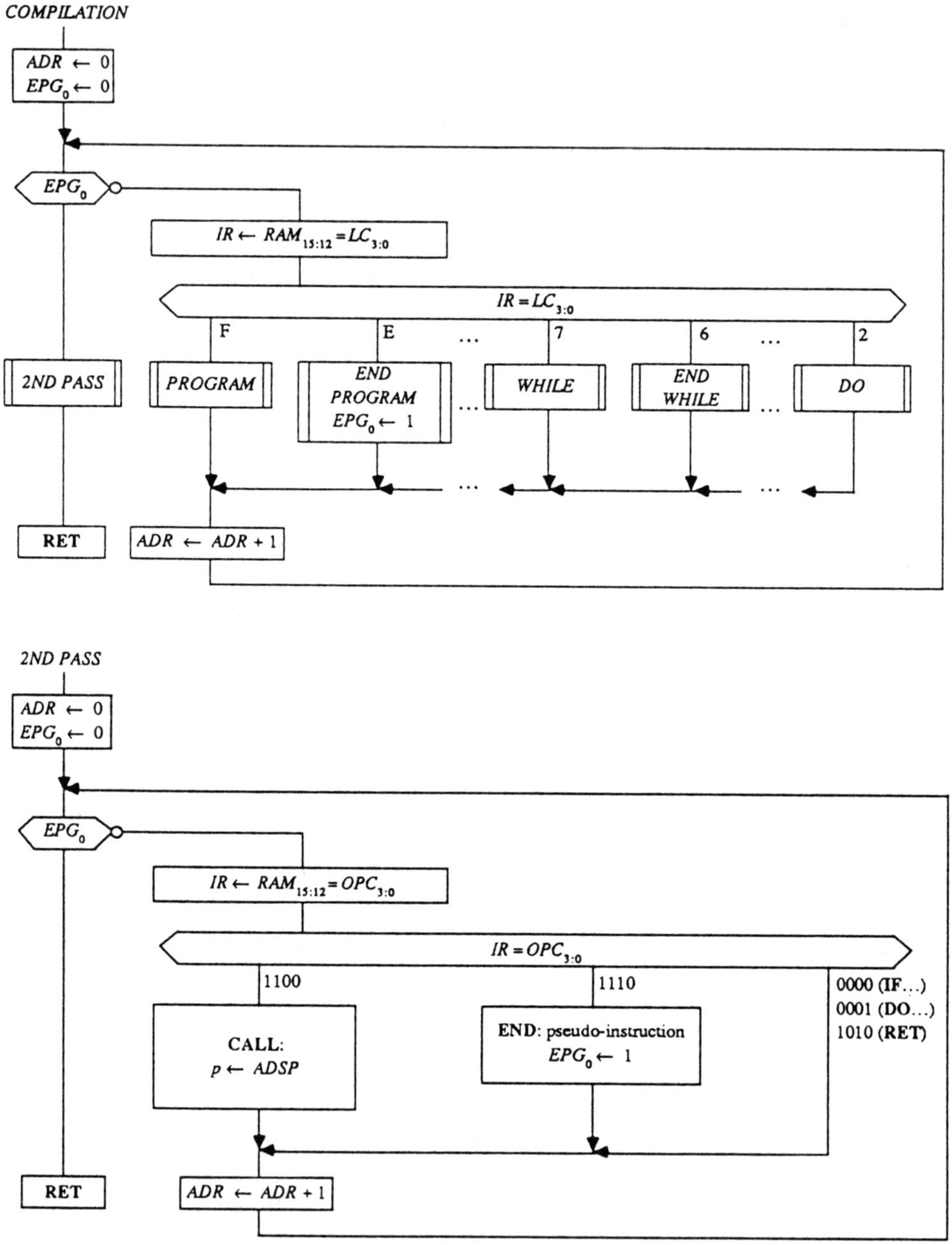
COMPILATION
ADR ← 0
EPG0 ← 0
EPG0
IR ← RAM15:12 = LC3:0
IR = LC3:0
F
E
7
6
2
2ND PASS
PROGRAM
END PROGRAM EPG0 ← 1
WHILE
END WHILE
DO
RET
ADR ← ADR + 1
2ND PASS
ADR ← 0
EPG0 ← 0
EPG0
IR ← RAM15:12 = OPC3:0
IR = OPC3:0
1100
1110
0000 (IF...)
0001 (DO...)
1010 (RET)
CALL:
p ← ADSP
END: pseudo-instruction
EPG0 ← 1
RET
ADR ← ADR + 1

Figure 7.31

$ROMA_{15:0}$	$ROM_{31:0}$	ADR	L4	L5: COMPILATION
			PROCEDURE FF	procedure FF {*COMPILATION*}
1007	104000E2	22	DO 007	do $BUS = Y, Y = 0, PC \leftarrow 0$
1402	1440005B	23	DO 402	do $ADR \leftarrow BUS, BUS = Y, Y = PC$
1008	104030E2	24	DO 008	do $BUS = Y, Y = 0, EPG \leftarrow 0$
0B27	0B....27	25	IF *SENDBAR* ELSE 27	while *SENDBAR*
0825	08....25	26	GO TO 25	end while
1009	1043209F	27	DO 009	do $BUS = Y, Y = EPG, IR \leftarrow BUS$
0C4D	0C....4D	28	IF *BUS0BAR* ELSE 4D	while *BUS0BAR*
100A	1010209F	29	DO 00A	do $BUS3{:}0 = RAM15{:}12, IR \leftarrow BUS$
003C	00....3C	2A	IF *BUS*0 ELSE 3C	if *BUS*0
0137	01....37	2B	IF *BUS*1 ELSE 37	if *BUS*1
0232	02....32	2C	IF *BUS*2 ELSE 32	if *BUS*2
0330	03....30	2D	IF *BUS*3 ELSE 30	if *BUS*3
C.4F	C.....4F	2E	CALL 4F	call FB {*PROGRAM*}
0831	08....31	2F	GO TO 31	else
C.53	C.....53	30	CALL 53	call FA {*WHILE, IF*}
			ENDIF	endif
0836	08....36	31	GO TO 36	else
0335	03....35	32	IF *BUS*3 ELSE 35	if *BUS*3
C.53	C.....53	33	CALL 53	call FA {*WHILE, IF*}
0836	08....36	34	GO TO 36	else
C.5A	C.....5A	35	CALL 5A	call F9 {*CALL*}
			ENDIF	endif
			ENDIF	endif
083B	08....3B	36	GO TO 3B	else
023A	02....3A	37	IF *BUS*2 ELSE 3A	if *BUS*2
C.62	C.....62	38	CALL 62	call F8 {*PROCEDURE*}
083B	08....3B	39	GO TO 3B	else
C.65	C.....65	3A	CALL 65	call F7 {*ENDIF*}
			ENDIF	endif
			ENDIF	endif
0849	08....49	3B	GO TO 49	else
0148	01....48	3C	IF *BUS*1 ELSE 48	if *BUS*1
0243	02....43	3D	IF *BUS*2 ELSE 43	if *BUS*2
0341	03....41	3E	IF *BUS*3 ELSE 41	if *BUS*3
C.69	C.....69	3F	CALL 69	call F6 {*END PROGRAM*}
0842	08....42	40	GO TO 42	else
C.6F	C.....6F	41	CALL 6F	call F5 {*END WHILE*}
			ENDIF	endif
0847	08....47	42	GO TO 47	else
0346	03....46	43	IF *BUS*3 ELSE 46	if *BUS*3
C.73	C.....73	44	CALL 73	call F4 {*ELSE*}
0847	08....47	45	GO TO 47	else
C.76	C.....76	46	CALL 76	call F3 {*DO*}
			ENDIF	endif
			ENDIF	endif
0849	08....49	47	GO TO 49	else
C.7F	C.....7F	48	CALL 7F	call F2 {*END PROCEDURE*}
			ENDIF	endif
			ENDIF	endif
1006	104002C3	49	DO 006	do $BUS = Y, Y = PC + 1, PC \leftarrow PC + 1$
1402	1440005B	4A	DO 402	do $ADR \leftarrow BUS, BUS = Y, Y = PC$
1009	1043209F	4B	DO 009	do $BUS = Y, Y = EPG, IR \leftarrow BUS$
0828	08....28	4C	GO TO 28	end while
C.95	C.....95	4D	CALL 95	call F1 {*2ND PASS*}
A...	A.......	4E	RET	end procedure

Figure 7.32

7.4.6 Random access memory RAM

Suppose the source program consists of h lines and np procedures (§7.3.8). Before the start of the compilation this will have been written into the memory RAM, which can then be described very simply by

- h words $RAM_{15:0}[ADR]$ with $0 \leqslant ADR \leqslant h - 1$ (7.43)

stating that the first h words of RAM contain the h lines of the source program (see Figure 7.33).

During the compilation each line of the source program is replaced by the corresponding instruction in the object language, as in Figure 7.24. We remarked in §7.3.11 that since in the particular case of an **L5** source program, **program . . . endif**, **procedure . . .** and **end program** lines do not give rise to any object-language instruction, the number of memory words needed for the object program is less than h. The last np words in RAM are reserved for the explicit addresses *ADSP* of the np procedures and s further words are needed for the processor *stack*, where s is the maximum number of nested **if. . .**and **while. . .**constructions in the source program:

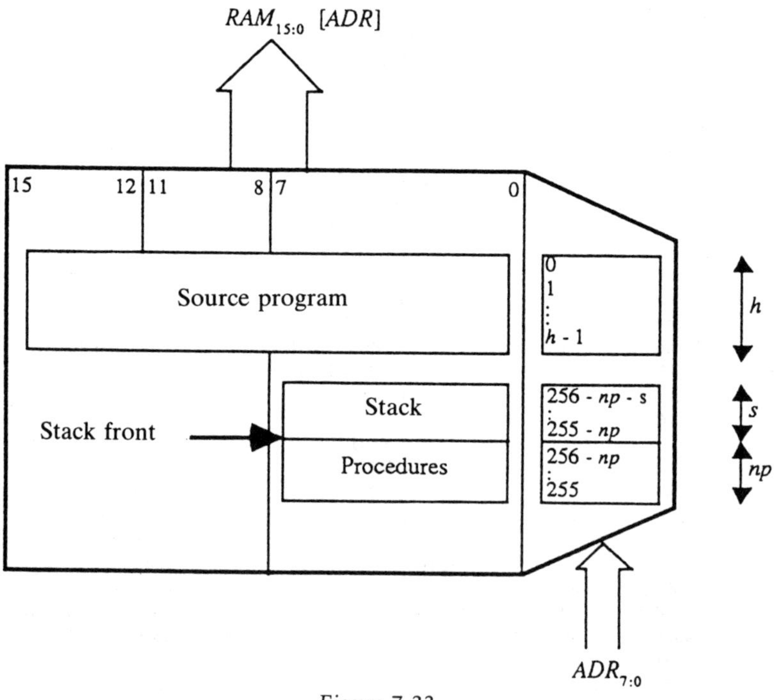

Figure 7.33

- np words $RAM_{7:0}[ADR]$ with $256 - np \leqslant ADR \leqslant 255$ (7.44)
- s words $RAM_{7:0}[ADR]$ with $256 - np - s \leqslant ADR \leqslant 255 - np$ (7.45)

Clearly, the lowest address in the stack ($256 - np - s$) must be above the highest in the source program ($h - 1$):

$$256 - np - s > h - 1 \tag{7.46}$$

When the compilation is completed the object program will occupy the first l words of RAM, where $l < h$:

- l words $RAM_{15:0}[ADR]$ with $0 \leqslant ADR \leqslant l - 1 < h - 1$ (7.47)

7.4.7 Procedures *WHILE, END WHILE*

As an example, we give here the details of the procedures *WHILE* and *END WHILE* which compile the **L5** construction **while . . . end while** respectively in accordance with §7.3.13 and Figure 7.26.

Figure 7.34 gives the formats of **while** and **end while** and also of the corresponding instructions **IF . . . ELSE . . .** and **GO TO . . . .** Figure 7.35 gives the compilation of **while . . .** (the procedure *WHILE*). The *temporary register* TEMP1 holds the index i, the *low level (object) program counter* LPC holds the present address $ADR = ADRWHILE$ of the object program instruction currently being processed and the *stack pointer* SP manages the part of RAM defined by (7.45) where it puts the address *ADRWHILE* to wait for the execution of the procedure *END WHILE*, given in Figure 7.36. When the writing of the preceding instruction **IF** xi **ELSE** *ADRENDWHILE*+1 is completed the next instruction **GO TO** *ADRWHILE* is generated in its turn.

The final procedures are given in Figure 7.37, where we observe:

- *WHILE* and *IF* are executed by the single procedure *WHILE, IF*, which itself calls a further common procedure *WHILE, IF, ELSE*;

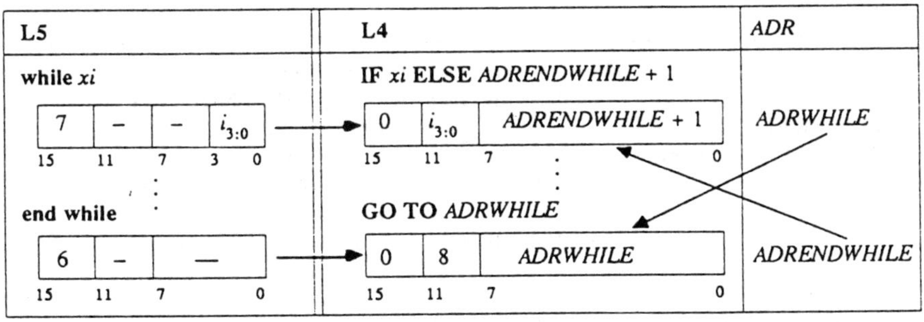

Figure 7.34

Comments	LLL code = $ROM_{31:0}$	HLL mnemonics
	—	PROCEDURE WHILE
Transfer of i into temporary register	10 30 50 9F	DO TEMP1 ← $RAM_{3:0}$ (= $i_{3:0}$)
Addressing RAM with actual LLL address	14 40 40 5B	DO ADR ← LPC (= ADRWHILE)
Writing IF x_i ELSE . . . instruction	18 — — 00 11 50 20 5B 12 40 50 5B	DO REG(8) ← 00 DO $RAM_{15:12}$ (ADRWHILE) ← REG(8) (= 0) DO $RAM_{11:8}$ (ADRWHILE) ← TEMP1 (= $i_{3:0}$)
Push ADRWHILE on stack for further calculation of IF x_i ELSE ADRENDWHILE + 1	14 40 10 5B 13 40 40 5B 10 40 10 CB	DO ADR ← SP (stack pointer) DO $RAM_{7:0}$ (SP) ← LPC (= ADRWHILE) DO SP ← SP − 1
Increment actual LLL program address	10 40 42 C3 A- — — —	DO LPC ← LPC + 1 END PROCEDURE

Figure 7.35

	—	PROCEDURE END WHILE
Pop stack and complete writing IF x_i ELSE ADRENDWHILE + 1 instruction	14 40 12 C3 10 30 50 9F 14 40 50 5B 13 40 42 43	DO ADR ← SP + 1; SP ← SP + 1 DO TEMP1 ← $RAM_{7:0}$ (SP + 1) (= ADRWHILE) DO ADR ← TEMP1 (= ADRWHILE) DO $RAM_{7:0}$ (ADRWHILE) ← LPC + 1 (= ADRENDWHILE + 1)
Addressing RAM with actual LLL program address	14 40 40 5B	DO ADR ← LPC (= ADRENDWHILE)
Writing GO TO ADRWHILE instruction	18 — — 00 11 50 20 5B 18 — — 08 12 50 20 5B 13 40 50 5B	DO REG(8) ← 00 DO $RAM_{15:12}$ (ADRENDWHILE) ← REG(8) (= 0) DO REG(8) ← 08 DO $RAM_{11:8}$ (ADRENDWHILE) ← REG(8) (= 8) DO $RAM_{7:0}$ (ADRENDWHILE) ← TEMP1 (= ADRWHILE)
Increment actual LLL program address	10 40 42 C3 A- — — —	DO LPC ← LPC + 1 END PROCEDURE

Figure 7.36

- *END WHILE* similarly calls a common procedure *END WHILE, ELSE*.

Thus we have the declarations:

- ***assignment register*** *REG*[*j*]: *REG*[8] = $REG_{7:0}$;
- **RALU** ***registers*** *RAM*[*B*]: *RAM*[1] = *SP*; *RAM*[4] = *LPC*;
  RAM[5] = *TEMP1*

7.4.8 Remaining procedures: *PROGRAM* to *END PROGRAM*

In addition to the procedures *WHILE, IF* and *END WHILE* just discussed there are eight further procedures corresponding to the remaining eight lines of Figure 7.21: *PROGRAM, DO, CALL, ELSE, ENDIF, PROCEDURE, END PROCEDURE, END PROGRAM*. These are shown in Figure 7.37; they give rise to the further declaration which describes a *temporary register* TEMP2:

- **RALU** ***register*** *RAM*[*B*]: *RAM*[6] = *TEMP2*

7.4.9 Procedure *2ND PASS*

After the registers MAR and EPG have been set to zero ($ADR \leftarrow 0$, $EPG_0 \leftarrow 0$) the procedure *2ND PASS* (Figure 7.31) reads each line in turn of the object program held in RAM, performs the transfer

$$IR \leftarrow RAM_{15:12} = OPC_{3:0} \qquad (7.48)$$

and then decodes the operating code $OPC_{3:0}$.

Three cases arise:

1. if $OPC_{3:0}$ = 0000, 0001 or 1010, corresponding respectively to **IF. . .**, **DO. . .** , **RET**, the address *ADR* is incremented and the next instruction taken;
2. if $OPC_{3:0}$ = 1110, corresponding to the *pseudo-instruction* **END** signalling the end of the program, EPG is set to 1 ($EPG_0 \leftarrow 1$), terminating the procedure;
3. if $OPC_{3:0}$ = 1100, corresponding to **CALL. . .** , the name *p* of the procedure called is replaced by the relevant address *ADSP* as shown in Figure 7.38.

7.4.10 Software realization

Figures 7.28, 7.29, 7.30, 7.32, 7.37 and 7.38 give the main program *PASCALINE* and the related procedures for the compiler. Apart from the micro-command instructions **DO** $ROM_{27:0}$ all the instructions can

ROMA$_{15:0}$	*ROM*$_{31:0}$	*ADR*	L4	L5: *PROGRAM..END PROGRAM*
			PROCEDURE FB	**procedure** FB {*PROGRAM*}
100B	104040E2	4F	**DO** 00B	**do** *BUS* = *Y*, *Y* = 0, *LPC* ← 0
100C	1030509F	50	**DO** 00C	**do** *BUS*7:0 = *RAM*7:0, *TEMP1* ← *BUS*
100D	104510D4	51	**DO** 00D	**do** *BUS* = *Y*, *Y* = FFH - *TEMP1*, *SP* ← FFH - *TEMP1*
A...	A.......	52	**RET**	**end procedure**
			PROCEDURE FA	**procedure** FA {*WHILE*, *IF*}
100C	1030509F	53	**DO** 00C	**do** *BUS*7:0 = *RAM*7:0, *TEMP1* ← *BUS*
1410	1440405B	54	**DO** 410	**do** *ADR* ← *BUS*, *BUS* = *Y*, *Y* = *LPC*
1800	18....00	55	**DO** 800	**do** *REG* ← 0
1111	1150205B	56	**DO** 111	**do** *RAM*15:12 ← *BUS*3:0, *BUS* = *REG*
1212	1240505B	57	**DO** 212	**do** *RAM*11:8 ← *BUS*3:0, *BUS* = *Y*, *Y* = *TEMP1*
C.86	C.....86	58	**CALL** 86	**call** F0 {*WHILE*, *IF*, *ELSE*}
A...	A.......	59	**RET**	**end procedure**
			PROCEDURE F9	**procedure** F9 {*CALL*}
100C	1030509F	5A	**DO** 00C	**do** *BUS*7:0 = *RAM*7:0, *TEMP1* ← *BUS*
1410	1440405B	5B	**DO** 410	**do** *ADR* ← *BUS*, *BUS* = *Y*, *Y* = *LPC*
180C	18....0C	5C	**DO** 80C	**do** *REG* ← 0C
1111	1150205B	5D	**DO** 111	**do** *RAM*15:12 ← *BUS*3:0, *BUS* = *REG*
1219	12400062	5E	**DO** 219	**do** *RAM*11:8 ← *BUS*3:0, *BUS* = *Y*, *Y* = 0
1312	1340505B	5F	**DO** 312	**do** *RAM*7:0 ← *BUS*7:0, *BUS* = *Y*, *Y* = *TEMP1*
1014	104042C3	60	**DO** 014	**do** *BUS* = *Y*, *Y* = *LPC* + 1, *LPC* ← *LPC* + 1
A...	A.......	61	**RET**	**end procedure**
			PROCEDURE F8	**procedure** F8 {*PROCEDURE*}
1418	1430205B	62	**DO** 418	**do** *ADR* ← *BUS*, *BUS*7:0 = *RAM*7:0
1310	1340405B	63	**DO** 310	**do** *RAM*7:0 ← *BUS*7:0, *BUS* = *Y*, *Y* = *LPC*
A...	A.......	64	**RET**	**end procedure**
			PROCEDURE F7	**procedure** F7 {*ENDIF*}
1417	144012C3	65	**DO** 417	**do** *ADR* ← *BUS*, *BUS* = *Y*, *Y* = *SP* + 1, *SP* ← *SP* + 1
1418	1430205B	66	**DO** 418	**do** *ADR* ← *BUS*, *BUS*7:0 = *RAM*7:0
1310	1340405B	67	**DO** 310	**do** *RAM*7:0 ← *BUS*7:0, *BUS* = *Y*, *Y* = *LPC*
A...	A.......	68	**RET**	**end procedure**
			PROCEDURE F6	**procedure** F6 {*END PROGRAM*}
1410	1440405B	69	**DO** 410	**do** *ADR* ← *BUS*, *BUS* = *Y*, *Y* = *LPC*
180E	18....0E	6A	**DO** 80E	**do** *REG* ← 0E
1111	1150205B	6B	**DO** 111	**do** *RAM*15:12 ← *BUS*3:0, *BUS* = *REG*
1801	18....01	6C	**DO** 801	**do** *REG* ← 01
101B	1050309F	6D	**DO** 01B	**do** *BUS* = *REG*, *EPG* ← *BUS*
A...	A.......	6E	**RET**	**end procedure**
			PROCEDURE F5	**procedure** F5 {*END WHILE*}
C.8B	C.....8B	6F	**CALL** 8B	**call** EF {*END WHILE*, *ELSE*}
1312	1340505B	70	**DO** 312	**do** *RAM*7:0 ← *BUS*7:0, *BUS* = *Y*, *Y* = *TEMP1*
1014	104042C3	71	**DO** 014	**do** *BUS* = *Y*, *Y* = *LPC* + 1, *LPC* ← *LPC* + 1
A...	A.......	72	**RET**	**end procedure**

Figure 7.37

$ROMA_{15:0}$	$ROM_{31:0}$	*ADR*	L4	L5: *PROGRAM..END PROGRAM*
			PROCEDURE F4	**procedure** F4 {*ELSE*}
C.8B	C.....8B	73	CALL 8B	**call** EF {*END WHILE, ELSE*}
C.86	C.....86	74	CALL 86	**call** F0 {*WHILE, IF, ELSE*}
A...	A.......	75	RET	**end procedure**
			PROCEDURE F3	**procedure** F3 {*DO*}
100E	1020509F	76	DO 00E	**do** *BUS*3:0 = *RAM*11:8, *TEMP1* ← *BUS*
100F	1030609F	77	DO 00F	**do** *BUS*7:0 = *RAM*7:0, *TEMP*2 ← *BUS*
1410	1440405B	78	DO 410	**do** *ADR* ← *BUS*, *BUS* = *Y*, *Y* = *LPC*
1801	18....01	79	DO 801	**do** *REG* ← 01
1111	1150205B	7A	DO 111	**do** *RAM*15:12 ← *BUS*3:0, *BUS* = *REG*
1212	1240505B	7B	DO 212	**do** *RAM*11:8 ← *BUS*3:0, *BUS* = *Y*, *Y* = *TEMP1*
1313	1340605B	7C	DO 313	**do** *RAM*7:0 ← *BUS*7:0, *BUS* = *Y*, *Y* = *TEMP*2
1014	104042C3	7D	DO 014	**do** *BUS* = *Y*, *Y* = *LPC* + 1, *LPC* ← *LPC* + 1
A...	A.......	7E	RET	**end procedure**
			PROCEDURE F2	**procedure** F2 {*END PROCEDURE*}
1410	1440405B	7F	DO 410	**do** *ADR* ← *BUS*, *BUS* = *Y*, *Y* = *LPC*
180A	18....0A	80	DO 80A	**do** *REG* ← 0A
1111	1150205B	81	DO 111	**do** *RAM*15:12 ← *BUS*3:0, *BUS* = *REG*
1219	12400062	82	DO 219	**do** *RAM*11:8 ← *BUS*3:0, *BUS* = *Y*, *Y* = 0
1319	13400062	83	DO 319	**do** *RAM*7:0 ← *BUS*7:0, *BUS* = *Y*, *Y* = 0
1014	104042C3	84	DO 014	**do** *BUS* = *Y*, *Y* = *LPC* + 1, *LPC* ← *LPC* + 1
A...	A.......	85	RET	**end procedure**
			PROCEDURE F0	**procedure** F0 {*WHILE, IF, ELSE*}
1415	1440105B	86	DO 415	**do** *ADR* ← *BUS*, *BUS* = *Y*, *Y* = *SP*
1310	1340405B	87	DO 310	**do** *RAM*7:0 ← *BUS*7:0, *BUS* = *Y*, *Y* = *LPC*
1016	104010CB	88	DO 016	**do** *BUS* = *Y*, *Y* = *SP* - 1, *SP* ← *SP* - 1
1014	104042C3	89	DO 014	**do** *BUS* = *Y*, *Y* = *LPC* + 1, *LPC* ← *LPC* + 1
A...	A.......	8A	RET	**end procedure**
			PROCEDURE EF	**procedure** EF {*END WHILE, ELSE*}
1417	144012C3	8B	DO 417	**do** *ADR* ← *BUS*, *BUS* = *Y*, *Y* = *SP* + 1, *SP* ← *SP* + 1
100C	1030509F	8C	DO 00C	**do** *BUS*7:0 = *RAM*7:0, *TEMP1* ← *BUS*
1412	1440505B	8D	DO 412	**do** *ADR* ← *BUS*, *BUS* = *Y*, *Y* = *TEMP1*
131A	13404243	8E	DO 31A	**do** *RAM*7:0 ← *BUS*7:0, *BUS* = *Y*, *Y* = *LPC* + 1
1410	1440405B	8F	DO 410	**do** *ADR* ← *BUS*, *BUS* = *Y*, *Y* = *LPC*
1800	18....00	90	DO 800	**do** *REG* ← 0
1111	1150205B	91	DO 111	**do** *RAM*15:12 ← *BUS*3:0, *BUS* = *REG*
1808	18....08	92	DO 808	**do** *REG* ← 08
1211	1250205B	93	DO 211	**do** *RAM*11:8 ← *BUS*3:0, *BUS* = *REG*
A...	A.......	94	RET	**end procedure**

Figure 7.37

$ROMA_{15:0}$	$ROM_{31:0}$	*ADR*	L4	L5: *2ND PASS*
			PROCEDURE F1	**procedure** F1 {*2ND PASS*}
100B	104040E2	95	DO 00B	**do** $BUS = Y, Y = 0, LPC \leftarrow 0$
1410	1440405B	96	DO 410	**do** $ADR \leftarrow BUS, BUS = Y, Y = LPC$
1008	104030E2	97	DO 008	**do** $BUS = Y, Y = 0, EPG \leftarrow 0$
1009	1043209F	98	DO 009	**do** $BUS = Y, Y = EPG, IR \leftarrow BUS$
0CA9	0C....A9	99	IF *BUSOBAR* ELSE A9	**while** *BUSOBAR*
100A	1010209F	9A	DO 00A	**do** $BUS3{:}0 = RAM15{:}12, IR \leftarrow BUS$
02A5	02....A5	9B	IF *BUS*2 ELSE A5	**if** *BUS*2
01A0	01....A0	9C	IF *BUS*1 ELSE A0	**if** *BUS*1
1801	18....01	9D	DO 801	**do** $REG \leftarrow 01$
101B	1050309F	9E	DO 01B	**do** $BUS = REG, EPG \leftarrow BUS$
08A4	08....A4	9F	GO TO A4	**else**
1418	1430205B	A0	DO 418	**do** $ADR \leftarrow BUS, BUS7{:}0 = RAM7{:}0$
100C	1030509F	A1	DO 00C	**do** $BUS7{:}0 = RAM7{:}0, TEMP1 \leftarrow BUS$
1410	1440405B	A2	DO 410	**do** $ADR \leftarrow BUS, BUS = Y, Y = LPC$
1312	1340505B	A3	DO 312	**do** $RAM7{:}0 \leftarrow BUS7{:}0, BUS = Y, Y = TEMP1$
			ENDIF	**endif**
08A5	08....A5	A4	GO TO A5	**else**
			ENDIF	**endif**
1014	104042C3	A5	DO 014	**do** $BUS = Y, Y = LPC + 1, LPC \leftarrow LPC + 1$
1410	1440405B	A6	DO 410	**do** $ADR \leftarrow BUS, BUS = Y, Y = LPC$
1009	1043209F	A7	DO 009	**do** $BUS = Y, Y = EPG, IR \leftarrow BUS$
0899	08....99	A8	GO TO 99	**end while**
A...	A.......	A9	RET	**end procedure**

Figure 7.38

be written in terms of the standard mnemonic expressions of **L4** and **L5**, and coded in hexadecimal as words in $ROM_{31:0}$, as in Figure 7.14; at least the 16 bits $ROM_{23:8}$ will remain undefined.

In the case of the micro-command instruction **DO** $ROM_{27:0}$ the **L5** mnemonic expressions state the relations of equality and synchronous assignment realized by the processor, whilst the word $ROM_{31:0}$ expresses in hexadecimal the execution of these relations, in the format of Figure 7.14 and according to the definitions of Figure 7.12, 7.13 and 7.16. Justification of the more compact code $ROMA_{15:0}$ and of the corresponding **L4** expressions is given later, in §7.4.14.

The final **L4** program, in the version developed here, consists of 170 instructions each of 32 bits, ADR = 00 to A9, with a maximum of three nested procedures; thus the depth of the sequencer stack is three.

7.4.11 Comment

Let us assume that in accordance with §7.4.6 and Figure 7.33 we have allocated *np* consecutive words of RAM for the *np* addresses of the object program procedures. In the interests of simplicity of the compilation algorithm we must ensure that the names of these procedures are compatible with the memory organization, so they must be numbered as follows:

$$FF, FF—1, \ldots FF - np + 1 \quad (FF_H = 255_D) \tag{7.49}$$

The **L5** source program for the *PASCALINE* compiler illustrates this principle: the 17 procedures ($np = 11_H$) are numbered from FF to FF $- np + 1 =$ EF. Further, this program has $h = 204$ lines of source code and a maximum of $s = 5$ sucessive nestings (**if. . .**and **while. . .**); substituting these values in (7.46) we have $234 > 203$, thus checking the inequality.

7.4.12 Hardware realization: interpreter INT4.1

We can now give the declarations for *PASCALINE*:

- ***test variables*** *xi*: BUS_0, BUS_1, BUS_2, BUS_3, 0, 1, *SEND*, *SENDBAR* = *SEND'*, *BUS0BAR* = BUS_0'
  (the test variable $xi = 0$ is needed by the **L4** instruction **GO TO** *ADR+*);
- ***assignment registers*** *REG*[*j*]:
  $REG[1] = RAM_{15:12}$; $REG[2] = RAM_{11:8}$; $REG[3] = RAM_{7:0}$;
  $REG[4] = ADR_{7:0}$; $REG[8] = REG_{7:0}$;
- **RALU** ***registers*** *RAM*[*B*]:
  RAM[0] = *PC* (source program counter)
  RAM[1] = *SP* (stack pointer)
  RAM[2] = *IR* (instruction register)
  RAM[3] = *EPG* (end-of-program register)
  RAM[4] = *LPC* (object program counter)
  RAM[5] = *TEMP1* (temporary register 1)
  RAM[6] = *TEMP2* (temporary register 2).

Thus for the interpreter INT4.1 (Figures 7.11, 7.14) to be able to execute the **L4** *PASCALINE* program it must be provided with:

- a control unit (CU) that can accept the nine test variables *xi*;
- a universal processing unit (PU) with at least five assignment registers, of which three are addressable and constitute the synchronized memory RAM; and seven internal registers in its RALU.

7.4.13 Hardware realization: interpreter INT4.2

From the *PASCALINE* program (Figures 7.28 to 7.38) a list of all the micro-commands $\mu C_{23:0} = ROM_{23:0}$ can be drawn up; there are 28 of these, as shown in Figure 7.39, and for their minimal coding, also shown in Figure 7.39, five variables $ADRB_4$ to $ADRB_0$ are required.

The small number of micro-commands $\mu C_{23:0}$, related to the inefficient use of the original memory ROM (§7.2.10), suggests that a new block diagram should be considered, for example Figure 7.40. This is derived from the control unit of Figure 7.14 by making the following changes.

1. The 32-bit ROM is replaced by the 16-bit ROMA.
2. The micro-command instruction field $ROM_{23:0}$ is replaced by $ROMA_{4:0} = ADRB_{4:0}$, giving the minimal code of Figure 7.39.
3. A new read only memory ROMB is added, to each address $ADRB_{4:0}$ of which there corresponds a micro-command $ROMB_{23:0} = ROM_{23:0}$, as in Figure 7.39.

$ADRB_{4:0}$	$ROM_{23:0} = ROMB_{23:0}$	DESCRIPTION
00	9 02 09F	*BUS*3:0 = *FLAG*3:0, *IR* ← *BUS*
01	6 00 09F	*BUS*7:0 = *INL*7:0, *PC* ← *BUS*
02	4 00 05B	*BUS* = *Y*, *Y* = *PC*
03	8 00 05B	*BUS*3:0 = *INL*15:12
04	7 00 05B	*BUS*3:0 = *INL*11:8
05	6 00 05B	*BUS*7:0 = *INL*7:0
06	4 00 2C3	*BUS* = *Y*, *Y* = *PC* + 1, *PC* ← *PC* + 1
07	4 00 0E2	*BUS* = *Y*, *Y* = 0, *PC* ← 0
08	4 03 0E2	*BUS* = *Y*, *Y* = 0, *EPG* ← 0
09	4 32 09F	*BUS* = *Y*, *Y* = *EPG*, *IR* ← *BUS*
0A	1 02 09F	*BUS*3:0 = *RAM*15:12, *IR* ← *BUS*
0B	4 04 0E2	*BUS* = *Y*, *Y* = 0, *LPC* ← 0
0C	3 05 09F	*BUS*7:0 = *RAM*7:0, *TEMP1* ← *BUS*
0D	4 51 0D4	*BUS* = *Y*, *Y* = FFH - *TEMP1*, *SP* ← FFH - *TEMP1*
0E	2 05 09F	*BUS*3:0 = *RAM*11:8, *TEMP1* ← *BUS*
0F	3 06 09F	*BUS*7:0 = *RAM*7:0, *TEMP2* ← *BUS*
10	4 04 05B	*BUS* = *Y*, *Y* = *LPC*
11	5 02 05B	*BUS* = *REG*
12	4 05 05B	*BUS* = *Y*, *Y* = *TEMP1*
13	4 06 05B	*BUS* = *Y*, *Y* = *TEMP2*
14	4 04 2C3	*BUS* = *Y*, *Y* = *LPC* + 1, *LPC* ← *LPC* + 1
15	4 01 05B	*BUS* = *Y*, *Y* = *SP*
16	4 01 0CB	*BUS* = *Y*, *Y* = *SP* - 1, *SP* ← *SP* - 1
17	4 01 2C3	*BUS* = *Y*, *Y* = *SP* + 1, *SP* ← *SP* + 1
18	3 02 05B	*BUS*7:0 = *RAM*7:0
19	4 00 062	*BUS* = *Y*, *Y* = 0
1A	4 04 243	*BUS* = *Y*, *Y* = *LPC* + 1
1B	5 03 09F	*BUS* = *REG*, *EPG* ← *BUS*

Figure 7.39

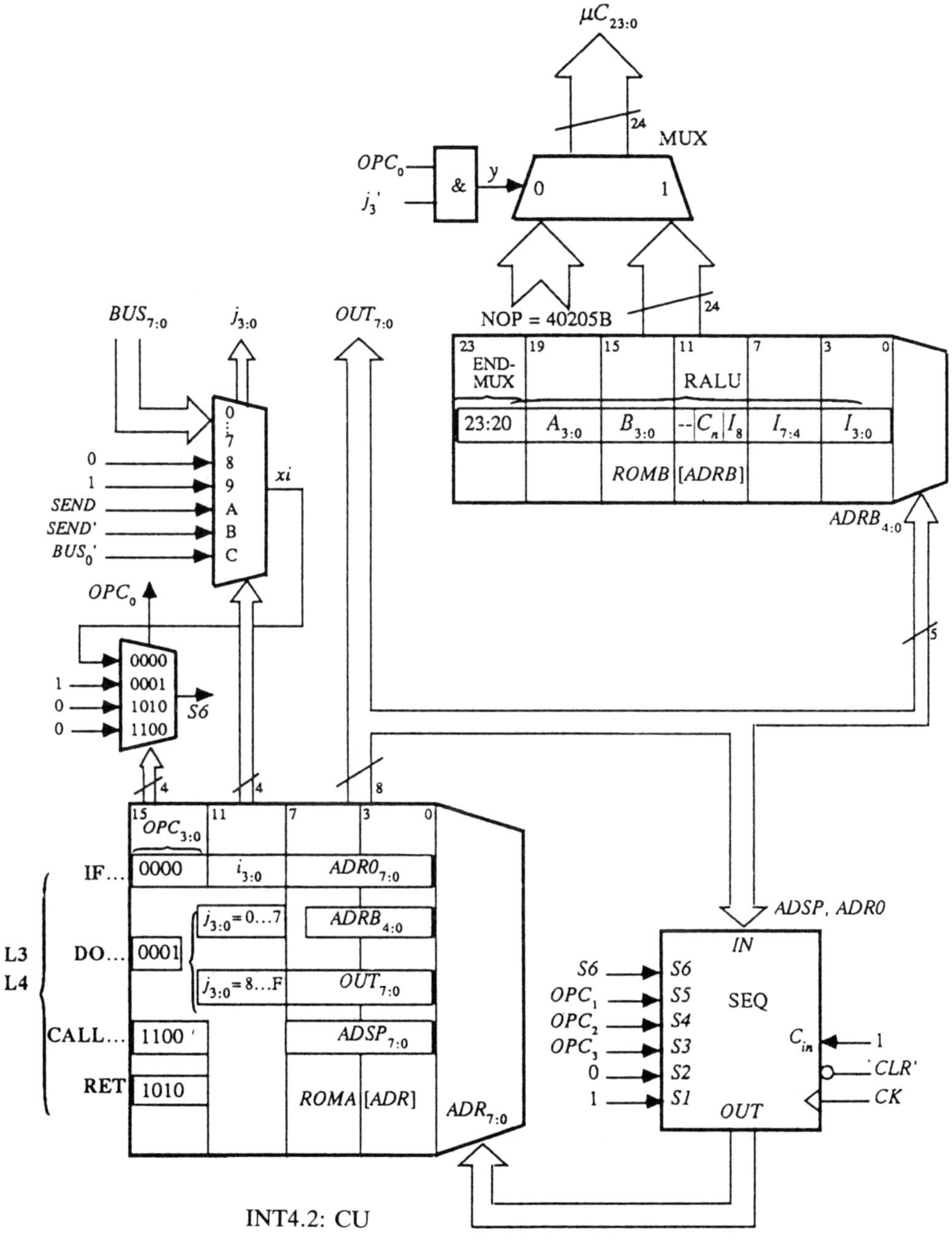

μC 23:0
24
MUX
OPC0
j3'
&
y
0
1
NOP = 40205B
24
BUS 7:0
j 3:0
OUT 7:0
23
END-
MUX
19
15
11
RALU
7
3
0
23:20
A 3:0
B 3:0
-- Cn I8
I 7:4
I 3:0
ROMB [ADRB]
ADRB 4:0
0 … 7
8
9
A
B
C
xi
0
1
SEND
SEND'
BUS0'
OPC0
0000
0001
1010
1100
S6
1
0
0
5
4
4
8
15
OPC 3:0
11
7
3
0
IF…
0000
i 3:0
ADR0 7:0
L3
L4
DO…
0001
j3:0 = 0…7
ADRB 4:0
j3:0 = 8…F
OUT 7:0
CALL…
1100
ADSP 7:0
RET
1010
ROMA [ADR]
ADR 7:0
ADSP, ADR0
IN
SEQ
S6
S6
OPC1
S5
OPC2
S4
OPC3
S3
0
S2
1
S1
Cin
1
CLR'
CK
OUT
INT4.2: CU

Figure 7.40

The combination of the universal processing unit of Figure 7.11 and the control unit of Figure 7.40 gives the new universal processor, INT4.2. In contrast to INT4.1, INT4.2 can execute **L3** and **L4** instructions in the normal 16-bit format. Some writers say that the architecture of Figure 7.40 constitutes a *2-level control unit*, and distinguish between the *micro-memory* ROMA and the *nano-memory* ROMB.

7.4.14 Software realization: micro-program and nano-program

In the *PASCALINE* program the new minimal code is in hexadecimal, $ROMA_{15:0}$; in the mnemonic **L4** expressions each micro-command instruction **DO** *REG*[*j*], $ADRB_{4:0}$ contains the minimal code *ADRB*. Such a software realization is called a *minimal-coding microprogram*; it is bound indissolubly to a program in the nano-memory, sometimes called a *nano-program*. This is shown in Figure 7.39 which, if $ADRB_{4:0}$ is considered as five input variables and $ROMB_{23:0}$ as 24 output variables, can be regarded as a truth table.

7.4.15 Comment

In this new layout the memory requirement has been reduced from the $256 \times 32 = 8192$ bits of the original ROM (Figure 7.14) to the total of 4864 bits of the two memories ROMA ($256 \times 16 = 4096$ bits), ROMB ($32 \times 24 = 768$ bits); whilst the decoding performed by ROMB introduces an extra delay into the execution of each instruction. This delay is the price that has to be paid for the economizing in memory.

7.4.16 Definitions: horizontal and vertical micro-programs

Figure 7.41 is an example of a *universal instruction*: this can execute any of the **L4** instructions **IF. . . , DO. . . , CALL. . . , RET**, in the formats of Figure 7.40, according to the value of the operating code *OPC*. Such an instruction has these characteristics:

- any field always holds the same function, meaning that it always has the same name: *ADR0* and *ADSP* are different names but play equivalent roles;
- each field feeds one bus and one only; thus each bus has a special purpose.

This guarantees the maximum parallelism because with these properties a test, an assignment to a register, the execution of a micro-command and the determination of the address of the next instruction

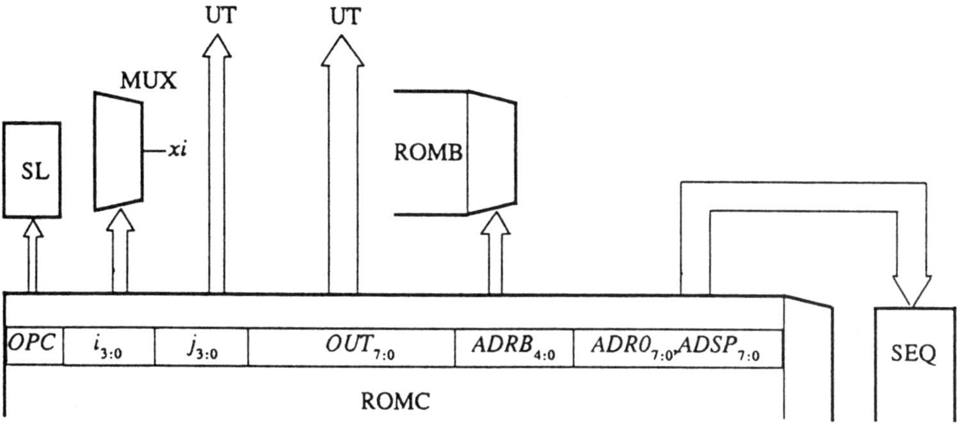

Figure 7.41

can all be performed simultaneously with each instruction execution. We call a micro-program written with such instructions a *horizontal micro-program*: it gives greater speed of execution, at the cost of greater width of memory.

The properties are not possessed by any of the languages discussed in this book, in particular **L3** and **L4** which can be executed by the control unit of Figure 7.40, because:

- each field of a memory word has its own particular function, depending on the type of instruction;
- the bus fed by any particular field thus plays different roles according to the type of instruction; thus the buses are general-purpose.

Micro-programs written with instructions of this type are called *vertical micro-programs*; here memory is economized, at the cost of the lower speed resulting from the sequential decomposition of the universal instruction.

Finally, the coding of the various fields can be either minimal, in the sense of §7.4.13, or not. The type of the coding is independent of the type of the micro-program (horizontal or vertical), although there is often confusion between the use of a horizontal micro-program with non-minimal coding, both leading to wide memories, and vertical micro-programming with minimal coding, both leading to narrow memories.

7.4.17 Conclusion

The *PASCALINE* compiler illustrates the designing of an **L4** program of significant complexity, intended for execution by a universal processor. The general method of solution will be seen to be similar both to that of successive refinements (§6.1.18), in that the initial specification is broken down so as to be realizable by the primitive instructions of the language; and to that of the construction of a specialized processor (§6.2.16), in that the RALU's computing resources and transfer registers can perform arithmetical and logical operations of significant complexity during the execution of a single micro-command instruction of type **DO. . . .**

Whilst it is easy to optimize the set of test instructions by the methods for reduction and simplification given in Chapter 2, this is not the case with the sequential decomposition of the micro-command instructions, optimization of which requires a detailed knowledge of the parallel computations performed by the processing unit. References to some methods that can be used for this optimization are given in the bibliography of §7.4.18.

We have said in this section, as in section 7.2, that the determination of the hexadecimal code from a high-level specification and the characteristics of the RALU is a difficult and tedious task. There is a need therefore for programming tools — micro-assemblers, simulators — to aid this task when the program to be developed is above a certain size; the bibliography of §7.4.18 gives references to some of the tools that are available.

7.4.18 Bibliography

The application of the general principles of top-down programming (successive refinements) to micro-programs that include complex micro-command instructions is dealt with in [63] (pp. 323–327).

Many studies have been made of coding of instructions, both minimal and otherwise, particularly in connection with 2-level and pipeline architectures aimed at increasing computing speeds: [63] (pp. 225–230, 239–241) and [114]. Study of these architectures necessarily involve the concepts of horizontal and vertical micro-programming, the relative merits of which are discussed in [63] (pp. 234–239), [67] (pp. 273–277) and [114].

Optimization of micro-programs in which there are sequences of micro-command instructions can be studied from two points of view:

- *horizontal optimization*, which aims to minimize the instruction width (number of bits), so as to economize on memory, that is, space;

- *vertical optimization*, which aims to minimize the length of the micro-program (number of instructions) so as to speed the execution, that is, to economize on time; and also to reduce the amount of memory needed, so again to economize on space.

Horizontal optimization was mentioned briefly in §6.2.12 in connection with the construction of a specialized processor; see also [105], [107] (pp. 96–117); more general methods are given in [67] (pp. 281–287), [117], [134] (pp. 100–105) and [148] (pp. 70–75). Vertical optimization aims to exploit as far as possible the parallelism available in the processing unit, by combining as many command states (micro-orders) as possible in a single instruction. This can be a process of either *local packing*, in which only sequences of instructions of type **DO**...are considered, or *global compaction*, in which sequences of intructions of all types are considered: see [118], [136] and [148] (pp. 76–81, 381–431).

A *micro-assembler* is a compiler of a special type: its source language is *symbolic micro-programming language* and its object language is binary code for loading into the memory ROM; it can be either universal or specialized, that is, applicable either to different source languages or to only one. Descriptions are given in [42], [63] (pp. 300–313) and [148] (pp. 337–379).

7.4.19 Exercise

The aim is to optimize the *PASCALINE* compiler by reducing still further the number of lines of the **L5** program. As a first step, apply the methods of simplification and reduction of Chapter 2 to the main tests:

- of $FLAG_{3:0} = BUS_{3:0}$ in the main program (Figures 7.27–8);
- of $IR = LC_{3:0} = BUS_{3:0}$ in the procedure *COMPILATION* (Figures 7.31–2);
- of $IR = OPC_{3:0} = BUS_{3:0}$ in the procedure *2ND PASS* (Figures 7.31, 7.38).

Next, attempt to introduce parallelism by arranging for several micro-command instructions to be executed during the same clock time. Taking note of §7.2.8, consider in particular the pairs of instructions with the following addresses:

11 & 12 in Figure 7.29
1A & 1B, 1F & 20 in Figure 7.30
22 & 23, 49 & 4A in Figure 7.32

Finally, derive two versions of the optimized compiler: one with non-minimal coding, for the memory ROM of Figure 7.14; and one with minimal coding, for the memories ROMA, ROMB of Figure 7.40. Give these in the form of tables similar to Figures 7.28 to 7.39.

7.4.20 Exercise

In a variant of the control unit of the minimally-coded INT4.2 of Figure 7.40 the neutral micro-command NOP = 40205B is stored in one particular word of ROMB. Show what changes to the original hardware this entails, and compare the two systems.

7.4.21 Project: digital clock

Figure 5.22 is a structured form of the clock algorithm of §5.1.14. This is to be written in **L4** for execution by the interpreter INT4.2, consisting of a processing unit (Figure 7.11) and a minimally-coded control unit (Figure 7.40). The registers $T[i]$, $G[i]$, i, s are to be positioned so that the time, as hours, minutes and seconds, is always displayed. Construct the programs for this in **L5** and **L4**, and the hexadecimal code for ROMA, ROMB. Finally, give the logic system that has to be added to the processing unit to provide this display.

7.4.22 Project

The interpreter INT4.2 (§7.4.13) can first execute the *PASCALINE* compiler and then execute the resulting compiled **L4** program: cf. Figure 7.18, with INT4.2 replacing the pair INT4.1 and INT3. Using as an example the **L5** program for the reversible counter of Figure 5.57, show how the architecture of INT4.2 must be modified to enable a new control variable *COMP* to be added, to have these effects:

- $COMP = 1$ gives *compilation mode,* in which the sequencer SEQ in the control unit receives the addresses *ADSP*, *ADR0* and the orders *S6*, $OPC_{3:1}$ from ROMA and generates the address *ADR* as shown in Figure 7.40;
- $COMP = 0$ gives *interpretation mode,* in which this sequencer receives these same addresses and orders from RAM in the processing unit, which holds the object program to be executed, and generates the address *ADR* of RAM.

Investigate the consequences of this modification for the construction of the **L5** counter program, in particular for the choice of test variables *xi* and of the assignment registers $REG[j]$. What are the fundamental limitations of the new architecture?

7.5 APPLICATIONS: BOOTSTRAPPING, SELF-COMPILATION, INTERPRETATION

7.5.1 Introduction

Writing a compiler in a low-level language such as **L4** can be a tedious task, so it is natural to look for a way of doing this in a high-level language such as **L5**. A process called *bootstrapping* is needed for this approach, and is the subject of the first part of this section.

A high-level language, **L5** say, can be executed without compilation, by writing an interpreter in a low-level language, **L4** say; an outline of such a program is given in the second part of the section. This provides an example of the classical problem of interpreting a high-level language program by a micro-program.

7.5.2 Definition: conditional repetition 'repeat . . . until . . .'

The *conditional repetition* of *P*, written **repeat** *P* **until** *xi* (Figure 7.42) is a structured program in the sense of §5.1.5. It can be realized directly in the language **L3** in the form of a program *P4*.

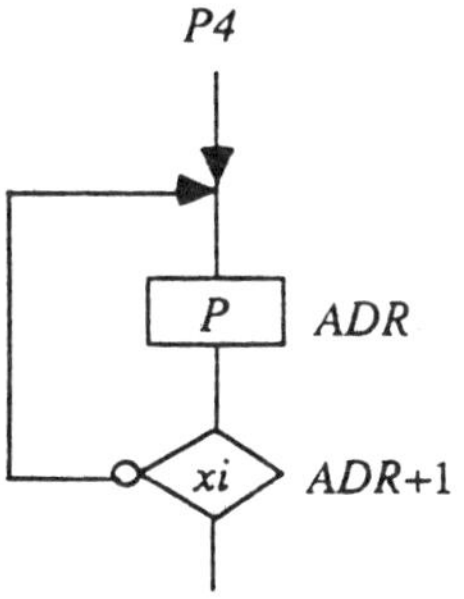

Figure 7.42

ADR	L4⁺	L5⁺
–	**PROGRAM** *P4*	**program** *P4*
–	**REPEAT**	**repeat**
ADR	**DO** *P*	**do** *P*
ADR+1	**IF** *xi* **ELSE** *ADR*	**until** *xi*
–	**END PROGRAM**	**end program**

Figure 7.43

7.5.3 Definitions: the languages $L4^+$, $L5^+$

$\mathbf{L4}^+$ is an extension of **L4** (§5.2.8) obtained by adding a new keyword:

$$\mathbf{L4}^+ = \mathbf{L4} + \{\mathbf{REPEAT}\} \qquad (7.50)$$

The syntax is that of **L4** (Figure 5.31) with the non-terminal symbol 'statement' replaced by Figure 7.44.

Correspondingly, $\mathbf{L5}^+$ is obtained from **L5** (§5.2.9) by adding two terminal symbols:

$$\mathbf{L5}^{+} = \mathbf{L5} + \{\mathbf{repeat},\ \mathbf{until}\ldots\} \tag{7.51}$$

and modifying the syntax of Figure 5.33 to read as in Figure 7.45.

Figure 7.43 gives the program *P4* in both **L4**$^+$ and **L5**$^+$ and Figure 7.46 gives a possible format for the two new lines of **L5**$^+$.

statement: **DO** | **CALL** | **IF** {statement} **GO TO** {statement} **ENDIF** | **IF** {statement} **GO TO** | **REPEAT** {statement} **IF;**

L4$^+$

Figure 7.44

statement: **do** | **call** | **if** {statement} **else** {statement} **endif** | **while** {statement} **end while** | **repeat** {statement} **until;**

L5$^+$

Figure 7.45

repeat :	5	–	–	–
until *xi* :	4	–	–	$i_{3:0}$

Figure 7.46

7.5.4 Definition: compiler *PASCALINE*$^+$

This is a new compiler, written in **L4**, which is to accept **L5**$^+$ as source language and translate it into **L4**$^+$ as object language (Figure 7.47), which is then directly executable by an interpreter for **L3** or **L4**.

7.5.5 Bootstrapping

We saw in section 7.4 that writing even a modest compiler in a low-level language such as **L4** is not a light task; we shall now show how the new compiler *PASCALINE*$^+$ can be written directly in **L5** itself. This is done as follows.

- The new compiler program *PASCALINE*$^+$ is written in **L5**, taking over all the material constructed for its predecessor *PASCALINE* and simply adding the procedures needed to compile the new lines **repeat** and **until**. . . .

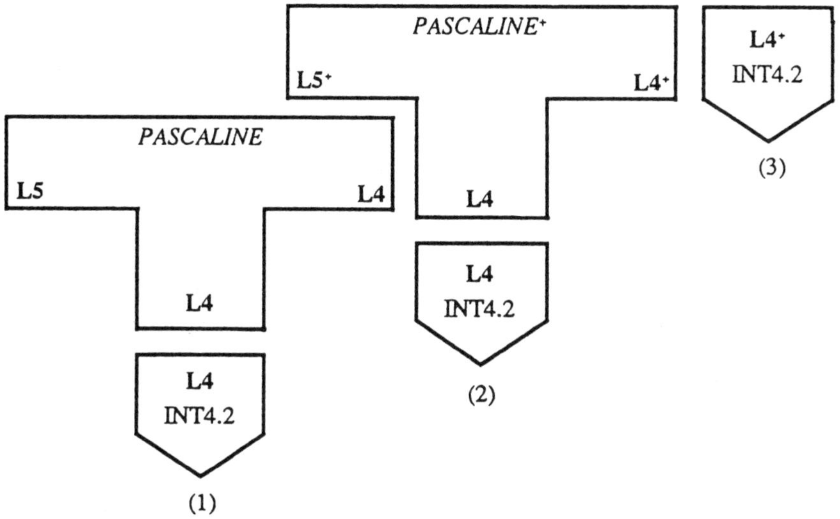

Figure 7.47

- This **L5** program is the source for the original *PASCALINE* compiler (stage 1 in Figure 7.47); after it has been executed by the interpreter INT4.2 the data in the memory RAM of Figure 7.11 are those of the object program in **L4**. Thus we have our new compiler *PASCALINE*$^+$, in **L4**.
- In order to use this we must transfer it from RAM in the processing unit to ROMA in the control unit (Figure 7.40), where it will replace the previous *PASCALINE* (stage 2 in Figure 7.47); this is easily done if RAM is an EEPROM (*electrically erasable programmable* ROM), for example the Xicor X2816A.
- When this transfer has been done the new compiler is operational. It will accept any **L5**$^+$ source program and produce the correponding object program in **L4**$^+$, which in turn can be executed by any interpreter for **L3** or **L4**, in particular by INT4.2 (stage 3 in Figure 7.47).

This process, in which a first compiler (*PASCALINE* in this case) is hand-written in a low-level language (**L4**), to compile a sub-set of the final language (**L5**), is called *bootstrapping*. It enables the second compiler program (*PASCALINE*$^+$), for the more complex language (**L5**$^+$), to be compiled automatically.

The technique of bootstrapping makes it practical to design complex compilers and write the programs for these in relatively high-level languages.

7.5.6 Comment

The compiler can be transferred from the processing unit (in RAM) to the control unit (in ROMA) only if the **L4** formats are identical; only then can INT4.2, with its minimally coded control unit (Figure 7.40), execute the object program obtained from RAM.

7.5.7 Definition: self-compiler

When a compiler is written in the source language that it is to compile — **Lc** = **Ls** in Figure 7.17 — we say we have a *self-compiler*. An example is the *PASCALINE* compiler written in **L5**.

7.5.8 Project

The task is to check the correctness of the *PASCALINE* program by making it compile itself: the interpreter INT4.2 (§7.4.13) can be assumed to be available. This means performing stage 1 of Figure 7.47, using as data (the source program) the self-compiler *PASCALINE*; the **L4** object program produced by the compilation must conform to the minimal code $ROMA_{15:0}$ of Figures 7.28 to 7.38.

7.5.9 Project

Again assuming the availability of INT4.2, and also of EEPROMs, the task here is to write the compiler $PASCALINE^{+}$ in **L5** and bootstrap this as described in §7.5.5.

7.5.10 Project

L4.3 is a version of **L4** in which the instructions **IF...ELSE...** and **CALL...** are given in the form of the relations (4.10), (4.11), that is, with relative addressing. Using the method sketched out in §7.5.5, write in **L5** a self-compiler *CALINE* that will translate an **L5** source program into an **L4.3** object program; *CALINE* in turn is to be compiled into **L4** by means of INT4.2 and *PASCALINE*. Compare the complexities of *CALINE* and *PASCALINE*.

7.5.11 Definition: the interpreter *PASCALINT*

The importance of high-level languages such as **L5** has already been emphasized (§5.2.10). However, execution of a program in such a language requires a preliminary compilation, performed by a program

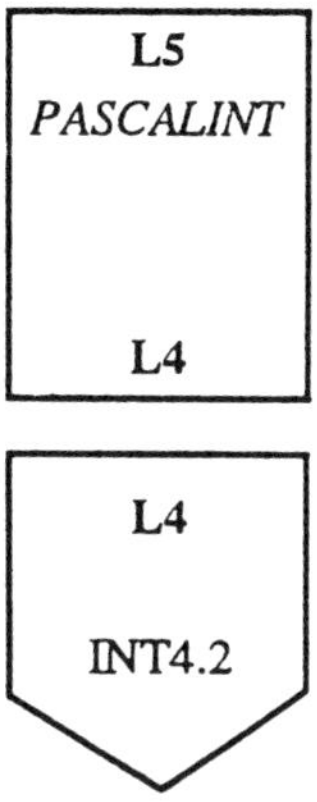

Figure 7.48

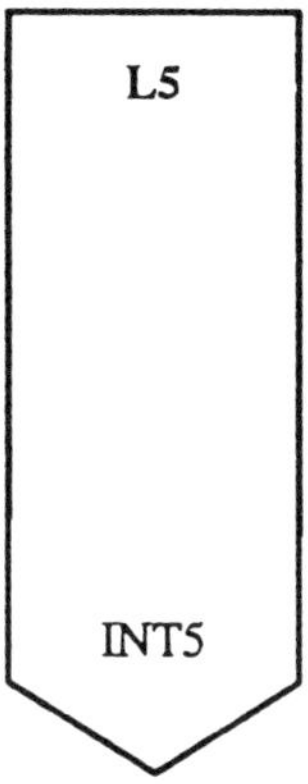

Figure 7.49

such as *PASCALINE*, whereas it would be simpler if the high-level program could be executed directly without any compilation. Therefore, keeping in mind the definitions of §§7.3.5–6, we attempt to write in **L4** an interpreter, which we shall call *PASCALINT* (Figure 7.48) which will accept **L5** as source language; and the **L4** will be executed by a hardware system, the interpreter INT4.2 of §7.4.13.

7.5.12 Description: the interpreter *PASCALINT*

Consider as an example the **L5** program for the reversible counter, Figure 5.57; we assume that **L4** and **L5** are defined by the formats of Figures 7.22, 7.21 respectively. The interpreter will consist of the following:

- a main program *PASCALINT*, identical to that of *PASCALINE*, Figure 7.27; this will provide the address, write and incrementation modes as before but compilation is replaced by *interpretation*, performed by a procedure *INTERPRETATION*;
- a procedure *INTERPRETATION* (Figure 7.50), closely similar to *COMPILATION* of Figure 7.31, except that the call to the procedure *2ND PASS* is omitted;
- eleven procedures *PROGRAM*, . . . , *DO* for execution respectively of the eleven lines **program**, . . . , **do** of **L5**: these constitute the heart of the interpreter.

Consider now the interpretation of the construction **if . . . else . . . endif**, which is typical of high-level languages. In Figure 5.57 the line **if** x is at ADR = 06 in the **L5** column; no next address is given, as there is

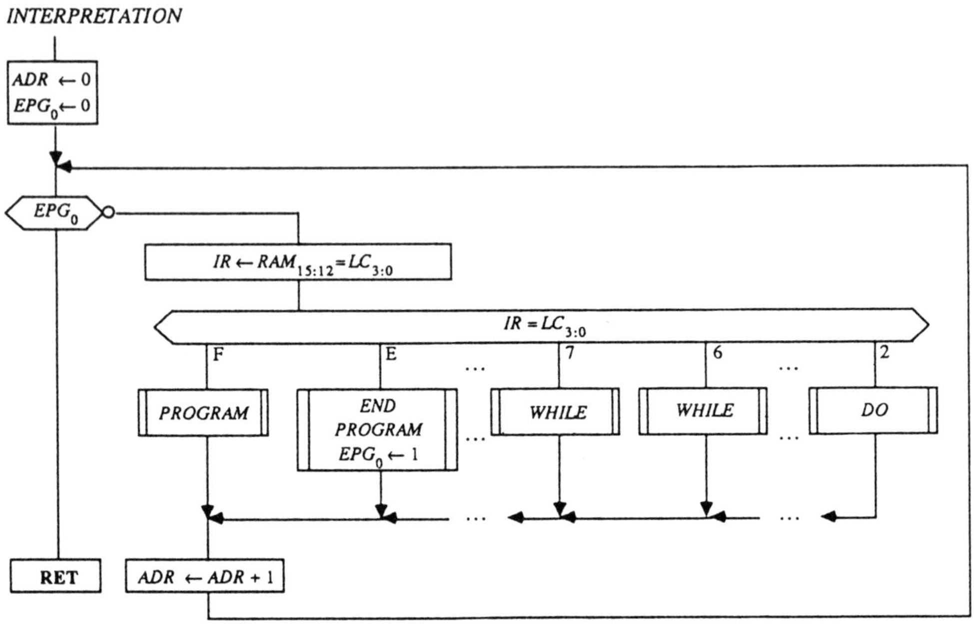

Figure 7.50

in the corresponding **L4** entry **IF** x **ELSE** 0B, so **the interpreter must work through the program line by line**. If $x = 1$ it executes the lines 07 to 0B in succession, reads **else** at 0C and then, since $x \neq 0$, skips 0D to 11.

Similarly, on reading a line such as **call** p the interpreter scans the succeeding lines without executing them until it detects the line **procedure** p, when it starts to execute the procedure. Assuming that the system has a stack on which the return address in the calling program has been placed, it will return to this address on reading the **end procedure** that terminates p.

7.5.13 Comment

Interpretation of **L5** by *PASCALINT* differs fundamentally from compilation by *PASCALINE*:

- the absence of future addresses from the **L5** program, in contrast to the *ADR0*, *ADSP* of **L4**, requires the interpreter to scan the program line by line; consequently execution is much slower than for the equivalent **L4** program;
- the hardware system INT4.2 is now dedicated to executing

PASCALINT, and consequently the processing unit required by the interpreted program — for example, the registers *REG*[*j*] — must be correspondingly specialized;
- compilation is a once-only operation: the **L5** source program is the data for the compiler which translates into **L4**, and this needs to be done only once; but interpretation has to be performed every time the **L5** program is run, since it is unchanged by the process.

7.5.14 Conclusion

The combination of interpreter program *PASCALINT* with the hardware interpreter INT4.2 (Figure 7.48) is an example of a *2-level interpretation processor*:

- the upper level, that is, the memory RAM of Figure 7.21, contains the *high-level program*, or simply the *program*, in this case in **L5**;
- the lower level, that is, the memory ROM of Figure 7.14 or 7.40, contains the interpreter, in this case *PASCALINT*; this is a *low-level program*, or *micro-program*, which expresses the *interpretation algorithm* of the source (**L5**) language in the object (**L4**) language. This object language can be executed directly by the processor's control unit.

Some writers contend that the decoding memory ROMB of Figure 7.40 constitutes a third level of interpretation, so that its contents (Figure 7.39) should be called a *nano-program*.

This 2-level structure of interpretation is typical of present-day standard universal processors, built from one or more complex integrated circuits and generally called *micro-processors*. In the case of *programmable micro-processors* the micro-program can be changed, and therefore the interpretation algorithm also.

7.5.15 Project

The task is to design the *PASCALINT* interpreter, in full detail; it can be written in **L4**, or in **L5** if a compiler is available, and is to be executed by INT4.2. Interpret the **L5** program for the reversible counter of Figure 5.57 and determine the execution time; what extra hardware is needed for the inputs *xi* and the outputs *REG*[*j*]?

7.5.16 Project

The task is to design and construct a hardware interpreter for **L5** (Figure 7.49), a specialized 1-level processor INT5. This must realize the interpretation algorithm of §7.5.12 directly, and is therefore equivalent to the INT4.2 processor with the addition of the *PASCALINT* interpreter. Make use of what was done for the design of the **L3** interpreters, and in particular aim to make maximum use of the resources provided by the sequencers, cf. §4.2.3.

7.5.17 Project: interpreter for an assembly language

An assembly language — cf. [139] (p. 219) — is specified by the instruction set of Figure 7.52, the instruction format of Figure 7.51, the addressing mode of Figure 7.53 and the test variable *FM* defined in Figure 7.54. Assuming the availability of INT4.2, construct the **L4** interpretation micro-program for this language. Give any modifications that may be needed to the INT4.2 hardware; give also the contents of the decoding memory ROMB.

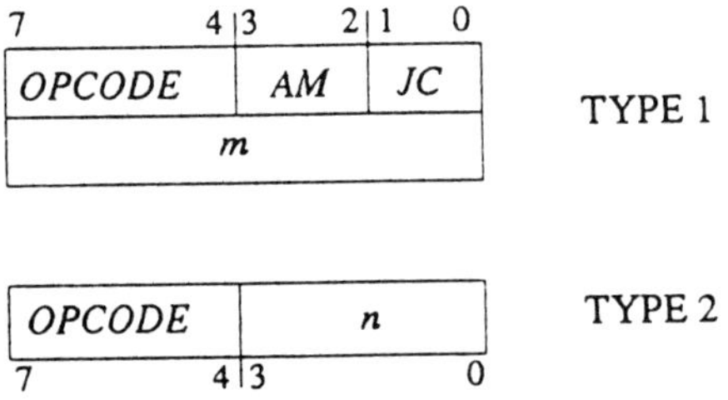

Figure 7.51

TYPE	INSTRUCTION	DESCRIPTION	*OPCODE*
1	LOAD *A*, *s*	$A \leftarrow s$	0000
1	LOAD *d*, *A*	$d \leftarrow A$	0001
1	ADD *A*, *s*	$C,A \leftarrow A + s,\ Z \leftarrow ZERO$	0010
1	AND *A*, *s*	$A \leftarrow A \wedge s,\ C \leftarrow 0,\ Z \leftarrow ZERO$	0011
1	JUMP *m*	$PC \leftarrow m$	0100
1	JUMP *tm*	$PC \leftarrow FM' \cdot (PC + 1) \vee FM \cdot m$	0101
2	CPL *A*	$A \leftarrow A'$	1000
2	RRC *A*	$A \leftarrow (C,A)/2,\ C \leftarrow A_0$	1001
2	LOAD *A*, $*n*	$A \leftarrow IN\,(n)$	1010
2	LOAD $*n*, *A*	$OUT\,(n) \leftarrow A$	1011

Figure 7.52

ADDRESSING	DESCRIPTION	*AM*
immediate	$s = m$	00
absolute	$s = d = RAM_{7:0}[m]$	01
indirect	$s = d = RAM_{7:0}[RAM_{7:0}[m]]$	11

Figure 7.53

CONDITION	DESCRIPTION	*JC*
CARRY SET	$FM = C$	00
CARRY CLEAR	$FM = C'$	01
ZERO SET	$FM = Z$	10
ZERO CLEAR	$FM = Z'$	11

Figure 7.54

7.5.18 First general conclusion: micro-programming and the CISC processor

The definition of micro-programming is due to Wilkes, who in 1951 suggested a method for designing the control unit of a processor, based on the use of a sequence of micro-instructions — a micro-program — held in a read only memory; in the 1960s micro-programming was taken up by industry and, for example, was used in most models of the IBM System/360 series. In this historical context micro-programming is generally understood as **the art and technique of producing interpreters for high-level languages**, as we have discussed in §7.5.14.

At that time random access memory that was available was much slower than the processors, a disparity that led to the use of complex instructions at the program level, interpreted by sequences of high-speed micro-instructions, the micro-program. Machines designed on this principle are now called *complex instruction set machines*, CISC.

To achieve high speed the micro-programs of CISC machines are organized horizontally; the need to control a complex processing unit requires each micro-instruction to consist of a large number of bits, often over 100. The requirements of parallelism then give rise to difficulties in optimization, as was illustrated to some extent by the design of the *PASCALINE* compiler. In these machines the application program, the data and the results are usually all held in a common random access memory, separate from the read-only memory in which the micro-program is held: this is called the *von Neumann architecture*.

7.5.19 Second general conclusion: firmware and the RISC processor

The approach of this book has been to emphasize an approach different from, but complementary to, that of classical micro-programming: that the specification for a micro-program is not an interpretation algorithm but a logic system, either combinational or sequential, whilst the interpreter is a 1-level processor, a binary decision machine. The concept of the vertically-organized micro-program follows from this, in which each micro-instruction is of fewer bits than in the horizontally-organized case. The resulting simplicity of the processing unit, often reduced to a few registers, together with the feasibility of applying the methods of the theory of logical systems, enable a true optimization of the software to be achieved. The micro-program, held in read only memory, is always distinct from the data and the results, these latter being generally held in registers or a random access memory; this gives what is called the *Harvard architecture*. This approach to micro-programming is summed up in the term *firmware*, which we can define as **the art and technique of transformation and equivalence between hardware (logic systems) and software (micro-programs)**. We must emphasize again that this hardware–software equivalence is a particular case of the equivalence between space and time.

This leads to the concept of the *reduced instruction set computer*, the RISC machine, with the characteristics that each instruction occupies only a single memory word and is executed by a hardware interpreter in a single clock time. Thus any RISC processor is a 1-level interpreter [120] and, in principle, can be designed and programmed by methods very similar to those developed here [144]. However, a new difficulty now arises in connection with the interpretation of high-level languages: the program, the data and the results are all held in the common memory (RAM), in accordance with the von Neumann architecture; the hardware interpreter has to read and execute an instruction and possibly also to write a result to memory, all of which will take several clock times; the need to overcome this potential disadvantage degrades the original simplicity of the architecture.

The technological advances of the 1980s have made available random access memories of very high speed and very large capacity at low cost; this has made it possible to have the program instructions, held in the main memory, interpreted directly by hardware. Thus the distinction between program and micro-program is blurred, and the 1-level interpretation of the RISC processor is displacing the 2-level interpretation of the CISC.

7.5.20 Bibliography

Wilkes's classical paper [113], reproduced in [130] (pp. 266–270) is the basis of standard organization of the micro programmed processor, described in particular in [66], [67] (pp. 271–273), [120], [132], [133] and [134] (pp. 1–24).

The construction of micro-programs for the interpretation of a given instruction set, together with the architecture of the associated 2-level processors, forms the core of most works on standard micro-programming: [18] (pp. 450–498), [67] (pp. 295–319), [114], [120], [127] (pp. 137–171, 290–327), [128] (pp. 275–423), [135] (pp. 137–172) and [148]. Some writers give accounts of commercially available processors and micro-programmable micro-processors, e.g. [2] (pp. 458–489), [3] (pp. 179–207), [18] (pp. 499–555), [129] (pp. 110–165) and [134]; or of extension to three levels of interpretation (to nano-programs): [126] (pp. 3–22) and [137]. A generalization to *m* levels is discussed in [131] (pp. 25–32), together with the problems of synchronization that arise; this describes also (pp. 181–212) the design of a small processor, with emphasis on the choice of architecture and its consequences for performance, considered from both space and time points of view.

The original concept of firmware is discussed in [146] and [147].

8

Appendices

8.1 SIMPLIFICATION OF DISCRETE FUNCTIONS

8.1.1 Example: 7-segment display

We want the minimal tree for the incompletely defined discrete function $Z = f, g$ given in Figures 2.18 and 2.19.

8.1.2 Method

We first determine all the branch products that have the separation property (§2.1.9), that is, that cover a single output state. We then form the minimal sets of products having both separation and coverage (§2.1.8) properties: a tree-structured search avoids the need to construct all possible sets and gives first those that are minimal. Construction of the tree finally checks the compatibility property [28].

8.1.3 Step 1

A systematic search of Figure 2.19 gives all the blocks that have the separation property, covering either a single output state 0, 1, 2 or 3 or a choice of states in the case of Φ conditions (0, 1, 2 or 0, 1, 2, 3). This gives 49 branch products, shown in the *coverage table* of Figure 8.1; the columns of this table give for each product the output state (or output states in the case of the Φ conditions) and the decimal numbers of the minterms covered (§1.1.7).

This is a tedious process and it may be preferable to resort to the systematic method due to McCluskey [30], [1], [59]; this starts from the following logical functions, given here in their canonical decimal form:

$$Z0\ (D,C,B,A) = \Sigma 1 + \Phi 7,10\ldots 15 \quad (8.1)$$

$$Z1\ (D,C,B,A) = \Sigma 2,3 + \Phi 7,10\ldots 15 \quad (8.2)$$

$$Z2\ (D,C,B,A) = \Sigma 0 + \Phi 7,10\ldots 15 \quad (8.3)$$

$$Z3\ (D,C,B,A) = \Sigma 4,5,6,8,9 + \Phi 10\ldots 15 \quad (8.4)$$

Branch products	Output states	0	1		2	3					0,1,2	0,1,2,3					
	Minterms D,C,B,A	1	2	3	0	4	5	6	8	9	7	10	11	12	13	14	15
D'C'B'A	0	x															
C'B	1		x	x								x	x				
BA	1			x							x		x				x
D'C'B	1		x	x													
D'BA	1			x							x						
C'BA	1			x									x				
C'BA'	1		x									x					
D'C'BA	1			x													
D'C'BA'	1		x														
D'C'B'A'	2				x												
D	3								x	x		x	x	x	x	x	x
DC'	3								x	x		x	x				
DB'	3								x	x				x	x		
DA'	3								x			x		x		x	
DA	3									x			x		x		x
CA'	3					x		x						x		x	
CB'	3					x	x							x	x		
DB'A'	3								x					x			
DC'B'	3								x	x							
D'C'A'	3								x			x					
DC'A	3									x			x				
DB'A	3									x					x		
CB'A'	3					x								x			
D'CB'	3					x	x										
DCA'	3					x		x									
CB'A	3						x								x		
CBA'	3							x								x	
D'CB'A'	3					x											
D'CB'A	3						x										
D'CBA'	3							x									
DC'B'A'	3								x								
DC'B'A	3									x							
CBA	0,1,2										x						x
D'CBA	0,1,2										x						
DC	0,1,2,3													x	x	x	x
DB	0,1,2,3											x	x			x	x
DCB'	0,1,2,3													x	x		
DCA'	0,1,2,3													x		x	
DCA	0,1,2,3														x		x
DCB	0,1,2,3															x	x
DBA	0,1,2,3												x				x
DBA'	0,1,2,3											x				x	
DC'B	0,1,2,3											x	x				
DC'BA'	0,1,2,3											x					
DC'BA	0,1,2,3												x				
DCB'A'	0,1,2,3													x			
DCB'A	0,1,2,3														x		
DCBA'	0,1,2,3															x	
DCBA	0,1,2,3																x
Score		1	4	6	1	6	4	4	8	8	4	10	11	11	10	10	10

Figure 8.1

$$Z0,1,2\ (D,C,B,A) = \Sigma\, 7 + \Phi\, 10\ldots 15 \tag{8.5}$$

$$Z0,1,2,3\ (D,C,B,A) = \Sigma 10\ldots 15 \tag{8.6}$$

where Zj is the logical function whose value is 1 for state j.

The 49 branch products are grouped horizontally into six classes according to their output state: 0, 1, 2, 3 and the Φ states 0, 1, 2, and 0, 1, 2, 3. In each class the products with the smallest number of variables are placed first. Finally, a score is calculated for each minterm of D, C, B, A, equal to the number of products that cover that minterm — in Figure 8.1 this is the number of crosses in the relevant column.

8.1.4 Step 2

Using a representation due to Meisel [31] a *coverage tree* (Figure 8.2), is constructed to determine the standard sets. The branch products are first checked for coverage and separation as follows.

1. The 16 minterms are put in increasing order of score, with an arbitrary order in the case of equal scores. This gives the following:

$$\begin{array}{l} \text{minterms } \underbrace{1 \to 0}_{} \to \underbrace{2 \to 5 \to 6 \to 7}_{} \to \underbrace{3 \to 4}_{} \to \underbrace{8 \to 9}_{} \\ \text{scores:} \quad\ \ 1 \qquad\qquad\quad 4 \qquad\qquad\quad 6 \qquad\quad 8 \\ \to \underbrace{10 \to 13 \to 14 \to 15}_{10} \to \underbrace{11 \to 12}_{11} \end{array} \tag{8.7}$$

2. Minterm 1 is taken first: this is covered by the single product $D'C'B'A$ which constitutes a unique branch in the coverage tree; to this we attach the corresponding output state (index 0) and the number of the covered minterm (1).
3. Minterm 0 is taken next, covered by $D'C'B'A_2'$: $D'C'B'A$ and $D'C'B'A'$ are essential branch products.
4. Minterm 2 has the four coverages $C'B$, $D'C'B$, $C'BA'$, $D'C'BA'$, giving four branches in the tree. A systematic search then requires the parallel development of all these branches; $C'B$ is taken first, since a product of two letters covers four minterms whilst a three letter product covers only two. Branches abandoned provisionally are reconsidered later.
5. Minterm 5 also is covered by four products, CB', $D'CB'$, $CB'A$, $D'CB'A$, and so gives four branches also; CB'_3 is the only product with two letters and is therefore the one chosen for further exploration.
6. Minterm 6 also is covered by four products, CA', DCA', CBA', $D'CBA'$; CA' covers minterms 4 and 12 which are already covered in this branch and DCA' covers 4, so these do not have the separation

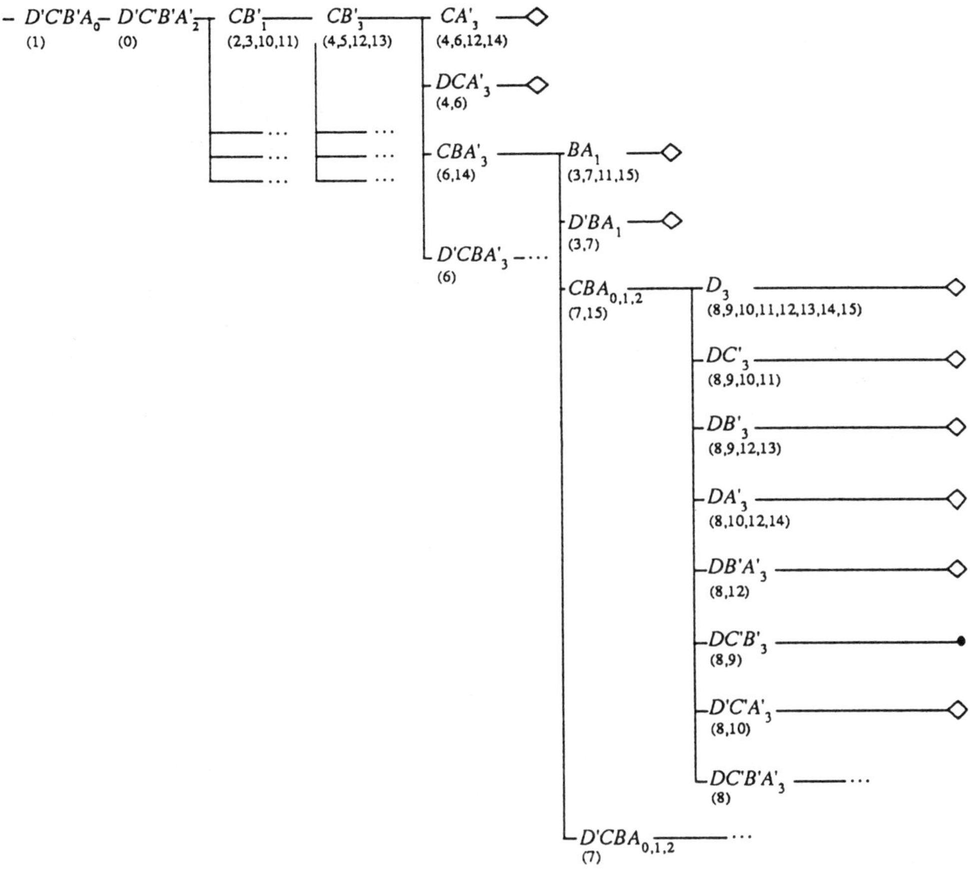

Figure 8.2

property. The corresponding branches are therefore rejected, as shown by the mark ◊ in Figure 8.2; CBA', being the simpler of the two remaining products, is chosen for further exploration.

7. Continuing in this way we finally obtain a branch that has both separation and coverage properties: this, marked • in Figure 8.2, gives the set of products of the branch $S2$:

$$S2 = \{D'C'B'A_0, D'C'B'A'_2, C'B_1, CB'_3, CBA'_3, CBA_{0,1,2}, DC'B'_3\} \tag{8.8}$$

8.1.5 Step 3

The process of constructing the binary decision tree provides a check that the set $S2$ has the compatibility property, that is, that it is a standard set (§2.1.12). Figure 2.21 gives its Karnaugh map and Figure 2.23 is the tree *Z2* that it produces.

It remains to prove that this tree is minimal. A systematic approach would require all the branches of Figure 8.2 to be developed in parallel and the consequential explosion would not only make the use of a computer essential but would also limit the study to small-scale problems. However, the rate of explosion can be reduced by:

(a) testing for compatibility as the construction of the coverage tree proceeds: that is, by checking that all the products in the branch being studied have at least one variable in common (§2.1.18);
(b) using the known bounds for the number of branch products: in [28] it is shown that this number cannot be less than the number of prime implicants of *Z*, which in this case is seven; it follows that both the set *S2* and the tree *Z2* are minimal.
(c) using heuristic algorithms, such as are given in [28].

8.2 REDUCTION OF DISCRETE FUNCTIONS

8.2.1 Definition: the P-function

Any binary decision tree, sub-tree or diagram can be defined by a *function pair* g, h which Thayse [2] (pp. 388–418), [3] (pp. 115–142), [41], [43], [44] has called the *P-function*, written $<g;h>$. Here g is a logical function called the *domain* of *P* and h is a discrete function, the *co-domain*.

8.2.2 Example: the comparator

The discrete function *Z* for the comparator of §2.1.2 can be represented either by a decision tree or by the Karnaugh map of Figure 2.12, with 16 cells and 10 blocks. By definition the domain of the tree is 1 (the unit domain) and the co-domain is *Z*, so the P-function is $<1;Z>$ (Figure 8.3).

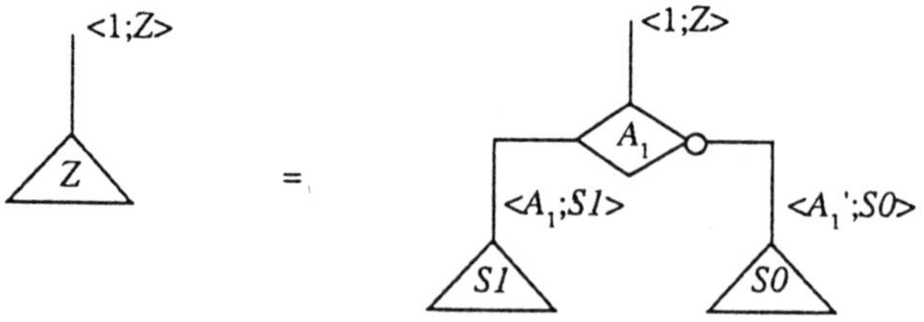

Figure 8.3

The tree Z can be decomposed into two sub-trees *S0*, *S1*, for $A_1 = 0, 1$ respectively, each described by a Karnaugh half-map of eight cells. The domains of *S0*, *S1* are, by definition, A_1', A_1 and their co-domains are the discrete functions *S0*, *S1* themselves, giving the P-functions $<A_1'; S0>$, $<A_1; S1>$, as in Figure 8.3. The general property is that in any sub-tree:

- the domain is a logical function that shows either the branch of the tree running from the root to this sub-tree, or the location of the sub-map in the complete Karnaught map;
- the co-domain is the discrete function realized by the sub-tree.

Continuing with the comparator, from Figure 2.34 we get the binary decision diagram of Figure 8.4, with the P-functions of all the possible sub-trees of Z. This shows:

- each confluence of branches, showing the existence of a common sub-tree, is expressed, for this sub-tree, by a domain that consists of the logical sum of the branches joining the root to the sub-tree. For

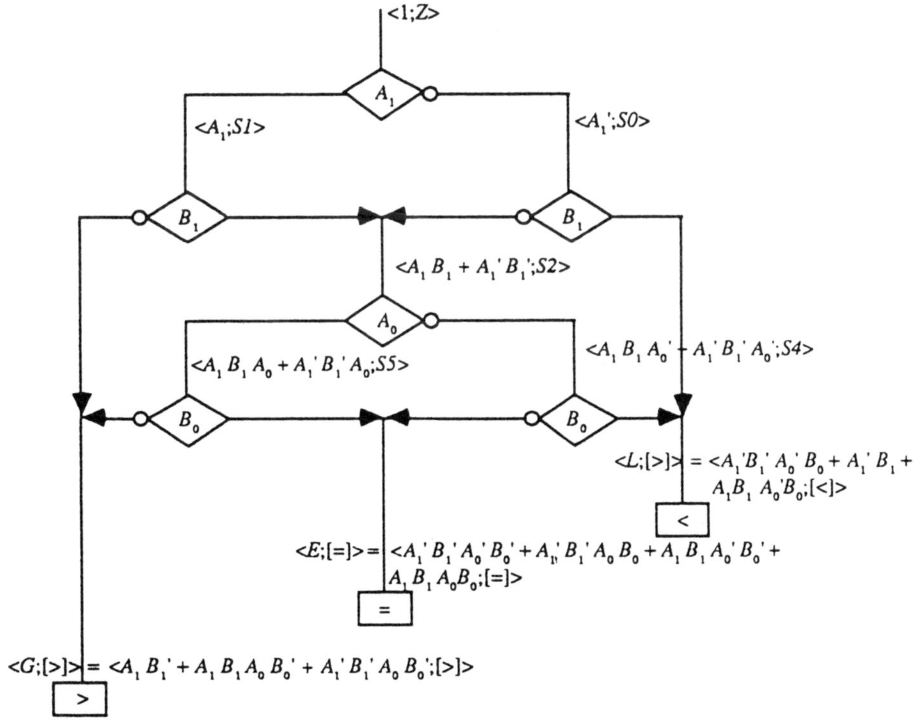

Figure 8.4

example, the common sub-tree that realizes the discrete function $S2$ is joined to the root by the two branches A_1B_1, $A_1'B_1'$ and its P-function is $<A_1B_1 + A_1'B_1'; S2>$;

- the domains of the leaves of the diagram, that is, of the trivial sub-trees consisting of a single assignment element [>], [=] or [<], are the logical functions G, E, L defined by (2.10) to (2.12).

8.2.3 P-function methods

P-function methods are of two types, top-down and bottom-up; both aim to provide a systematic procedure for determining a binary decision diagram that will realize a discrete function under certain constraints — in particular, the constraint of using the minimum number of test elements. The procedure involves finding the P-functions for all possible sub-trees of the diagram.

- *Top-down method* (from root to leaves): this starts with the P-function $<1; Z>$, of the discrete function Z in the unit domain (the complete Karnaugh map). All the P-functions are computed until the r domains (G, E, L in §8.2.2) of the r discrete constants ([>], [=], [<]) are reached: that is, the r trivial sub-trees with a single assignment element.
- *Bottom-up method* (from leaves to root): this starts with the r domains G, E, L associated with the r discrete constants [>], [=], [<] and computes all the P-functions up to that for the complete diagram $<1; Z>$.

Because of its greater convenience in practice we shall use the second, bottom-up, method; in general, this is a matter of determining a tree S with P-function $<g; h>$, from a given pair of P-functions $<g_0; h_0>$, $<g_1; h_1>$ for sub-trees $S0$, $S1$, as in Figure 8.5.

Thayse has shown that this can be achieved by the use of a *general composition law* ***Tx***, where x is the test variable. This is defined by

$$<g; h> = <g_1(x = 1) \cdot g_0(x = 0) \leqslant g \leqslant g_1 \cdot x + g_0 \cdot x'; \quad h_1 \cdot x + h_0 \cdot x' > \tag{8.9}$$

written symbolically

$$<g; h> = <g_1; h_1> \boldsymbol{Tx} <g_0; h_0> \tag{8.10}$$

The co-domain h is a completely-defined discrete function, since h_0 and h_1 are both discrete; the domain g is a logical function, since g_0 and g_1 are logical, and is incompletely defined, its value lying between a lower bound $g_{min} = g_1(x = 1) \cdot g_0(x = 0)$ and an upper bound $g_{max} = g_1 \cdot x + g_0 \cdot x'$.

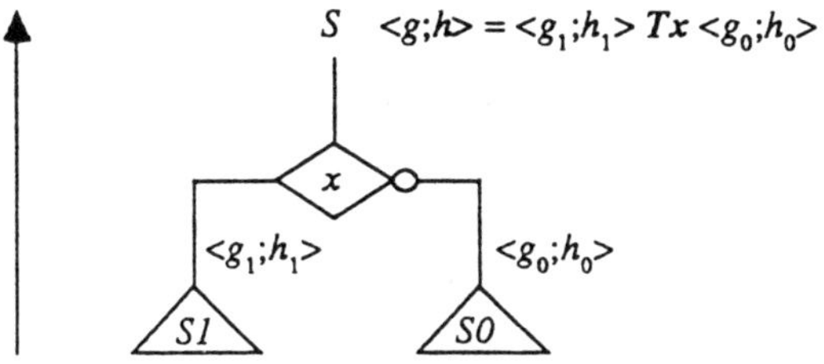

Figure 8.5

Thayse has shown also that the choice $g = g_{\min}$ produces all the minimal binary decision diagrams for a discrete function Z, defined in §2.2.17; it is expressed by a particular case of the general law ***Tx*** which we call the *composition law*, ***T1x***:

$$<g; h> = <g_1(x = 1) \cdot g_0(x = 0); h_1 \cdot x + h_0 \cdot x' > \quad (8.11)$$

The choice $g = g_{\min}$, that is, of the composition law ***T1x***, is made for two reasons:

- first, it leads to relatively simple calculations involving only the domains;
- second, it does not eliminate any solution that is minimal in the sense of §2.2.17; it does however eliminate certain solutions constituted by *non-simple diagrams*, in which the same variable appears at several different locations in the same branch; this is acceptable, since non-simple trees, and therefore non-simple diagram, also, have already been eliminated from the general study (cf. §2.1.6).

8.2.4 Example: binary adder

The arithmetical sum of two m-bit binary numbers A, B can be found by an iterative system in which each of m sub-systems adds one bit a of A, one bit b of B and a 1-bit carry c from the preceding stage to give a 1-bit sum s and a 1-bit carry r to the next stage. These bits are shown in the Karnaugh map of Figure 8.6 and are described by the pseudo-boolean polynomial

$$Z = Z0 \cdot [0] + Z1 \cdot [1] + Z2 \cdot [2] + Z3 \cdot [3] \quad (8.12)$$

where

$$Z0 = a'b'c', \; Z1 = a'b'c + a'bc' + ab'c', \\ Z2 = a'bc + abc' + ab'c, \; Z3 = abc \quad (8.13)$$

In this example the discrete function Z is completely defined.

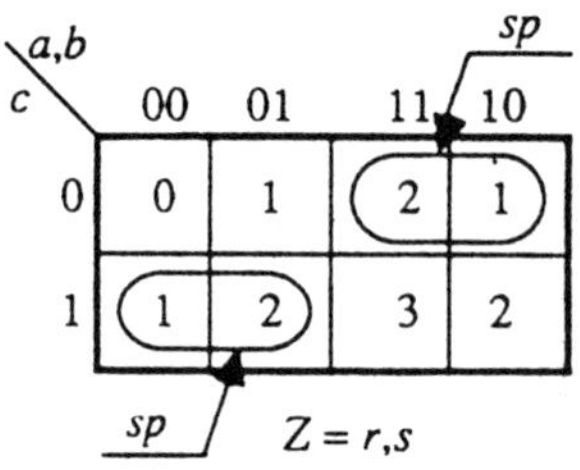

Figure 8.6

8.2.5 Stage 1

The four logical functions Zj, $j \in \{0, 1, 2, 3\}$, form the four domains of Class 1 in the table of Figure 8.7; in the general method each is simplified and represented by a minimal polynomial, but in this example no simplification is possible, each function being given by its canonical algebraic form.

For each variable x of the problem, here $x \in \{a, b, c\}$, all the functions $Zj(x = 1)$, $Zj(x = 0)$ are computed, giving the set of *factors* for Class 1, as in Figure 8.7. From this set all those factors F are eliminated which are included in the domains Zj of Class 1, that is, which satisfy either of the relations

$$F \leqslant Zj, \; F + Zj = Zj \tag{8.14}$$

In this example none are eliminated.

The new domains that will form Class 2 are now computed, using the composition law ***T1x***: by (8.11) the new domain is

$$g = g_1(x = 1) \cdot g_0(x = 0) \tag{8.15}$$

This is applied by forming all possible products $Zj(x = 1) \cdot Zk(x = 0)$, with $j, k \in \{0, 1, 2, 3\}$, $j \neq k$ and taking $x \in \{a, b, c\}$; this gives, for example, the following domain:

$$R0 = Z1(a = 1) \cdot Z0(a = 0) = b'c' \cdot b'c' = b'c' \tag{8.16}$$

which can be written in the abridged formula

$$R0 = Z1 \; \boldsymbol{Ta} \; Z0 \tag{8.17}$$

where ***Ta*** is the composition law ***T1x*** with $x = a$.

The final set of Class 2 domains is obtained by:

- expressing each domain by its simplified algebraic form, that is, by a minimal polynomial: e.g. $R0 = b'c'$;
- giving for each domain the abridged formula, e.g. $R0 = b'c' = Z1 \; \boldsymbol{Ta} \; Z0$;

when the same domain can be expressed by several different formulae all are given: this happens only in Class 3 in Figure 8.7;
- eliminating from Class 2 any factors included in the Class 1 domains, including the trivial case of the logical constant 0: in this example there are no deletions.

The result here is the set of nine Class 2 domains, *R0* to *R8*, shown in Figure 8.7.

Class	Domain	Factors					
		a = 1	*a* = 0	*b* = 1	*b* = 0	*c* = 1	*c* = 0
1	*Z0 = a'b'c'*	0	(b'c')	0	(a'c')	0	(a'b')
	Z1 = a'b'c + a'bc' + ab'c'	(b'c')	(b'c + bc')	(a'c')	(a'c + ac')	(a'b')	(ab' + a'b)
	Z2 = a'bc + ab'c + abc'	(bc' + b'c)	(bc)	(a'c + ac')	(ac)	(a'b + ab')	(ab)
	Z3 = abc	(bc)	0	(ac)	0	(ab)	0
2	*R0 = b'c' = Z1* ***Ta*** *Z0*	(b'c')	(b'c')	0	[c']	0	[b']
	R1 = bc' + b'c = Z2 ***Ta*** *Z1*	(bc' + b'c)	(bc' + b'c)	[c']	[c]	[b']	[b]
	R2 = bc = Z3 ***Ta*** *Z2*	(bc)	(bc)	[c]	0	[b]	0
	R3 = a'c' = Z1 ***Tb*** *Z0*	0	[c']	(a'c')	(a'c')	0	[a']
	R4 = a'c + ac' = Z2 ***Tb*** *Z1*	[c']	[c]	(a'c + ac')	(a'c + ac')	[a']	[a]
	R5 = ac = Z3 ***Tb*** *Z2*	[c]	0	(ac)	(ac)	[a]	0
	R6 = a'b' = Z1 ***Tc*** *Z0*	0	[b']	0	[a']	(a'b')	(a'b')
	R7 = a'b + ab' = Z2 ***Tc*** *Z1*	[b']	[b]	[a']	[a]	(a'b + ab')	(a'b + ab')
	R8 = ab = Z3 ***Tc*** *Z2*	[b]	0	[a]	0	(ab)	(ab)
3	*U0 = c' = R4* ***Ta*** *R3 = R1* ***Tb*** *R0*	[c']	[c']	[c']	[c']	0	1
	U1 = c = R5 ***Ta*** *R4 = R2* ***Tb*** *R1*	[c]	[c]	[c]	[c]	1	0
	U2 = b' = R7 ***Ta*** *R6 = R1* ***Tc*** *R0*	[b']	[b']	0	1	[b']	[b']
	U3 = b = R8 ***Ta*** *R7 = R2* ***Tc*** *R1*	[b]	[b]	1	0	[b]	[b]
	U4 = a' = R7 ***Tb*** *R6 = R4* ***Tc*** *R3*	0	1	[a']	[a']	[a']	[a']
	U5 = a = R8 ***Tb*** *R7 = R5* ***Tc*** *R4*	1	0	[a]	[a]	[a]	[a]
4	*V = 1 = U5* ***Ta*** *U4 = U3* ***Tb*** *U2 = U1* ***Tc*** *U0*						

Figure 8.7

8.2.6 Stage 2

This starts with the nine Class 2 domains just found, *R0* to *R8* of Figure 8.7. The Class 2 factors are calculated as in Stage 1 and entered in the table of Figure 8.7; and all those Clase 1 and Class 2 factors are eliminated that are included in any domain *Zj* or *Ri* of Classes 1 and 2: there are 36 such factors, shown in parentheses in Figure 8.7.

The Class 3 domains are now computed as before, by applying the composition law ***T1x*** to all possible products among the remaining factors, formed as follows:

- of Class 1 with Class 2: in this example there are none, since all the Class 1 factors are either null or are in parentheses and therefore are eliminated;

- within Class 2: this gives the six products *U0–U5*, after elimination of all those already included in Class 1 and Class 2.

These remaining factors are expressed in their simplified algebraic form and also by one or more abridged formulae, as (8.17); in this example there are two such formulae for each domain, as shown in Figure 8.7.

8.2.7 Stage 3

The procedure continues as before: from the Class 3 domains *U0–U5* the Class 3 factors are computed and all Class 1, 2 or 3 factors are eliminated that are included in any domain *Zj*, *Ri*, *Uk*; these are shown in square brackets in Figure 8.7.

The computation of the Class 4 domains, performed as before with the law ***T1x***, gives a single term, the logical constant 1, together with three abridged formulae.

8.2.8 Stage 4

The exhaustive search through all the compositions $g = g_1(x = 1) \cdot g_0(x = 0)$ is now completed, resulting in the logical constant $V = 1$ as the single domain and therefore the single row of Class 4.

The set of domains 1 to 4 gives a family of solutions, that is, of equivalent binary decision diagrams. To find those that are minimal, in the sense of using the minimum number of test elements, we proceed as follows:

- the first test element in a minimal diagram will have 1 as its domain (cf. Figure 8.3), and therefore the domain $V = 1$ of Figure 8.7; this is represented in the *diagram graph* of Figure 8.8 by *V* enclosed in a diamond;
- Figure 8.7 (Class 4) shows that this domain *V* can be realized by any of three different compositions: *U5* ***Ta*** *U4*, *U3* ***Tb*** *U2*, *U1* ***Tc*** *U0*; each of these compositions starts a branch in the graph. These three branches contain respectively *U5* and *U4* (upper branch), *U3* and *U2* (middle branch), *U1* and *U0* (lower branch);
- taking as an example the upper branch, *U5* can be realized either by *R8* ***Tb*** *R7* or by *R5* ***Tc*** *R4*, giving the two parallel continuations of the branch labelled *b′*, *b″* respectively; *U4*, realized either by *R7* ***Tb*** *R6* or *R4* ***Tc*** *R3*, then gives rise to two further parallel continuations of each of these first continuations, labelled *b1*, *b2* (from *b′*) and *b3*, *b4* (from *b″*). No domain is repeated in the graph, so that for example *R7*, arising from *U5* (= *R8* ***Tb*** *R7*), is not repeated when it arises also from *U4* (= *R7* ***Tb*** *R6*);

- in the branch $b1$ the three domains $R8 = Z3\ \mathbf{Tc}\ Z2$, $R7 = Z2\ \mathbf{Tc}\ Z1$, $R6 = Z1\ \mathbf{Tc}\ Z0$ of Class 2 lead to the four domains $Z3$, $Z2$, $Z1$, $Z0$ of Class 1; these domains specify the output elements and are therefore shown in rectangles in Figure 8.8;
- development of the complete graph in this way gives 12 branches, each of which is a solution to the original problem; and those with the smallest number of diamond symbols (test elements) are the minimal solutions.

The minimal solutions here all have six test elements, that given by the branch $b9$, for example, consisting of ten domains: $\{V, U1, U0, R5, R4, R3, Z3, Z2, Z1\}$; it is represented by the following relations and the minimal diagram of Figure 8.9.

$$V = 1 = U1\ \mathbf{Tc}\ U0 \tag{8.18}$$

$$U1 = c = R5\ \mathbf{Ta}\ R4 \tag{8.19}$$

$$U0 = c' = R4\ \mathbf{Ta}\ R3 \tag{8.20}$$

$$R5 = ac = Z3\ \mathbf{Tb}\ Z2 \tag{8.21}$$

$$R4 = a'c + ac' = Z2\ \mathbf{Tb}\ Z1 \tag{8.22}$$

$$R3 = a'c' = Z1\ \mathbf{Tb}\ Z0 \tag{8.23}$$

$$Z3 = abc \tag{8.24}$$

$$Z2 = a'bc + ab'c + abc' \tag{8.25}$$

$$Z1 = a'b'c + a'bc' + ab'c' \tag{8.26}$$

$$Z0 = a'b'c' \tag{8.27}$$

8.2.9 Comments

The search for a minimal diagram by this process is best conducted by developing all the branches in parallel, for then a solution is obtained as soon as a branch ends and longer branches need not be considered further.

A study of Figure 8.9 reveals two trivial sub-trees with a single assignment element (the domains $Z2$, $Z1$) and a non-trivial sub-tree sp defined by the domain $R4 = a'c + ac'$. Representation of $R4$ in the Karnaugh map of Figure 8.6 is equivalent to the graphical method of §2.2.13 for finding the common sub-trees sp.

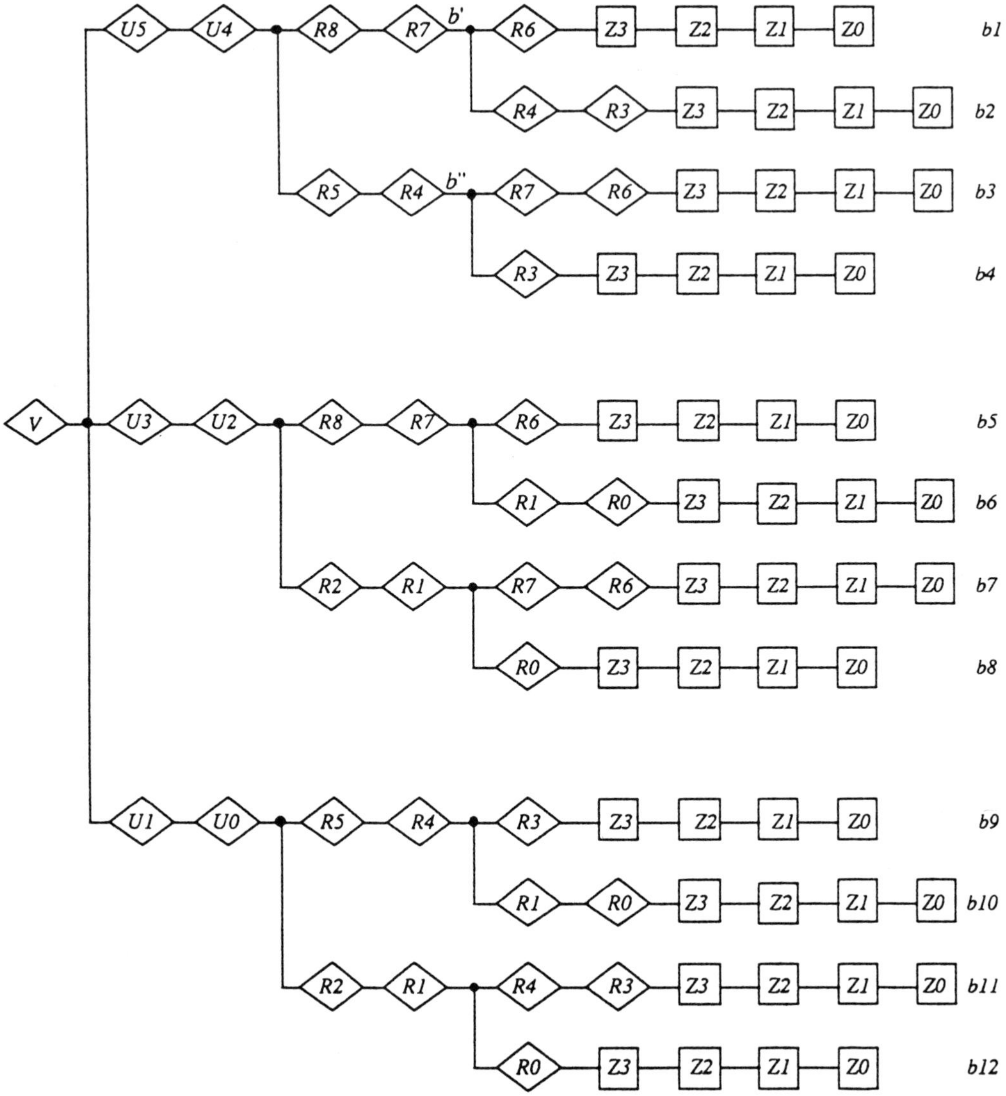
V
U5
U4
U3
U2
U1
U0
R8
R7
b'
R6
Z3
Z2
Z1
Z0
b1
R4
R3
b2
R5
b''
b3
b4
b5
R1
R0
b6
R2
b7
b8
b9
b10
b11
b12

Figure 8.8

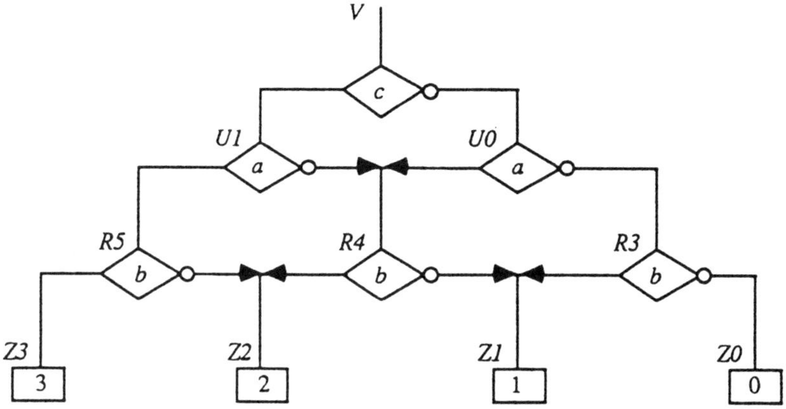

Figure 8.9

8.2.10 Application: incompletely defined function

The discriminator for the calendar months discussed in §§2.1.19–20 can be described by a discrete function Z which is incompletely defined. This is a function of four variables M_4, M_3, M_2, M_0, given by the Karnaugh map of Figure 8.10 and by the pseudo-boolean polynomial

$$Z = ZF \cdot [\mathrm{F}] + Z30 \cdot [30] + Z31 \cdot [31] \tag{8.28}$$

Each Φ state can take the value F, 30 or 31:

$$\Phi = \{\mathrm{F}, 30, 31\}$$

Each logical function Zj, $j \in \{\mathrm{F},30,31\}$, takes the value 1 for the output state j and for the set of states Φ; so the following canonical decimal forms and simplified forms can be deduced from Figure 8.10:

$$\begin{aligned} ZF(M_3, M_2, M_4, M_0) &= \Sigma 0, 6, 7, 10 \ldots 15 \\ &= M_2M_3 + M_2M_4 + M_3M_4 + M_3'M_2'M_4'M_0' \end{aligned} \tag{8.29}$$

$$\begin{aligned} Z30(M_3, M_2, M_4, M_0) &= \Sigma 3, 4, 6, 7, 9, 10 \ldots 15 \\ &= M_0M_4 + M_3M_0 + M_3M_4 + M_2M_0' \end{aligned} \tag{8.30}$$

$$\begin{aligned} Z31(M_3, M_2, M_4, M_0) &= \Sigma 1, 2, 5 \ldots 8, 10 \ldots 15 \\ &= M_4M_0' + M_3M_4 + M_2M_0 + M_3M_0' \\ &\quad + M_3'M_4'M_0 \end{aligned} \tag{8.31}$$

M_4,M_0 \ M_3,M_2	00	01	11	10
00	F	30	Φ	31
01	31	31	Φ	30
11	30	Φ	Φ	Φ
10	31	Φ	Φ	Φ

Z

Figure 8.10

The logical functions *ZF, Z30, Z31* all take the value 1 for the state Φ; therefore, by the definition of §2.1.3, the value of *Z* for this state cannot be determined, so Z is an incompletely defined function. These three logical functions constitute the three Class 1 domains of the P-function method just described; application of the method then gives the minimal solution with five test elements, shown in Figure 2.41.

8.2.11 Application: multiple functions

The car starter of §5.3.2 is a 2-state sequential system represented by the two partial tables *A, B* of Figure 8.11, which in turn are described by the completely defined discrete functions *ZA, ZB*:

$$ZA = x1'x2'[\mathrm{A},0] + x1'x2[\mathrm{B},0] + x1x2'[\mathrm{A},3] + x1x2[\mathrm{A},2] \tag{8.32}$$

$$ZB = x1'x2'[\mathrm{A},0] + x1'x2[\mathrm{B},0] + x1x2'[\mathrm{B},6] + x1x2[\mathrm{B},4] \tag{8.33}$$

Multiplication of the domains of *ZA, ZB* by the logical functions *fA, fB* respectively gives the following six Class 1 domains:

$$\text{for the constant } [\mathrm{A},0]\text{: } Z0 = fA \cdot x1'x2' + fB \cdot x1'x2' \tag{8.34}$$

$$\text{for the constant } [\mathrm{B},0]\text{: } Z1 = fA \cdot x1'x2 + fB \cdot x1'x2 \tag{8.35}$$

$$\text{for the constant } [\mathrm{A},3]\text{: } Z2 = fA \cdot x1x2' \tag{8.36}$$

$$\text{for the constant } [\mathrm{A},2]\text{: } Z3 = fA \cdot x1x2 \tag{8.37}$$

$$\text{for the constant } [\mathrm{B},6]\text{: } Z4 = fB \cdot x1x2' \tag{8.38}$$

$$\text{for the constant } [\mathrm{B},4]\text{: } Z5 = fB \cdot x1x2 \tag{8.39}$$

Application of the P-function method to these logical functions gives the table of Figure 8.12; and in Class 3 we get the logical functions *fA, fB* which constitute the unit domains of *ZA, ZB* respectively.

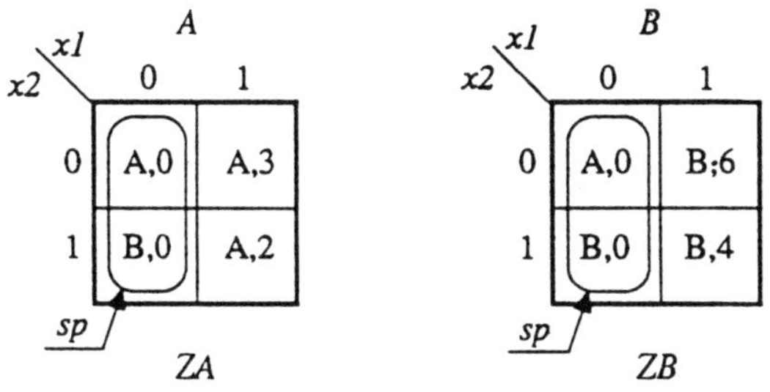

Figure 8.11

Class	Domain	x1 = 1	x1 = 0	x2 = 1	x2 = 0
1	Z0 = fA · x1'x2' + fB · x1'x2'	0	fA · x2' + fB · x2'	0	(fA · x1' + fB · x1')
	Z1 = fA · x1'x2 + fB · x1'x2	0	fA · x2 + fB · x2	(fA · x1' + fB · x1')	0
	Z2 = fA · x1x2'	(fA · x2')	0	0	(fA · x1)
	Z3 = fA · x1x2	(fA · x2)	0	(fA · x1)	0
	Z4 = fB · x1x2'	(fB · x2')	0	0	(fB · x1)
	Z5 = fB · x1x2	(fB · x2)	0	(fB · x1)	0
2	R0 = fA · x2' = Z2 T1 Z0			0	fA
	R1 = fA · x2 = Z3 T1 Z1			fA	0
	R2 = fB · x2' = Z4 T1 Z0			0	fB
	R3 = fB · x2 = Z5 T1 Z1			fB	0
	R4 = fA · x1' + fB · x1' = Z1 T2 Z0	0	fA + fB		
	R5 = fA · x1 = Z3 T2 Z2	fA	0		
	R6 = fAfB · x1 = Z3 T2 Z4 = Z5 T2 Z2	fA · fB	0		
	R7 = fB · x1 = Z5 T2 Z4	fB	0		
3	fA = R5 T1 R4 = R1 T2 R0				
	fB = R7 T1 R4 = R3 T2 R2				

Figure 8.12

The diagram graph, with the output elements omitted, is given in Figure 8.13; this shows a single minimal solution, with five test elements. Figure 8.14 gives the binary decision diagrams for *ZA*, *ZB*, with five test elements; the common sub-tree *sp* can be seen in the two tables of Figure 8.11.

8.2.12 Conclusion

Because of the inherent combinatorial explosion, application of the P-function method requires the use of computers and has to be restricted to problems with a small number of variables. A program for generating all the P-functions for a given function, and thus for generating a table such a Figure 8.7 or 8.12, is described in [40] and [42].

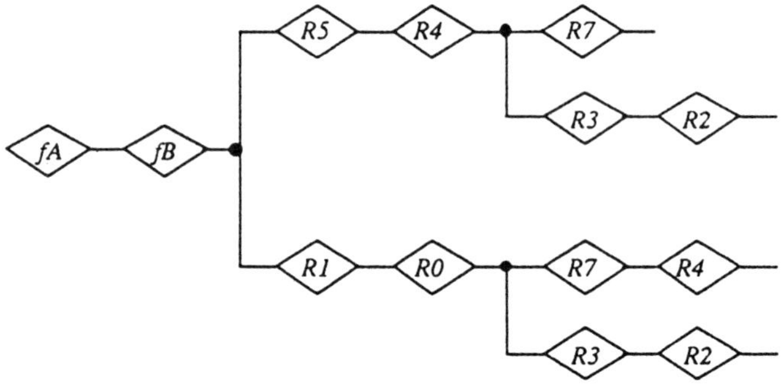

Figure 8.13

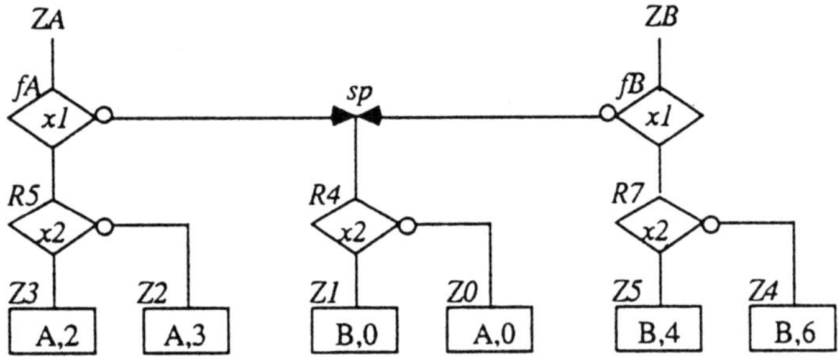

Figure 8.14

8.3 REDUCTION OF BINARY DECISION TREES

8.3.1 Example: partial tree for the comparator

The problem is to construct a minimal binary decision diagram for the partial tree for the comparator, Figure 2.8.

8.3.2 Representation: test list

In the tree Z of Figure 2.8 each test element is identified by a number in the range 1 to 9, its *address ADR*. The tree can then be represented in tabular form, Figure 8.15, as follows.

1. For a tree with n test elements, n rows are allocated: in this case 9, $1 \leqslant ADR \leqslant 9$.
2. Each row consists of the address ADR of an element, the variable x

tested, the address *ADR1* of the next element if $x = 1$ and *ADR0* if $x = 0$.
3. If the next element is an assignment its address is replaced by its assignment value *s* (*s1* for $x = 1$, *s0* for $x = 0$).

This table is called the *test list* for *Z*.

8.3.3 Reduction of the test list

Two test elements with addresses *ADRi*, *ADRj* are said to be *identical* or *equivalent*, written $ADRi \equiv ADRj$, if they concern the same variable ($xi = xj$) and give either the same next addresses or the same assignments for both $x = 1$ and $x = 0$: that is, $ADR1i = ADR1j$ or $s1i = s1j$ and $ADR0i = ADR0j$ or $s0i = s0j$. In such a case a single one of the two, *ADRi* say, can replace the pair.

In Figure 8.15 elements 6 and 8 are identical: they have the same variable ($x = B_0$) and lead to the same assignments for $x = 1$ ($s1 = [=]$) and for $x = 0$ ($s0 = [>]$); and similarly 7 and 9 are identical. Thus the pair 6, 8 can be replaced by 6 and 7, 9 by 7; this is shown in Figure 8.15, and the suppression of the elements 8, 9 shown by putting these numbers in parentheses. Elements 4 and 5 also are seen to be identical, and can be replaced by 4: this is shown by the square brackets.

Study now shows that no further reduction is possible; the original list of nine tests has been transformed to an equivalent shorter one of six tests, the *minimal* or *reduced* test list for the tree *Z*. This gives an exact description of the diagrams of Figures 2.33 and 2.34.

ADR	*x*	*ADR1* *s1*	*ADR0* *s0*
1	A_1	2	3
2	B_1	4	>
3	B_1	<	[5] 4
4 [≡ 5]	A_0	6	7
[5	A_0	(8) 6	(9) 7]
6 (≡ 8)	B_0	=	>
7 (≡ 9)	B_0	<	=
(8	B_0	=	>)
(9	B_0	<	=)

Figure 8.15

8.3.4 Example: the complete tree for the comparator

Figure 8.16 is the test list for the complete tree for the comparator, Figure 2.4. To simplify the reduction process we have grouped the test elements according to the variable tested, so that in searching for identical elements we need only compare those within the same group.

There can be *trivial test elements*, giving the same output (next address or assignment) for $x = 1$ and $x = 0$; such an element can be eliminated and its address *ADRj* replaced wherever it occurs in the list by the unique output (*ADR1* = *ADR0* or *s1* = *s0*). *ADR* = 13 is an example here, and can be replaced by the single assignment [<].

The identical and the trivial elements are shown by the brackets in the table of Figure 8.16: parentheses for those testing B_0, square brackets for A_0. The minimal list has six elements and is identical with Figure 8.15 except for the addresses for $x = B_0$.

ADR	*x*	*ADR1* *s1*	*ADR0* *s0*
1	A_1	2	3
2	B_1	4	[5] >
3	B_1	[6] <	[7] 4
4 [≡ 7]	A_0	8	9
[5	A_0	(10) >	(11) >]
[6	A_0	(12) <	(13) <]
[7	A_0	(14) 8	(15) 9]
8 (≡14)	B_0	=	>
9 (≡ 15)	B_0	<	=
(10	B_0	>	>)
(11	B_0	>	>)
(12	B_0	<	<)
(13	B_0	<	<)
(14	B_0	=	>)
(15	B_0	<	=)

Figure 8.16

8.3.5 Reduction of a binary decision tree

The reduction of a tree is a matter of finding the identical sub-trees that it contains (§2.2.6). A method derived from that for reducing a test list can be summarized as follows, cf. [28], [45] and [145].

1. Each test element is given an identifying address.
2. The test list is constructed, grouping the addresses according to the variable tested.
3. The trivial elements are identified and eliminated, each being replaced by its unique output, either an address or an assignment.
4. In each group each pair of identical elements $ADRi \equiv ADRj$ is replaced by a single one of the pair, say *ADRi*, and the list corrected by replacing every occurrence of *ADRj* by *ADRi*.
5. The search for trivial elements and identical pairs is continued until all possibilities have been exhausted.
6. The resulting list gives the required minimal diagram.

In the general case for a completely defined discrete function the solution is unique; the proof of this depends on the theory of state reduction of a finite state machine, and is given in [35] (pp. 175–219), [36] (pp. 127–141) and [37] (pp. 282–300). The unique reduced form is called the *canonical diagram* for the given tree [145].

Whilst the method is exhaustive, what it gives is the unique minimal diagram for a given *tree*, that is, for a particular representation of a discrete function. Finding the minimal diagram for the function is the much more general problem studied in section 8.2.

8.3.6 Example: the function *MAJORITY*

The logical function *MAJORITY* of five variables, $MAJ(E, D, C, B, A)$, is defined in §2.2.11 as the function that takes the value 1 when any three or more of its arguments are 1, and zero otherwise; it can be represented by the truth table of Figure 8.18 or by the Karnaugh map of Figure 2.42. From the map a partial tree with 19 test elements can be derived, described by the test list of Figure 8.17, reduction of which by the method of §8.3.5 gives the minimal diagram with nine test elements, as Figure 2.46.

8.3.7 Comment

In the reduced test list of Figure 8.17 the assignment elements are not shown in detail — their number and their position in the final diagram are not given. In a binary decision diagram it is usual, in accordance with §2.2.4, to show the common sub-trees that have a single assignment element; thus in this example Figure 2.46 represents the two output states of $MAJ(E, D, C, B, A)$ by two such elements, $MAJ = 0$ and $MAJ = 1$.

ADR	*x*	*ADR1* *s1*	*ADR0* *s0*
1	*E*	2	3
2	*D*	4	5
3	*D*	{6} 5	7
4	*C*	*MAJ* = 1	8
5{≡ 6}	*C*	[9] 8	10
{6	*C*	[11] 8	[12] 10}
7	*C*	[13] 10	*MAJ* = 0
8 [≡ 9,11]	*B*	*MAJ* = 1	14
[9	*B*	*MAJ* = 1	(15) 14]
10 [≡ 12,13]	*B*	(16) 14	*MAJ* = 0
[11	*B*	*MAJ* = 1	(17) 14]
[12	*B*	(18) 14	*MAJ* = 0]
[13	*B*	(19) 14	*MAJ* = 0]
14 (≡ 15...19)	*A*	*MAJ* = 1	*MAJ* = 0
(15	*A*	*MAJ* = 1	*MAJ* = 0)
(16	*A*	*MAJ* = 1	*MAJ* = 0)
(17	*A*	*MAJ* = 1	*MAJ* = 0)
(18	*A*	*MAJ* = 1	*MAJ* = 0)
(19	*A*	*MAJ* = 1	*MAJ* = 0)

Figure 8.17

8.3.8 Definition: symmetric functions

For the function *MAJ* we can determine the number of 1s in any input state of the variables; this is called the *index* of the state and in this example (Figure 8.18) it varies from 0 to 5. As the table of Figure 8.19 shows, the value of *MAJ* depends solely on the value of i.

A logical function whose value is determined completely by the value of the index is called a *symmetric function*; so *MAJ* is symmetric and we write

$$MAJ(E, D, C, B, A) = S_{3,4,5}(E, D, C, B, A) \tag{8.40}$$

stating that $MAJ = 1$ if $i = 3, 4$ or 5; $MAJ = 0$ otherwise.

Symmetric functions were studied by Shannon and Caldwell [37] (pp. 548–553), [38] (pp. 271–310) and [39]; a fundamental property of such a function is that any permutation of two variables leaves the function unchanged, that is, the resulting function has the same truth table as the original. It follows that any decision tree for a symmetric

E = 0					
i	*D*	*C*	*B*	*A*	*MAJ* (*E*, *D*, *C*, *B*, *A*)
0	0	0	0	0	0
1	0	0	0	1	0
1	0	0	1	0	0
2	0	0	1	1	0
1	0	1	0	0	0
2	0	1	0	1	0
2	0	1	1	0	0
3	0	1	1	1	1
1	1	0	0	0	0
2	1	0	0	1	0
2	1	0	1	0	0
3	1	0	1	1	1
2	1	1	0	0	0
3	1	1	0	1	1
3	1	1	1	0	1
4	1	1	1	1	1

E = 1					
i	*D*	*C*	*B*	*A*	*MAJ* (*E*, *D*, *C*, *B*, *A*)
1	0	0	0	0	0
2	0	0	0	1	0
2	0	0	1	0	0
3	0	0	1	1	1
2	0	1	0	0	0
3	0	1	0	1	1
3	0	1	1	0	1
4	0	1	1	1	1
2	1	0	0	0	0
3	1	0	0	1	1
3	1	0	1	0	1
4	1	0	1	1	1
3	1	1	0	0	1
4	1	1	0	1	1
4	1	1	1	0	1
5	1	1	1	1	1

Figure 8.18

i	*MAJ* (*E*, *D*, *C*, *B*, *A*)
0, 1, 2	0
3, 4, 5	1

Figure 8.19

function can be transformed into an equivalent tree by simply permuting any pair of its variables; and therefore that **the reduction of a tree of a symmetric function gives the minimal diagram not only for that tree but also for all the trees that can be derived from the original by permuting any pair of variables**.

Thus the method of reduction given in §8.3.5 is particularly well suited to symmetric functions.

8.3.9 Application: a discrete function

The discrete function defined in §2.2.16 can be expressed as a pseudo-boolean polynomial:

$$Z = G \cdot [>] + E \cdot [=] + L \cdot [<] \tag{8.41}$$

where G, E, L are disjoint logical functions, in a 1-out-of-3 code. The reader should check that they are symmetric:

$$G = S_{3,4}(a, b, c, d) \quad E = S_2(a, b, c, d) \quad L = S_{0,1}(a, b, c, d) \tag{8.42}$$

and that therefore Z also is symmetric.

This generalizes immediately: any discrete function Z with r output states can be represented by a pseudo-boolean polynomial in a 1-out-of-r code, in which each of r disjoint logical functions multiplies one of the r non-logical constants (§2.1.3); and if these logical functions are symmetric then Z also is symmetric. A discrete symmetric function is easily reduced by the method of §8.3.5.

8.4 COMPOSITION OF BINARY DECISION DIAGRAMS

8.4.1 Representation: composition of diagrams

Let Y, Z be binary decision diagrams that realize the logical functions $Y1$, $Z1$. The diagram Y is described by the discrete function Y (§2.1.16):

$$Y = Y1 \cdot [1] + Y0 \cdot [0] = Y1 \cdot [1] + Y1' \cdot [0] \tag{8.43}$$

where $Y1$, $Y1'$ are logical functions and [1], [0] are discrete constants. Similarly

$$Z = Z1 \cdot [1] + Z0 \cdot [0] = Z1 \cdot [1] + Z1' \cdot [0] \tag{8.44}$$

Any diagram that realizes a logical function such as $Y1$ or $Z1$ can be represented by a schema such as Figure 8.20, with a single input terminal and the two assignment elements [1], [0]. The inverse, e.g. $Y1'$ of $Y1$, is represented by a simple interchange of the discrete constants [1] and [0] in the diagram for Y.

Any assemblage of binary decision diagrams, as for example Figure 8.21, constitutes a *composition of diagrams*.

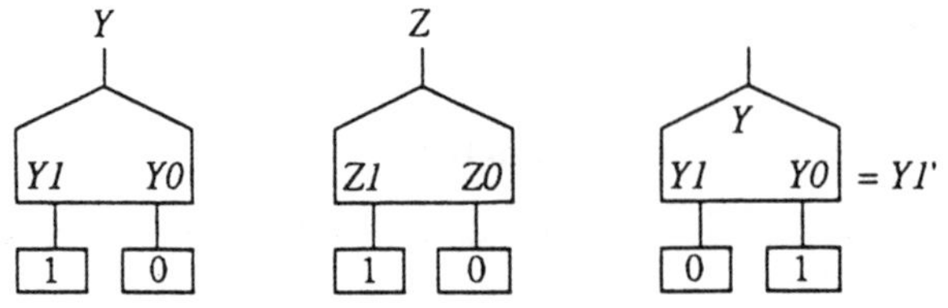

Figure 8.20

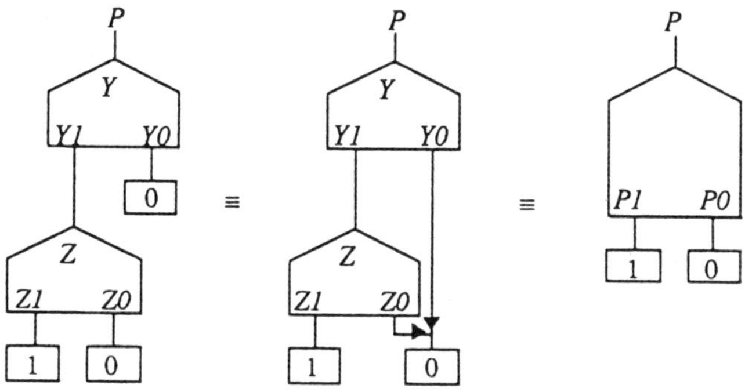

Figure 8.21

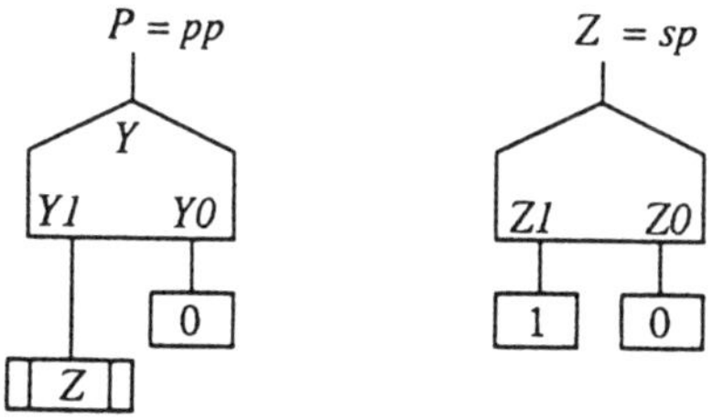

Figure 8.22

8.4.2 The product composition

The logical product $P1 = Y1 \cdot Z1$ of the logical functions $Y1$, $Z1$ can be realized by either of the following compositions of the diagrams for Y and Z:

1. the assignment [1] in Y is replaced by the diagram for Z, as in Figure 8.21;
2. the assignment [1] in Z is replaced by the diagram for Y.

The three schemas of Figure 8.21 are all equivalent and can be described by the relation

$$P = Y1 \cdot Z + Y1' \cdot [0] \tag{8.45}$$

and substituting for Z its expression (8.44)

$$P = Y1 \cdot Z1 \cdot [1] + Y1 \cdot Z1' \cdot [0] + Y1' \cdot [0] \tag{8.46}$$

Thus the final diagram represents the discrete function

$$P = P1 \cdot [1] + P1' \cdot [0] = Y1 \cdot Z1 \cdot [1] + (Y1 \cdot Z1)' \cdot [0] \tag{8.47}$$

which realizes the logical product $P1 = Y1 \cdot Z1$: such an assemblage is called a *product composition* of the diagrams Y, Z or the logical functions $Y1, Z1$.

The schema of Figure 8.22, which includes a sub-tree call element for the diagram Z, is an equivalent representation to Figure 8.21.

8.4.3 The sum composition

The logical sum $S1 = Y1 + Z1$ can be realized by either of the following compositions of the diagrams for Y and Z:

1. the assignment [0] in Y is replaced by the diagram for Z as in Figure 8.23;
2. the assignment [0] in Z is replaced by the diagram for Y.

The four schemas of Fig. 8.23 are all equivalent; the following relations hold:

$$S = Y1 \cdot [1] + Y1' \cdot Z \tag{8.48}$$

$$S = Y1 \cdot [1] + Y1' \cdot Z1 \cdot [1] + Y1' \cdot Z1' \cdot [0] \tag{8.49}$$

$$S = S1 \cdot [1] + S1' \cdot [0] = (Y1 + Z1) \cdot [1] + (Y1 + Z1)' \cdot [0] \tag{8.50}$$

where S is the *sum composition* of the diagrams Y, Z or the logical functions $Y1, Z1$.

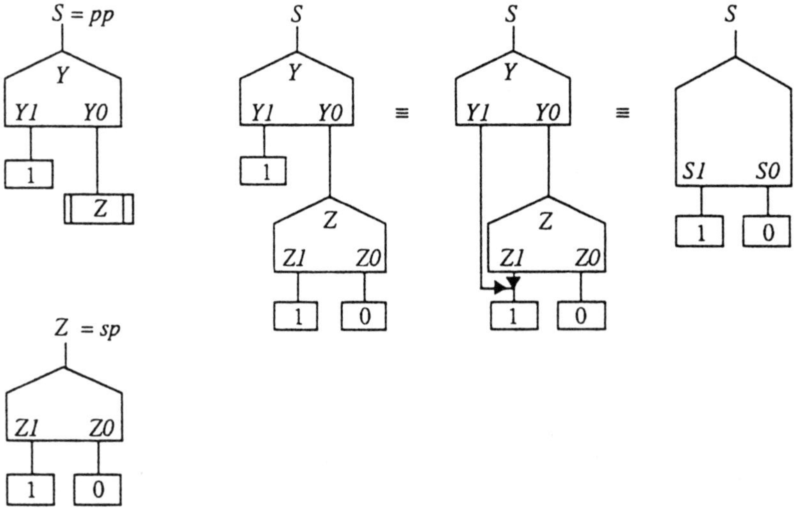

Figure 8.23

8.4.4 Example

We want to construct a binary decision diagram, minimal if possible, for the logical function

$$Z(a, b, c, d, e, f, g, h, i) = (ab'c + de)f(g' + hi) \tag{8.51}$$

The required diagram can be constructed by first decomposing Z into partial functions and then forming the appropriate compositions of the separate diagrams for these. The decomposition is as follows:

$$Z1 = ab'c \tag{8.52}$$

$$Z2 = de \tag{8.53}$$

$$Z3 = g' \tag{8.54}$$

$$Z4 = hi \tag{8.55}$$

$$Z5 = Z1 + Z2 \tag{8.56}$$

$$Z6 = Z3 + Z4 \tag{8.57}$$

$$Z = Z5 \cdot f \cdot Z6 \tag{8.58}$$

Here:

- $Z1$, $Z2$, $Z4$ are obtained either by the graphical method of simplification decribed in §2.1.14 or by forming product compositions of the elementary variables, cf. Figure 8.24;
- $Z5$, $Z6$ are obtained by means of sum compositions, as in Figure 8.25;

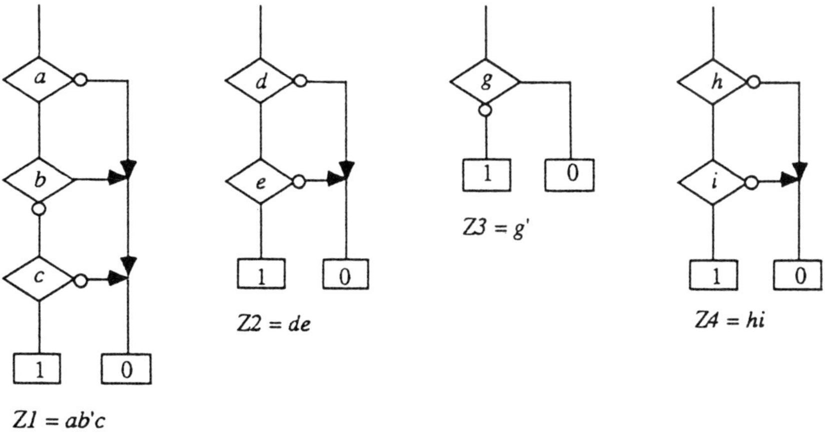

Figure 8.24

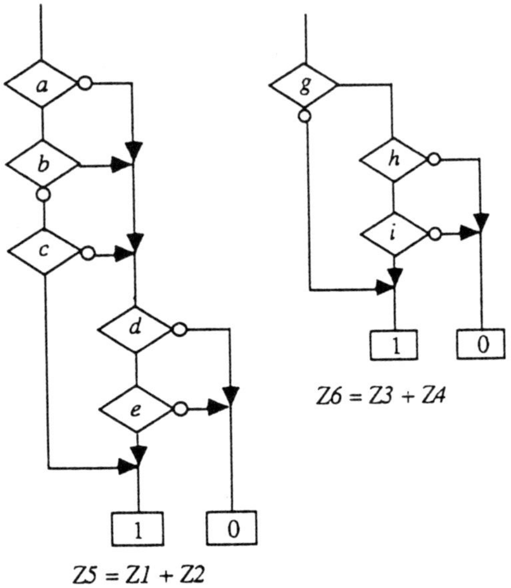

Figure 8.25

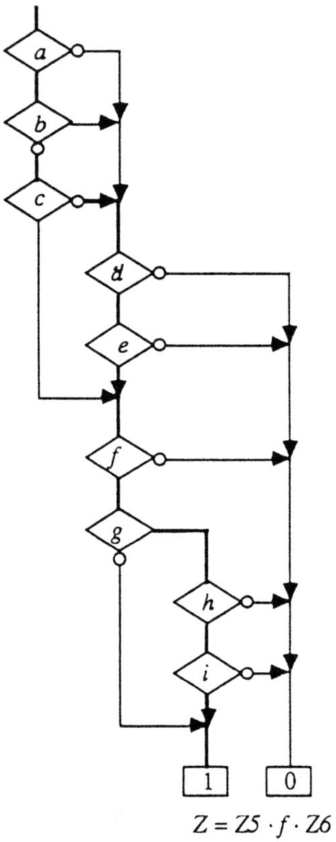

Figure 8.26

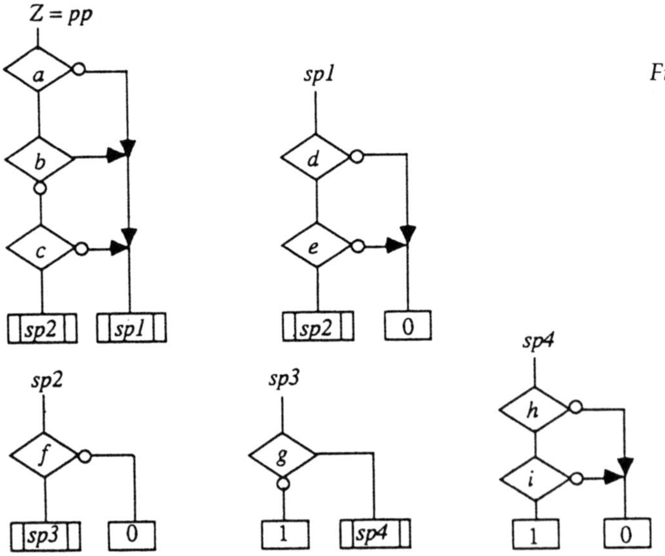

Figure 8.27

- finally, Z is formed by means of two successive product compositions, as in Figure 8.26.

Use of the sub-tree call elements gives the five diagrams of Figure 8.27: this set is equivalent to the single diagram of Figure 8.26 and has the same number of test elements.

8.4.5 Definition: atomic binary decision diagram

An *atomic binary decision diagram* is a diagram in which at least one branch (path from the root to an assignment element) contains all the test elements. Figure 8.26 is such a diagram, in which all the nine test elements lie on the branch shown by a heavy line.

It can be shown [58] that if a logical expression {NOT, AND, OR} of l letters is realized entirely by compositions — products, sums and possibly inversions — then:

- the final diagram is atomic;
- it has as many test elements as there are letters in the expression: thus in the preceding example the expression (8.51) for Z has nine letters and the atomic diagram Figure 8.26 has nine test elements;
- if the expression has repeated variables it follows that one variable must occur more than once in at least one branch: this is the case of a *non-simple diagram*, already mentioned in §8.2.3.

If only simple diagrams, that is, with no repeated variables in any branch, are considered then other composition methods become available [145].

8.4.6 Comment

In the theory of hardwired logic systems [1], [59] any sum of products that realizes a logical function Z with the minimum number of letters is called a *minimal polynomial* for Z. If this number is l then by §8.4.5 there is an atomic diagram with l test elements that realizes Z; from which it follows that no diagram for Z, whether atomic or not, simple or not, with more than l test elements can be minimal.

More generally, the result holds if l is the number of letters in any logical expression whatever, constructed with the functions NOT, AND, OR, variables and many number of parentheses: an example is the expression (8.51).

8.4.7 Method: composition of binary decision diagrams

The binary decision diagram for an arbitrary logical function given by a {NOT, AND, OR} expression of l letters can be realized by:

- realizing each logical product as a product composition, using the rules of §8.4.2;
- realizing each logical sum as sum composition, using the rules of §8.4.3;
- realizing each logical inversion as a permutation of the discrete logical constants, as in §8.4.1.

The result will be an atomic diagram with l test elements and two assignment elements, [0] and [1].

This is the method that must be used when the original expression has a relatively large number of different variables — in practice, more than five or six — and about the same (not significantly more) letters.

8.5 METHODS FOR STRUCTURING PROGRAMS

8.5.1 Introduction

In this section we give two variants of the global structuring method of §5.1.18 for determining the minimal or quasi-minimal number k of branches of the decision tree T (Figure 5.20): that is, the number of essential loops in the unstructured flowchart. Both methods are systematic and replace the intuitive approach of §5.1.21.

8.5.2 Representation: program equation

Figures 8.28 and 8.29 represent a control and an action instruction respectively, with address $ADR = i$. For each of these we have an *unstructured program equation ti,* where *ti* is the algebraic expression for the program that starts at *i*, or the flowchart representing this program. The program equation for the control instruction of Figure 8.28 is

$$ti = <_a tp \,|\, tq> \qquad (8.59)$$

and for the action instruction of Figure 8.29 is

$$ti = t\, tj \qquad (8.60)$$

There is a fundamental difference between the program equation and the characteristic equation (§5.1.6): (8.59) describes a program that is not necessarily structured, whilst the characteristic equation $<_a P \,|\, Q>$ describes the structured program for Figure 5.7.

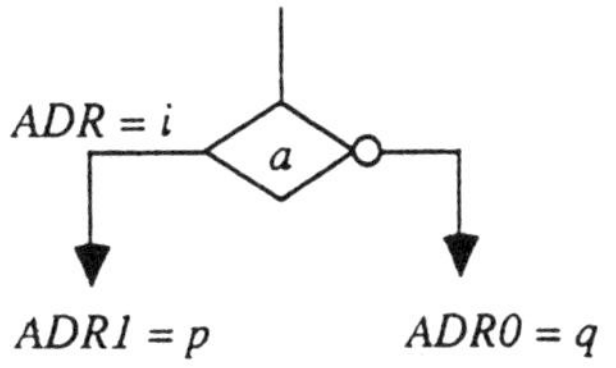

Figure 8.28

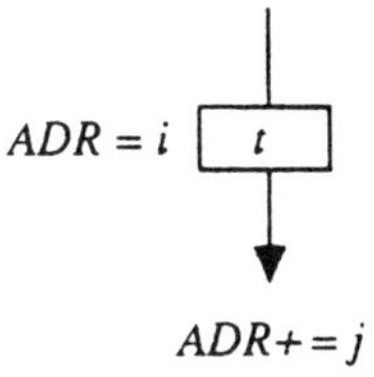

Figure 8.29

8.5.3 Example

Figure 8.30 is a proper, unstructured flowchart with ten instructions; it can be described by the following system of ten equations:

$$t1 = A\ t2 \tag{8.61}$$

$$t2 = <_P t3 \,|\, t4> \tag{8.62}$$

$$t3 = B\ t5 \tag{8.63}$$

$$t4 = C\ t7 \tag{8.64}$$

$$t5 = <_Q t2 \,|\, t7> \tag{8.65}$$

$$t6 = D\ t2 \tag{8.66}$$

$$t7 = <_R t9 \,|\, t6> \tag{8.67}$$

$$t8 = E\ t7 \tag{8.68}$$

$$t9 = <_S t10 \,|\, t8> \tag{8.69}$$

$$t10 = F\ t0 \tag{8.70}$$

The instruction addresses have been assigned arbitrarily except for the entry and exit, which always have $ADR = 1, 0$ respectively.

Application of the global structuring method of §5.1.18 to the example of Figure 8.30 gives a canonical structured flowchart with a single **while . . . do . . .** element (i.e. a single loop), a decision tree with $n = 10$ branches and $n - 1 = 9$ test elements, and a discrete $n + 1 =$ 11-valued auxiliary variable s, $0 \leqslant s \leqslant 10$. We wish to simplify the tree T in the sense of reducing the number of tests; this number being equal to the number of instructions in the original flowchart, or the number of equations ti minus 1, we attempt to reduce the last by a process of successive replacements.

Consider for example equations (8.61) to (8.64): from these we get

$$t1 = A\ t2 = A<_P t3 \,|\, t4> = A<_P B\ t5 \,|\, C\ t7> \tag{8.71}$$

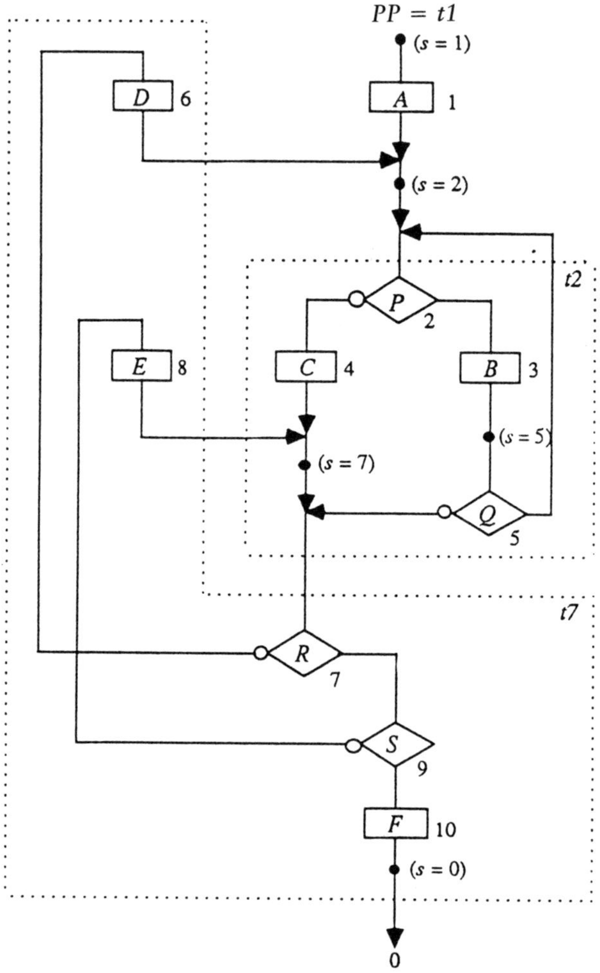

Figure 8.30

Thus we attempt to solve the equations (8.61) to (8.70) by eliminating as many variables *ti* as possible; when we have reduced the number to the minimum possible (among which will be *t0*, which is never eliminated) we can be certain that we have found a structured flowchart with the minimal number of tests.

8.5.4 Representation: graph of equations

The process of systematic solution of these equations is helped by constructing a *graph of equations*, e.g. Figure 8.31, as follows:

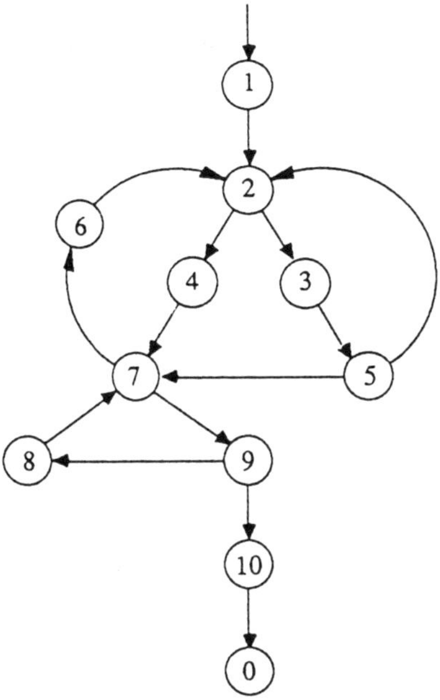

Figure 8.31

- each instruction in the flowchart, e.g. Figure 8.30, is represented by a vertex numbered with the address of that instruction; vertex 0 represents the exit;
- each connection in the flowchart is represented by a directed arc.

A *circuit* in the graph is any closed directed path through any number of vertices; a circuit is *elementary* if it contains no other cicuits. Thus

$$B2 = \{2, 3, 5\} \quad \text{and} \quad B7 = \{2, 3, 5, 7, 6\}$$

are circuits, of which only B2 is elementary since B2 $\in$ B7.

8.5.5 Determining the circuits in a graph

We first look for the circuits in the graph of equations, and then for the elementary circuits among these. For this we compute for each vertex j a logical proposition Pj that gives the conditions under which one or more circuits can pass through that vertex: the non-negated occurrence of a vertex number in the expression for a proposition means that at least one circuit contains that vertex.

Consider the vertex $j = 2$ in Figure 8.31. Any circuit into this must go through either 1, 5 or 6 immediately before reaching 2 and any circuit leading from it must go immediately through 3 or 4. Therefore if there is a circuit through 2 there must also be one through 1 OR 5 OR 6 AND one through 3 OR 4; which is expressed by

$$P2 = 2 \rightarrow (1 + 5 + 6)(3 + 4) \tag{8.72}$$

where '+' is the logical sum OR, juxtaposition is the logical product AND and '→' is logical *implication*, equivalent to

$$a \rightarrow b = a' + b \tag{8.73}$$

Application of (8.73) to (8.72) gives

$$P2 = 2' + (1 + 5 + 6)(3 + 4) \tag{8.74}$$

which states that either there is no circuit through 2 or, if there is, there is also a circuit through at least one of 1, 5, 6 and also through at least one of 3, 4.

The complete set of circuits is described by the logical proposition

$$\begin{aligned} P &= \Pi_j\, Pj,\ j = 0, 1, \ldots 10 \\ &= 0' \cdot 1' \cdot [2' + (1 + 5 + 6)(3 + 4)] \cdot [3' + 2 \cdot 5] \cdot [4' + 2 \cdot 7] \cdot \\ &\quad [5' + 3 \cdot (2 + 7)] \cdot [6' + 2 \cdot 7] \cdot [7' + (4 + 5 + 8) \cdot (6 + 9)] \cdot \\ &\quad [8' + 7 \cdot 9] \cdot [9' + 7 \cdot (10 + 8)] \cdot [10' + 9 \cdot 0] \end{aligned}$$

Evaluation of this, using the rules of logical algebra [1], [59], gives the polynomial sought:

$$\begin{aligned} P = {} & 2'3'4'5'6'7'8'9' + 2'3'4'5'6'7\,8\,9 + 2\,3\,4'5\,6'7'8'9' + 2\,3\,4'5\,6'7\,8\,9 \\ & + 2\,3'4\,5'6\,7\,8\,9 + 2\,3'4\,5'6\,7\,8'9' + 2\,3\,5\,7\,8\,9 \\ & + 2\,3\,4\,5\,6\,7\,8'9' + 2\,3\,5\,6\,7\,8'9' \end{aligned} \tag{8.75}$$

Each of the products in P is a possible circuit, each true variable representing a vertex; thus there are seven distinct circuits:

$$\begin{aligned} &B1 = \{7, 8, 9\} \quad B2 = \{2, 3, 5\} \quad B3 = \{2, 3, 5, 7, 8, 9\} \\ &B4 = \{2, 4, 6, 7, 8, 9\} \quad B5 = \{2, 4, 6, 7\} \quad B6 = \{2, 3, 4, 5, 6, 7\} \\ &B7 = \{2, 3, 5, 6, 7\} \end{aligned}$$

of which the only elementary circuits are

$$B1 = \{7, 8, 9\} \quad B2 = \{2, 3, 5\} \quad B5 = \{2, 4, 6, 7\} \tag{8.76}$$

8.5.6 Solution of the equations

Reflection shows that structuring a flowchart implies breaking all the feedback paths, and therefore breaking all the elementary circuits in the equation graph as for example Figure 8.31. Every vertex in a circuit is a possible break point; we define a *minimal set* E of vertices by:

1. every circuit is broken at a vertex belonging to E;
2. the cardinality of E is minimal.

We again use the rules of logical algebra to find the minimal sets: [1] (pp. 291–293), [59] (pp. 357–359). For the present example we have the elementary circuits B1, B2, B5 of (8.76); the logical product of these is

$$F = (7 + 8 + 9)(2 + 3 + 5)(2 + 4 + 6 + 7) \tag{8.77}$$

and the minimal sets are the minimal length products in the development of *F*: these are

2.7, 2.8, 2.9, 3.7, 5.7

giving the five minimal sets

$$\begin{aligned} &\mathrm{E1} = \{2, 7\} \quad \mathrm{E2} = \{2, 8\} \quad \mathrm{E3} = \{2, 9\} \quad \mathrm{E4} = \{3, 7\} \\ &\mathrm{E5} = \{5, 7\} \end{aligned} \tag{8.78}$$

Thus the set of 10 equations (8.61) to (8.70) can be solved in terms of two variables only, from which it follows that the number of essential loops (§5.1.21) is $k = 2$.

Take for example *t2* and *t7*, from E1; successive replacements give the following:

$$t2 = <_P B <_Q t2 \,|\, t7 > |\, C\, t7 > \tag{8.79}$$

$$t7 = <_R <_S F\, t0 \,|\, E\, t7 > |\, D\, t2 > \tag{8.80}$$

in which, apart from the output variable *t0* which is never eliminated, only *t2* and *t7* appear.

Finally, there is an initial condition that ensures that the program starts with the instruction $ADR = 1$; this is given by the equation for *t1*, which involves only *t2*, *t7* and *t0*:

$$t1 = A\, t2 \tag{8.81}$$

We have now broken the original flowchart of Figure 8.30 into three blocks, described by the equations (8.79) to (8.81), the last representing the starting condition.

8.5.7 Software realization: simplified structured flowchart

We now return to the general method of §5.1.21 and proceed as follows:

1. to each equation *ti* of the unstructured program there corresponds the characteristic equation *Ri* of the equivalent structured program;
2. for each occurrence of an action *tj* on the right in any equation of the

unstructured program there is an assignment $sj = s \leftarrow j$ in the corresponding member of the characteristic equation.

Thus from (8.79) and (8.80) we derive the characteristic equations *R2*, *R7* for the specialized part of the final flowchart, Figure 8.32:

$$R2 = <_P B <_Q s2 \mid s7 > \mid C\, s7 > \tag{8.82}$$

$$R7 = <_R <_S F\, s0 \mid E\, s7 > \mid D\, s2 > \tag{8.83}$$

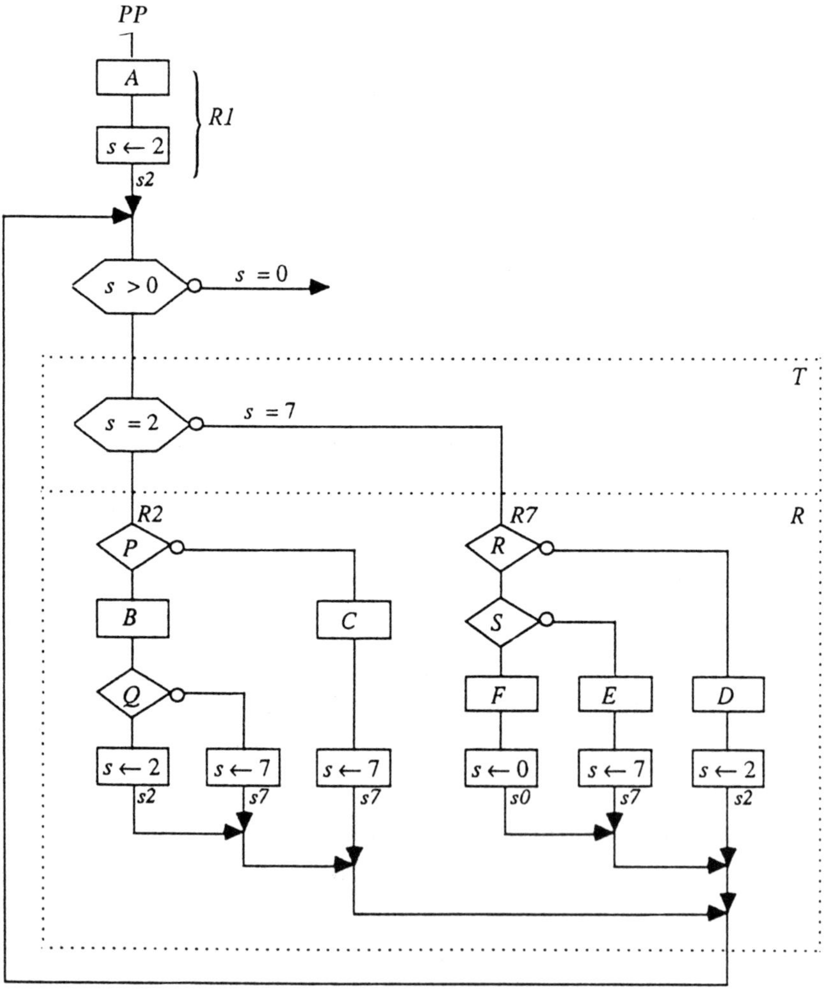

Figure 8.32

and from (8.81) the characteristic equation $R1$ for the starting condition, replacing the assignment $s \leftarrow 1$ in the standard part:

$$R1 = A\ s2 \tag{8.84}$$

It can be checked that in the final flowchart:

- there is only a single **while . . . do . . .** element, and therefore only a single feedback loop;
- the decision tree T has $k = 2$ branches and $k - 1 = 1$ test element;
- the auxiliary variable s is $k + 1 = 3$-valued, with $s \in \{0, 2, 7\}$; k is the number of essential loops, which is also the minimal number of independent variables in terms of which the solution of the set of equations ti can be expressed.

8.5.8 Method 1: graph of equations

We start with a proper, unstructured flowchart with n instructions and proceed as follows.

1. Number the instructions from 1 to n, in any order, assigning address 1 to the initial instruction and 0 to the exit.
2. Construct the graph of the equations, with a numbered vertex for each instruction and a directed arc for each connection.
3. Find all the elementary circuits in the graph, say bi, $i = 1 \ldots l$; if bi consists of the vertices bix, $x = 1 \ldots K$ it can be represented by the logical sum

$$Si = \sum_{x=1}^{K} bix$$

4. Form the logical product of the sums Si, $i = 1 \ldots l$ derived from the complete set of elementary circuits:

$$F = \prod_{i=1}^{l} Si = \prod_{i=1}^{l} \sum_{x=1}^{K} bix$$

5. Find the minimal length products in the development of F; these give the minimal sets E which determine the k independent variables for the set tj.

This gives the final system of k equations, with, in general, a further equation for the starting condition $t1$.

If the method of global structuring is applied to the $k + 1$ partial flowcharts it gives a structured flowchart containing a single **while . . . do . . .** element, a decision tree with k branches and $k - 1$ test elements and a discrete $(k + 1)$–valued auxiliary variable.

8.5.9 Conclusion

If the problem is to analyse an asynchronous sequential logic system then again the approach is to find the minimal number of independent internal variables, which is the same as the least number of vertices of the equations graph that must be removed so as to break all the elementary circuits. The complete analogy of this with the problem treated in this section allows much use to be made of the results obtained here and proved in [94] (pp. 253–258, 267–271).

8.5.10 Representation: state diagram

As an example we take Figure 8.30 again. Since, as we know, there is an equivalence between a program, described by a flowchart, and a sequential system, described by a state diagram and/or a state table, we can construct a *state graph* for the system as follows (cf. the bibliography of §5.4.16 and the definitions of §5.3.1).

1. The test variables of the program are the input variables xi of the sequential system.
2. The assignments of the program are the output states Z of the sequential system.
3. After executing any single assignment the state s of the system is always one of those shown by a mark • in Figure 8.30; also there is always an *initial state* preceding the initial instruction, the address of this instruction being always $ADR = 1$. Each state s is labelled with the address of the immediately following instruction, thus

   $$s \in \{1, 2, 5, 7, 0\}$$

4. For an input state or set of input states, e.g. $x = Q'R'$, each internal state s (e.g. $s = 5$) leads to an output state Z ($Z = D$) and a future state s^+ ($s^+ = 2$): this change from a present state s to the next state s^+ is a *state transition*, $s \to s^+$.
5. Figure 8.33 is the state diagram for this example; the five internal states s are represented by five vertices and the state transitions by directed arcs. Each arc is labelled with the relevant input state x and the output state Z.

To enable the internal states to be determined correctly we should add the neutral operation (NOP instruction) to any loop that contained no action instruction or to any flowchart in which the output was realized by a control or a test instruction: this latter eventuality arises in Figure 5.14. In this connection, see the exercise of §5.1.31.

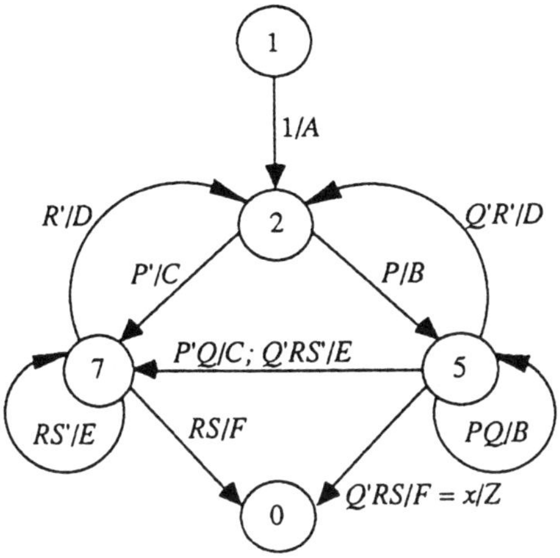

Figure 8.33

8.5.11 Representation: state table

Figure 8.34 is the state table for the system we are considering, derived from the state diagram of Figure 8.33 as follows (cf. §5.3.4):

1. the $2^4 = 16$ columns correspond to the 16 input states of the four variables P, Q, R, S;
2. the five rows correspond to the five internal states s;
3. each of the $16 \times 5 = 80$ cells of the table formed by the intersection of a column (an input state x) with a row (an internal state s) specifies a resultant state s^+, Z; these are grouped in blocks in the figure, with all the cells in a block corresponding to the same resultant state, as shown;

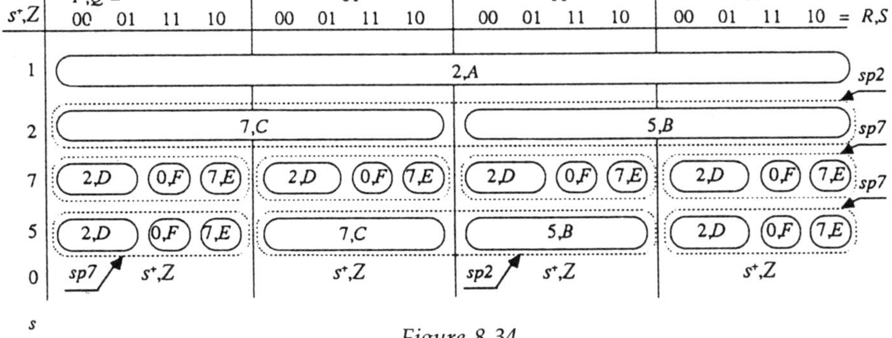

Figure 8.34

4. for the *final state* $s = 0$ there is no next state, nor is the output state known; thus the values s^+, Z for this state are unknown rather than undefined (Φ, Φ) and therefore are shown symbolically as s^+, Z.

8.5.12 Comment

The state diagram (Figure 8.33) and state table (Figure 8.34) differ from the usual diagrams and tables for hardwired synchronous sequential systems [1], [59] as follows:

- there is an initial state $s = 1$ that is not accessible from any other state s;
- there is a final state $s = 0$ for which the resultant states s^+, Z is unknown; thus this cannot be involved in any reduction of the table.

These properties follow immediately from the flowchart of Figure 8.30; we have assumed that this is a proper flowchart in the sense of §5.1.4 and therefore that it has a single input and a single output terminal.

8.5.13 Software realization: simplified structured flowchart

In Chapter 5 we described two methods for realizing a sequential system, that is, a state tables, by means of a structured program: the method of the state table tree (§5.3.15) and that of separation of the variables (§5.3.22). If we can assume, as in §8.5.12, that we are dealing with proper flowcharts we can use either method without restriction; here we choose separation of variables since with this it is easy to compare the results of the two variants of the global structuring method described in the present section.

1. The primitive state table, derived from the graph, is that of Figure 8.34.
2. Recalling that the final state $s = 0$ cannot be involved in any reduction, we can say that this table of $Ns = 5$ states is minimal; for convenience in making the comparison we adopt a 1-out-of-*Ns* code and associate with each state a *Ns*-valued variable.
3. We perform a simplification or reduction on each row of the table (i.e. for each of the *Ns* partial trees), using the methods of Chapter 2; this gives, for this example, two common sub-trees *sp2, sp7*.
4. We construct the main tree, with $Ns = 5$ branches and $Ns - 1 = 4$ test elements, each selecting one of the *Ns* partial trees.
5. The assemblage of the main tree and the $Ns = 5$ partial trees (decomposed in this example) gives the final tree, which is decomposed; for the sake of clarity, in each partial tree we have

separated the original assigments $A \ldots F$ from those of the internal state, $s \leftarrow 0 \ldots s \leftarrow 7$.

6. The special features of a proper flowchart are expressed by the assignment $s \leftarrow 1$, the initial condition essential for reaching the initial state $s = 1$, and the exit labelled $s = 0$ which realizes the partial tree for the state $s = 0$ for which the resultant states s^+, Z are unknown.

This gives the final structured flowchart of Figure 8.35, for which we can check:

- it contains a single **while . . . do . . .** element and therefore a single loop;
- the decision tree T has $Ns - 1 = 4$ branches and $Ns - 2 = 3$ test elements;
- the auxiliary variable s is $Ns = 5$-valued, with $s \in \{1, 2, 5, 7, 0\}$

where Ns is the number of states in the minimal reduced table, which is equivalent to the original proper program.

8.5.14 Method 2: state table

Starting with a proper, unstructured flowchart of n instructions the procedure is as follows.

1. Construct the state diagram for the equivalent sequential system; this will have as many vertices as there are states.
2. Construct the state table for this system and if necessary reduce it; let Ns be the number of rows in the minimal table.
3. Code the table in terms of a 1-out-of-Ns code, using either Ns logical variables or a single Ns-valued discrete variable s.
4. Construct the main tree that tests s, with Ns branches and Ns-1 tests; precede this tree with an assignment giving the starting condition $s \leftarrow 1$.
5. For each of these Ns branches except that for the final state $s = 0$ construct the corresponding partial tree, possibly decomposed.

This gives the required flowchart, consisting of a single **while . . . do . . .** element, a main tree with Ns branches and $Ns - 1$ test elements, and a discrete Ns-valued auxiliary variable.

8.5.15 Comments

The properties of sequential systems have dictated the construction of the state diagram and table (Figures 8.33 and 8.34) in this way:

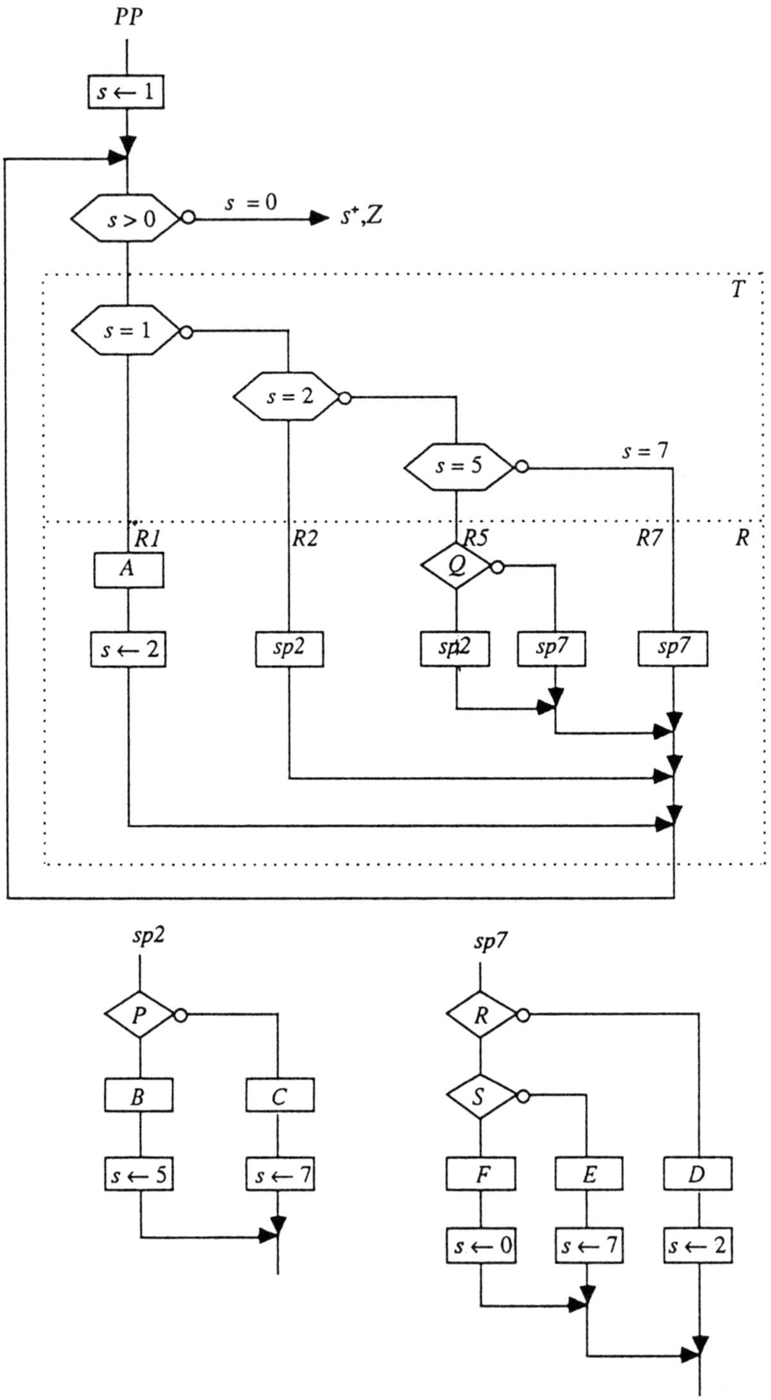

PP
s ← 1
s > 0
s = 0
s⁺,Z
T
s = 1
s = 2
s = 5
s = 7
R1
R2
R5
R7
R
A
Q
s ← 2
sp2
sp2
sp7
sp7
sp2
P
B
C
s ← 5
s ← 7
sp7
R
S
F
E
D
s ← 0
s ← 7
s ← 2

Figure 8.35

- every internal state s determines, for every input state x, a unique output state Z (and therefore a unique action instruction) and a unique next state s^+.

In Figure 8.30 each of the five states s is represented by a mark • placed before a decision tree that acts on the input variables P, Q, R, S which together form the input states; each branch of the tree is followed by a single action instruction which gives the output state Z. Ignoring the undefined state $s = 0$, the four states $s \in \{1, 2, 5, 7\}$ are thus four partial programs, given by the following equations:

$$t1 = A\ t2 \tag{8.85}$$

$$t2 = <_P B\ t5 \,|\, C\ t7> \tag{8.86}$$

$$t5 = <_Q t2 \,|\, t7> \tag{8.87}$$

$$t7 = <_R <_S F\ t0 \,|\, E\ t7> \,|\, D\ t2> \tag{8.88}$$

If we apply the method of global structuring (§§5.1.18, 8.5.7) to these equations we recover the flowchart of Figure 8.35.

The solution obtained by Method 2 (the state table method) results from a particular solution of the equations (8.61) to (8.70) of the Method 1 (graph of equations); the choice of the variables *t1*, *t2*, *t5*, *t7* gives a possible solution, but not a minimal one. The flowchart of Figure 8.35:

- requires more tests of the auxiliary variable s than does the previous minimal solution — four against the three of Figure 8.32;
- in contrast to the previous solution, allows the control instructions and the action instructions to be organized into separate groups.

To summarize, any proper unstructured program can be represented by the state table of the equivalent sequential system; the coding of these states by means of internal variables is equivalent to the introduction of auxiliary variables in Method 1 (§8.5.8). The decision tree finally obtained is a possible realization of Method 1, that is, a solution of the equations that in general is not minimal.

8.5.16 General conclusion

The two variants given here of the method of global structuring both give a structured flowchart having a single **while . . . do . . .** element and therefore a single feedback loop.

In the first variant the minimum number of breakings of the elementary circuits (the essential loops) is determined by a systematic process, giving a structured schema with the minimum number of tests of the auxiliary variable; in this schema the control and action instructions are mingled, as in Figure 8.32. In the second a decision tree is constructed, derived from the state table equivalent to the program; the resulting structured schema does not necessarily have the minimum number of tests but does offer the possibility of separating the control and action instructions into two groups, as Figure 8.35.

These methods can be applied to any proper unstructured program. The example we have been discussing, Figure 8.30, might give the erroneous impression that from any unstructured flowchart they would produce a structured equivalent with a single feedback loop, but it is clear that in practice this example should be viewed from two quite different angles:

1. either it is a part (a sub-program) of a much larger program, in which case any sub-program that either precedes or follows Figure 8.30 (or its structured equivalent Figure 8.32) in the complete program may itself have several feedback loops;
2. or it is the complete structure of a program in which each action instruction *A*, *B*, . . . *F* is itself realized by a proper program with its own feedback loops and its own control and action instructions.

The method of local structuring given in §5.1.8 tries in the first instance to structure all parts of the flowchart that lend themselves to this, without introducing auxiliary variables; these are to be used only as a last resort, when they constitute a necessary evil.

Figure 8.36 shows the main links between the two variants, and also the extent of their field of application. For example, from a specification for a sequential system expressed as a state diagram or table it is possible to generate either an unstructured flowchart for a direct realization without auxiliary variables, or, after coding of the internal states, a structured flowchart for realization with auxiliary variables.

8.5.17 Bibliography

The structuring methods given in this section are due to Mange [97], [98]. Reference [101] describes a representation for an unstructured flowchart by a state diagram and also by a particular form of the state table, the *decision table*.

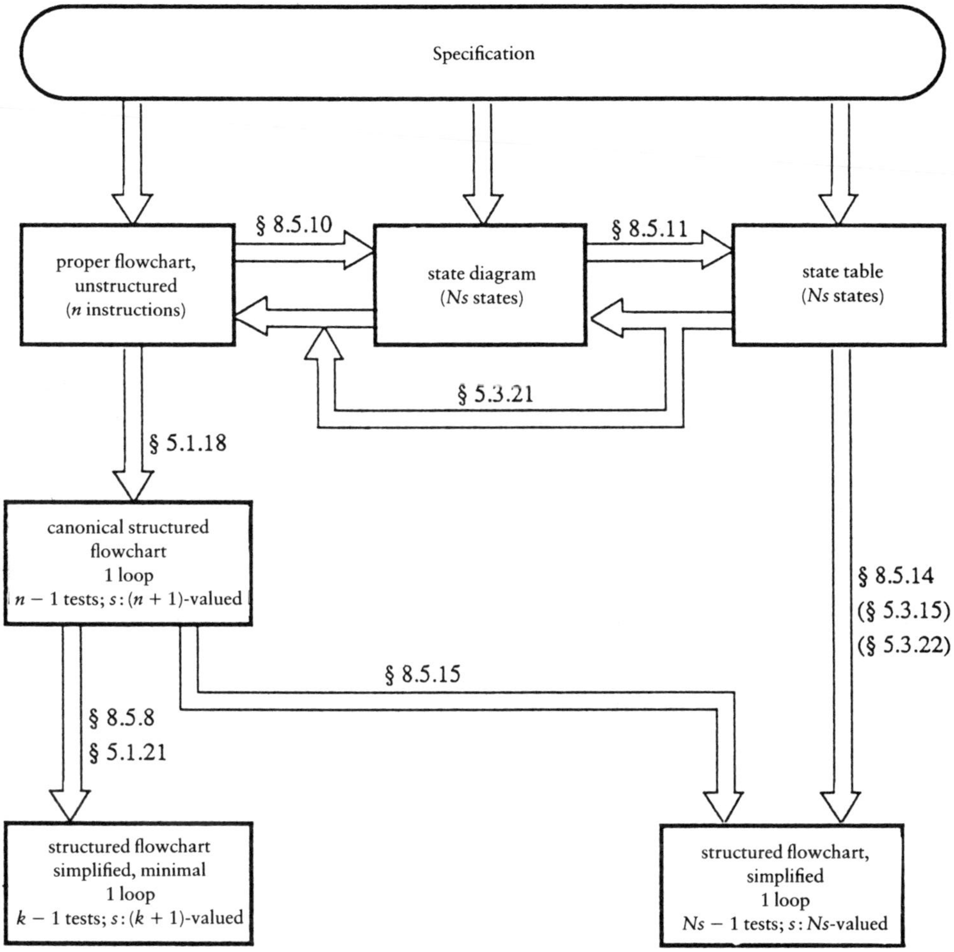

$n > Ns > k$

Figure 8.36

8.6 NUMBER SYSTEMS

8.6.1 Definition: decimal system

A number written in the ordinary way

$$N = 1975 \quad (8.89)$$

is equivalent to the arithmetical expression

$$N = 1.10^3 + 9 \cdot 10^2 + 7 \cdot 10^1 + 5 \cdot 10^0 \quad (8.90)$$

in which the signs '·' (product) and '+' (sum) have their normal arithmetical meanings. We say the N is expressed in the *decimal number system*, or, briefly, is a *decimal number*. The successive powers of 10 are the *weights*, whose values are understood in (8.89); 10 is the *base* of the system and in this system there are ten symbols $0, 1, \ldots 9$ which constitute the *digits*. These are shown in heavy type in the column N_D of Figure 8.37. When necessary, the base is indicated by a suffix, as N_D here.

8.6.2 Definition: binary system

A number N can also be expressed as a sum of weights that are powers of 2, in which can we say that it is expressed in the *binary system*, or is a *binary number*. The base is now 2, and there are only two symbols, 0, 1: these are the *binary digits* or *bits*, shown in heavy type in the column N_B in Figure 8.37. The compact notation of a binary number is of the form

$$N = 110101 \quad (8.91)$$

which is equivalent to

$$N = 1 \cdot 2^5 + 1 \cdot 2^4 + 0 \cdot 2^3 + 1 \cdot 2^2 + 0 \cdot 2^1 + 1 \cdot 2^0 \quad (8.92)$$

with '·' and '+' meaning as before.

8.6.3 Method

Conversion of a binary number to its decimal equivalent is trivial, simply a matter of evaluating the powers of 2 as decimal numbers and summing the terms as in (8.92): thus

$$N = 110101_B = 2^5 + 2^4 + 2^2 + 2^0 = 53_D \quad (8.93)$$

N_B	N_D	N_H
0	0	0
1	1	1
10	2	2
11	3	3
100	4	4
101	5	5
110	6	6
111	7	7
1000	8	8
1001	9	9
1010	10	A
1011	11	B
1100	12	C
1101	13	D
1110	14	E
1111	15	F
10000	16	10
10001	17	11
10010	18	12
10011	19	13
10100	20	14
10101	21	15
10110	22	16
10111	23	17
11000	24	18
11001	25	19
11010	26	1A
11011	27	1B
11100	28	1C
11101	29	1D
11110	30	1E
11111	31	1F

Figure 8.37

8.6.4 Definition: hexadecimal system

This uses 16 for its base, with the 16 symbols: the ten digits 0 . . . 9 followed by the six letters A . . . F. These are shown in heavy type in the column N_H in Figure 8.37.

Thus the hexadecimal number

$$N = 35 \tag{8.94}$$

is equivalent to

$$N = 3 \cdot 16^1 + 5 \cdot 16^0 = 53_D \tag{8.95}$$

Conversion of a binary number to its hexadecimal form is trivial: each group of four bits, starting from the right, is converted independently, thus

$$N_B = 110101_B = (11)(0101)_B = 35_H \tag{8.96}$$

8.6.5 Representation of negative numbers

With the three bits N_2, N_1, N_0 multiplying the respective weights 2^2, 2^1, 2^0 we can represent the $2^3 = 8$ positive numbers from $000_B = 0_D$ to $111_B = 7_D$ (Figure 8.38); the decimal value N_D is found from

$$N_D = N_2 \cdot 2^2 + N_1 \cdot 2^1 + N_0 \cdot 2^0 \tag{8.97}$$

If we introduce a fourth bit N_3, called the *sign bit* and associated with the negative weight -2^3, we can represent the $2^4 = 16$ numbers from $1000_B = -8_D$ to $0111_B = +7_D$, as in Figure 8.38. The decimal value is now found from

$$N_D = N_3 \cdot (-2^3) + N_2 \cdot 2^2 + N_1 \cdot 2^1 + N_0 \cdot 2^0 \tag{8.98}$$

Thus the decimal number N_D repesented by (8.98) is *negative* if $N_3 = 1$.

8.6.6 Properties

These properties follow from (8.98) and Figure 8.38:

1. the bit N_3 gives the sign of the equivalent decimal number N_D: if $N_3 = 1$, N_D is negative, and is positive if $N_3 = 0$;
2. the number 0 (zero) is positive;
3. a positive decimal number is changed to a negative number of the same absolute value by means of two binary operations: inversion of each bit followed by the addition of 1; thus

$$+N_D = +6_D = 0110_B$$

N_3 (-2^3)	N_2 $(+2^2)$	N_1 $(+2^1)$	N_0 $(+2^0)$	N_D
1	0	0	0	−8
1	0	0	1	−7
1	0	1	0	−6
1	0	1	1	−5
1	1	0	0	−4
1	1	0	1	−3
1	1	1	0	−2
1	1	1	1	−1
0	0	0	0	+0
0	0	0	1	+1
0	0	1	0	+2
0	0	1	1	+3
0	1	0	0	+4
0	1	0	1	+5
0	1	1	0	+6
0	1	1	1	+7

Figure 8.38

inversion of 0110 gives 1001_B

$1001_B + 1 = 1010_B$

$1010_B = -6_D = -N_D$

The binary number 1010 computed by this process is called the *2s-complement* of the original number.

8.6.7 Binary subtraction

Binary subtraction is performed by adding the 2s-complement; thus

$5 - 3 = 2$

$(+5) + (-3) = 2$

$(0101) + (1101) = 10010$

and neglecting the 1 on the extreme left — the 'carry bit' — we get $0010 = +2_D$.

The general process is that to perform the binary subtraction $A - B$, where $A > B$, we

1. invert B (i.e. replace 1s by 0s, and 0s by 1s — the straight complement) to give B';
2. add 1 to B', giving the 2s-complement;
3. add this to A and neglect the carry bit.

$$\text{Thus} \quad A - B = A + B' + 1 \tag{8.99}$$

A particular case of subtraction is *decrementation*, subtracting 1:

$$A - 1 = A + 11\ldots110 + 1 = A + 11\ldots111 \tag{8.100}$$

8.6.8 Bibliography

Number systems in general, and conversion from any one system to any other, are treated in [139] (pp. 21–34, 112–120); and representation of negative numbers and the subtraction operation in [18] (pp. 10–16, 322–328, 362–382) and [139] (pp. 44–68).

8.7 CONVENTIONS

8.7.1 Operations on free variables

The three basic logical functions AND, OR, NOT are represented by the operators '·' (which can be omitted and taken as understood), '+' and ''', with the definitions of §§1.1.3, 1.1.4: thus

- AND: $a \cdot b = ab$
- OR: $a + b$
- NOT: a'

Here OR is *inclusive*, i.e. meaning a or b or both; it is often convenient to use the exclusive OR, meaning either a or b but not both, written EXOR or XOR and represented by the symbol ⊕ (§2.2.17):

- EXOR/XOR: $a \oplus b = a'b + ab'$

8.7.2 Operations on words

First, we distinguish between the relations

- equality, represented by '='
- asynchronous assignment, represented by ':='
- synchronous assignment, represented by '←'

Next, suppose we have the 4-bit words $A = A_{3:0}$, $B = B_{3:0}$, $C = C_{3:0}$. The operations AND, OR, NOT, EXOR on these are represented by the symbols $\wedge$, $\vee$, $'$, $\oplus$ respectively ('$\cdot$' and '+' are used only with free variables):

- AND: $C = A \wedge B = [A_3 \cdot B_3, A_2 \cdot B_2, A_1 \cdot B_1, A_0 \cdot B_0]$
- OR: $C = A \vee B = [A_3 + B_3, A_2 + B_2, A_1 + B_1, A_0 + B_0]$
- NOT: $A' = A_3', A_2', A_1', A_0'$
- EXOR: $C = A \oplus B = [A_3 \oplus B_3, A_2 \oplus B_2, A_1 \oplus B_1, A_0 \oplus B_0]$

The arithmetical operations of addition (ADD) and subtraction (SUB) are distinguished from these logical operations by being represented by the normal arithmetical symbols '+', '−':, together with a symbol (here R) for a possible carry:

- ADD: $R, C = A + B$
- SUB: $R, C = A - B$

Incrementation (INC) is the addition of 1 and decrementation (DEC) is the subtraction of 1:

- INC: $A \leftarrow A + 1$
- DEC: $A \leftarrow A - 1$

and counting by ns (COUNT) can be regarded as incrementation modulo n.

- COUNT: $A \leftarrow A + 1 \pmod{n}$

Shifts of one bit to the right (SHIFT RIGHT) or to the left (SHIFT LEFT) are expressed by divisions (symbol /) or multiplications (symbol ∗) by 2, respectively:

- SHIFT RIGHT: $A \leftarrow A/2$, i.e. $A_3, A_2, A_1, A_0 \leftarrow \Phi A_3, A_2, A_1$
- SHIFT LEFT: $A \leftarrow A*2$, i.e. $A_3, A_2, A_1, A_0 \leftarrow A_2, A_1, A_0, \Phi$

Rotations of one bit to right or left are derived from the shift operations:

- ROT RIGHT: $A \leftarrow A/2$, $A_3 \leftarrow A_0$
- ROT LEFT: $A \leftarrow A*2$, $A_0 \leftarrow A_3$

It is to be understood that synchronous assignments on the same line, separated by a comma, are performed simultaneously.

Bibliography

[1] D. MANGE, *Analyse et synthèse des systèmes logiques*, Traité d'électricité, volume V, Presses polytechniques romandes, Lausanne, 1985.
[2] M. DAVIO, J.-P. DESCHAMPS, A. THAYSE, *Digital systems with algorithm implementation*, John Wiley, Chichester, 1983.
[3] M. DAVIO, J.-P. DESCHAMPS, A. THAYSE, *Machines algorithmiques*, Presses polytechniques romandes, Lausanne, 1982.
[4] B.R. DEEM, K. MUCHOW, A. ZEPPA, *Digital Computer Circuits and Concepts*, 2nd edition, Reston Publishing Company, Reston (Virginia), 1977.
[5] K.L. SHORT, *Microprocessors and Programmed Logic*, Prentice-Hall, Englewood Cliffs, 1981.
[6] J. FLORINE, *Logique transitionnelle microprogrammée*, InterEditions, Paris, 1983.
[7] J. EIMBINDER, Editor, *Semiconductor Memories*, Wiley-Interscience, New York, 1971.
[8] J.P. HAYES, *Digital System Design and Microprocessors*, McGraw-Hill, New York, 1984.
[9] W.N. CARR, J.P. MIZE, *MOS/LSI Design and Application*, McGraw-Hill, New York, 1972.
[10] G. LUECKE, J.P. MIZE, W.N. CARR, *Semiconductor Memory Design and Application*, McGraw-Hill, New York, 1973.
[11] A. BARNA, D.I. PORAT, *Integrated Circuits in Digital Electronics*, John Wiley, New York, 1973.
[12] S. MUROGA, *VLSI System Design*, John Wiley, New York, 1982.
[13] S.G. SHIVA, *Computer Design and Architecture*, Little, Brown and Company, Boston, 1985.
[14] *IBM Journal of research and development*, vol. 28, No. 2, March 1984, pp. 123–230.
[15] R.M. TANNER, Fault-Tolerant 256K Memory Designs, *IEEE Transactions on Computers*, vol. C-33, No. 4, April 1984, pp. 314–322.
[16] C.R. CLARE, *Designing logic systems using state machines*, McGraw-Hill, New York, 1973.
[17] *The TTL Data Book for Design Engineers* (LCC 4112), 2nd edition, Texas Instruments Incorporated, Dallas, 1981.
[18] M.M. MANO, *Digital Logic and Computer Design*, Prentice-Hall, Englewood Cliffs, 1979.
[19] J. DUCHENE, Simplification d'un circuit logique par utilisation des

circuits à 3 états, *L'onde électrique*, vol. 57, No. 2, février 1977, pp. 126–129.

[20] *MOS Memory Data Book*, 1984-European Edition, Texas Instruments, 1984.

[21] *Mitsubishi Data Book*, 1982, LSI, Mitsubishi Electric, 1982.

[22] B.M.E. MORET, Decision Trees and Diagrams, *Computing Surveys*, vol. 14, No. 4, December 1982, pp. 593–623.

[23] S.B. AKERS, Binary Decision Diagrams, *IEEE Transactions on Computers*, vol. C-27, No. 6, June 1978, pp. 509–516.

[24] R.T. BOUTE, The Binary Decision Machine as Programmable Controller, *Euromicro Newsletter*, vol. 2, No. 1, January 1976, pp. 16–22.

[25] C.Y. LEE, Representation of Switching Circuits by Binary-Decision Programs, *The Bell System Technical Journal*, vol. 38, No. 4, July 1959, pp. 985–999.

[26] M. SILVA, R. DAVID, Binary-decision graphs for implementation of Boolean functions, *IEE Proceedings*, vol. 132, Pt. E, No. 3, May 1985, pp. 175–185.

[27] M. DAVIO, A. THAYSE, *Sequential evaluation of Boolean functions, MBLE Report R341*, Manufacture Belge de Lampes et de Matériel Electronique, Bruxelles, 1977.

[28] E. CERNY, D. MANGE, E. SANCHEZ, Synthesis of Minimal Binary Decision Trees, *IEEE Transactions on Computers*, vol. C-28, No. 7, July 1979, pp. 472–482.

[29] D. MANGE, E. SANCHEZ, Synthèse des fonctions logiques avec des multiplexeurs, *Digital Processes*, vol. 4, No. 1, 1978, pp. 29–44.

[30] E.J. McCLUSKEY, Minimization of Boolean Functions, *The Bell System Technical Journal*, vol. 35, No. 6, November 1956, pp. 1417–1444.

[31] W.S. MEISEL, A Note on Internal State Minimization in Incompletely Specified Sequential Networks, *IEEE Transactions on Electronic Computers*, vol. EC-16, No. 4, August 1967, pp. 508–509.

[32] P.J. ZSOMBOR-MURRAY, L.J. VROOMEN, Logical choice and the discriminating designer, *IEEE Micro*, vol. 5, No. 3, June 1985, pp. 63–68.

[33] M.D. ERCEGOVAC, T. LANG, *Digital Systems and Hardware/Firmware Algorithms*, John Wiley, New York, 1985.

[34] J.L. BENTLEY, An Introduction to Algorithm Design, *Computer*, vol. 12, No. 2, February 1979, pp. 66–78.

[35] J. ZAHND, *Machines séquentielles*, Traité d'électricité, volume XI, Georgi, Saint-Saphorin, 1980.

[36] D. LEWIN, L. MARET, *Systèmes logiques*, Spes, Lausanne, 1972.

[37] F.J. HILL, G.R. PETERSON, *Introduction to Switching Theory and Logical Design*, 3rd edition, John Wiley, New York, 1981.

[38] S.H. CALDWELL, *Les circuits de commutation et leur conception*, Eyrolles, Paris, 1967.

[39] S.H. CALDWELL, The Recognition and Identification of Symmetric Switching Functions, *A.I.E.E. Transactions, Part II, Communications and Electronics*, vol. 73, May 1954, pp. 142–147.

[40] E. SANCHEZ, A. THAYSE, Implementation and transformation of

algorithms based on automata, Part III, *Philips Journal of Research*, vol. 36, No. 3, 1981, pp. 159–172.

[41] A. THAYSE, Synthesis and Optimization of Programs by Means of P-Functions, *IEEE Transactions on Computers*, vol. C-31, No. 1, January 1982, pp. 34–40.

[42] E. SANCHEZ, *Horloge microprogrammée à l'aide des algorithmes de décision binaire*, thèse No. 568, Ecole polytechnique fédérale de Lausanne, Lausanne, 1985.

[43] A. THAYSE, *P-Functions and Boolean Matrix Factorization*, Springer-Verlag, Berlin, 1984.

[44] A. THAYSE, P-Functions: A New Tool for the Analysis and Synthesis of Binary Programs, *IEEE Transactions on Computers*, vol. C-30, No. 2, February 1981, pp. 126–134.

[45] D. MANGE, Arbres de décision pour systèmes logiques câblés ou programmés, *Bulletin ASE/UCS*, vol. 69, No. 22, 18 novembre 1978, pp. 1238–1243.

[46] J.-D. WARNIER, *Logical Construction of Programs*, H.E. Stenfert Kroese B.V., Leiden, 1974.

[47] D. MANGE, La programmation structurée dans les automatismes numériques, *Revue générale de l'électricité*, 1985, No. 6, juin 1985, pp. 510–517.

[48] D.A. MANGE, A High-Level-Language Programmable Controller, Part I, *IEEE Micro*, vol. 6, No. 1, February 1986, pp. 25–41.

[49] D.A. MANGE, A High-Level-Language Programmable Controller, Part II, *IEEE Micro*, vol. 6, No. 2, April 1986, pp. 47–63.

[50] R.S. PRESSMAN, *Software Engineering: A Practitioner's Approach*, McGraw-Hill International, Auckland, 1982.

[51] D. MANGE, E. SANCHEZ, A. THAYSE, P.J. ZSOMBOR-MURRAY, L.J. VROOMEN, R. HUDSON, T. LE-NGOC, Comments on binary-decision-based programmable controllers, *IEEE Micro*, vol. 5, No. 3, June 1985, pp. 58–63.

[52] P.J.A. ZSOMBOR-MURRAY, L.J. VROOMEN, R.D. HUDSON, T. LE-NGOC, P.H. HOLCK, Binary-Decision-Based Programmable Controllers, Part I-III, *IEEE Micro*, vol. 3, No. 4, August 1983, pp. 67–83, No. 5, October 1983, pp. 16–26, No. 6, December 1983, pp. 24–39.

[53] M. ANDREWS, *Principles of firmware engineering in microprogram control*, Pitman, London, 1981.

[54] W.I. FLETCHER, *An Engineering Approach to Digital Design*, Prentice-Hall, Englewood Cliffs, 1980.

[55] T. MAURIN, M. ROBIN, *Les systèmes microprogrammés*, Dunod, Paris, 1978.

[56] J.B. PEATMAN, *Microcomputer-Based Design*, McGraw-Hill, New York, 1977.

[57] C.C. FOSTER, T. IBERALL, *Computer Architecture*, 3rd edition, Van Nostrand Reinhold, New York, 1985.

[58] R.E. PRATHER, H.T. CASSTEVENS, Realization of Boolean Expressions by Atomic Digraphs, *IEEE Transactions on Computers*, vol. C-27, No. 8, August 1978, pp. 681–688.

[59] D. MANGE, *Analysis and Synthesis of Logic Systems*, Artech House, Norwood (MA), 1986.
[60] D. MANGE, Compteurs microprogrammés, *Bulletin ASE/UCS*, vol. 70, No. 19, 6 octobre 1979, pp. 1087–1095.
[61] E. SANCHEZ, A. STAUFFER, Horloge microprogrammée MICROM, *Actes du 10ème Congrès international de chronométrie*, Société suisse de chronométrie, Büren, 1979, No. 3, pp. 279–284.
[62] C. PIGUET, J.-F. PEROTTO, N. PEGUIRON, J.-J. MONBARON, E. SANCHEZ, R. SAINT-GIRONS, Microcomputer Design for Digital Watches, *Implementing Functions: Microprocessors and Firmware*, pp. 431–442, L. Richter, P. Le Beux, G. Chroust, G. Noguez (eds.), North-Holland, Amsterdam, 1981.
[63] G.J. MYERS, *Digital System Design with LSI Bit-Slice Logic*, John Wiley, New York, 1980.
[64] C. BRIE, R. GERBER, *Les microprocesseurs en tranches*, Technique & Documentation, Paris, 1979.
[65] J. MICK, J. BRICK, *Bit-Slice Microprocessor Design*, McGraw-Hill, New York, 1980.
[66] N.A. ALEXANDRIDIS, Bit-Sliced Microprocessor Architecture, *Computer*, vol. 11, No. 6, June 1978, pp. 56–80.
[67] J.P. HAYES, *Computer Architecture and Organization*, McGraw-Hill, New York, 1978.
[68] K. TRUÖL, U. VIEBEG, *Strukturierter Programmentwurf*, R. Oldenbourg, München, 1985.
[69] R.C. LINGER, H.D. MILLS, B.I. WITT, *Structured Programming: Theory and Practice*, Addison-Wesley, Reading, 1979.
[70] G.G. BOULAYE, *Logique et organes des calculatrices numériques*, Dunod, Paris, 1970.
[71] E.N. YOURDON, Editor, *Classics in Software Engineering*, Yourdon Press, New York, 1979.
[72] E. YOURDON, *Techniques of Program Structure and Design*, Prentice-Hall, Englewood Cliffs, 1975.
[73] N. WIRTH, *Programmer en MODULA-2*, Presses polytechniques romandes, Lausanne, 1984.
[74] C. BÖHM, G. JACOPINI, Flow Diagrams, Turing Machines and Languages with only two Formation Rules, *Communications of the ACM*, vol. 9, No. 5, May 1966, pp. 366–371.
[75] J.-M. BERNARD, Il faut en finir avec la méthode d'Huffman!, *Le Nouvel Automatisme*, vol. XXIV, No. 8, septembre-octobre 1979, pp. 41–50.
[76] Y. TABOURIER, A. ROCHEFELD, C. FRANK, *La programmation structurée en informatique*, Les éditions d'organisation, Paris, 1975.
[77] B. MEYER, C. BAUDOIN, *Méthodes de programmation*, Eyrolles, Paris, 1978.
[78] N. WIRTH, *Introduction à la programmation systématique*, Masson, Paris, 1977.
[79] B.J. CAREY, Formal Methods Expedite Microprocessor-Based System Design, *Computer Design*, vol. 16, No. 2, February 1977, pp. 97–105.
[80] D.A. HUFFMAN, The Synthesis of Sequential Switching Circuits, *Journal*

of The Franklin Institute, vol. 257, No. 3, March 1954, pp. 161–190, No. 4, April 1954, pp. 275–303.

[81] P. NASLIN, *Circuits logiques et automatismes à séquences, 3e édition*, Dunod, Paris, 1970.

[82] D. MANGE, E. SANCHEZ, Simplicité ou structuration? Deux méthodes pour la réalisation microprogrammée d'automatismes séquentiels, *Le Nouvel Automatisme*, vol. XXVI, No. 26, novembre-décembre 1981, pp. 43–49.

[83] D. MANGE, Programmation structurée, *Bulletin ASE/UCS*, vol. 72, No. 7, 11 avril 1981, pp. 339–345.

[84] D. MANGE, Microprogrammation structurée, *Le Nouvel Automatisme*, vol. XXV, No. 13, avril 1980, pp. 45–54.

[85] L.H. JONES, Instruction sequencing in microprogrammed computers, *AFIPS Conference Proceedings*, vol. 44, 1975.

[86] L.D. CORAOR, P.T. HULINA, O.A. MOREAN, A General Model for Memory-Based Finite-State Machines, *IEEE Transactions on Computers*, vol. C-36, No. 2, February 1987, pp. 175–184.

[87] J.B. PEATMAN, *Digital Hardware Design*, McGraw-Hill International, Auckland, 1980.

[88] O.J. DAHL, E.W. DIJKSTRA, C.A.R. HOARE, *Structured Programming*, Academic Press, London, 1972.

[89] D. HAREL, On Folk Theorems, *Communications of the ACM*, vol. 23, No. 7, July 1980, pp. 379–389.

[90] A.W. BURKS, H.H. GOLDSTINE, J. VON NEUMANN, Preliminary discussion of the logical design of an electronic computing instrument, *J. von Neumann, Collected Works*, vol. V, pp. 34–79, A.H. Taub, Ed., MacMillan, New York, 1963.

[91] S.C. KLEENE, General recursive functions of natural numbers, *Math. Annalen 112*, 1936, pp. 727–742.

[92] S.R. KOSARAJU, Analysis of Structured Programs, *Journal of Computer and System Sciences*, vol. 9, No. 3, December 1974, pp. 232–255.

[93] C. PIGUET, J.-F. PEROTTO, J.-J. MONBARON, Conception d'un microprocesseur horloger, *Actes du 10ème Congrès international de chronométrie*, Société suisse de chronométrie, Büren, 1979, No. 3, pp. 271–278.

[94] J.-P. PERRIN, M. DENOUETTE, E. DACLIN, *Systèmes logiques, tome 1*, Dunod, Paris, 1967.

[95] S. THELLIEZ, J.-M. TOULOTTE, *GRAFCET et logique industrielle programmée*, Eyrolles, Paris, 1980.

[96] W.A. WULF, M. SHAW, P.N. HILFINGER, *Fundamental Structures of Computer Science*, Addison-Wesley, Reading, 1981.

[97] D. MANGE, Applications de la théorie des systèmes logiques à la structuration des programmes, *Technique et Science Informatiques*, vol. 2, No. 3, mai-juin 1983, pp. 167–177.

[98] D. MANGE, Applications of switching theory to program structuring, *Technology and Science of Informatics*, vol. 2, No. 3, 1983, pp. 159–168.

[99] E. ASHCROFT, Z. MANNA, The Translation of "Go to" Programs to

"While" Programs, *Information Processing 71*, pp. 250–255, North-Holland Publishing Company, 1972.

[100] H.F. LEDGARD, M. MARCOTTY, A Genealogy of Control Structures, *Communications of the ACM*, vol. 18, No. 11, November 1975, pp. 629–639.

[101] A. LEW, On the Emulation of Flowcharts by Decision Tables, *Communications of the ACM*, vol. 25, No. 12, December 1982, pp. 895–905.

[102] S.S. YAU, J.J.-P. TSAI, A Survey of Software Design Techniques, *IEEE Transactions on Software Engineering*, vol. SE-12, No. 6, June 1986, pp. 713–721.

[103] M.A. JACKSON, *Principles of Program Design*, Academic Press, London, 1975.

[104] A. STAUFFER, Méthode de synthèse des systèmes digitaux. Première partie: l'unité de traitement, *Bulletin ASE/UCS*, vol. 71, No. 3, 9 février 1980, pp. 143–150.

[105] A. STAUFFER, Méthode de synthèse des systèmes digitaux. Seconde partie: l'unité de commande, *Bulletin ASE/UCS*, vol. 71, No. 7, 12 avril 1980, pp. 341–348.

[106] J.-M. BERNARD, *Conception structurée des systèmes logiques*, Eyrolles, Paris, 1987.

[107] W. GRASS, *Steuerwerke, Entwurf von Schaltwerken mit Festwertspeichern*, Springer-Verlag, Berlin, 1978.

[108] O. SPANIOL, *Computer Arithmetic, Logic and Design*, John Wiley, Chichester, 1981.

[109] S.C. LEE, *Modern Switching Theory and Digital Design*, Prentice-Hall, Englewood Cliffs, 1978.

[110] G. SAUCIER, Conception descendante et choix de l'architecture des circuits à très haute intégration, *R.A.I.R.O. Automatique*, vol. 16, No. 3, 1982, pp. 233–257.

[111] J.P. HAYES, Component Expansion Techniques in Computer Design, *Digital Processes*, vol. 4, No. 3–4, Autumn-Winter 1978, pp. 295–312.

[112] P.M. KOGGE, *The Architecture of Pipelined Computers*, McGraw-Hill, New York, 1981.

[113] M.V. WILKES, The best way to design an automatic calculating machine, *Report of the Manchester University Computer Inaugural Conference*, Electrical Engineering Department of Manchester University, Manchester, England, July 1951, pp. 16–18.

[114] T.G. RAUSCHER, P.M. ADAMS, Microprogramming: A Tutorial and Survey of Recent Developments, *IEEE Transactions on Computers*, vol. C-29, No. 1, January 1980, pp. 2–20.

[115] S. DAVIDSON, Progress in High-Level Microprogramming, *IEEE Software*, vol. 3, No. 4, July 1986, pp. 18–26.

[116] A.T. SCHREINER, H.G. FRIEDMAN, *Introduction to Compiler Construction with UNIX*, Prentice-Hall, Englewood Cliffs, 1985.

[117] S.S.S.P. RAO, V. RAMESH, Micro-Store Optimization based on Microoperation Utilisation Profile, *Microprocessing and Microprogramming*, vol. 13, 1984, pp. 115–120.

[118] S.U. RAO, A.K. MAJUMDAR, An Algorithm for Global Compaction of Horizontal Microprograms, *SIGMICRO Newsletter*, vol. 17, No. 2, July 1986, pp. 19–30.
[119] P. PRINETTO, Control Part Descriptions and Languages for Microprogramming in R.W. HARTENSTEIN, ed., *Hardware Description Languages*, North-Holland, Amsterdam, 1987, pp. 75–110.
[120] D. PATTERSON, La microprogrammation, *Pour la Science*, No. 67, mai 1983, pp. 50–59.
[121] D.A. PATTERSON, STRUM: Structured Microprogram Development System for Correct Firmware, *IEEE Transactions on Computers*, vol. C-25, No. 10, October 1976, pp. 974–985.
[122] B. HANSEN, *Brinch Hansen on Pascal Compilers*, Prentice-Hall International, London, 1985.
[123] C. RAPIN, *Compilation, tome 1*, Ecole polytechnique fédérale, Lausanne, 1980.
[124] A.V. AHO, R. SETHI, J.D. ULLMAN, *Compilers: Principles, Techniques and Tools*, Addison-Wesley, Reading, 1986.
[125] *Bipolar Microprocessor Logic and Interface Data Book*, Advanced Micro Devices, Sunnyvale, 1985.
[126] G.D. KRAFT, W.N. TOY, *Microprogrammed Control and Reliable Design of Small Computers*, Prentice-Hall, Englewood Cliffs, 1981.
[127] M.M. MANO, *Computer System Architecture, Second Edition*, Prentice-Hall, Englewood Cliffs, 1982.
[128] G.G. LANGDON, Jr, *Computer Design*, Computeach Press, San Jose, 1982.
[129] G.W. GORSLINE, *Computer Organization: Hardware/Software, Second Edition*, Prentice-Hall, Englewood Cliffs, 1986.
[130] E.E. SWARTZLANDER, Jr, ed., *Computer Design Development-Principal Papers*, Hayden Book, Rochelle Park, 1976.
[131] F. ANCEAU, *The Architecture of Microprocessors*, Addison-Wesley, Wokingham, 1986.
[132] G. BOULAYE, *La microprogrammation*, Dunod, Paris, 1971.
[133] G.G. BOULAYE, *Microprogramming*, MacMillan, London, 1975.
[134] D.K. BANERJI, J. RAYMOND, *Elements of Microprogramming*, Prentice-Hall, Englewood Cliffs, 1982.
[135] V.C. HAMACHER, Z.G. VRANESIC, S.G. ZAKY, *Computer Organization, Second Edition*, McGraw-Hill, Auckland, 1984.
[136] S.U. RAO, A.K. MAJUMDAR, Global Microcode Compaction — A Performance Evaluation by Simulation, *Microprocessing and Microprogramming*, vol. 22, No. 3, May 1988, pp. 159–174.
[137] C. PIGUET, E. DIJKSTRA, A. THEYSE, M. STAUFFER, J.-F. PEROTTO, A Design Methodology of Microprogrammed Controllers for Custom CMOS ICs, *Microprocessing and Microprogramming*, vol. 21, No. 1–5, August 1987, pp. 463–470.
[138] M. ANSORGE, C. PIGUET, E. DIJKSTRA, Design Methodology for Low-power Full Custom RISC Microprocessors, *Microprocessing and Microprogramming*, vol. 18, No. 1–5, December 1986, pp. 427–434.

[139] J.-D. NICOUD, *Calculatrices*, Traité d'électricité, volume XIV, Presses polytechniques romandes, Lausanne, 1983.

[140] *PAL Device Data Book*, Advanced Micro Devices, Sunnyvale, 1988.

[141] *PAL Device Handbook*, Advanced Micro Devices, Sunnyvale, 1988.

[142] J.-D. WARNIER, *Construction et transformation des programmes*, Les éditions d'organisation, Paris, 1985.

[143] M. GINDRE, D. ROUX, *Electronique numérique: logique séquentielle*, McGraw-Hill, Paris, 1987.

[144] C. PIGUET et al., De la machine séquentielle synchronisée au processeur RISC, *Bulletin ASE/UCS*, vol. 79, No. 11, 4 juin 1988, pp. 619–628.

[145] R.E. BRYANT, Graph-Based Algorithms for Boolean Function Manipulation, *IEEE Transactions on Computers*, vol. C-35, No. 8, August 1986, pp. 677–691.

[146] D. MANGE, Le MAGICIEL: un pont entre le MAtériel et le loGICIEL, *Technique et Science Informatiques*, vol. 4, No. 1, janvier-février 1985, pp. 165–169.

[147] D. MANGE, Le matin du magiciel, *Polyrama*, No. 80, novembre 1988, pp. 18–23.

[148] S. HABIB, ed., *Microprogramming and Firmware Engineering Methods*, Van Nostrand Reinhold, New York, 1988.

Index